Chapter 9   A Procedure for Selecting Program Activities   256
A Group Task Recording Form   269

Chapter 10   The Process of Observational Learning   290
Uses of Unstructured Role-Play Procedures   292–293
A Social Network Chart   297

Chapter 11   The Problem-Solving Process in Task Groups   332
Two Cycles of a Problem-Solving Process   333

Chapter 12   A Group Member's Decision Rules for Choosing among
    Applicants for Assistant Program Director   359
Procedures for Acting on Motions during a Parliamentary
    Meeting   365–366

Chapter 14   Group Recording Form   407
The Self-Monitoring Process   410
Session Evaluation Form   411
Steps in the Developmental Research Process   413
Changes in Baseline Data after an Intervention in a Group   414
Graphed Data from a Single-System Evaluation   415
Example of Goal Attainment Scaling   418
An Efficiency Evaluation of a Group Program for Smoking
    Cessation   420

An Introduction to
Group Work Practice

SIXTH
EDITION

An Introduction to Group Work Practice

Ronald W. Toseland

*University at Albany,
State University of New York*

Robert F. Rivas

Siena College

PEARSON

Boston | New York | San Francisco
Mexico City | Montreal | Toronto | London | Madrid | Munich | Paris
Hong Kong | Singapore | Tokyo | Cape Town | Sydney

Senior Acquisitions Editor: Patricia Quinlin
Editorial Assistant: Carly Czech
Marketing Manager: Wendy Albert
Production Supervisor: Roberta Sherman
Editorial-Production and
  Electronic Composition Services: TexTech International
Composition Buyer: Linda Cox
Manufacturing Buyer: Debbie Rossi
Interior Design: Carol Somberg
Cover Administrator: Elena Sidorova

For related titles and support materials, visit our online catalog at www.ablongman.com.

Between the time website information is gathered and then published, it is not unusual for some sites to have closed. Also, the transcription of URLs can result in typographical errors. The publisher would appreciate notification where these errors occur so that they may be corrected in subsequent editions.

Library of Congress Cataloging-in-Publication Data

Toseland, Ronald W.
      An introduction to group work practice / Ronald W. Toseland, Robert F. Rivas. — 6th ed.
         p. cm.
      Includes bibliographical references and index.
         ISBN-13: 978-0-205-59382-8
         ISBN-10: 0-205-59382-8
         1. Social group work.   I. Rivas, Robert F.   II. Title.
      HV45.T68 2009
      361.4—dc22   2007045628

Printed in the United States of America

10   9   8   7   6   5   4   3   V069   12   11   10

To our parents
Stella and Ed
Marg and Al

Contents

Preface   xvii

part I
The Knowledge Base of Group Work Practice   1

chapter 1

Introduction   3

Organization of the Text   3

The Focus of Group Work Practice   4

Values and Ethics in Group Work Practice   6

Practice Values   6

Practice Ethics   9

Definition of Group Work   11

Classifying Groups   13

Formed and Natural Groups   13

Purpose and Group Work   13

Treatment and Task Groups   14

Group versus Individual Efforts   16

Advantages and Disadvantages of Treatment Groups   16

Advantages and Disadvantages of Task Groups   18

A Typology of Treatment and Task Groups   19

Treatment Groups   20

Support Groups   *20*

Educational Groups   *23*

Growth Groups   *24*

Therapy Groups   *25*

Socialization Groups   *26*

Self-Help Groups   *27*

Task Groups   29

Groups to Meet Client Needs   *29*

Groups to Meet Organizational Needs   *36*

Groups to Meet Community Needs   *40*

chapter 2

Historical Developments   45

Knowledge from Group Work Practice: Treatment Groups   45

Differences between Casework and Group Work   *46*

Intervention Targets   *47*

The Weakening of Group Work   *48*

Current Practice Trends   *49*

Divergent and Unified Practice Models   *51*

Knowledge from Group Work Practice: Task Groups   53

Knowledge from Social Science Research   53

Influential Theories   56

Systems Theory   *56*

Psychodynamic Theory   *58*

Learning Theory   *59*

Field Theory   *61*

Social Exchange Theory   *62*

chapter 3

Understanding Group Dynamics   64

The Development of Helpful Group Dynamics   64

Group Dynamics   65

Communication and Interaction Patterns   *65*

Group Cohesion   74

Social Integration and Influence   78

Group Culture   83

Stages of Group Development   86

chapter 4

Leadership   92

Leadership and Power   93

Theories of Group Leadership   95

Factors Influencing Group Leadership   95

Effective Leadership   97

An Interactional Model of Leadership   98

Purposes of the Group   99

Type of Problem   99

The Environment   100

The Group as a Whole   101

The Group Members   102

The Group Leader   103

Group Leadership Skills   104

Facilitating Group Processes   105

Data Gathering and Assessment   109

Action Skills   111

Learning Group Leadership Skills   118

Leadership Style   119

Coleadership   123

chapter 5

Leadership and Diversity   128

Approaches to Multicultural Group Work   128

Developing Cultural Sensitivity   129

Assessing Cultural Influences on Group Behavior   133

Intervening with Sensitivity to Diversity   139

part II
The Planning Stage   149

chapter 6

Planning the Group   151

Planning Focus   151
Planning Model for Group Work   152
Establishing the Group's Purpose   153
Assessing Potential Sponsorship and Membership   154
Recruiting Members   160
Composing the Group   163
Orienting Members   170
Contracting   171
Preparing the Environment   173
Planning for Virtual Groups   175
Preparing a Written Group Proposal   181

part III
The Beginning Stage   185

chapter 7

The Group Begins   187

Objectives in the Beginning Stage   188

Introducing New Members   189

Defining the Purpose of the Group   193

Confidentiality   195

Helping Members Feel a Part of the Group   197

Guiding the Development of the Group   197

Task and Socioemotional Focus   202

Goal Setting in Group Work   203

Contracting   205

Facilitating Members' Motivation   207

Addressing Ambivalence and Resistance   207

Working with Involuntary Clients   211

Anticipating Obstacles   213

chapter 8

Assessment   216

Definition of Assessment   216

Relationship to Individual Assessment   217

The Assessment Process   218

How Much Information?   218

Diagnostic Labels   219

Assessment Focus   220

Assessing the Functioning of Group Members   221

Methods for Assessing Group Members   222

Assessing the Functioning of the Group as a Whole   229

Methods for Assessing the Group as a Whole   235

Assessing the Group's Environment   241

Assessing the Sponsoring Organization   242

Assessing the Interorganizational Environment   244

Assessing the Community Environment   244

Linking Assessment to Intervention   246

part IV
The Middle Stage   251

chapter 9

Treatment Groups: Foundation Methods   253

Middle-Stage Skills   253
Preparing for Group Meetings   254
Structuring the Group's Work   257
Involving and Empowering Group Members   261
Helping Members Achieve Their Goals   263
Working with Reluctant and Resistant Group Members during the Middle Phase   272
Monitoring and Evaluating the Group's Progress   275

chapter 10

Treatment Groups: Specialized Methods   279

Intervening with Group Members   279
Intrapersonal Interventions   279
Interpersonal Interventions   288
Environmental Interventions   295
Intervening in the Group as a Whole   301
Changing Communication and Interaction Patterns   302
Changing the Group's Attraction for Its Members   303
Using Social Integration Dynamics Effectively   305
Changing Group Culture   306
Changing the Group Environment   307
Increasing Agency Support for Group Work Services   308
Links with Interagency Networks   309
Increasing Community Awareness   310

chapter 11

Task Groups: Foundation Methods   313

The Ubiquitous Task Group   313

Leading Task Groups   314

Preparing for Group Meetings   315

Sharing Information   318

Enhancing Involvement and Commitment   320

Developing Information   321

Dealing with Conflict   323

Making Effective Decisions   326

Understanding Task Groups' Political Ramifications   329

Monitoring and Evaluating   330

Problem Solving   331

A Model for Effective Problem Solving   331

Identifying a Problem   332

Developing Goals   337

Collecting Data   338

Developing Plans   339

Selecting the Best Plan   339

Implementing the Plan   340

chapter 12

Task Groups: Specialized Methods   344

Small Organizational Groups   344

Brainstorming   344

Variations on Brainstorming   348

Focus Groups   349

Nominal Group Technique   353

Multiattribute Utility Analysis   357

Quality Circles, Quality Improvement Teams, and Self-Managed Work Teams   361

Large Organizational Groups   364

Parliamentary Procedure   364

Phillips' 66   367

Methods for Working with Community Groups   370

Mobilization Strategies   370

Capacity-Building Strategies   372

Social Action Strategies   373

part V
The Ending Stage   377

chapter 13

Ending the Group's Work   379

Factors That Influence Group Endings   379

The Process of Ending   380

Planned and Unplanned Termination   380

Member Termination   381

Worker Termination   383

Ending Group Meetings   383

Ending the Group as a Whole   385

Learning from Members   386

Maintaining and Generalizing Change Efforts   386

Reducing Group Attraction   392

Feelings about Ending   393

Planning for the Future   395

Making Referrals   396

chapter 14

Evaluation   400

The Practitioner's Dilemma   400

Why Evaluate? The Group Worker's View   401

Reasons for Conducting Evaluations   401

Organizational Encouragement and Support   402

Time Considerations   *402*

Selecting an Evaluation Method   *402*

Evaluation Methods   403

Evaluations for Planning a Group   403

Obtaining Program Information   *403*

Needs Assessment   *404*

Evaluations for Monitoring a Group   405

Monitoring Methods   *405*

Evaluations for Developing a Group   412

Single-System Methods   *413*

Case Study Methods   *416*

Evaluations for Determining Effectiveness and Efficiency   417

Evaluation Measures   420

Choosing Measures   *421*

Types of Measures   *422*

chapter 15

Case Examples   427

A Caregiver Support Group   427

The Support Component   *427*

The Educational Component   *428*

The Coping-Skills Component   *428*

The Problem-Solving Component   *429*

A Community Coalition   439

The Planning Stage   *440*

The Beginning Stage   *441*

The Middle Stage   *446*

The Ending Stage   *450*

appendix a

1. Guidelines for Ethics   453

2. Ethical Guidelines for Group Counselors   456

3. Standards for Social Work Practice with Groups   458

appendix b

Films and Videotapes   471

appendix c

Group Announcements   474

appendix d

Outline for a Group Proposal   476

appendix e

An Example of a Treatment Group Proposal   477

appendix f

An Example of a Task Group Proposal   479

appendix g

Suggested Readings on Program Activities   481

Bibliography   *485*
Name Index   *523*
Subject Index   *533*

Preface

We continue to be gratified by the wide use of this text by professionals, as well as by educators and students in undergraduate and graduate courses in schools of social work throughout the United States and the world. The third edition of the book has been translated into Japanese. In preparing the sixth edition, we have revised each chapter, thoroughly updated reference material, and added new content.

Because we remain committed to presenting a coherent and organized overview of group work practice from a generalist practice perspective, the sixth edition continues to include typologies illustrating group work practice with task and treatment groups at the micro-, meso-, and macrolevel. In this edition, we have added self-help groups to the treatment typology, reflecting their popularity in today's society. Our research and practice focus mostly on treatment groups, and the sixth edition continues to present our interest in improving practice with these types of groups. In recent years, for example, we have done research on the uses of virtual group formats (teleconference and Internet groups) and have included an updated and expanded section on virtual groups in this edition.

Over the years, we have been especially pleased that our text has been used by educators who are dedicated to improving task group practice within social work. Group work is a neglected area of social work practice, especially practice with task groups. Most social workers spend a great deal of time in meetings of various sorts, and many social workers have leadership responsibilities in these groups. Group work is also essential for effective macro social work practice, and therefore, we have continued to emphasize practice with community groups. The sixth edition also continues our focus on three focal areas of practice: (1) the individual group member, (2) the group as a whole, and (3) the environment in which the group functions. We continue to emphasize the importance of the latter two focal areas because our experiences in supervising group workers and students and conducting workshops for professionals have revealed that the dynamics of a group as a whole and the environment in which groups function are often a neglected aspect of group work practice.

We are aware that students and practitioners want practical suggestions about how to proceed when facilitating treatment and task groups during each state of their development. Thus, we expanded our emphasis on practice principles and leadership skills and have highlighted some practice principles. We have also added case examples within many of the chapters in order to illustrate some of the practice principles used in each stage of social group work. Also included is an expanded section on working with reluctant and involuntary group members and sharing leadership power with members.

NEW TO THIS EDITION

- New section on working with self-help groups.

- Expanded and updated research-based literature throughout exposes students to more evidence-based practice and includes many examples from the authors' own practice.

- Contains many more short case examples throughout the text, allowing students to see how content can be applied in practice settings, helping to reinforce chapter content.

- Greater focus on short-term psycho-educational groups.

- New techniques such as visualization and deep breathing added to the working stage of treatment groups.

- Changes the order of the group development stage model so that the chapter on evaluation follows the chapter on ending the group.

- A new section on working with involuntary group members prepares students for leadership roles in groups with mandated clients in the beginning as well as the middle stages of group work.

- New second color makes the interior of the book more visually appealing and helps to highlight charts, graphs, etc.

- NEW for students: MyHelpingKit—a Media Supplement that contains chapter by chapter Learning Objectives, Chapter Summaries, Flashcards with Key Terms, Interactive Video Clips, Cases, Career Explorations, and Research Navigator™. Available at no additional cost to the student when value-packaged with a new text. Contact your local Pearson rep for more details, www.ablongman.com/replocator.

FOR INSTRUCTORS

- An Instructor's Manual/Test Bank is available with this text. Please contact your local Pearson rep to obtain this.

- Appendix B: Contains suggestions for group work films and videotapes.

- Appendix G: Contains Program Activities for groups of children and adolescents.

FOR STUDENTS

- MyHelpingKit—a new Media Supplement that contains chapter by chapter Learning Objectives, Chapter Summaries, Flashcards with Key Terms, Interactive Video Clips, Cases, Career Explorations, and Research Navigator. Available at no additional cost to the student, when value-packaged with a new text.

The ideas expressed in this book have evolved during many years of study, practice, and research. Some of the earliest and most powerful influences that have shaped this effort have come about through our relationships with Bernard Hill, Alan Klein, Sheldon Rose, and Max Siporin. Their contributions to the development of our thinking are evident throughout this book. Perhaps even more important, however, was their support and encouragement in the early years of our professional development and their belief in our ability to make a contribution to knowledge about group work practice.

The ideas in this book were also greatly influenced by Albert Alissi, Martin Birnbaum, Leonard Brown, Burton Gummer, Margaret Hartford, Motier Haskins, Grafton Hull, Jr., Norma Lang, Catherine Papell, William Reid, Beulah Rothman, Jarrold Shapiro, and Peter Vaughan. We would also like to thank the reviewers: Cheryl K. Brandsen, Calvin College; Jacqueline Corcoran, Virginia Commonwealth University; Susan Jakubowicz, New York University; Nancy P. Kropf, Georgia State University; and Matthew T. Theriot, University of Tennessee-Knoxville. Their comments, suggestions, and reactions were invaluable in improving the quality of the book. We are also indebted to the many practitioners and students with whom we have worked over the years. Reviewing practice experiences, discussing and analyzing audiotapes of group meetings, and providing consultation and supervision to the practitioners with whom we work on group research projects have helped us to clarify and improve the ideas presented in this text.

We would also like to acknowledge the material support and encouragement given to us by our respective educational institutions. The administrative staff of the School of Social Welfare, University at Albany, State University of New York, and Siena College have played important roles in helping us to accomplish this project. In particular, we would like to acknowledge the support of Dean Katharine Briar-Lawson, University at Albany. We are also deeply grateful to Pam Laverty and to Michelle Zinoman, MSW, for their help with the preparation of this new edition.

Most of all, however, we are indebted to our spouses, Sheryl Holland and Donna Allingham Rivas. Their personal and professional insights have done much to enrich this book. Without their continuous support and encouragement, we would not have been able to complete this work. A special note of thanks also goes to Rebecca, Stacey, and Heather for sacrificing some of their dads' time.

R. W. T.
R. F. R.

An Introduction to
Group Work Practice

part I

The Knowledge Base of Group Work Practice

chapter **1**

Introduction

chapter **2**

Historical Developments

chapter **3**

Understanding Group Dynamics

chapter **4**

Leadership

chapter **5**

Leadership and Diversity

Introduction

This text focuses on the practice of group work by professional social workers. Group work entails the deliberate use of intervention strategies and group processes to accomplish individual, group, and community goals using the value base and ethical practice principles of the social work profession. As one prepares to become an effective social work practitioner, it is important to realize the effect that groups have on people's lives. It is not possible to be a member of society without becoming a member of numerous groups and being influenced by others (Falck, 1988). Although it is possible to live in an isolated manner on the fringes of groups, our social nature makes this neither desirable nor healthy.

Groups provide the structure on which communities and the larger society are built. They provide formal and informal structure in the workplace. But more important, they provide a means through which relationships with significant others are carried out. Participation in family groups, peer groups, and classroom groups helps members learn acceptable norms of social behavior, engage in satisfying social relationships, identify personal goals, and derive a variety of other benefits that result from participating in closely knit social systems. Experiences in social, church, recreation, and other work groups are essential in the development and maintenance of people and society. Yet Putnam (2000) points out that there has been a sharp decline in participation in clubs and other civic organizations, and that social capital is not valued in contemporary society. One goal of this book is to underscore the importance of groups as fundamental building blocks for a connected, vibrant society.

ORGANIZATION OF THE TEXT

Group work can be understood as a series of activities carried out by the worker during the life of a group. We have found that it is helpful to conceptualize these activities as being a part of six developmental stages:

1. Planning
2. Beginning

3. Assessment
4. Middle
5. Ending
6. Evaluation

Groups exhibit certain properties and processes during each stage of their development. The group worker's task is to engage in activities that facilitate the growth and development of the group and its members during each developmental stage. This book is divided into five parts. Part I focuses on the knowledge base needed to practice with groups. The remaining four parts are organized around each of these six stages of group work. Practice examples illustrating each developmental stage can be found at the end of Chapters 6 through 14.

THE FOCUS OF GROUP WORK PRACTICE

Social work practitioners use group work skills to help meet the needs of individual group members, the group as a whole, and the community. In this text, group work is conceptualized from a generalist practice perspective. Group work involves the following aspects.

Group Work Practice

- Practice with a broad range of treatment and task groups
- A focus on individual group members, the group as a whole, and the group's environment
- Application of foundation knowledge and skills from generalist social work practice to a broad range of leadership and membership situations
- Integration and use of specialized knowledge and skills based on a comprehensive assessment of the needs of a particular group
- A recognition of the interactional and situational nature of leadership

This text is firmly grounded in a generalist approach to practice. To accomplish the broad mission and goals of the social work profession, generalist practitioners are expected to possess basic competencies that enable them to intervene effectively with individuals, families, groups, organizations, and communities. This text is designed to help generalist practitioners understand how group work can be used to help individuals, families, groups, organizations, and communities function as effectively as possible. This text is also grounded in an evidenced based approach to practice. To the extent possible, all suggestions made are based on evidence accumulated from research studies in the literature.

Most group work texts are focused on the use of groups for clinical practice, and many focus only on therapy or support groups, with little attention to social, recreational, or educational purposes. Also, scant mention is made of committees, teams, and other administrative groups that social workers are expected to participate in as members and leaders. Despite the distinctive emphasis of the social work profession on the interface between individuals and their social environment, in most group work texts, even less attention is paid to social action groups, coalitions, and other community groups. This text examines work with a broad range of groups in generalist practice with individuals, organizations, and communities.

Some prominent group workers (Hartford, 1971; Klein, 1972) focus on the group as a whole as the unit of intervention and place less emphasis on work with individuals in the group. Others place their emphasis on changing individual group members within the group context (Rose, 1998; Sundel, Glasser, Sarri, & Vinter, 1985). Both perspectives are useful. When leading any group, workers should direct their attention to individuals, the group as a whole, and the community in which the group functions. The worker focuses on individual members to help them accomplish their goals. The worker intervenes with the group as a whole to achieve an optimal level of group functioning and to ensure that the group accomplishes its purposes. The worker also assesses the group's environment and decides whether to help the group adapt to it or change it.

The purpose of the group helps determine the emphasis that each focal area should receive. For example, in a support group for recently separated people, the worker might focus on the development of mutual aid among members of the group as a whole. In an assertion training group, the worker might focus on assessing members' specific skills and deficits and developing individualized treatment plans.

In both cases, however, other focal areas should not be neglected. For example, in the support group it is necessary to help individual members develop plans for dealing with specific problems they are facing. In the assertion training group, it is important to enhance group cohesion, mutual sharing, and mutual aid in the group as a whole.

In both groups, attention must also be given to the community in which the groups function. For example, a close examination of the community in which members of the assertion training group function might suggest a need to make community services more responsive to members of the group. This may, in turn, lead to the development of a social action group to address this problem. Later, this text examines in detail these three focal areas.

Another aspect of group work practice is that workers draw on a broad base of knowledge and skills from generalist practice, which they apply to their work with a broad range of groups. The generalist approach emphasizes that social workers are called on to perform many roles in their professional lives. It suggests that there are foundation knowledge and skills that transcend specific roles. For example, in-depth knowledge about human development and skill in empathic responding are essential for effective work with individuals, families, groups, and communities. Although foundation knowledge and skills are described throughout this text, specialized knowledge and skills are often needed when practicing with special populations such as children, adolescents, and older adults. Therefore, this text also presents specialized knowledge and skills useful for practice with these populations.

Most experienced practitioners continue to learn by exposure to different approaches to group work. Although some approaches, such as behavioral and humanistic, are not easily integrated with one another, aspects of divergent approaches can often be integrated in a particular practice situation. A major tenet of the generalist approach is that practice should be based on a comprehensive assessment of the needs of a particular group in a particular situation. An integration of practice approaches is often preferable to using a single approach. Exclusive adherence to one approach may work well for a group with a particular set of needs, but it may not work well when leading a group with other needs. Rigid adherence to one approach tends to make a worker oblivious to other potentially useful methods and to distort a worker's assessment of a situation. A worker might mistakenly attempt to fit data from a situation to a particular practice approach rather than choosing the practice approach to fit the situation. For these reasons, group workers can be most effective when they are familiar with several approaches to group work and when they apply specialized knowledge and skills differentially depending on the particular group work endeavor.

This approach also recognizes the interactional nature of the helping process. A static, prescriptive approach to group work practice often appeals to novice practitioners because of its simplicity but does not match the complexity and diversity of the real world of group work practice. The leadership model presented in Chapter 4 presents some of the factors that workers should consider when deciding how to proceed with a group.

VALUES AND ETHICS IN GROUP WORK PRACTICE

Practice Values

In social work, the focus of group work practice is influenced by a system of personal and professional values. These values affect workers' styles of intervention and the skills they use in working with clients. They also affect clients' reactions to the worker's efforts. Despite the emphasis on ethics and values in the new *Curriculum Standards* published by the Council on Social Work Education (Commission on Accreditation. 2001) found that few social group work course syllabi gave any emphasis to the topic of values or ethics in group work practice.

Values are beliefs that delineate preferences about how one ought to behave. They refer to a goal that is worth attaining (Rokeach, 1968). There is no such thing as value-free group work practice. All group workers operate on the basis of certain specific assumptions and values regarding the nature of human beings, the role of members, and the role of the group leader. Values influence the methods used to accomplish group and individual goals. Even a leader who is completely permissive and nondirective reveals the values embodied in such a stance.

A worker's actions in the group are affected by contextual values, client value systems, and the worker's personal value system. The context in which the group functions affects the values exhibited in the group. Contextual sources of values include the values of society, values of the agency sponsoring the group, and values of the social work profession. Brill and Levine (2005) have identified these values that are dominant in American society.

American Values

- Judeo-Christian doctrine with its emphasis on the dignity and worth of people and people's responsibility for their neighbor
- Democratic values that emphasize equality and participation, including men's and women's rights to life, liberty, and the pursuit of happiness
- The Puritan ethic, which emphasizes men's and women's responsibility for themselves, and the central role of work in a moral life
- Social Darwinism, which emphasizes the survival of the strongest and the fittest in a long-term evolutionary process

The organization and the community that are sponsoring the group are also part of the contextual value system that can influence a worker's stance toward the group. The health and social service organizations sponsoring the group have a history and a tradition with regard to the services they provide.

Before proposing to begin a group, the worker should become familiar with the agency's formal and informal values, which are embodied in its mission, goals, policies, procedures, and practices. Are treatment groups a preferred method of delivering therapeutic services? Are decisions often made in task groups consisting of staff members, or are most decisions made by agency administrators without staff input? Becoming aware of the policies, procedures, and practices regarding the use of groups in a particular agency can help the worker prepare for possible resistance and evaluate and use sources of support within the agency.

The community where the group conducts its business can also influence the functioning of the group. For example, community standards and traditions, as well as racial, ethnic, and socioeconomic composition, differ widely among communities. When planning a group, the worker needs to consider how these aspects of communities are likely to influence the group and its members.

The worker and the group are also affected by professional values. Important social work values summarized by Siporin (1975) include respecting the worth and dignity of the individual, respecting a person's autonomy and self-direction, facilitating a person's participation in the helping process, maintaining a nonjudgmental attitude, ensuring equal access to services and social provisions, and affirming the interdependence of the individual and society.

Beyond the values held by all professional social work practitioners, group workers share a special concern and interest in values that are basic to group work practice. Some of the key values of group work have been stated by Gisela Konopka (1983). She suggests that all group workers should agree on the importance of the following values.

Group Work Values

- Participation of and positive relations among people of different color, creed, age, national origin, and social class in the group
- The value of cooperation and mutual decision making embodied in the principles of a participatory democracy
- The importance of individual initiative within the group
- The importance of freedom to participate, including expressing thoughts and feelings about matters of concern to individual members or the group as a whole, and having the right to be involved in the decision-making process of the group
- The value of high individualization in the group so that each member's unique concerns are addressed

These values are not absent in other aspects of social work practice, but in group work they are of central importance. In addition to these five core values, we have found four additional values to be fundamental to practice with any type of task or treatment group.

Four Key Values

- Respect and dignity—We value the worth and dignity of all group members no matter how devalued or stigmatized they may be by society. This includes valuing members' contributions to the life of the group and adhering to all aspects of the National Association of Social Workers (NASW) code of ethics.

- Solidarity and mutual aid—We value the power and promise of relationships to help members grow and develop, to help them heal, to satisfy their needs for human contact and connectedness, and to promote a sense of unity and community.
- Empowerment—We value the power of the group to help members feel good about themselves and to enable them to use their abilities to help themselves and to make a difference in their communities.
- Understanding, respect, and camaraderie among people from diverse backgrounds—We value the ability of groups to help enrich members by acquainting them to people from other backgrounds. Members' respect and appreciation for each other grow as their relationships deepen over the life of a group. Thus, one powerful aspect of social group work is that it helps to decrease ignorance, misunderstanding, and prejudice among people from diverse backgrounds.

In addition to these core values, the worker and the members bring their own unique set of values to the group. Part of the worker's task is to help members clarify their values and to identify and resolve value conflicts between the leader and members, among members, and among members and the larger society. More information about resolving conflicts is discussed in Chapters 4 and 11.

The worker should be especially sensitive to the effects that cultural diversity have on valued behavior in groups. For example, Lewis and Ho (1975) point out that in Native American culture, although cooperation is an important value, it is considered impolite to offer advice, help, or opinion to someone unless it is solicited. Giordano (1973) suggests that group members with Irish ethnic backgrounds often prefer not to express their feelings openly, whereas Italian Americans are more likely to express their feelings freely.

Workers' personal value systems also affect how they practice. If workers are uncomfortable discussing certain value-laden topics, or if they impose their own values on the group, their work will be seriously impaired. Similarly, if they are not aware of the implications of their values, they are likely to get into conflicts with members who have different values.

Workers who are not aware of their own values will also have difficulty when faced with ambiguous and value-laden situations. Sometimes the goals of the worker, the agency, the community, and the group members differ. This often occurs with involuntary clients who are receiving the service of a worker at the request of law-enforcement officials or others in the community who find the client's behavior unacceptable. The clearer workers are about their own values and their own purposes and stances in relation to working with the group, the easier it will be for them to sort through conflicting goals and make their own purposes known to group members.

One of the best ways for workers to become aware of their own values and their own stance in working with a group is to obtain supervision. Although workers will never become value-free, supervision can help them become aware of the values they bring to the group. Supervision can help workers modify or change values that are not consistent with those of the social work profession or helpful in their practice with groups of people. Value-clarification exercises can also help workers identify personal and professional values that might influence their work with a group (Gibbs & Gambrill, 1998; Loewenberg & Dolgoff, 1996; Smith, 1977).

Practice Ethics

The NASW has developed a code of ethics to guide the practice of its members. The code of ethics is an operational statement of the central values of the social work profession. Social workers who lead groups should be thoroughly familiar with it. It is available directly from NASW and is reproduced in many social work practice textbooks.

Corey and Corey (2006) point out that a code of ethics specifically for group workers is a helpful adjunct to the more general codes of ethics developed by professional associations. Unfortunately, a code of ethics specifically for social work practice with groups has not been developed (Dolgoff & Skolnik, 1992; Commission on Accreditation. 2001). Two organizations, the Association for Specialists in Group Work (ASGW) and the American Group Psychotherapy Association (AGPA), have taken the lead in developing specific codes of ethics for interdisciplinary group work practice. The codes of ethics of these associations appear in Appendixes A1 and A2. Both codes focus on three main areas: (1) informed consent, (2) leader competence and training, and (3) the appropriate conduct of group meetings.

The first area includes telling members about the purpose and goals of the group and giving them information such as the potential risks of participation; the cost, timing, and duration of sessions; whether participation is voluntary; what is expected of group members during meetings; procedures to ensure confidentiality; and screening and termination procedures. Social workers who provide services to groups face special confidentiality challenges when attempting to comply with standard 1.07 of the NASW code of ethics, which focuses on confidentiality issues. Workers should inform members that they cannot guarantee that group members will not share confidential material outside the group. (Fallon, 2006; Lasky & Riva, 2006) Nevertheless, workers should be aware that breaches of confidentiality in groups increase their liability (Reamer, 2001). They should guard against breaches of confidentiality by having all members of the group pledge that they will adhere to confidentiality policies. Reamer (1998) also suggests that workers have a firm policy not to talk individually about any other group member outside of the group context. This policy builds trust and avoids perceptions of favoritism or special alliances with certain members. Some ethical dilemmas faced by group workers are described cogently by Bergeron and Gray (2003).

In a survey of 300 group psychotherapists, Roback, Ochoa, Bloch, and Purdon (1992) found that the limits of confidentiality are rarely discussed with potential group members even though breaches of confidentiality by members are fairly common. Group leaders may also be required to report certain information, such as child abuse, even without the permission of a group member. To avoid ethical and legal problems associated with a group leader's failure to provide sufficient information about the limits of confidentiality, Roback, Moore, Bloch, and Shelton (1996), Reamer (1998) and Fallon (2006) suggest having members and the leader sign an informed consent form (Table 1.1).

The second area covered in codes of ethics for group practitioners includes ensuring that workers have the proper education, training, and experience to lead a particular group. Practitioners should not offer a group, or use a procedure or technique within a group, without sufficient education, experience, and supervision to ensure that it is implemented properly. Practitioners should seek out additional supervision when they anticipate or encounter difficulties with a particular group.

As they continue to practice, group workers have the additional responsibility to engage in ongoing professional development activities including workshops, seminars, and other

TABLE 1.1 ● *Informed Consent Form*

INFORMED CONSENT FORM

1. The law may require the therapist to notify the authorities if you reveal that you are abusing children or if you express an intent to harm yourself or to harm other people.

2. If you reveal secrets in the group, the secrets may be told outside the group by other members of the group. If your secrets are told outside the group, people you know may learn your secrets. You could be hurt emotionally and economically if your secrets are told outside the group.

3. Other group members may tell their secrets to you. If you tell the secrets outside the group, the member whose secrets you tell might have legal grounds to sue you for money for telling the secrets.

4. If you violate the confidentiality rules of the group, the group leader may expel you from the group.

I have read and fully understand the information provided above about the risks of group psychotherapy. I have discussed the risks with the group leader, and I have had the chance to ask all the questions that I wished to ask about the matters listed above and about all other matters. The group leader has answered all my questions in a way that satisfies me. I understand that I can leave the group at any time. By signing this document, I agree to accept the risks listed in this form and the risks explained to me by the group leader.

SIGNATURE OF THE GROUP MEMBER	DATE
SIGNATURE OF GROUP LEADER	DATE
SIGNATURE OF WITNESS	DATE

Reprinted by permission from the American Group Psychotherapy Association, Inc.

professional educational opportunities. They should also keep up with current clinical and empirical findings that relate to their ongoing work with group members.

The third broad area in both codes of ethics focuses on ethical principles for the conduct of group meetings.

Ethical Principles

- Screening procedures lead to the selection of members whose needs and goals can be met by the group
- Workers help members develop and pursue therapeutic goals
- Workers discuss whether the proceedings of the group are confidential and make provisions so that they are kept confidential

- Members are protected from physical threats, intimidation, the imposition of worker and member values, and other forms of coercion and peer pressure that are not therapeutic
- Members are treated fairly and equitably
- Workers avoid exploiting members for their own gain
- Appropriate referrals are made when the needs of a particular member cannot be met in the group
- The worker engages in ongoing assessment, evaluation, and follow-up of members to ensure that the group meets their needs

Galinsky and Schopler (1977) point out that violation of these ethical principles can be damaging to group members. They suggest, for example, that the harm encounter groups do to some members can be traced to inappropriate screening procedures and the failure of group workers to describe the risks and requirements of group membership. Similarly, Harold Lewis (1982) points out that although the NASW code of ethics indicates the primacy of clients' interests, workers sometimes choose to give primacy to their own definitions of clients' needs or to give some group members' needs primacy over the needs of other members. For example, it has been found that both unsolicited aggressive confrontation and passive abdication of authority are associated with damaging group experiences (Smokowski, Rose, & Bacallao, 2001; Smokowski, Rose, Todar, & Reardon, 1999). Overall, a safe, low-conflict environment is related to positive outcomes in treatment groups (Kivlighan & Tarrant, 2001).

Lakin (1991) suggests that even well-intentioned, enthusiastic group workers can subtly violate ethical principles and that these violations can be harmful to members. He presents evidence, for example, that pressures to conform can lead members to suppress particular opinions, thoughts, or points of view simply because they clash with the dominant ideology expressed in the group. To guard against these potential ethical violations, he suggests that all group workers should consider the extent to which (1) workers' values are consonant with the needs and problems of group members, (2) workers are pushing their own agendas without regard to the needs and wishes of group members, and (3) each member's needs are individualized rather than treated as identical to needs of other members.

In 2006, the Association for the Advancement of Social Work with Groups adopted a revised set of standards for social work groups. The standards include (1) the essential knowledge and values that underlie social work practice with groups, (2) the tasks that should be accomplished in each phase of group work, and (3) the knowledge that is needed to carry out the tasks in each phase. The standards provide social workers with needed guidance for the effective and ethical practice of social group work, and they help group workers to avoid unintended ethical violations. The standards have been reprinted in Appendix A3.

DEFINITION OF GROUP WORK

Although there are divergent approaches to group work within the social work profession and allied disciplines, a generalist approach suggests that each approach has its merits and particular practice applications. The broad definition offered in this chapter allows beginning practitioners to understand the boundaries of group work, specialized approaches, and many practice applications. *Group work* can be defined as

> *Goal-directed activity with small treatment and task groups aimed at meeting socioemotional needs and accomplishing tasks. This activity is directed to individual members of a group and to the group as a whole within a system of service delivery.*

The definition describes group work as goal-directed activity, which refers to planned, orderly worker activities carried out in the context of professional practice with people. Goal-directed activity has many purposes. For example, group workers may aim to support or educate members, help them socialize and achieve personal growth, or provide treatment for their problems and concerns.

Workers may also help members of a group develop leadership skills so that they can take increasing responsibility for the group's development. Workers should also enable their groups to change the social environment. This includes helping members gain greater control over the organizations and communities that affect their lives. Some writers advocate a person-in-situation view of practice (Anderson, 1997; Glassman & Kates, 1990; Shulman, 1999). Others focus on techniques of individual change within small groups (MacKenzie, 1990, 1996; Rose, 1989, 1998; Rose & LeCroy, 1991). Both approaches are valuable, and attention should be given to both when groups set their goals.

The next component of the definition of group work refers to working with small groups of people. In this text, the term *small group* implies the ability of members to identify themselves as members, to engage in interaction, and to exchange thoughts and feelings among themselves through verbal, nonverbal, and written communication processes. Members can meet face-to-face, by telephone or video, or through computer networks.

The definition of group work also indicates that workers practice with both treatment and task groups. Most workers are called on to help clients meet their personal needs and to help their agency or organization accomplish its tasks. For example, most direct service workers have many opportunities to work with both treatment and task groups. Within treatment and task groups, attention should be paid to meeting members' socioemotional needs as well as to accomplishing tasks.

Our definition of group work also emphasizes that the worker should have a dual focus within any group: goal-directed activities with individual members and with the group as a whole. Although some writers favor working with the goals of individual members (Rose, 1989, 1998; Rose & LeCroy, 1991), and others emphasize working with the group as a whole as the primary focus of attention (Klein, 1972), few hold views that are mutually exclusive. Writers who emphasize individual members as the primary client system usually note the importance of the group as a whole. Those who focus on the group as the primary client system frequently note the importance of individualizing the members' needs, concerns, and goals. Both individuals and groups have life histories, developmental patterns, needs, goals, and characteristic behavior patterns that should be of concern to the worker. Therefore, both individual members and the group as a whole should receive the attention of the worker.

The final portion of the definition of group work emphasizes that groups do not exist in a vacuum. They exist in relation to a community that sponsors, legitimizes, and influences their purposes and in relation to an existing service delivery system. Even self-help groups and groups conducted in private practice are influenced by organizational and community support, sponsorship, and sanction.

There is an exchange of influence between a group and its sponsoring agency. A group is often influenced by its sponsoring organization's resources, mission, goals, and policies.

At the same time, a group may be the catalyst for a needed change in agency policies or procedures.

● **CASE EXAMPLE** *A Support Group for New Parents*

A Catholic Family Service Agency decided to form a group for new parents. However, because of the large number of parents that could possibly attend, the agency decided to limit membership in the support group for new parents to a specific geographic area served by the agency. Because of the large number of single parents interested in attending the group meetings, the agency decided to offer child care during meetings.

In this example, the agency influences the composition of the group by limiting the parents attending to a specific geographic area. At the same time, the group influences the agency by ensuring that child care is available during meetings.

CLASSIFYING GROUPS

To understand the breadth of group work practice, it is helpful to become familiar with the variety of groups in practice settings. Because there are so many kinds of groups that workers may be called on to lead, it is helpful to distinguish among them. In the following two sections, distinctions are made among groups on the basis of whether they are formed or occur naturally and whether they are treatment or task oriented.

Formed and Natural Groups

Formed groups are those that come together through some outside influence or intervention. They usually have some sponsorship or affiliation and are convened for a particular purpose. Some examples of formed groups are therapy groups, educational groups, committees, social action groups, and teams. *Natural groups* come together spontaneously on the basis of naturally occurring events, interpersonal attraction, or the mutually perceived needs of members. They often lack formal sponsorship. Natural groups include family groups, peer groups, friendship networks, street gangs, and cliques.

This text is primarily concerned with formed groups. Natural groups such as families are neither planned nor constructed by a group worker. Generally, natural groups have a longer developmental history, which has unique implications for the relationships among members and the interventions used by workers. For these reasons, a separate body of knowledge has been developed for work with natural groups such as families.

Despite the differences between formed and natural groups, many of the skills and techniques presented in this text are readily applicable to work with natural groups, and we encourage group work practitioners to use them. Some efforts have already been made in this regard, such as attempts to use group work skills in working with the family unit (Bell, 1981), working with gangs (Klein, 1997), and enhancing the social networks of persons who are socially isolated (Maguire, 1991).

Purpose and Group Work

Formed groups can be classified according to the purposes for which they are organized. The term *purpose* can be defined as the general aims of a group. The importance of purpose in group work cannot be overemphasized. According to Wilson (1976), "the nature of the framework for the practice of group work depends on the purpose of the group [that is] served" (p. 41). A group's purpose identifies the reasons for bringing members together. As Klein (1972) notes, "purpose guides group composition" (pp. 31–32). It also helps guide the group's selection of goal-directed activities and define the broad parameters of the services to be delivered.

In this text, the term *treatment group* is used to signify a group whose major purpose is to meet members' socioemotional needs. The purposes for forming treatment groups might include meeting members' needs for support, education, therapy, growth, and socialization. In contrast, the term *task group* is used to signify any group in which the overriding purpose is to accomplish a goal that is neither intrinsically nor immediately linked to the needs of the members of the group. Although the work of a task group may ultimately affect the members of the group, the primary purpose of task groups is to accomplish a goal that will affect a broader constituency, not just the members of the group.

Treatment and Task Groups

In classifying groups as either treatment or task oriented, it is important to consider how the two types differ. Table 1.2 points out some of the major differences between treatment and task groups in terms of selected characteristics. These include the following:

- The bond present in a group is based on the purpose for which it is convened. Members of treatment groups are bonded by their common needs and common situations. Task group members create a common bond by working together to accomplish a task, carry out a mandate, or produce a product. In both types of groups, common cultural, gender, racial, or ethnic characteristics can also help to form bonds among members.

- In treatment groups, roles are not set before the group forms, but develop through interaction among members. In task groups, members may take on roles through a process of interaction, but roles are more likely to be based on members' positions within the organization. Also, roles are frequently assigned by the group based on the tasks to be accomplished. Roles that may be assigned include chair or team leader, secretary, and fact finder.

- Communication patterns in treatment groups are open. Members are usually encouraged to interact with one another. Task group members are more likely to address their communications to the leader and to keep their communication focused on the task to be accomplished. In some task groups, the amount that members communicate on a particular agenda item may be limited by the worker. In other task groups, members may limit their own communication because they believe they will not be well received by the group.

- Treatment groups often have flexible procedures for meetings, including a warm-up period, a period for working on members' concerns, and a period for summarizing the group's work. Task groups are more likely to have formalized rules such as parliamentary procedure that govern how members conduct group business and reach decisions.

- Treatment groups are often composed of members with similar concerns, problems, and abilities. Task groups are often composed of members with the necessary resources and expertise to accomplish the group's mission.

- In treatment groups, members are expected to disclose their own concerns and problems. Therefore, self-disclosures may contain emotionally charged, personal concerns. In task groups, member self-disclosure is relatively infrequent. It is generally expected that

**TABLE 1.2 ● ** *A Comparison of Task and Treatment Groups*

Selected Characteristics	Type of Group	
	Treatment	**Task**
Bond	Members' personal needs	Task to be completed
Roles	Develop through interaction	Develop through interaction or are assigned
Communication patterns	Open, back-and-forth interaction based on members' needs	Focused on a task to be accomplished
Procedures	Flexible or formal, depending on the group	Formal agenda and rules
Composition	Based on common concerns, problems, or characteristics	Based on needed talents, expertise, or division of labor
Self-disclosure	Expected to be high	Expected to be low
Confidentiality	Proceedings usually private and kept within the group	Proceedings may be private but are sometimes open to the public
Evaluation	Success based on members' meeting treatment goals	Success based on members' accomplishing task or mandate, or producing a product

members will confine themselves to discussions about accomplishing the group's task and will not share intimate, personal concerns.

● Treatment group meetings are often confidential. Some task group meetings, such as the meetings of treatment conferences and cabinets, may be confidential, but the meetings of other task groups, such as committees and delegate councils, are often described in minutes that are circulated to interested persons and organizations.

● The criteria for evaluating success differ between treatment and task groups. Treatment groups are successful to the extent that they help members meet their individual treatment goals. Task groups are successful when they accomplish group goals, such as generating solutions to problems and making decisions, or when they develop group products, such as a report, a set of regulations, or a series of recommendations concerning a particular community issue.

● CASE EXAMPLE *Treatment and Task Group*

In one group, the worker meets with adults who have recently become parents for the first time. The purpose of this parenting group is to provide a forum for discussion about their adjustment to parenthood. In a second group, the worker brings together community representatives from several different social service agencies and school districts to study day-care resources for the purpose of making recommendations to a government agency regarding changes in government support for day-care for low-income children is to provide a forum for discussion about their adjustment to parenthood. In the second group, the worker brings together several community representatives to study day-care resources and make recommendations to a government agency regarding changes in government support for day care.

The parents' group is classified as a treatment group because it is convened to meet the personal needs of its members. The group is bonded by its common purpose and the common needs and concerns of its members. It is expected that friendships may develop among group members and that members will help each other in their adjustment to parenthood. It is also expected that the feeling level and the level of self-disclosure will be high because of the similar characteristics of the members and the problems they face. Because members may self-disclose about personal issues, the proceedings of the group are confidential. Roles develop on the basis of how members assist in accomplishing the purpose of the group and how members meet each other's needs.

Because parenting is a developmental phenomenon involving constant discovery and change, the procedures of the group are flexible to allow members to share their immediate weekly concerns. The parents' group is composed with the similarity of members' needs in mind. Patterns of communication focus on members' needs, such as adjusting to parenthood and becoming effective parents. To evaluate the success of the group, the worker focuses on members' satisfaction with the group experience and whether the group has met their needs.

In the group discussing day-care services, the focus is task oriented, and the purpose is external to the personal needs of the members. Members are bonded by the common cause of improving day-care services. They are expected to reveal their personal viewpoints only to the extent that they contribute to the group's task. Personal feelings are occasionally shared, but factual data are given greater weight. The group is publicized and seeks outside, expert testimony to contribute to its deliberations. Confidentiality is impractical because it would hinder the accomplishment of the group's task. Roles are assigned by the worker on the basis of members' preferences. For example, members are appointed to subcommittees to collect needed data. Roles develop on the basis of how each member contributes to the task of the group.

To facilitate an organized approach to the task, the group works from an agenda, which is published in advance to give participants time to prepare for the proceedings. To facilitate a division of labor and encourage different perspectives, the group is composed by selecting members who have some knowledge of day-care programs and other needed areas of expertise, such as zoning restrictions, local, state, and federal child-care regulations, and financing. Patterns of communication focus on the task rather than on members' personal concerns. In evaluating the effectiveness of the group, the worker examines the group's decisions, actions, written reports, and recommendations for clarity, thoroughness, and feasibility.

GROUP VERSUS INDIVIDUAL EFFORTS

There are several advantages and disadvantages to using a group rather than an individual effort to meet individual, organizational, and community needs. In describing these advantages and disadvantages, it is important to distinguish between the effectiveness and efficiency of treatment and task groups.

Advantages and Disadvantages of Treatment Groups

There are many advantages of social group work. The advantages of group treatment stem from the fact that in addition to the worker, members can be helpful to each other. Members provide opportunities for socialization and for validation and normalization of problems and concerns. The presence of others also gives members an opportunity to learn from the experience of peers, to receive feedback, and to have role models and practice partners who can help with efforts to change. Feedback from peers is often seen as more grounded and less coercive than when it is received from a paid professional worker who may not have experienced similar concerns or who may be viewed as an authority figure by reluctant or involuntary clients. Coining the term *helper-therapy principle,* Lieberman and Borman (1979) noted that those who provide help derive therapeutic benefit themselves. Mutual aid gives members an opportunity to share experiential knowledge and to gain insights vicariously.

Advantages of Group Treatment

- Empathy from multiple sources—vicarious identification with and understanding of members' situations by peers and the worker
- Feedback—multiple points of view shared by group members
- Helper-therapy—providing help and mutual support to other group members is therapeutic for the member who shares experiences and knowledge
- Hope—instillation of hope by other group members who have coped effectively with similar situations
- Mutual aid—members give and receive help
- Normalization—removal of stigma from problems seen as socially unacceptable by the larger society
- Practice of new behaviors—other members provide opportunities to try out new behaviors in the safe environment of the group
- Reality testing—sharing ways of being and getting feedback about whether they are realistic and socially acceptable
- Recapitulation—working through previously unsatisfactory relationships with family members, peers, and friends with the help of group members
- Recreation of the family of origin—group members serve as surrogate family and symbolically represent family members
- Resources—a wide pool of knowledge about concerns and the resources and services to help with these concerns
- Role models—members and the leader serve as models
- Solidarity—connectedness with other members
- Socialization—opportunities to overcome isolation and learn social skills from others
- Social support—support from other members of the group
- Transcendence—members sharing how they adapted to and compensated for disabilities
- Validation—group members confirming similar experiences, problems, and concerns
- Vicarious learning—learning by hearing about other members' coping responses

Although these advantages provide justification for using group work in treatment, several potential disadvantages of group treatment should be considered. Groups can encourage member conformity (Corey & Corey, 2006) and member dependency (Klein, 1972). When members open themselves to other members through self-disclosure, they are vulnerable to breaches of confidentiality and other harmful responses (Corey & Corey, 2006). Groups can scapegoat individual members (Konopka, 1983). Groups sometimes focus on a few particularly assertive or talkative members, which creates a danger that these members' problems will receive attention and other, less assertive or less talkative members will receive little help (Yalom, 1995).

Members can benefit from treatment groups when they have some ability to communicate with others and when their concerns or problems lend themselves to group discussion. To the extent that certain group members, such as autistic children and schizophrenic adults, cannot communicate effectively, group work must be modified to include nonverbal program activities and, where appropriate, simple, brief verbal activities that are consistent with those members' skill levels. People who have an extreme need for privacy or confidentiality may also be unable to take part in group treatment without considerable support or reassurance. Groups are contraindicated for people whose behavior is so alien to others' that it results in negative rather than positive interactions or when it leads to the failure of others to continue with the group.

Empirical studies tend to support clinical reports of the effectiveness of treatment groups. In a comprehensive review of well-designed studies comparing group and individual treatment, Toseland and Siporin (1986) found that group treatment was more effective than individual treatment in 25 percent of the studies that were reviewed, but individual treatment was not found to be more effective than group treatment in any of the studies. Group work was also found to be more efficient than individual treatment and to produce fewer dropouts from treatment. Other reviews of group treatment also confirm that it is as effective as individual treatment (Fuhriman & Burlingame, 1994; Piper & Joyce, 1996). For example, in a meta-analysis of 23 studies comparing group and individual treatment, group and individual treatment were equally effective (McRoberts, Burlingame, & Hoag, 1998).

Although the empirical literature does not yield a clear pattern of the types of problems most effectively treated in groups, group treatment may be more effective than individual treatment for enhancing social supports and less effective for dealing with intense, highly personal, psychological problems, but more research is needed (Toseland, Rossiter, Peak, & Smith, 1990). Overall, findings from both the clinical and the empirical literature suggest that social workers should consider recommending group treatment for individuals who suffer from isolation or who have other difficulties with interpersonal relationships, and individual treatment for those with highly personal psychological problems.

Advantages and Disadvantages of Task Groups

A group approach, as compared with an individual effort, has advantages in helping individuals, organizations, and communities accomplish tasks. In working with groups of people in organizations and communities, democratic participation is highly desirable (Gummer, 1991, 1995). Participation through group interaction helps members feel they have a stake in their organization or community. Also, resistance to change is minimized when those who are to be affected are given the opportunity to participate in the change through group discussion and shared decision making.

Group discussion, deliberation, and decision making can have other benefits. The increased quantity of information available in groups can be beneficial for generating alternative action plans, for problem solving, and for making decisions. Certain tasks are complex, requiring a pool of talents, expertise, or opinions for them to be completed in a satisfactory manner (Hare, Blumberg, Davies, & Kent, 1995). The division of labor that occurs in well-run groups can help members complete tasks quickly and efficiently (Tropman, 1995).

Some disadvantages should be kept in mind when considering selecting a group approach for accomplishing tasks. For example, group problem solving may take more time than individual problem solving, and the presence of others may interfere with the effectiveness of best members' problem-solving abilities (Hare et al., 1995). Napier and Gershenfeld (1993) note that poorly run groups can make members feel frustrated, bored, or unappreciated and often accomplish little. Groups are also sometimes used to make simple decisions or solve simple problems that could be dealt with more easily by individuals. Under these conditions, group meetings can be costly to an organization and frustrating and unnecessary for group members.

Findings about the effectiveness of group versus individual problem solving and decision making suggest that groups are more effective than the average individual, but rarely more effective than the best individual (Hare et al., 1995). Groups tend to be more effective than individuals when dealing with problems with known solutions rather than with problems where there is no clear right or wrong answer, what Forsyth refers to as *intellective* versus *judgmental* tasks (Forsyth, 2006, p. 366). Groups tend to be more effective than individuals on difficult and complex tasks requiring high levels of creativity (Hare et al., 1995).

Overall, the advantages and disadvantages of using a task group for problem solving and decision making should be evaluated within the context of a particular situation and in reference to the types of goals to be achieved. For example, shared decision making may be more important than the time it takes to make a decision or even the quality of the decision.

Although this text suggests that group work methods have a fairly wide applicability for many different types of individual, organizational, and community problems, these problems are sometimes best approached by using several practice methods. Thus, although group work is a valuable method by itself, within a generalist practice framework, it is also valuable as part of a larger, planned change effort that may use additional methods such as social casework or community organization to achieve particular goals.

A TYPOLOGY OF TREATMENT AND TASK GROUPS

The broad distinctions between formed and natural groups and between treatment and task groups can be further refined and developed into a classification system of the many types of groups workers may encounter in practice settings. One way to develop a classification system is to categorize treatment and task groups according to their primary purpose. According to Klein (1972), a number of group purposes are possible.

Group Work Purposes

- Rehabilitation—restoring members to their former level of functioning
- Habilitation—helping members grow and develop
- Correction—helping members who are having problems with social laws or mores

- Socialization—helping members learn how to get along with others and do what is socially acceptable
- Prevention—helping members develop and function at an optimal level and helping them prepare for events that are likely to occur
- Social action—helping members change their environment
- Problem solving—helping members resolve complex issues and concerns
- Developing social values—helping members develop a humanistic approach to living

The rest of this chapter presents typologies of treatment groups and task groups that social workers encounter in practice. The typologies are based on the primary purposes of each type of treatment and task group. Although groups with only one purpose rarely exist in practice, developing pure categories—that is, groups with a single purpose—is useful in illustrating differences between groups and in demonstrating the many ways that groups can be used in practice settings.

TREATMENT GROUPS

Six primary purposes for treatment groups are (1) support, (2) education, (3) growth, (4) therapy, (5) socialization, and (6) self-help. In practice settings, there are innumerable variations of treatment groups that combine these six primary purposes. For example, a group for parents of children with Down syndrome might be oriented toward both education and growth. A group for alcoholics might have all five primary purposes. Table 1.3 is designed to show clearly the similarities and differences among groups with different purposes. Table 1.3 can be used as a guide by workers who are planning to lead groups with only one purpose or to lead groups that combine several purposes.

Support Groups

The description of the treatment typology begins with support groups because support is a common ingredient of many successful treatment groups. Support groups can be distinguished from other groups using supportive intervention strategies by their primary goals: to foster mutual aid, to help members cope with stressful life events, and to revitalize and enhance members' coping abilities so they can effectively adapt to and cope with future stressful life events. Examples of support groups include the following:

- A group of children meeting at school to discuss the effects of divorce on their lives
- A group of people diagnosed with cancer, and their families, discussing the effects of the disease and how to cope with it
- A group of recently discharged psychiatric patients discussing their adjustment to community living
- A group of single parents sharing the difficulties of raising children alone

Leadership of support groups is characterized by a facilitative approach that emphasizes helping members share their collective experiences in coping with a stressful event. The

TABLE 1.3 ● *A Typology of Treatment Groups*

Selected Characteristics	Purpose of the Group					
	Support	Education	Growth	Therapy	Socialization	Self-Help
Purpose	To help members cope with stressful life events and revitalize existing coping abilities	To educate through presentations, discussion, and experience	To develop members' potential, awareness, insight	To change behavior Correction, rehabilitation, coping, and problem solving through behavior change interventions	To increase communication and social skills Improved interpersonal relationships through program activities, structured exercises, role plays, etc.	To help members solve their own problems
Leadership	A facilitator of empathic understanding and mutual aid	Leader as teacher and provider of structure for group discussion	Leader as facilitator and role model	Leader as expert, authority figure, or facilitator, depending on approach	Leader as director of the group's actions or programs	Leader is often a lay person with the problem shared by the other group members, but can sometimes be a professional who shares the problem
Focus	The ability of the individual to cope with a stressful life experience Communication and mutual aid	Individual learning Structuring of the group for learning	Either member or group focus, depending on the approach Individual growth through the group experience	Individual members' problems, concerns, or goals	The group as a medium for activity, participation, and involvement	Members working together to help each other solve their own problems
Bond	Shared stressful experience, often stigmatizing	Common interest in learning, skills development	Common goals among members Contract to use group to grow	Common purpose with separate member goals Relationship of member with worker, group, or other members	A common activity, enterprise, or situation	Acceptance that all members are equal and valued and can help each other

(continued)

TABLE 1.3 ● *Continued*

Selected Characteristics		Purpose of the Group				
	Support	Education	Growth	Therapy	Socialization	Self-Help
Composition	Based on a shared life experience Often diverse	Similarity of education or skill level	Can be diverse Based on members' ability to work toward growth and development	Can be diverse or can be composed of people with similar problems or concerns	Depending on location of group and purpose, can be diverse or homogeneous	Based solely on shared problem or concern
Communication	Much sharing of information, experiences, and coping strategies Frequent self-disclosure of emotionally charged material	Frequently leader-to-member, didactic Sometimes member-to-member during discussions Self-disclosure low	Highly interactive Members often take responsibility for communication in the group Self-disclosure moderate to high	Leader-to-member or member-to-member, depending on approach Self-disclosure moderate to high	Often represented in activity or nonverbal behavior Self-disclosure low to moderate and often nonverbal	Diverse and open membership welcoming to all who share the problem Member-to-member communication with high level of self-disclosure

group worker helps members share their experiences and empathically respond to each other. Simply recounting events, ventilating feelings, and reflecting on efforts to cope can promote self-understanding and help overcome loneliness, isolation, and despair. The group worker also helps members overcome feelings of alienation, stigmatization, and isolation by validating, affirming, and normalizing their experiences.

A major role of the worker is to facilitate hope in the future and motivate members to improve coping skills through self-help and mutual aid (Steinberg, 1997). The worker fosters group norms that encourage members to share information and suggestions for more effective coping and to try out new coping strategies. Because support is basic to many types of groups, these strategies for assisting members are also used, to varying degrees, in other treatment and task groups.

Strong emotional bonds often develop quickly in support groups because of members' shared experiences. Emotional bonding may also occur because members are stigmatized by the larger community and find comfort and power in their association with each other. Frequently, there is a high level of self-disclosure of emotionally charged material in support groups.

In addition to directly facilitating support groups, workers are often called on to provide indirect assistance to support groups led by lay leaders. A worker might be asked to consult with the lay leader, serve as a referral source, or provide material assistance. Consultation may take the form of speaking at a meeting, helping the group resolve a problem in its functioning, or assisting members with specific problems or issues. The worker may be asked to refer appropriate individuals to a support group, provide a meeting place, or offer other support, such as help with printing a newsletter or distributing publicity.

Some writers have pointed out that professionals might interfere with the effective functioning of lay-led, self-help support groups (Katz et al., 1992; Katz & Bender, 1987). The potential does exist for professionals to dominate, interfere with, or take over the functioning of such groups. Members of self-help groups are sometimes wary of professional involvement because they fear it will compromise the autonomy and confidentiality of the group. This is particularly true of self-help groups such as Parents Anonymous, in which members share concerns about child abuse or neglect—situations often considered socially stigmatizing.

Most evidence, however, suggests that there are strong connections between self-help support groups and professionals and that both professionals and lay leaders benefit by cooperating with each other (Kurtz, 1997; Powell, 1987; Toseland & Hacker, 1982, 1985). Professionals gain an additional treatment resource that is often more flexible and responsive than the formal service system. Lay leaders have someone to turn to when they need particular types of expertise, resources, or assistance. Both can join forces when lobbying for additional community resources and services.

Educational Groups

The primary purpose of educational groups is to help members learn new information and skills. Educational groups are used in a variety of settings, including treatment agencies, schools, nursing homes, correctional institutions, and hospitals. Examples of educational groups include the following:

- An adolescent sexuality group sponsored by a family planning agency
- A wellness-in-the-workplace group designed by a social worker directing an employee assistance program

- A group for prospective foster parents sponsored by a child welfare agency
- A group sponsored by a community planning agency to help board members become more effective

All educational groups are aimed at increasing members' information or skills. Most groups routinely involve presentations of information and knowledge by experts. They also often include opportunities for group discussion to foster learning. When leading educational groups, workers concentrate on both the individual learner and the group as a whole as vehicles for learning, reinforcement, and discussion.

Members of educational groups are bonded by a common interest in the material to be learned and by common characteristics, such as being an adolescent, a prospective foster parent, a union worker, or a board member. In composing educational groups, workers consider each member's knowledge of the subject matter and level of skills and experience so that all members can derive the most benefit from the learning process.

Some educational groups seek members with different levels of exposure to the subject matter so that beginners can learn from advanced members. When the group is small, there are usually opportunities for member-to-member communication and group discussion. Depending on the norms of the group and the subject matter, member self-disclosure varies from low to moderate. In general, a relatively low level of self-disclosure is expected in an educational group because the group is often structured around a presentation of material by the worker, a guest speaker, or a member. Usually, the material to be learned is seen as more important than the needs of members to self-disclose. However, workers often use a personalized approach to learning that emphasizes the developmental learning needs of individual members. This is especially true in residential and institutional settings in which members' emotional or social functioning is impaired.

Other approaches to leading educational groups emphasize learning as a social experience. Workers who use this approach focus on group discussion and group activities rather than on didactic methods. Community center workers often use this approach to attract and hold the interest of members who participate in educational groups for personal enjoyment and enrichment.

Growth Groups

Growth-oriented groups offer opportunities for members to become aware of, expand, and change their thoughts, feelings, and behaviors regarding themselves and others. The group is used as a vehicle to develop members' capabilities to the fullest. Growth groups focus on promoting socioemotional health rather than remediating socioemotional illness. Examples of growth groups include the following:

- An encounter group for married couples
- A values-clarification group for adolescents
- A consciousness-raising group sponsored by a women's community center
- A gay-pride group sponsored by a community health clinic serving the gay community in a large urban area

Growth groups generally stress self-improvement and the potential of human beings to live a full and rewarding life, especially through improved relationships with others. They provide a supportive atmosphere in which individuals can gain insights, experiment with new behaviors, get feedback, and grow as human beings. The bond in growth groups stems from members' commitment to help one another develop and maximize their potential.

When composing growth groups, workers often select members who have diverse backgrounds and the potential to enrich and broaden each other's experiences. However, some growth groups are composed of members with similar characteristics to enhance empathy and support within the group. In most growth-oriented groups, self-disclosure is moderate to high.

Communication in growth groups is member centered and highly interactive. In-depth self-disclosure is expected, with members encouraged to reveal more about themselves as they become comfortable with their participation in the group.

Therapy Groups

Therapy groups help members change their behavior, cope with and ameliorate personal problems, or rehabilitate themselves after physical, psychological, or social trauma. Although there is often an emphasis on support, therapy groups are distinguished from support groups by their focus on remediation and rehabilitation.

In group work practice, particular importance is often accorded to leading therapy groups, even to the exclusion of other types of group work, possibly because of the traditional importance attributed to the medical model, which stresses therapy and treatment to bring sick or dysfunctional people back to health. Konopka (1983) noted that the high status of psychiatry on the North American continent helped to make the term *therapy* more precious and more important than the terms *casework* and *group work* (terms used by the social work profession). Thus, therapy groups are often associated with the professionalism of group work as a method of practice. Examples of therapy groups include the following:

- A psychotherapy group for outpatients at a community mental health center
- A group, sponsored by a voluntary health association, for people who want to stop smoking
- A first-offenders group in a juvenile diversion program sponsored by a probation department
- A hospital-sponsored group for people addicted to drugs

In therapy groups, members come together to solve their problems. The group leader is often viewed as an expert, an authority figure, and a change agent. Members' problems are assessed and treatment goals are developed with the help of the worker. Although the group has a common purpose, each member may have a different problem with different symptoms. In addition, the etiology and development of each member's problem is unique. Therefore, to achieve individual goals, the worker often focuses on one member at a time. Depending on the approach or stance of the worker, the members of a therapy group may be expected to help each other work on problems. The level of member self-disclosure is usually quite high but can depend somewhat on the types of problems experienced by group members.

Members of therapy groups have much to gain: relief from symptoms, loss of emotional pain, or resolution of a problem. Still, to ensure that members' needs are met, much planning usually takes place before the beginning of a therapy group. Therapeutic interventions are selected after a careful assessment of individual members, and the group is composed in relation to the members' problems. Often, members participate in an intake procedure so the worker can assess their interest in participating in the group, determine their suitability for group treatment, and explain the purpose of the group. Although these procedures are also used with other types of groups, they are often given greater emphasis in therapy groups.

Socialization Groups

Socialization groups help members learn social skills and socially accepted behavior patterns so they can function effectively in the community. Socialization groups frequently use program activities such as games, role plays, or outings to help members accomplish individual goals (Barlow, Blythe, & Edmonds, 1999; Middleman, 1978, 1980, 1982).

The personal needs of members and the goals of the group are often met through program activities rather than exclusively through group discussion. Thus, socialization groups feature a learning-through-doing approach in which members improve their interpersonal skills by participating in program activities. Examples of socialization groups include the following:

- A Catholic Youth Organization (CYO) activity group
- A social club for outpatients of a psychiatric center
- A monthly Vietnam Veterans evening social at a rural Veterans of Foreign Wars (VFW) post
- A Parents Without Partners group, which includes picnics, dances, and other social activities

Leadership of socialization groups can be directive or nondirective, depending on the complexity of program activities and the competencies of group members. Member participation is the key to successful individual and group outcomes. The group is a medium for activity, participation, and involvement, and members are bonded to each other through these activities. The composition of socialization groups can be based on the similar interests and needs of members or on the common experiences offered by a particular program activity.

There are at least three common forms of socialization groups: (1) social skills groups, (2) governance groups, and (3) recreation groups. Some social skills groups, such as assertiveness training groups, are formed for adults who wish to improve their existing skills. Unlike the other types of groups in our typology, social skills groups can be particularly useful for individuals who are unable or unwilling to communicate effectively and for those who have difficulty engaging in satisfying social relationships. Young children, shy adolescents, and mildly retarded adults are examples of client populations that can benefit from social skills groups. Program activities can help draw out these types of group members by helping them form meaningful relationships and learn social skills. Activities provide the basis for interaction and communication without the need for direct, verbal communication. Thus, by using program activities, group work can take place through nonverbal means.

In other cases, role plays, psychodrama, and other activities requiring both verbal and nonverbal communication can be used to increase members' skills and promote socialization. The behavior displayed during these activities can help a worker assess members' problems and plan effective interventions.

Governance groups are often found in residential settings such as group homes, psychiatric hospitals, and congregate housing. The purpose of these groups is to involve residents (of the unit, ward, floor, or house) in the daily governance of the institution. Although governance groups are closely related to task groups because they solve problems and make decisions, they have been classified as treatment groups because their primary focus is on the needs of their members.

Through their participation in the governance process, members learn advocacy, communication, conflict resolution, and empowerment skills. They also learn to share with others, take responsibility for their actions, and participate in decision-making processes. The concept of a governance group is borrowed, in part, from the idea of the therapeutic community in which members have input into the rules that govern their behavior. Examples of governance groups include house meetings, ward meetings, resident councils, family meetings, and patient-rights meetings.

Participation in governance groups provides a method for members to identify with and become committed to the goals of the therapeutic community. It helps clarify members' roles, responsibilities, and rights within the community. All members of therapeutic communities are encouraged to attend meetings so that they have a voice in the way the community functions. In some settings, such as residential treatment centers, attendance may be required.

A third type of socialization group focuses on recreational activities. Much of the recent group work literature has understated the importance of recreational groups in meeting members' personal needs. The roots of group work can be traced to recreational groups like scouting, camping, sports, and club groups (Boyd, 1935; Slavson, 1945, 1946; Smith, 1935; Wilson, 1976). Recreation can be both an end and a means to an end. As an end, recreation can be a desirable leisure time activity. As a means, recreation can help a particular population become involved in an activity that has therapeutic benefits, such as increasing social skills.

Recreational groups are particularly important for working with children, adolescents, and older adults in neighborhood centers. Because the groups are enjoyable, they are often helpful in engaging resistant clients such as gang members and predelinquent, latency-age children. They can help members learn community values and accepted norms of behavior, develop interpersonal skills, and feel a sense of belonging. In addition, recreational groups help members develop confidence in their ability to function as a part of a group and to function in other social situations. To carry out these important purposes, recreation groups require leaders who are skilled in both group work and the featured recreational mode or program activity.

Self-Help Groups

Although they share many characteristics with support, educational, and socialization groups, the distinguishing character of self-help groups are that they are led by members who share the problem experienced by the other member of the group. We decided to include self-help groups as a separate type of treatment groups because self-help groups are so widely available in today's society and professionals often play vital roles in them. Although it is often thought that self-help groups are led by lay people, in actual practice, many self-help groups are actually led by professionals who have experienced the problem shared by the other members of the group (Riessman & Carroll, 1995; Toseland & Hacker, 1982).

Examples of self-help groups include the following:

- An Alcoholics Anonymous Group
- Mended Hearts, a group for patients that have undergone bypass or other heart surgery procedures
- Make Today Count, a group for cancer survivors
- A Gamblers Anonymous Group

Although there is no accurate estimate of the number of self-help groups in the United States or throughout the world, they are very numerous. For example, the *Self-Help Group Sourcebook* alone lists over 1,000 national and international headquarters of self-help groups in the United States and Canada (White & Madara, 2002), and includes 33 separate clearinghouses for self-help information in 22 different countries. These organization, in turn, sponsor many self-help groups in local communities.

Leadership patterns can be quite diverse in self-help groups. In some self-help groups, leadership is rotated among members whereas in other self-help groups, members take turns taking responsibility for leading the group. There are also some self-help groups who have one or two members who take leadership responsibility. Some self-help groups such as Alcoholics Anonymous are very explicit that the groups are composed and run by lay leaders who are chosen from the membership. Such groups welcome professional members but treat professionals as ordinary members. These self-help groups may seek the assistance of professionals outside of the context of meeting as needed, but accord professional social workers no special status within the Alcoholics Anonymous fellowship. Other self-help groups welcome professional involvement as leaders and as speakers, and the role between professional and lay person may be blurred.

Self-help group may be focused on helping members change or on social change and advocacy, although many groups combine different foci. Kurtz (2004), for example, organized self-help groups into five categories (1) groups that are peer-led and oriented to individual change and nonprofessionally led, such as Alcoholics Anonymous, (2) groups that are peer-led and social change oriented that focus on support, education, and advocacy, such as the National Alliance for the Mentally Ill, (3) groups that are support oriented, advocacy oriented, and professionally led that are part of national organizations, such as the Alzheimer's Foundation, (4) smaller, local, professionally-led groups that are held in hospitals, social service organizations or other community organizations, and (5) change-oriented groups that have peer leadership combined with professional involvement as independent sponsors or co-leaders, such as Parents Anonymous. Clearly, self-help groups are so diverse and numerous that they almost defy any simple classification system.

Most self-help groups are characterized by an open membership policy. Anyone can attend a group meeting who shares the problem or concern being addressed. Because of their policy of open membership, self-help groups often have set formats that are repeated each meeting. For example, there may be a brief statement of the purpose of the group at the beginning followed by a speaker and then a time for members to share concerns and issues. This set structure enables members to feel comfortable attending quickly, even if they are new to the group or if they have missed meetings. New members quickly learn the structure, and feel comfortable with what is going to happen during the meeting and what is expected of them. The focus of self-help groups is on members helping members. Members are seen as equals who share similar problems and concerns. Self-help groups place a great deal of emphasis on de-stigmatizing the problems shared and faced by members. There is a strong sense of empathy and support accompanied by a sense of empowerment that members can help themselves to overcome problems. issues, and concerns and lead better, more fulfilled lives through their own efforts to help each other. Usually there are no special requirements for attendance except that members share the problem that is the main focus or purpose of the group and that members limit what they say in the group to the purpose of the group. Members, therefore, may come and go freely, deciding when they would like to attend. Most self-help groups are self-supporting, although they may receive some support from a sponsoring organization that may provide a meeting room, or may help with guest speakers or refreshments.

TASK GROUPS

Task groups are common in most agencies and organizations. They are used to find solutions to organizational problems, to generate new ideas, and to make decisions. Task groups can have three primary purposes: (1) meeting client needs, (2) meeting organizational needs, and (3) meeting community needs.

Task groups with the primary purpose of serving client needs include teams, treatment conferences, and staff-development groups. Task groups with the primary purpose of serving organizational needs include committees, cabinets, and boards of directors. Task groups with a primary purpose of serving community needs include social action groups, coalitions, and delegate councils.

Selected characteristics of each type of group are presented in Table 1.4. As with the typology for treatment groups, there is often some overlap between different types of task groups in actual practice situations. Thus, instead of a rigid classification system, the typology is intended as a guide for workers who may be called on to lead different types of task groups.

Groups to Meet Client Needs

Teams

Over the years, a growing body of evidence has accumulated about the effectiveness of teams in social service and business settings (Abramson, 2002; Abramson & Bronstein, 2004; Banker, Field, Schroeder, & Sinha, 1996; Cohen & Bailey, 1997; Gummer, 1995; Hackman, 2002; Halstead, 1976; Heinemann & Zeiss, 2002; Keith, 1991; Levi, 2007; Schmitt, Farrell, & Heinemann, 1988; Stewart, Manz, & Sims, 1999). By bringing together the knowledge and skills of different categories of professionals and paraprofessionals, team work is often considered the most effective method of delivering comprehensive social and health services to those in need (Abramson & Bronstein, 2004; Brill, 1976;

TABLE 1.4 ● *A Typology of Task Groups*

Selected Characteristics	Client Needs		
	Teams	**Treatment Conferences**	**Staff Development**
Purpose	To engage in collaborative work on behalf of a client system	To develop, coordinate, and monitor treatment plans	To educate members for better practice with clients
Leadership	Appointed by sponsoring agency	Neutral chair or chaired by member with most responsibility	Leader, supervisor, consultant, or educator
Focus	Build team to function smoothly High member focus	Decision-oriented Low member focus High client focus	Focus on staff members' needs and their performance with clients
Bond	Team spirit Needs of organization and client	Client system Treatment plan Inter- or intra-agency agreement	Continuing education needs Interest in client welfare Professional development
Composition	Often heterogeneous	Diversity by function, specialty, and expertise	Individuals with similar educational needs
Communication	Theoretically close, sometimes artificial or inspirational Low to moderate self-disclosure	Consideration of all points of view about the client system High disclosure	Leader-to-member Didactic and experiential instruction Member-to-member

(continued)

TABLE 1.4 ● Continued

Selected Characteristics	Organizational Needs		
	Committees	Cabinets	Board of Directors
Purpose	To discuss issues and accomplish tasks	To advise an executive officer about future directions or current policies and procedures	To govern an organization
Leadership	Appointed or elected	Appointed by chief executive officer of an organization	Officers designated by bylaws are nominated by subcommittee and approved by vote of the membership
Focus	A specific task or charge	The development of procedures and policies for organizational management	Policy making Governance Monitoring Fiscal control Fundraising
Bond	Interest in a task	Loyalty to the organization and the chief executive officer	Commitment to the mission of the organization Service orientation
Composition	Diversity to aid decision making and division of labor	Appointment based on administrative responsibilities and expertise	Diverse members often selected for their status, power, influence in the community, expertise, representation of particular interest groups and constituencies
Communication	Relative to task Low member self-disclosure	Members present points of view based on their position in an organization To build a power base	Formal communication Parliamentary procedures Less formal in subcommittees Low member self-disclosure

(continued)

TABLE 1.4 ● Continued

Selected Characteristics	Community Needs		
	Social Action Groups	**Coalitions**	**Delegate Councils**
Purpose	To devise and implement social change tactics and strategies	To exert greater influence by sharing resources, expertise, and power bases of social action groups with common goals	To represent different organizations, chapters, or other units
Leadership	Indigenous leadership emerging from the groups Practitioner often is staffer or adviser	Often a charismatic or dedicated individual leading by consensus or elected by vote of the membership	Representatives appointed by the sponsoring organization
Focus	Consumer, community, social justice	Building consensus and a partnership for maximum influence	Collective input and action Equality of representation Focus on larger issues, concerns, and positions
Bond	Perception of injustice, inequity, or need for change	Interest in an issue Commitment to an ideological position	Larger purpose or community concern, rather than individual or agency concern
Composition	Based on common interest, shared purpose, and investment in community	Loose, temporary confederation of groups or organizations working in partnership to achieve a common goal	Diverse by definition Represents interest of sponsoring organization
Communication	Informal member-to-member discussion Formulation and implementation of tactics and strategies for change High member self-disclosure in relation to social problems	Formal or informal, depending on type of coalition Less formal in caucuses and subgroups Moderate member self-disclosure representing group interests	Provides a forum for communication among organizations Delegates are communication links between council and the sponsoring organization Low member self-disclosure

Fatout & Rose, 1995; Gummer, 1995; Kane, 1975a, 1975b; Levi, 2007; Scholtes, Joiner, & Streibel, 1996). A *team* can be defined as

> *A number of individual staff members, each of whom possesses particular knowledge and skills, who come together to share their expertise with one another for a particular purpose. (Toseland, Palmer-Ganeles, & Chapman, 1986, p. 46)*

Team members coordinate their efforts and work together on behalf of a particular client group. Examples of teams include the following:

- A group of professionals working with stroke victims and their family members in a rehabilitation hospital
- A group of professionals who deliver home-based hospice care
- Professional and paraprofessional helpers trained in crisis intervention sponsored by a county mental health agency
- A group of professionals and aides who work with patients in a psychiatric hospital

According to Abramson and Bronstein (2004), social workers have not always done a good job communicating their role on the team. Social workers need to make a strong case for their roles in resource procurement, counseling, advocacy, and coordination of service delivery. They also need to make a strong case for their skills in maintaining and building the smooth functioning of teams.

The functioning of the team is the responsibility of the team leader. Team leaders are often appointed by an administrator from the team's sponsoring agency, but in some settings they are elected or nominated by team members. The team leader is a facilitator and coordinator for the group and is accountable to the agency for the actions of the team. The team leader is responsible for conducting meetings, motivating team members, coordinating individual efforts, and ensuring effective team functioning.

In most, if not all, cases an agency sanctions the mutual involvement of team members on behalf of a particular client population. Often, the team is composed of members with different professional orientations, such as social work, nursing, physical and occupational therapy, and medicine. The team might also be composed of paraprofessionals, such as mental health therapy aides. There is also a growing body of evidence that it is important to involve clients and family members as members of team (Abramson & Bronstein, 2004), yet this often does not happen in practice.

Usually, particular attention is paid to how team members work together as a group, frequently referred to as *team building*. Meetings should avoid focusing solely on service delivery—some time should be devoted to how members function as a group (Toseland, Palmer-Ganeles, & Chapman, 1986). Neglecting team functioning can lead to a variety of problems such as interpersonal conflict and rivalry, duplication of effort, and uncoordinated or incomplete service (Levi, 2007).

Members are bonded by a team spirit that assists them in their work as a group rather than being a collection of individuals representing disparate concerns and professional agendas. When building and maintaining an effective team, the worker must foster the organization's support of teamwork, encourage members' personal and professional orientations toward collaboration, and help members to develop skills to clarify roles and negotiate conflicts (Steckler & Fondas, 1995).

Ideally, team members should meet regularly to discuss their service delivery efforts and their functioning as a team (Abramson, 1989; Gruenfeld, 1998). Communication among team members varies according to the working situation of the team (Fatout & Rose, 1995; Levi, 2007). Sometimes team members work independently of each other. For example, within a residential program for children, child-care workers might be considered important team members although they work different shifts. To promote adequate communication and a coordinated team effort in such situations, it is a good practice to schedule meeting times when shifts overlap.

Treatment Conferences

Treatment conferences meet for the purpose of developing, monitoring, and coordinating treatment plans for a particular client or client system. Members consider the client's situation and decide on a plan for working with the client. Examples of treatment conferences include the following:

- An interdisciplinary group of professionals planning the discharge of a patient in a mental health facility
- A group of child-care workers, social workers, nurses, and a psychiatrist determining a treatment plan for a child in residential treatment
- A parole board considering testimony regarding the release of a prisoner from a correctional facility
- A group of community mental health professionals considering treatment methods for a young man experiencing severe depression

Although treatment conferences may at first appear similar to team meetings, they differ in five respects:

1. Members of a treatment conference might not all work together as do members of teams. They may be employees of different organizations who come to a treatment conference to discuss ways to coordinate their efforts on behalf of a particular client.

2. Participants may not have the same close working relationships and shared sense of purpose that are essential in teamwork. Members may not work together from day to day. In fact, they may never have met before the treatment conference.

3. Treatment conference groups often meet less frequently than teams; they gather as the need arises in particular situations.

4. The composition of teams is relatively stable, but the composition of treatment conference groups varies depending on the clients being discussed.

5. The plan of action might be carried out by only one member who is entirely responsible for the client's care. For example, during a treatment conference in a family service agency, a worker gets advice from colleagues about how to help a group member with a particularly difficult issue. The other members of the treatment conference have no direct contact with the client. In contrast, all members of a team usually have some contact with clients served by the team.

In treatment conferences, participants generally focus on one client at a time. Members who are familiar with the client contribute information that may be helpful in developing or improving a treatment plan. Other members, who might not be familiar with the client, can also contribute their expertise about how to most effectively treat the type of problem the client is experiencing. On the basis of this information, the group discusses the client's overall circumstances and considers alternative treatment plans. The group decides on one plan that all members agree will be the most helpful for the client.

Treatment conferences are oriented toward decision making, problem solving, and coordinating the actions of members. The group focuses its attention on the needs of the client rather than on the needs of the group members. The bond that group members feel is based on their concern for a client and their commitment to an agreed-on treatment plan.

Treatment conferences usually include all helping professionals who are working with a client. The group can also include consultants or experts who do not work directly with the client but who can contribute to the treatment plan by offering insight, resources, or advice. Treatment conference membership is diverse by design. Participants are invited because they have new insights and treatment opportunities based on their area of expertise and their unique experiences with a client.

It is the policy of some agencies to have clients and their spouses, parents, guardians, or significant others participate in treatment conferences. However, the staff of some agencies believe that inviting clients to treatment conferences may inhibit open discussion. Also, some staff believe that the conflicting facts, multiple options in treatment planning, or emotionally charged issues that are sometimes discussed during treatment conferences can confuse or upset clients. These agencies sometimes invite the client and significant others to the portion of the treatment conference that occurs after treatment staff have had a private discussion about the client's situation. However, these agencies are in a minority. Most agencies simply opt not to have the client present at treatment conferences (Toseland, Ivanoff, & Rose, 1987).

No data are available to address when, or even if, it is best to invite clients and their significant others to treatment conferences, but there is a growing consensus that it is important to do so (Abramson & Bronstein, 2004). Because a client's right to self-determination is an important part of the value base of social work practice, careful consideration should be given to soliciting clients' input into the treatment-planning decisions that will affect their lives.

Treatment conference leadership can be determined in a variety of ways. In some agencies, the conferences are always led by the same person. This person might be the program director or a member of the staff, such as the social worker whose job includes responsibility for treatment coordination. Commonly, the designated leader is the worker with the most responsibility for, or involvement with, the client's care. In some agencies, leadership is rotated or a supervisor leads the meeting. In these situations, the leader can lend objectivity to the proceedings because he or she does not work directly with the client. For a detailed description of the functioning of a treatment conference see Jacobsen and Jacobsen (1996).

Staff Development Groups

The purpose of staff development groups is to improve services to clients by developing, updating, and refreshing workers' skills. Staff development groups provide workers with an opportunity to learn about new treatment approaches, resources, and community services; to practice new skills; and to review and learn from their previous work with clients. Examples of staff development groups include the following:

- A group of professionals who attend a series of seminars about pharmacology offered by a regional psychiatric center
- An in-service development seminar on codependency for the staff of an alcoholism treatment agency
- Group supervision offered by an experienced social worker for social workers who work in school districts in which there are no supervisors
- A program director who conducts a weekly supervisory group for paraprofessionals who work in a community outreach program for isolated elderly people

Ideally, leaders of staff development groups are experts in a particular field. Often they also possess extensive experience and knowledge gathered through specialized training, study, and reflection on difficult practice issues.

The focus of staff development groups is on improving workers' skills so they can perform more effectively on behalf of their clients. The trainer or leader can use many methods to aid learning, such as lectures, discussions, audio- and videotape presentations, simulations, and live demonstrations. Members may be given the opportunity to practice new skills in the group and to receive feedback from the trainer and the other members.

Members are bonded by their desire to improve their skills. Often they share an interest in a similar client population or treatment method. They may also share in the camaraderie that comes from being at similar stages in their professional development.

In some staff development groups, the leader takes primary responsibility for the content of each session. The leader may make presentations, arrange for guest speakers, or prepare and conduct simulations and other staff development exercises. In other groups, members are responsible for structuring the group by taking turns presenting their work with particular clients.

Members are expected to risk opening their work to the scrutiny and critique of the rest of the group and to participate in staff development exercises and discussions. They are also expected to learn from their own mistakes and the mistakes of others in the group. Honest, frank, constructive communication and feedback among members is valued, as is a high level of self-disclosure.

Groups to Meet Organizational Needs

Committees

The most common type of task group is the committee. A committee is made up of people who are appointed or elected to the group. Their task is to "accomplish a charge" (Pincus & Minahan, 1973, p. 61) that is delegated to the committee from a higher authority such as organizational bylaws or an agency executive. Committees may be temporary creations (ad hoc committees) or more permanent parts of the structure of an organization (standing committees). Examples of committees include the following:

- A group of young people responsible for recommending activities for the local community center
- A group of employees assigned the task of studying and recommending changes in the agency's personnel policy

- A group of social workers considering ways to improve service delivery to pregnant teenagers
- A group of staff members developing recommendations for an employee assistance program

In these examples, members are concerned with producing reports, accomplishing tasks, issuing recommendations, or making decisions. In each example, the committee's work requires the collective wisdom of a number of people with varied viewpoints, expertise, and abilities.

Although members are expected to share their personal views during deliberations, the level of self-disclosure in committees is frequently low. In some cases, however, there are variations in the level of self-disclosure, depending on the norms that have developed in the committee and on the nature of the issues being discussed. For example, when the subject matter is of a sensitive nature, discussing personal viewpoints may require a high level of members' self-disclosure.

Most committees tend to follow a standard set of procedures. Sometimes committees rely on parliamentary procedure to conduct their meetings. In other cases, committees develop their own rules and regulations that control how members introduce and discuss issues and how decisions are reached.

It is useful for each meeting to have an agenda so committee members can follow the activity of the group and know what to expect during the rest of the meeting. The agenda provides structure, focus, and direction for the group. The chairperson is responsible for seeing that the agenda and the formalized procedures are carried out. The chairperson may be appointed by the authority that has given the committee its mandate or may be elected by committee or organization members.

Committees frequently deal with complex issues, requiring the group to divide large tasks into a series of smaller subtasks. To deal with these subtasks, a committee often authorizes the formation of one or more subcommittees from its membership. Subcommittees report back to the larger committee, which coordinates subcommittee reports and activities and deliberates about any recommendations made by the subcommittees.

The composition of subcommittees is sometimes the responsibility of the chairperson, who considers the qualifications and abilities of each committee member and selects subcommittee members on the basis of their ability to complete a particular task. The chairperson may also ask for volunteers rather than appoint members. This is particularly true when the subcommittee deals with a particularly onerous task and highly motivated members are needed. In other cases, subcommittee members are elected by members of the full committee.

Committees are generally accountable to an administrator or other individual or group who gave the committee its charge. The power vested in a committee depends on the group's mandate and the extent to which its actions are binding. It is common, however, for committees to be given the power to make recommendations rather than issue binding decisions.

The importance of the committee as a type of task group cannot be overemphasized. Most other types of task groups mentioned in our typology use elements of committee structure to complete their tasks. It can be argued that other forms of task groups, such as cabinets and treatment conferences, are special forms of committees.

Cabinets

Cabinets are designed to provide advice and expertise about policy issues to chief executive officers or other high-level administrators. Policies, procedures, and practices that affect the entire organization are discussed, developed, or modified in cabinets before being announced by a senior administrative officer. Cabinets enable formal communications among senior administrators in an organization and help garner support for particular policies and procedures among senior and midlevel administrators. Examples of cabinet groups include the following:

- A meeting of section heads in a large state health department to discuss long-term care reimbursement policies
- A weekly meeting of supervisory social work staff and the director of social services in a large municipal hospital
- A series of meetings of senior United Way staff to discuss potential changes in methods of allocating money among member agencies
- A meeting of department heads in a county social services department

Cabinets focus their efforts on administrative and policy issues that may have important implications for the entire organization or subdivisions within it. Although committees often make recommendations to a high-level administrator who is not part of the group, cabinet members often give advice about developing and changing policies and procedures directly to the chief executive officer or other administrator who leads the meeting. In some organizations, cabinets are delegated the authority to make decisions by the chief executive officer.

Unlike committee members, who may be elected or appointed, cabinet members are often appointed by the chief executive officer. Cabinet members are typically supervisors, department heads, or senior managers with powerful positions within the organization. Occasionally, the executive might ask an outside consultant to join the group because of that person's background and knowledge.

Authority and power are particularly important in cabinets. Members often vie for the chief executive's attention and for the chance to influence policy decisions. Members sometimes take stances on policy issues that will benefit the program or section they lead within the larger organization.

The proceedings of cabinet meetings are often kept confidential. Self-disclosure is typically low, with members thinking strategically about how their statements on issues will affect their own standing within the group and the likelihood that they will be able to influence current and future policy decisions.

Boards of Directors

There are two primary types of boards: the governing board and the advisory board (Conrad & Glenn, 1976). Under the articles of incorporation and the bylaws of not-for-profit organizations, governing boards—sometimes referred to as boards of trustees—are legally and financially responsible for the conduct of the organization.

The members of governing boards are stewards of the public trust and are accountable to the state government that granted the organization its charter; to the federal government, which granted tax-exempt status; and, ultimately, to the public, whom the organization serves (Wolf, 1990). Members of advisory boards provide counsel and guidance to the management of an organization. However, they have no official power to make policy or fiscal decisions. Examples of board groups include the following:

- Trustees of a large public hospital
- Members of the governing board of a family service agency
- Individuals on the citizens' advisory board of a county department of social services
- Members of the board of a corporation that includes several affiliated social service and health agencies

The primary functions of boards of directors are policy making, oversight of agency operations, ensuring the financial integrity and stability of the organization, and public relations (Tropman, 1995). Boards of directors determine the mission and short- and long-range goals of the organization. They set personnel and operating policies. They offer counsel and advice to the chief executive officer and monitor the organization's operations. They establish fiscal policy, set budgets, and install monitoring and auditing mechanisms. They also engage in fundraising, hire the chief executive officer, and manage public relations (Howe, 2002). Boards, however, are not supposed to engage in the day-to-day operations of the organization, the hiring of staff (other than the executive director), or the details of programmatic decisions (Wolf, 1990).

The position and duties of the president, vice-president, secretary, treasurer, and any other officers of a board of directors are generally specified in the articles of incorporation and bylaws of the organization. The terms of these officers and how they are selected are specified in the board's operating procedures. Usually, officers are nominated by a subcommittee of the board and are elected to specified terms by the entire membership.

It has been estimated that 11.5 million people sit on the boards of not-for-profit agencies in the United States (Waldo, 1986). Board members are bonded by their commitment to the mission and goals of the organization and by their commitment to community service.

They are often a diverse group of individuals who are selected on the basis of their power, status, and influence in the community; their expertise; and their representation of particular interest groups and constituencies. For example, a board might contain lawyers who can provide advice on legal matters, accountants or bankers who can provide advice on fiscal matters, business people who can assist with fundraising and advertising, other media experts who can help with public relations, and policy experts and consumers who can provide guidance on programmatic and service issues.

Written agendas are usually circulated before board meetings. Communication is often formal, following the rules of parliamentary procedure. Much of the actual work, however, is often conducted in less formal subcommittee meetings. Boards often have several standing and ad hoc committees that report at board meetings and recommend actions in the form of motions. For example, the finance committee might recommend that the board approve the annual budget of the agency, the personnel committee might recommend a change in health benefits for employees of the organization, or the nominating committee might present a slate of new officers for board approval. For more information about boards see Blackmon and Holland (2000); Chait, Holland, and Taylor (1993); and Hughes, Lakey, and Bobowick (2000).

Groups to Meet Community Needs

Social Action Groups

Social action groups empower members to engage in collective action and planned change efforts to alter some aspect of their social or physical environment (Staples, 2004). They are often referred to as "grass roots" organizations because they arise from the concerns of individuals in the community who may have little individual power or status. Although the goals of social action groups are frequently linked to the needs of the individual members of the group, goal achievement generally also benefits people outside the group. Thus, social action groups serve the common good of both members and nonmembers. Examples of social action groups include the following:

- A citizens' group advocating increased police protection on behalf of the elderly population in a neighborhood
- A group of social workers lobbying for increased funding for social services
- A tenants' group seeking support for a playground area in their housing complex
- A group of community leaders working to increase the access of African Americans to a mental health agency

Staples (2004) points out that there are a variety of vehicles through which small groups take on social action efforts. There include organizing committees composed of well-respected opinion leaders who come together to organize a social movement, house meetings where a group of individuals get together to recruit others and to discuss controversial issues, issue committees that identify, prioritize, and select issues for action, lobbying committees that bring issues to elected officials, and negotiating teams that work at the bargaining table to bring about a change. Small groups are also used for many other social action purposes such as fund raising and developing and coordinating special events.

A worker involved in a social action group can assume one of many leadership roles, depending on the nature of the change effort and the needs of the group. A worker assumes an enabler role to help the group acquire information or resources, determine priorities and procedures, and plan a strategy for action. For example, in working with tenants concerned about their rights, the worker might help organize a tenant-rights group to help the individuals pursue their common goals.

Alternatively, workers might take a directive role because of their expertise regarding the change effort. In a lobbying effort, for example, a worker might be particularly knowledgeable about techniques for influencing legislators. In this instance, the worker might be asked to speak for the social action group or might encourage the group to examine particular issues or use particular strategies, such as collaboration, bargaining, or conflict.

Although directive approaches to leading social action groups are sometimes useful and appropriate, the worker should be guided by the purpose of the group and the preferences of group members. The worker should make sure that a directive approach does not inhibit indigenous leadership from developing among members. Abels (1980) suggests that the worker should assume the role of an "instructed" advocate for the group. Using this approach, the worker's role is defined and limited by the social action group and includes four major goals: "(1) to help the group achieve its purpose, (2) to help the group remain together as a unit long enough to achieve these purposes, (3) to enable members to function in an autonomous manner, and (4) to help the group to come to terms with its community" (Abels, 1980, p. 327).

The bond that holds members of action groups together is a shared perception of injustice, inequity, and a need for a change in the current social structure. Yet, Mondros and Wilson (1994) point out that less than 2 percent of a potential constituency ever becomes involved in a social action group and that large numbers of individuals drop out after their initial enthusiasm fades. Five factors that help people stay involved in social action groups are (1) the importance of the work of the group, (2) the group's effectiveness, (3) a sense of community and peer support, (4) interest in the task, and (5) the feeling of making a contribution (Mondros & Wilson, 1994). Methods to enhance and sustain membership based on these and other factors are described in Chapters 3 and 12.

The composition of social action groups can vary depending on the nature and circumstances of the change effort. Sometimes workers take a leadership role in composing social action groups; in other cases, groups may form as a result of the interests of one or more concerned citizens. In the latter case, the worker is often asked to be a facilitator, enabler, or consultant to lend expertise to the change effort without necessarily influencing the composition of the group.

When the worker does have a role in composing the group, consideration should be given to the level of support for the change effort among key community leaders. In some instances, the worker may seek members who can exert influence in the environment or who have the diverse skills and resources needed to empower the group.

Communication patterns in social action groups vary with the circumstances of the group. The worker helps the group develop open communication patterns so that all members have a chance to become involved. The worker also helps the group establish communication links with its environment. Good communication helps avoid misunderstandings and promotes a cooperative effort among all those who may have some stake in the change effort (Mondros & Wilson, 1994).

Coalitions

Coalitions—or alliances, as they are sometimes called—are groups of organizations, social action groups, or individuals that come together to exert influence by sharing resources and expertise. Coalition members agree to pursue common goals, which they believe cannot be achieved by any of the members acting alone.

Examples of coalitions include the following:

- A group of family planning and community health-care clinics who have formed a pro-choice coalition to influence state and federal legislation on abortion
- Not-for-profit home-care agencies who gather to lobby for greater access to community care for the chronically ill elderly
- Community agencies that want to bring public attention to the need for a community teen center
- Business, community, and civic leaders who team up to explore ways to reduce racial tensions in a large urban area

The formation of coalitions as political and social forces to improve the responsiveness of the social environment to human beings has a long tradition in social group work

(Mizrahi & Rosenthal, 1998). For example, Newstetter (1948) described principles for interagency collaboration that have formed the basis for more recent writings on the formation and development of coalitions (Bailey & Koney, 1996; Dluhy, 1990; Gentry, 1987; Hula, 1999; Mayer et al., 1998; Merenda, 1997; Mondros & Wilson, 1994; Prigmore, 1974; Schopler, 1994; Weisner, 1983; Winer & Ray, 1996).

Coalitions are often formed by a charismatic or dedicated individual who has high visibility and respect within the community. This individual helps organizations, groups, and individuals understand that they have common goals and purposes that could be better served by working together.

Because members of coalitions are often concerned about preserving their autonomy while joining with others in the group, coalitions sometimes experience conflict in establishing mutual goals, working agreements, plans of action, and equitable ways of sharing resources and accomplishments. Therefore, a primary task throughout coalition formation and development is building and maintaining consensus and a smooth partnership in which efforts can be focused on the goals to be achieved rather than on intragroup rivalry. Charismatic leaders are helped in their efforts by the coalition members, who are bonded by their ideals, common ideology, and interest in a particular issue or set of issues.

Coalitions take many forms (Dluhy, 1990). Frequently, they are loose, temporary confederations of organizations or social action groups that coalesce to share resources and gain strength in numbers. In such informal coalitions, the autonomy of the individual members is strictly protected. Over time, however, some coalitions become stable, long-term organizations with centralized staff and resources.

Meetings may be characterized by ideologically fervent speechmaking and position taking. Much emphasis is placed on developing strategies to accomplish specific goals and coordinating activities involved in the action plan. Sometimes, coalition meetings are characterized by formal interactions following the rules of parliamentary procedure. Although parliamentary procedures are often not as strictly adhered to as they are in board meetings or delegate councils, they are used in coalitions to promote a sense of inclusion and belonging so that members feel they have the opportunity to fully participate in the collective deliberations and decision making of the coalition. Still, Dluhy (1990) notes that coalitions often have one or more elite decision makers who may have considerable influence on the decision making and operation of the group.

Although parliamentary procedure is frequently used during formal meetings of the members, freewheeling interaction often occurs during caucuses, and in subgroup and one-to-one discussions between coalition meetings. Less formal procedures are also frequently used in ad hoc, single-issue coalitions that do not have a long history of operation.

Delegate Councils

Delegate councils are composed for the purposes of facilitating interagency communication and cooperation, studying communitywide social issues or social problems, engaging in collective social action, and governing large organizations. Members of delegate councils are appointed or elected by a sponsoring unit. The members' primary function is to represent the interests of their sponsoring unit during council meetings. A variation of the delegate council is the delegate assembly, which is usually larger. Examples of delegate councils include the following:

- A number of agency representatives who meet monthly to improve interagency communication
- A group of elected representatives from local chapters of a professional organization who meet to approve the organization's budget
- A state task force to study family violence composed of members appointed from each county
- A yearly meeting of representatives from family service agencies throughout the county

Representation is an important issue in delegate councils. A member represents a group of people, an agency, or another system. The member is often given authority to speak for the represented unit. Because the unit has agreed to participate by sending a representative, the represented unit generally agrees to abide by decisions made by the delegate council.

There are differing ways to achieve representation. The number of representatives for each sponsoring unit can vary with the size or importance of the unit. For example, legislative bodies frequently determine the number of representatives by considering the population of each voting district, county, or state, and apportioning an appropriate number of representatives for each district.

Other councils' representation may be dictated by a sanctioning authority to ensure control over policy decisions. For example, a consumer council for a large department of social services may have more employees than clients to ensure departmental control over the decisions made by the group.

Delegate councils are usually concerned with broad issues that affect several agencies, a large segment of a population, or a group of people in a wide geographic area. Delegate councils provide an effective communications link among groups of people who otherwise might not be able to communicate in a formal way. For example, delegate councils frequently serve as a forum for communication among diverse human service agencies within a city, state, or nation. Such agencies might not otherwise communicate effectively with each other. They may also form part of the governance structure of unions or professional organizations that represent a diverse and geographically dispersed membership.

Delegate councils can be either discussion oriented or action oriented, or they may have components of both orientations. White House Conferences on Aging, for example, involve a series of delegate councils that discuss issues of concern to older U.S. citizens and make recommendations for government action.

Delegate councils are formed in a number of ways. Some councils are the product of ad hoc task forces or coalitions that have been meeting informally for some time. Other councils begin with the support and sponsorship of a particular agency and gradually establish their own identities, rules and procedures, and sources of funding. Representatives to delegate councils are either elected or appointed, and leadership is usually determined through an election.

Because council members are responsible for representing the views, interests, and positions of their sponsors to the delegate council, members often act formally on behalf of their constituencies. Delegates communicate with their sponsors regarding the proceedings of the council. The effectiveness of the delegate council depends on the ability of each delegate to achieve two-way communication between the council and the represented unit. The individual delegates are not expected to engage in a high level of personal self-disclosure because they are bound by a mandate to present the collective views of the group of people they represent.

SUMMARY

This introductory chapter provides a framework for studying and working with groups. Group work is a broad field of practice conducted by professional social workers with, and on behalf of, many different client groups in many different settings. A definition of group work is offered that encompasses the breadth of group work practice and is sufficiently flexible to allow specialized approaches and objectives. To understand the types of groups that exist in practice, a distinction is made between treatment and task groups. Although some functions and objectives of task and treatment groups overlap, they are distinguished by a variety of characteristics.

This chapter also helps clarify the kinds of task and treatment groups often encountered in practice and illustrates the commonalities and differences among these groups. The typology of treatment groups distinguishes among those with five primary purposes: (1) support, (2) education, (3) growth, (4) therapy, and (5) socialization.

The typology of task groups distinguishes among nine types of task groups that are organized to serve three primary purposes: (1) meeting client needs, (2) meeting organizational needs, and (3) meeting community needs. Types of task groups that serve client needs include teams, treatment conferences, and staff development groups. Types of task groups that serve organizational needs include committees, cabinets, and boards of directors. Types of task groups that serve community needs include social action groups, coalitions, and delegate councils.

chapter 2

Historical Developments

To develop a broad perspective concerning the potential uses of groups in practice settings, it is helpful to understand the developments that have occurred in the study of groups and in the practice of group work over the years. This historical perspective also gives the group worker a firm foundation on which to build a knowledge base for effective group work practice.

Two general types of inquiries have enhanced the understanding of groups. One type has come from social scientists who have experimented with groups in laboratories. This inquiry has led to social science findings about basic properties and processes of groups. The other type of inquiry has been made for over 100 years by group work practitioners from disciplines including but not limited to adult education, psychology, social work, recreation, theater, and medicine. The results of both inquiries have led to improved methods for working with groups.

KNOWLEDGE FROM GROUP WORK PRACTICE: TREATMENT GROUPS

Although casework began in England and the United States in charity organizations in the late nineteenth century, group work grew up mainly in British and American settlement houses. The use of group work in settlement houses and casework in charity organizations was not by accident. Group work—and the settlement houses in which it was practiced—offered citizens the opportunity for education, recreation, socialization, and community involvement. Unlike the charity organizations, which focused on the diagnosis and treatment of the problems of the poor, settlement houses offered groups as an opportunity for citizens to gather to share their views, gain mutual support, and exercise the power derived from their association for social change. Alissi (2001) points out that groups were a central component of clubs and social settlements. The focus was on promoting the well-being of individual members through acceptance, companionship, and solidarity, while at the same time promoting democratic participation, social justice, and social action in civic, industrial, and social institutions.

There were some exceptions to this trend. For example, as early as 1895, some people in the charity organization movement realized there was a need to organize the poor for social change as well as to work with them one-to-one (Brackett, 1895). Boyd (1935) reported how social group work was used for therapeutic purposes in state mental institutions.

Contributions to social group work have also made by many other disciplines. For example, Dr. Pratt, a physician who worked with tuberculosis patients in 1905, is often attributed with being the first to use a group as a treatment modality. Early contributors with mental health backgrounds include Lazell (1921), who reported using psychoeducational methods in the treatment of inpatients, Marsh (1931, 1933, 1935), who reported using milieu therapy, and Syz (1928), who reported using a here-and-now focus with patients with dementia. There were also early psychodynamic group therapists such as Wender (1936), Schilder (1937), and Slavson (1940), who reported the results of their clinical work.

Interest in group work also stemmed from those who had led socialization groups, adult education groups, and recreation groups in settlement houses and youth service agencies (McCaskill, 1930). In fact, during these early years, the term *club work* was often used interchangeably with the term *group work* (Slavson, 1939a, p. 126).

It is often believed that group work is considerably younger than casework, but group work agencies actually started only a few years after casework agencies. There were courses for group workers in schools of social work in the early 1900s (Maloney, 1963), and both casework and group work were used by social workers in the early twentieth century.

Casework soon became identified with the social work profession, but group work did not become formally linked with social work until the National Conference of Social Work in 1935. The identification of group work with the social work profession increased during the 1940s (American Association of Group Workers, 1947), although group workers continued to maintain loose ties with recreation, adult education, and mental hygiene until 1955, when group workers joined with six other professional groups to form the National Association of Social Workers.

Differences between Casework and Group Work

Compared with caseworkers, who relied on insight developed from psychodynamic approaches and on the provision of concrete resources, group workers relied on program activities to spur members to action. Program activities of all types were the media through which groups attained their goals (Addams, 1909, 1926; Boyd, 1935, 1938; Smith, 1935). Activities such as camping, singing, group discussion, games, and arts and crafts were used for recreation, socialization, education, support, and rehabilitation. Unlike casework, which was mainly focused on problem solving and rehabilitation, group work activities were used for enjoyment as well as to solve problems. Thus, the group work methods that developed from settlement house work had a different focus and a different goal than did casework methods.

Differences between casework and group work can also be clearly seen in the helping relationship. Caseworkers sought out the most underprivileged victims of industrialization and diagnosed and treated worthy clients by providing them with resources and acting as examples of virtuous, hardworking citizens.

Although group workers also worked with the poor and impaired, they did not focus solely on the poorest people nor on those with the most problems. They preferred the word *members* rather than *clients* (Bowman, 1935). They emphasized members' strengths rather than their weaknesses. Helping was seen as a shared relationship in which the group worker and the group members worked together for mutual understanding and action regarding their common concerns for their community. As concerns were identified, group members supported and helped one another, and the worker mediated between the demands of society and the needs of group members (Schwartz, 1981).

Shared interaction, shared power, and shared decision making placed demands on group workers that were not experienced by caseworkers. The number of group members, the fact that they could turn to one another for help, and the democratic decision-making processes that were encouraged meant that group workers had to develop skills different from those of caseworkers. Group workers used their skills to intervene in complex and often fast-paced group interactions but remained aware of the welfare of all group members. Schwartz (1966) summed up the feelings engendered by the new group work method very well in the statement "there are so many of them and only one of me" (p. 572).

Unlike the early writings of caseworkers, which emphasized improving practice outcomes by careful study, diagnosis, and treatment (Richmond, 1917), the early writings of group workers (Coyle, 1930, 1935) emphasized the processes that occurred during group meetings. For example, Grace Coyle, one of the first social workers to publish a text on groups, titled her 1930 work *Social Process in Organized Groups,* whereas the first text on casework, published in 1917 by Mary Richmond, was called *Social Diagnosis.*

The emphasis on group processes has remained throughout the history of group work. Group workers have always been concerned with how best to use the unique possibilities offered by the interaction of different people in a group. Thus, workers focus on the group as a whole as well as on individual members.

Intervention Targets

The importance of group work for enlightened collective action (Follett, 1926) and democratic living (Slavson, 1939b) was an essential part of social group work's early roots. Grace Coyle's work, for example, focused heavily on social action, social change, and social justice (Coyle, 1935, 1938). Thus, social group work has its roots in both the individual change focus of early group therapists and the educational and social change foci of group workers with educational, recreational, club, and settlement house settings. Today, group work in the settlement house tradition is best seen in community centers, especially in developing countries (Yan, 2001).

During the 1940s and 1950s, group workers began to use groups more frequently to provide therapy and remediation in mental health settings. Therapy groups were insight oriented, relying less on program activities and more on diagnosis and treatment of members' problems (Konopka, 1949, 1954; Redl, 1944; Trecker, 1956).

The emphasis on the use of groups for therapy and remediation was the result, in part, of the influence of Freudian psychoanalysis and ego psychology and, in part, of World War II, which created a severe shortage of trained workers to deal with mentally disabled war veterans. It was also spurred on by Fritz Redl and Gisela Konopka, who helped make group services an integral part of child guidance clinics. Interest in the use of groups in psychiatric settings continued into the 1950s, as can be seen in the proceedings of a national institute on this topic in 1955 (Trecker, 1956).

Although there was an increased emphasis in the 1940s and 1950s on using groups to improve the functioning of individual members, interest remained in using groups for recreational and educational purposes, especially in Jewish community centers and in youth organizations such as the Girl Scouts and the YWCA. During the 1950s and 1960s, groups were also used for community development and social action in neighborhood centers and community agencies. At the same time, there was an increase in the study of small groups as a social phenomenon. For example, in 1947, Kurt Lewin and others founded the National Training Laboratories (NTL), which focused on group dynamics, using t-groups (training groups), to help executives and other group leaders to understand the power of group dynamics and to learn how to facilitate groups more effectively. NTL flourished during the 1950s and 1960s and, after a period of decline during the 1970s, is effectively carrying out its mission today. According to Hare (1976), the 1950s were the golden age of the study of groups.

The Weakening of Group Work

During the 1960s the popularity of group services declined. This can be seen in accounts of well-known projects such as the Mobilization for Youth experiment (Weissman, 1969). Weissman stated, "the planners of Mobilization for Youth did not accord group work services a major role in the fight against delinquency" (p. 180). Work training programs and educational opportunities were viewed as more significant than group work services—except in the area of community organization, in which the skill of group workers played an important role in organizing youths and adults around important social concerns.

Also, during the 1960s, the push toward a generic view of practice in schools of social work and the movement away from specializations in casework, group work, and community organization tended to weaken group work specializations in professional schools and reduce the number of professionals trained in group work as their primary mode of practice. Taken together, these factors contributed to the decline of group work in the 1960s.

During the 1970s interest in group work continued to wane. Fewer professional schools offered advanced courses in group work, and fewer practitioners used it as a practice method. To increase awareness among practitioners about the potential benefits of groups, group workers throughout the United States and Canada came together in 1979 for the First Annual Symposium for the Advancement of Group Work. Each year since then, an annual group work symposium has been convened. The symposia bring together social group workers from the United States and other countries, who present clinical findings, research results, and workshops based on the work they have done with groups in their own communities.

During the last two decades, attempts to revitalize group work within social work have continued unabated. The Association for the Advancement of Social Work with Groups (AASWG) has expanded into an international association with many affiliated local chapters. In addition to the annual symposia it sponsors, the AASWG has a person who is a liaison to the Council on Social Work Education to promote group work curriculum in schools of social work. The AASWG has also developed standards on group work education and submitted testimony to the Commission on Educational Policy of the Council on Social Work Education.

Despite the attempts at revitalization, Putnam (2001) points out that the decline of civic engagement in voluntary associations and participation in formed and natural groups of all sorts has continued into the twenty-first century. Putnam (2001) attributes this to a number of factors including (1) time and money pressures, (2) mobility and sprawl, and (3) the availability of technology and the mass media. In describing the harm that this has caused, he stresses the importance of human capital and reengagement in all of our social institutions.

Current Practice Trends

Treatment Groups

In an article that has had a profound effect on social work practice with groups, Papell and Rothman (1962) outlined three historically important models of group work practice, shown in Table 2.1, that are still widely used today. These three models are (1) the social goals model, (2) the remedial model, and (3) the reciprocal model.

Social Goals Model

The social goals model focuses on socializing members to democratic societal values. It values cultural diversity and the power of group action. It was used, and continues to be used, in settlement houses and in group work with youth organizations such as the Girl Scouts, the YWCA, and Jewish community centers. It also has been used by community development agencies to change societal norms and structures and improve the social welfare of all citizens.

The worker acts as an enabler who uses program activities, such as camping, discussions, and instructions about democratic processes, to socialize members. The worker also acts to empower members by helping them make collective decisions and use their collective strength to make society more responsive to their needs. For example, Macgowan and Pennell (2001) demonstrate how they use the social goals model to empower family members to make a plan for change in a model they refer to as *family group conferencing.*

The writings of Klein (1953, 1970, 1972) and Tropp (1968, 1976) helped to refine the social goals model. Tropp focused on how group development can be used to empower members to achieve the goals they have set for themselves. He was strongly opposed to the worker's establishing goals for members, believing instead that groups could promote growth only when the worker encouraged group self-direction toward common goals. Klein's writings emphasized the importance of matching members' needs to environmental opportunities for growth. Like Tropp, Klein emphasized the autonomy of group members and their freedom to pursue their own self-defined goals. Middleman (1980, 1982) has also made important contributions to the model by emphasizing the importance of program activities. Breton (1994, 1995, 1999; Nosko & Breton, 1997–1998), Cohen and Mullender (1999), Cox (1988), Cox and Parsons (1994), Lee (2001), Mondros and Wilson (1994), Mullender and Ward (1991), Parsons (1991), and Pernell (1986) have also made significant contributions by focusing on empowerment strategies in social group work.

Remedial Model

The remedial model focuses on restoring or rehabilitating individuals by helping them change their behavior. The worker acts as a change agent and intervenes in the group to achieve specific purposes determined by group members, the group worker, and society. The remedial model uses a leader-centered approach to group work, with the worker actively intervening in the group's process, often using step-by-step problem solving and task-centered or behavioral methods. Garvin (1997), Rose (1998), and Vinter (1967) are often associated with this approach to group work. With the increased attention to time-limited, goal-directed practice

TABLE 2.1 ● *Three Models of Social Group Work*

Selected Characteristics	Social Goals Model	Remedial Model	Reciprocal Model
Purpose and goals	Social consciousness, social responsibility, informed citizenship, and informed political and social action	To restore and rehabilitate group members who are behaving dysfunctionally	To form a mutual aid system among group members to achieve optimum adaptation and socialization
Agency	Settlement houses and neighborhood center settings	Formal agency setting, clinical outpatient or inpatient settings	Compatible with clinical inpatient and outpatient settings and neighborhood and community centers
Focus of work	Larger society, individuals within the context of the neighborhood and the social environment	Alleviating problems or concerns Improving coping skills	Creating a self-help, mutual aid system among all group members
Role of the group worker	Role model and enabler for responsible citizenship	Change agent who engages in study, diagnosis, and treatment to help group members attain individual treatment goals	Mediator between needs of members and needs of the group and the larger society Enabler contributing data not available to the members
Type of group	Citizens, neighborhood, and community residents	Clients who are not functioning adequately and need help coping with life's tasks	Partners who work together sharing common concerns
Methods used in the group	Discussion, participation, consensus, developing and carrying out a group task, community organizing, and other program and action skills to help group members acquire instrumental skills about social action and communal living and change	Structured exercises, direct and indirect influence—within and outside of the group—to help members change behavior patterns	Shared authority where members discuss concerns, support one another, and form a cohesive social system to benefit one another

Adapted from Papell and Rothman, 1980.

and measurable treatment outcomes, this model has received increasing attention in the group work literature in recent years (Clifford, 1998; Edleson & Syers, 1990; Ellis, 1992; MacKenzie, 1990, 1996; Magen, 1999; Piper & Joyce, 1996; Rose & LeCroy, 1991; Shapiro, Peltz, & Bernadett-Shapiro, 1998; Spitz & Spitz, 1999). It is used widely in inpatient and community-based settings with individuals who have severe behavioral problems and social skills deficits.

Time-limited, highly structured remedial groups are also being used with increasing frequency in managed care settings as cost effective alternatives to long-term individual and group psychotherapy (MacKenzie, 1995). A recent survey of directors and providers in managed care companies suggests that this trend is likely to accelerate in future years (Taylor & Burlingame, 2001). Although the survey indicated that social workers were more familiar than psychologists and psychiatrists with short-term structured group work approaches, it also indicated that practitioners from all disciplines tended to be more familiar and more comfortable with the traditional process-oriented, long-term group models, suggesting that more graduate and undergraduate education and more in-service training are needed about how to conduct short-term, structured, remedial model groups (Taylor & Burlingame, 2001).

Reciprocal Model

The third model presented by Papell and Rothman (1962), the reciprocal model, is sometimes referred to as the *interactional model* (Reid, 1997). The model derives its name from the emphasis on the reciprocal relationship that exists between group members and society. Members both influence and are influenced by the environment. The worker acts as a mediator, helping group members find the common ground between their needs and societal demands. The worker also acts as a resource person who facilitates the functioning of the group and helps members form a mutual-aid system and explore new ways of coping with and adapting to environmental demands.

As contrasted with the remedial model, in which the work of the group is often focused on helping individual members with specific problems, the reciprocal model encourages workers to use group processes to foster a therapeutic environment in the group as a whole. The reciprocal model also encourages the worker to help the agency and the wider community better understand and meet individual members' needs. Gitterman and Shulman (2005), Schwartz (1976), and Shulman (1999) are best known for the group-centered, process-oriented approach to group work practice, but other authors such as Brown (1991), Falck (1988), Glassman and Kates (1990), and Wasserman and Danforth (1988) have made important contributions to this model of group work practice.

The reciprocal model is closely aligned with ecological systems theory, which has received criticism for being too vague to guide practice (Wakefield, 1996). Despite this criticism, the reciprocal model has wide appeal because of its humanistic orientation, which emphasizes the potential for growth and development of group members, the activation of members' adaptive capacities through mutual-aid efforts, and the attempt at making the social environment more responsive to members' needs.

Divergent and Unified Practice Models

The different foci of current practice models are equally valid, depending on the purposes, practice situations, and tasks facing the group. Group work practice has an eclectic base, which developed as a response to diverse needs for educational, recreational, mental health, and social services (Alissi, 1980; Lang, 1972, 1979a, 1979b; Papell & Rothman, 1980; Roberts & Northen, 1976). A remedial purpose, for example, may be particularly appropriate for some populations and in some settings, such as alcohol and drug treatment centers and residential centers for delinquent youth. In contrast, the reciprocal model is ideally suited for support groups designed to help members cope with distressing life events. It is also ideally suited to the facilitation of self-help groups in which reciprocal sharing of mutual concerns and the giving and receiving of support are central. For example, in Make Today Count, a medical self-help group for cancer patients, members are encouraged to share their concerns, experiences, and the reactions of their family members to help each other cope with their illness.

The usefulness and appropriateness of different practice models suggest that group workers should make differential use of group work methods, depending on the purposes, objectives, and goals of the groups they are leading. In a comprehensive review of the history of group work, Reid (1981) concludes that there has always been more than one model of group work operating in the United States and that there will continue to be several models in use to meet the many purposes and goals of group work.

In recent years, there has also been a greater attempt to integrate different models of group work practice (Papell, 1997). For example, Papell and Rothman (1980) proposed a "mainstream model" of group work practice that incorporates elements of many different practice models. They suggested that this model was characterized by "common goals, mutual aid, and nonsynthetic experiences" (p. 7). They pointed out that the fostering of a mutual-aid system among members is a common ingredient of many seemingly polarized approaches to group work practice. They suggested that group development and the creation of group structures for increasing the autonomy of members as the group develops are also common elements of most current conceptualizations of group work practice.

Alissi (2001) has described what he believes to be the central tenants of the mainstream model. These include a commitment to (1) democratic values, including voluntary group association, collective deliberation, decision making and action, cultural pluralism, individual freedom and liberty, and social responsibility to promote the common good; (2) the welfare of the individual and the betterment of society; (3) program activities that reflect the needs, interests, and aspirations of members; (4) the power of small group processes; and (5) the influence of the group worker doing *with* rather than *for* the members of the group.

Similarly, in considering the past, present, and future of group work in social work, Middleman and Wood (1990) also conclude that, in practice, there is a blending of models of group work. They suggested that a mainstream model of social work with groups should include the worker (1) helping members develop a system of mutual aid; (2) understanding, valuing, and respecting group processes as powerful dynamics for change; (3) helping members become empowered for autonomous functioning within and outside the group; and (4) helping members "re-experience their groupness at the point of termination" (p. 11). Thus, they concluded that some clinical work with groups, especially when it focuses exclusively on one-to-one work with individual members within a group context, would be excluded from a mainstream model of social work with groups.

In recent years there has been a growing emphasis on short-term structured groups for persons with specific problems such as depression, eating disorders, and a variety of other problems (see, for example, Bieling, McCabe, & Antony, 2006; Kaduson & Schaefer,

2000; Kellner, 2001; Langelier, 2001; McFarlane, 2002; Riess and Dockray Miller, 2002; Roffman, 2004; Rose, 2004; Velasquez, Maurer, Crouch, & DiClemente, 2001; Waterman & Walker, 2001; White & Freeman, 2000). Some of these authors such as Bieling and colleagues (2006) make a real effort to pay attention to how group dynamics can be used when working on individual problems. Others, however, do not fit into the mainstream model because they use the group only as a vehicle for treating multiple individuals, rather than making use of the group and its dynamics as a vehicle for change.

In the first edition of this book, Toseland and Rivas (1984) had as a primary goal bridging the chasm between the reciprocal, remedial, and social goals approaches to group work. The intent of the first edition, and this edition, is to elucidate a core body of knowledge, values, skills, and procedures that are essential for professional, competent group work practice, regardless of ideological orientation. The intent of this book is also to show how the group as a whole can facilitate change. Working with individuals for a time on a one-on-one basis in the context of a group is sometimes desirable, but only when the worker pays attention to the group as a whole, and invites and encourages all the members to get involved in the work being done with a single individual.

KNOWLEDGE FROM GROUP WORK PRACTICE: TASK GROUPS

Task groups have operated in social agencies since settlement houses and charity organizations began more than 100 years ago. The distinction between task groups and treatment groups made today was not made in the earlier history of group work. Groups were used simultaneously for both task and treatment purposes. Earlier in the history of group work, the journals *The Group,* published from 1939 to 1955, and *Adult Leadership,* published from 1952 to 1977, devoted much space to articles about leading task groups.

With a few notable exceptions (Brill, 1976; Trecker, 1980) during the 1960s and 1970s, interest in task groups waned. However, interest was rekindled during the 1980s and 1990s with the renewed emphasis on the value of participatory management practices (Gummer, 1991, 1995). For example, Dluhy (1990), Ephross and Vassil (2005), Fatout and Rose (1995), Toseland and Ephross (1987), and Tropman (1996) have all made outstanding contributions to the task group literature. Still, the current need for expertise in task group practices is becoming critical as more and more agencies are using participatory management practices and team approaches to service delivery. This text is designed, in part, to address this gap in the literature.

KNOWLEDGE FROM SOCIAL SCIENCE RESEARCH

Practitioners sometimes criticize the findings of social scientists as not being generalizable to real-world practice settings. Some social scientists conducting their research in laboratory settings use analogue designs, which may include short-term groups, artificial problems, and students who are not always motivated. Despite these limitations, the precision of laboratory studies enables social scientists to examine how different group dynamics operate. Findings from these studies increase practitioners' understanding of how helpful and harmful group dynamics develop.

Social scientists also use naturalistic observations to study the functioning of community groups. Some classic observational studies are those conducted by Bales (1955), Lewin (1947, 1948), Roethlisberger and Dickson (1939), Thrasher (1927), and Whyte (1943). Although not as precise as laboratory studies, naturalistic studies overcome some of the limitations of laboratory studies and provide many insights into the way groups develop.

According to Hare (1976), the scientific study of groups began at the turn of the century. A basic research question, which was asked at that time and continues to receive much attention today, concerns the extent to which being a part of a group influences the individual group member. Triplett (1898), for example, examined the effect that cyclists had on each other during races and found that a racer's competitiveness appeared to depend on the activities of others on the track. Taylor (1903) found that productivity increased among workers who were freed from the pressure to conform to the standards of other workers. Those early findings suggest that the presence of others has a significant influence on an individual group member. The presence of others tends to generate pressure to conform to the standards of behavior that are expected of those who belong to the group.

Other early social scientists also recognized the influence of groups on individual behavior. LeBon (1910) referred to the forces that were generated by group interaction as "group contagion" and "group mind," recognizing that people in groups react differently than do individuals. McDougall (1920) extended the concept of the group mind. He noted the existence of groups as entities and pointed out a number of group-as-a-whole properties that could be studied as phenomena separate and distinct from properties affecting individuals working outside of a group.

The concept of a primary group was also an important contribution to the study of groups. Cooley (1909) defined a *primary group* as a small, informal group—such as a family or a friendship group—that has a tremendous influence on members' values, moral standards, and normative behaviors. The primary group was therefore viewed as essential in understanding socialization and development.

Few studies of small-group processes were published between 1905 and 1920, but activity in this area increased after World War I (Hare, 1976). Several experiments conducted during that time illustrated the powerful effects of group forces on the judgments and behavior of group members. Allport (1924), for example, found that the presence of others improved task performance, and Sherif (1936) and Asch (1957) found that members were highly influenced by the opinions of others in the group.

After World War I, social scientists began to study groups operating in the community. One of the earliest social scientists to study groups in their natural environments was Frederick Thrasher (1927). He studied gangs of delinquents in the Chicago area by becoming friendly with gang members and observing the internal operations of gangs. He noted that every member of a gang had a status within the group that was attached to a functional role in the gang. Thrasher also drew attention to the culture that developed within a gang, suggesting there was a common code that all members followed. The code was enforced by group opinion, coercion, and physical punishment. Thrasher's work and the works of Shaw (1930) and Whyte (1943) have influenced how group work is practiced with youths in settlement houses, neighborhood centers, and youth organizations. The naturalistic studies of boys in camp settings by Newstetter, Feldstein, and Newcomb (1938) were also influential in the development of group work services.

Later, Sherif and colleagues (Sherif, 1956; Sherif & Sherif, 1953; Sherif, White, & Harvey, 1955) relied on naturalistic observations of boys in a summer camp program to demonstrate how cohesion and intergroup hostility develop in groups. Groups of boys who spent time together and had common goals, such as winning a tug-of-war, became more cooperative, developed a liking for one another, and felt solidarity with their teammates. At the same time, antagonism between groups increased. Bringing boys from different groups together only increased the tension until tasks were assigned that required the joint efforts of boys from different groups.

Social scientists also learned more about people's behavior in groups from studies done in industry and in the U.S. Army. Perhaps the most famous of all industrial studies is the classic series of studies at Western Electric's Hawthorne Plant in Chicago (Roethlisberger, 1941; Roethlisberger & Dickson, 1939, 1975). These studies were designed to test whether piece-rate wage incentives increased the output of workers who assembled telephone equipment. The incentives were designed in such a way that wage increases gained by one team member would also benefit other team members. Management believed such a system would encourage individual productivity and increase group spirit and morale because all team members would benefit from the increase in productivity.

It was found that an informal group had developed among team members. Despite the opportunity to improve individual and group wages, workers did not produce more under the new incentive system. Results of the studies suggest that informal norms of what constituted a fair day's work governed the workers' behavior. Members of a work group that produced too much were ridiculed as "rate busters" and those who produced too little were called "chiselers." Occasionally, more severe sanctions called "binging" were applied by team members when a worker did not conform to the team's notion of a fair day's work. Binging consisted of striking a fellow worker as hard as possible on the upper arm while verbally asking the worker to comply with the group's norms.

Studies conducted on combat units during World War II also helped identify the powerful effects that small groups can have on the behavior of their members. For example, in describing the fighting ability of combat soldiers, Shils (1950) and Stouffer (1949) found that the courage of the average soldier was only partially sustained by hatred of the enemy and the patriotic ideas of a democratic society. Their studies revealed that soldiers' loyalty to their particular unit strengthened their morale and supported them during periods of intense combat stress.

During the 1950s, an explosion of knowledge about small groups took place. Earlier experiments by Bales (1950), Jennings (1947, 1950), Lewin, Lippitt, and White (1939), and Moreno (1934) spurred interest in the study of both task and treatment groups. Some of the most important findings from this period are summarized in the work of Cartwright and Zander (1968), Hare (1976), Kiesler (1978), McGrath (1984), Nixon (1979), and Shaw (1976). Because these viewpoints are reflected in a discussion of group dynamics and leadership in Chapters 3 and 4, they are not presented here.

The major themes of small-group research that were initially developed in the first half of the twentieth century—that is, cohesion, conformity, communication and interaction patterns, group development, leadership, and social cognition and perception—continue to dominate the research efforts of social scientists investigating the dynamics of small groups today (Forsyth, 2006; McGrath, Arrow, & Berdahl, 2000). But Garvin (1998) also notes that new themes have emerged. These include an increased emphasis on the effects of gender and diversity on group development. Horne and Rosenthal (1997) note that in recent years there has been a greater emphasis on research on teamwork (see, e.g., Abramson & Bronstein, 2004; Levi, 2007; Payne, 2000). There has also been an increased interest in the use of computer technology both for decision support systems (Forsyth, 2006), as well as to form virtual groups through telephone, video, and internet, for people who do not get together in-person (Toseland, Naccarato, & Wray, 2007).

INFLUENTIAL THEORIES

From knowledge about small groups accumulated over the years in laboratory and natural settings, investigators of group phenomena began to develop comprehensive theories to explain group functioning. An enormous variety of these theories exist (Douglas, 1979). This chapter considers five of the most important theories: (1) systems theory, (2) psychodynamic theory, (3) learning theory, (4) field theory, and (5) social exchange theory. Although a thorough knowledge of systems theory is basic to all group work practice, the text also summarizes four additional theories that have had an important influence on group work practice. As they become more experienced, group workers should consider learning more about these theories.

Systems Theory

Systems theory attempts to understand the group as a system of interacting elements. It is probably the most widely used and broadly applied theory of group functioning (Anderson, 1979; Olsen, 1968). Several influential theorists have developed conceptualizations of groups as social systems.

To Parsons (1951), groups are social systems with several interdependent members attempting to maintain order and a stable equilibrium while they function as a unified whole. Groups are constantly facing changing demands in their quest to attain goals and to maintain a stable equilibrium. Groups must mobilize their resources and act to meet changing demands if they are to survive. According to Parsons, Bales, and Shils (1953), there are four major functional tasks for systems such as a group: (1) integration—ensuring that members of groups fit together; (2) adaptation—ensuring that groups change to cope with the demands of their environment; (3) pattern maintenance—ensuring that groups define and sustain their basic purposes, identities, and procedures; and (4) goal attainment—ensuring that groups pursue and accomplish their tasks.

Groups must accomplish these four functional tasks to remain in equilibrium. The work of carrying out these tasks is left to the group's leader and its members. The leader and members act to help their group survive so they can be gratified as the group reaches its goal (Mills, 1967). To do this, group members observe and assess the group's progress toward its goals and take action to avoid problems. The likelihood that a group will survive depends on the demands of the environment, the extent to which members identify with group goals, and the degree to which members believe goals are attainable. By overcoming obstacles and successfully handling the functional tasks confronting them, groups strive to remain in a state of equilibrium.

Robert Bales, another important systems theorist, has a somewhat different conception of groups as social systems. Whereas Parsons was interested in developing a generalizable systems model to explain societal as well as group functioning, Bales concentrated his efforts on observing and theorizing about small task groups in laboratory settings. According to Bales (1950), groups must solve two general types of problems to maintain themselves. These include (1) instrumental problems, such as the group's reaching its goals, and (2) socioemotional problems, which include interpersonal difficulties, problems of coordination, and member satisfaction. Instrumental problems are caused by demands placed on the group by the outside environment; socioemotional problems arise from within the group.

The implications of Bales' work is that the worker should be concerned about group processes and outcomes, that is, members' social and emotional needs and the task accomplishments expected of the group. Exclusive attention to tasks leads to dissatisfaction and conflict within the group. Exclusive attention to members' socioemotional needs leads to the group's failure to accomplish its objectives and goals.

Because instrumental and socioemotional needs often conflict, it is usually impossible to attend to both sets of problems simultaneously. Therefore, the worker is placed in the precarious position of attending alternately to task and socioemotional needs to maintain the group's optimal functioning.

In contrast with Parsons, who emphasized harmony and equilibrium, Bales' systems model emphasizes tension and antagonism. Groups tend to vacillate between adaptation to the outside environment and attention to internal integration. Bales (1950) calls this the group's "dynamic equilibrium." Swings in attention are the result of the functional needs of the group in its struggle to maintain itself.

To study this "dynamic equilibrium," Bales observed interactions in several different kinds of task groups such as juries and teams (Bales, 1950, 1954, 1955). Bales found that, to deal with instrumental problems, group members asked for or gave opinions, asked for or gave information, and asked for or made suggestions. To handle socioemotional problems, group members expressed agreement or disagreement, showed tension or released tension, and showed solidarity or antagonism. Through these interactions, group members dealt with problems of communication, evaluation, control, decision making, tension reduction, and integration.

Bales (1954, 1955) also suggests that groups go through a natural process of evolution and development. Analysis of the distribution of interactions in each category in problem-solving groups suggests that typical task groups emphasize giving and receiving information early in group meetings, giving and asking for opinions in the middle stage, and giving and asking for suggestions in later stages (Shepard, 1964).

Bales (1950) developed a scheme for analyzing group interaction on the basis of his theory about how group members deal with instrumental and expressive tasks. This scheme is called Interaction Process Analysis. It puts members' interactions into 12 categories. Bales, Cohen, and Williamson (1979) have continued to develop and refine this system of analyzing group interactions. The new system, Systematic Multiple Level Observation of Groups (SYMLOG), is explained in Chapter 8.

The final conception of systems theory relevant to our understanding of group dynamics has been presented in Homans' (1950) early work, *The Human Group.* It is also evident in the writings of Germain and Gitterman (1996) and Siporin (1980) on ecological systems theory. According to these writers, groups are in constant interaction with their environments. They occupy an ecological niche. Homans suggests that groups have an external system and an internal system. The external system represents a group's way of handling the adaptive problems that result from its relationship with its social and physical environment. The internal system consists of the patterns of activities, interactions, and norms occurring within the group as it attempts to function.

Like Bales, Homans notes that the relative dominance of the internal system or the external system depends on the demands of the external and the internal environment of the group. Homans, however, denies the homeostatic idea of equilibrium proposed by Parsons and Bales, preferring to conceive of groups as ever changing entities. Change and the constant struggle for equilibrium are ever present.

The different conceptualizations of systems theory may at first appear confusing. However, when one considers the vast array of groups in modern society and people's different experiences in them, it becomes easier to understand how different conceptualizations of systems theory have developed. It is important to recognize that each conceptualization represents a unique attempt to understand the processes that occur in all social systems.

Concepts derived from these differing views of systems theory that are particularly relevant for group workers include the following:

- The existence of properties of the group as a whole that arise from the interactions of individual group members
- The powerful effects of group forces on members' behavior
- The struggle of groups to maintain themselves as entities when confronted with conflicts
- The awareness that groups must relate to an external environment as well as attend to their internal functioning
- The idea that groups are in a constant state of becoming, developing, and changing, which influences their equilibrium and continued existence
- The notion that groups have a developmental life cycle

Workers can use these concepts to facilitate the development of group processes that help treatment and task groups achieve their goals and help members satisfy their socioemotional needs.

Psychodynamic Theory

Psychodynamic theory has had an important influence on group work practice. In his work *Group Psychology and the Analysis of the Ego,* Freud (1922) set forth his theoretical formulations about groups and their influence on human behavior. Many of Freud's other works have also influenced group work practice. For example, commonly used terms such as *insight, ego strength,* and *defense mechanisms* originated in Freud's work. Although psychodynamic theory focuses primarily on the individual, and Freud did not practice group psychotherapy, many of his followers, including Bion (1991), Klein, Bernard, and Singer (2000), Redl (1942, 1944), Rutan (1992), Rutan and Stone (2001), and Yalom (1995), have adapted psychodynamic theory for working with groups. Psychodynamic theory has also influenced the founders of other practice theories used in groups, such as Eric Berne's transactional analysis, Fritz Perl's gestalt therapy, and Jacob Moreno's psychodrama.

According to psychodynamic theory, group members act out in the group unresolved conflicts from early life experiences. In many ways, the group becomes a reenactment of the family situation. Freud (1922), for example, describes the group leader as the all-powerful father figure who reigns supreme over group members. Group members identify with the group leader as the "ego ideal" (Wyss, 1973). Members form transference reactions to the group leader and to each other on the basis of their early life experiences. Thus, the interactions that occur in the group reflect personality structures and defense mechanisms that members began to develop early in life.

The group leader uses transference and countertransference reactions to help members work through unresolved conflicts by exploring past behavior patterns and linking these patterns to current behaviors. The group leader might, for example, interpret the behavior of two group members who are struggling for the leader's attention as unresolved sibling rivalry. When interpretations made by the group worker are timed appropriately, members gain insight into their own behavior. According to psychodynamic theory, insight is the essential ingredient in modifying and changing behavior patterns inside and outside the group.

Conceptions of psychodynamic group treatment (Yalom, 1995) have adapted and modified classical psychodynamic theory to include a greater emphasis on the here-and-now experiences of group interaction. Because of this emphasis this application is often referred to in the literature as *interpersonal group therapy* (Leszcz, 1992). Emphasizing the here-and-now experiences of group members is useful in ensuring that members deal with issues of immediate concern to them. From an analysis of here-and-now behavior patterns in the microcosm of the group, the leader can help members reconstruct unresolved childhood conflicts and have "corrective emotional experiences" (Leszcz, 1992, p. 48). Through direct, mutual interpersonal communications, members build interpersonal skills, adaptive capacities, and ego strength, as well as gain insight into their behavior. The cohesiveness of the group encourages members to reveal intimate details about their personal lives and to describe and act out their conflicts in a safe, supportive environment.

Psychodynamic theory has also been influential in furthering our understanding of how individuals behave in groups. Wilford Bion, who was psychodynamically trained, developed the Tavastock approach to help people understand the primitive emotional processes that occur in groups. He suggested that group members often avoid the work of the group by reacting to the leader's authority with flight-fight responses and dependency (Bion, 1991).

A thorough discussion of psychodynamic theory of group functioning is beyond the scope of this book. For further explanation of modern adaptations of psychodynamic theory to group work practice, see Janssen (1994), Konig (1994), Piper, Ogrodniczuk, and Duncan (2002), Rice (1987), Rutan (1992), Rutan and Stone (2001), and Yalom (1995).

Learning Theory

Perhaps no theory has stirred more controversy within social group work than learning theory. As with psychodynamic theory, the primary focus of learning theory is on the behavior of individuals rather than on the behavior of groups. Thus, learning theory has generally ignored the importance of group dynamics. Also, like the early emphasis on primitive drives in psychodynamic theory, the early emphasis on environmental contingencies and the de-emphasis of free will has led some group workers to conclude that learning theory is deterministic. For these reasons, some view learning theory as antithetical to the values and traditions of growth, autonomy, and self-determination that are so much a part of the heritage of group work practice.

Despite the controversy, learning theory has had an important influence on current methods of group work practice. The emphasis on clear and specific goal setting, contracting, the influence of the environment on the group and its members, step-by-step treatment planning, measurable treatment outcomes, and evaluation can be traced, at least in part, to the influence of learning theory. The growing importance of short-term, structured psychoeducational groups attests to the important influence that learning theory principles have had on group work practice (Budman, Simeone, Reilly, & Demby, 1994; Grayson, 1993; MacKenzie, 1990; Piper, 1992; Piper & Joyce, 1996; Rose, 1998; Wells, 1994).

According to social learning theory (Bandura, 1977), the behavior of group members can be explained by one of three methods of learning. In the classical approach to learning theory, behavior becomes associated with a stimulus. For example, a worker responds by making a negative verbal comment each time a member turns and speaks to another member while the worker or other group members are speaking. After several times, the mere stimulus of the member's turning, without speaking, will be enough to cue the worker to respond with a negative verbal comment.

A second and more common method of learning is called operant conditioning. In this paradigm, the behaviors of the group members and the worker are governed by the consequences of their actions. Thus, if member A acts in a certain way and member B reacts positively, member A is likely to continue the behavior. Similarly, if a group worker receives negative feedback from group members about a particular behavior, the worker will be less likely to behave that way in the future.

In the group, the worker might use praise to increase member-to-member communications and negative verbal comments to decrease member-to-leader communications. To help a member with a problem he or she has experienced in the outside environment, such as being overweight, the group leader might ask the member to develop a plan that specifies self-imposed rewards for behavior that decreases caloric intake and self-imposed sanctions for behavior that increases caloric intake.

Several writers (Feldman, Caplinger, & Wodarski, 1983; Feldman & Wodarski, 1975; Rose, 1989, 1998, 2006; Rose & Edleson, 1987) use operant learning theory principles in their approach to group work. For example, Rose (1989) suggests that tokens, praise, or other reinforcers can be used to increase desired behavior and decrease undesired behavior in the group or in the external environment. Groups that focus on themes such as social skills training, assertiveness, relaxation, and parenting skills also frequently rely heavily on learning theory principles.

Bandura (1977) has developed a third learning paradigm called social learning theory. If group members or the group worker were to wait for classical or operant conditioning to occur, behavior in groups would be learned very slowly. Bandura proposed that most learning takes place through observation and vicarious reinforcement or punishment. For example, when a group member is praised for a certain behavior, that group member and other group members reproduce the behavior later, hoping to receive similar praise. When a group member who performs a certain behavior is ignored or punished by social sanctions, other group members learn not to behave in that manner because such behavior results in a negative outcome.

In response to concerns that learning theory has not taken into consideration motivations, expectations, and other cognitive aspects of behavior, Ellis (1992) and others have described cognitive-behavioral approaches to treatment (Beck, 1995; Leahy, 1996; Sheldon, 1995). Although learning theorists have not attempted to explain the functioning of groups as a whole, learning theory principles have been shown to be useful in helping members make desired changes. All group workers should be familiar with the basic principles of learning theory and cognitive behavior modification. Because of their particular relevance to treatment groups, some principles of classical, operant, social learning theory and cognitive-behavioral approaches are used in the discussion of specialized methods for leading treatment groups in Chapter 10.

Field Theory

Kurt Lewin, more than any other social scientist, has come to be associated with the study of group dynamics. He conducted numerous experiments on the forces that account for behavior in small groups. For example, in an early study investigating leadership, Lewin, Lippitt, and White (1939) created three types of groups with authoritarian, democratic, and laissez-faire leadership. The results of this study are reported in Chapter 4. Lewin and his colleagues were the first to apply the scientific method in developing a theory of groups. In 1944, he and his colleagues set up laboratories and formed the Research Center for Group Dynamics at the Massachusetts Institute of Technology.

According to Lewin's field theory, "a group has a life space, it occupies a position relative to other objects in this space, it is oriented toward goals, it locomotes in pursuit of these goals, and it may encounter barriers in the process of locomotion" (Shepard, 1964, p. 25). The unique contribution of field theory is that it views the group as a gestalt, that is, an evolving entity of opposing forces that act to hold members in the group and to move the group along in its quest for goal achievement. According to Lewin (1947), groups are constantly changing to cope with their social situation, although there are times in which a "quasi-stationary equilibrium" exists for all groups. In all cases, however, the behavior of individual group members and the group itself must be seen as a function of the total situation (Lewin, 1946).

In developing field theory, Lewin introduced several concepts to aid in understanding the forces at work in a group. Among these are (1) roles, which refer to the status, rights, and duties of group members; (2) norms, which are rules governing the behavior of group members; (3) power, which is the ability of members to influence one another; (4) cohesion, which is the amount of attraction the members of the group feel for one another and for the group; (5) consensus, which is the degree of agreement regarding goals and other group phenomena; and (6) valence, which is the potency of goals and objects in the life space of the group.

Lewin sought to understand the forces occurring in the group as a whole from the perspective of individual group members. He did this mathematically and topographically, using vectors to describe group forces. Emphasizing the importance of properties of the group that act on the individual member, most field theorists have focused their research efforts on *cohesion*, which they define as the totality of forces acting on individual members to keep them in the group. Studies by field theorists have shown that cohesion is related to agreement on goals and norms, shared understanding, and similar demographic backgrounds of members, as well as to productivity, satisfaction, and cooperative interaction patterns (Cartwright, 1951; Cartwright & Zander, 1968; Lippitt, 1957).

Along with his interest in formulating a theoretical model of group dynamics, Lewin was interested in the effect of groups on individuals' psychological makeup. Before his death in 1947, Lewin developed the t-group as a way to observe the effects of group processes on group members and as a means to help individual group members change their own behavior. Although he was not directly involved, he helped found the first National Training Laboratory in Group Development in 1947. Since then, t-groups have been used extensively at the National Training Laboratories as an experiential means to train group facilitators, to teach individuals about the effects of group dynamics, and to help individuals examine and change their own behavior.

Relying on a principle in Lewin's field theory that suggests individuals will not change their own behavior unless they see their behavior and their attitudes as others see them, the t-group experience attempts to provide participants with extensive feedback about their own behavior. Members are confronted with the effects of their behavior on other group members and on the group's facilitator. Role plays, simulations, and other experiential program activities are often used to illustrate how group processes develop and how they affect members.

Social Exchange Theory

Although field theory emphasizes the group as a whole, social exchange theory focuses on the behavior of individual group members. Blau (1964), Homans (1961), and Thibaut and Kelley (1959) are the principal developers of this approach to groups. Deriving their theory from animal psychology, economic analysis, and game theory, social exchange theorists suggest that when people interact in groups, each attempts to behave in a way that will maximize rewards and minimize punishments. Group members initiate interactions because the social exchanges provide them with something of value, such as approval. According to social exchange theorists, because ordinarily nothing is gained unless something is given in return, there is an exchange implied in all human relationships.

In social exchange theory, group behavior is analyzed by observing how individual members seek rewards while dealing with the sustained social interaction occurring in a group. For an individual in a group, the decision to express a given behavior is based on a comparison of the rewards and punishments that are expected to be derived from the behavior. Group members act to increase positive consequences and decrease negative consequences. Social exchange theory also focuses on the way members influence one another during social interactions. The result of any social exchange is based on the amount of social power and the amount of social dependence in a particular interaction.

Guided Group Interaction (Empey & Erikson, 1972; McCorkle, Elias, & Bixby, 1958) and Positive Peer Culture (Vorrath & Brendtro, 1985) are two specialized group work methods that rely heavily on principles from social exchange theory. They are frequently used with delinquent adolescents in residential and institutional settings. In both approaches, structured groups are used to confront, challenge, and eliminate antisocial peer-group norms and to replace them with prosocial norms through guided peer-group interaction.

Social exchange theory has been criticized as being mechanistic because it assumes people are always rational beings who act according to their analysis of rewards and punishments (Shepard, 1964). For the most part, these criticisms are unfounded. Social exchange theorists are aware that cognitive processes affect how people behave in groups (Keller & Dansereau, 1995; Knottnerus, 1994). Group members' perceptions of rewards and punishments are influenced by cognitive processes such as intentions and expectations. Thus, the work of social exchange theorists in psychology and of symbolic interaction theorists in sociology has helped to account for the role of cognitive processes in the behavior of individuals in groups and other social interactions. The influence of symbolic interaction theory and social exchange theory on social work practice with groups can be seen in the work of Balgopal and Vassil (1983) and Early (1992).

SUMMARY

This chapter describes historical developments in the practice of group work and in the social sciences. A historical perspective is presented to help workers develop a broad understanding of the uses of groups in practice settings and develop a knowledge base they can use to practice effectively with different types of groups.

The historical overview of group work practice presented in this chapter suggests that throughout the twentieth century, groups were used for a variety of purposes, such as education, recreation, socialization, support, and therapy. The early emphasis on the use of groups for education, recreation, and socialization has waned in recent years in favor of an increased interest in the use of groups for support, mutual aid, and therapy. This trend parallels the gradual transition during the 1930s and 1940s away from group work's amorphous roots in adult education, recreation, and social work to its formal incorporation into the social work profession during the 1950s.

Currently, social group work is being revitalized in schools of social work and in practice settings. As current trends indicate, in recent years there has also been an increased recognition of the roots of social group work and the multiple purposes group work can serve.

This chapter also briefly explores historical developments in social science research that have relevance for understanding group processes. Findings from these studies emphasize the powerful influence that the group as a whole has on individual group members. The chapter closes with a review of five theories: (1) systems theory, (2) psychodynamic theory, (3) learning theory, (4) field theory, and (5) social exchange theory, all of which have had an important influence on group work practice.

chapter 3

Understanding Group Dynamics

The forces that result from the interactions of group members are often referred to as *group dynamics.* Because group dynamics influence the behavior of both individual group members and the group as a whole, they have been of considerable interest to group workers for many years (Coyle, 1930, 1937; Elliott, 1928).

A thorough understanding of group dynamics is useful for practicing effectively with any type of group. Although many theories have been developed to conceptualize group functioning, fundamental to all of them is an understanding of groups as social systems (Anderson, 1979). A system is made up of elements and their interactions. As social systems, therefore, task and treatment groups can be conceptualized as individuals in interaction with each other.

THE DEVELOPMENT OF HELPFUL GROUP DYNAMICS

One of the worker's most important tasks is to help groups develop dynamics that promote the satisfaction of members' socioemotional needs while facilitating the accomplishment of group tasks. Some years ago, Northen (1969) reminded group workers that this is not an automatic process.

Inattention to group dynamics can have a negative effect on the meeting of members' socioemotional needs and on goal attainment. Groups can unleash both harmful and helpful forces. The Hitler youth movement of the 1920s and 1930s, the Ku Klux Klan, the religious groups in Jonestown and at the Branch Davidians' ranch in Waco, Texas, and other harmful cults are familiar examples of group dynamics gone awry. Studies over the past thirty years have clearly shown that harmful group dynamics can be very traumatic for group members, with some emotional effects lasting years after the group experience (Galinsky & Schopler, 1977; Lieberman, Yalom, & Miles, 1973; Smokowski, Rose, & Bacallao, 2001; Smokowski, Rose, Todar, & Reardon, 1999). Two extremes of group leadership, aggressive confrontation and extreme passivity, seem to have particularly pernicious effects on members (Smokowski, Rose, & Bacallao, 2001; Smokowski et al., 1999). In contrast, appropriate development of group dynamics can lead to positive outcomes for the group and its members (Bednar & Kaul, 1994).

This chapter seeks to help group workers recognize and understand the dynamics generated through the group process. People who are familiar with group dynamics are less likely to be victimized by harmful leaders and groups. The chapter is also designed to help workers establish and promote group dynamics that satisfy members' socioemotional needs and that help groups achieve goals consistent with the humanistic value base of the social work profession. Some strategies for doing this follow.

Strategies for Promoting Helpful Group Dynamics

- Identify group dynamics as they emerge during ongoing group interaction
- Assess the impact of group dynamics on group members and the group as a whole
- Assess the impact of current group dynamics on future group functioning
- Examine the impact of group dynamics on members from different racial/ethnic and socioeconomic backgrounds
- Facilitate and guide the development of group dynamics that lead to members' satisfaction with their participation and that enable the group to achieve its goals

GROUP DYNAMICS

In this text, four dimensions of group dynamics are of particular importance to group workers in understanding and working effectively with all types of task and treatment groups:

1. Communication and interaction patterns
2. Cohesion
3. Social integration and influence
4. Group culture

In-depth knowledge of group dynamics is essential for understanding the social structure of groups and for developing beginning-level skills in group work practice.

Communication and Interaction Patterns

According to Northen (1969), "Social interaction is a term for the dynamic interplay of forces in which contact between persons results in a modification of the behavior and attitudes of the participants" (p. 17). Verbal and nonverbal communications are the components of social interaction. Communication is the process by which people convey meanings to each other by using symbols. Communication entails (1) the encoding of a person's perceptions, thoughts, and feelings into language and other symbols, (2) the transmission of these symbols or language, and (3) the decoding of the transmission by another person. This process is shown in Figure 3.1. As members of a group communicate to one another, a reciprocal pattern of interaction emerges. The interaction patterns that develop can be beneficial or harmful to the group. A group worker who is knowledgeable about helpful communications and interactions can intervene in the patterns that are established to help the group achieve desired goals and to ensure the socioemotional satisfaction of members.

Communication can be verbal, nonverbal, or written. Whereas members of face-to-face groups experience verbal and nonverbal communications, members of telephone groups experience only verbal communications, and members of computer groups experience only written messages. Communication can also be synchronous, that is, back and forth in real time, or asynchronous, that is, not within the same time frame. Asynchronous communications occur in computer groups where members may respond to messages after they are posted on bulletin boards or in chat rooms.

Communication as a Process

The first step in understanding and intervening in interaction patterns is for the worker to be aware that, whenever people are together in face-to-face groups, they are communicating. Even if they are not communicating verbally, their nonverbal behaviors communicate intended and unintended messages.

As shown in Figure 3.1, all communications are intended to convey a message. Silence, for example, can communicate sorrow, thoughtfulness, anger, or lack of interest. In addition, every group member communicates not only to transmit information but also for many other reasons. Kiesler (1978) has suggested that people communicate with such interpersonal concerns as (1) understanding other people, (2) finding out where they stand in relation to other people, (3) persuading others, (4) gaining or maintaining power, (5) defending themselves, (6) provoking a reaction from others, (7) making an impression on others, (8) gaining or maintaining relationships, and (9) presenting a unified image to the group. Many other important reasons for communication could be added to this list. For example, Barker and colleagues (2000) highlight the importance of relational aspects of communication such as cooperation, connection, autonomy, similarity, flexibility, harmony, and stigmatization.

Workers who are aware that group members communicate for many reasons can observe, assess, and understand communication and interaction patterns. Because patterns of communication are often consistent across different situations, group workers can use this information to work with individual members and the group as a whole. For example, a worker observes that one member is consistently unassertive in the group. The worker might help the member practice responding assertively to situations in the group. Because the pattern of a lack of assertiveness is likely to occur in situations outside the group, the worker suggests that the member consider practicing the skills in situations encountered between meetings.

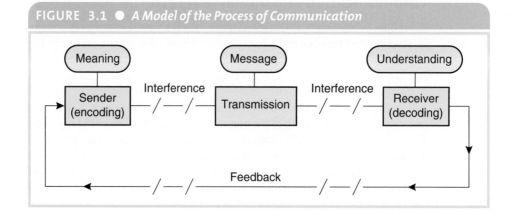

FIGURE 3.1 ● *A Model of the Process of Communication*

In addition to meanings transmitted in every communication, the worker should also be aware that messages are often received selectively. *Selective perception* refers to the screening of messages so they are congruent with one's belief system. As shown in Figure 3.1, messages are decoded and their meanings are received. Individual group members have a unique understanding of communications on the basis of their selective perception. Selected screening sometimes results in the blocking of messages so that they are not decoded and received. Napier and Gershenfeld (1993) suggest that the perception of a communication can be influenced by (1) life positions that result from experiences in early childhood, (2) stereotypes, (3) the status and position of the communicator, (4) previous experiences, and (5) assumptions and values. Thus, what might appear to a naive observer as a simple, straightforward, and objective social interaction might have considerable hidden meaning for both the sender and the receiver.

● **CASE EXAMPLE** *Selective Perception In a Parenting Group*

In a parenting group one member began to talk about the differences between her son and her daughter. The member mentioned that her daughter was much more difficult for her to handle than her son. Another member of the group said in an angry voice, "you just never think your daughter can do anything good." The group became silent and the original member said that even though her daughter was difficult it was not true that she "could never do anything right." The worker asked the other members about their reactions to the interaction but no one volunteered. The worker than asked the second member to talk about her own relationship with her mother and her daughter. As the member talked it became clear that she had a lot of resentment about the way her mother had treated her as a child, and now as an adult she had compensated for that in her interactions with her own daughter. The worker then asked the member if the way she perceived the first member's interaction with her daughter could have anything to do with how she was treated by her own mother. Before the member could answer, other members of the group began to talk about how they were treated by their own parents and how it made them especially sensitive to the way they interacted with their own children. Later, in the same session the member who had gotten angry said to the member that she had confronted that she apologized if she had over reacted. The member who had been confronted said that she had learned a lot from the discussion and was going to think of some new ways that she could interact with her daughter when her daughter "pushed her buttons." This led to a discussion of the things that triggered members to act in angry ways toward their children and what they might do differently to avoid getting angry.

It is not possible, or even desirable, for workers to analyze each interpersonal communication that occurs in a group. However, with a little practice, workers can develop a "third ear," that is, become aware of the meanings behind messages and their effect on a particular group member and on the group as a whole. Group workers are in a much better position to intervene in the group when they have a full understanding of the meanings of the messages being communicated and received by each member.

It is particularly important for the worker to pay attention to the nonverbal messages that are communicated by members. Body language, gestures, and facial expressions can provide important clues about how members are reacting to verbal communications. Members may not want to verbalize negative feelings, or they may just not know how to express their feelings. When workers are attuned to nonverbal messages, they can verbalize the feelings conveyed in them. This, in turn, may encourage members to talk about issues that they were previously only able to express nonverbally. For example, without identifying particular members who may be uncomfortable being associated with a particular sentiment, the worker might say "I noticed some tension in the group when we began to talk about. . . . I am wondering if anyone would like to share their feelings about this." Similarly, the worker might say "I thought I noticed a little boredom when we began talking about. . . . Has that topic been exhausted? Would you like to move on to the other issues we were going to discuss?"

Communications can also be distorted in transmission. In Figure 3.1, distortion is represented as interference. Among the most common transmission problems are language barriers. In the United States, workers frequently conduct groups with members from different cultural backgrounds and for whom English is a second language. In addition to problems of understanding accents and dialects, the meanings of many words are culturally defined and may not be interpreted as the communicator intended. Special care must be taken in these situations to avoid distorting the meanings intended by the communicator (Kadushin & Kadushin, 1997).

Noise and other distortions inside or outside the meeting room can interfere with effective communication. Similarly, hearing or eyesight problems can create difficulties in receiving messages. For example, almost one third of older people suffer from hearing impairments (Jette, 2001), and 25 percent suffer from visual impairments (Lighthouse International, 1995). Thus, when working with groups, the practitioner should be alert to physical problems that may impair communication. Some strategies for working with members with visual impairments and hearing impairments are presented in Tables 3.1 and 3.2.

Although meaning is communicated in every verbal and nonverbal message, it is also important for workers to be aware that problems in sending or receiving messages can distort or obfuscate intended meanings. Even when messages are clear, language barriers and

---

TABLE 3.1 ● *Techniques for Communicating with Group Members Who Have Hearing Impairments*

1. Position yourself so you are in full view of the person and your face is illuminated.

2. Speak in a normal voice.

3. Speak slowly and clearly. Stress key words. Pause between sentences.

4. Make sure no one else is talking when a group member is speaking to a hearing-impaired person or when a hearing-impaired person is speaking to a group member.

5. Make sure the room is free of background noises and has good acoustics.

6. Look for cues, such as facial expressions or inappropriate responses, that indicate the individual has misunderstood.

7. If you suspect that the individual has misunderstood, restate what has been said.

8. Speak *to* the individual, not *about* the person.

Adapted from Blazer, 1978.

TABLE 3.2 ● *Techniques for Communicating with Group Members Who Have Visual impairments*

1. Ask the individual whether assistance is needed to get to the meeting room. If the reply is yes, offer your elbow. Walk a half step ahead so your body indicates a change in direction, when to stop, and so forth.

2. Introduce yourself and all group members when the meeting begins. Go around the group clockwise or counterclockwise. This will help the group member learn where each member is located.

3. When you accompany a visually impaired person into a new meeting room, describe the layout of the room, the furniture placement, and any obstacles. This will help orient the individual.

4. Try not to disturb the placement of objects in the meeting room. If this is unavoidable, be sure to inform the person about the changes. Similarly, let the individual know if someone leaves or enters the room.

5. When guiding visually impaired individuals to their seat, place their hand on the back of the chair and allow them to seat themselves.

6. Speak directly to the visually impaired person, not through an intermediary.

7. Look at the individual when you speak.

8. Don't be afraid to use words such as *look* and *see*.

9. Speak in a normal voice. Do not shout.

10. Visually impaired people value independence just as sighted people do. Do not be overprotective.

11. Give explicit instructions about the location of coffee or snacks, and during program activities. For example, state, "The coffee pot is 10 feet to the left of your chair," rather than "The coffee pot is right over there on your left."

Adapted from a handout prepared by Lighthouse International, 111 E. 59th St., New York, NY 10222.

---

cultural interpretations of the meaning conveyed in a message may mean that it is not received as intended (Anderson & Carter, 2003). This can be a particularly vexing problem for members from bilingual backgrounds for whom English is a second language (Sue & Sue, 1999). It has been pointed out, for example, that white Americans have a significantly higher rate of verbal participation in groups than Asian Americans, Native Americans, and Mexican Americans of similar educational background (Gray-Little & Kaplan, 2000). Because higher rates of verbal participation in groups are associated with reduced attrition and other therapeutic benefits, lower levels of participation by minority members of multi-cultural groups is troubling (Gray-Little & Kaplan, 2000). Therefore, when English is a second language, care should be taken to ensure that members understand what is being said and that they feel comfortable contributing to the group discussion. Workers can often help by ensuring that minority members have ample opportunity to speak and that their points of view are carefully considered by the group.

To prevent distortions in communications from causing misunderstandings and conflict, it is also important that members receive feedback about their communications. Feedback is a way of checking that the meanings of the communicated messages are understood correctly.

For feedback to be used appropriately it should (1) describe the content of the communication or the behavior as it is perceived by the group member, (2) be given to the member who sent the message as soon as the message is received, and (3) be expressed in a tentative manner so that those who send messages understand that the feedback is designed to check for distortions rather than to confront or attack them.

Examples of feedback are "John, I understood you to say . . ." or "Mary, if I understand you correctly, you are saying. . . ." Feedback and clarification can help to prevent communications from being interpreted in unintended ways. For an in-depth discussion about the effects of feedback on task group behavior, see Nadler (1979); for the effect of feedback on members of treatment groups, see Rhode and Stockton (1992).

Interaction Patterns

In addition to becoming aware of communication processes, the worker must also consider patterns of interaction that develop in a group.

Patterns of Group Interaction

- Maypole—when the leader is the central figure and communication occurs from the leader to the member and from the member to the leader
- Round robin—when members take turns talking
- Hot seat—when there is an extended back-and-forth between the leader and one member as the other members watch
- Free floating—when all members take responsibility for communicating, taking into consideration their ability to contribute meaningfully to the particular topic

The first three patterns are leader centered because the leader structures them. The fourth pattern is group centered because it emerges from the initiative of group members.

In most situations, workers should strive to facilitate the development of group-centered rather than leader-centered interaction patterns. In group-centered patterns, members freely interact with each other. Communication channels between members of the group are open. In leader-centered patterns, communications are directed from members to the worker or from the worker to group members, thereby reducing members' opportunities to communicate freely with each other.

Group-centered communication patterns tend to increase social interaction, group morale, members' commitment to group goals, and innovative decision making (Carletta, Garrod, & Fraser-Krauss, 1998). However, such patterns can be less efficient than leader-centered patterns because communication may be superfluous or extraneous to group tasks (Shaw, 1964). Sorting out useful communications can take a tremendous amount of group time. Therefore, in task groups that are making routine decisions, when time constraints are important and when there is little need for creative problem solving, the worker may deliberately choose to encourage leader-centered rather than group-centered interaction patterns.

To establish and maintain appropriate interaction patterns, the worker should be familiar with the factors that can change communication patterns, such as:

- Cues and the reinforcement that members receive for specific interactional exchanges
- The emotional bonds that develop between group members

- The subgroups that develop in the group
- The size and physical arrangements of the group
- The power and status relationships in the group

Workers can change interaction patterns by modifying these important factors.

CUES AND REINFORCERS.   Cues such as words or gestures can act as signals to group members to talk more or less frequently to one another or to the worker. Workers and members can also use selective attention and other reinforcers to encourage beneficial interactions. For example, praise and other supportive comments, eye contact, and smiles tend to elicit more communication, whereas inattention tends to elicit less communication. So that all members may have a chance to participate fully in the life of a group, workers may want to reduce communication from particularly talkative members or encourage reserved members to talk more. Often, pointing out interaction patterns is all that is needed to change them. At other times, verbal and nonverbal cues may be needed. Sometimes, however, more active intervention is needed. For example, reserved members may benefit from group go-rounds where they are provided an opportunity to speak when it is their turn. Similarly, directing communication to others may help to reduce the amount of time dominant group members talk. When these strategies do not work, other strategies may be used with the permission of members. For example, to ensure that a dominant member does not monopolize all the group time, the worker may seek permission to interrupt any member who talks for more than two or three minutes and to redirect the communication to other members. This can be done with the understanding of "giving all members a chance to participate." The worker can say things like "Your thoughts are important, but other members need time to share their thoughts as well. If it is okay with you, I would like to find out who else has something they would like to talk about," or "That's a good thought . . . but you have been talking for a while. Can you hold that thought for later and let someone else have a turn to share their thoughts now?" When this is done consistently by the worker, it is often sufficient to reduce the dominance of a single member.

EMOTIONAL BONDS.   Positive emotional bonds such as interpersonal liking and attraction increase interpersonal interaction, and negative emotional bonds reduce solidarity between members and result in decreased interpersonal interaction. Attraction and interpersonal liking between two members may occur because they share common interests, similar values and ideologies, complementary personality characteristics, or similar demographic characteristics (Hare et al., 1995).

Hartford (1971) calls alignments based on emotional bonds *interest alliances*. For example, two members of a planning council might vote the same way on certain issues and they may communicate similar thoughts and feelings to other members of the council on the basis of their common interests in the needs of the business community. Similarly, members of a minority group might form an interest alliance based on similar concerns about the lack of community services for minority groups.

SUBGROUPS.   Subgroups also affect the interaction patterns in a group. Subgroups form from the emotional bonds and interest alliances among subsets of group members. They occur naturally in all groups. They help make the group attractive to its members because individuals look forward to interacting with those to whom they are particularly close. The practitioner should not view subgroups as a threat to the integrity of the group unless the attraction of members within a subgroup becomes greater than their attraction to the group as a whole.

There are a variety of subgroup types, including the dyad, triad, and clique. Also, there are isolates, who do not interact with the group, and scapegoats, who receive negative attention and criticism from the group. More information about these roles, and other roles, is presented in Chapter 8.

In some situations the worker may actively encourage members to form subgroups, particularly in groups that are too large and cumbersome for detailed work to be accomplished. For example, subgroup formation is often useful in large task groups such as committees, delegate councils, and some teams. Members are assigned to a particular subgroup to work on a specific task or subtask. The results of the subgroup's work are then brought back to the larger group for consideration and action.

Regardless of whether the worker actively encourages members to form subgroups, they occur naturally because not everyone in a group interacts with equal valence. The formation of intense subgroup attraction, however, can be a problem. Subgroup members may challenge the worker's authority. They may substitute their own goals and methods of attaining them for the goals of the larger group. They can disrupt the group by communicating among themselves while others are speaking. Subgroup members may fail to listen to members who are not a part of the subgroup. Ultimately, intense and consistent subgroup formation can negatively affect the performance of the group as a whole (Gebhardt & Meyers, 1995).

When intense subgroup attraction appears to be interfering with the group as a whole, a number of steps can be taken.

Strategies for Addressing Intense Subgroup Attraction

- Examine whether the group as a whole is sufficiently attractive to members
- Promote the development of norms that emphasize the importance of members' listening to and respecting each other
- Promote the development of norms restricting communication to one member at a time
- Change seating arrangements
- Ask for certain members to interact more frequently with other members
- Use program materials and exercises that separate subgroup members
- Assign tasks for members to do outside of the group in subgroups composed of different members

If intense subgroup loyalties persist, it can be helpful to facilitate a discussion of the reasons for them and their effect on the group as a whole. A frank discussion of the reasons for subgroup formation can often benefit the entire group because it can reveal problems in the group's communication patterns and in its goal-setting and decision-making processes. After the discussion, the worker should try to increase the attraction of the group for its members and help them reach out to one another to reopen channels of communication.

In some cases, the worker may wish to use subgroups for therapeutic purposes. For example, Yalom (1995) suggests that the worker can use relationships between members to recapitulate the family group experience. Transference and countertransference reactions among members may be interpreted to help members gain insight into the impact of their early development on their current way of relating to others in the group and their broader social environment.

SIZE AND PHYSICAL ARRANGEMENTS.

Other factors that influence interaction patterns are the size and physical arrangement of the group. As the size of the group increases, the possibilities for potential relationships increase dramatically. For example, with three people there are six potential combinations of relationships, but in a group with seven people there are 966 possible relationships (Kephart, 1951). Thus, as groups grow larger, each member has more social relationships to be aware of and to maintain, but less opportunity to maintain them.

With increased group size there are also fewer opportunities and less time for members to communicate. In some groups, the lack of opportunity to participate might not be much of a problem. It should not be assumed that members who are not actively participating are uninvolved in the group, although this may be true. Some group members welcome a chance for active involvement but speak only when they have an important contribution that might otherwise be overlooked. Often, however, a reduced chance to participate leads to dissatisfaction and a lack of commitment to decisions made by the group. Increased group size also tends to lead to subgroup formation as members strive to get to know those seated near them.

The physical arrangement of group members also influences interaction patterns. For example, members who sit in circles have an easier time communicating with each other than do members who sit in rows. Even members' positions within a circular pattern influence interaction patterns. Members who sit across from each other, for example, have an easier time communicating than do members on the same side of a circle who are separated by one or two members.

Because circular seating arrangements promote face-to-face interaction, they are often preferred to other arrangements. There may be times, however, when the group leader prefers a different arrangement. For example, the leader of a task group may wish to sit at the head of a rectangular table to convey his or her status or power. The leader may also wish to seat a particularly important member in close proximity. In an educational group, a leader may choose to stand before a group seated in rows, an arrangement that facilitates members' communications with the leader and tends to minimize interactions among members of the group.

Physical arrangements can also be used to help assess relationships among members and potential problems in group interaction. For example, members who are fond of each other often sit next to each other and as far away as possible from members they do not like. Similarly, members who pull chairs out from a circle, or sit behind other members, may be expressing their lack of investment in the group.

An interesting physical arrangement that often occurs in groups results from members' tendency to sit in the same seat from meeting to meeting. This physical arrangement persists because members feel secure in "their own" seat near familiar members. When seating arrangements are modified by the leader, or by circumstance, communication patterns are often affected.

POWER AND STATUS.

Two other factors affecting communication and interaction patterns are the relative power and status of the group members. Initially, members are accorded power and status on the basis of their position and prestige in the community, their physical attributes, and their position in the agency sponsoring the group. As a group develops, members' status and power change, depending on how important a member is in helping the group accomplish its tasks or in helping other members meet their socioemotional needs. When members carry out roles that are important to the group, their power and status increase. When a member enjoys high status and power, other members are likely to direct their communications to that member (Napier & Gershenfeld, 1993).

Principles for Practice

With basic information about the nature of communication and interaction patterns in groups, workers can intervene in any group to modify or change the patterns that develop. Workers may find the following principles about communication and interaction patterns helpful:

- Members of the group are always communicating. Workers should assess communication processes continually and help members communicate effectively throughout the life of a group.

- Communication patterns can be changed. Strategies for doing this start with identifying patterns during the group or at the end of group meetings during a brief time set aside to discuss group process. Workers then can reinforce desired interaction patterns; increase or decrease emotional bonds between members; change subgroups, group size, or group structure; or alter the power or status relationships in a group.

- Members communicate for a purpose. Workers should help members understand each other's intentions by clarifying them through group discussion.

- There is meaning in all communication. Workers should help members understand and appreciate the meaning of different communications.

- Messages are often perceived selectively. Workers should help members listen to what others are communicating.

- Messages may be distorted in transmission. Workers should help members clarify verbal and nonverbal communications that are unclear or ambiguous.

- Feedback and clarification enhances accurate understanding of communications. The worker should educate members about how to give and receive effective feedback and model these methods in the group.

- Open, group-centered communications are often, but not always, the preferred pattern of interaction. The worker should encourage communication patterns that are appropriate to the purpose of the group.

Workers who follow these principles can intervene to help groups develop patterns of communication and interaction that meet members' socioemotional needs while accomplishing group purposes.

Group Cohesion

Group cohesion is the result of all forces acting on members to remain in a group (Festinger, 1950). According to Forsyth (2006) cohesion is made up of three components: (1) member-to-member attraction and a liking for the group as a whole, (2) a sense of unity and community so that the group is seen as a single entity, and (3) a sense of teamwork and *esprit de corps* with the group successfully performing as a coordinated unit.

People are attracted to groups for a variety of reasons. According to Cartwright (1968), the following interacting sets of variables determine a member's attraction to a group.

Reasons for Members' Attraction to the Group

- The need for affiliation, recognition, and security
- The resources and prestige available through group participation
- Expectations of the beneficial and detrimental consequences of the group
- The comparison of the group with other group experiences

Cohesive groups satisfy members' need for affiliation. Some members have a need to socialize because their relationships outside the group are unsatisfactory or nonexistent. For example, Toseland, Decker, and Bliesner (1979) have shown that group work can be effective in meeting the needs of socially isolated older persons. Cohesive groups recognize members' accomplishments, and promote members' sense of competence. Members are attracted to the group when they feel that their participation is valued and when they feel they are well-liked. Groups are also more cohesive when they provide members with a sense of security. Schachter (1959), for example, has shown that fear and anxiety increase people's needs for affiliation. When group members have confidence in the group's ability to perform a specific task, it has also been found that the group is more cohesive and performs more effectively (Gibson, 1999; Pescosolido, 2001, 2003; Silver & Bufiano, 1996). Similarly, feelings of collective self-efficacy also have been shown to have an important impact on actual performance (Bandura, 1997a, 1997b).

The cohesion of a group can also be accounted for by incentives that are sometimes provided for group membership. Many people join groups because of the people they expect to meet and get to know. Opportunities for making new contacts and associating with high-status members are also incentives. In some groups, the tasks to be performed are enjoyable. Other groups might enable a member to accomplish tasks that require the help of others. Prestige may also be an incentive. For example, being nominated to a delegate council or other task group may enhance a member's prestige and status in an organization or the community. Another inducement to group membership may be access to services or resources not otherwise available.

Expectations of gratification and favorable comparisons with previous group experiences are two other factors that help make groups cohesive. For example, members with high expectations for a group experience and little hope of attaining similar satisfactions elsewhere will be attracted to a group. Thibaut and Kelley (1959) have found that members' continued attraction to a group depends on the "comparison level for alternatives"—that is, the satisfaction derived from the current group experience compared with that derived from other possible experiences.

Members' reasons for being attracted to a group affect how they perform in the group. For example, Back (1951) found that members who were attracted to a group primarily because they perceived other members as similar or as potential friends related on a personal level in the group and more frequently engaged in conversations not focused on the group's task. Members attracted by the group's task wanted to complete it quickly and efficiently and maintained task-relevant conversations. Members attracted by the prestige of group membership were cautious not to risk their status in the group. They initiated few controversial topics and focused on their own actions rather than on those of other group members.

Cohesion can affect the functioning of individual members and the group as a whole in many ways. Research and clinical observations have documented that cohesion tends to increase many beneficial dynamics.

Effects of Cohesion

- Expression of positive and negative feelings (Pepitone & Reichling, 1955; Yalom, 1995)
- Willingness to listen (Yalom, 1995)
- Effective use of other members' feedback and evaluations (Yalom, 1995)
- Members' influence over each other (Cartwright, 1968)
- Feelings of self-confidence and self-esteem, and personal adjustment (Seashore, 1954; Yalom, 1995)
- Satisfaction with the group experience (Widmeyer & Williams, 1991)
- Perseverance toward goals (Cartwright, 1968; Spink & Carron, 1994)
- Willingness to take responsibility for group functioning (Dion, Miller, & Magnan, 1970)
- Goal attainment, individual and group performance, and organizational commitment (Evans & Dion, 1991; Gully, Devine, & Whitney, 1995; Mullen & Cooper, 1994; Wech, Mossholder, Steel, & Bennett, 1998)
- Attendance, membership maintenance, and length of participation (Prapavessis & Carron, 1997)

Although cohesion can have many beneficial effects, workers should be aware that cohesion operates in complex interaction with other group properties. For example, although cohesive groups tend to perform better than less cohesive groups, the quality of decisions made by cohesive groups is moderated by the nature of the task (Gully et al., 1995) and by the size of the group (Mullen & Cooper, 1994). Cohesion has more influence on outcomes, for example, when task interdependence is high rather than when it is low (Gully et al.). Cohesion also varies over the course of a group's development. For example, Budman, Soldz, Demby, Davis, and Merry (1993) have shown that what is viewed as cohesive behavior early in the life of a group may not be viewed that way later in the group's development.

It also should be pointed out that cohesion can have some negative effects on the functioning of a group. Although group cohesion often leads to a higher level of group performance, Forsyth (2006) points out that cohesion does not always lead to this effect. In cohesive groups that have mediocre or low standards of performance, the cohesion of the group can actually foster a lower level of performance rather than a higher level of performance. Cohesion is a necessary, albeit not sufficient, ingredient in the development of "group think." According to Janis (1972) *group think* is "a mode of thinking that people engage in when they are deeply involved in a cohesive ingroup, when the members' strivings for unanimity override their motivation to realistically appraise alternative courses of action" (p. 9) When *group think* occurs groups become close minded and the pressure for conformity limits methodical search and appraisal procedures (Forsyth, 2006).

In addition to encouraging pathological conformity, cohesion can lead to dependence on the group. This can be a particularly vexing problem in intensive therapy groups with members who started the group experience with severe problems and poor self-images. Thus, while promoting the development of cohesion in groups, the worker should ensure that members' individuality is not sacrificed. Members should be encouraged to express divergent opinions and to respect divergent opinions expressed by other group members. It is also important to adequately prepare members for group termination and independent functioning. Methods for this preparation are discussed in Chapter 14.

Principles for Practice

Because cohesion has many benefits, workers should strive to make groups attractive to members. Workers may find the following principles helpful when trying to enhance a group's cohesiveness:

- A high level of open interaction promotes cohesiveness. The worker should use group discussions and program activities to encourage interaction among members.
- When members' needs are met, they want to continue participating. Therefore, the worker should help members identify their needs and how they can be met in the group.
- Achieving group goals makes the group more attractive to its members. The worker should help members focus on and achieve goals.
- Noncompetitive intragroup relationships that affirm members' perceptions and points of view increase group cohesion. The worker should help group members to cooperate rather than compete with each other.
- Competitive intergroup relationships help to define a group's identity and purpose, thereby heightening members' cohesion. The worker can use naturally occurring intergroup competition to build intragroup bonds.
- A group that is too large can decrease members' attraction to the group by obstructing their full participation. The worker should compose a group that gives all members the opportunity to be fully involved.
- When members' expectations are understood and addressed, members feel as if they are part of the group. The worker should help members clarify their expectations, and should strive for congruence between members' expectations and the purposes of the group.
- Groups that offer rewards, resources, status, or prestige that members would not obtain by themselves tend to be attractive. Therefore, workers should help groups to be rewarding experiences for members.
- Pride in being a member of a group can increase cohesion. The worker should help the group develop pride in its identity and purpose.

If the costs of participation in a group exceed the benefits, members may stop attending (Thibaut & Kelley, 1954). Although workers cannot ensure that all factors are present in every group, they should strive to make sure that the group is as attractive as possible to each member who participates.

Social Integration and Influence

Social integration refers to how members fit together and are accepted in a group. Groups are not able to function effectively unless there is a fairly high level of social integration among members. Social order and stability are prerequisites for the formation and maintenance of a cohesive group. Social integration builds unanimity about the purposes and goals of the group, helping members to move forward in an orderly and efficient manner to accomplish work and achieve goals.

Norms, roles, and status hierarchies promote social integration by influencing how members behave in relationship to each other and by delineating members' places within the group. They lend order and familiarity to group processes, helping to make members' individual behaviors predictable and comfortable for all. Norms, roles, and status dynamics help groups to avoid unpredictability and excessive conflict that, in turn, could lead to chaos and the disintegration of the group. Too much conformity and compliance resulting from overly rigid and restrictive norms, roles, and status hierarchies can lead to the suppression of individual members' initiative, creativity, and intellectual contributions. At the same time, a certain amount of predictability, conformity, and compliance is necessary to enable members to work together to achieve group goals. Therefore, it is important for workers to guide the development of norms, roles, and status hierarchies that achieve a balance between too little and too much conformity.

The extent of social integration and influence varies from group to group. In groups with strong social influences, members give up a great deal of their freedom and individuality. In some groups this is necessary for effective functioning. For example, in a delegate council in which members are representing the views of their organization, there is generally little room for individual preferences and viewpoints. Norms and roles clearly spell out how individual delegates should behave. In other groups, however, members may have a great deal of freedom within a broad range of acceptable behavior. The following sections describe how the worker can achieve a balance so that norms, roles, and status hierarchies can satisfy members' socioemotional needs while simultaneously promoting effective and efficient group functioning.

Norms

Norms are shared expectations and beliefs about appropriate ways to act in a social situation such as a group. They refer to specific member behaviors and to the overall pattern of behavior that is acceptable in a group. Norms stabilize and regulate behavior in groups. By providing guidelines for acceptable and appropriate behavior, norms increase predictability, stability, and security for members and help to encourage organized and coordinated action to reach goals.

Norms result from what is valued, preferred, and accepted behavior in the group. The preferences of certain high-status members might be given greater consideration in the development of group norms than the preferences of low-status members, but all members share to some extent in the development of group norms.

Norms develop as the group develops. Norms develop directly as members observe one another's behavior in the group and vicariously as members express their views and opinions during the course of group interaction. As members express preferences, share views, and behave in certain ways, norms become clarified. Soon it becomes clear that sanctions and social disapproval result from some behaviors and that praise and social approval result from other behaviors. Structure in early group meetings is associated with increased cohesion, reduced conflict, and higher member satisfaction (Stockton, Rohde, & Haughey, 1992). The emergence of norms as the group progresses, however, reduces the need for structure and control by the worker.

Because norms are developed through the interactions of group members, they discourage the capricious use of power by the leader or by any one group member. They also reduce the need for excessive controls to be imposed on the group from external forces.

Norms vary in important ways. Norms may be overt and explicit or covert and implicit. Overt norms are those that can be clearly articulated by the leader and the members. In contrast, covert norms exert important influences on the way members behave and interact without ever being talked about or discussed. For example, a group leader who states that the group will begin and end on time, and then follows through on that "rule" each week, has articulated an explicit group norm in an overt fashion. In contrast, a covert, implicit norm might be for members of a couples group to avoid any talk of intimate behavior or infidelity. The implicit norm is that these topics are not discussed in this group.

● CASE EXAMPLE *A Couple's Group*

In the fourth meeting of a couple's group, the leader noticed that the members had not mentioned anything about their sexual lives. At one point during the group meeting, the leader observed that although members had talked about the conflicts that they were having in their lives about money, household chores, and other issues, no one had brought up the topic of sex. The leader asked if anyone would like to talk about their satisfaction or dissatisfaction with their sex life. After a pause, one woman volunteered that she and her husband had not had sex for several months, and that her husband seemed to be resentful about that. Her husband did not respond at first, but other members of the group began to talk about their sex lives and eventually, the husband who had not responded talked about his feelings. Later in the group, the leader used the taboo topic of sex to lead a productive discussion of how safe and secure members of the group were feeling about bringing up difficult topics in the group, and what could be done to make members feel more comfortable. One agreement that came out of this discussion was that members would try not to get angry at each other between meetings for things said in the group and instead would bring any feelings they had back into the group during the next meeting.

Norms vary according to the extent that people consider them binding. Some norms are strictly enforced whereas others are rarely enforced. Some norms are more elastic than others; that is, some permit a great deal of leeway in behavior, but others prescribe narrow and specific behaviors.

Norms also have various degrees of saliency for group members. For some members, a particular norm may exert great influence, but for others it may exert little influence.

Deviations from group norms are not necessarily harmful to a group. Deviations can often help groups move in new directions or challenge old ways of accomplishing tasks that are no longer functional. Norms may be dysfunctional or unethical, and it may be beneficial for members to deviate from them. For example, in a treatment group, norms develop that make it difficult for members to express intense emotions. Members who deviate from this norm help the group reexamine its norms and enable members to deepen their level of communication. The worker should try to understand the meaning of deviations from group norms and the implications for group functioning. It can also be helpful to point out covert norms and to help groups examine whether these contribute to the effective functioning of the group.

Because they are so pervasive and powerful, norms are somewhat more difficult to change than role expectations or status hierarchies. Therefore, a worker should strive to ensure that the developing norms are beneficial for the group. Recognizing the difficulty of changing norms, Lewin (1947) suggested that three stages are necessary for changing the equilibrium and the status quo that hold norms constant. There must first be disequilibrium or unfreezing caused by a crisis or other tension-producing situation. During this period, group members reexamine the current group norms. Sometimes a crisis may be induced by the worker through a discussion or demonstration of how current norms will affect the group in the future. In other cases, dysfunctional norms lead to a crisis.

In the second stage, members return to equilibrium with new norms replacing previous ones. According to Lewin, the second stage is called *freezing.* In the third stage, called *refreezing,* the new equilibrium is stabilized. New norms become the recognized and accepted rules by which the group functions. Napier and Gershenfeld (1993) have suggested ways that norms can be changed.

Changing Norms

- Discussing, diagnosing, and making explicit decisions about group norms
- Directly intervening in the group to change a norm
- Deviating from a norm and helping a group to adapt a new response
- Helping the group become aware of external influences and their effect on the group's norms
- Hiring a consultant to work with the group to change its norms

Roles

Like norms, roles can also be an important influence on group members. Roles are closely related to norms. Whereas norms are shared expectations held, to some extent, by everyone in the group, *roles* are shared expectations about the functions of individuals in the group. Unlike norms, which define behavior in a wide range of situations, roles define behavior in relation to a specific function or task that the group member is expected to perform. Roles continue to emerge and evolve as the work of the group changes over time (Salazar, 1996).

● **CASE EXAMPLE** *A Cancer Survivor's Group*

In a group for cancer survivors, one member, Mary, took on the role of socioemotional leader, comforting members when they brought up difficult topics and also drawing out quiet members who seemed like they were feeling particularly down or vulnerable. Joe, on the other hand took on the role of task leader making sure that the group stayed on topic when the conversation moved away from issues dealing with cancer or how to cope with the effects of the disease. Jenny was the humorist, the person who saw the bright side of things, making positive remarks and seeing the bright side of things when the tone of the group became somber. June took on the role of the indigenous leader, offering to help the leader Dorothy set up the meeting room, bringing in baked goodies and other treats for the group, and helping members between meetings when they needed transportation to medical appointments or someone to talk to when they were feeling down.

Roles are important for groups because they allow for division of labor and appropriate use of power. They ensure that someone will be designated to take care of vital group functions. Roles provide social control in groups by prescribing how members should behave in certain situations. Performing in a certain role not only prescribes certain behavior but also limits members' freedom to deviate from the expected behavior of someone who performs that role. For example, it would be viewed as inappropriate for an educational group leader to express feelings and emotional reactions about a personal issue that was not relevant to the topic.

Changes or modifications of roles are best undertaken by discussing members' roles, clarifying the responsibilities and the privileges of existing roles, asking members to assume new roles, or adding new roles according to preferences expressed during the group's discussion.

Status

Along with norms and role expectations, social controls are also exerted through members' status in a group. *Status* refers to an evaluation and ranking of each member's position in the group relative to all other members. A person's status within a group is partially determined by his or her prestige, position, and recognized expertise outside the group. To some extent, however, status is also dependent on the situation. In one group, status may be determined by a member's position in the agency sponsoring the group. In another group, status may be determined by how well a member is liked by other group members, how much the group relies on the member's expertise or how much responsibility the member has in the group. It is also determined by how a person acts once he or she becomes a member of a group. Because status is defined relative to other group members, a person's status in a group is also affected by the other members who comprise the group.

Status serves a social integration function in a rather complex manner. Low-status members are the least likely to conform to group norms because they have little to lose by deviating. For this reason, low-status members have the potential to be disruptive of productive group processes. Disruptive behavior is less likely if low-status members have hopes of gaining a higher status. Medium-status group members tend to conform to group norms so that they can retain their status and perhaps gain a higher status. Therefore, workers should provide opportunities for low-status members to contribute to the group so that they can become more socially integrated and achieve a higher status. High-status members perform many valued services for the group and generally conform to valued group norms when they are establishing their position. However, because of their position, high-status members have more freedom to deviate from accepted norms. They are often expected to do something special and creative when the group is in a crisis situation (Nixon, 1979). If medium- or low-status members consistently deviate from group norms, they are threatened with severe sanctions or forced to leave the group. If high-status members consistently deviate from group norms, their status in the group is diminished, but they are rarely threatened with severe sanctions or forced to leave the group.

● **CASE EXAMPLE** *A Psychiatric Team on an Inpatient Setting*

In a psychiatric team in an adolescent ward of a state mental hospital, the psychiatrist was clearly viewed as the highest status member of the team. The other team members, the social worker and nurse held middle status positions, and the mental health therapy aides and the student intern held lower status positions. Gradually, over time, however, the status of the social worker and one of the mental health therapy aides rose because they seemed to be able to develop a special rapport with some of the adolescents with the most difficult problems. At the same time, the status of the psychiatrist diminished somewhat as he was called away from meetings and missed some meetings entirely, and also was perceived as rather rigid in his theoretical perspectives and demanding in his views of what he expected of other team members. The nurse's role on the team also increased somewhat because she became the person who could meet with the psychiatrist and make needed adjustments to medications. One of the mental health therapy aides continued to maintain a rather low status on the team as he seemed not very engaged in his work, often talking disparagingly about patients, and contributing little that was positive to the overall team meeting.

Status hierarchies are most easily changed by the addition or removal of group members. If this is not possible, group discussion may help members express their opinions and feelings about the effects of the current status hierarchy and how to modify it. Changing members' roles in the group and helping them to achieve a more visible or responsible position within the group can also increase members' status.

Overall, norms, roles, and status are important components of the social influence groups have on members. Pioneering studies by Sherif (1936), Newcomb (1943), Asch (1952, 1955, 1957), and Milgram (1974) clearly demonstrated the power influence that the group has on the individual. It has also been shown, however, that individual group members with minority opinions can influence the majority (Moscovici, 1985, 1994; Moscovici & Lage, 1976; Moscovici, Lage, & Naffrechoux, 1969). Some methods that members with minority opinions can use to get their opinions heard and paid attention to follow.

Expressing and Getting Minority Opinions Adopted by the Majority

- Offer compelling and consistent arguments
- Ask the group to carefully listen to and consider your thoughts
- Appear confident
- Do not rigidly cling to a viewpoint or be close-minded about other points of view
- Take a flexible stand, consider compromise
- Use uncertainties and flawed logic in the majority's opinions to inform your own approach

Principles for Practice

Norms, roles, and status are interrelated concepts that affect the social integration of individuals in the group. They limit individuality, freedom, and independence, but at the same time stabilize and regulate the operation of the group, helping members to feel comfortable and secure in their positions within the group and with each other. Therefore, in working with task and treatment groups, workers should balance the needs of individuals and of the group as a whole, managing conformity and deviation, while ensuring that norms, roles, and status hierarchies are working to benefit rather than hinder or limit individual members and the whole group. Workers may find the following principles about these dynamics helpful when facilitating a group:

- The worker should help group members to assess the extent to which norms, roles, and status hierarchies are helping members feel socially integrated while helping the group to accomplish its goals.

- The worker should facilitate norms, roles, and status hierarchies that give the group sufficient structure so that interaction does not become disorganized, chaotic, unsafe, or unduly anxiety producing.

- The worker should avoid facilitating norms, roles, and status hierarchies that restrict members' ability to exercise their own judgment and free will, and to accomplish agreed-on goals. The worker should ensure that there is freedom and independence within the range of acceptable behaviors agreed on by the group.

- Members choose to adhere to norms, roles, and status hierarchies in groups that are attractive and cohesive. Workers should help make the group a satisfying experience for members.

- Members choose to adhere to norms, roles, and status hierarchies when they consider the group's goals important and meaningful. Therefore, workers should emphasize the importance of the group's work and the meaningfulness of each member's contributions.

- Members choose to adhere to norms, roles, and status hierarchies when they desire continued membership because of their own needs or because of pressure from sources within or outside the group. Therefore, workers should consider the incentives for members to participate in a group.

- Rewards and sanctions can help members adhere to norms, roles, and status expectations. Workers should assess whether rewards and sanctions are applied fairly and equitably to promote healthy social integration that benefits each member and the group as a whole.

By following these principles, workers can ensure that the norms, role expectations, and status hierarchy that develop in a group satisfy members' needs while helping to accomplish individual and group goals.

Group Culture

Although it has often been overlooked in discussions of group dynamics, group culture is an important force in the group as a whole. *Group culture* refers to values, beliefs, customs, and traditions held in common by group members (Olmsted, 1959). According to Levi (2007), culture can be viewed as having three levels. At the surface, symbols and rituals display the culture of the group. For example, in Alcoholics Anonymous groups, members usually begin an interaction by saying their first name and by stating that they are an alcoholic. At a deeper level, culture is displayed in the way members interact with one another. For example, the way conflict is handled in a group says much about its culture. The deepest level of culture includes the core beliefs, ideologies, and values held in common by members.

Multicultural differences within the group can have an important impact on the development of group culture and the social integration of all members. For example, individualism, competitiveness, and achievement are more valued in American and European cultures than are humility and modesty, which are more prevalent in some non-Western cultures. Similarly, experiences of group survival, social hierarchy, inclusiveness, and ethnic identification can powerfully influence the beliefs, ideologies, and values that are held by racially and ethnically diverse members, but these same experiences may have little salience for members of majority groups who have long been acculturated to dominant societal values (Hopps & Pinderhughes, 1999; Matsukawa, 2001). Insensitivity to these values, however, can isolate and alienate minority members and reduce their opportunity for social integration within the group.

● **CASE EXAMPLE** *A Caregivers' Group For Latinos*

In a caregiver support group for Latinos sponsored by a community agency, the worker, who was experienced in leading many caregiver groups, most for non-Latinos, noticed that when the members of this group talked about their elders there was even more respect accorded to the elders' status in the family than was true in groups of Anglo caregivers. The group leader also noticed that members were reluctant to volunteer comments unless specifically invited to do so by the leader. The leader decided to ask members about this and she learned that among some Latinos the traditional norm of respect for the leader precluded them from volunteering comments. The leader explained to the group that in this context spontaneity was welcome and they should feel free to voice their opinions about caregiving issues and needs. The worker also noticed that the members would sometimes use Spanish language words to describe their feelings to one another even though the group was being conducted in English. The worker had a discussion with the members about what to do when this happened because she was afraid that all the members might not understand what was being said between two members. The group decided that this practice was acceptable and came to an agreement about how this would be handled. In this particular group, because some of the members did not speak fluent Spanish, it was decided that any member could ask for a translation of what was being said between members when they lapsed into Spanish.

When the membership of a group is diverse, group culture emerges slowly. Members contribute unique sets of values that originate from their past experiences as well as from their ethnic, cultural, and racial heritages. These values are blended through group communications and interactions. In early meetings, members explore each other's unique value systems and attempt to find a common ground on which they can relate to each other. By later meetings, members have had a chance to share and understand each other's value systems. As a result, a common set of values develops, which becomes the group's culture. The group's culture continues to evolve throughout the life of the group.

Group culture emerges more quickly in groups with a homogeneous membership. When members share common life experiences and similar sets of values, their unique perspectives blend more quickly into a group culture. For example, members of groups sponsored by culturally based organizations, such as the Urban League or Centro Civico, and groups that represent a particular point of view, such as the National Organization for Women (NOW), are more likely to share similar life experiences and similar values than are groups with more diverse memberships. One of the attractions of these homogeneous groups is that they provide an affirming and supportive atmosphere.

Culture is also influenced by the environment in which a group functions. As part of the organizational structure of an agency, a community, and a society, groups share the values, traditions, and heritage of these larger social systems. The extent to which these systems influence the group depends on the degree of interaction the group has with them. For example, on one end of the continuum, an administrative team's operational procedures are often greatly influenced by agency policies and practices. On the other end, gangs tend to isolate themselves from the dominant values of society, the community, and local youth organizations. Group workers can learn a great deal about groups by examining how they interact with their environment.

Groups that address community needs often have much interaction with their environment. When analyzing a change opportunity, building a constituency, or deciding how to implement an action plan, groups that set out to address community needs must carefully consider dominant community values and traditions. The receptivity of powerful individuals within a community will be determined to some extent by how consistent a group's actions are with the values and traditions they hold in high regard. Whenever possible, groups attempting to address community needs should frame their efforts within the context of dominant community values. The practitioner can help by attempting to find the common ground in the values of the community and the group. When a group's actions are perceived to be in conflict with dominant community values, it is unlikely to receive the support of influential community leaders. In these situations, the group may rely on conflict strategies (described in Chapters 9 and 11), to achieve its objectives.

Once a culture has developed, members who endorse and share in the culture feel secure and at home, whereas those who do not are likely to feel isolated or even alienated. For isolated members the group is often not a satisfying experience. It is demoralizing and depressing to feel misunderstood and left out. Feelings of oppression can be exacerbated. Those who do not feel comfortable with the culture that has developed are more likely to drop out of the group or become disruptive. More extreme feelings of alienation can lead to rebellious, acting-out behavior. Subgroups that feel alienated from the dominant group culture may rebel in various ways against the norms, roles, and status hierarchies that have developed in the group. This can be avoided by providing individual attention to isolated members, and by stimulating all members to incorporate beliefs, ideologies, and values that celebrate difference and transcend individual differences. The worker can also help by fostering the full participation and integration of all group members into the life of the group.

Principles for Practice

The culture that a group develops has a powerful influence on its ability to achieve its goals while satisfying members' socioemotional needs. A culture that emphasizes values of self-determination, openness, fairness, and diversity of opinion can do much to facilitate the achievement of group and individual goals. Sometimes members bring ethnic, cultural, or social stereotypes to the group and thus inhibit the group's development and effective functioning. Through interaction and discussion, workers can help members confront stereotypes and learn to understand and appreciate persons who bring different values and cultural and ethnic heritages to the group.

In helping the group build a positive culture, the worker should consider the following principles:

- Group culture emerges from the mix of values that members bring to the group. The worker should help members examine, compare, and respect each other's value systems.
- Group culture is also affected by the values of the agency, the community, and the society that sponsor and sanction the group. The worker should help members identify and understand these values.
- Group members and workers can hold stereotypes that interfere with their ability to interact with each other. Workers should help members eliminate stereotypical ways of relating to each other and develop an awareness of their own stereotypes.
- Value conflicts can reduce group cohesion and, in extreme cases, lead to the demise of the group. The worker should mediate value conflicts among members and between members and the larger society.
- Group culture can exert a powerful influence on members' values. The worker should model values such as openness, self-determination, fairness, and acceptance of difference, which are fundamental to social group work and the social work profession.
- Groups are most satisfying when they meet members' socioemotional and instrumental needs. Therefore, the worker should balance members' needs for emotional expressiveness with their needs to accomplish specific goals.

STAGES OF GROUP DEVELOPMENT

According to Northen (1969), "a stage is a differentiable period or a discernible degree in the process of growth and development" (p. 49). The rest of this text is organized around the skills that workers can use during each stage of a group's development. A group's entire social structure, its communication and interaction patterns, cohesion, social controls, and culture evolve as it develops. Therefore, an in-depth understanding of group development is essential for the effective practice of group work. This section reviews some of the ways that group development has been conceptualized by other group work theoreticians.

Many attempts have been made to classify stages of group development. Table 3.3 lists some of the models of group development that have appeared in the literature. Most are based on descriptions of groups that the authors of each model have worked with or observed. Most models propose that all groups pass through similar stages of development. As can be seen in Table 3.3, however, different writers have different ideas about the number and types of stages through which all groups pass. For example, Bales' (1950) model of group development has only three stages, but the model presented by Sarri and Galinsky (1985) has seven stages.

Relatively few empirical studies have been conducted of particular models, and little empirical evidence exists to support the notion that any one model accurately describes the stages through which all groups pass. The studies that have been conducted suggest that groups move through stages, but that the stages are not constant across different groups (Shaw, 1976; Smith, 1978). MacKenzie (1994), Wheelan (1994), and Worchell (1994) point out that both progressive and cyclical processes exist in groups; that is, although groups often move through stages of development from beginning to end, they also often come back to readdress certain basic process issues in a cyclical or oscillating fashion. For example,

TABLE 3.3 ● *Stages of Group Development*

Development Stage	Beginning	Middle	End
Bales (1950)	Orientation	Evaluation	Decision making
Tuckman (1963)	Forming	Storming Norming Performing	Termination
Northen (1969)	Planning and Orientation	Exploring and testing Problem solving	Pretermination
Hartford (1971)	Pregroup planning Convening Group formation	Dislategration and conflict Group formation and maintenances	Termination
Klein (1972)	Orientation Resistance	Negotiation Intimacy	Termination

Trecker (1972)	Beginning
	Emergence of some group
	  feeling
		Development of bond, purpose, and
		  cohesion
		Strong group feeling
		Decline in group feeling
			Ending

Sarri & Galinsky (1985)	Origin phase Formative phase	Intermediate phase 1 Revision phase Intermediate phase II Maturation phase	Termination
Garland, Jones, & Kolodny (1976)	Preaffiliation Power and control	Intimacy Differentiation	Separation
Henry (1992)	Initiating Convening	Conflict Maintenance	Termination
Wheelan (1994)	Dependency and Delusion	Counterdependency and flight Trust and structure Work	Termination
Schiller (1995)	Preaffiliation	Establishing a relational base Mutuality and interpersonal empathy Mutuality and change	Separation

there is often a cyclical movement of group members from feeling (1) invested in the task to emotionally displaced from the task, (2) part of the group to autonomous, (3) defended to open, and (4) isolated to enmeshed.

There is some evidence that stages of group development may be affected by the needs of group members, the type of group, the goals of the group, the setting in which the group meets, and the orientation of the leader (Shaw, 1976; Smith, 1978). For example, a study of open-membership groups (Schopler & Galinsky, 1990) revealed that few moved beyond a beginning stage of development. *Open-membership* groups that are able to move beyond a beginning level of development are those that have a membership change less frequently than every other meeting and those with less than a 50 percent change in membership (Galinsky & Schopler, 1989).

Groups with frequent and extensive membership changes almost always remain at a formative stage. Such groups cope with problems in continuity and development by following highly ritualistic and structured procedures for group meetings. For example, a group in a stroke rehabilitation unit in a large teaching hospital in which a patient's typical stay is three to four weeks might be structured to begin with a half-hour educational presentation, followed by a half-hour discussion. The group would meet three times a week. Eight different topics could be presented before they are repeated. Therefore, patients with typical hospital stay of three to four weeks could learn about all eight topics, yet begin and end their participation at any time. However, the intimacy that can be achieved during the middle stage of groups with closed memberships is rarely achieved in groups in which members are continually entering and leaving the group.

Despite the variable nature of the stages of group development described by different writers, many of the models contain similar stages. As can be seen in Table 3.3, the various phases of group development can be divided into three stages: beginning, middle, and end. Each model of group development is placed in relationship to these three broad stages.

Most writers suggest that the beginning stages of groups are concerned with planning, organizing, and convening. The beginnings of groups are characterized by an emergence of group feeling. Group feeling, however, often does not emerge without a struggle. For example, Klein (1972) emphasizes the resistance of members to group pressure; Garland, Jones, and Kolodny (1976) emphasize the desire of group members to become a part of the group while maintaining their autonomy. Thus, along with the tendency to approach one another, there is also a tendency for members to maintain their distance. Garland, Jones, and Kolodny (1976) identified this tendency as an approach-avoidance conflict. As the beginning stage progresses and norms and roles are differentiated, members explore and test the roles they are beginning to assume in the group. Conflict may emerge. The leader can help by encouraging members to discuss and resolve conflicts as they emerge during the group process. It is also helpful to point out that encountering conflict and dealing with it are normal steps in the development of smooth-working relationships in preparation for the intense work to come in the middle stage. More information about conflict among members and how to resolve it is provided in Chapters 4, 7, and 11.

Although some work is accomplished in all stages of a group's development, most occurs in the middle stage. At the beginning of this stage, the conflicts over norms, roles, and other group dynamics found in the later part of the beginning stage give way to established patterns of interaction. A deepening of interpersonal relationships and greater group cohesion begin to appear. After this occurs, groups concern themselves with the work necessary to accomplish the specific tasks and goals that have been agreed on. The terms used to describe this stage include *problem solving, performing, maintenance, intimacy, work,* and *maturity.* Task accomplishment is preceded by a differentiation of roles and accompanied by the development of feedback and evaluation mechanisms.

The ending stage of a group is characterized by the completion and evaluation of the group's efforts. Bales' (1950) model of group development suggests that during this stage, task groups make decisions, finish their business, and produce the results of their efforts. Treatment groups, which have emphasized socioemotional functioning as well as task accomplishment, begin a process of separation, during which group feeling and cohesion decline. Often members mark termination by summarizing the accomplishments of the group and celebrating together.

Models of group development provide a framework to describe worker roles and appropriate interventions during each stage of a group. They also help workers organize and systematize strategies of intervention. For example, in the beginning stage, a worker's interventions are directed at helping the group define its purpose and helping members feel comfortable with one another. Models of group development can also prepare the leader for what to expect from different types of groups during each stage of development. For example models such as the one by Schiller (1995), shown in Table 3.3, help the worker to focus on the development of dynamics in women's groups.

The usefulness of theories of group development for group work practice, however, is limited by the uniqueness of each group experience. The developmental stages of groups vary significantly across the broad range of task and treatment groups that a worker might lead. It should not be assumed that all groups follow the same pattern of development or that an intervention that is effective in one group will automatically be effective in another group that is in the same developmental stage. Nevertheless, organizing content into specific developmental stages is a useful heuristic device when teaching students and practitioners how to lead and be effective members of treatment and task groups.

The model of group development presented in this text includes four broad stages: (1) planning, (2) beginning, (3) middle, and (4) ending. The beginning stage includes separate chapters on beginning groups and assessment. The middle stage includes four chapters focused on generic and specialized skills for leading task and treatment groups. The ending stage includes chapters on evaluating the work of the group and on terminating with individual members and the group as a whole. The rest of this text is organized around the skills, procedures, and techniques that help groups function effectively during each stage.

Principles for Practice

The worker should be knowledgeable about the theoretical constructs that have been proposed about the stages of group development. Knowing what is normative behavior for members at each stage can help the worker to assess whether the group is making progress toward achieving its goals. It can also help workers to identify dysfunctional behavior in an individual group member and problems that are the responsibility of the group as a whole. The following practice principles are derived from an understanding of group development:

- Closed-membership groups develop in discernible and predictable stages. The worker should use systematic methods of observing and assessing the development of the group and should teach group members about the predictable stages of group development.

- The development of open-membership groups depends on member turnover. The worker should help open-membership groups develop a simple structure and a clear culture to help new members integrate rapidly into the group.

- Groups generally begin with members exploring the purpose of the group and the roles of the worker and each member. The worker should provide a safe and positive group environment so that members can fully explore the group's purpose and the resources available to accomplish the group's goals.

- After the initial stage of development, groups often experience a period of norm development, role testing, and status awareness that results in expressions of difference among members and the leader. The worker should help members understand that these expressions of difference are a normal part of group development.

- Structure has been demonstrated to increase member satisfaction, increase feelings of safety, and reduce conflict in early group meetings. A lack of structure can lead to feelings of anxiety, insecurity, and can lead to acting out and projection. Therefore, the worker should provide sufficient structure for group interaction, particularly in early group meetings.

- Tension or conflict sometimes develops from differences among members. The worker should help the group resolve the conflict by helping the group develop norms emphasizing the importance of respect and tolerance and by mediating the differences and finding a common ground for productive work together.

- Groups enter a middle stage characterized by increased group cohesion and a focus on task accomplishment. To encourage movement toward this stage, the worker should help members stay focused on the purpose of the group, challenge members to develop an appropriate culture for work, and help the group overcome obstacles to goal achievement.

- In the ending stage, the group finishes its work. The worker should help members review and evaluate their work together by highlighting accomplishments and pointing out areas that need further work.

- Groups sometimes experience strong feelings about endings. The worker should help members recognize these feelings, review what they accomplished in the group, and help members plan for termination.

SUMMARY

Groups are social systems made up of people in interaction. This chapter describes some of the most important forces that result from the interaction of group members. In working with task and treatment groups, it is essential to understand group dynamics and be able to use them to accomplish group goals. Without a thorough understanding of group dynamics, workers will not be able to help members satisfy their needs or help the group accomplish its tasks.

Group workers should be familiar with four dimensions of group dynamics: (1) communication and interaction patterns; (2) the cohesion of the group and its attraction for its members; (3) social controls such as norms, roles, and status; and (4) the group's culture. Communication and interaction patterns are basic to the formation of all groups. Through communication and interaction, properties of the group as a whole develop, and the work of the group is accomplished. This chapter presents a model of the communication process.

Groups are maintained because of the attraction they hold for their members. Members join groups for many reasons. The extent to which the group meets members' needs and expectations determines the attraction of the group for its members and the extent to which a group becomes a cohesive unit. As cohesion develops, group structures are elaborated and norms, roles, and status hierarchies form. Norms, roles, and status hierarchies are social controls that help to form and shape shared expectations about appropriate behavior in the group. Conformity to expected behavior patterns results in rewards, and deviation results in sanctions. Social controls help to maintain a group's equilibrium as it confronts internal and external pressure to change during its development. However, social controls can be harmful if they are too rigid, too stringent, or if they foster behavior that is contrary to the value base of the social work profession.

As the group evolves, it develops a culture derived from the environment in which it functions as well as from the beliefs, customs, and values of its members. The culture of a group has a pervasive effect on its functioning. For example, a group's culture affects the objectives of the group, which task the group decides to work on, how members interact, and which methods the group uses to conduct its business.

Although properties of groups are often discussed as if they were static, they change constantly throughout the life of a group. Many writers have attempted to describe typical stages through which all groups pass. Although no single model of group development is universally accepted, some of the major characteristics that distinguish group process during each stage of group development are discussed in this chapter. These characteristics can be a useful guide for group practitioners in the beginning, middle, and ending stages of group work, which are described in later portions of this text.

This chapter points out the power of group dynamics in influencing group members and in contributing to or detracting from the success of a group. As workers become familiar with properties of groups as a whole, their appreciation of the effects that natural and formed groups have on the lives of their clients is enhanced. In addition, workers can use their understanding of group dynamics to enhance their ability to work effectively with both task and treatment groups.

chapter 4

Leadership

Leadership is the process of guiding the development of the group and its members. The goal of effective leadership is twofold: (1) to help the group and its members to achieve goals that are consistent with the value base of social work practice, and (2) to meet the socio-emotional needs of members. According to Forsyth (2006) 80 percent of leadership can be explained by two factors (1) task leadership focusing on the group's work and its goals, and (2) relationship leadership focusing on the interpersonal relations within the group. Task leadership includes defining a structure for the group, setting standards, identifying roles, planning and coordinating activities, proposing solutions, monitoring compliance, and stressing the need for efficiency and productivity (Yukl, 2002), Relationship leadership includes giving support and encouragement, boosting morale, establishing rapport, showing concern and consideration for members, and reducing tension and conflict (Yukl, 2002).

Leadership should not be viewed as a static process performed only by one person. Rather, leadership is a reciprocal, transactional, transformational, cooperative, and adaptive process involving members (Forsyth, 2006). Leadership is reciprocal, because the leader does not just influence the members, but rather leaders and members influence each other. Leadership is transactional because leaders and members work together exchanging ideas, skills, and effort to increase rewards and attain goals. Leadership is transformational because effective leaders motivate members, build their confidence and trust in one another, and unite them in common beliefs, values, and goals. Leadership is also a cooperative process during which leaders do not just use sheer power but gain the cooperation and mutual respect of members in shared goal-seeking activities. Leadership is an adaptive goal-seeking process whereby the leader helps members to change course and adapt to new situations to attain personal and group goals. Although the leadership role is most often associated with the designated leader—that is, the worker—it is important to distinguish between the worker as the designated leader and the indigenous leadership that emerges among members as the group develops. Leadership is rarely exercised solely by the worker. As the group unfolds, members take on leadership roles.

Workers should do as much as possible to stimulate and support indigenous leadership. Encouraging indigenous leadership helps to empower members. Members begin to feel that they have some influence, control, and stake in the group situation. Exercising leadership skills in the group increases members' self-esteem and the likelihood that they will advocate for themselves and for others outside of the group context.

Encouraging indigenous leadership also helps members to exercise their own skills and abilities. This, in turn, promotes autonomous functioning and ensures that members' existing skills do not atrophy. Thus, this chapter emphasizes both the importance of the worker as group leader and the importance of members' sharing in leadership functions as the group develops.

There is an increasing amount of evidence that gender roles play an important role in emerging leadership. In studies of emerging leaders, males are generally viewed more positively than females (Kolb, 1997). Also, the same leadership behaviors are often viewed more positively when attributed to males than to females (Shimanoff & Jenkins, 1991). Group leaders who are aware of this evidence will be better prepared to provide females with opportunities to assert their leadership abilities, and to guard against male dominance of leadership roles within task and treatment groups.

LEADERSHIP AND POWER

Workers who are new to the leadership role are sometimes uncomfortable with their power and influence and react by denying their power or by trying to take too much control. These strategies are rarely effective. Especially in early group meetings, members look to the leader for guidance about how to proceed. Experienced leaders are comfortable with their power and influence. They use it to empower members, which gradually enables members to take increasing responsibility for the group as it develops.

Workers use their influence as leaders within and outside the group to facilitate group and individual efforts to achieve desired goals. Within the group, the worker intervenes by guiding the dynamics of the group as a whole or by helping individual members change. In exercising leadership outside the group, the worker intervenes to influence the environment in which the group and its members function. For example, the worker might try to change organizational policies that influence the group or obtain additional resources from a sponsor so the group can complete its work. In exerting leadership inside or outside the group, the worker is responsible for the group's processes, actions, and task accomplishments.

In considering a worker's power, it is helpful to distinguish between attributed power and actual power. *Attributed power* comes from the perception among group members or others outside the group of the worker's ability to lead. Workers who take on the responsibilities inherent in leading a group are rewarded by having attributed to them the power to influence and the ability to lead. Such power is attributed by group members, peers, superiors, the sponsoring agency, and the larger social system.

The attributed power of the worker comes from a variety of sources. Among these sources are professional status, education, organizational position, experience, defined boundaries between worker and group members' roles, fees for service, and the commonly held view that a group's success or failure is the result of its leadership. Workers should recognize that attributed leadership ability is as important as actual power in facilitating the development of the group and its members.

Workers can increase the power attributed to them by group members. Studies have shown that members' expectations about the group and its leader influence the group's performance (Bednar & Kaul, 1994; Karakowsky & McBey, 2001; Piper, 1994). Preparing members with films, brochures, or personal interviews that offer information about the group, its leader, and the success of previous groups has been shown to be effective in increasing the change-oriented expectations of members and in helping individuals and groups accomplish their goals (Bednar & Kaul, 1994; Karakowsky & McBey, 2001; Kaul & Bednar, 1994). When formal preparation is impossible, informal preparation by word of mouth or reputation can be used.

As their attributed power increases, workers are more likely to be regarded with esteem by group members and to be looked to as models of effective coping skills whose behaviors are emulated and whose guidance is followed. Workers should not, however, attempt to gain power for its own sake or unilaterally impose their own values, standards, and rules concerning conduct inside or outside the group.

Actual power refers to the worker's resources for changing conditions inside and outside the group. Actual power depends on the sources of a worker's influence. The power bases first described by French and Raven (1959) follow.

Power Bases

- Connection power—being able to call on and use influential people or resources
- Expert power—having the knowledge or skill to facilitate the work of the group
- Information power—possessing information that is valuable to and needed by others
- Legitimate power—holding a position of authority and the rights that accrue to that position in the organization or larger social system
- Reference power—being liked and admired; the group members want to be identified with the worker
- Reward power—being able to offer social or tangible rewards
- Coercive power—being able to sanction, punish, or deny access to resources and privileges

Use of power can have both negative and positive consequences. For example, coercive power is sometimes used to compel clients to receive treatment. However, coercion can have negative effects such as hostility, anger, rebellion, and absence from group meetings. Therefore, the worker should exercise power judiciously, in a manner consistent with personal, professional, and societal values.

At the same time, the worker's power as leader cannot, and should not, be denied, which sometimes occurs when suggestions are made that members should take total responsibility for leading the group. Groups need leaders to avoid disorganization and chaos; leadership and power are inseparable (Etzioni, 1961).

Anyone who has attended the first meeting of a new group recognizes the power the worker has as the designated leader. This power can be illustrated most vividly by examining members' behaviors and feelings during the initial portion of the first group meeting. Members direct most of their communications to the worker or communicate through the worker to other group members. Members are often anxious and inquisitive, wondering what they can expect from the group and its leader. They comply readily with requests made by the worker. Although members may wonder about the worker's ability to help them and the group as a whole, they usually give the worker latitude in choosing methods and procedures to help the group achieve its objectives.

Beginning with the first group meeting, it is essential that workers move as rapidly as possible to share their power with members and the group as a whole. This encourages members to begin to take responsibility for the group and makes the group more potent. Some methods for sharing power are presented here.

Methods for Sharing Power with the Group

- Encourage member-to-member rather than member-to-leader communications
- Ask for members' input into the agenda for the meeting and the direction the group should take in future meetings
- Support indigenous leadership when members make their first, tentative attempts at exerting their own influence in the group
- Encourage attempts at mutual sharing and mutual aid among members
- Model and teach members selected leadership skills early in the life of the group
- Use naturally occurring events in the life of the group to "process" information about leadership skills and style

Theories of Group Leadership

Early theories about the best method to use in leading a group focused primarily on leadership style. Leadership was considered a trait rather than a cluster of behaviors that could be learned (Halpin, 1961). More recent evidence, however, clearly indicates that although certain personality factors may foster effective leadership, that leadership can also be learned (Forsyth, 2006).

Three positions on a continuum of leadership behavior—laissez-faire, democratic, and autocratic—were the subject of early investigations (Lewin & Lippitt, 1938; Lewin et al., 1939). The continuum can be seen in Figure 4.1. Findings from these studies indicated that there were more aggression, hostility, and scapegoating in autocratic groups than in democratic groups. There were no differences in the tasks completed by the groups, although there was some indication that the products of democratic groups were qualitatively superior to those of groups that used autocratic or laissez-faire styles of leadership. Group members also preferred the democratic group's process—that is, they liked the leader better and felt freer and more willing to make suggestions. These early findings seemed to suggest that allowing members to participate in the group's decision-making process was the preferred leadership style.

Factors Influencing Group Leadership

The early theories that focused on leadership styles were found to be too simplistic to explain leadership in most situations (Chemers, 2000). Gradually, contingency theories became more popular. These theories emphasized that situational factors helped to determine what skills and leadership style are most appropriate and effective for a particular group. For example, Nixon (1979) has suggested that at least seven factors must be assessed before predicting what leadership styles or behaviors are most effective.

Influences on Leadership

- The leadership expectations held by group members
- The way leadership has been attained
- Whether there is competition between designated leaders and the leaders that emerge as groups develop

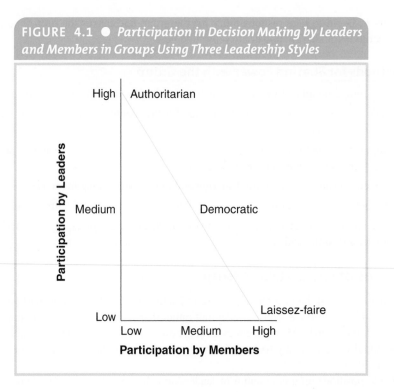

FIGURE 4.1 ● *Participation in Decision Making by Leaders and Members in Groups Using Three Leadership Styles*

- The needs, tasks, and goals of the group as a whole
- The task and socioemotional skills of members
- The nature of authority within and outside of the group
- The environmental demands placed on the group and its leadership

To understand the dynamics of leadership in diverse treatment and task groups, several factors in addition to the personality and leadership style of the worker should be considered. For example, in analyzing leadership in task groups, a number of investigators have shown that leaders develop different relationships with different members of a group (Dienesch & Liden, 1986; Graen & Schiemann, 1978; McClane, 1991). For example, an "individualized consideration" of each member is one of the central components of Bass's (1985, 1998) transformational leadership theory.

Others have suggested that leadership must be seen as a process within the context of the group and its environment. For example, Garvin (1997) emphasizes the role of the agency in influencing the work of treatment groups. When studying group leadership, Heap (1979) observed that the degree of activity of a worker is directly related to the social health of the group's members. Thus, a worker should be more active in groups in which members are "out of touch with reality" or "withdrawn or very aggressive" (p. 50). For example, a worker might need to be directive and structured in a remedial group for severely mentally ill inpatients of a state hospital. The worker, as "expert," may work with each member in turn for 5 or 10 minutes. Other members may be asked to offer opinions or provide feedback, but the primary focus is on helping an individual achieve particular treatment goals.

Similarly, Toseland (1995) notes that group workers have to be active when working with the frail elderly in groups. The energy level of these group members is often low, and they are often preoccupied with their own physical functioning. Also, frail, older group members tend to relate to the group leader rather than to each other. Being energetic and working hard to establish connections among members can counteract these tendencies.

In contrast, when working with interested, eager, competent members, the worker should take on a less active, enabler role. For example, a group-centered leadership approach is usually more effective in support, growth, and socialization groups in which members are eager, competent, and not severely impaired. In using a group-centered method, the worker facilitates communication, interaction, understanding, and mutual aid and encourages members to help one another rather than to look to the worker as an expert who can solve their concerns or problems.

Overall, one conclusion that can be drawn from social science findings and from data accumulated from group work practice is that one method of leadership is not effective in all situations. The worker's leadership skills and intervention strategies should vary depending on the degree to which the group as a whole and its individual members can function autonomously. The less autonomous the group, the more the worker must play a central role in leading the group. Conversely, the more autonomous the group, the more the worker can facilitate the members' own self-direction and indigenous leadership abilities.

Effective Leadership

Although research on contingency theories of leadership has continued, research on "transformational" leadership has taken preeminence in recent years. A major contribution to leadership theory was made by Burns in 1978 when he distinguished between transactional (contingency-based leadership) and transformational leadership. Transformational leaders are those who (1) display high levels of competency and trustworthiness, (2) inspire and motivate members with their vision, (3) stimulate independent and creative thinking among members, and (4) individualize members by understanding their personal needs and goals (Bass, 1985, 1998; Bass & Avolio, 1990a, 1990b, 1993). Transformational leadership models suggest that the leader should be a charismatic role model with vision who helps members to align their own goals with group and organizational goals (Alimo-Metcalfe & Alban-Metcalfe, 2001; Bass & Avolio, 1994). Transformational leaders empower members by affirming and reinforcing their autonomy and individuality as they pursue individual, group, and organizational goals. Members are encouraged to question assumptions and to approach problems in new ways so that they are creative and innovative problem solvers (Alimo-Metcalfe & Alban-Metcalfe, 2001). Thus, transformational leaders use the power bases available to them, but the focus is on inspiring and empowering members rather than inducing compliance (Sosik & Jung, 2002). Transformations occur as members embrace group and organizational goals, and view their own personal goals as a part of these larger goals.

In an attempt to unify contingency theories and transformational theories of leadership, Chemers (2000) suggests that effective leaders first have to establish the legitimacy of their leadership by being competent and trustworthy. He refers to this as "image management." Thus, effective leaders are highly respected individuals who have a vision. They promote safe, welcoming environments that avoid the extremes of aggressive confrontation of members or passive abdication of leadership to members who attempt to dominate groups (Kivlighan & Tarrant, 2001; Smokowski, Rose, & Bacallao, 2001). Next, leaders have to understand the abilities, values, and personalities of members. They use this understanding to encourage and guide members as they contribute to group goal attainment, while at the same time helping members to satisfy their own needs and achieve their own personal goals. Effective leaders must also skillfully deploy the resources they have at their disposal. This includes empowering members and reinforcing feelings of confidence and individual and group efficacy (Bandura, 1995, 1997b). It also includes making sure that the group engages in good information processing and decision making, so that when resources are deployed, the environmental demands on members and the group are carefully considered (Chemers, 2000).

AN INTERACTIONAL MODEL OF LEADERSHIP

Unlike contingency and transactional leadership theories that focus exclusively on the leader, the model of leadership presented in this book focuses on the group, the worker as designated leader, the members, and the environment in which the group functions. This "interactional model" is presented in Figure 4.2. Because this model views leadership as being derived from the interactions of the group, its members, the designated leader, and the environment, the model is closely related to the ecological systems perspective of social

FIGURE 4.2 ● *An Interactional Model of Group Leadership*

casework proposed by Germain and Gitterman (1996) and Siporin (1980) as well as the interactional perspective presented by Gitterman and Shulman (2005).

The interactional model represents leadership as a shared function that is not lodged solely in the designated group leader. In addition to the worker's role as designated leader, the model in Figure 4.2 clearly shows that leadership emerges from a variety of interacting factors as the group develops. These factors are (1) the purposes of the group, (2) the type of problem the group is working on, (3) the environment in which the group works, (4) the group as a whole, (5) the members of the group, and (6) the leader of the group.

Purposes of the Group

When one considers how leadership emerges in a group, it is essential to consider the purposes of the group. According to Browning (1977), a group may be formed (1) to perform tasks that require more than one or two people, (2) to meet individual needs, (3) to bring people together who are involved in the same or similar problems, (4) to represent a larger collection of people, (5) to form the largest collection of people that can be managed together, (6) to help maintain an organization more economically than individuals, (7) to increase motivation, or (8) as a result of physical factors such as working together in the same office. To this list can be added the purpose of using the group to change conditions or situations outside the group in an organization, a service delivery system, or an entire social system.

A group may have a single purpose or several purposes. The worker should consider how a group's purposes are interpreted by all systems that interact with it. The worker should ensure that the purpose of the group and the type of problem to be worked on are consistent. For example, if the purpose of a group is to meet the needs of socially isolated individuals, the types of problems on which the group works should be related to group members' needs for increased social interaction; that is, the group should not be working on problems of housing or finances unless they are linked to the primary purpose of decreasing isolation.

The purpose of a group helps determine how workers guide group processes. For example, in a group whose purpose is solely to complete a task or solve a problem, a worker might choose to encourage members to structure and focus the interactions more than in a group whose purpose is to have members share common concerns and ideas about an issue.

Type of Problem

The type of problem or task a group works on also has important implications for leadership. It has been found that groups do better than individuals on certain types of tasks, but individuals working alone do better on others (Hare et al., 1995). Generally, groups do better when the task is additive, such as collecting information. Thus, it would be better to form a treatment conference group to collect information about a client from all the professionals working with the client rather than to get the information from each professional separately. Groups are also more effective when they are choosing between clearly delineated alternatives. For example, Toseland, Rivas, and Chapman (1984) found that groups were more effective than individuals working alone when making decisions about funding priorities for medically underserved counties.

Groups also do better on tasks requiring a wide range of responses (Thorndike, 1938). For example, it is preferable to have group members and the leader generate alternative solutions with a woman who is having trouble expressing her anger rather than to have the woman generate the alternatives with one worker. For these kinds of tasks, the worker should promote interaction, input, and feedback from all group members so that a wide range of responses is generated and evaluated.

Individuals working alone solve some problems or accomplish some tasks faster and better than they would working in a group. Individuals working alone more readily solve complex problems requiring many variables to be synthesized into a whole. In these cases, the group's product is no better than the best performance of a member of the group (Thorndike, 1938).

● **CASE EXAMPLE** *Individual and Group Problem Solving*

In preparing a countywide plan for distributing emergency allocation funds to communities affected by a recent tornado, a worker decided to use a nominal group procedure that encouraged members to work alone before sharing their ideas with the group. In addition, the worker formed subgroups to work on specific ideas generated by the individual before they were considered in formal group discussion. By using both individual work and group interaction, the worker helped the group deal with a complex problem more efficiently.

Several other aspects of problems should be considered when leading a group. One is whether the problem is of concern to the group as a whole, to a subgroup, or to an individual. All members of the group might not be affected to the same extent by a particular problem or task being considered by a group. For example, when leading a group to teach parenting skills to foster parents, the worker should try to get all members involved in discussing parenting problems that are of interest to everyone in the group. When a member raises a problem unique to his or her particular situation, the worker should try to develop from this information generalized principles of child rearing of interest to all group members. This technique is often called *universalizing.*

When considering the type of problem confronting a group, workers should also be aware of where their legitimate influence ends. It may not be appropriate for the worker to encourage discussion of certain topics. For example, a worker leading a task group planning for an emergency housing shelter should not encourage a group member to talk about personal family life. In other situations, however, workers may want to encourage discussion of taboo areas. For example, when the problem being discussed is child abuse, it might be helpful for the worker to encourage all members to talk about how they were disciplined during their early childhood.

The Environment

The environment in which the group conducts its work has a profound effect on how leadership emerges in the group. Environmental influences come primarily from three interrelated sources: (1) the immediate physical setting, (2) the agency or organization in which the group functions, and (3) other social systems and the social environment.

The Setting

The worker should ensure that the setting facilitates the group's work. The decor and comfort of the waiting room and meeting area and the availability of equipment and supplies such as tables, blackboard, or newsprint all influence the group's leadership. It is important for the worker to match group members' needs and preferences to a setting that facilitates the group's work. For example, sitting around a table may facilitate the work of a task group because members can spread out papers and write more easily. In contrast, a table may interfere with the observation of nonverbal communication in a therapy group, and it may also hamper role playing and engagement in other program activities.

The Agency Context

In addition to the physical environment, the agency influences the group and its leader in several ways. The worker, for example, must be aware of agency policies, rules, and regulations that govern the group's behavior, its process, and its product. The worker is given legitimate authority by the agency or organization to help the group perform its tasks. The agency's delegation of this authority to the worker often assumes the worker will use the method of service delivery that currently exists in the agency. For example, two group workers trying to help pregnant women stop abusing alcohol may use quite different means, depending on the type of program sponsored by each agency. One group leader may use a reality-therapy group approach; the other may use a group format based on cognitive-behavioral self-control procedures.

Other Social Systems

The third way the environment influences group leadership is through large social systems, such as the community in which the group operates. The worker's behavior is influenced by norms established by society. For example, in a group for abusive parents, the worker intervenes to help members comply with societal norms and values concerning appropriate parenting behaviors. Smaller social systems can also affect a group's work. For example, an agency committee might hesitate to become involved in a search for additional emergency housing if a delegate council formed by a community planning agency is already looking at ways to develop additional emergency housing resources.

The Group as a Whole

At least four properties of the group as a whole influence how leadership emerges. These are (1) the size of the group, (2) the time limit in which the group is expected to accomplish its goals, (3) group dynamics, and (4) the stage of a group's development.

Group Size

As the size of a group increases, the opportunity for member participation decreases. The number of rules may increase as workers use them to maintain order and control in the group. Subgroups are more likely to form. The leader is more likely to be in the front of a large group, and leader-to-member and member-to-leader interactions are more likely than member-to-member interactions to occur.

Time Limits

Time limits may be voluntary or mandatory. A treatment group, for example, might decide to use a time-limited method such as a behavioral group approach or a task-centered group approach. A task group, such as a delegate council, might feel responsible for making a speedy decision on an issue for an upcoming statewide meeting. In either case, time limits affect leadership behavior. Generally, time limits are associated with greater structuring of interactions, an increase in task-focused behavior, and fewer opportunities for indigenous leadership to emerge.

Group Dynamics

Another property that can influence leadership is the dynamics that operate in a group. As discussed in Chapter 3, these include communication and interaction patterns, cohesion, social control, and group culture. Workers should use their skills to foster the development of group dynamics that help the group accomplish its tasks and contribute to members' satisfaction. Interventions to change the dynamics of the group as a whole are discussed in Chapter 10.

Stage of Development

The stage of a group's development also affects leadership behavior. If the group is to develop successfully, the worker must be aware of the developmental tasks that face the group during each stage. A large portion of this text focuses on the specific skills and methods that workers can use during each stage of a group's development.

The Group Members

Group members influence how leadership emerges in three important ways: (1) through the unique characteristics and life experiences they bring to the group, (2) by the extent that they participate in the group, and (3) by the extent that they share in leading the group.

Member Characteristics

Several characteristics of members affect their ability to influence the group. These include members' interpersonal skills, access to information, perceived responsibility for the work of the group, motivations, and expectations about the process and outcome of the group. The importance of these characteristics should not be overlooked when considering how leadership develops in a group. It has been shown, for example, that members' expectations influence outcomes in both treatment (Piper, 1994) and task groups (Gibb, 1969) and that interpersonal skill level and knowledge about a particular problem also help determine how well a group functions (Browning, 1977; Hersey, Blanchard, & Natemeyer, 1979).

Because members' attributes differ, one member who is knowledgeable about a particular topic may become the task leader while that topic is being discussed. Another member may serve as the group's socioemotional leader by expressing feelings and responding to other members' feelings. This suggests that the worker should remain aware of each member's leadership potential as the group progresses and help members to take on appropriate leadership roles that match their interests and skills. This is in keeping with the transformational leadership model mentioned earlier in this chapter, in which the leader individualizes and empowers members, helping them to use their unique interests and strengths and to view personal goals within the context of the larger group goal.

Extent of Participation

The extent of members' participation also influences how a worker leads a group. Some members' lack of interpersonal skills or motivation may prevent them from participating fully. In these situations the worker may want to take on a more active stance by encouraging members to interact by using go-rounds to get each member's feedback about particular topics and by using program activities and other expressive therapies such as music, movement, or art to involve and draw out members. In some groups, for example in school settings, members may also have developmental disabilities that limit their ability to participate.

● **CASE EXAMPLE**   *Group Activities for Children with Autism*

In a self-contained classroom, with eight children with autistic spectrum disorders, in order to help the children understand others' feelings, a school social worker might use feelings charades. For example, the worker might first show pictures of people with different feelings, and then act out or model the feelings. Then the social worker would ask for volunteers to role play a person with a feeling and to have another child guess the feeling. The worker might also play a movement game called the mirror to help students pay attention to each other and to practice following the lead of another child in a social situation. In this game, the worker might bring in a mirror and show the children how it reflects whatever action is performed in front of it. Then the worker asks the children to form pairs and for one child to follow or *"mirror"* the movements of the other. Then, the children reverse roles, and the child who initially was the mirror, acts out or *"mirrors"* what the first child does.

Sharing Leadership

Members' willingness to share leadership responsibilities is determined by their feelings of competency, their previous leadership experiences, and their perceptions of the openness of the designated leader to sharing leadership functions. It is also affected, in part, by the amount of time the member has been a part of the group. A new group member often has difficulty exerting leadership in a group in which the relationship among members has been established. Similarly, a member of a street gang that has been together for several years has more influence with the gang than a worker who is just beginning to interact with the gang.

The Group Leader

When one examines how leadership emerges in a group, the power base, skill level, personality, and choice of service technology of the designated leader all play important roles. As indicated earlier, seven types of power bases can be used to influence a group: connection, expert, information, legitimate, referent, reward, and coercive. Most workers draw on a variety of power bases; workers should realize the power bases at their disposal when they are considering leading a group.

● **CASE EXAMPLE**   *A Group of Persons with Alcoholism*

A worker planning to lead a group of individuals referred from the court for driving-while-intoxicated offenses has several power bases to draw on in leading the group. The leader can present information about the harmful effects of alcohol and can connect the members of the group to other treatment resources such as Alcoholics Anonymous (AA) and may even be able to connect members to sponsors within the AA program. The leader can also use some other power bases such as the role of an expert who can certify if the person has completed the group successfully, which may have implications for the person getting their license back or on their probation status.

The level of skill that workers possess also influences their ability to lead. Experience and training of workers have been correlated with effectiveness in working with individuals and groups (Dies, 1994).

A worker's personality, interpersonal style, and preferences for how to lead, all influence how leadership emerges in the group. For example, a worker who is shy and sensitive about others' feelings is less likely to use confrontation as a technique when leading a group. Therefore, it is important for workers to be aware of how their interpersonal style affects their attempts to objectively analyze what the group needs as they attempt to exert effective leadership. This is often referred to as *effective use of self* in social work practice. Some methods for becoming more aware of one's leadership style and how to modify it for the good of the group are described later in this chapter.

The service technology that workers use also affects how they conduct their groups. *Service technology* refers to particular theories or methods of intervention used by a worker. Three leaders of groups for alcoholics, for example, may intervene in quite different ways—by using transactional analysis or behavior therapy or, perhaps, reality therapy. Workers' choice of service technologies may be influenced by their personal preferences, their training, or the ideology of the agency in which they work.

A worker's technological and ideological stance often helps in organizing interventions. Workers may wish to receive specialized instruction in a particular service technology, such as behavior modification; however, it is essential that they become familiar with basic practice principles of leading groups before they receive specialized training.

GROUP LEADERSHIP SKILLS

Group leadership skills are behaviors or activities that help the group achieve its purpose and accomplish its tasks and help members achieve their personal goals. Both workers and members use leadership skills, although the worker ordinarily uses them more than any other member of the group. Leadership skills are combined when conducting group meetings. For example, in using a problem-solving method, a worker calls on numerous leadership skills to help a committee arrive at a decision concerning personnel practices in a family service agency. Similarly, in an aftercare treatment group for recovering drug addicts, a worker relies on many different skills to help members remain drug free.

There has been long-standing interest in the *skillful use of self* in social work practice (Goldstein, 1983). Most evidence concerning the effect of skill level on desired outcomes has been gathered from the evaluation of work with individuals rather than from work with groups (Dies, 1994). Reviews of the literature suggest that skills can be learned and that skill level makes a difference in performance (Dies, 1994). There is some evidence that specific skills such as attending intently and responding empathically are directly connected to positive outcomes (Shulman, 1978; Toseland, Rossiter, Peak, & Hill, 1990). Results are tentative, however, because it is difficult to design studies to assess the independent effect of one particular skill.

Group leadership skills are somewhat different from skills used in working with an individual. Both members and the worker have greater choice regarding the level and focus of their interaction. For example, they may choose to be active or passive, and they may decide to interact with some members more than others. There is also a greater possibility of shared leadership and the delegation of various leadership responsibilities.

Some of the basic skills necessary for group leadership are categorized in Table 4.1. Skills are listed in three categories: (1) facilitating group processes, (2) data gathering and assessment, and (3) action. Skills are classified on the basis of their most likely function within the group. Skills listed under one category may, however, be used in another category, particularly if they are combined with other skills. For example, responding is classified as a skill in facilitating group processes. Although responding to another group member's actions or words facilitates communication, responding may also lead to additional data gathering, assessment, or action.

Facilitating Group Processes

Table 4.1 lists several different skills in the category of facilitating group processes. All these skills can be used by workers differentially, depending on their intentions when attempting to influence various group processes. In general, however, skills in facilitating group processes contribute to positive group outcome when they improve understanding among group members, build open communication channels, and encourage the development of trust so

TABLE 4.1 ● *A Functional Classification of Group Leadership Skills*

Facilitating Group Processes	Data Gathering and Assessment	Action
1. Involving group members	1. Identifying and describing thoughts, feelings, and behaviors	1. Supporting
2. Attending to others		2. Reframing and redefining
3. Expressing self	2. Requesting information, questioning, and probing	3. Linking members' communications
4. Responding to others	3. Summarizing and partializing information	4. Directing
5. Focusing group communication	4. Synthesizing thoughts, feelings, and actions	5. Giving advice, suggestions, or instructions
6. Making group processes explicit	5. Analyzing information	6. Providing resources
7. Clarifying content		7. Disclosure
8. Cuing, blocking, and guiding group interactions		8. Modeling, role playing, rehearsing, and coaching
		9. Confronting
		10. Resolving conflicts

that all members are willing to contribute as much as they can to the problem on which the group is working.

Involving Group Members

Ideally, all members should be involved and interested in what is being discussed in the group. Yalom (1995) has called this universalizing a group member's experience. Involving members who have been silent helps identify commonalities and differences in their life experiences. As members become involved they realize how particular problems affect them and how a solution to one member's problem can directly or indirectly help them. Involving others is also essential for building group cohesiveness, developing a sense of mutual aid, and encouraging shared decision making.

Involving group members also means helping them take on leadership roles within the group. The worker should be cautious about doing too much for members and thereby stifling individual initiative. Instead of jealously guarding the leadership role, workers should encourage members to contribute to the content of group meetings and help shape group dynamic processes. This can be done by providing members with opportunities for leadership roles during program activities, by praising members for their leadership efforts, and by inviting and encouraging members' participation and initiative during group interaction. For example, the worker might say "Mary, I know that you are knowledgeable about that; do you have anything to add to what Tom has said?" Similarly, the worker might say, "Tom, you did such an excellent job in the role play last week. Would you be willing to play the part of the angry storekeeper?"

Attending Skills

Attending skills are nonverbal behaviors, such as eye contact and body position, and verbal behavior that convey empathy, respect, warmth, trust, genuineness, and honesty. Attending skills are useful in establishing rapport as well as a climate of acceptance and cohesiveness among group members. Egan (2002) suggests that, in addition to body position and eye contact, skills that indicate that a worker has heard and understood a member are part of effective attending. Research has shown that effective attending skills are an important characteristic of successful leaders (Johnson & Bechler, 1998). Effective attending skills include repeating or paraphrasing what a member says and responding empathically and enthusiastically to the meaning behind members' communications. They also include what Middleman (1978) has referred to as "scanning" skills. When scanning the group, the worker makes eye contact with all group members, which lets them know that the worker is concerned about them as individuals. Scanning also helps reduce the tendency of workers to focus on one or two group members.

Expressive Skills

Expressive skills are also important for facilitating group processes. Workers should be able to help participants express thoughts and feelings about important problems, tasks, or issues facing the group and to reiterate and summarize them when necessary. Members should also be helped to express their thoughts and feelings as freely as possible in an appropriate and goal-oriented manner. Members of task and treatment groups can often benefit from an open discussion of formerly taboo areas that affect the group or its members. Self-disclosure is an expressive skill that can be used effectively for this purpose.

Although self-disclosures should be made judiciously, according to their appropriateness for particular situations, they can often be useful in helping the worker promote open communication about difficult subjects. For example, a worker might say, "I just lost my mother, who also had been ill for a long time. I know what you mean, Bea, when you say that watching a loved one slowly decline right before your eyes is so hard. Your situation is different than mine, because it's your husband, but I can just imagine how terribly difficult it is for you. Do you want to share with us how you have been coping?"

Responding Skills

Skillful responses help the group as a whole and individual members accomplish tasks. The worker might, for example, amplify subtle messages or soften overpowering messages (Middleman & Wood, 1990). The worker can also redirect messages that may be more appropriate for a particular member or the group as a whole.

Workers can use responding skills selectively to elicit specific reactions that will affect future group processes. For example, if a worker's response supports a group member's efforts, the member is more likely to continue to work on a task or a concern. If the worker disagrees with a member's statement or action, the member is likely to react either by responding to the worker's statement or by remaining silent. The member is not likely to continue to pursue the original statement. Thus, by responding selectively to particular communications, the worker can exert influence over subsequent communication patterns.

Focusing Skills

The worker can facilitate group processes by focusing them in a particular direction. This can be done by clarifying, asking a member to elaborate, repeating a particular communication or sequence of communications, or suggesting that group members limit their discussion to a particular topic. Helping the group maintain its focus can promote efficient work by reducing irrelevant communications and by encouraging a full exploration of issues and problems.

Making Group Processes Explicit

The skill of making group processes explicit helps members to become aware of how they are interacting. For example, a worker may point out implicit group norms, particular member roles, or specific interaction patterns. The worker may ask members whether they observed a particular pattern or type of interaction, whether they are comfortable with the interaction, and whether they would like to see changes in the ways members interact. Middleman and Wood (1990) point out that it is important for the worker to verbalize therapeutic group norms and to encourage the development of traditions and rituals. For example, pointing out that at the beginning of each group meeting members seem to take turns "telling their story" and receiving feedback about how they handled a particular situation encourages members to consider whether they want to continue this pattern of interaction.

Pointing out the here-and-now of group interaction is an underused skill. Sometimes, workers get so caught up in the content of interaction that they forget to pay attention to group processes. Other workers are reluctant to make their observations public. Workers who have difficulty directing the group's attention to group processes should consider practicing this skill by setting aside a few minutes at the beginning or end of each meeting for a discussion of group processes or by making a conscious effort to point out group processes in brief summary statements at intervals during meetings. Clinical and supervisory experience suggests that the process of pointing out here-and-now group interaction becomes easier with practice. A brief example of how to point out here-and-now interactions during group meetings follows.

● **CASE EXAMPLE** *Pointing Out Group Dynamics*

In order to help members understand how their interactions affected the group-as-a-whole, the leader of a support group for recovering alcoholics often took time out from discussion of members' issues to bring up group dynamics and processes. He noted that members sometimes ignored nonverbal reactions of other members and often asked members to observe what was going on with the group-as-a-whole. Eventually, members became more skilled at observing this and other communication dynamics within the group. The leader frequently asked members to evaluate the leadership behavior of other members, using this "processing" time to discuss both member and group strengths. As the group progressed, the leader and members structured these discussions into the final few minutes of the session, giving them time each week to discuss group processes.

Clarifying Content

Just as it can be beneficial to make group processes explicit, it can also be beneficial to point out the content of members' interactions. The worker's purpose in clarifying content is to help members communicate effectively. The skill of clarifying content includes checking that a particular message was understood by members of the group and helping members express themselves more clearly. It also includes pointing out when group interaction has become unfocused or has been sidetracked by an irrelevant issue.

The skill of clarifying content can also be used to point out the possible avoidance of taboo subjects. For example, in a support group for caregivers of the frail elderly, the worker might point out that the subject of nursing home placement has not arisen.

Cuing, Blocking, and Guiding Group Interactions

To help a group accomplish the goals it has set for itself, the worker will often find it helpful to guide the group's interaction in a particular direction. To start this process it is helpful to constantly scan the group to look for verbal and nonverbal cues about group processes. The worker should avoid getting too caught up in the content of the group and instead should focus on the processes that are occurring among members. Cuing can be used to invite a member to speak so that the group stays focused on a topic. It can also be used when the worker wants to move the group in a new direction by focusing on or cuing a member, who has brought up an important new topic, for the group to discuss. Blocking can also be used when a member is getting off topic or is saying something that is inappropriate. By encouraging a member to speak or by limiting or blocking a group member's communication, the worker can guide the group's interaction patterns. This method has been referred to as selecting communications patterns purposely (Middleman & Wood, 1990).

● **CASE EXAMPLE** *A Bereavement Support Group*

In a support group for recently widowed persons, members are talking about what to do about the personal belongings of their loved one who has died. One member, John, starts to talk about giving things to the Salvation Army. However, the worker scanning the group notices that two of the other members, Mary and Helen, are having strong personal reactions to the topic of disposing of their loved ones' personal belongings. The worker turns to John who had started to talk about the Salvation Army, mentions that that is a good resource, but asks if he would mind holding on to that thought until later in the group. The worker than asks if Mary, Helen, or anyone else would like to share what they are feeling or thinking before getting into the specifics of how to dispose of the belongings.

The skill of guiding group interactions has many uses. For example, the worker may want to correct a dysfunctional aspect of the group's process, such as the development of a subgroup that disrupts other members. A worker who can skillfully guide group interaction patterns can limit the communication between subgroup members and increase their communication with other group members. The worker may also want to use guiding skills to explore a particular problem or help members sustain their efforts in solving a problem or completing a task. At other times, the worker may want to encourage open communication. For example, by redirecting a communication, the worker can help members speak to one another. The worker might say, "John, your message is really intended for Jill. Why don't you share your message directly with her rather than through me?"

Data Gathering and Assessment

Data-gathering and assessment skills are useful in developing a plan for influencing communication patterns as well as in deciding on the action skills to use to accomplish the group's purposes. These skills provide a bridge between the process-oriented approach of facilitating group processes and the task-oriented approach of using action skills to achieve goals and satisfy members' needs. Without effective data-gathering and assessment skills, workers' interventions are not grounded in a complete understanding of the situation. This can result in the use of premature, oversimplified, or previously attempted solutions that have not been carefully analyzed and weighed.

Identifying and Describing Skills

Perhaps the most basic data-gathering skill is helping members identify and describe a particular situation. This skill allows elaboration of pertinent factors influencing a problem or task facing the group. In using this skill, workers should attempt to elicit descriptions that specify the problem attributes as clearly and concretely as possible. To understand the problem, it is often useful for the worker to identify or describe historical as well as current aspects of the problem. It may also be helpful to share alternative ways of viewing the situation to obtain diverse frames of reference, alternative interpretations of events, and potential solutions to a problem. For example, the worker might say, "You have given us a pretty complete description of what happened, Amy, but I wonder, what do you think Jim would say if I asked him to give an account of the same situation? How do you think he would view this?"

Requesting Information, Questioning, and Probing

The skills of identifying and describing a situation are essential to workers' attempts to gather data by requesting information, questioning, and probing. Using these skills, workers can clarify the problem or concern and broaden the scope of the group's work by obtaining additional information that may be useful to all members. The worker should be careful to ask questions that are clear and answerable. Double questions or value-laden questions may be met with resistance, passivity, anger, or misunderstanding. For some issues and for some group members, questioning or probing may be seen as a confrontation or a challenge to what has already been stated, particularly in areas in which the member is reluctant to give additional information, because the information is perceived as emotionally charged or potentially damaging to the member's status in the group. The worker should be particularly sensitive to these concerns when seeking additional information from a member. Helping the member explore fears or concerns about the potentially damaging effect of a disclosure can be a helpful intervention. Another is asking for feedback from other members about the realistic basis of personal fears.

● CASE EXAMPLE *A Single Parents Group*

In a single parents group, the worker asks John, a member of the group with partial custody of an eleven year old son who has Attention Deficit Hyperactivity Disorder to elaborate on his feelings about his son, who has a lot of behavior problems both at school and at home. In response, John says spontaneously, "sometimes I get so frustrated I just feel like bashing his head in," but then immediately says he would not do such a thing. Sensing that John feels awkward about what he just said, the worker asks other members if they have had similar feelings in dealing with their own children. Several members talk about their frustrations and how they sometimes feel like they are about to lose control. A good interaction follows where members talk about how they handle situations where they fear they may lose control. The worker decides to join in and self-disclose a particular occasion on which she became so frustrated with her child that she had to leave the room before she did or said something she would regret later. In this way, John and the other members were able to disclose strong feelings without fear of how they would be perceived in the group.

Summarizing and Partializing

When information has been discussed about the problems or concerns facing the group, a worker can use summarizing or partializing skills. Summarizing skills enable a worker to present the core of what has been said in the group and provide members an opportunity to reflect on the problem. Summarizing skills give members and the worker an opportunity to consider the next steps in solving the problem and allow members to compare with the worker's summary their perceptions about what has gone on in the group. Partializing skills are useful for breaking down a complex problem or issue into manageable bits. Partializing is also helpful in determining group members' motivation to work on various aspects of the problem. For example, the worker might say, "John, I heard you talk a lot about your frustration with the group's not sticking to its purpose here. Would you tell us briefly what you would like to see the group do that we aren't doing right now? . . . Okay, so you are suggesting that we could take three steps to stay on track better during future discussions. . . . Am I paraphrasing you correctly? Are these the three things you think would keep us on track?"

Synthesizing

Another useful data-gathering and assessment skill is synthesizing verbal and nonverbal communications. Examples of synthesizing skills include making connections among the meanings behind a member's actions or words, expressing hidden agendas, making implicit feelings or thoughts explicit, and making connections between communications to point out themes and trends in members' actions or words.

Synthesizing skills can be useful in providing feedback to members about how they are perceived by others. Because these skills often involve a considerable amount of judgment and conjecture about the facts available to the worker, they should be used cautiously, and all members should have the opportunity for input into the synthesis. Ideally, when the worker synthesizes a number of interactions or points out similarities in group problem solving or in group communication patterns, all members should be able to give feedback about their perceptions of the situation. For example, during a weekly staff meeting of an adolescent unit in a state mental hospital, a worker might mention the patterns of interactions that have developed among team members. In describing these patterns, the worker would ask members for feedback on how they perceived the group's interaction.

Analyzing Skills

Once the data have been gathered and organized, the worker can use analyzing skills to synthesize the information and assess how to proceed. Analyzing skills include pointing out patterns in the data, identifying gaps in the data, and establishing mechanisms or plans for obtaining data to complete an assessment. For example, in a treatment conference at a group home for adolescents, the worker can use analyzing skills to point out patterns used by staff members in previous work with a particular youngster. The group can then explore new methods and techniques for future efforts to work with the youngster. In an educational treatment group for potentially abusive parents, the worker can use analyzing skills to link parents' behavior patterns to the onset of physical abuse of their children.

Action Skills

Supporting Group Members

Action skills are most often used by the worker to help the group accomplish its tasks. Perhaps the most basic skill in this area is supporting group members in their efforts to help themselves and each other. Skills to support group members will not be effective unless members perceive the group to be a safe place in which their thoughts and feelings will be accepted. Thus, it is essential to begin by helping the group develop a culture in which all members' experiences and opinions are valued. The worker supports members by encouraging them to express their thoughts and feelings on topics relevant to the group, by providing them the opportunity to ventilate their concerns, by soliciting their opinions, and by responding to their requests and comments.

Support also means helping members respond empathically to each other and validate and affirm shared experiences. Skills in supporting members often involve pointing out their strengths and indicating how their participation in the group can help to resolve their problems. It also means providing hope for continued progress or success.

Ventilation and support are the primary goals of some groups. For example, support groups are sometimes formed for the staff of neonatal intensive care units and burn units of regional hospitals. Such groups give staff a chance to talk about and reflect on the emotionally draining situations they frequently face. Medical social workers who form and facilitate these groups encourage staff to ventilate pent-up emotions and provide peer support for one another. Similarly, the therapeutic elements of a treatment group for recently widowed people include the ventilation of feelings about the loss of a loved one, the affirmation of similar feelings and experiences, and the encouragement to cope effectively with the transition despite feelings of grief.

Reframing and Redefining

Often, one of the greatest obstacles to the work of a group or an individual is failure to view a problem from different perspectives to find a creative solution (Clark, 1998). Redefining and reframing the problem can help members examine the problem from a new perspective. Thus, a worker may want to reframe or redefine an issue or concern facing the group. For example, in a group in which one member is being made a scapegoat, the worker might help members redefine their relationship to that member. Redefining can be done by having members talk about how they relate to the person who is being scapegoated and how they might improve their relationship with that person. In this case, reframing the problem from one that focuses on the scapegoated member to one that is shared by all members is a useful way to change members' interactions with this particular member. As the problem is redefined and group members change their relationship with the member being scapegoated, the problem often diminishes or disappears. Reframing is described in greater detail in Chapter 9.

Linking Members' Communications

The skill of linking members' communications involves asking members to share their reactions to the messages communicated by others in the group. Middleman and Wood (1990) refer to this skill as reaching for a feeling link or an information link. Members have a tendency to communicate with the worker rather than with other members, especially in early group meetings. The worker can prevent this from becoming a pattern by asking members about their reactions to a particular communication. For example, in a group in a psychiatric inpatient setting designed to prepare the members for independent living, the worker might say, "Mary, how do you feel about what Joe just said? I recall that during our last meeting, you expressed feeling anxious about living on your own." Alternatively, the worker might say, "Have any of you had the same feeling?" When members of the group validate and affirm each other's experiences and feelings, they develop a sense of belonging. Members no longer feel isolated or alone with their concerns. They stop questioning and doubting their own interpretations of a situation and their own reactions to it.

The skill of linking members' communications also involves asking members to respond to requests for help by other members. Helping members respond to each other fosters information sharing, mutual aid, and the building of a consensus about how to approach a particular problem. For example, in response to a query from a group member about whether the worker knows of a resource for helping her take care of her frail father while she is at work, the worker might ask whether any other members have used adult day care or respite care. Workers find that members are often more receptive to using a service or a resource when they hear positive reports about it from other members of the group.

Particularly when working with mandated and reluctant clients, workers who suggest use of a particular resource may be viewed with skepticism. Members sometimes believe that the worker has a vested interest in getting them to use a particular service. In contrast, the testimonials of one or more group members about the benefits of a particular service are often viewed with less skepticism. Workers should also be aware that once they provide a response, other members are less likely to provide their own perspective. Thus, although a direct response to a member's communication is often warranted, it is often a good practice for workers to turn to other members of the group for their input before jumping in with their own responses.

Directing

Whether the worker is clarifying the group's goal, helping members participate in a particular program activity, leading a discussion, sharing new information, or making an assessment of a particular problem, the worker is directing the group's action. Directing skills are most effective when coupled with efforts to increase members' participation and input (Stogdill, 1974). The worker should not use directing skills without obtaining members' approval or without involving them in decisions about the direction the group should take to accomplish its goals. The worker should be aware of how each member reacts to being directed in a new component of the group's work. For example, when directing a role play in a remedial group designed to help teenagers learn how to handle angry feelings more effectively, the worker should be aware of how the action will affect each member. Depending on the way they express their anger, some group members may benefit more than others from playing certain roles.

Advice, Suggestions, and Instructions

Workers give advice, suggestions, and instructions to help group members acquire new behaviors, understand problems, or change problematic situations. Advice should only be given, however, after a careful assessment of what the member has tried in a situation. This avoids awkward situations where the worker provides advice or suggestions only to find that it has been tried and has not worked. Advice should also be given in a tentative manner such as, "have you considered . . ." This type of phrasing enables members to express their opinion about the advice and whether they are ready to accept it. Group work experts have suggested being cautious about giving advice especially if it is not solicited by a member (Kottler, 2001), and process analyses of treatment and support groups indicate that it is not given often by professionals (Smith, Tobin, & Toseland, 1992). Nonetheless, advice is expected and wanted by many clients, especially those of lower socioeconomic status (Aronson & Overall, 1966; Davis, 1975; Mayer & Timms, 1970). Further, these skills appear to have some beneficial effect in helping clients formulate new ideas and approaches to resolving problems (Davis, 1975; Ewalt & Kutz, 1976; Fortune, 1979; Reid & Shapiro, 1969; Smith et al., 1992). For example, in a review of studies of various therapeutic mechanisms of change, Emrick, Lassen, and Edwards (1977) reported that advice giving was strongly associated with positive changes in clients. Effective ways to give advice, suggestions, and instructions follow.

Giving Advice, Suggestions, and Instructions

- Should be appropriately timed
- Should be clear and geared to comprehension level of members
- Should be sensitive to the language and culture of members
- Should encourage members to share in the process
- Should facilitate helping networks among members

Advice, suggestions, and instructions should be timed appropriately so that group members are ready to accept them. They should also be clear and geared to the comprehension level of the members for whom they are intended. A group of teenage parents who have not completed high school requires a presentation of ideas, advice, suggestions, and instructions quite different from a presentation to a group of highly educated women who have delayed child rearing until their early thirties.

Workers should also be sensitive to the language and culture of the members of their groups. Certain words in English might not translate appropriately or with the same meaning in another language. Further, the cultural heritage of a population may influence how such individuals receive and decode messages sent from the worker.

The worker should not act alone in giving advice, suggestions, and instructions. This sets the worker off as an expert who may be seen as too directive. The worker should encourage members to share information, advice, and instructions with each other. Middleman (1978) and Shulman (1999) refer to this as the worker's reaching for feelings and information that members may be hesitant to disclose.

To encourage members to share information and advice with each other, the worker should facilitate the development of helping networks where members feel free to share their life experiences, information, and resources, as well as their opinions and views. One of the distinct advantages of group work over individual work is the ability of group members to rely on one another for help in solving problems and accomplishing goals. Experience suggests that well-established helping networks often continue outside the group long after the group experience has ended. For example, a worker who formed a support and parenting skills education group for single parents in an inner city area later helped the group members form a child-care cooperative that flourished for years after the 12-week parenting skills group ended. Similarly, the members of a support group for family members of patients recently discharged from inpatient settings in the inner city were helped by a worker to form a local chapter of a national welfare rights organization.

Providing Resources

Organizations that sponsor groups have access to a wide variety of resources such as medical treatment, home health care, financial assistance, job and rehabilitation counseling, family planning, and financial management consultation, which the worker can make available to members. Making skillful use of these resources through accurate assessment and referral can be helpful to members. The worker can also encourage members to talk about the resources and services they have found to be effective. In this way, the cumulative knowledge of all group members can be used for mutual aid. Members who talk enthusiastically about a resource or service can be more convincing than a worker providing the very same information.

In task groups, workers can also provide a variety of resources for members. They can influence the environment in which a group works, either directly or indirectly, to make it easier for the group to accomplish its tasks. Workers may have access to important people or action groups that can give the group's work proper consideration. In addition, because task groups are often composed of members with a variety of skills and resources, members can also help one another achieve the group's goals.

Disclosure

Disclosure is an action skill that should be used sparingly by the worker for the specific purpose of deepening the communication within the group. Too often, novice workers disclose to join in and be a part of the group. Workers should remember, however, that their main role is to facilitate communication among members. Therefore, it is often more important to pay attention to the processes that are occurring in the group among members rather than to get involved directly in the content of the discussion. Getting pulled into the content can have negative consequences as the worker can be seen to be taking sides. It also distracts the worker from focusing on the verbal and non-verbal interaction occurring among members. The value of disclosure is in deepening communication occurring in the group, empathizing with members, and letting the members know that the worker understands their situation. Disclosure can also model openness and risk-taking, demonstrating that the group is a safe place to talk about difficult emotional issues.

● **CASE EXAMPLE** *Disclosure in a Couple's Group*

During the interaction in a couple's group, members began to talk about how difficult it was for them to take responsibility for their own actions within their marriage and how it was easier to blame their partner for situations. Members went on to talk about how they could carry around anger at their spouse for hours and even days at a time. At one point the worker stepped in and said that he had had similar experiences in his own relationship with his wife, and how hard it was for him to step back and think about his role in the situation. The worker then asked the members to think about what happened when they stepped back and took a look at the situation and their role in it. This led to a productive discussion of how to step back from situations when one blamed one's partner for a situation, and how this could be done without holding the anger in for hours or even days.

Modeling, Role Playing, Rehearsing, and Coaching

The action skills of modeling, role playing, and rehearsing situations in the group can be helpful in both task and treatment groups. *Modeling* refers to the worker or a member demonstrating behaviors in a particular situation so that others in the group can observe what to do and how to do it. For example, the worker in an assertion training group might demonstrate how to respond to a spouse who has become quite angry. In another group, the worker might model caring and concern by going over to a group member who has begun to cry and placing an arm around the member's shoulder.

Role playing refers to having group members act out a situation with each other's help. The two primary purposes of role playing are to assess members' skill in responding to an interpersonal situation and to help members improve particular responses. Responses can be improved through feedback, rehearsal of a new response, or coaching (Etcheverry, Siporin, & Toseland, 1987).

Role playing can be a very useful tool when trying to help members improve responses to stressful situations. For example, in a group for couples trying to improve their relationships, the worker might ask each couple to role play an argument they had during the past week. During the role play, the worker asks each couple to switch roles so that each partner could experience how the other felt, thought, and acted in the situation. Role play can help members understand their partner's behavior and how their own behavior influenced their partner. The couples can use the feedback they received to experiment with new and better ways to communicate during an argument. In this way, the couples learn new communication skills and begin to use improved ways of responding to each other during disagreements.

Rehearsing refers to practicing a new behavior or response based on the feedback received after a role play. Because it is difficult to learn new behaviors or to diminish less adaptive but habituated behavior patterns, a member may have to practice a new response several times.

Coaching is the use of verbal and physical instructions to help members reproduce a particular response. For example, members of a group for the mentally retarded might practice expressing their feelings during interpersonal interactions. As members practice, the worker coaches them by giving instructions and demonstrating how to improve their responses. Additional information about different role-playing techniques is presented in Chapter 9.

Confrontation Skills

Confrontation is a useful action skill for overcoming resistance and motivating members. Confrontation is the ability to clarify, examine, and challenge behaviors to help members overcome distortions and discrepancies among behaviors, thoughts, and feelings (Egan, 2002; Toseland & Spielberg, 1982). Confrontation skills should be used only when the worker has carefully assessed the situation and decided that what is said will not be rejected by a member. If a member is not ready to examine thoughts, behaviors, or feelings, the member may react negatively to a confrontation by becoming passive, angry, or hostile.

Because confrontations are potent and emotionally charged, workers should be prepared for strong reactions. In certain circumstances, workers may want to make gentle or tentative confrontations to explore a member's reactions before making direct, full-scale confrontation. Although confrontations are often associated with pointing out a member's flaws or weaknesses, they can be used to help members recognize strengths and assets. For example, in a remedial group for psychiatric inpatients, a depressed group member who is self-deprecating might be confronted and challenged to begin to recognize his strengths and assets. Similarly, a member of a growth group might be confronted by pointing out how her words differ from her actions.

Resolving Conflicts

One of the most important action skills is helping resolve conflicts among the members of the group and with individuals and social systems outside the group. Group members may conflict with one another for a variety of reasons. For example, in a delegate council, members may represent constituencies that have quite different concerns, interests, and goals. In a treatment team, group members' responsibilities for different work functions and tasks may cause conflict or competition, particularly if resources for accomplishing a task are limited.

Many of the models of group development described in the previous chapter indicate that conflict may arise among members as the group develops. The worker should help the group view conflict as a healthy process that can clarify the purposes and goals of the group and the way members can work together.

Although conflicts inevitably arise, skillful group facilitation can help avoid unnecessary conflicts and resolve disagreements before they turn into hostile disputes. To help avoid unnecessary conflicts, workers can suggest that the group develop and maintain rules for participation. These rules are frequently expressed in early contractual discussions with members. Sometimes these rules, which should be developed with the participation of all group members, are stated in a written agreement that all members sign at the beginning of a new group. An example of such a written agreement is shown in Figure 4.3. Having agreed-on rules clearly written and displayed on a blackboard or flip chart is particularly helpful in children's groups. Children enjoy setting rules for their group, and, with the guidance of a leader, they can help each other follow rules they have made.

When conflicts arise among members, the worker may also use moderating, negotiating, mediating, or arbitrating skills to resolve disagreements before they turn into hostile disputes. Moderating skills help workers keep meetings within specified bounds so that conflict is avoided. Negotiating skills are used to help members come to an agreement or an understanding when initial opinions differ. Mediating skills are used when two or more members are in conflict and action is necessary to help them reach an agreement and resolve the dispute. Arbitration skills involve having an authoritative third person meet with the group. This person listens to the dispute and binds the members to a settlement. Arbitration is sometimes used in task groups that have reached an impasse when working on a labor contract. Specific methods that workers can use to help resolve conflicts in groups are described more fully in Chapter 11.

Members may also come into conflict with forces outside the group. The members of therapy groups, for example, often expect workers to provide guidance about how to resolve conflicts with spouses, other family members, friends, fellow workers, and acquaintances. In attempting to be more assertive, a member of a therapy group might receive hostile, angry, or aggressive responses from family members or friends. In such a case, the worker might attempt to reduce the conflict by intervening directly in the situation or by helping the member develop the skills necessary to overcome the conflict alone. When the conflict is an inevitable by-product of a change the member wishes to make outside the group, the worker can help the member feel comfortable with the conflict until a new state of equilibrium is achieved.

Sometimes it is helpful for the worker to meet with people outside the group to resolve a member's conflict. For example, a worker might meet with the parents of an adolescent group member to discuss how the parents set limits and rules for their child. In other cases, workers can prepare members for the reactions they may encounter outside the group. For example, a worker can help members learn how to respond to potential rejection or hostility when they are more assertive than usual with a particular person. Preparing members for

FIGURE 4.3 ● *Rules for Group Participation*

I, the undersigned, agree to:

1. Attend each group session or call one day before the group meeting to explain my absence.

2. Not talk about anything that occurs in the group to anyone outside the group, unless it applies only to myself and no other group member.

3. Carry out all assignments agreed to in the group between group sessions.

4. Speak in turn so that everyone gets a chance to talk.

5. Give the group two weeks' notice before terminating my participation.

_____   _____
         Name   Date

what to expect in a wide range of situations and settings also helps ensure their success when they are using newly learned behaviors in unfamiliar settings or situations.

Workers may also need to resolve conflicts between the group as a whole and the larger society. For example, workers may help resolve conflicts between tenants' associations and housing authorities, welfare rights groups and county departments of social services, or support groups for individuals with chronic illnesses and health-care providers. Moderating, negotiating, mediating, and arbitrating skills can often be used successfully in these situations. However, in some situations, mobilization and social action skills (described in Chapter 11) may have to be used to resolve a conflict.

Learning Group Leadership Skills

Persons who are training to become group workers should begin by becoming thoroughly familiar with the theoretical knowledge about groups as a whole and the way members and leaders function in groups. However, to integrate theoretical knowledge about group dynamics with practical experience, trainees should (1) participate in exercises and role plays illustrating how group dynamics operate, (2) observe others leading and being members of groups, (3) examine their participation as members of natural or formed groups, and (4) lead or colead a group in a supervised field practicum.

In the classroom, trainees can learn to lead groups under a variety of conditions and circumstances by combining didactic and experiential methods of learning. Didactic material should expose trainees to the array of groups they may be called on to lead. Therefore, lectures, discussions, and examples should include groups in several settings with different purposes and clientele. Lecture material can be supplemented with films and videotapes of different social work groups in action. A list of available films is presented in Appendix B.

Cognitive knowledge is, by itself, insufficient for effective group work practice. Training should include exercises and role plays to illustrate and demonstrate the material presented during lectures. Often laboratory groups can be formed to help trainees practice the material that has been presented. Lab groups give trainees a sense of what it is like to be a member of a group. Also, leadership can be rotated in a lab group so that all members are responsible for leading a group at least once. Exercises to illustrate the concepts in each chapter of this book can be found in a manual entitled *Student Workbook: An Introduction to Group Work Practice* that accompanies this book (Furman, 2005), and other interactive group exercises can be found in Barlow, Blythe, and Edmonds (1999).

Laboratory group experiences can be enhanced by the use of video and audio equipment. These devices give trainees feedback about their verbal and nonverbal behavior as they participate in or lead a meeting. Tapes made during labs can be reviewed by trainees and the lab leader during supervisory sessions to help members develop their leadership skills.

Trainees can also learn how to lead a group by observing a group or by becoming a member of an existing group in the community. The trainee learns vicariously by observing the leader's behavior. The leader acts as a model of leadership skills for the member.

Learning also occurs through critiques of the group's process. Critiquing the group helps ensure that trainees do not accept all the activities of the group's leader without question. It gives trainees an opportunity to examine the development of a group over time and to observe the effects of leadership skills in action. It is relatively easy to structure lab groups so that part of the group's time is spent analyzing the group process, but trainees may not have this opportunity in community groups. Therefore, to achieve maximum benefit from participation in a community group, trainees should have an opportunity to discuss their experiences in supervisory sessions or in the classroom.

When trainees become familiar with basic skills in leading a group through these experiences, they are ready for a field practicum. The field practicum may include leading several sessions of a group, coleading a group, or leading an entire group while receiving supervision. For purposes of learning about group leadership skills, group supervision is preferable to individual supervision because the supervisor models group leadership skills while reviewing a trainee's work with a group. Rivas and Toseland (1981) have found that a training group is an effective way to provide supervision. Methods for conducting group supervision are discussed by Rose (1989). If not enough practicum sites are available, trainees can form their own task or treatment groups by providing group services to students or community residents (Rivas & Toseland, 1981).

Before leading a group, it is helpful for trainees to discuss their concerns about the first meeting. Lonergan (1989) reports that these concerns can include (1) unmanageable resistance exhibited by members, such as not talking; (2) losing control of the group because of members' excessive hostility or acting out; (3) inability to deal with specific behaviors such as a member dropping out of the group capriciously, members dating each other, or individuals making sexual advances within the group or between group meetings; (4) overwhelming dependency demands by members; and (5) lack of attendance and the disintegration of the group. Because trainees react differently to their first group experience, supervisors should explore each individual's concerns and help them deal with their anxiety by discussing likely group reactions and reviewing what could be done in the unlikely event that a trainee's worst concern is realized. For additional information about effective methods for learning group leadership skills, see Berger (1996) or Barlow and others (1999).

Leadership Style

It is important to recognize that, although leadership skills can be learned, they are not applied in a mechanical, objective fashion. Group work is a subjective encounter among the members of the group, all of whom have distinct personalities, viewpoints, and methods of relating to objective reality. Workers and members bring expectations, preferences, and styles of relating to the group. Although these may be modified during the course of interaction, they continuously color and shape the evolving interaction and the skills that workers use to facilitate the group. As Goldstein (1988) states, "As people enter into a group and take part in shaping its purpose and goals, the underlying premises that they bring to the encounter and their ways of perceiving, thinking and interpreting will inexorably determine how the process unfolds" (p. 25). Reid (1997) aptly points out that in therapy groups, "each [person] brings to the [group] experience a history of relating to others, sometimes with success and at other times without. In this therapeutic alliance group members may react to the therapist as if he or she were a significant figure from their own family. Similarly, the leader may react in exactly the same way, projecting onto others his or her own unresolved feelings and conflicts" (pp. 105–106). In the psychoanalytic tradition, projection of feelings by members onto the leader is called *transference*. Projection of feelings onto members by the leader is called *countertransference*.

To become an effective group leader it is not sufficient, therefore, to learn group leadership skills without paying attention to how they are applied. It is essential for leaders to become self-reflective practitioners who consider carefully the meaning of their interactions with all members of the group. One of the hallmarks of an effective leader is the ability and willingness to examine the effect of personal beliefs, expectations, preferences, personality, style of relating, and subjective experience of reality on a particular group. Effective leaders are not afraid to explore with members, supervisors, or colleagues the possible ramifications of their behavior in a group. They observe carefully and think deeply about the meaning of members' reactions to particular interaction.

The first step in helping leaders become more aware of the effect of their style of interaction is for them to do a self-assessment of their strengths and weaknesses as a leader. One way to do this is by asking participants to complete the Leadership Comfort Scale (LCS) shown in Figure 4.4. The LCS allows participants to rate their degree of comfort with 10 situations that group leaders frequently experience. Participants are also asked to write down their responses to a series of open-ended questions, such as:

- Describe what you perceive to be your major strengths and weaknesses as a leader.
- What types of group members make you feel uncomfortable?
- What situations or events during group meetings do you find particularly difficult to deal with?
- What feedback have you received from others about your leadership skills?
- What steps have you taken to improve your leadership skills? What steps have you considered but not yet taken?

Participants' anonymous answers to the LCS are tabulated and the aggregate answers are presented on a flip chart or blackboard. Volunteers who are willing are asked to share their answers to the open-ended questions, which inevitably leads to a lively discussion of difficult leadership situations and participants' strengths and weaknesses in dealing with them. The discussion also helps point out the diversity of responses to challenging leadership situations.

FIGURE 4.4 ● *Leadership Comfort Scale*

Indicate your feelings when the following situations arise in the group. Circle the appropriate feeling.

1. Dealing with silence	Comfortable	Uncomfortable
2. Dealing with negative feelings from members	Comfortable	Uncomfortable
3. Having little structure in a group	Comfortable	Uncomfortable
4. Dealing with ambiguity of purpose	Comfortable	Uncomfortable
5. Having to self-disclose your feelings to the group	Comfortable	Uncomfortable
6. Experiencing high self-disclosure among members	Comfortable	Uncomfortable
7. Dealing with conflict in the group	Comfortable	Uncomfortable
8. Having your leadership authority questioned	Comfortable	Uncomfortable
9. Being evaluated by group members	Comfortable	Uncomfortable
10. Allowing members to take responsibility for the group	Comfortable	Uncomfortable

Completing the Beliefs About Structure Scale (BASS), shown in Figure 4.5, can further the process of self-assessment. When completing the BASS, participants sometimes state that their answers depend on the purpose of the group, the types of group members, and so forth. Leadership is interactive, but individuals have preferences about the degree of structure they are most comfortable with. Participants should be asked to respond to the inventory in a way that best describes their natural tendencies and preferences.

After completing the BASS, participants can be asked to total the number of items they circled in column A and column B and to form two groups—one for those who had higher column A scores favoring a higher level of structure, and one for those who had higher column B scores favoring a lower level of structure. Participants in each group are asked to discuss why they preferred a higher or lower level of structure. They may also be asked to prepare for a debate with members of the other group about the benefits of their approach to structuring the work of the group.

Participants can also be asked to complete the How Members Achieve Change Scale, which is presented in Figure 4.6. Once this scale is completed, different approaches to helping members change are discussed. For example, the importance of insight in psychoanalytic group psychotherapy is contrasted with the importance of identifying here-and-now feelings in gestalt therapy. Similarly, the importance of cognition in cognitive therapy is contrasted with the importance of action in behavior therapy. Participants can also be asked to provide examples of the methods they use to help members change. For example,

---

FIGURE 4.5 ● *Beliefs About Structure Scale (BASS)*

Circle the statement in Column A or B that best describes your preference when running a group.

Column A	Column B
Time-limited group	Open-ended group
High structure/rules	Low structure/rules
Formal contract	Informal contract
Leader sets group purpose	Members decide purpose
Focus on member goals	Focus on group process
Leader-centered authority	Shared authority
Closed membership	Open membership
Homogeneous membership	Heterogeneous membership
Use of program activities	Use of open discussion
Focus on member behavior	Focus on meaning of communication
Directive leadership	Nondirective leadership

Summarize what you have learned about your style from the above choices. What are the major themes that emerge about your preferences for a particular level of structure within a group?

FIGURE 4.6 ● *How Members Achieve Change Scale*

Group leadership style is partly a function of how one believes members achieve change in their lives and how one believes the group should take responsibility for helping members change. Answer the following questions about these dynamics. Avoid using the term *it all depends*. Instead, choose the answer that best expresses your natural preference or inclination.

1. Do people achieve change best through insight or action?
2. Do people achieve change best by focusing on their affect (feelings) or their cognition (thoughts)?
3. When helping a member to achieve change, would you concentrate on changing the member's behavior or the member's thoughts?
4. When evaluating whether a member was making progress in the change efforts, would you assess whether the member did what the member wanted, what you wanted, or what society wanted?
5. Is it more important to give your attention to group content or group process?
6. Do you think the responsibility for the functioning of the group rests with the leader or the members?

Choose the statement that best characterizes your opinion. (circle one)

7. The purpose for group work is:
   a. Raising social consciousness, social responsibility, informed citizenship, and social and political action.
   b. Restoring and rehabilitating group members who are behaving dysfunctionally.
   c. Forming a mutual aid system among members to achieve maximum adaptation and socialization.
8. The role of the worker is to be a:
   a. Role model and enabler for responsible citizenship.
   b. Change agent, problem solving with members to meet their goals.
   c. Mediator between the needs of the members and the needs of the group and larger society.
9. Which methods would you tend to use in the group?
   a. Discussion, participation, consensus, group task
   b. Structured exercises, direct influence in and out of group
   c. Shared authority, support, building a positive group culture

Based on your responses to the previous nine questions, summarize your preferences for how to help members change.

---

participants who prefer to help group members change through action strategies might describe role-playing or psychodrama procedures that they have found to be particularly effective.

Participants can also discuss preferences for process-oriented or outcome-oriented leadership styles and preferences for member-centered or leader-centered leadership styles. Discussion is not intended to promote a particular style of leadership or even to help leaders identify what style of leadership they are most comfortable with. Rather, the aim is to encourage participants to become more self-reflective, to consider their natural tendencies and preferences, and to gain greater insight into how their natural tendencies and preferences affect their interaction with group members.

COLEADERSHIP

Coleadership presents a dilemma for the practicing group worker (Kolodny, 1980). Do the benefits of coleadership exceed its potential disadvantages? An entire issue of the journal *Social Work with Groups* has been devoted to this topic.[1] Although there is little empirical evidence to suggest that two leaders are better than one (Yalom, 1995), there are many clinical reports of the benefits of having two leaders (Cooper, 1976; Davis & Lohr, 1971; Levine, 1980; MacLennon, 1965; McGee & Schuman, 1970; Roller & Nelson, 1991; Schlenoff & Busa, 1981; Starak, 1981).

Coleadership allows greater coverage of the dynamics of the groups, especially if coleaders sit opposite each other. Because it is hard to see what is going on with members to your immediate right and left, coleaders who sit across from each other can more easily monitor members on both sides of the group. Also, coleaders can specialize in attending to some facets of group behavior over others, for example, coleaders can take turns focusing on process and content issues. Some of the other most frequently cited benefits of having a coleader follow.

Benefits of Coleadership

- Leaders have a source of support.
- Leaders have a source of feedback and an opportunity for professional development.
- A leader's objectivity is increased through alternative frames of references.
- Inexperienced leaders can receive training.
- Group members are provided with models for appropriate communication, interaction, and resolution of disputes.
- Leaders have assistance during therapeutic interventions, particularly during role plays, simulations, and program activities.
- Leaders have help setting limits and structuring the group experience.

This list suggests several ways in which coleadership can be helpful. For the novice worker, probably the greatest benefit of coleadership is having a supportive partner who understands how difficult it is to be an effective leader. As Galinsky and Schopler (1980) point out, "The support of a compatible co-leader lessens the strains of dealing with difficult and often complicated group interactions" (p. 54). During group meetings, coleaders help each other facilitate the work of the group. Between group meetings, they share their feelings about the group and their roles in it. In addition to supporting each other's efforts at group

---

[1]*Social Work with Groups* (1980), 3 (4).

leadership, coleaders can share feedback with each other about their mutual strengths and weaknesses and thereby foster each other's professional growth and development.

Coleadership can also be helpful because it allows workers to share alternative frames of reference regarding the interaction that has taken place in the group. This helps fill in gaps in each worker's memory of events and helps each view the interaction from a different perspective. This process, in turn, may lead to a more complete and accurate assessment as well as to more adequate planning when the coleaders prepare for future group meetings.

Coleadership provides a group with the benefit of having two experts who can help with problem solving. It provides two models of behavior for members to identify with and helps in role plays, simulation, and program activities engaged in by the group. Coleaders can increase workers' abilities to establish and enforce limits as long as they share common goals (Davis & Lohr, 1971). Coleaders also have the opportunity to structure their roles to meet the needs of members. For example, one worker can focus on members' socioemotional needs and the other worker can focus on members' task needs. In its most refined form, coleadership can be used strategically to promote therapeutic goals in a powerful and effective fashion. For example, when describing the benefits of male and female coleadership of spouse abuse groups, Nosko and Wallace (1997) point out that male and female coleaders who are perceived as different but equal can be effective at structuring their leadership and interaction to promote the resolution of faulty gender socialization among members. Effective coleaders use their relationship with each other to model effective interpersonal interactions that members can emulate both within and outside of the group.

Despite the benefits, coleadership has some potential disadvantages.

Disadvantages of Coleadership

- Can be more expensive than solo leadership
- Need to coordinate planning between meetings
- If leaders do not function well together they may not serve as role models for members
- Training new leaders by placing them in groups with experienced leaders may create conflict and tension
- Conflict between leaders can negatively affect group outcomes

Because it requires the time of two leaders, coleadership is expensive. Leaders must coordinate their actions in planning for the group. Between group sessions, communication can be a problem if workers do not make a concerted effort to find the time to discuss their work together (Herzog, 1980). If leaders do not function well together, they may not serve as therapeutic role models for members (Davis & Lohr, 1971). Yalom (1995) recommends that coleaders have equal status and experience. He suggests that the apprenticeship format—that is, training new group leaders by placing them in groups with experienced leaders—may create conflict and tension.

Conflict between coleaders can have detrimental effects on the outcome of a group (Cooper, 1976; Edelwich & Brodsky, 1992; Yalom, 1995). Members may be able to side with one leader against the other or avoid working on difficult issues. When coleaders experience conflict with one another, it can be helpful to resolve the conflict in the group. This lets members know that the leaders are comfortable with conflict and are able to work together to resolve it. It also enables the coleaders to act as models by demonstrating appropriate conflict-resolution strategies. Galinsky and Schopler (1980) caution however, that in some situations, it may not be helpful to resolve a conflict between coleaders in the group. For example, when conflicts are deep-seated and when there is little hope of a successful resolution, they may be better handled in supervisory sessions. The decision about whether to resolve a conflict in a group should depend on its potential effect on members. Because members are usually aware of conflicts between coleaders, it is generally preferable to resolve them within the group, especially if the resolution process is amicable and not too distressing for members. When conflict is resolved outside the group, some members may not be aware that resolution has occurred. Also, resolving a conflict outside the group does not enhance members' conflict-resolution skills.

Because of the lack of empirical evidence about its effectiveness, the benefits and drawbacks of coleadership should be carefully considered before two leaders are used in a group. In an article about coleadership, Wright (2002) points out that the decision to have cofacilitators should be based on the needs of the group rather than on worker preferences for solo or coleadership. In situations in which it is especially important to have models who represent different points of view, it may be important to have coleaders. For example, in a group of couples, it can be useful to have both male and female leaders. In other situations, however, the expense of coleadership or the incompatibility of potential coleaders may negate any potential benefits.

When the decision is reached to colead a group, it is essential that coleaders meet together regularly to plan for the group and to discuss group process issues that arise as the group develops (Davis & Lohr, 1971). To avoid coleaders' becoming too busy to meet together, it is helpful if they schedule a specific time to meet after each group meeting. During these meetings, coleaders should review what they did well in working together, what difficulties they experienced, how they plan to work together during the next meeting, and how members and the group as a whole are progressing. In particular, they should discuss their reactions to members and their perceptions of any difficulties or resistance that members may be experiencing. They should review the overall development of the group as it moves through the phases of group development to hopefully more cohesive and productive forms of interaction. Coleaders should also discuss their own relationship such as their division of responsibility in the group and their feelings about their equitable contributions in the group. In a recent article, Antieno Okech and Kline (2006) point out that competency concerns strongly influence coleaders' relationship and performance in a group. Therefore, it is essential for coleaders to talk about their respective roles in the group between meetings. Coleaders should be particularly aware of any attempts to divide their effort that could result in working toward different purposes or on behalf of different group factions. Coleaders should schedule their review meeting soon after a group meeting because they are more likely to remember what has occurred, and they have more time to prepare for the next meeting.

Experience has shown that it is worse to have a coleader with whom one does not agree than to lead a group alone. Therefore, group workers should be cautious in choosing a coleader. Difficulties may arise when workers agree to colead a group without carefully considering whether they can work together effectively. Potential coleaders may want to examine each other's styles while leading a group or during team meetings before agreeing to colead a group. Figure 4.7 presents some issues to discuss before deciding to colead a group.

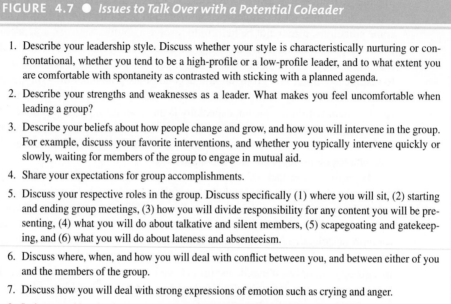

FIGURE 4.7 ● *Issues to Talk Over with a Potential Coleader*

1. Describe your leadership style. Discuss whether your style is characteristically nurturing or confrontational, whether you tend to be a high-profile or a low-profile leader, and to what extent you are comfortable with spontaneity as contrasted with sticking with a planned agenda.

2. Describe your strengths and weaknesses as a leader. What makes you feel uncomfortable when leading a group?

3. Describe your beliefs about how people change and grow, and how you will intervene in the group. For example, discuss your favorite interventions, and whether you typically intervene quickly or slowly, waiting for members of the group to engage in mutual aid.

4. Share your expectations for group accomplishments.

5. Discuss your respective roles in the group. Discuss specifically (1) where you will sit, (2) starting and ending group meetings, (3) how you will divide responsibility for any content you will be presenting, (4) what you will do about talkative and silent members, (5) scapegoating and gatekeeping, and (6) what you will do about lateness and absenteeism.

6. Discuss where, when, and how you will deal with conflict between you, and between either of you and the members of the group.

7. Discuss how you will deal with strong expressions of emotion such as crying and anger.

8. Is there anything that is nonnegotiable regarding your coleadership of a group?

SUMMARY

This chapter focuses on leading task and treatment groups effectively. Although leadership is sometimes viewed as a function executed exclusively by the worker, leadership functions should be shared with group members. In this regard, the text distinguishes between the worker's role as the designated leader of the group and the leadership roles of group members that emerge as the group develops.

Leadership has been defined as the process of guiding the development of the group and its members to achieve goals that are consistent with the value base of social work practice. A worker's ability to guide group members depends on the power attributed to the worker by group members, by the supporting agency or organization, and by the larger society that sanctions the work of the group.

The power bases that can be used to guide the development of the group and its members include (1) connection power, (2) expert power, (3) information power, (4) legitimate power, (5) referent power, (6) reward power, and (7) coercive power. Leaders vary in the degree to which they have access to each power base and the extent to which they use the power bases to guide the group.

Leadership is affected by a variety of situational factors that act in combination. Thus, there is no one correct way to lead all groups. Rather, leadership methods should vary according to the particular group a worker is leading. This chapter reviews the remedial, social goals, and reciprocal models of group leadership and examines several variables that affect group leadership. To help workers examine situational variables, the text describes an interactional model of group leadership. The model includes (1) the purpose of the group, (2) the type of problem the group is working on, (3) the environment in which the group is working, (4) the group as a whole, (5) the members of the group, and (6) the leader of the group.

It is essential that workers be familiar with a range of leadership skills that can be applied in many different types of groups and in many different settings. Skills include (1) facilitating group processes, (2) data gathering and assessment, and (3) action. Together, these skills constitute the core skills needed for effective leadership of task and treatment groups.

It is also essential that workers be aware of their leadership styles. A number of exercises are presented to help workers identify their preference for a particular leadership style and understand how their preferences influence their practice with treatment and task groups.

The chapter ends with an examination of coleadership. The benefits, drawbacks, and pitfalls of coleadership are described.

Leadership and Diversity

Group leaders often work with people from a wide range of backgrounds. Diversity within the group can be based on a variety of characteristics such as race, ethnicity, culture, national origin, religion, social class, gender, sexual orientation, and disability. When differences exist among members or between the leader and members, leadership can be particularly challenging.

APPROACHES TO MULTICULTURAL GROUP WORK

It is helpful for leaders to develop a perspective on how to work with people whose backgrounds are different from their own. Such a perspective has been referred to as anti-oppressive group work (Brown & Mistry, 1994), ethnic-sensitive practice (Devore & Schlesinger, 1999), minority practice (Lum, 2003), a cross-cultural approach (Green, 1999; Pinderhughes, 1979; Sue & Sue, 1999), and cultural/multicultural competence (Diller, 1999; Vasquez & Han, 1995). According to Pinderhughes (1995), cultural competence includes (1) the ability to perceive others through their own cultural lens, (2) knowledge of specific beliefs and values in the client's community, (3) personal comfort with differences, (4) a willingness to change previous ideas and stereotypes, (5) the ability to be flexible and adapt one's thinking and behavior in novel settings, and (6) the skill to sort through diverse information about a community to understand how it might apply to particular individuals. Green (1999) points out that cultural competence can be learned. An empirically based approach for learning about issues of race, gender, and class in groups is presented by Davis and Proctor (1989). More recently, Davis, Galinsky, and Schopler (1995) developed a comprehensive framework for leadership of multiracial groups that highlights areas of potential difficulty for group workers and suggests practice guidelines for selecting appropriate intervention techniques. Important aspects of their framework, recognize, anticipate, problem-solve (RAP), follow.

Leadership of Multiracial Groups

- Engage in ongoing self-assessment and assessment of the group, its members, and their environment

- Anticipate potential sources of tension in composing the group, in formulating the purpose, and in structuring the group's work together
- Intervene at the individual, group, and environmental levels to promote harmony and understanding; to resolve racial, ethnic, and cultural issues; and to involve members in confronting and resolving problems within and outside the group

Understanding the dynamics of race, ethnicity, and culture is essential for effective group work practice, but people also differ from each other in gender, social class, geographic background, educational and disability level, language, level of acculturation and assimilation, and age. Thus, in addition to learning practice principles for use with particular groups such as Native Americans (Marsiglia, Cross, & Mitchell-Enos, 1998; Weaver, 1999), African Americans (Aponte, Rivers, & Wohl, 2000; McRoy, 2003) or other groups (Lum, 2005), leaders can benefit from using a broader conceptual framework about diversity within groups, which includes:

- Developing cultural sensitivity
- Assessing cultural influences on group behavior
- Intervening with sensitivity to diversity

Developing Cultural Sensitivity

The terms *identity* and *culture* are often used to refer to the many ways people can differ. To develop a perspective on effective work with people of diverse cultural backgrounds, the group leader should engage in a process of self-exploration. Green (1999) describes this process as developing "cultural competence" (pp. 88–108) and suggests that workers who are culturally competent have an awareness of their own cultural limitations, are open to cultural differences, and acknowledge the integrity of other cultures. Steps in the process of developing cultural sensitivity follow.

Developing Cultural Sensitivity in Groups

- Explore your own cultural identity
- Learn how members define and identify themselves culturally
- Frame discussions of differences by emphasizing the strengths of various cultures
- Provide members with opportunities to describe how they experience their cultural backgrounds and identities
- Become familiar with the backgrounds of client groups with whom you frequently work
- Gain knowledge about particular cultural communities
- Become immersed in a particular culture
- Model acceptance and a nonjudgmental attitude about the values, lifestyles, beliefs, and behaviors of others by recognizing the value of diversity
- Acknowledge the effect of societal attitudes on members of diverse groups
- Honestly explore prejudices, biases, and stereotypical assumptions about working with people from diverse backgrounds

Workers can become more culturally sensitive by exploring their feelings about their own identity. Sometimes leaders fail to take into account how they experience their identity and how this might affect their interactions with members from other backgrounds. Among both leaders and members, there may be little acknowledgment of identity issues and how these issues affect values, beliefs, and skills, perhaps because of discomfort with the subject of identity or because leaders fear that raising identity issues may reduce cohesion within the group. However, to ignore differences within the group denies the background and self-identity of each member. Davis, Galinsky, and Schopler (1995) note, for example, that "whenever people of different races come together in groups, leaders can assume that race is an issue, but not necessarily a problem" (p. 155).

Leaders can also benefit from knowledge about how members define and identify themselves. Because the manifestation of racial, cultural, ethnic, and other identity variables is the prerogative of the member rather than of the leader, the leader should provide opportunities for members to discuss their identities. For example, the leader can ask, "How do our cultural backgrounds affect how assertive we are in our daily lives?" or "How can we use our differing ethnic backgrounds to brainstorm some innovative solutions to the problem we are discussing here?"

Level of acculturation and assimilation are also important factors to consider. The theory of assimilation views minority status as temporary with everyone living in the United States, regardless of ethnicity or race, gradually acquiring the cultural values of the mainstream culture. Although the assumption that everyone eventually assimilates is deeply rooted in U.S. society, it is clear that some minority groups continue to practice traditional, culturally bound norms for generations. Therefore, cultural pluralism theory may provide a better theoretical framework for culturally competent workers (Pillari, 2002). Cultural pluralism's main premise is that different ethnic and racial groups can interact in the larger society while maintaining their cultural distinctiveness and integrity (Parrillo, 2006). The cultural pluralism framework encourages workers and members to view differences in attitudes, norms, structures, and values positively as distinctive and defining elements of a person's identity.

It is often helpful for the worker to frame the discussion of differences in ways that help members to see the strengths in their backgrounds. Diversity should be viewed as an asset to the group. After reviewing the empirical evidence about the performance of homogeneous versus heterogeneous groups, Forsyth (2006) points out that "diverse groups may be better at coping with changing work conditions, because their wider range of talents and traits enhances their flexibility. Diversity should also help groups seek alternative solutions to problems and increase creativity and innovation" (p. 307). McLeod, Lobel, and Cox (1996), for example, found that groups that included Asian Americans, African Americans, Latinos, and whites outperformed groups that included only whites. Similarly, Watson, Johnson, and Merritt (1998) found that diverse teams performed better than nondiverse teams. A heterogeneity of member characteristics is associated with a variety of perspectives, and a variety of perspectives is associated with high-quality idea production. It is important to keep in mind, however, that "diverse teams that actually utilized the variety of perspectives . . . outperformed the homogeneous teams, whereas diverse teams that did not utilize their diversity performed worse than the homogeneous teams" (McLeod et al., 1996, p. 261). Superior performance by groups utilizing the perspectives of a culturally and racially diverse membership clearly suggests that group leaders should promote diversity in group composition. The findings also suggest that workers should develop skills in helping members to understand and work with members with different perspectives and experiences. Levi (2007) points out that the issue of the effectiveness of homogeneous and heterogeneous teams is complicated by several issues. For example, diversity in personal attributes and diversity in functional attributes can interact with the type of task being performed by a team. Personal attributes include differences in values, attitudes, and demographic variables such as age, gender, and race. Functional attributes include knowledge, abilities, and skills relating to the work environment. In a meta-analysis of many homogeneous and heterogeneous groups that distinguished between personal and functional attributes, Jackson (1992) found that in most situations heterogeneous teams performed better. However, diversity in personal attributes can create problems such as a lack of cohesion and conflict in group processes. These need to be addressed to ensure the effectiveness of diverse teams. Thus, while diverse teams generally prove to be more effective at problem solving, creativity, and overall effectiveness, conflict and a lack of cohesiveness need to be skillfully handled by the worker as group processes emerge, in order for the teams and other work groups to function effectively.

Members may also have a variety of self-identity issues that affect their participation in the group (Vasquez & Han, 1995). Some members may have clear self-identification with one race, ethnicity, or background or may identify with more than one. Others may have little knowledge about their racial, ethnic, or cultural heritage. It can be helpful if the leader provides members with opportunities to describe how they experience their cultural background and whether they experience any identity conflicts. The case example illustrates this point.

● **CASE EXAMPLE** *Cultural Sensitivity*

The group worker was concerned about a member's participation in a support group for women preparing to return to the workforce. The member often showed up for the meetings late and appeared tired. Although the worker suspected that the member was stressed by family responsibilities, she sensed there were other factors involved in her situation. During a group meeting, the leader asked members to discuss how their cultural backgrounds influenced their return to work. The member explained that her family duties posed considerable time constraints on her ability to look for work, and she was unsure how her family would react to her holding a full-time job. She explained that as a Latina, there were specific expectations placed on her by her cultural upbringing. These included putting her family first in all of her activities and adhering to specific role expectations about what women should do within and outside the home. The member's disclosure to the group of this aspect of her self-identity and the subsequent discussion facilitated by the worker helped other members to explore their own cultural identities and its impact on their job seeking behavior. The discussion also provided new insights for members about how their background and development affected their job readiness.

Self-identity issues are also important in group work with gay, lesbian, bisexual, and transgendered group members. Groups can provide an important support network and can be helpful in problem solving regarding issues of isolation, prejudice, stereotyping, and coming out. Groups can also be helpful in addressing interpersonal issues that arise with initiation and integration into gay organizations and communities. Getzel (1998); Nystrom (2005); Peters (1997); and Walters, Longres, Han, and Icard (2003) present useful information for working with gay, lesbian, bisexual, and transgendered individuals in groups.

Although it is not possible for a group leader to know all the complexities of diverse cultures and backgrounds, it is helpful for leaders to become familiar with the backgrounds of client groups with whom they frequently work. Green (1999) suggests that knowledge can be gained through several methods. For example, the leader can research literature and other information to develop a personal knowledge base about people from different cultures. When working with a group composed of members from a particular culture, the leader can visit that cultural community, interview leaders and key informants, and become a participant observer.

The leader can also gain knowledge about a particular cultural community through the process of *social mapping,* in which formal and informal relationships among members of a community are systematically observed and analyzed. For example, a leader assigned to conduct an afterschool group that included several Hispanic members visited the local parish priest serving the Hispanic community and interviewed several members of the parish to gain a better understanding of the needs of young people in the community. In addition, the leader attended several social functions sponsored by the church and met with parents and other community members who provided the worker with new insights into the needs of Hispanic youth.

When a leader has little knowledge about a particular culture or background, it is helpful to become immersed in that culture. Living or spending a concentrated period of time in a cultural community can help the leader better understand the common values, norms of behavior, and worldviews held by members of that culture. Immersion also assists the leader in establishing credibility among members of the community, in developing relationships important for connecting members to resources outside the group, and in understanding the importance of natural helping networks.

Leaders should be open to the differences exhibited by diverse cultures. It is particularly important for leaders to be accepting and nonjudgmental about the values, lifestyles, beliefs, and behaviors of others and to recognize the value of difference and diversity (Diller, 1999). Leaders who suspend judgment can learn a great deal about other cultures simply by asking members to describe their own backgrounds. Members are in the best position to describe how they experience their own self-identity. By asking members, leaders express their interest in members and their desire to get to know them individually. Because members are in the best position to describe how they experience their self-identity, the leader can learn much about other cultures by asking members for information about their backgrounds.

It is also important to acknowledge the effect of societal attitudes on members of diverse groups. Leaders should keep in mind that members of minority groups continually experience prejudice, stereotyping, and overt and institutional discrimination. The reality of ethnic and racial superiority themes in our society, as well as classism, sexism, and the history of depriving certain groups of rights and resources, should all be considered when attempting to develop a perspective on diversity. This case example illustrates how one worker attempted to help a group discuss discrimination and to develop a perspective on diversity.

● **CASE EXAMPLE** *Discrimination and Diversity*

During an educational group for parents of children with developmental disabilities, the worker asked members to discuss the effects on themselves and their children of societal attitudes toward children with disabilities. Members were very willing to discuss examples of prejudice and incidents of discrimination. The worker used these discussions to help members share experiences about other forms of discrimination based on race, ethnicity, culture, and sexual orientation. These discussions helped the group understand the universality of such experiences in the group and the dynamics behind prejudice and discrimination. The worker helped the group to examine the strengths in their backgrounds and how negative experiences had helped them to grow strong and cope more effectively. The discussion also helped to empower members who began to talk about how they could best confront stereotypes and challenge discriminatory practices when they encountered them outside of the group.

It can be helpful for leaders to honestly explore their prejudices, biases, and stereotypical assumptions in working with people from diverse backgrounds. Williams (1994) suggests leaders themselves may go through stages of ethnocultural development in which they experience cultural resistance and "color blindness" before acknowledging the importance of cultural influences and achieving cultural sensitivity. Leaders should acknowledge such thoughts and feelings and work on correcting them. Attending workshops on cultural sensitivity, doing self-inventories, researching one's own cultural heritage, attending specific cultural activities in the community, and joining cultural associations and organizations can help the leader achieve a fuller sense of cultural self-awareness. These activities can also help leaders gain a sense of their strengths and weaknesses in dealing with diversity. McGrath and Axelson (1999) and Hogan-Garcia (1999), for example, describe many exercises that can be used to increase leaders' awareness, knowledge, and sensitivity when working with multicultural groups.

Assessing Cultural Influences on Group Behavior

It is important for the group leader to recognize that the cultural backgrounds of members can have a profound effect on how they participate in the group. Assessing the cultural influences on group behavior requires constant vigilance throughout the life of a group. Diversity among members from differing cultural backgrounds as well as among members from the same cultural background requires careful consideration. Stereotyping members on the basis of preconceived notions of cultural behavior is an ineffective approach. Members must be individualized and differentially assessed. As Chau (1992) suggests, cultural sensitivity in assessing members is a prerequisite for becoming an effective group leader. Some issues that should be considered when assessing cultural influences on group behavior are described below.

Factors to Consider When Assessing Cultural Influences on Group Behavior

- The match between member and leader backgrounds
- The influence of member backgrounds on group participation
- Members' views of the agency sponsoring the group
- The cultural sensitivity of outreach and recruiting efforts
- The formation of relationships among persons from diverse backgrounds
- The influence of the larger environmental context where members live on their behavior in the group

- Preferred patterns of behavior, values, and languages within the group
- Members' experiences with oppression and their feelings about themselves, their group identity, and the larger society

Early in the planning stage of a group, the benefits of matching member and leader backgrounds should be considered. There is some evidence that minority clients express a preference for ethnically similar workers (Atkinson & Lowe, 1995; D'Andrea, 2004). However, there is mixed evidence about whether matching client and worker backgrounds leads to more effective treatment (Atkinson & Lowe, 1995; D'Andrea, 2004; Proctor & Davis, 1994; Sexton & Whiston, 1994; Sue, Zane, & Young, 1994; Ricker, Nystul, & Waldo, 1999). Also, there are benefits to having persons with different backgrounds interact, and practical difficulties often limit supervisors' choices in matching leaders and members (Gruenfeld, 1998).

Regardless of whether matching is attempted, some differences in the backgrounds of members and between members and the leader are likely. Therefore, when one plans a group, it is important for the leader to consider how members' backgrounds are likely to affect their participation in it. For example, it is helpful to assess how potential members' differing cultural backgrounds and levels of acculturation and assimilation affect their understanding of the purpose of the group. Members with different backgrounds bring differing expectations and experiences and that can affect how they view the group's purposes and the way work is conducted in the group. Confusion about the purpose of the group can lead to members' frustration and anxiety in the group's early stages.

The leader should also consider how members' backgrounds are likely to interact with the sponsorship of the group. The worker should consider, for example, how the sponsoring agency is viewed by members from different backgrounds. It is also important to consider how accessible the agency is, both physically and psychologically, to potential members. As Davis, Galinsky, and Schopler (1995) note, ethnic and socioeconomic boundaries of neighborhoods may be difficult for members to cross. When the sponsoring agency is perceived as being in a neighborhood that does not welcome persons from differing cultures, the leader may need to reach out to members or deal with members' perceptions of institutional or neighborhood prejudice and discrimination before continuing with further planning efforts.

When recruiting members, the leader should consider how to optimize outreach efforts. For example, in certain ethnic neighborhoods, key community members such as clergy, political leaders, and neighborhood elders may play an important part in helping the worker to gain support for the group and to reach potential members.

When composing a diverse group, the worker should consider how members from differing cultural groups are likely to relate to each other and to the leader. The literature on group composition gives suggestions for composing a diverse group (Brown & Mistry, 1994; Davis, Galinsky, & Schopler, 1995; Davis, Strube, & Cheng, 1995; McLeod, Loebel, & Cox, 1996; Mistry & Brown, 1997). Davis, Galinsky, and Schopler (1995) suggest that workers need to be sensitive to racial composition to overcome tension. In addition, they warn that marked imbalance among members with one type of characteristic can cause problems of subgrouping or domination by members of one particular background. When reviewing the strengths of same-sex or same-race groups, Brown and Mistry (1994) noted that same-sex groups have advantages when the group task is associated with issues of personal identity, social oppression, and empowerment or issues of personal and political change.

A complete assessment of group members should consider the larger environmental context in which members live and how that context can influence behavior within the group (Chau, 1992; Lum, 2004; Ramos, Jones, & Toseland, 2005). Davis, Galinsky, and Schopler (1995) list several environmental factors that can be considered sources of tension among members from diverse backgrounds—the climate of society, events in the members' neighborhoods, and the sponsoring organization's reputation for responsiveness to racial concerns. In addition, the direct experience of racism, sexism, and other forms of oppression can have profound effects on members' behavior. Still, some commonalities are often present among members with similar backgrounds. This case example describes the impact of one type of experience on open communication and self-disclosure among a group of resettled refugees from Cambodia.

● **CASE EXAMPLE** *Communication and Self-Disclosure*

Despite his efforts to model the skills of open communication and self-disclosure, the leader of a group for resettled refugees from Cambodia often encountered members who were silent when discussions turned to conditions in their homeland. During these discussions, several members had difficulty talking about their experiences and seemed unable to confide in other members of the group. Through encouragement and honest interest, the worker helped several quiet members identify that they had been exposed to a variety of extreme conditions in their homeland, including torture, civil unrest, and government-sponsored violence. One member bravely told her story of watching members of a revolutionary group kill her parents. Her courage in disclosing this to the group helped other silent members to develop trust in the group and to gradually share their own stories. The worker learned how external oppression can profoundly influence communication and interaction within a group.

It is also wise to keep in mind that members bring preferred patterns of behavior, values, and language to the group (Axelson, 1999; Devore & Schlesinger, 1999). They also bring with them experiences with oppression and particular feelings about themselves, their group identity, and the larger society. When problems such as member dissatisfaction or conflict among members occur, the leader should keep in mind that the problems may be caused by cultural differences, not by an individual member's characteristics or flaws in group processes. For example, some members of a group became upset when two African American group members became animated when talking about oppression. The other members talked about their reactions to the anger expressed by these two members. The worker helped the group to discuss what it was like to live with racism and prejudice on a daily basis and the anger that this causes. She acknowledged the white members' difficulty in knowing how to react when this anger is expressed. The worker also helped the group to see that, in some ways, the group reflected difficult and unresolved issues in the community. The interaction that followed the worker's intervention helped all members to become more empathic and understanding, and increased group cohesion.

Several factors can interfere with the process of learning about how cultural background affects members' behavior in the group. The leader may fail to recognize that cultural differences exist or may diminish their importance. Facing difference is a difficult process, and leaders may think recognizing and expressing difference among members will cause conflict within the group. The leader may also fail to recognize differences among members of the same cultural group by assuming that all members of that culture have common behavioral characteristics and thereby overgeneralize and stereotype members with a common cultural heritage. Among Hispanic Americans, for example, there are wide differences in life experiences for people from a Mexican American background and people from Puerto Rico (Moreno & Guido, 2005). Similarly, there are differences between African Americans with ancestry from different regions of Africa and African Americans with ancestry from Jamaica, Puerto Rico, and South America. It should not be assumed that all members of a common heritage share all perceptions, abilities, and characteristics. It should also be noted that even if members share a common cultural background, major differences in economic status may influence how the members experience the group. Different patterns and degrees of acculturation and assimilation also have a profound impact on the way cultural heritages are expressed in a group (Berry, 1997; Brook, Gordon, & Meadow, 1998; Granrose & Oskamp, 1997). Information on how culture can influence group dynamics follows.

Cultural Influences on Group Dynamics

Communication and Interaction

- Language, symbols, and nonverbal communication patterns of persons from different cultural backgrounds
- Language sensitivity and knowledge of words appropriate to various cultural contexts
- Stylistic elements of communication among diverse groups
- Nonverbal communications and how cultural groups differ in their use of space and distance
- Interaction patterns specific to different cultural groups

Cohesion

- Subgroup patterns among various cultural groups
- Expectations and motivations among persons from diverse backgrounds
- Cultural characteristics that influence common group goals

Social Integration

- Culturally determined normative behavior
- Influence of culture on task and socioemotional role development in groups
- Influence of discrimination and oppression on how members experience power and control within the group

Group Culture

- Shared ideas, beliefs, and values held by members from diverse cultural backgrounds
- Level of group feeling expressed by members as influenced by cultural norms

The leader should assess how members' backgrounds are likely to affect the way they experience communication and interaction patterns, cohesion, social integration, and the overall group culture. To assess communication and interaction patterns, it is important for the leader to understand the language, symbols, and nonverbal communication patterns of people from different cultural backgrounds (Lum, 2004; Ramos, Jones, & Toseland, 2005).

For example, in leading her first group with Chinese American members, a worker learned that group members from this cultural background felt uncomfortable with some of the attending behaviors she had learned in her social work education. Through some gentle probing and consultation with persons from that community, she learned that her direct eye contact, forward body position, and open body position were intimidating and communicated a level of disrespect to some members.

D. W. Johnson (2003) suggests that assessing communication and interaction patterns requires language sensitivity and knowledge of words and expressions that are appropriate and inappropriate in communicating with diverse groups. The leader should also have an awareness of the stylistic elements of communication, including how members of diverse cultural backgrounds communicate. For example, because of their respect for the authority of the leader's status and position in the group, some Asian Americans rely heavily on the group leader, especially in the first few sessions. Some groups of Native Americans may consider it impolite to give opinions in the group, and such attitudes may be mislabeled as resistance by the leader or by non-Native American members.

The group leader should strive to become aware of the nuances of messages sent by members, including how nonverbal messages differ across various cultures (Ramos, Jones, & Toseland, 2005). People from different backgrounds use body language, gestures, and expressions to accompany and define the meaning of the verbal messages they send. In addition, the leader should consider how cultural groups differ in their use of space, that is, whether distance or closeness is the norm, and what other nonverbal communication norms govern interaction in the culture. It is also helpful for leaders to learn the language of members from diverse cultures. Earnest attempts to learn even rudimentary language skills are often respected by group members, an important factor in developing a trusting, professional helping relationship with members.

The leader should be aware of differing interaction patterns used by members of diverse cultural groups. Members from some cultural backgrounds may favor a member-to-leader pattern of interaction; others may favor a member-to-member pattern that supports mutual aid among members in the group. In task groups, members from diverse groups may have differing views of status hierarchies, which can affect interaction patterns between members and the leader. This case example illustrates how culture can influence interaction in a group.

● **CASE EXAMPLE** *Culture and Group Interaction*

A committee in a community center in a Chinese American section of the city was charged with planning a fundraising event. The leader observed that the Chinese American members of the group hesitated to criticize the behavior of a member who was monopolizing the group. The leader, who was not Chinese American, asked a member after a group meeting about this behavior. The leader learned that the Chinese American members were hesitant to bring up their feelings because the monopolizing member was a person of advanced age and status in the community. According to Chinese American cultural heritage, interactions with older, high-status persons require respect. Criticism was not an acceptable behavior. The leader asked the member for advice about how to handle the situation, and it was suggested that using go-rounds and an agenda that designated other members to give reports could help to reduce the elderly member's dominance because he would then not feel that he had to fill voids or take the lead in loosely structured group discussions. This was tried successfully in subsequent meetings.

When the group has a membership drawn from many cultural groups, the leader should assess how subgrouping patterns may affect the group processes. Sociometric patterns can be influenced by cultural background, and this information is useful in assessing the behavior of members in the group and the behavior of the group as a whole. In a training group for college peer counselors, some members expressed their concerns about why most African American members sat together and communicated among themselves. The leader pointed out that cultural, racial, and ethnic groups often form informal subgroups on the basis of mutual interests and on common characteristics and experiences. The leader helped members to understand that members from minority groups on campus may also have needs for grouping as a protective, security-giving behavior. Through program activities and discussions, the leader helped all members of the group interact and become better acquainted.

Culturally sensitive workers consider the expectations and motivations that members from different cultural backgrounds bring to the group. For example, cohesion can be influenced by member expectations, which, in turn, can be influenced by the cultural background of members. In a support group for caregivers, some members with Hispanic backgrounds did not expect to divulge private family matters or publicly complain about their role as caregivers, and this affected how they bonded with other group members. If the cultural characteristics of members differ widely and are not explicitly taken into consideration, a climate of togetherness and a common sense of group goals can be difficult to achieve and the overall cohesion of the group is affected.

The leader should explore how members' cultural characteristics can affect their views of norms, roles, status, and power within the group. Group norms are often the result of the expectations that members bring to the group from previous experiences. The leader should assess how members' cultural backgrounds influence the norms that are developed in the group. For example, in many African American communities there is a strong belief in the power of spirituality and the "good" Christian life as antidotes to problems such as substance abuse, marital disharmony, difficulties in child rearing, depression, and alienation (Diller, 1999). Members' role expectations, developed within their particular cultural context, also often guide their behavior within the group. Gender-specific role expectations, for example, are prominent among certain ethnic groups. Thus, the leader should consider how members' culture influences their role expectations.

It is also important for the leader to be sensitive to how members from diverse backgrounds experience power and control within the group. Many members from minority groups have had direct experience with oppression, discrimination, and prejudice, which can affect how members feel about the use of power within the group. The leader should understand that these experiences are likely to influence how some members may deal with power and control. It is also imperative for the leader to ensure that patterns of discrimination are not repeated within the group.

The leader should assess how the cultural backgrounds of members contribute to the overall group culture. Shared ideas, beliefs, and values held by group members are, in part, a reflection of what experiences individual members bring to the group. The group culture can include, for example, a heightened sense of spirituality when the group is composed of Native Americans or Hispanic Americans. The strengths of some cultural backgrounds can reinforce other important aspects of group culture. For example, in a caregivers group composed of African Americans, the cultural strength of the extended family as a natural helping network can help create a group culture of networking and mutual aid among members.

The level of group feeling and group morale may also be a function of the cultural context of the group's members. In a group composed of Hispanic Americans, one might expect the expression of a higher level of group feelings and emotions than that in a group composed of Asian Americans because in the latter group, members may believe strong expressions of emotion outside the family are not appropriate (Gray-Little & Kaplan, 2000).

In addition to having an impact on group dynamics such as the culture of the group, it is important for workers to be aware that members' backgrounds can have a profound impact on group development and how leadership emerges in the group. Consider, for example, the impact of gender. Regarding group development, Schiller (1997) points out that affiliation and intimacy often appear earlier in women's groups and that conflict occurs later. Using Garland, Jones, and Kolodney's (1976) model of group development, Schiller (1995, 1997) proposes that the first and last stages of group development—preaffiliation and termination—remain the same, but that the three middle stages of group development—power and control, intimacy, and differentiation—would be conceptualized better as establishing a relational base, mutuality and interpersonal empathy, and challenge and change. Schiller (1997) goes on to describe the implications for practice of this alternative conceptualization of group development, which she refers to as the *relational model.*

Regarding leadership, Forsyth (2006) points out that women's leadership skills are often undervalued because they are viewed as socioemotional experts rather than as instrumental experts. (Dodge, Gilroy, & Fenzel, 1995; Nye & Forsyth, 1991). Because of gender stereotypes and leadership prototypes, therefore, men are often viewed by both men and women as having more leadership potential, and men more often emerge as leaders of groups, even in groups that are composed largely of women (Forsyth, 2006). There is evidence, however, that by pointing out these dynamics in both task and treatment groups, workers can provide greater opportunities for women to take on leadership roles (Forsyth, 2006).

Intervening with Sensitivity to Diversity

There are many ways for a group leader to intervene with sensitivity to issues of diversity in the group. Many of these are based on established principles of social work practice. Others are culturally specific practices that can be especially helpful in culturally competent group work practice. Some of these methods follow.

Intervening with Sensitivity to Diversity

- Using social work values and skills
- Using a strengths perspective
- Exploring common and different experiences among members
- Exploring meanings and language
- Challenging prejudice and discrimination
- Advocating for members
- Empowering members
- Using culturally appropriate techniques and program activities

Using Social Work Values and Skills

Developing a culturally sensitive approach to group leadership means using social work values to guide interventions. The values of being nonjudgmental, genuine, and accepting can often compensate for wide differences in cultural backgrounds between the leader and members. Effective communication skills can also make a big difference. For example, good questioning skills, which stress open, nonjudgmental questions, can encourage members to respond in their own cultural styles. Similarly, the leader should be aware that for listening skills to be effective, the skills should be tailored to the cultural background of members. This is illustrated in the following case example.

● **CASE EXAMPLE** *Culture and Communication*

A leader in a group for substance abusers used active listening skills with a Native American member, often paraphrasing and summarizing the content of the member's statements. When the member's participation became less frequent, the leader wondered if the member was experiencing a relapse of his substance abuse. Despite these initial impressions, the leader learned from his supervisor that his paraphrasing and summarizing might be viewed as offensive by the Native American member. Recognizing that his leadership style might not be the most effective in this situation, he used passive listening skills that conveyed to the member that he was being heard and that his participation was being carefully considered. The member's participation in the group increased. The leader learned that depending on the cultural style of the member, the leader might use active listening skills for some members and passive listening skills for others.

Using a Strengths Perspective

The leader should explore and use the strengths inherent in the cultural backgrounds of members (Appleby, Colon, & Hamilton, 2001). All cultures have strengths, which can be tapped to empower members. A case example of a leader using a strengths-based approach with a group of older adults follows.

● **CASE EXAMPLE** *A Strengths-Based Approach*

In a group for adults who care for relatives with Alzheimer's disease, the leader discussed the strong natural helping networks of several African American members and how these networks supported the efforts of the caregivers. The African American members acknowledged that their networks were resources that they could use for respite care for their relatives. Other members learned about some of the strengths of the African American extended family and realized they could explore some of these arrangements for respite care and emotional support for their own situation. Thus, the understanding of strengths of African Americans greatly contributed to the overall success of the group.

In the same group, a woman of Latino background was criticized by another member for passively accepting the sole responsibility for caregiver in her family. The leader intervened, stressing that the role of caregiver was a culturally assigned one, usually given to a female in the household (Phillips, Torres de Ardon, Komnenich, Killeen, & Rusinak, 2000; Purdy & Arguello, 1992). The leader pointed out that commitment to the care of family members by Latinas was viewed as a core value in Latino culture. Such strong familism in taking care of frail older Latinos was viewed as a strength both within and outside the Latino community (Flores, 2000; Sanchez-Ayende, 1998). Other group members agreed with the leader's perspective. Because she felt her cultural heritage had been acknowledged positively, the woman became more active in the group.

In both task and treatment groups, it is important to point out how the group is strengthened by having members with diverse experiences and perspectives. Unfortunately, although ratings by external evaluations found no differences based on team composition, there is evidence that members of teams that are heterogeneous with regard to gender, racial, and other characteristics perceive themselves to be less effective than teams with homogeneous membership (Baugh & Graen, 1997). It can be helpful, therefore, for workers to emphasize to members the accumulating evidence supporting the notion that diverse perspectives lead to more effective problem solving in groups (Forsyth, 2006). The worker can then go on to encourage members to express diverse perspectives, and to help the group to consider fully and grapple with the implications of each perspective. The worker's ultimate aim is to frame alternative perspectives as benefitting all members by enhancing the information exchange in the group. This will, in turn, enhance the group's ability to accomplish individual member and group goals. For a detailed discussion of how to work with multicultural task groups, see Granrose and Oskamp (1997); and for a review of multicultural work with treatment groups see Brook, Gordon, and Meadow (1998), Gray-Little and Kaplan (2000), and Hopps and Pinderhughes (1999).

Exploring Common and Different Experiences among Members

In working with members from diverse backgrounds it is often useful to acknowledge the differences that exist in the group and to explore the experiences that members may have in common. This process can begin by acknowledging diversity in the group and exploring how the cultural backgrounds of members may contribute to that diversity. For example, in a support group for parents who have experienced the death of a child, the leader began by self-disclosing that she was of Irish American background. She explained that, in her family, death was characteristically dealt with by planning large family gatherings, which sometimes took on a festive atmosphere. She also acknowledged that it may be particularly difficult for Irish American men to verbally express their grief. The members used this opportunity to explore their own cultural reactions to death and grieving by noting how different cultures express their feelings about death. The worker's initial disclosure and modeling helped the group explore their differing views of death and grieving and deal with difficult issues held in common by the members.

Exploring common and different experiences can also help overcome barriers to members' self-disclosure. Members are sometimes reluctant to disclose when they believe others may be judgmental about their cultural values, behavior, and lifestyle. As described in the case study, exploring cultural differences and fostering cultural appreciation can help members feel more secure in disclosing their thoughts and feelings.

● **CASE EXAMPLE** *Exploring Cultural Differences*

In a support group for parents, it seemed particularly difficult for participants who came from a Chinese American background to share intimate details of their family life. The worker tried to model self disclosure and also encouraged other members to openly discuss difficult issues that they faced with their children. The developing norm of high self disclosure continued to be difficult for the Chinese American parents. After one meeting, the father met briefly with the worker and noted that in his culture, certain family matters were considered private, to be discussed only among close family members. The worker acknowledged this and promised to help members show sensitivity to this cultural difference during the meetings. The Chinese American family felt more comfortable after that and participated more frequently in some of the group's discussions.

The leader can also model the skill of empathy for members, which, in turn, can increase their responsiveness to differences. Helping members develop empathy allows them to comprehend more fully the experiences that result from diverse lifestyles.

Exploring Meanings and Language

Meaning is expressed through language. Many cultures do not attach common meanings to certain phenomena such as social problems or medical diseases (Dinges & Cherry, 1995). There may be no clear equivalent in the Spanish language, for example, for some psychiatric diagnoses. Likewise, an illness such as Alzheimer's disease may be defined in Spanish using nonmedical terms. The leader should help group members explore the differences in meaning reflected in different languages. Although some rudimentary knowledge of other languages is an asset, the leader should realize that language helps to shape reality. There are instances in which common terms and idiomatic expressions in English have no clear equivalent in another language. The leader should realize that members who speak English as a second language can define social situations, problems, and other conditions in culturally bound ways. It can be very helpful and interesting for all group members to discuss and explore culturally bound definitions, as the case example indicates.

● **CASE EXAMPLE** *The Impact of Language*

In a socialization group for new parents, one of the members had a mobility disability that required her to use a wheelchair. Although other members seemed to be sensitive to the needs of the member with the mobility disability, they used a variety of terms to refer to her during group discussions, including "the handicapped person" and "the disabled person." The leader asked the members to consider using a "person-first" formulation when referring to the member. She suggested that the member was a person with a disability, rather than a disabled or handicapped person. In group discussions, the leader noted that most persons with disabilities are offended when language suggests that they should be primarily defined by the nature of their disability rather than as people first, with all of the same strengths, capabilities, and potential as others. Members became more sensitive to the meanings inherent in language and how language can promote the strengths or weaknesses of people with disabilities.

The leader can help members interpret the significance of certain aspects of their culture to members of the group. In some instances, members may not understand the reasoning behind a cultural practice or phenomenon, which can lead to criticism or insensitivity among members. For example, in a rehabilitation group for spine-injured people, a member from Central America noted that he had visited the local *curandero,* who prescribed native herbs and other remedies. The initial reaction of several members was to discount this practice and accuse the member of going outside the traditional medical establishment. However, the leader and other members explained the importance of folk medicine and traditional healing in the member's culture and how the local healer contributed to the member's mental and physical well-being. Members learned the importance of this cultural practice and the significance of different sources of folk healing for some members (Koss-Chioino, 1995).

Similarly, spirituality may contribute significantly to the well-being of members of a group. It is important to acknowledge the importance of spirituality for particular members of a group and to explain the significance of different religious orientations. Group workers sometimes ignore spirituality because of the belief that it is linked to a specific religious denomination. It is important to take an ecumenical view and emphasize how spirituality transcends organized religion. The worker should avoid proselytizing about a particular religion but should acknowledge the importance of spirituality in the lives of some, if not all, the group members.

Challenging Prejudice and Discrimination

For members of diverse cultures, the realities of prejudice and discrimination can be heightened in a group. Challenging stereotypes and biases is an important leader skill. Some members may deny their individual biases, prejudices, or stereotypes, and it is important for the leader to challenge them to more realistically understand how they feel about people who are different from themselves. There is some evidence, for example, that suggests that psychoeducational group experiences can help members overcome stereotypes and biases (Rittner & Nakanishi, 1993).

Experience also suggests that task groups can help to overcome prejudice. Differences in cultural beliefs (Maznevski & Peterson, 1997a; Diaz, 2002), attitudes towards interpersonal interactions (Goto, 1997), differences in attitudes and judgments about the self and others (Earley & Randel, 1997), and language differences (Orasanu, Fischer, & Davison, 1997) can all be addressed in task groups. The following case example focuses on attitudes towards and judgments about group members based on age stereotypes.

● **CASE EXAMPLE** *Overcoming Prejudice*

In a coalition planning a homeless shelter, several younger members discounted or ignored the suggestions made by older members. This developed as a pattern over the course of the early meetings of the group. Noting this, the leader asked members to spend time giving attention to the group's processes, particularly asking that members discuss how differences in the group might inhibit the group's work. After discussing what she had observed in the group, the leader helped younger members confront their prejudices about the older members and the group became more cohesive and goal oriented.

It is important for the leader to help members understand the discrimination that members have experienced in the past. Almost all minority groups have experienced discrimination and attempts to undermine their power and sense of positive self-identity. Burwell (1998) notes that extermination, expulsion, exclusion, and assimilation have all been used against minority group members. On a more subtle level, society often ignores the views of minorities and marginalizes their contributions. Schriver (1998) suggests, for example, that minorities do not partake of the privileges often accorded to members of the majority group. Access to a privileged status results in unearned advantages accruing to a particular group because of race, gender, socioeconomic status, or some other characteristic. In the United States, for example, white males have a more privileged status than do African American males, which has profound consequences for both groups.

The leader can help members to understand the effects of privilege and discrimination by asking members to identify a situation in which they felt discriminated against and to discuss the experience with other group members. After this exercise, members are better able to appreciate each other's experiences in dealing with discrimination and the effect it has had on their views of themselves, others, and their life position.

Advocating for Members

Members from minority groups may need special assistance in negotiating difficult service systems. Also, they may need help obtaining benefits and services. In a parenting skills group, for example, the leader became concerned about the absence of several Native American members. In investigating the reasons for their absence, she noted that these group members felt guilty about leaving their child-care duties to attend group sessions. The leader secured the support of her agency in providing child care at the agency during group meetings. Because of her efforts, members attended more regularly and their commitment and bond to the parenting group was greatly enhanced. Similarly, Brown (1995) points out that group process considerations are necessary for creating groups that are accessible for members with disabilities.

Leaders may wish to consider engaging in other advocacy activities on behalf of group members such as working with family members and community support systems. For example, in a socialization group for the frail elderly, the leader experienced a good deal of absenteeism from members who nevertheless seemed to enjoy the group. It was discovered that for many members transportation depended on family or friends who were often busy. The leader used this information to advocate on members' behalf with the local Office for the Aging. Eventually, a senior van was assigned to provide transportation for group members. In another instance, a worker built a coalition of members from various gay, lesbian, and bisexual support groups to bring political pressure on city officials to pass adequate antidiscrimination legislation.

Advocating for group members, within and outside the group, is especially important for populations and groups who experience prejudice and discrimination. Persons who are diagnosed with AIDS, for example, often have difficulty obtaining housing, health care, social services, and other community-based services to which they are entitled. Leaders of groups for members experiencing high levels of discrimination should be prepared to spend time outside group sessions to help members gain access to needed services.

Empowering Members

Group intervention can help empower members by raising their cultural consciousness and by developing mutual aid within the group (Chau, 1992; Hopps & Pinderhughes, 1999). Personal, interpersonal, and political power can be fostered by constructive dialogue among all members and by discussions that foster cultural identity and consciousness (Gutierrez & Ortega, 1991; Hopps & Pinderhughes, 1999). The leader can help members obtain a sense of personal power and self-worth by reinforcing positive feelings about their identity and encouraging all members to interact with each other. All levels of system intervention, including larger systems such as institutions and communities, should be included in these efforts. The case example provides a brief illustration of how a social support group engaged larger systems.

● **CASE EXAMPLE** *Engaging the Community*

A social support group sponsored by Centro Civico decided to sponsor a "senior expo" featuring the contributions of Latino elderly to the local community. The senior expo included ethnic foods, arts and crafts, exhibitions, workshops, and volunteer opportunities. Two other important aspects of the senior expo were a voter registration drive and an opportunity for members of the community to discuss their concerns about public transportation and safety with city council members.

Using Culturally Appropriate Techniques and Program Activities

Culturally sensitive techniques and program activities value diversity within the group, acknowledge how members of minority groups have unique sets of experiences, and allow members to appreciate both minority and majority cultural contexts (Vasquez & Han, 1995). The use of culturally sensitive program activities and other intervention techniques helps members to develop mutual respect for each other. It has been noted, for example, that several curative factors at work in groups for women apply equally to members of other minority groups (Vasquez & Han, 1995). When members have ethnicity or some other characteristic in common, they often feel understood by each other and gain validation for a similar heritage and a similar experience. In addition, such groups help members have compassion for themselves, accept the reality of human frailty, and develop positive perceptions of others.

Developing culturally sensitive intervention skills can be fostered by reviewing specialized formats reported in the literature for groups composed of members from specific cultures. Pearson (1991), for example, suggests that leadership skills need to reflect a more structured approach for some Asian and Asian American people. Adopting a traditional Western style, with less structure and reliance on members to take responsibility for group interactions, would cause discomfort for these types of members. In contrast, Rittenhouse (1997) suggests that feminist group work often encourages unstructured out-of-group contact, the minimization of the power distance between leader and member, and a focus on the societal and political factors that contribute to members' problems.

Other writers have also developed culturally sensitive formats for particular minority groups. For example, Mistry and Brown (1997) focus on practice with groupings composed of members from mixed racial backgrounds. Gutierrez and Ortega (1991) report the success of ethnic identity groups and consciousness-raising groups in empowering Latinos. Lopez (1991) suggests that structured activity groups in which members work together on tasks can be helpful for Latino youth. Ramos, Jones, and Toseland (2005) describe how a health education group program for caregivers of the frail elderly can be adapted for Latino caregivers. Lewis and Ford (1990) describe how group leaders can help African American group members use social networks by incorporating traditional strengths of African American families into group work practice. Ashby, Gilchrist, and Miramontez (1987) demonstrate how incorporating traditional Native American "talking circles" into group meetings can be effective in group work with Native American adolescents. Similarly, Kim, Omizo, and D'Andrea (1998) present evidence that culturally consonant group work using a Native Hawaiian healing method and a culturally indigenous form of communication had a more beneficial effect on Native American adolescents' self-esteem than did group work that did not use this approach.

Overall, Chau (1992) suggests that group interventions should be directed at helping members enhance ethnic consciousness and pride, develop ethnic resource bases and sources of power, and develop leadership potential. Hopps and Pinderhughes (1999) have developed a model for working with poor and oppressed populations from various racial and ethnic backgrounds, and textbooks by Appleby, Colon, and Hamilton (2001) and Lum (2003, 2005) contain chapters focused on work with Latino, African American, Asian, and other racial/ethnic groups. The following case example provides a brief illustration of how one agency adapted treatment services for Native Americans.

● CASE EXAMPLE *Culturally Sensitive Treatment Services*

Despite many years of working with persons who experienced alcohol and substance abuse, a substance abuse treatment agency recognized that it was less effective when working with persons from Native American backgrounds than with persons from other backgrounds. The executive director of the agency contacted a Native American social worker who had experience in leading a culturally oriented group experience called "The Red Road." This program employed an intensive three-day experience for participants using many aspects of Native American traditions and spirituality, including traditional talking circles, prayers and discussions, traditional drumming and music, and other spiritual aspects such as smudging, pipe ceremonies, and participating in a sweat lodge. In addition, members were able to discuss their people's history of oppression and discrimination, including U.S. social policy toward Native Americans and the effects of the boarding school experience and the reservation system on various Native American nations. This turned out to be a powerful experience for participants, and later qualitative evaluations supported the effectiveness of this culturally relevant treatment method.

Principles for Practice

The group leader has a dual responsibility with regard to diversity. The leader should differentiate among members and individualize each member's strengths but also universalize members' common human characteristics and goals. The leader should help to ensure cultural pluralism, that is, the right of persons from all cultures to adhere to their practices and worldviews. In addition, the leader should seek to promote harmony among members who are different from each other.

The research literature on working with persons from diverse backgrounds is characterized by suggestions for working with particular categories of persons. Group work practitioners can benefit from studying this body of knowledge and applying specific suggestions to their practice with particular groups of people. More broadly, however, the group leader should challenge the group to discover, acknowledge, and deal with its diversity. Often, members are the best source of teaching and learning about diversity. Although this should not be seen as the sole responsibility of members who are from different backgrounds, they can be invited to share their experiences.

To understand diversity and be sensitive to working with persons who come from different backgrounds, group workers should consider the following practice principles:

- Some form of diversity is always present in groups. Workers should acknowledge the diversity in the groups they lead and help members to explore the differences they bring to the group experience.

- Sensitivity to diversity is important for both leaders and members of groups. Leaders who engage in their own process of self-assessment and exploration of feelings about their own identity are in a better position to deliver culturally sensitive intervention than are those with less self-awareness.

- The process of becoming culturally sensitive is an ongoing obligation of all group leaders. Thus, it is important for leaders to continuously seek knowledge about how members define themselves and how their identities affect their participation in the group.

- Being culturally sensitive requires an open mind. Leaders should be nonjudgmental about the differences they encounter among group members and should welcome the richness and positive potential that diversity offers to the group as a whole.

- Persons from diverse backgrounds often have firsthand experience with prejudice, stereotyping, discrimination, and oppression. Leaders should understand and acknowledge the effects of these phenomena and help members to understand how such treatment can affect group participation.

- Diversity and difference can have a profound effect on how groups function. Leaders should recognize that the dynamics of groups vary because of differences in the identities and backgrounds of their members and should consider how diversity is likely to effect the development of groups.

- Member identity and background affects how members work toward their goals. A complete assessment—of group members, the group as a whole, and the group's environment—should consider the diverse characteristics of members and the cultural context in which they have developed.

- Differences in communication styles and language affect the members' overall ability to communicate. Leaders should monitor effects that language and communication have on the conduct of the group and attempt to understand how members from differing cultural groups communicate.

- On the basis of their experiences with environments outside the group, certain members may lack power and may be denied access to society's resources. Empowering members on both an individual and a communitywide basis by using empathy, individualization, support, and advocacy is an important group work skill.

- Persons from differing backgrounds are sustained by their cultural and spiritual traditions. It is important for leaders to acknowledge this and attempt to understand the place of spirituality as well as traditional concepts surrounding illness and healing and should use these factors as much as possible.

- Members who stereotype each other or discriminate against each other should be challenged to confront their biases, prejudices, and stereotypes. These behaviors should not be allowed to continue within the group.

> • There are a variety of specialized cultural formats appropriate for use in groups. It is helpful for leaders to develop a repertoire of intervention techniques and program activities relevant to particular cultural groups with whom they are likely to work.

SUMMARY

This chapter focuses on leading task and treatment groups with members from diverse backgrounds. It is important for the group leader to develop a perspective from which to work effectively with members from differing backgrounds. The group leader should develop cultural sensitivity through a process of self-exploration. The leader can also benefit from exploring the identity of others and by gaining knowledge about differing cultural and ethnic groups. An important prerequisite to these activities is openness to differences exhibited by diverse cultures. In planning and composing groups, the leader should consider how persons of differing backgrounds will experience the group and how the group will be affected by their membership. The cultural backgrounds of members can have a profound effect on how members participate in the group. A complete assessment of the group and its members should consider the larger environmental context in which members live and how that context can influence group dynamics.

This chapter also discusses how leaders can intervene with sensitivity to diversity. Suggestions developed in this regard include using social work values and skills, emphasizing a strengths perspective, exploring common and different experiences among members, exploring meanings and language, challenging prejudice and discrimination, advocating for members, empowering members, and using culturally appropriate techniques and program activities. The chapter ends with a description of practice principles to assist leaders working with diverse groups of people.

The Planning Stage

Planning the Group

chapter **6**

Planning the Group

Planning marks the beginning of the worker's involvement in the group endeavor. The planning process has two distinct parts. The first is directed at forming the group, the aspect with which this chapter is primarily concerned. The second part of planning includes the ongoing adjustments and forward-looking arrangements that are made by the leader and the members as the group progresses through its beginning, middle, and ending stages.

In forming the group, the worker focuses on the individual member, the group as a whole, and the environment. In focusing on individual members, the worker considers each person's motivations, expectations, and goals for entering the group. The worker focuses on the group as a whole by considering the purpose for the group and the dynamics that may develop as a result of the members' interaction. The worker also focuses on the environment of the group by considering the likely influence on the group of the sponsoring organization, the community, and the larger society.

The second aspect of planning is carried out throughout the life of the group. During the beginning stage, the worker and the members plan in more detail how to accomplish the overall group purpose. The worker carries out detailed assessments of individual members of the group. These assessments lead to additional planning activities in the middle and ending stages of the group. For example, in treatment groups, the worker and the members engage in an ongoing assessment of the extent to which the group is helping members accomplish their goals. This assessment, in turn, leads to the refinement, adjustment, and reformulation of treatment plans and to recontracting with individual members for modified treatment goals.

In task groups, the worker uses data collected during assessments to formulate procedures for accomplishing the group's work, such as developing session agendas, dividing labor and responsibility, and determining methods to be used in making decisions and solving problems.

Although this chapter emphasizes the need for pregroup planning, there are many times when the worker's ability to plan a group is constrained. It is common, for example, for the recruitment process to yield a pool of potential group members that is large enough to form only a single group. In this case, a worker faces the choice of accepting all applicants, delaying the group for additional recruitment, or screening out some applicants and beginning a group with few members. It is also common for workers to inherit leadership of existing groups or to form a single group from all clients of a particular program or residential setting.

The planning of task groups may be constrained for a variety of reasons. For example, recruitment may be constrained by organizational bylaws or dictated by administrative structure. Likewise, the members of a delegate council are often selected by the organizations who are represented by the council, thereby constraining pregroup planning about the composition of the group. Despite constraints, workers still have the responsibility to think carefully about how they will guide the group's development to ensure that it is productive and that it provides a satisfying experience for members. Workers should plan for the group as carefully as possible within any existing constraints. Such planning helps foster the achievement of positive group and member outcomes and avoids unanticipated difficulties later in the life of the group.

● **CASE EXAMPLE**   *Planning for an Advisory Group*

The First Methodist Church of River Falls decided to begin an initiative to resettle refugees from the war-torn country of Kosovo. Although church members had a strong desire to help and a good knowledge of the resources in their community, they had little knowledge about professional helping methods or the administration of a volunteer program. Further, they had very little knowledge about Kosovo and the persons who were fleeing from there to seek refuge in the United States.

Members of the church decided to develop a committee to assist in carrying out the resettlement initiative. Members began by spending a good deal of time deciding on the specific goals of the committee. They decided that the group's goals would include: (1) providing the church with advice on how to set up and administer a volunteer program, (2) locating persons who could provide culturally appropriate consultation about refugees from Kosovo, and (3) assisting the church in securing funding for the initiative through grants and other fund-raising activities.

Next, church members spent time discussing who should be invited to join the committee. They decided that the group would need a membership that had diverse resources at its command. For example, it was suggested that some of the members be recruited from social work organizations, particularly those that had volunteer programs. Other members should have knowledge of persons from Kosovo, including persons who were knowledgeable about the Muslim religion. They also decided that the committee should have members with experience in writing grants and in fund-raising.

In addition to these planning considerations, church members discussed what would occur during the first meeting. They agreed on a meeting agenda and a list of resources that the group would need to conduct its work.

PLANNING MODEL FOR GROUP WORK

We have developed a model of planning that can be used for both treatment and task groups. This model includes the following:

- Establishing the group's purpose
- Assessing the potential sponsorship and membership of the group

- Recruiting members
- Composing the group
- Orienting members to the group
- Contracting
- Preparing the group's environment
- Securing financial arrangements
- Preparing a written group proposal

This planning model describes an orderly set of procedures to guide workers. In actual practice, however, workers may not plan for the group in a step-by-step fashion. Instead, the worker may find that it is necessary to engage in several aspects of planning at the same time. For example, recruiting, contracting, and preparing the environment can occur simultaneously. Similarly, determining purpose and assessing potential membership can sometimes be done together. Carrying out one step may also influence how another step is handled. For example, in assessing the potential membership of a committee, the worker may realize that a budget item for travel is required for certain members of the group. Thus, the information gained in carrying out one procedure (assessing membership) influences action taken in another (securing financial arrangements).

Establishing the Group's Purpose

The first and most important question that can be asked about a proposed group is "What is the group's purpose?" A statement of the purpose should be broad enough to encompass different individual goals, yet specific enough to define the common nature of the group's purpose. A clear statement of purpose helps members answer the question "What are we doing here together?" It can help prevent a lack of direction that can be frustrating for group members and lead to an unproductive group experience.

A brief statement of the group's purpose generally includes information on the problems or issues the group is designed to address, the range of individual and group goals to be accomplished, and how individual members and the group as a whole might work together. Some examples of statements of purpose follow.

- The group will provide a forum for discussing parenting skills; each member is encouraged to bring up specific issues about being a parent and to provide feedback about the issues that are brought up.
- The group will study the problem of domestic violence in our community, and each member will contribute to a final task force report on how to address the issue.
- The group will review and assess all proposals for improving services to youth from minority communities and decide what projects to fund.

These statements are broad, but they provide information that will help members understand the nature of the group endeavor. As discussed in Chapter 7, the members of the group usually discuss and clarify the group's purpose in early group sessions and produce more specific aims and goals through their interaction with each other and with the worker. It is nonetheless helpful for the worker to prepare for the early discussions by anticipating questions that members might raise, identifying potential agenda items, clarifying the roles that the members and the worker will play in the group, and identifying potential obstacles to effective group functioning.

The purpose of a group can frequently be clarified by considering how the idea for establishing it was generated. The idea may have come from several sources, such as the group worker, agency staff members, potential clients, or the larger community. The following examples illustrate how ideas for groups are generated.

Group-Worker-Generated

- The worker proposes an educational group for children on the basis of the worker's perception of the need for adolescent sex education.
- The worker proposes an advising delegate council in a hospital on the basis of a survey of employees' job satisfaction, which indicates the need for better communication among professional departments.

Agency-Staff-Generated

- Several agency caseworkers, concerned with rising rates of family violence, suggest that clients from their caseloads participate in a remedial group for child abusers.
- The chairperson of the agency board of directors requests that a committee be established to study and suggest alternative sources of funding for the agency.

Member-Generated

- The parents of children in a day-care center request a series of educational group meetings to discuss concerns about their children's behavior at home.
- Several clients receiving subsidized housing suggest to the director of the agency that a social action group be formed to combat poor housing conditions in a neighborhood.

Community-Generated

- A group of ministers representing community churches approach a community center about developing an afterschool program for children of the working poor.
- A coalition of community groups requests a meeting with the administrator of a community center to explore ways to reach out to young people before they are recruited by gangs.

Assessing Potential Sponsorship and Membership

Although assessment of potential sponsorship and membership for the group might be seen as separate, in reality, the agency and its clients are intrinsically linked. The worker must assess both the sponsoring agency and the potential membership base to plan for the group. Agency sponsorship determines the level of support and resources available to the group. The assessment of potential membership helps the worker make an early estimate of the group's potential viability.

Assessing Potential Sponsorship

In Chapter 1, it was noted that group work is carried out in conjunction with a system of service delivery, such as a social service agency. The nature of the sponsoring organization has a significant effect on the formation of the group. The following presents aspects of the potential that should be considered when planning a group.

Elements in Assessing the Potential Sponsorship of a Group

- The mission, goals, objectives, and resources of the organization
- The fit between the policies of the organization and the goals of the proposed group
- The level of potential support for the group within the organization
- The nature of the unmet and ongoing needs of the group
- The costs and benefits of the group in relation to the sponsoring organization
- The level of community need for the group and the level of community interest and support

Hartford (1971) suggests that the purpose, focus, goals, and sanctions of the group service are conditioned by the setting and the clientele. Wilson and Ryland (1980) also emphasize the effect of the sponsoring organization, particularly its effect on task groups, and note that "whatever is defined as the purpose of the agency has a direct bearing on the decision-making process within the agency's constituent groups" (p. 172). For example, treatment groups rely on agency administrators and staff for sanctions, financial support, member referrals, and physical facilities. Similarly, task groups are intrinsically linked to the functioning of their sponsoring agencies and must continually refer to the agency's mission, bylaws, and policies for clarification of their task, charge, and mandate.

In assessing an organization as sponsor for the group, the worker should pay careful attention to the fit between the organization's policies and goals and the purpose of the proposed group. The proposed group should fit within the overall operating goals of the organization. If the group represents a new form of service or suggests a problem area or a population that has not been the focus of the potential sponsor, the worker will have to be prepared to justify the request to begin a group.

It is important to recognize that the worker's assessment of the sponsoring organization is carried out not only to determine the overall level of support for the proposed group service, but also to garner any additional support that may be needed to begin the group. Abramson (1983) has pointed out that it is essential to identify key areas of interest and perceived need within the entire organizational community. She suggests that it is often helpful to meet with line staff and program administrators to obtain their ideas about the need for a particular group service. In interdisciplinary settings, it is important to test the idea for a new group service beyond the social work staff. The idea for a new group service should be presented to staff from other disciplines by highlighting common perceptions of unmet needs and pointing out how the new group service could support and enhance the work of other disciplines. This process has the added benefit of breaking down interdisciplinary competition, fostering a sense of mutual mission, and developing a bond with staff on whom the new group program will ultimately depend for referrals.

The worker may also wish to carry out a needs assessment or gather data to document unmet needs. Administrators and boards of directors may be particularly interested in the costs and potential benefits of the proposed group service. A brief review of similar group work efforts can help clarify the possible costs or benefits associated with proposing a particular group program. In other situations, an organization may decide to offer the group service on a trial basis while conducting a cost analysis, such as the one described in Chapter 13.

It is also helpful to gather support for the idea for a new group service from the larger community. This can be done by encouraging consumers within a geographical region to express their interest in a new group service or by urging community leaders and others who have influence within community social service organizations to express their interest in and support for the new service. The relevance of the proposed group program to the sponsoring organization's mission and the visibility it could bring to the organization should also be highlighted.

In some instances, the potential sponsoring organization may decide the proposed group is not central enough to its core mission. In a county-funded rape crisis center, for example, the worker may propose a group service for battered women who have been victims of family violence but who have not been raped. Such an expansion of services, although appropriate and related to the agency's purpose, may be viewed as beyond the scope of the agency's mission, beyond staff resources, or not reimbursable within the agency's current funding sources.

When workers encounter a lack of support or resistance to a proposed group service, they should determine whether the proposal could be modified to increase support and alleviate the concerns that have been expressed or whether a different sponsor should be sought. For example, with the previously mentioned domestic violence group, the worker might work with supervisors and other administrators within the agency to highlight the need for the group and to seek additional funding for the service. Alternatively, the worker might decide to explore the idea for the group service with a family service agency or a community center that has expressed interest in providing service for domestic violence victims.

Garnering support for the idea of a new group service both within and outside the organization helps ensure the success of the group when it is implemented. A summary of elements in assessing the potential sponsorship of the group follows.

Elements in Assessing the Potential Sponsorship of a Group

- Identify the extent to which the problem or issue that the group intends to work on fits the mission and goals of the sponsoring organization
- Identify the extent to which a resolution of the problem or issue to be addressed by the group is valued by the sponsoring organization and the larger community
- Obtain the support of the administration of the organization to explore the possibility of a new group service
- Find out if the need is being met, or should be met, by any other organization in the community and contact that organization to avoid any possible duplication of service and to check the possibility of joining forces for co-sponsoring a group service
- Identify and resolve any differences in perspectives among staff that may lead to hidden agendas and thereby jeopardize a group service being planned

- Obtain staff consensus about the goals of the program and the group work methods that will be used to achieve them
- Assess the willingness of the sponsor to provide external support such as transportation, child care, or funding for supplies that might be needed to conduct the group

Assessing Potential Membership

Along with assessing agency sponsorship and garnering support for a new group work endeavor, the worker should begin to assess the potential membership of a group. Such a beginning assessment does not involve extensive procedures, such as arriving at goals for members or agreeing on individual contracts. Rather, in this early assessment, the worker is thinking about who should be recruited to participate in a planned group. A summary of elements in assessing the potential membership of a group follows.

Elements in Assessing the Potential Membership of a Group

- The extent of the problem or need addressed by the group
- Members' recognition and shared perceptions about the purpose of the group
- Cultural and other differences that could influence perceptions about the purpose of the group
- Members' perceptions of the sponsoring organization
- Potential affects of ambivalence, resistance, or involuntary nature of the group on members' participation
- Specialized knowledge needed for understanding and working with members
- Demographic differences and commonalities of potential members
- Potential benefits to members of participating in the group
- Barriers, obstacles, and drawbacks to member participation
- Resources needed from the organization and community to ensure members' interest and participation

When assessing the potential members of a treatment group, the worker can begin by collecting data about the extent of the problem and the need for a new group service. As potential clients are identified, the worker can collect data about them by direct observation, by personal or telephone interview, or by talking with collateral contacts such as family members or agency staff. The worker relates this information to the proposed group's purpose and decides whether the extent of the problem justifies the need for a new group service.

When planning task groups, the worker considers potential members according to their interest in the task, their expertise, and their power and position to help the group accomplish its purposes. Members might also be sought on the basis of their importance to the sponsoring agency, their status in the community, or their political influence.

An important aspect of assessing potential membership is determining whether potential members share the worker's perception of the tasks facing the group. Shared perceptions lead to group cohesion and increase members' satisfaction with group functioning. In addition, the worker spends less time overcoming obstacles and resistance to accomplishing the group's goals when members share similar perceptions of the concerns facing the group.

Information should be gathered about the extent to which potential members recognize the need for the group, its purpose, tasks, and goals. This process helps workers anticipate the degree of member commitment to the group. It also helps to coalesce divergent views of the purpose of the group and the methods used to accomplish the work of the group. Shulman (1999) refers to this as "tuning in" to the members of the group.

In groups in which the membership is culturally diverse, the worker may need to give particular attention to the differences in perception of the group's purpose. Members from differing backgrounds can have divergent opinions about the meaning of the group and the purpose for meeting together.

It is also important to assess potential members' view of the sponsor. Is there any stigma attached to receiving service from a particular organization? Is the organization known to the potential client group? What is the organization's reputation with the group to be served? The worker should carefully consider what qualities of the potential sponsor are likely to attract clients and what obstacles may interfere with the successful initiation of a group program. For example, a family service agency may have the resources to sponsor a group for African American single mothers but may have difficulty recruiting members because potential members perceive the staff of the agency to be culturally insensitive. If the agency sponsoring the group is perceived to be unable to relate to particular segments of the community, it will encounter considerable resistance when trying to initiate a group service.

● CASE EXAMPLE *A Parenting Group for Single Mothers*

The previously mentioned family service agency contacted local community leaders, a community center, and a health clinic serving primarily African Americans. The family service agency also reached out to a coalition of Ministers from Baptist Churches in the area serving the African American community. After meeting with individuals from these organizations separately, a series of three planning meetings were held. It was decided to host the group for single mothers in the health clinic and that each of the organizations at the meeting would publicize the group and encourage single mothers to attend. A worker from the family service agency led the group, but speakers on educational topics related to health and nutrition came from the health-care clinic, and a worker from the community center provided child care while the members attended the group.

Often the worker must plan for leading a group of reluctant participants. The extent of reluctance can range from ambivalence about seeking assistance, to active resistance. The term *involuntary* is often applied to individuals who are ordered by the courts to receive treatment. Working with involuntary clients requires special expertise. During the planning stage, the worker should become thoroughly familiar with the legal statutes and ethical issues that apply and with the rights of individuals who find themselves in these situations (Rooney, 1992).

Workers may also be called on to plan groups for reluctant members who are given the choice between treatment and a negative alternative such as incarceration, probation, or the suspension of driving privileges. In these situations, the worker should become thoroughly familiar with the specialized methods developed to motivate clients to make productive use of the group experience. For example, Brekke (1989) describes the use of a five-session orientation group designed to prepare men who batter their wives for a more structured and lengthier cognitive behavioral group. Similarly, in a residential program for substance abusers, information and techniques to confront denial may be used in combination with powerful incentives such as the return of driving privileges. Within the residential setting, information about the damaging effects of alcohol, peer interaction focused on sobriety, and access to certain privileges may be combined to help members make productive use of a group program. More information about working with reluctant and resistant clients is presented in Chapters 7 and 9.

Workers planning a group for a new population are unlikely to have information at their fingertips about what strategies are most effective for working with individuals who have specialized problems. Gathering information by reviewing the literature and from practitioners experienced with the population can be invaluable in preparing for the group. Obtaining information about specialized groups is particularly important when planning groups for people from diverse cultural backgrounds and when the worker's background differs significantly from that of group members. Such information helps workers to recognize their own biases, develop tolerance for their own and others' perceptions, and enhance their abilities to accurately perceive clients' needs.

In assessing potential membership, the worker should consider the demographic differences and commonalities of potential members and how such characteristics will affect other steps in the planning process. For example, in assessing potential membership of a support group for Latino caregivers of elderly parents, the worker might learn that special recruiting techniques are indicated, such as printing announcements in Spanish, advertising in newspapers for speakers of Spanish, or contacting Hispanic community leaders.

To prepare for recruiting and orienting members in both voluntary and mandatory groups, it can be helpful to list the potential benefits of participating and to share them with potential members. Some workers are reluctant to describe the potential benefits of participating in a group because they fear they will be perceived as boasting about their own skills or because they fear raising the expectation for service among members of vulnerable groups. However, individuals who are considering whether to participate in a group welcome a clear description of the potential benefits of participation. A worker's enthusiasm and optimism can be contagious, increasing members' motivation to participate and their enthusiasm for what might be accomplished. Yalom (1995) refers to this process as the "instillation of hope."

When assessing membership, workers should also identify barriers, obstacles, and drawbacks to group participation. In their zest to recruit members, workers sometimes minimize the difficulties individuals might encounter in joining a group. Experience suggests that it is better to acknowledge disadvantages to participation and try whenever possible to resolve them so they do not prevent individuals from participating. Often, discussing disadvantages with potential members during an orientation interview and planning ways to resolve them can be helpful.

At other times, it may be necessary to find additional resources or to increase incentives from the sponsoring agency or the larger community. For example, practical barriers may be overcome if the sponsoring agency offers to provide transportation, child care, or a sliding fee schedule. Similarly, an organization in the larger community might offer a meeting site with less stigma or a group of organizations might lobby with a funding body to provide additional resources for a group program that has wide community support. The following case example illustrates how a worker can help resistant or reluctant group members.

● CASE EXAMPLE *Planning for Resistant and Reluctant Members*

Although she was enthused about starting a new group for college students who had vio-lated the college dormitory's alcohol policy, Beth was worried about how members would feel about being mandated to attend this short-term group. During preparations for the group, she became familiar with the college policies that prohibited alcohol use in the dorms. She hoped that knowledge of the policies would prepare her to answer members' questions about why they needed to attend the group. She also prepared a clear state-ment about her role in the group and what the expectations would be for attendance and participation. In addition, Beth prepared a list of group goals for members' consideration during the first meeting. Beth also consulted the literature about how to deal with invol-untary group members. Based on what she learned, she prepared what she would say dur-ing the opening of the first meeting. The statement acknowledged the mandatory nature of the group and members' ambivalence about participating. She noted that it was ulti-mately up to members to decide how they would participate in the group and whether the group would be a positive and productive experience for each of them. She hoped that these beginning preparations, along with her enthusiasm and genuine desire to help, would assist in overcoming the resistance she anticipated from the members during the beginning stage of the group.

Recruiting Members

Recruitment procedures should ensure an adequate number of potential members for the group. In recruiting members, the worker considers sources from which potential members can be identified and referred to the group. Members can be recruited within the worker's agency or in other organizations or the community.

Within a social service agency, potential members can be identified from the caseloads of colleagues, from records, or from mailing lists. In some groups, current members may be able to identify potential members. Potential members might also introduce themselves to the worker, individually or in a group, to suggest that the agency initiate a particular group service. Finally, the worker might consider reviewing the agency's waiting list to determine whether any persons waiting for service would benefit from group treatment.

For certain treatment groups, such as for men who batter, the worker's own agency may not have a large enough potential membership base. In planning for these groups, the worker can contact other social service and health agencies to obtain referrals. In contact-ing other social service agencies for referrals, the worker may want to contact line staff with whom they are familiar. It is also helpful to contact supervisory and administrative staff to inform them of the purpose of the proposed group, to elicit their support, and to gain access to other line workers who can identify potential group members.

The worker also can assess the community to locate concentrations of potential members. Census data can be helpful in finding people with certain demographic charac-teristics (Toseland, 1981). The worker might also talk to community leaders, politicians, police officials, schoolteachers, or clergy.

For task groups, the type of group and its purpose often determine the best sources for recruiting members. For example, members of a committee to study an agency's employee benefit package can be recruited from employees of the agency and from the agency's board of directors. A task force to study the problem of refugee resettlement can recruit members from all agencies serving that population in the community.

Occasionally, membership recruitment is determined by the nature of the task group. The members of teams, for example, are selected for their specific expertise and professional background. Boards recruit members from community constituents because the board "stands in" for the community and is accountable to the community for the services the agency provides.

Methods of Recruiting Members

When the worker has identified recruitment sources, decisions must be made about how to reach them. A variety of recruitment techniques will help potential members understand the purpose of the group and help them decide whether to join.

Methods of Recruiting Members

- Contacting potential members directly through interviews and telephone contacts
- Contacting key people in the networks of potential members
- Sending announcements through direct mail
- Posting announcements in community organizations
- Using websites to advertise the group
- Speaking at public meetings and appearing on radio and television shows
- Issuing press releases, publishing announcements in organizational and association newsletters, and working with reporters to prepare feature newspaper articles

Some evidence suggests that direct contact with potential clients is the most effective recruitment method (Toseland, 1981). When potential group members can be identified from agency records or from caseloads of colleagues, the worker may wish to set up initial appointments by letter or by telephone. The worker can then interview prospective members in the office or at home. However, person-to-person contact, particularly in-home contact, can be quite expensive in terms of the worker's time and therefore may not be feasible.

In some situations, the worker may recruit potential group members by contacting key people in the informal networks of a particular population. For example, in recruiting for a group composed of Native Americans, the worker may first discuss the idea with important Native American community elders to gain their acceptance for the group. When recruiting Chinese Americans, the worker might identify cultural associations that provide support for this population, which could provide the worker with a means for assessing the viability of the group and the potential for recruiting members. Since trust is a key issue when recruiting members of culturally diverse groups, workers also should spend time getting to know the community and to become known to its members before attempting to organize and lead a group.

Brief, written announcements also can be an effective recruitment tool. However, care must be taken to ensure that announcements are sent to the correct audience. To be effective, mailed and posted announcements must be seen by potential members or potential referral sources. Therefore, careful targeting of the pool of potential group members is essential. Too often, workers rely on existing mailing lists developed for other purposes or post announcements where they will not be noticed by the target group. Computerized record systems and internet listservs are becoming more widely available and can be useful in identifying and targeting individuals who may need a particular service.

If the worker has a list of potential members, announcements can be mailed directly to them. The worker may also mail announcements to workers in other social service agencies who are likely to have contact with potential group members. Experience suggests that a follow-up phone call to those who have received announcements increases the probability that referrals will be made. Announcements can also be posted on community bulletin boards, in housing projects, public gathering places, and in local businesses. In rural locations, announcements can be posted at firehouses, church halls, schools, general stores, and post offices. Such locations are usually the best places to post announcements because people gather in those places to discuss information about their community. The worker also can ask that announcements be read at meetings of community service groups, church groups, business associations, and fraternal organizations.

The increase in computer literacy, the availability of local area networks, and the Internet have improved accessibility for potential members. Group announcements can be posted on local area networks or community computer bulletin boards or be sent to targeted users of particular computing services. It is also possible for organizations or nationally federated groups to create their own web pages that are accessible to millions of persons who may be interested in learning more about particular services.

Appendix C contains two examples of announcements for groups. An announcement should include a clear statement of the group's purpose. The proposed meeting place, dates, times, length and frequency of meetings, and any service fees should also be clearly specified. The sponsoring agency and the group leader's name should be listed along with telephone numbers for potential members to call for more information. It is sometimes helpful to list any special arrangements that are planned, such as child-care services, transportation, or refreshments.

The worker might also want to make information about the group available through public speaking and through local television or radio stations. Many civic and religious organizations welcome guest speakers. A presentation on the need for the group, its purpose, and how it would operate can be an effective recruitment tool. Commercial television and radio stations broadcast public service announcements deemed to be in the public interest, and the proposed group program might be eligible for inclusion in such broadcasts.

Commercial television and radio stations frequently produce their own local public interest programs, such as talk shows, public discussions, special news reports, and community news announcements. Although public access cable television channels generally have smaller audiences, they can also be used by the worker to describe a group service and to invite members to join.

Press releases and newsletter articles are another way to recruit members. Many newspapers publish a calendar of events for a specified week or month; brief announcements can be placed in the calendar. An article in the features section of a newspaper also can reach many potential members. Newspapers frequently publish stories about new group services or particular social problems. The worker should consider whether the group is newsworthy and, if so, contact a local editor and request an interview with a reporter. We have found that feature newspaper stories are the single most important source for recruiting new members to groups in community settings.

Composing the Group

When composing the groups, the worker chooses members according to their needs and the needs of the whole group for accomplishing its goals. Group composition is carried out according to a set of established principles that the worker decides on beforehand.

Principles of Group Composition

- A homogeneity of members' purposes and certain personal characteristics
- A heterogeneity of member coping skills, life experiences, and expertise
- An overall structure that includes a range of the members' qualities, skills, and expertise

In addition to these principles, the worker should consider the issues of diversity, group size, and whether the membership will be open or closed.

Homogeneity

The principle of homogeneity suggests that members should have a similar purpose for being in the group and have some personal characteristics in common. Homogeneity facilitates communication and bonding and helps members to identify and relate to each other's concerns.

Members should accept and identify with the major purpose for the group so they can use the meetings to their full advantage. The worker should assess the extent to which members' purposes coincide with one another and with the purpose of the group. Without some common purposes for being in the group, members will have little basis for interacting.

Members should share some personal characteristics, such as age, level of education, cultural background, degree of expertise relative to the group task, communication ability, or type of problem. The worker should determine that all members have enough characteristics in common to facilitate the work of the group. The extent to which members should possess common characteristics varies with the type of group. In an educational group for new parents, it might be important that all members be able to read English at a sixth-grade level to understand program materials recommended for reading at home. In a program-oriented group for youngsters in a treatment center, the most important common characteristic may be their living situation. Groups of alcoholics, drug abusers, and delinquents all have a problem in common.

In a study of selection criteria for new members of treatment groups, Riva, Lippert, and Tackett (2000) found that a national sample of leaders mentioned compatibility with the group theme as the most important variable, followed by client's motivation for personal change, enthusiasm about being in the group, and expectations that the group would help. Other important selection criteria included clients' (1) reality testing, (2) self awareness, (3) ability to express feelings, (4) ability to tolerate anxiety, (5) ability to self-disclose, and (6) sensitivity to others' needs. In studies that compared those who dropped out of group treatment to those who completed, it was found that ability to express oneself and ability to trust and relate to others were the important predictive factors (Blouin et al., 1995; Oei & Kazmierczak, 1997). Thus, it appears that personality factors are important in screening and selecting members.

Heterogeneity

For most groups, there should be some diversity of members' coping skills, life experiences, and levels of expertise. It has been noted that the existence of differences in members' coping patterns "opens the eyes of members to options, choices, and alternatives, and makes it possible for them to learn from one another" (Klein, 1972, p. 6). In support groups, for example, it is helpful for members to learn what coping skills other members have found to be effective and what strategies they have used to solve problems.

In some groups, the worker chooses members with differing life experiences or diverse characteristics to foster learning among members. A growth group, for example, might be composed of members from different cultures, social classes, occupations, or geographic areas to expose individuals to the benefits of differing viewpoints and lifestyles. Differences among members can provide multiple opportunities for support, validation, mutual aid, and learning.

Workers should also consider building heterogeneity into the membership of task groups to ensure an adequate range of resources and provide an efficient division of labor when dealing with complex tasks. For example, agency boards of directors are usually composed of members who represent a variety of professions, agencies, and occupations. These members bring legal, financial, marketing, and other kinds of expertise to the board. Other task groups, such as delegate councils, are also often composed of members who represent differing constituencies with diverse interests and needs. For example, a coalition formed to study the problem of juvenile delinquency might be composed of members from diverse parts of a city, that is, members from the business district, the inner city, and suburban neighborhoods. Such heterogeneity can be an important asset to the group in accomplishing its tasks.

Group Structure

The worker structures a group by selecting members who are able to meet each other's needs and are able to accomplish the group's purposes. Guidelines include selecting members who:

- Have the ability and desire to communicate with others in the group
- Can accept each other's behavior
- Can get along with each other despite differences of opinions, viewpoints, or positions
- Have some capacity to understand their own behavior
- Be motivated to contribute to and work in the group

A member who is grossly ineffective in communicating with peers could engender more antagonism than support from fellow members and is thus best excluded from group treatment. Similarly, people who cannot accept or use feedback and those who are highly opinionated and unwilling to consider other viewpoints are poor candidates for treatment groups. Ideally, it is helpful to have highly motivated members. Social workers, however, are often confronted with reluctant or involuntary clients. Methods to work with these clients are described in Chapters 7 and 9.

Guidelines for composing task groups have also been proposed. Likert (1961), for example, suggested that task groups be composed of members who are (1) skilled in various roles of membership and leadership, (2) attracted to the group, (3) highly motivated to abide by the group's values and to achieve group goals, and (4) strongly motivated to communicate fully and frankly all information that is relevant to the group's activity. Put more simply, Scheidel and Crowell (1979) suggest that members of task groups should "together possess all the information necessary to the performance of their task plus the ability to interpret and use it" (p. 122).

The worker should choose members who will be able to put the needs of the group or the requirements of the task before their own personal needs. Klein (1972) notes, for example, that "committee productivity is curtailed when members use the committee for the meeting of personal needs rather than the fulfillment of group goals" (p. 335).

The worker also should seek members who demonstrate ability to cooperate with one another. No matter what the level of expertise or ability of members, task groups can be hampered by a lack of cooperative effort. Although it is not always possible to predict how people will work together, it is necessary to give this concept some consideration when composing a group.

Diversity and Demographic Characteristics

Although demographic characteristics alone are not predictive of successful group outcomes (Yalom, 1995), they are important to consider when composing a group. In selecting members, the worker usually considers three major characteristics: age, gender, and sociocultural factors.

It is not sufficient to consider only age when composing a group. The worker should seek members who are similar in their stage of development and their life tasks. The level of maturity, self-insight, and social skills can vary considerably within age groups. Neither children nor adults acquire these characteristics solely on the basis of age, but rather through multiple experiences with their environment, family, peer group, and culture. For example, in composing a children's group, it is helpful to consider the level of members' social and emotional development as well as the childrens' ages.

Research suggests that the behavior of members varies with the gender composition of the group (Forsyth, 2006). In a men's or women's support group, for example, an atmosphere of support and openness can often be enhanced through homogeneity of gender composition. In a remedial group for children, a mixed-gender group may interfere with interaction because of the tendency of children at certain ages either to impress or ignore members of the opposite sex.

In other situations, mixed groups are more effective. For example, in a task group such as a teen-club planning meeting, a mixed group is most appropriate to help members of the opposite sex learn to relate to one another. Similarly, an assertiveness group might include both men and women so that members can realistically role play exercises.

The sociocultural background of potential members can also have a profound effect on group processes and outcomes. The worker should assess differences and commonalities among members based on sociocultural factors and should be sensitive to the needs of each member as well as to the overall needs of the group. Hopps and Pinderhughes (1999) describe how groups can be effectively used to empower poor and oppressed individuals.

The level of support and interaction is often increased when members have a common sociocultural background. Support groups for foreign-born students in U.S. colleges, for example, are frequently based on the similar cultural backgrounds of the members. Thus, in some situations, the worker may decide that similar backgrounds will help members deal with certain problems or issues. For example, a worker may restrict membership in a cultural awareness group to members of a single ethnic group. Similarly, in a support group for parents of terminally ill children, the worker may restrict membership to people from the same cultural background to ensure that members will have similar belief systems and values about death, loss, and grieving.

In other situations, the worker may deliberately plan a group composed of members with diverse sociocultural backgrounds. Diversity can foster mutual understanding and learning among members. Socialization groups in neighborhood centers and youth organizations might be composed by the worker so they encourage members from different ethnic, cultural, and racial groups to interact. Sometimes differences among members can be a real source of strength. For example, in planning for a social action group concerned with increasing neighborhood police protection, membership drawn from people of different cultural backgrounds can demonstrate a broad base of support for the group's cause. Common mistakes in composing a group are presented in this case example.

● CASE EXAMPLE *Composing a Group*

David, a new school social worker, was asked by the assistant principal to compose a group for seventh grade students who were experiencing difficulties at school because their parents were in the process of separation or divorce. Students were identified by teachers, the school nurse, and the school guidance counselor as potentially benefiting from a group experience. After the first meeting, David didn't understand why the group was such a disaster. The members didn't want to follow his directions and wouldn't work on the tasks and activities he had prepared for them. Members teased each other and failed to follow the group rules. In addition, the group divided into subgroups that interfered with meaningful discussion. David had followed all of the rules of composition, as far as he could tell. Nevertheless, the group just wasn't cohesive. He assumed that members would have a common bond based on their home situation. He also felt that since they were in the same grade that they would have sufficient homogeneity to work well together. Their ages were all within one year of each other and they all lived in the same affluent suburban community. After thinking more about it, he realized his mistakes. He had composed a coed group, without considering the differences that might be influential between girls and boys at that grade, age, and stage of life. Same sex groups are often preferable for middle school students. He also failed to ask students if they wanted to be in the group. He also failed to screen out two verbally and physically aggressive students who had really acted out in the group and who were much better behaved when they were seen individually by David. David also planned shorter program activities that would engage and interest members more effectively than the activities used in the first session.

Size

The worker determines the size of the group according to several criteria. Bertcher and Maple (1985) suggest that size "depends on the objectives of the group and the attributes of its members" (p. 190). The group should be small enough to allow it to accomplish its purpose, yet large enough to permit members to have a satisfying experience.

Studies of committees have shown that the most common sizes are five, seven, and nine members (Brilhart, 1974). With the exception of large task groups, such as delegate councils, the optimal range for task groups appears to be from five to seven members. Bales (1954) suggests that five is the optimal number of members for task groups; for decision-making groups, Scheidel and Crowell (1979) suggest that seven members are desirable. When determining the size of task groups, the worker must consider how many members are needed to accomplish the tasks efficiently and effectively. Although smaller groups are not always best for accomplishing complex tasks, Thelen (1954) suggests that the worker compose the smallest group "in which it is possible to have represented at a functional level all the social and achievement skills required for the particular activity" (p. 187).

When determining the size of treatment groups, the worker should consider how the members will be affected. Will members feel satisfied with the attention given to their concerns or problems? This is an issue for the worker, because "as group size increases, the complexity increases rapidly; the number of interpersonal relationships increases geometrically as the number of members increases arithmetically" (Brilhart, 1974, p. 30). Bertcher and Maple (1985) suggest a range of more than 3 but less than 15 members. Klein (1972) notes, "Five to seven is often given as ideal . . . developmental groups of fifteen are viable" (p. 65). In general, the literature indicates that seven members are ideal (Garvin, 1997; Yalom, 1995). Despite suggestions about the ideal size for treatment groups, little empirical research has been conducted about the relationship between treatment group size and effectiveness.

The worker should consider the advantages and disadvantages inherent in different group sizes. Larger groups offer more ideas, skills, and resources to members than do smaller groups (Douglas, 1979). In general, larger groups can handle more complex tasks (Bertcher & Maple, 1985). Members have greater potential for learning because of the presence of additional role models. Members have more opportunity for support, feedback, and friendship, yet there is also less pressure to speak or to perform. Members can occasionally withdraw and reflect on their participation. Also, in larger groups, fewer difficulties arise when one or more members are absent. There is less danger that the group will fall below the size needed for meaningful interaction (Yalom, 1995).

Larger groups also have disadvantages. The larger the group, the less individualized attention each member can receive. Close, face-to-face interaction is more difficult. There is more danger of harmful subgroups forming. Large groups also encourage withdrawal and anonymity by silent members. They create less pressure to attend because members' absence is less conspicuous than in smaller groups. Larger groups are also more difficult for the worker to manage. They frequently require more formalized procedures to accomplish their meeting agendas. Large groups have more difficulty achieving cohesiveness and more difficulty reaching consensus (Carron & Spink, 1995). Also, as size increases, task groups are less productive (Mullen & Cooper, 1994).

Overall, decisions about the number of members to include in a treatment or task group should be based on the purpose of the group, the needs of the members, their ability to contribute to the work of the group, practical considerations such as whether a potential member will be able to attend meetings, and any constraints imposed by the sponsor. Following is a summary of some of the major planning considerations related to deciding on the size of the group.

Group Size: Large versus Small

Large Groups

- Offer more ideas, skills, and resources to members
- Can handle more complex tasks
- Offer members more potential for learning through role models
- Provide members with more potential for support, feedback, and friendship
- Allow members to occasionally withdraw and reflect on their participation
- Help to ensure that there will be enough members for meaningful interaction even if some members fail to attend

Small Groups

- Provide members with a greater level of individualized attention
- Enable closer face-to-face interaction
- Present less opportunity for the formation of harmful subgroups
- Present fewer opportunities for members to withdraw from participation
- Allow for easier management by the worker
- Tend to have more informal operating procedures
- Provide more opportunities for achieving cohesiveness
- Can achieve consensus more easily

Open and Closed Membership

During the planning process, the worker should determine whether the group will be open or closed to new members. Open groups maintain a constant size by replacing members as they leave (Yalom, 1995). Members enter and terminate throughout the life of the group, ensuring the group's continuance. Closed groups begin and end with the same membership and frequently meet for a predetermined number of sessions (Yalom, 1995).

Often the choice between open or closed membership is affected by the purpose of the group or by practical considerations. A treatment group based in a residential treatment facility, for example, adds members as they become residents. Similarly, a committee formed to study the deinstitutionalization of psychiatric patients might discover it needs to add representatives from local community group homes to make more comprehensive recommendations.

In some situations, closed groups are preferable to open groups. An educational group for those who wish to learn to be more assertive might find it helpful to begin and end with the same membership so that new members will not impede the progress of the original members. A closed group might also be helpful for teenage mothers learning parenting skills so that a prescribed curriculum that covers the content in a competency-based, step-by-step manner can be followed.

In other situations, open group membership is preferable. Members of Alcoholics Anonymous (AA), for example, are comforted by the knowledge that they can, without notice, attend any open AA meeting in the community. Open-membership groups also can provide people who are experiencing crises in their lives with a timely alternative to treatment—they do not have to wait for a new group to form.

In many situations, open membership is the only practical alternative. Because of rapid patient turnover in hospitals, for example, workers would find it impractical to form a group and expect the same patients to attend a fixed number of meetings and then be discharged all together.

What modifications should the worker consider when planning for an open-membership group? If the worker can control when members begin and leave a group, the worker should consider during the planning process when it is optimal to add new members. For example, the worker may decide it is best to add new members during the first few sessions and then close group membership. Alternatively, the worker might plan to add no more than one or two new members in any given meeting.

In Chapter 3, it was mentioned that when membership change is frequent and extensive, group development is adversely affected. To cope with the effects of a changing membership, planners of open groups should consider ensuring that there is a well-publicized, fixed structure for every group meeting (Galinsky & Schopler, 1989; Schopler & Galinsky, 1984, 1990). Each meeting, for example, might feature a guest speaker followed by small-group discussion. It is helpful to publicize the topic for each meeting and to stress that meetings are open to new members. In groups with high turnover, each meeting should be independent; that is, an individual should not need to have attended a previous meeting to understand or participate in a current meeting. Also, consideration should be given to rotating a cycle of topics in a fixed period of time so that all clients or patients who have an average length of stay in inpatient or outpatient programs can attend a full cycle of meetings before their discharge.

When workers have the opportunity to decide whether to form an open or a closed group, they should be guided by reviewing some of the following advantages and disadvantages of each membership option. Open membership allows new ideas and new resources to be brought to the group through new members. Hartford (1971) notes that the "influx of new ideas, beliefs, and values" (p. 135) can make open groups more creative than closed groups. New members can change the entire character of the group.

The difficulties involved in adding new members to an already functioning group are not insurmountable. Yalom (1995), for example, notes that members can join a group, learn the group norms, and participate in meaningful ways without requiring the group to regress to an earlier stage of its development.

There are, however, potential disadvantages to open group membership. Hartford (1971) suggested that "instability is the basic shortcoming of the open group, resulting from loss of leadership, turnover in personnel, exodus of members, loss of group identity" (p. 135). Adding new members can disrupt members' work and delay or arrest the development of the group as a whole (Galinsky & Schopler, 1989; Schopler & Galinsky, 1990). Members of closed groups may form a greater sense of cohesion because they have all attended the group since its beginning. There is often a greater stability of roles and norms in closed groups. The benefits of a stable membership include higher group morale, more predictability of role behaviors, and an increased sense of cooperation among members. The stability of membership also makes planning for group sessions easier.

A disadvantage of closed groups is that when members drop out or are absent, the number of members in the group may become too small for meaningful group interaction.

Without the benefit of new ideas, viewpoints, and skills from new members, a closed group runs the risk of engaging in what Janis (1972) refers to as "group think," or what Kiesler (1978) calls "the avoidance of minority or outside opinions" (p. 322). Such avoidance can create an extreme form of conformity within the group that can reduce its effectiveness (Janis & Mann, 1977).

Orienting Members

After potential members have been recruited, the worker should screen them for appropriateness and orient them to the group. The primary orientation method for treatment groups is the intake interview. Generally, intake interviews are conducted individually. Intake interviews are important because they offer workers and members their first impressions of each other.

Alternatively, members of treatment groups can be oriented by listening to an audiotape of a group meeting, by viewing videotapes of a previous group, through didactic instruction, or by rehearsal of membership skills, such as how to effectively communicate one's thoughts and opinions. Role-induction strategies, often referred to as *pregroup training,* can take a single half-hour session or several sessions lasting several hours. Pregroup training can enhance group outcomes, reduce dropout rates, and increase members' satisfaction with the subsequent group experience (Bednar & Kaul, 1994; Kaul & Bednar, 1994).

Orientation for new members of task groups is sometimes done in small groups. For example, new board members may be asked to participate in a board training program that consists of several small group sessions on governance and the bylaws of the organization, fiduciary responsibilities, fund-raising, and public relations.

Orientations may be designed for many purposes, but three primary ones are (1) explaining the purpose of the group, (2) familiarizing members with group procedures, and (3) screening members for appropriateness.

Explaining the Purpose of the Group

The worker should begin orienting members by stating the group's purpose. The statement should be specific enough to allow members to ask questions about the group and clarify what will be expected of them. However, the statement should also be broad enough and tentative enough to encourage input and feedback. This can help potential members discuss and work through any ambivalence they might have about participating in the group.

Familiarizing Members with Group Procedures

Group members frequently have questions about how the group will work. Through these questions, members try to understand some of the general rules of group functioning. During the orientation interview, it is helpful for the worker to explain procedures for member participation and for how the group will conduct its business.

Leaders of both treatment and task groups often establish routine procedures for meetings during either the planning stage or the beginning stage of the group. Some treatment group meetings, for example, use a short review period for the first few minutes to discuss the major points of the last session. Time is then allotted for identifying particular member concerns to be discussed during the current session. Some groups use the final few minutes to summarize, to discuss between-meeting assignments, or to talk about the group's progress.

Task groups frequently follow routine procedures such as reading the minutes of the previous meeting, discussing old business, and bringing up new business. Many of these procedures are decided on by the group in its early meetings, but discussion of group procedures during the planning stage helps members see how they can participate in and contribute to the group.

Screening Members for Appropriateness

During the orientation, the worker screens members to ensure that their needs are matched with the purposes of the group. The worker observes members and collects impressions and information about them. Workers also apply any criteria developed for inclusion or exclusion of potential members. Members with impaired functioning can often be identified during the orientation interview, which gives the worker a chance to decide whether their membership in the group is appropriate.

Factors that may render people inappropriate for group membership include (1) problems with scheduling transportation or other practical considerations; (2) personal qualities, such as level of social skills, that are extremely dissimilar to those of other group members; and (3) needs, expectations, or goals that are not congruent with those of the other group members. Such factors have been linked to members' dropping out of treatment prematurely (Yalom, 1995). In considering members' appropriateness for a group, Klein (1972) takes a pragmatic view, suggesting that members should have "the ability to communicate with each other, motivation to work on their problems, no behavior so bizarre as to frighten the others, and no wide differences that are personally or culturally beyond acceptance" (p. 60). Such a view is helpful because it focuses on behavior that is observed during the orientation process rather than on labels or classifications of disorders that are difficult to observe.

Contracting

During the planning stage, the worker begins the contracting process. Contracts usually result from the dynamic interaction of the worker and the members during the beginning stage of the group, but certain contracting procedures are initiated before the group begins.

Two forms of contracting take place during the planning stage: contracting for group procedures and contracting for individual member goals. The worker should make some preliminary decisions about group procedures before beginning. These decisions include the duration and frequency of group meetings, attendance requirements, procedures to ensure confidentiality, and other considerations such as time, place, and any fees for meetings. The worker should also begin the process of contracting for individual member goals although most of this type of contracting takes place during the beginning stage of group work.

A *contract* is a verbal or written agreement between two or more members of a group. In a legal contract, each party agrees to provide something, although what is provided by each does not have to be equal, and penalties are specified if either party does not fulfill the contract.

In most task and treatment groups, contracts are verbal agreements. For example, the leader of an educational treatment group for foster parents may agree to meet with the group for five two-hour sessions to explain the process of becoming a foster parent and parents' ongoing responsibilities. The leader may also agree to explain the help that the agency can offer and how the legal rights of foster children can be safeguarded. Members may agree to attend each session and to use the information that is provided to become effective foster parents. Similarly, the leader of a treatment conference may verbally agree with group members about the procedures for reviewing cases, the responsibility of each staff member in the review process, and the ways in which the information presented during the meeting will be used in case planning.

At times, a written contract may be used. A written contract helps to clarify the group's purpose. It also helps members clarify expectations about the worker and the agency and allows the worker to specify what is expected of group members (Figure 6.1). A written contract can be referred to in group meetings if either the members or the worker needs to be reminded of the purpose, expectations, or obligations to which they agreed. Generally,

---

FIGURE 6.1 ● *Example of a Treatment Group Contract*

As a group member I agree to:

1. Attend all group sessions.
2. Arrive on time for each group session.
3. Refrain from repeating anything that is said during group sessions to anyone outside of the group meeting.
4. Complete any readings, exercises, treatment plans, or other obligations that I agree to in the group before the next group session.
5. Participate in exercises, role plays, demonstrations, and other simulations conducted during group meetings.

As the group leader I agree to:

1. Be prepared for each group session.
2. Begin and end all group sessions on time.
3. Provide refreshments and program material needed for each session.
4. Discuss the group only with my colleagues at work and not outside of the work context.
5. Evaluate each group session to ensure that the group is helping all members resolve their problems and is personally satisfying to all group members.
6. Provide members with appropriate agency and community resources to help them resolve their problems.

_____   _____
      Group member   Date

_____   _____
      Group leader   Date

written contracts specify ground rules for participation that do not change during the life of the group. However, contracts can be renegotiated by mutual agreement at any time during the group's life.

Written contracts are rarely used in task groups. The meeting agenda and the bylaws or other governance structure under which the task group operates are usually the only written agreements binding group members. Ordinarily, task groups rely on verbal contracts about the tasks to be accomplished, the roles of group members, and the division of labor in the group.

Contracting for Group Procedures

The worker begins to determine group procedures by deciding on the duration and frequency of meetings. These decisions are closely related to the group's purpose and the needs of its members. In treatment groups, the optimal length of time for each meeting varies. Meetings of groups of individuals with dementia in a nursing home may last only 30 to 45 minutes, but meetings of outpatient support groups often last one to two hours. Some groups, such as encounter or sensitivity training groups, meet for longer time periods and within a short time frame to achieve high communication levels and reduce member defensiveness.

The frequency of group meetings should also be considered when contracting for group procedures. In general, weekly sessions are recommended for treatment groups, although this does not preclude meeting more often when needed. The frequency of task group meetings depends on the requirements of the task and any time limits or deadlines that need to be considered. The worker must also consider how much time each member can devote to the group.

Specification of other group procedures should also be considered. The worker can specify attendance requirements, confidentiality of discussions, or other rules governing behavior in the group, such as how discussions will take place and how decisions will be made. Additional details include the time and place for meetings, any attendance fees involved, and the monitoring and evaluation procedures to be used by the worker.

Contracting for Member Goals

During the planning stage, workers also begin contractual arrangements with individual members. During orientation meetings workers should help members to describe what they would like to accomplish through group participation. Workers should describe the broad goals they have for the group and invite members to do the same. Questions such as "What do you hope to accomplish through your participation in the group?" can stimulate members to think about their roles in a group, what goals they want to accomplish, and how the goals fit with the broad purposes described by the worker. Methods that can be used when contracting with members of both treatment and task groups are explained in more detail in Chapter 7.

Preparing the Environment

Three factors that should be considered when preparing a group's environment include the physical setting, making arrangements to accommodate members who have special needs, and securing financial support. The extent of worker control over these factors is sometimes limited, but incorporating them into the planning process whenever possible enhances the chances for successful group development. Environmental factors to consider are presented in the following checklist.

Checklist for Preparing the Environment

- Room size: adequate for size of group and activities associated with meetings
- Furnishings: seating requirements, work and activity spaces, population specific needs
- Technology: audiovisual, computer, and telecommunications needs
- Atmosphere: lighting, heating and air conditioning, overall effect created by the meeting space
- Special needs: physical accessibility of meeting space, assistive technology, child care, transportation, interpreter
- Financial support: cost of group activities and materials, technology, duplicating, advertising, mailing, hospitality (food, beverages), other special arrangements

Preparing the Physical Setting

The setting for the group can have a profound effect on the behavior of group members and the conduct of group meetings. Room size, space, seating arrangements, furnishings, and atmosphere should all be considered. Difficulties encountered in early meetings, inappropriate behavior by members, and unanticipated problems in the development of the group can sometimes result from inadequate attention to the group's physical environment.

Room size can influence how active or involved members become with the business of the group. Generally, a small room engenders positive feelings of closeness among members and limits potential distractions. A large room can put too much distance among members and thus encourage some members to tune out. A small group of people meeting in a large room may be distracted by the open space around them and have difficulty concentrating on the group process.

On the other hand, a room may be too small and not allow enough space between members, which can lead to discomfort, irritability, anxiety, or acting out. Certain populations are particularly reactive to the size of the meeting room. Young children, for example, often benefit from a large, open area in which to engage in activities. Similarly, disabled older adults benefit from a room with wheelchair access; comfortable, high-back chairs that are not difficult to get in and out of; bright, glare-free lighting; and good acoustics (Toseland, 1995).

Comfortable seating should be available. Sometimes group members prefer to sit on the floor to create an informal atmosphere. Carpets, lamps, work tables, and other furnishings can also help create a comfortable atmosphere. A comfortable physical environment conveys a message to group members about the agency's regard for them as clients.

Overall, the worker should consider the total effect of the physical setting on a group's ability to accomplish its tasks. If a group is to engage in informal discussion, the worker can create an informal atmosphere with comfortable couches or pillows for sitting on the floor. If a group is to work on formal tasks, such as reviewing priorities for a five-year plan, the worker should create a more formal atmosphere. For example, a room in which the group can sit around a well-lighted table may be most appropriate.

Making Special Arrangements

The worker should be particularly sensitive to any special needs of group members and should be sure that special needs will not prevent members from being able to attend meetings. For example, when working with the physically challenged, the worker should plan a barrier-free location for meetings or should consider phone or computer groups as an alternative to face-to-face meetings. When planning a group for parents, the worker should consider child-care arrangements. For a children's group, the worker should discuss transportation arrangements and obtain parental consent for the children's involvement in the group. When working with individuals for whom English is a second language, the worker may wish to arrange for the services of an interpreter or may wish to cofacilitate the group with a bilingual worker.

The worker should pay particular attention to the resources needed by members who experience specific forms of disability. For example, the worker might want to ensure that persons who have hearing impairments have access to interpreters. In an educational group, it might be necessary for a person with severe physical disabilities to include his or her personal care attendant in meetings to ensure the member's full participation in discussions and activities. Members who have visual impairments may need reading materials converted to Braille.

The worker may not know that a potential member experiences a particular disability. For example, certain hidden disabilities such as asthma might preclude a member from participation in certain group activities or in certain environments. Insofar as possible, the worker should assess all potential members of a group during the intake process to determine their special needs.

Securing Financial Support

The worker should be concerned about how the expenses associated with the group will be met. For this reason, the worker should explore the financing arrangements with the group's sponsoring agency, beginning with an assessment of the agency's total financial statement. The costs associated with treatment and task groups vary, but major items include the salary of the worker, the use of the meeting room, and the expense of supervision for the worker. Other expenses may include duplicating, telephone, mailings, refreshments, and transportation.

Using information about costs and income, the worker can determine what financial support must be obtained for the proposed group. Expenses such as the worker's salary and the meeting room are often routinely paid by the agency. For expenses requiring an outlay of cash, the worker should submit a budget request to the sponsoring agency. A petty-cash fund can provide a flexible means to cover expenses incurred by the group.

For some treatment groups, income may be generated by fees collected from members, or it may be produced from contracts or grants. Although most task groups do not usually generate income, some are formed specifically to generate money for new programs or to raise funds for the agency. Others generate financial savings for their sponsoring organization through creative problem solving or decision making.

Planning for Virtual Groups

Virtual groups are those where members do not meet face-to-face. Instead, they meet over the telephone or through the Internet.

Virtual groups are an important alternative to face-to-face groups for many reasons. In some situations, it is just not possible for people who could benefit from social group work to meet face-to-face. For example, people who suffer from debilitating illnesses, such as the frail elderly and persons with terminal illnesses, often are not able to attend group meetings. Also, it is often very difficult for those with rare diseases to find face-to-face support groups composed of people with the same illnesses.

Transportation and distance can also be barriers to attending face-to-face meetings. In many rural and suburban areas, public transportation is poor and people who lack private transportation find it is difficult or impossible to attend face-to-face group meetings. Others find it difficult to avail themselves of a group service because they live such a long distance from the organization offering the service. For example, in rural communities, health and social service agencies often serve large geographic areas. Even in urban and suburban communities, some health and social service agencies, such as regional hospitals, serve the needs of special populations dispersed over a large area. The inconvenience of the meeting location along with time pressures and transportation costs can make attending face-to-face meetings difficult.

There are also many situations where it is possible for individuals to attend face-to-face groups, but they prefer not to attend. For example, some issues are socially stigmatizing, and members may not want to take the risk of disclosing in a face-to-face group. Hectic schedules and time constraints can make attending face-to-face groups unattractive for many potential members (McKenna & Green, 2002). For others, social anxiety and high levels of introversion can make attending face-to-face groups excruciatingly difficult. Some also see virtual groups as safer, because they offer greater control over the timing and pace of written and verbal interactions and direct physical contact (McKenna & Bargh, 1999; McKenna & Bargh, 2000).

Contrary to what is commonly expected, recent research suggests that in some situations virtual groups are actually more cohesive than face-to-face groups, and they exert greater influence on members' behavior (McKenna, Green, & Gleason, 2002; Postmes, Spears, & Lea, 1999; Postmes, Spears, Sakhel, & de Groot, 2001). Because members are anonymous, there are no visual cues to distract them from the core interests and values that motivated them to participate in the group (McKenna & Green, 2002). Members no longer focus on personal features such as skin color, or social status cues such as the way members are dressed or the cars they drive to the group (McKenna & Bargh, 2000). They focus more on the shared issues that bring them into contact. For example, a research project studied the impact of psychoeducational telephone support groups on caregivers to frail and disabled older adults. It was found that the caregivers—adult children and their spouses from very different socioeconomic backgrounds—were able to interact easily with each other. Bonds were formed because of similiar caregiving issues and concerns, rather than because of personal appearance or socioeconomic status (Smith & Toseland, 2006).

The presence of others who self-categorize and self-identify in a particular way can also increase group identification and social influence (Postmes et al., 2001). The fact that members of virtual groups are able to identify with the issues that brought them all to the group means that the salience of the group is enhanced and norms are more likely to be followed (Postmes et al., 1999).

Although there are many advantages to virtual groups, there are also disadvantages that should be carefully considered. Some research suggests that there may be greater hostility and aggression in virtual groups (Siegel, Dubrovsky, Kiesler, & McGuire, 1986;

Weinberg, 2001). For example, the term *flaming* is often used by Internet users to describe the activity of sending emotionally charged, hostile messages without clear provocation or advance warning (Oravec, 2000). It may be that the anonymity of these groups encourages this type of behavior. Text-only messages without nonverbal cues in Internet groups and tonal inflections and verbal messages without visual cues in telephone groups enable group members to unwittingly project negative meanings onto messages that were intended to have more positive connotations (Smokowski, Galinsky, & Harlow, 2001).

Privacy can also be an issue, particularly in online interactions that are open to the public (Oravec, 2000; Smokowski et al., 2001). Even in groups that use passwords, "lurkers" may sign up, but not interact. Active members may leave computer messages on screens that are open to public viewing. It is also easier for members of virtual groups to conceal or mask their true identities in order to form relationships with vulnerable group members who are seeking interaction with those who have similar life experiences.

Another concern is the quality of the information and services that are received during virtual group interaction (Bowman & Bowman, 1998). Information shared on the Internet is not subject to the same standards as information printed in scientific journals. Online and telephone counseling and support can be given by individuals without professional degrees who have not agreed to abide by the professional standards of accrediting bodies. Virtual group leaders may respond too quickly to text messages with little context or background. Exacerbating this problem, some members of virtual groups may expect quick fixes. Because of the open nature of the medium, it is not always feasible to prevent harmful interactions or to provide valid information that tempers or contradicts bad advice.

Despite these disadvantages, telephone and Internet groups have experienced a surge in interest. For many individuals, the advantages of these groups outweigh the disadvantages.

Telephone-Mediated Groups

In recent years, technological advances have made it possible to have telephone conversations among a number of individuals. This is often referred to as *teleconferencing* or making a *conference call* (Kelleher & Cross, 1990). Until recently, the use of this technology was largely limited to task group meetings in large organizations with members who were geographically dispersed but it is being used more widely now in social service agencies who are trying to reach out to individuals who either can not get to in-person groups, or prefer telephone groups.

Some of the special considerations in setting up a telephone group are (1) teleconferencing capacity in the organization's telephone system or sufficient funds to purchase the service, (2) a speaker phone if there will be more than one leader, (3) *teleconferencing* equipment, and (4) a willingness of participants to stay on the telephone for a long duration. We have explored the use of hands-free headsets for participants, but we have found that these are not necessary, and some participants find purchasing the headsets and installing them with existing telephone equipment difficult.

A comprehensive review of the literature revealed 19 studies focused on the use of telephone support groups for people with many types of disability ranging from those with AIDS to those with visual impairments. Although there were few rigorously controlled studies, the results and conclusions of these studies were overwhelmingly positive. There are a number of advantages of telephone groups some of which follow.

Advantages of Telephone Groups

- Convenience and accessibility of meeting in one's own home
- Reduced time needed to participate because there is no travel time
- Reduction of stigma because of greater privacy
- Ability to reach persons living in rural areas and those who lack transportation
- Ability to reach people who are homebound or caring for someone who can't be left alone
- Greater willingness to share issues that might be taboo in-person groups

At the same time, telephone groups have potential disadvantages. Perhaps the biggest disadvantage is cost. One way to reduce costs is to use a low-cost internet voice-over tele-conference provider. Another way is to purchase the equipment called a "bridge" necessary to make conference calls and to have sufficient telephone lines to run a call center. Costs can then be spread over many employees who may use the technology for administrative and clinical purposes. To help defray costs, teleconferencing capabilities can also be rented to other organizations and private practitioners. The following is a list of potential disadvantages of telephone groups.

Disadvantages of Telephone Groups

- Cost
- Difficulties in assessing members' needs and the impact of interactions without the benefit of facial expressions and other nonverbal clues
- The difficulty of including members with hearing problems
- Distortions caused by technological problems, call waiting, or background noises from other persons in the household
- Concerns about confidentiality because of a lack of privacy within callers' households
- Changes in group dynamics caused by the lack of visual and nonverbal clues
- The difficulty of using program activities, flip charts, and other visual media
- Expressions of hostility or insensitivity that can sometimes be greater when members are not meeting face-to-face

Some disadvantages of telephone groups are not inherent in the technology itself but rather in how it is used. For example, telephone groups that last over an hour can lead to fatigue, especially when members are frail (Stein, Rothman, & Nakanishi, 1993; Wiener, Spencer, Davidson, & Fair, 1993). For this reason, and because the amount of time for a telephone conference is often predetermined by arrangements with the teleconference provider, leaders must be vigilant about preparing members properly for the ending of each meeting.

Another disadvantage of telephone groups is that they offer no informal time for members to get together with each other before or after the meeting (Rounds, Galinsky, & Stevens, 1991). With members' consent, swapping telephone numbers for between-session contact is one solution. In our current research on telephone support groups for caregivers, members have gotten together between meetings, after the time-limited groups ended over coffee at a diner, and in members' homes.

Because members lack visual cues during telephone meetings, the worker must be particularly attentive to tone of voice, inflection, silences, and other cues such as members becoming less responsive or completely dropping out of the discussion over time. It is also helpful to (1) have members identify themselves each time they communicate, (2) help members to anticipate frustrations such as missed cues or interruptions during group meeting times, while at the same time appreciating the benefits of the medium, (3) prompt members to clarify statements and to give clear feedback to each other, and (4) check on members' emotional reactions and make these clear to all group members (Schopler et al., 1997). In general, leaders of telephone groups should plan to be more active than in in-person groups, helping members to communicate effectively without visual cues. Despite these limitations, telephone groups offer a promising alternative to face-to-face interacting groups for frail or isolated individuals.

Workers who are planning telephone groups may also consider some of the following things that we have learned from our recent experience with telephone groups. For example, we have found that it works better for the leader to call each member than to have members call in to the group using an access code. When members call in, they are more apt to call late or call from inconvenient locations. If members know they are going to be called at a certain time, our experience suggests that the ability to start a group on time with all members present is enhanced. The Internet provider that we use enables us to set amplification for each caller so that the voices of callers with soft voices can be amplified and those with loud voices can be softened. However, we still occasionally have to remind members not to use speaker phones or some cordless phones with poor voice quality. We have also found that, although it is a good practice for members to identify each other each time they speak, members get to know each other's situations and voices quickly and can frequently identify each other without the need for self-identification. Our experience also suggests that the leader has to take a more active role in directing the action than in face-to-face groups. For example, in an opening go-round, the leader has to indicate who should introduce themselves next, because the physical cues that indicate a particular member is next in line to introduce themselves are not present in telephone groups. Similarly, telephone group leaders often have to take a more active role in directing questions from one member to another member, and questions sometimes have to be repeated because the member to whom the question is directed may not have expected to be asked to respond.

It is a good practice to meet with each member of a telephone group at least once before the start of the group. Sometimes, however this is not practical because of the long distances separating members. In these cases, we have found that it is helpful to mail each member of a telephone group a workbook with all the handouts, worksheets, and other materials that will be used during meetings. In that way, members can follow along in their workbook when the leader is speaking about a particular topic, or asking the members to engage in an exercise. This helps to overcome the inability to use flip charts or other visual media that are commonly used in in-person groups. We have also found that members of telephone groups like to get together in-person after the group has been meeting for a while. Therefore, if a series of telephone groups is planned, it is a good idea to try and have members from similar geographic locations in the same group. This not only enables them to get together in person more easily, but it also helps the leader to know what services to link members to in particular communities.

We have not found distractions within members' home environments to be a major problem. Most members are good about explicitly stating when they have to stop their participation for a brief period when they have to deal with an interruption or a chore that could not be avoided, and they also readily let the group know when they have returned and are reengaged in the teleconference. Overall, we have found that participants really enjoy telephone groups, and few have experienced any problems with being on the telephone for the hour and fifteen minutes it takes us to start and conduct a group session.

Telephone groups are still not widely used and there are some issues that will need to be resolved in coming years. For example, reimbursement for telephone group services is not widely available and practitioners will have to check prior to starting a group whether private or public insurers will reimburse for the service. There has also been little discussion in the literature about the professional standards for delivering telephone services (Glueckauf, Pickett, Ketterson, Loomis, & Rozensky, 2003; Maheu, Whitten, & Allen, 2001; Nickelson, 2000). The American Psychological Association has developed an ethics statement about telephone psychotherapy (Haas, Benedict, & Kobos, 1996), but the focus is more on one-on-one telephone therapy with patients with mental health problems than on group intervention focused on support, education, or coping skills for dealing with chronic illnesses. For more information about telephone groups see Glueckauf and Ketterson (2004); Glueckauf and Loomis (2003); Glueckauf, Nickelson, Whitton, and Loomis (2004); Kaslyn (1999); Martindale-Adams, Nichols, Burns, and Malone (2002); Rosswurm, Larrabee, and Zhang (2002); Schopler, Galinsky, and Abell (1997); Schopler, Abell, and Galinsky (1998); Toseland, Naccarato, and Wray (2007).

Computer-Mediated Groups

There has been a sharp increase in the popularity of computer-mediated groups in recent years. There are now literally thousands of computer-mediated groups for persons with many different types of health, mental health, and social concerns. Research on computer-mediated groups has also increased in recent years. In a search of the literature we found over 40 articles on computer groups, focused on many different types of group members.

To access or develop a computer-mediated group, an individual must have access to a computer and an online service. The online service is used to access search services such as Google or Yahoo, which are, in turn, used to find the desired site on the Internet. For example, Alcoholics Anonymous groups can be accessed at http://aa-intergroup.org or www.12stepforums.net.

Four ways that computer-mediated groups can be formed using the Internet are (1) chat rooms, (2) bulletin boards, (3) e-mail, and (4) listservs (Santhiveeran, 1998). Chat rooms are virtual spaces, opened during specified time periods, where individuals can post messages and receive feedback interactively in a short time frame. In contrast, bulletin boards are usually open 24 hours a day. They enable individuals to post messages that can be answered at any time. E-mail allows an individual to write messages to particular individuals who can respond at any time. Listservs allow a large group of individuals to present and receive information and news. Thus, some computer-assisted group meetings occur in real time; that is, everyone participates at a specific time and the discussion is interactive. Other group meetings require members to post messages to which other members can respond at any time. Sites on the Internet are also excellent sources of information and education for group members. For example, members of a computer-mediated, real-time support group for cancer patients might be encouraged to visit a site sponsored by a reputable source such as the National Cancer Institute to obtain current information about diagnoses and treatment options.

Computer-mediated groups offer many advantages to participants. Like telephone groups, they offer a variety and diversity of support, especially for frail group members and persons with very specialized concerns who may not be sufficiently numerous in any one geographic area to form a group (Finn, 1995). They also offer the same anonymity as telephone groups but have particular appeal to those who enjoy written communication or the convenience of 24-hour access. Although they require an initial investment in hardware and software, online service charges are less expensive than telephone conference services. In addition, they eliminate time and distance barriers even more effectively than do telephone groups.

Glueckauf and Loomis (2003) report that members of computer-mediated support groups experience many of the same therapeutic factors commonly associated with face-to-face support groups. However, Finn and Lavitt (1994) point out that computer-mediated groups often lack clear and accountable leadership and that this factor, in turn, has the potential to lead to destructive interactions, superficial self-disclosure, and the compounding of isolation by persons with interpersonal difficulties. In addition to a lack of formal facilitation by social workers and other helping professionals, there is a lack of professional standards regulating how to conduct these groups and how to bill for services that are rendered (Glueckauf, Pickett, Ketterson, Loomis, & Rozensky, 2003). Computer-mediated groups tend to limit access by individuals in lower socioeconomic groups who have less access to computer hardware and software, and the service is not covered by Medicare or Medicaid.

It has been speculated that computer-mediated groups might replace in-person support group services (Alemi et al., 1996). Although there is some evidence that current users of support groups substitute computer-mediated groups for attendance at some support group meetings, there is also evidence that the use of computer-mediated groups increases participation in in-person support groups by persons who have not previously attended in-person support group meetings (Bass, McClendon, Brennan, & McCarthy, 1998). More research on the benefits and limitations of computer groups needs to be conducted, however, before any definitive conclusions can be drawn about their effectiveness. More research and policy discussions are also needed about professional facilitation, professional standards and accountability, record keeping, and reimbursement rates for services rendered to online group members.

Preparing a Written Group Proposal

In planning for a group, the worker might find it useful to prepare a written proposal. Such a proposal is sometimes required for obtaining agency sponsorship or for obtaining funding from various sources. A written proposal can also inform potential members about the group. Spending time to organize and write a group proposal can also aid the worker in preparing for meetings. For most groups, a brief summary of one or two pages, following the outline presented in Appendix D, is sufficient. Two sample proposals, one for a treatment group and one for a task group, are presented in Appendices E and F.

SUMMARY

This chapter stresses the need for planning in group work. Workers consider many variables and exercise control over as many of them as possible. The planning process should be guided by the purposes of the group, the needs of the members, and the requirements of the task.

The chapter presents a model for planning treatment and task groups. Steps in the model include (1) establishing the group's purpose, (2) assessing the potential sponsorship and membership, (3) recruiting members, (4) composing the group, (5) orienting members, (6) contracting, (7) preparing the group's environment, (8) planning of virtual groups, and (9) preparing a written group proposal. The model can be useful in planning for the many different types of groups a worker may lead. All planning models represent an idealized, step-by-step set of procedures that may vary, depending on the realities of agency practice, but following a logical planning model can assist workers in helping groups meet members' needs and accomplish established goals.

● CASE EXAMPLE

Cathy worked for a university counseling center that stressed preventive services. She perceived that there were an increasing number of women being referred to her by the university's health center with symptoms of depression and anxiety. Many had successfully raised children and were seeking further education to start a new career after their children had left home. In addition to having concerns about returning to school as nontraditional-age students, many did not receive much encouragement from their spouses or partners, rendering their efforts to seek a new career even more difficult. Cathy wondered if a support group would be the best way to help these women. She conveyed her plans for a possible group to her supervisor in the form of a group proposal and began planning for the group.

She talked with colleagues in the counseling center and the health center about their experiences with older students to assess the need for a support group. She found that they too had been seeing a number of women who were beginning second careers and who were in need

of supportive services. To learn more about the types of problems older students might be encountering, she called the local community college and discussed the group with several academic advisors from Start Again, an educational program designed to assist nontraditional-age students. In addition, she spoke with a few women on her caseload to see if they shared her perception of the need for a support group. They seemed very interested. Cathy also spoke to her supervisor and discussed her preliminary ideas about the group. Her supervisor said that a support group would fit the mission and goals of the organization. She thought the group could help Cathy's clients with the transition back to school and prevent more serious psychological, social, and physical problems later, as the women pursued life changes associated with starting a second career.

Informed by her initial assessment, Cathy concentrated on defining the purpose of the group. She recognized that the initial statement of purpose should provide basic information that would help members understand the nature of the group and how it would work. She decided that the purpose would be "to bring women together to discuss issues about starting a second career, going to college as a nontraditional-age student, and dealing with family issues related to life changes." Members would share their experiences and support each other through discussion and social activities. Cathy hoped that the group would help eliminate or reduce members' depression and anxiety and increase their coping skills.

Cathy developed a two-pronged recruitment plan that she hoped would ensure the group had an adequate number of members. She described the purposes of the proposed group during weekly staff meetings in both the counseling center and the health center and asked her colleagues to refer potential members to her. In addition, she wrote a short article about the group for a monthly student newsletter that was widely distributed on campus. In it, she listed the purpose of the group and suggested that potential members call her at the office to discuss their interest in attending.

Despite these efforts, only a few persons contacted her about the group. In her telephone conversations with potential members, she learned that many felt overwhelmed by the demands of returning to school. Despite their perception that the group could be helpful, they seemed reluctant to commit their time to another new endeavor. Cathy suggested that potential members meet once to assess whether the group would meet their needs and be worth attending. Twelve women agreed to a first meeting, but the most convenient meeting time for the majority accommodated only nine women's schedules.

During the first orientation meeting, Cathy took notes on the women's individual situations. She noted that all potential members were over forty years old and all but one had children who were either in high school or college. All seemed to be having some difficulty balancing the academic demands of college with the time demands of their families. They displayed an interesting range of diversity based on income level as well as racial, ethnic, and cultural backgrounds. They also seemed to use differing coping strategies for dealing with their spouses' and partners' lack of supportiveness, suggesting that they could learn much from each other. Cathy also felt that all potential members were articulate, had good insight into their personal and family situations, and had potential for helping others in the group. Despite having only eight members attending the orientation session, Cathy felt that the composition of the group would promote the development of therapeutic group processes.

Cathy described the purpose of the group, answered members' questions about how the group would work, and helped members to discuss and shape how the group would function. After this discussion, members seemed genuinely interested in attending more sessions, and they seemed relieved to meet others who were experiencing similar life transitions. Cathy and the members agreed that the group could be an open one, adding members from time to time, but that the size of the group should not exceed eight members. In addition, members discussed some initial thoughts about attendance, confidentiality, length and time of meetings, and Cathy's role in the group. After this discussion, Cathy noted that they had started to form the elements of an informal contract that could be discussed more fully in the next meeting of the group. She added that in the early sessions, members could also begin to work on their individual goals and contracts with the group and with each other. Overall, the orientation session seemed quite successful.

Behind the scenes, Cathy made arrangements with the counseling center for supporting the new group. She identified a comfortable meeting space for the group, one that was accessible and private. Although members had no special child care or transportation needs, she asked the counseling center to provide some funds for refreshments.

PART III

The Beginning Stage

chapter 7

The Group Begins

chapter 8

Assessment

The Group Begins

The beginning of a group is often characterized by caution and tentativeness. The members have certain expectations about the group based on experiences in other groups. Also, they may have met with the worker before the first group meeting or received information on the purpose of the group through other agency workers or from other group members. Nevertheless, at the beginning of any group, members are not fully certain about its purposes. Members wonder about what will be expected of them and what the leader and the other members will be like. Thus, from the very first contact, participants assess each other, mainly on the basis of nonverbal cues such as dress and personal appearance. The first interchanges are often stereotyped conversations in which participants attempt to become familiar with one another through mutual interests in places, people, events, leisure and work pursuits, and other common experiences (Hartford, 1971).

As the group meeting progresses, an approach-avoidance conflict often becomes more evident (Garland, Jones, & Kolodny, 1976). Members approach each other in their striving to connect with one another, but they avoid getting too close because they fear the vulnerability that such intimacy implies. Members are concerned about the way they present themselves early in a group and often prefer to proceed with caution. Members often do not feel secure about what they can expect from the group or their own ability to perform in the group. Therefore, they are often cautious about what they reveal.

Discussion of emotionally charged issues can be detrimental in the beginning of a group. When a member self-discloses emotionally charged issues very early in the group's development, other members sometimes feel threatened and may disclose little for a time. This occurs because few norms have developed about how to behave, and members are unsure about how to respond. Members may feel threatened if they think they will be asked to self-disclose at similar levels. They may not be ready to do so, or they may think others will not be receptive or supportive.

Through their initial interactions, members attempt to find their places within the group. As the group develops norms, members begin to find out what is acceptable and unacceptable behavior. The tentative interactions found at the beginning of most groups are a testing ground for developing relationships. Group members attempt to reach out to find who in the group they can trust with their thoughts and feelings and with whom they can form continuing relationships.

Members' past experiences can affect their reactions in a new group. A useful exercise that can be done early in the group's life is to have all members describe an experience they had in a previous group and emphasize how that group experience affects their participation in the current group.

Members react in different ways to groups. Some remain silent, taking a wait-and-see stance. Others try to reduce their anxiety by engaging in conversation or by asking questions to help them clarify their position in a group. Gradually, a pattern of relating develops within the group, and the pattern crystallizes as the group develops.

Workers should try to remain aware of the patterns of relating as the group develops. The worker can point out patterns of relating as they form and encourage the development of patterns that will help to accomplish group and individual goals. For example, the worker may want to model and reinforce open-interaction patterns that encourage all members to participate.

OBJECTIVES IN THE BEGINNING STAGE

The beginning stage is often considered, by both novice and experienced workers, to be a difficult stage of group work because members often seek direction about how to proceed but are ambivalent about following any suggestions. Members struggle to maintain their autonomy but, at the same time, fit in and get along with others in the group. The worker's primary goals are to help members to work together in a cooperative and productive manner and to feel that their unique contribution to the group is respected and appreciated. To accomplish these goals it is helpful to:

- Facilitate member introductions
- Clarify the purpose and function of the group as it is perceived by the worker, the members, and the sponsoring organization
- Discuss and clarify the limits of confidentiality within the group
- Help members to feel that they are a part of the group
- Guide the development of the group
- Balance task and socioemotional aspects of the group process
- Set goals
- Contract for work
- Facilitate members' motivation and ability to work in the group
- Address ambivalence and resistance
- Working with mandated clients
- Anticipate obstacles to achieving individual and group goals

In the following pages, these tasks and the corresponding skills necessary to carry them out are presented sequentially. In actual practice, of course, the group worker should be concerned about these tasks simultaneously.

Introducing New Members

When the participants have arrived and the group is ready to begin, the first task of the worker is to introduce members to one another. Introductions help members share their mutual concerns and interests and develop trust. The worker should decide what information is important for members to share with the group. Beyond each member's name, the information revealed by each member should depend on the purpose of the group. For example, if the group is an interagency task force to study the problem of battered women, members might be expected to share their position in their agency, their experiences with services for battered women, and their reasons for becoming involved in the task force. If the group is for parents with children who have behavior problems, in addition to information about themselves, members might briefly describe their children and the behavior problems they are experiencing.

Introductions can give members a starting point for interaction. Therefore, the information that is shared should attempt to bring out commonalities. The worker can facilitate this process by noting common characteristics and shared concerns disclosed by different members. Rather than proceeding through the introduction mechanically, the worker should encourage members to discuss commonalities. This process helps members feel at ease with one another. It also helps develop group cohesion and demonstrates to members that they are not alone with their problems and concerns.

● **CASE EXAMPLE** *A Support Group For Caregivers of Persons With Dementia*

The worker asked each member in turn to talk about themselves, the person for whom they were caring, and the problems they were experiencing. One member, Mary, mentioned how concerned she was about her husband driving even though he refused to give it up. The worker stopped the group introductions at this point and asked if anyone else had experienced a similar problem and how they were handling it. Several members began to talk about the problem and their concerns about it. The worker suggested that since this seemed to be a concern for many members that they continue with the introductions, but take up the topic of driving later during the group meeting. Later during the group introductions another member brought up the topic of her husband's agitated behavior, and how he paced and followed her from room to room. Again the worker asked if any other group members had experienced that problem, and several said they had. The worker said that that they would also talk about that behavior later in the group meeting or during the next group meeting if there was not time to get to it in today's meeting.

The opportunity for members to share common concerns and issues with one another is one of the unique aspects of social group work practice. Yalom (1995) has called this phenomenon *universality*. People who come to treatment groups often believe that they are alone with their problems. In reality, although they may have been experiencing their problems in isolation, other people experience similar concerns. The first group meeting provides them with feelings of support and comfort as they realize they are not alone.

A similar process occurs in task groups. For example, workers from different community agencies often experience the same frustrations and problems in serving clients with particular social service needs. Alone, workers may think they can do little to make the system more responsive to clients. But together, in a task force, a treatment conference, or in any other task group, workers can share their concerns, coordinate their efforts, and work to change problematic situations.

Round Robin

The most common method of introducing members to one another is to have them speak in round robin fashion. If this method is used, it is helpful for the worker to go first. In the early stages of the group, members take many of their cues from the worker, who can serve as a model by disclosing personal characteristics. Once members hear the worker's introduction, they are likely to focus on the disclosures as they introduce themselves.

Sometimes, the worker may want members to disclose information about areas of concern that the worker does not share. For example, in a group of parents, the worker may not have children. Workers should note the absence of this characteristic in their own lives, state how it might affect their work in the group, and ask members to comment on this factor in their introductions. For example, the worker might say, "I don't have any children of my own, but I've worked with children in the past at summer camp, in foster care, and for the past four years in my current position."

When they introduce themselves, members rarely disclose more than the worker has disclosed. In fact, they initially tend to disclose to a lesser extent than the worker. Therefore, if workers expect a certain level of self-disclosure or want to foster disclosures in a certain area, their introductions should reflect what is expected. This is not to suggest that the introduction should call on members to reveal in-depth, personal life experiences. Pressing for such disclosures at the beginning of a group is likely to increase rather than decrease barriers to open communication.

Communication styles and expectations about self-disclosure are influenced by our cultural heritage. Pearson (1991) suggests, for example, that clients who identify with the cultural imperatives in Chinese society may believe that close, personal relationships are usually reserved for family and that high levels of self-disclosure are not as desirable as a "balance and restraint in the experience and expression of emotions" (p. 51).

Variations on Round Robin

Several variations on the round robin may be useful in opening different types of groups. To increase interaction, for example, members can be divided into pairs. One member of each pair interviews the other for five minutes by asking for details specified by the worker. When time is up, members reverse roles and continue for another five minutes. When the group reconvenes, members introduce their partners to the group by recalling the facts learned during their conversation. In addition to helping members develop a relationship with a partner, group workers find that this method of introduction sometimes leads to a greater depth of self-disclosure than round robin because new group members are likely to reveal more about themselves on a one-to-one basis than when they face the entire group.

A variation on this opening is what Shulman (1999) has called "problem swapping" (p. 348). Members volunteer to discuss their problems or concerns openly before the group. This opening promotes group interaction, leads to the identification of shared problems and concerns, and helps members to consider how they might proceed.

An opening that is useful in growth-oriented groups is known as *top secret*. Members are asked to write down one thing about themselves that they have not or would not ordinarily reveal to new acquaintances. The leader collects the top secrets and reads them to the group. Members attempt to identify the person who made each revelation, giving a reason for their choice. This exercise can be repeated in a later group session to illustrate the extent to which trust and cohesion have increased in the group. Members often reveal more intimate or personal top secrets after they come to know and feel comfortable with the members of their group. Variations on this opening exercise are "my most embarrassing experience" and "my greatest success."

Another opening exercise that can help members to disclose something about themselves or their family of origin is called *my name.* Members can be asked to discuss how they got their names and what meaning the name has for them and for their family of origin. For example, a member might state that his father felt strongly that he should be named Samuel, after an uncle who had died. The member goes on to discuss the uncle and other facts about his family of origin. He might also mention that he disliked being called Sam by his parents and decided at age 13 to insist that his parents and friends call him by his middle name, Allen. This exercise can often lead to interesting discussions of members' feelings about themselves now and in the past. It also helps members learn each other's names, which is important for open and personal interaction.

Other openings such as *treasure hunt* can be useful. Members are asked to find out two or three facts about each of the other group members. This activity offers much structured, but informal, group interaction to help members overcome initial anxieties. The facts obtained are shared when the group reconvenes.

Program activities can also be used in opening a group. Such activities help members share important information about themselves while working on an assigned task or activity. In addition to increasing members' self-disclosure, program activities can build cohesion in the group. For example, in children's groups, members may be asked to pick an animal that represents them. When introducing themselves, members can name the animal they have selected and state what characteristics of the animal they identify with. Another program activity for children or adolescent groups is to have members stand in a circle and hold hands with two members who are not next to them. Members are then asked to untangle themselves and form a circle without letting go of each other's hands. Additional program activities that can be used to open a group can be found in Barlow, Blythe, and Edmonds (1999); Bufe and DeNunzio (1998); Furman (2005); Middleman (1982); or in the annual handbook on developing human resources by Pfeiffer and Goodstein (1984–1996) (published annually since 1984).

Variations in Group Beginnings

A number of factors can change the way a worker begins a group. Sometimes workers become involved with groups of people who have known each other before the group was formed. This can occur when the members are clients of a neighborhood center, a residential treatment facility, or are friends in the community. Similarly, in task groups, members may be familiar with one another as coworkers in the same agency or as coworkers in a network of agencies working with similar clients or a similar social problem. When members know one another, the challenges for the worker are different from the challenges that occur in a group of strangers.

Members who have had previous contact with one another are more likely to relate in ways that are characteristic of their previously established patterns. Roles and relationships established earlier may be carried into the new group, regardless of their functional or dysfunctional nature in the current group situation. In groups in which only a few members know one another or in which previous relationships between members vary from friendly to neutral or unfriendly, subgroups are likely to develop more often than they would in groups composed of strangers. There is also a natural tendency for friends or acquaintances to interact with one another and exclude strangers.

When it is possible to obtain information about potential group members, the worker should try to find out about any relationships that may exist among potential members. This will give the worker some indication of what form members' relationships are likely to take as they begin the group. It also gives the worker an opportunity to plan strategies to intervene in dysfunctional relationship patterns. The worker may wish to use information about members' previous relationships to reconsider the composition of the group and to understand members' interactions as the group unfolds. For example, a worker in a group home might use knowledge about the relationships that have developed among residents when deciding how to intervene to change communication patterns in a group that has just been established within the facility.

Another common variation in beginning a group occurs when the worker becomes involved in a previously formed group (see, e. g., the following case example). This can happen when a worker (1) reaches out and works with a gang of adolescents, (2) is a consultant for a self-help group, (3) is asked to staff a previously formed committee, or (4) is asked to replace the leader of an intact treatment group. These situations are different from one in which all members are new to the group. Instead of members looking to the leader for direction, as in a new group, the worker in a previously formed group is the newcomer in a group with established patterns of relating. Members of previously formed groups are concerned with how the worker will affect the group, what they will have to do to accommodate the worker, and what the worker will expect of them. Members may also act on feelings resulting from termination with a previous worker. This is demonstrated in the following case example.

● CASE EXAMPLE   *Dealing with Feelings About a Worker Leaving the Group*

In assuming leadership for an existing substance abuse prevention group, the new worker began the meeting by asking members to discuss how they felt about her replacing their former worker. Because the group had been meeting together for over a year, members freely discussed their concerns about changing group leaders. They also asked very direct questions about the new worker's credentials, experiences, and leadership style. During these discussions, the new worker listened carefully to what members were saying. She chose to be less verbal so that members had more opportunities to talk. By encouraging members to be more verbal, the worker was able to make a preliminary assessment of the group's structure and was able to identify the informal leadership structure that had previously developed in the group.

In working with previously formed groups, the worker should become familiar with the group's structure and its current functions and processes. It is especially important that the worker become familiar with the formal and informal leadership of the group, with members' relationships with one another, and with the tasks that face the group. Information obtained from a previous leader or from agency records may offer some indication of how to approach the group. In working with gangs or other community groups for which little information is available, the worker may find it helpful to gather information about the group. Any information obtained before contact with the group should be considered tentatively, however, because it is difficult to predict how an ongoing group is likely to react to a new worker. The worker may also want to observe the group before attempting to intervene.

The worker's presence in a previously formed group will cause adjustments. A process of accommodation to the new worker and assimilation of the worker into the culture of the group will occur. In general, cohesive and autonomous groups that have functioned together for some time will find it difficult to accommodate a new worker and will expect the worker to become assimilated into the ongoing process of the group. For example, a worker from a neighborhood center who is interested in working with a closely knit gang of adolescents who grew up together may have to spend a considerable amount of time developing trust and rapport with the group before members will seriously consider participating in a recreational activity at the neighborhood center.

Defining the Purpose of the Group

Opening Statement

After introductions, the worker should make a brief statement about the group's purpose and the worker's function in the group. When members are not clear about the purpose of the group or the motives of the worker, their anxiety increases and they are less likely to become involved in working toward group goals. Evidence suggests that workers often fail to define the purposes of the group they are leading (Fuhriman & Burlingame, 1994). Even if the purpose has been explained to members during pregroup intake interviews, the worker should be sure to restate the purpose during the first meeting.

Helping the Group Define Its Purpose

- Construct a brief statement of purpose and clearly articulate it to the group
- Present the purpose as a positive statement that includes what members can accomplish
- When possible, have members present and discuss their views of the group's purpose, especially when orienting new members to the group
- Discuss the role of the group in relation to its sponsoring agency, stressing the mutual contributions that can be made by both the group and the agency
- Involve members by asking for feedback and use this feedback to refine or modify the purpose

The group's purpose should be presented in as positive a way as possible. Frank (1961) and other cognitive psychologists have pointed out the importance of persuasion, expectancy, and placebo effects in psychotherapy. These factors are also present in group work practice. Presenting a positive, hopeful image of what can be accomplished in the group makes use of the beneficial effects of these cognitive expectancies. Rather than focusing on members' problems or concerns, the worker can express the group's purpose in terms of the goals to be accomplished. Thus, statements that focus on positive objectives and goals, such as "Through this group experience you can learn to . . . " "You can stop . . . " or

"Through all of our efforts in this task force we can . . . " are preferable to statements that focus on the negative aspects of problems or concerns.

If the worker has successfully led a previous group that focused on similar concerns, the worker can mention this success. In treatment groups, such a statement by the leader offers members the hope that the group will help them to achieve their goals. In task groups, members are more likely to be motivated and to persist in goal achievement.

In open-ended treatment groups where new members replace old ones, it is often helpful to have those who have been in the group for some time state how the group has been helpful to them. Professional group workers can learn from the way that self-help groups such as Alcoholics Anonymous and Recovery Incorporated rely on the testimony of successful members as a major component of their group program. In task groups, members who have had some experience in the group can be asked to orient new members.

The opening statement about the group's purpose should include a brief description of the functions of the agency sponsoring the group. In treatment groups, the opening statement should define the limits of service so that members will have a clear notion of what services they can expect and what services are beyond the scope of the agency. There is nothing more frustrating for members than having their expectations go unfulfilled. The opening statement should include a brief statement about how the worker will help the members to accomplish their goals.

In task groups, relating the agency's function and mission to the group's purpose helps members understand why they were called together to participate in the group. The opening statement allows members to see how the agency's functions are related to the group's task. It is not uncommon, for example, for members of task groups to ask about how the results of their work will be used. Task group members may be interested, for example, in the extent to which their group can make permanent changes in policies, procedures, and practices through its findings and recommendations.

Involving Members

The opening statement focuses the group on considering the purposes for meeting. It should be presented as a starting point for further discussion rather than as an immutable definition that is not open to negotiation, modification, or change. Attempting to impose a definition of the group without input from members tends to reduce members' commitment and motivation and to increase members suspicions that their autonomy is threatened.

The stated purposes and goals should be broad enough that members can formulate their own purposes and their own goals (Northen, 1969). This does not mean that the worker's opening statement should be so broad that almost any purpose or goal can be contained within it. Statements about improving members' social functioning or coping ability may be too abstract for members to comprehend. Opening statements should be presented in clear, jargon-free language. However, the leader should avoid being overly specific. Instead, the worker should solicit members' ideas and suggestions about how to operationalize particular purposes and goals.

Open communication, particularly when it may conflict with the purposes or goals articulated by the worker, is often difficult to achieve. In the beginning stage, members are reluctant to risk their own tentative position within the group or to express opinions that may differ from those expressed by the worker or other members. Therefore, in addition to providing members with opportunities to express their opinions and concerns regarding the group's purpose and goals, the worker should reach out for members' input.

This can be done in a variety of ways. First, the worker should state clearly that the group is meant to serve the needs of its members, who ultimately determine the group's purpose and goals. Members can then be asked to state their own purposes and goals and to comment on the broad purposes and goals articulated by the worker. During this process, workers can encourage feedback by taking comments seriously and praising the members for sharing their feelings and thoughts.

● **CASE EXAMPLE**   *A Mandated Group for Men who Batter*

During the opening statement the worker mentioned that one of the primary goals of the group was to help the men in the group control their tempers. The worker asked the members what else they wanted to accomplish. This was first met by silence. The worker did not say anything and after a couple of minutes, one member stated that he wanted to get back together with his girlfriend. Another member began to talk about how he had done things that he regretted, and wanted to "make things right." At the same time, several members said that they felt backed into a corner by their partners and finally "exploded" and that they had tried to get out of the situation but their partner kept at them. The worker acknowledged these statements and indicated that the group was there to give them the tools to help them deal with these situations.

Members can sense whether the worker's call for feedback is genuine or perfunctory. If the worker makes a continuous effort to solicit feedback by encouraging all members to express their thoughts and feelings, members are more likely to feel that their input is welcome. For example, members can be asked to make a statement about how the group's purposes and goals meet their needs and to suggest how the group could be improved.

Confidentiality

In treatment groups and certain task groups, it is important for the worker to lead a discussion of confidentiality during the opening portion of the group meeting. This will be the first time that many of the members may have been asked to keep the proceedings of a group meeting confidential. Therefore, it is important for workers to emphasize the need for confidentiality and the harmful and destructive effects that can result when breaches occur. Trust among group members is essential for cohesion and the smooth functioning of the group. When workers reassure members that the group is a safe haven, a place where they can discuss emotionally charged issues in confidence and without fear of reprisal, trust deepens and cohesion develops. In treatment groups, members are often concerned about how information they share with the group will be used outside the group meeting by the worker and other group members. Members cannot be expected to disclose intimate concerns or develop a sense of trust unless they can be assured that discussions within the group will not be shared outside of meetings. It can be helpful to remind members about the confidentiality of meetings periodically throughout the life of the group. This is particularly important in residential settings because frequent interaction outside the group may promote violations of confidentiality.

As mentioned in Chapter 1, in some cases, the worker may be obligated to share information discussed in the group with law-enforcement officials. Workers are also likely to share information with supervisors and with fellow staff members during treatment conferences. Therefore, workers have an ethical obligation to be clear about the limits of confidentiality and with whom and under what circumstances data may be shared.

Confidentiality is also an important issue in many task groups. Members are often unsure about what issues, proposals, and facts can be shared with colleagues and others outside of the group. Because sensitive personal information is usually not discussed in task groups it is especially important for the leader to mention if the content of group meetings should be kept confidential, or if it can be shared with others outside the group to get their input.

● CASE EXAMPLE   *A State-Level Task Force*

A state-level task force designed to study ways to improve services to older people trying to live independently in the community deliberated for six months about a single-point-of-entry system that could be used to assess all individuals who might need long-term care services in the community or in a nursing home. The leader of the task force emphasized the confidential nature of the proceedings, letting members know that premature or partial release of the information discussed in the task force could hinder its work and upset various stakeholders who now screened older people for long-term care services. The worker emphasized that the report of the task force was advisory only and would not be released until it was approved after extensive deliberation and hearings by the legislature and the governor's office.

The time set aside for the discussion of confidentiality also provides an ideal opportunity for the worker to bring related value issues to the attention of the group. For example, the worker might engage the group in a discussion of how social group work values such as democratic participation, respect for the individuality of each member, self-determination, cooperation and mutual decision making, and the importance of individual initiative will be operationalized in the group. Depending on the type of group, workers might also talk about the problems that may arise when group members form intimate relationships outside of group meetings. These dangers include (1) distraction from the group's purpose, (2) side conversations, alliances, and other effects of being a couple on group dynamics, and (3) dealing with conflict and the breakup of relationships that developed in earlier group sessions.

It is helpful for the worker to assist the group in formulating a set of principles—a code of behavior for its operation—to which each member agrees to adhere. These are sometimes referred to as *group rules*. For example, members might agree to the following group rules.

Group Rules

- Come to the group on time
- Give the worker prior notice if I am unable to attend
- Listen without interruption when another group member is talking
- Avoid dominating the group discussion
- Be respectful of each other's thoughts and feelings
- Be sincere and honest when communicating thoughts and feelings
- Make positive, cooperative, helpful, and trustworthy contributions in response to each other's comments

Group rules should not be imposed unilaterally by the worker. Instead, members should help formulate the rules so that they take ownership of them.

Helping Members Feel a Part of the Group

When a group begins, there is little sense of belonging or cohesion. An important objective for the worker during the beginning stage is to help a diverse collection of individuals, who may be apprehensive and ambivalent, begin to identify themselves as a collective of supportive partners in a common enterprise. The worker aims to build cohesion while respecting individuality. To achieve this objective in early meetings, it is important to help members feel safe and comfortable in the group. Given a pregroup assessment of each member, the worker is in the best position to ensure that the demands of participating in the group do not exceed members' abilities. Thus, workers may tone down expectations for intimate disclosures suggested by a member or scale down unrealistic expectations about what can be accomplished in a given time frame.

To help members feel that they are a part of the group, it is a good practice to point out shared interests and common goals among members. Members are comforted by the familiar. Knowing that they are not alone with their concerns or issues helps them to feel closer to other participants in the group.

Pointing out commonalities does not mean the worker should overlook differences, however. The leader can use several techniques to help members acknowledge and begin to appreciate differences in the beginning stage of the group. The leader can point out the contributions that different backgrounds and different perspectives make to the group and can encourage members to explore differences and welcome new perspectives. The leader can ask nonthreatening, direct questions that help members explore, understand, and appreciate the different perspectives that are presented within the group.

The leader can also use program activities or exercises to help members explore differences in an entertaining and lively fashion. For example, a leader might help the group plan a dinner to which members would bring a dish representative of their culture, ethnicity, or nationality. Another activity is for each member to design a coat of arms that represents something about their personal background and to present the coat of arms to the group for discussion. The leader might also ask each member to create a "self-disclosure collage" that artistically represents elements of themselves not known to other members of the group. Overall, differences among members in their backgrounds and life experiences should be neither magnified nor ignored. Instead, the worker's task is to help members appreciate and respect differences.

The worker also helps members feel that they are a part of the group by protecting them from injury. Thus, misinformation should be corrected, and personal attacks should not be condoned. Also, the worker should continually scan the group to ensure that the content of the meeting is not having an adverse emotional effect on members.

Guiding the Development of the Group

Different theoretical writings suggest a range of possibilities for guiding the development of a group. Some writers suggest that the worker should provide little or no direction at the beginning of a group and prefer an approach that encourages members of the group to struggle with purposes and goals until mutual agreements about them can be achieved

(Klein, 1970). Unstructured approaches to group beginnings are often used in t-groups and other growth groups where the purpose of meeting is to learn about group dynamics and one's own interpersonal interaction style. The process of struggling to develop purposes and goals without any direction from the leader, however, is often anxiety provoking. Therefore, workers should be cautious about using unstructured approaches with members who are not functioning at optimal levels, when time to achieve particular outcomes is limited, and when exploration of one's interpersonal style is not a primary goal.

Other writers suggest that techniques to guide the development of the group should be used only to empower members to make democratic decisions and to actualize the purposes and goals that members, rather than leaders, have agreed to accomplish (Hopps & Pinderhughes, 1999). For example, in describing a humanistic approach to group work, Glassman and Kates (1990) suggest that the workers use techniques "in shaping the group members' processes of interaction and self-expression" (p. 121), but take care not to manipulate, coerce, or control members. A humanistic approach to leadership during the beginning stage is especially appropriate in support groups, social action groups, and coalitions in which the empowerment of members and the mobilization of their collective energy and wisdom are primary goals. However, elements of a humanistic approach, such as respect for the dignity and individuality of each member and belief in each member's potential for growth and development, are essential in all group work efforts.

Writers within the humanistic tradition point out that techniques such as "directing" and making a "demand for work" can help members develop and implement mutually agreed-on purposes (Gitterman & Shulman, 2005; Glassman & Kates, 1990; Hopps & Pinderhughes, 1999; Shulman, 1999). Yet, few writers within the humanistic tradition spend time addressing issues of limit setting and socialization in groups of severely impaired individuals and in groups with members who have been ordered into treatment because of delinquent or criminal behavior. Clearly, however, there are many practice situations in which the sponsoring organization and the larger society expect that workers will use their authority to help members function as more productive members of society. Yalom (1983), for example, points out the need for limit setting and a clear structure when working with psychiatric inpatients. Similarly, Levine and Gallogly (1985) suggest methods for dealing with challenges to the worker's authority when working with groups of alcoholics in inpatient and outpatient settings.

In many practice settings, short-term groups, such as social skills and life skills training groups for psychiatric inpatients, groups to help new parents learn parenting skills, assertion training groups, and anger control groups, are offered because workers have specific information and specific skills they think will benefit members. In these groups, the worker is designated by society and the sponsoring organization as an expert who provides direction and structure so that the members can learn new skills. Of course, even in these groups, members should have the opportunity to shape individual goals, group goals, and meeting agendas and to share their concerns and learn from one another.

An example of a session agenda for a time-limited, structured, parenting group is presented in Figure 7.1. The agenda provides the organizing framework for the first meeting. It indicates the goals for the session, the material to be covered during the group meeting, and the reading assignments and tasks required of each parent during the following week. Similar session agendas are prepared by the worker for each of the 10 sessions in the time-limited parenting group.

In structured, time-limited groups, it is quite common for the agenda to be developed before the group session. As compared with less structured, process-centered approaches,

FIGURE 7.1 ● *Sample Session Agenda for a Time-Limited, Structured Parenting Group*

AGENDA

Date_____

Session I

Goals

By the end of this session, each parent will be able to

1. Describe the purpose of the group program
2. State how behavior is learned
3. Describe specifically one behavior of his or her child
4. State the behavior he/she will monitor during the next week
5. Describe how each behavior will be monitored

Agenda

1. Introduction
   A. Leader introduces self to group
   B. Each member introduces self to group (name, number of children, current problems you would like to work on)
2. Orientation to the group program
   A. Purpose of the group session
      1. Goals
      2. Why should parents be trained in parenting skills?
      3. Who is responsible for what?
   B. Group contracts—read, modify, sign
3. Introduction to behavior modification—lecture
   A. Behavior is learned
      1. Reinforcement
      2. Extinction
      3. Punishment
   B. Role-play demonstration
4. Break
5. Assessment
   A. Discussion of behavior checklist
   B. Describe one behavior of your child
   C. Develop monitoring plan: what, who, how, when
6. Buddy system
   A. Description
   B. Choose buddy, exchange numbers, arrange calling time
7. Assignment
   A. Monitor chosen behavior and begin to chart it
   B. Call buddy
   C. Read units 1 and 2 (exercises at the end of each chapter are optional)
8. Evaluation

structured group approaches give the worker greater responsibility for group goals and the way the group conducts its work (Papell & Rothman, 1980). Although in process-centered approaches members are encouraged to take informal leadership roles and develop their own goals, agendas, and contracts, in time-limited groups the members' input is generally limited to modifying goals, agendas, and contracts that the worker has already developed.

Bauer and McBride (2003); Bieling, McCabe and Antony (2006); Budman, Soldz, Demby, Davis, and Merry (1993); McKay and Paleg (1992); Passi (1998); Rose (1989, 1998); Shapiro and colleagues (1998); White and Freeman (2000); and others describe a variety of time-limited, structured groups for acquiring skills, managing anxiety, coping with life transitions, and learning parenting skills. These groups usually meet for 6 to 16 meetings. Meetings usually contain a mixture of (1) educational material; (2) exercises, role play, and simulations to help members practice the material; (3) discussion of the material and the problems members are experiencing outside the group; (4) a brief period to go over weekly assignments for members to do outside the group; and (5) an evaluation of the meeting.

Because they focus on educating members and on providing emotional support, these groups are sometimes referred to as *psychoeducational* treatment groups. Psychoeducational groups are an increasingly popular and important source of help for many clients (Bieling, McCabe, & Antony, 2006). Perhaps the greatest asset of these groups is that they provide a planned framework that can be replicated intact or modified and adapted to fit different types of client groups. For example, a worker who decides there is a need for a social skills training group in a particular setting can use the framework presented by Rose (1989) to lead this type of time-limited, structured group. Other agendas for psychoeducational groups appear in Drum and Knott (1977); Asher-Svanum (1991); and Bauer and McBride (2003).

Studies about the efficacy of group work found that groups with specific purposes, homogeneous concerns, clear agendas, and structured group meetings were more effective than groups with less structure (Bauer & McBride, 2003; Budman, Simeone, Reilly, & Demby, 1994). Members reported appreciating that the leader provided specific information and effective strategies to help them with their concerns as the next case example illustrates.

● CASE EXAMPLE *A Healthy Heart Group in a Medical Setting*

A medical social worker decided to form a group for patients who had recently undergone heart bypass surgery. Family members were invited. This six session weekly group meeting was structured so that there was a speaker followed by a discussion period. Topics included nutrition, diet, exercise, keeping a positive mood, engaging in sexual activity, and other lifestyle issues, such as a moderation in drinking alcoholic beverages, and stress reduction techniques. After the speaker's presentation, each meeting provided the members with a chance to talk about their specific concerns and issues and to practice stress reduction techniques.

Workers should keep in mind that members' concerns and needs are not always most appropriately served by a time-limited, structured group approach. In support groups, for example, a flexible structure that maximized member input was found to be more effective than was a structured approach in helping members to ventilate their concerns and to give and receive help from fellow group members (Toseland, Decker, & Bliesner, 1979; Toseland & Hacker, 1982; Toseland, Sherman, & Bliven, 1981). In these groups, members were encouraged to reach out to one another as much as possible. Goals and specific agendas for each meeting were determined on the basis of feedback and mutual agreement among all members during meetings.

It is unfortunate that there is not more dialogue between authors who promote short-term, structured, behavioral, and task-centered approaches to treatment groups and authors who promote long-term, process-oriented, humanistic approaches. Authors who promote one approach over another often fail to acknowledge the value of alternative approaches, actively dismiss important contributions of alternative approaches, and ignore the core skills that form the base for all group work. It is the thesis of this text that both approaches have much to offer and that social work practice situations fall along a continuum. At the ends of the continuum, pure approaches may be effectively applied, but in most practice situations, a blending of approaches makes the most sense. Structure should be viewed as a tool to be used differentially in practice situations to help members and the group as a whole achieve agreed-on objectives.

Structure in Task Groups

Written agendas are frequently used in task groups to keep groups focused on the work that is to be accomplished. Figure 7.2 is an example of an agenda for a meeting of a delegate council. In this example, it is standard procedure to follow the agenda listed here.

Meeting Agenda Outline

- Approve the minutes of the previous meeting
- Call for new agenda items
- Announcements
- Receive reports from standing committees and administrative officers
- Work on current business
- Discuss any new agenda items that might have been introduced earlier in the group meeting
- Adjourn

Agenda items can be divided into three categories: information, discussion, and action. Often, agendas are accompanied by attachments to explain the agenda items. Agendas with their attachments are usually given to all group members several days before the meeting so they can become familiar with the business that will be discussed during the meeting.

In task groups, feedback is encouraged in several ways. Members might be encouraged to submit formal agenda items before group meetings. The items are then placed on the agenda. When the item is considered by the group, it is often helpful for the member who submitted the item to present it to the group. During meetings, members' feedback is usually limited to a discussion of the specific task or agenda item currently being discussed. Members have a chance to add new agenda items during a meeting only if the group's predetermined order of business can be concluded in time to discuss new business at the end of the meeting.

FIGURE 7.2 ● *Sample Agenda for a Delegate Council*

Meeting date _____

CYPRUS HILLS DELEGATE COUNCIL

Order of Business

	Information	Discussion	Action
1. Call to order			X
2. Approval of the minutes of the previous meeting			X
3. Call for new agenda item			X
4. Announcements	X		
5. Treasurer's report	X		
6. Program committee's report	X		
7. Director's report	X		
8. Emergency housing proposal		X	
9. Proposed changes in bylaws (see attachment A)			X
10. Election of members of the women's issues task force (see attachment B for slate of candidates)		X	
11. Proposal to develop an ad hoc committee on community health care		X	
12. New business		X	

Task and Socioemotional Focus

Another objective of the worker in the beginning stage is to balance the task and socioemotional aspects of the group process. Through systematic observation of leadership training groups, committees, juries, classes, therapy groups, and labor relations teams, Bales (1950) established a set of 12 categories to describe group interactions. Half the categories are in problem-solving or task-focused areas, and the other half pertain to socioemotional areas. Bales' scheme for observing a group is instructive because it points out that in all groups the worker must be conscious of both the task and socioemotional aspects of group process.

In task groups, it has been found that about two thirds of group interactions are focused on task accomplishment and one third on socioemotional aspects, such as giving support and releasing tension (Bales, 1955). Evidence concerning treatment groups suggests that they often spend more time on socioemotional aspects than on task-focused discussion (Munzer & Greenwald, 1957). Despite the difference in emphasis, pioneering studies by Bales (1950, 1955) and more recent studies by other researchers (Forsyth, 2006) suggest that in both task and treatment groups, neither the task nor the socioemotional aspects of group process can be neglected. An exclusive focus on tasks in any group may lead to members' dissatisfaction with their social and emotional interaction in the group. Focusing exclusively on tasks can lead to conflict among members and may result in a less effective group.

An exclusive focus on the social and emotional aspects of group interaction leads to a group whose members will be satisfied with their relationships with one another but will be dissatisfied about what has been accomplished. Thus, a balance between the task and the socioemotional aspects of group process is essential. No magic formula exists for achieving the appropriate balance between task and socioemotional aspects of the group. Only through a careful assessment of group and member needs, can the worker determine the appropriate balance.

Goal Setting in Group Work

In the first few meetings, groups often spend a considerable amount of time discussing goals. When the worker discusses the group's purposes, the process of goal formulation begins. Goals emerge from the interaction of individual members, the worker, and the system in which the group functions.

Workers' goals are influenced by the values and aims of the social work profession. As members of social service organizations, workers are aware of the aims and the limitations of the services they provide. Workers should also be cognizant of their function in the larger society, which sanctions and supports their work. Workers' formulation of goals reflects what they believe can be accomplished with the support, resources, and limitations within the environment where the group operates.

Workers' goals also are affected by what they know about the group members. In treatment groups, workers often have an opportunity to meet each member during the planning stage. Potential members are selected, in part, because of their compatibility with the purposes and goals developed for the group. Workers make preliminary assessments of members' needs and the capacities of each group member, as well as the tasks that face them. Goals are formulated on the basis of the assessment process.

In task groups, a similar process occurs. Goals are formulated by the worker in relation to the charge of the group from the sponsoring organization and the roles and status of the members who compose the task group. The following case example of a task group illustrates that the roles and the status of committee members limits their ability to make binding recommendations.

CASE EXAMPLE *Task Group to Examine Interdepartmental Coordination.*

A worker is charged with leading a committee to examine interdepartmental coordination of client services. Representatives from various departments throughout the agency are represented, but not the department heads. The committee meets a number of times and comes up with a series of goals and recommendations for better coordination. However, given the status and the roles of the members of the committee, the recommendations about improving coordination between departments are not adopted. Instead, a report is prepared and sent to the executive committee of the agency for additional action, because the members of the committee do not have the authority to implement the recommendations without approval from top level management.

Goals are formulated by individual group members who have their own perspective on the particular concerns, problems, and issues that affect them and their fellow group members. In previously formed or natural groups, members have the advantage of knowing more than the worker does about the concerns of the other group members.

In formed groups in which members do not know each other before the first group meeting, members' goals are based on a variety of factors.

Factors Affecting Members' Goals

- An assessment of their own needs
- Their previous attempts to accomplish a particular goal
- The environmental, social, and familial demands placed upon them
- Their assessment of their own capacities and capabilities
- Their impressions or experiences of what the social service agency sponsoring the group has to offer

Goals for the group are formulated through a process of exploration and negotiation in which the worker and the group members share their perspectives. In this process, members and the worker should communicate openly about the goals they have formulated individually.

The extent to which common goals can be developed for all group members varies from group to group. In some groups, members have one, overriding concern in common. For example, a group of cigarette smokers suffering from chronic lung disease may be able to move quickly to a discussion of a specific contract to reduce cigarette smoking. In groups that are more diverse, such as outpatients in a mental health setting, it is often more difficult to develop common goals. In these groups, common goals are often formulated on a general level, for example, to improve the interpersonal social skills of members. Goals for individuals in the group are formulated at a more specific level. For example, an individual goal might be "To improve my skills when confronting others about behaviors I find unacceptable."

The process of goal setting, therefore, is one in which the goals of the worker and the members are explored and clarified. Three types of goals emerge from this process: (1) group-centered goals that focus on the proper functioning and maintenance of the group; (2) common group goals that focus on the problems, concerns, and tasks faced by all group members; and (3) individual goals that focus on the specific concerns of each group member. In an educational treatment group for parents of young children, a group-centered goal might be to increase the group's attraction for its members. A common group goal might call for the parents to learn about the normal growth and development patterns of young children. An individual goal for the parents of one child might be to reduce their son's temper tantrums.

In task groups, three levels of goals can also be identified. For example, in a committee mandated to review intake procedures in a family service agency, a group-centered goal might be to establish open, member-centered interaction patterns. A common group goal might be to make several recommendations to the program director to improve admission procedures. An individual goal for a committee member might be to interview workers in two other agencies about different approaches to intake procedures that can be shared with the committee at the next meeting.

The worker should help members develop clear, specific goals. Early in the process, members formulate general goals they would like to achieve. Examples include statements such as "I would like to be less depressed" or "The group should try to reduce the paperwork involved in serving our clients."

After members have stated their goals for the group, workers can help to clarify them and make them as specific as possible. Workers help members identify objective and subjective indicators of their goals and the criteria that will be used to evaluate them. The case example on page 209 illustrates this process.

Defining goals clearly helps both workers and members focus on what they are attempting to achieve in the group. Developing clear goals is a prerequisite for entering the middle stage of group work. Before goals can be prioritized and a contract between worker and members developed, goals should be stated as clearly as possible. All members should have input into the development of goals and an opportunity to influence the direction the group will take to accomplish them.

● **CASE EXAMPLE** *Clarifying Goals and the Criteria for Evaluating Them*

For the goal statement "I would like to be less depressed," a member might be helped by the worker and the other group members to define indicators of depression such as sleeplessness, lack of appetite, lack of energy, depressed affect, and so forth. The worker can then lead the group's efforts to help the member identify criteria that would indicate goal achievement. For the depressed member this might include: (1) sleeping through the night and not waking up early in the morning, (2) eating three meals a day, (3) having the energy to do things, and (4) smiling and laughing more often.

In previously formed groups with preexisting goals, the worker has a different role in goal formulation. In some groups, goals may not have been clearly defined, and the worker's task is to help members clarify their goals. This is often the case with groups of teenagers and children who have not carefully considered their goals. In other previously formed groups, clear goals may exist. The worker's task in these groups is to help members achieve the goals that can be accomplished and modify or abandon those that are not likely to be achieved.

Achieving consensus about purposes and goals can be particularly difficult with involuntary members who are often pressured into participating in a group. Still, there is usually some common ground on which mutually agreed-on goals can be developed. For example, youthful offenders are sometimes given the choice of participating in group treatment or being sentenced through the juvenile court system. The worker can begin by stating the conditions and standards for continued participation and then encourage members to develop their own goals within these minimally acceptable conditions and standards. Trust takes longer to develop in such groups, but if the worker consistently shows interest in the members' goals, concerns, and aspirations, the group can be a useful treatment modality (Bauer & McBride, 2003).

Contracting

In group work, *contracts* are mutual agreements that specify expectations, obligations, and duties. The types of contracts that can be developed are presented in the following list. Contracts involving the group as a whole are usually developed around group procedures. Individual members' contracts are usually developed around individual treatment goals or individual task assignments.

Types of Contracts

- The group as a whole and the agency
- The group as a whole and the worker
- The worker and the group member
- Two or more group members
- The group as a whole and a member

The most common form of an individual-member contract is between a member and the worker. For example, a member may contract with the worker to stop smoking, to become more assertive, or to make more friends.

Contracts can also be developed between two or more group members to help each other achieve particular goals. For example, in an assertiveness training group, one member might decide to practice being assertive in two situations during the group meeting and in one situation during the week. The member may ask another member to praise her if she is assertive in the group and to telephone her during the week to see if she has been assertive in a situation outside the group. In return, she agrees to help the other member achieve a particular goal.

A third form of individual contracting occurs between a member and the group. The member, for example, can agree to obtain information about a resource for the group or can promise to report back to the group about the results of a particular meeting. In a cohesive group, member-to-group contracts can be quite effective because members do not want to let each other down by failing to follow through on the contract.

When contracting with individual members for goals or tasks, it is important to be as specific as possible about formulating behaviorally specific outcome goals. Goals specified in a written or verbal contract should state briefly who will do what, under what circumstances, and how results will be measured. The following examples contain outcome goals for a treatment group and a task group:

Examples of Outcome Goals

Treatment Group (to help members stop smoking)

Who:	Mary Jane
Will do what:	will refuse the offer of a cigarette
Under what circumstances:	when it is offered at a social gathering
How will it be measured:	and will report this offer to the group.

Who:	John Franks
Will do what:	will smoke less than three cigarettes
Under what circumstances:	at home, during each day of next week
How will it be measured:	as reported by spouse.

Task Group (committee to study juvenile crime)

Who:	Bill Evans
Will do what:	will interview the local family court judge
Under what circumstances:	prior to the next meeting
How will it be measured:	and prepare a written report for the committee.

Who:	Ann Murphy
Will do what:	will read five articles on juvenile crime
Under what circumstances:	within the next two weeks
How will it be measured:	and report significant findings to the committee.

Facilitating Members' Motivation

After an initial clarification of the purposes and goals of the group, the worker helps members increase their motivation for accomplishing the goals that have been mutually agreed on. Motivation is the key to the successful achievement of group and member goals. To a large extent, such motivation is determined by members' expectations about (1) the worker's role in the group, (2) the processes that will occur in the group, and (3) what can be accomplished through the work of the group. Members bring a set of expectations to any group experience, and the expectations have a powerful influence on the way the members behave in the group. For example, if a member expects the worker to tell him or her how to proceed, it is unlikely that the member will take much initiative in the group. If the member has been involved in a previous group experience in which little was accomplished, the member's expectations and motivations to work hard to achieve individual and group goals are likely to be diminished.

As the worker and the members begin to explore how they can work together, the worker should help members identify their expectations and motivations. The worker can do this by asking members direct questions about what they think they can accomplish in the group and how they expect the group to function. These questions often uncover ambivalence about giving up old ways of doing things and fear about what new and unknown changes may bring.

Addressing Ambivalence and Resistance

Sometimes members respond evasively to direct questions about their motivations and expectations, particularly when the worker has made an early and clear "demand for work" before assessing members' expectations and motivations (Schwartz, 1971, p. 11). Members may be reluctant to state ambivalent feelings about their ability to accomplish the goals for which they have contracted because they fear that the worker will disapprove. Mandated clients may not be prepared to acknowledge problems others have identified. The following list summarizes some techniques for dealing with ambivalence and resistance.

Addressing Ambivalence and Resistance in the Group

- Pay attention to overt and covert messages about accomplishing the group's work
- Acknowledge members' ambivalence and provide a realistic appraisal of members' chances for accomplishing successful change
- Help members work through their ambivalence and resistance
- Assist members to recognize the range of choices they have for participating in the group
- Help members work with each other to recognize where points of resistance may occur and to overcome challenges to their full participation

Before the worker states expectations about what members need to do to accomplish their goals, the worker should notice the overt and covert messages members give about accomplishing the group's work. If the worker picks up signals indicating a lack of motivation to accomplish goals, the worker should check the perception of the meaning of the message with the group members.

Ambivalent feelings about change are common and should not be viewed as an obstacle to accomplishing the group's work. It is rare for changes to be proposed and worked on without ambivalent feelings, and it is often difficult and painful to change problematic areas of one's life. At the very least, it requires giving up the security of old ways of doing things. Rather than ignoring, playing down, or attacking the ambivalence, workers should help members work through it. Acknowledging members' ambivalence is a helpful way to get members to recognize their reactions to change. A frank discussion of a member's ambivalence about change and the perceived ability to achieve a goal helps all members see that this is a common reaction to the changes they are planning to make. Also, a realistic appraisal of the chances for success is much preferred to covering up barriers to task achievement.

One exercise that can help uncover ambivalence is to have each member focus on a goal and list psychological, social, and environmental factors that hinder and promote its achievement. A variation on this exercise done with individual clients has been called "force field analysis" (Egan, 2002). In task groups, all members focus on one group goal. In treatment groups, it is more common for members to focus on one member's goal, but occasionally it is possible to select a common group goal on which to focus. The exercise can be done by all group members, in pairs, or at home between sessions.

In a force field analysis, the worker helps members list on paper or a blackboard the positive and negative aspects of attaining a goal and displays the results before all group members. This process facilitates an organized discussion of the factors that can help members achieve goals and the factors that may hinder them. Such a visual display helps members realize, often with surprise, that, despite their verbal assertions about achieving a goal, many factors may be detracting from their motivation.

An example of a list of positive and negative factors that could influence a group member's decision is shown in Figure 7.3. The decision involves whether the member should separate from her husband. An examination of a list of factors can help group members decide whether there are sufficient positive motivations for achieving a particular goal.

If a member reaches a decision to pursue a goal despite numerous factors that reduce motivation, the task of the worker and the other group members is to suggest ways to decrease the negative factors and increase the positive factors. For example, in the situation in Figure 7.3, the member decides to separate from her husband. To change some of the factors that reduce her motivation, the group helps the member to (1) overcome her fear about the effects of the separation on her children by suggesting that the children may be harmed more by seeing Mom and Dad constantly fighting than by experiencing their parents' separation; (2) examine her finances, her plans for child care, and other practical needs that she may have as she considers living independently; and (3) build her self-confidence and self-esteem by providing support and positive feedback during the separation process. Through this process, the group helps the member become motivated to achieve her goal with as little ambivalence, fear, and anguish as possible.

In some groups, workers encounter members who feel pressured or coerced into coming to the group. Members who feel pressured or coerced often are not ready to engage in the work of the group. They may delay or obstruct other members' work.

In an excellent text on dealing with resistant group members, Edelwich and Brodsky (1992) suggest that, in such a situation, the worker can point out that the members chose to participate in the group. Although some individuals may have chosen to participate in the group to avoid other less desirable choices, that choice was an agreement made with a referring agency. For example, in the case of being found guilty of driving while intoxicated, the member may have agreed to participate in a group treatment program instead of losing his driver's license. The worker should acknowledge that the member may not want to be in the group, but also note that the person freely chose the group over an alternative. The worker should also state that members are free to terminate their participation at any

FIGURE 7.3 ● Analysis of Factors that Increase and Decrease the Motivation of a Member of a Treatment Group

Problem: Whether to separate from my husband

Factors Increasing Motivation	Factors Decreasing Motivation
1. Tom drinks too much.	1. Concern about what breaking up will do to the kids.
2. Tom has been physically abusive twice in the last year.	2. Worried about whether I can live on only my salary.
3. There is almost daily verbal conflict between Tom and me.	3. Wonder if I can care for three kids and keep working 40 hours a week.
4. Staying in the relationship causes me to feel angry and depressed.	4. Feeling as if I would be breaking my commitment to Tom.
5. My relationship is interfering with the quality of my work at my job.	5. I'll have to explain the separation to my parents, friends, etc.
6. Tom and I have infrequent sexual relations.	
7. The kids are being affected by our constant fighting.	

time, but their decision to participate implies that they will adhere to the group norms and contractual obligations agreed to during the intake interview or the first group session.

As the group progresses, it may be necessary to remind members that it was their choice to participate rather than experience a serious consequence such as going to jail or being put on probation. The group also needs to help reluctant and resistant members to find reasons to participate. For example, the leader can encourage members to help each other to figure out what is positive and negative about their current lifestyle, and what they want to change. Then, members can decide how they want the group to support them and help them to accomplish these changes. It can also be helpful for the worker to use "I" statements while making a clear demand for work (Edelwich & Brodsky, 1992).

● CASE EXAMPLE *Use of "I" Statements*

I have a problem. Some of you don't seem to want to be here. If you don't want to be here, you don't have to be here. I don't want you to get the wrong impression—I'd rather you stay. But if you don't like being in the group, you can take it up with the agency that sent you and deal with the consequences of not continuing your participation. My job is to help you use your time in this group productively. Therefore, I would like those of you who choose to stay to think now about how you will use the group—what you want to accomplish. Think about the problems and issues in your life and what you'd like to work on in this group. I'll give you a few minutes. Then, let's go around and see what we can do together. I suggest that we begin the go-round by saying what we like and do not like about our current lifestyles, and what changes we want to make. Then later, we can focus on creating a plan to make these changes, and how the group can help you to accomplish the changes you want to make.

Expectations about Role Performance

In addition to ambivalence about changing a way of doing things, members often are concerned at the beginning of the group that they will not be able to contribute in the way they think is expected of them. For example, members of a committee may think they will be asked to do too much to prepare for group meetings or they may fear they have nothing to contribute. Similarly, members of educational groups are often apprehensive about their ability to learn new material, and members of support groups are fearful that members will not understand or share their concerns. Because expectations about role performance can interfere with a member's participation in the group, it is helpful for workers to describe their expectations of members and solicit feedback and input. Role clarification is a key leader skill in working with mandated clients (Trotter, 1999). This process provides a forum for members to air their fears about the challenges they face. It also helps clarify any mistaken or distorted expectations that members may have and provides an opportunity for workers to modify or change their own expectations.

Role clarification also helps members to understand the dual role of the worker as an agent of social control as well as a helper (Trotter, 1999). With respect to members' behavior in and outside of the group, the worker can clarify what is negotiable and what is not negotiable. Workers can also help members to think about their own expectations versus the expectations held by other constituencies, such as the referral source that suggested members attend the group as an alternative to a harsher punishment, the worker, the member's family, and so forth. Clarifying roles in this way can create greater empathy and understanding, and ensure that all parties are clear about what goals are shared in common, and what goals are not. Work can then proceed on the basis of tackling shared goals. The worker might also discuss the consequences, if any, of not working on the goal expectations of the referring agency, the worker, or the member's family. This helps to clarify the choices members are making and the likely consequences in their lives.

Authentic Communication about Purposes and Goals

Ambivalence about changing and fears about the demands that may be placed on them may lead members to be less than candid in early group meetings. Shulman (1999) points out that members of treatment groups may begin by sharing "near" problems "that do not bear directly on some of the more difficult and hard-to-talk-about issues" (p. 348). In task groups, members may bring up peripheral issues that could potentially sidetrack the group.

To increase authentic communication as the group develops, the worker can take several steps:

- Always treat members' suggestions and ideas about how to proceed with respect. The worker should not dismiss or ignore what a member says or treat it as a "smoke screen" or a "red herring." This will only alienate members and certainly will not encourage them to open up and reveal more meaningful issues. Instead, the worker should strive to understand the deeper issues implied by the member's message.

- Link the member's statements with the larger purposes of the group. The worker can do this by asking members how the suggestions or ideas fit in with the agreed-on purposes of the group.

- Place the relevant parts of the member's message in the context of themes or issues that have been previously discussed in the group.

- Support the initiative the member demonstrated by speaking up without endorsing the message. Statements such as "I'm glad to see that you are thinking about what you want to accomplish in the group" or "I'm happy to see that you care enough about the direction of the group to make that suggestion" let members know that their perspectives are welcome and valued without indicating that the worker supports the content of the message.

Promoting Prosocial Behaviors

Trotter (1999) also points out that it is important to promote prosocial behavior when working with mandated clients. He suggests doing this by (1) pointing out prosocial comments made during group interaction, (2) praising prosocial comments, suggesting that others emulate these comments, and rewarding prosocial comments in other ways, (3) acting as a model by using problem solving skills and coping skills that are prosocial, and (4) identifying and challenging antisocial or procriminal comments or behaviors. Prosocial comments can be rewarded, for example, by sending a note to members' probation officers about how well they are doing in the group. Members can also be encouraged to discuss their attempts at engaging in prosocial behaviors between meetings, the successfulness of these attempts, and obstacles to engaging in prosocial behaviors outside of the group.

Working with Involuntary Clients

There are many situations where group workers are called upon to work with involuntary clients who are mandated to attend groups. Involuntary clients are those that are pressured or required to attend a group in lieu of some worse punishment such as going to jail, losing a license, or as a condition of probation. Involuntary clients may also be those who are forced into a group by a school system, a therapeutic community, or some other entity with the notion that it will do them some good to participate. In these latter situations, the consequences of not following through by attending the group may not be clear, although the members know that they simply have to attend the group. Involuntary and mandated clients put workers in an awkward position, because they are being asked to help members make changes that they may not want to make.

One of the first steps in working with involuntary clients is to assess their readiness for change. Prochaska, DiClimente, and Norcross (1992) have developed a five part model of change (1) pre-contemplation, (2) contemplation, (3) preparation, (4) action, and (5) maintenance. Mandated clients often start off in the pre-contemplation stage which may take on many forms. According to Goldstein (2001), there are reluctant pre-contemplators who do not want to consider change because they do not have sufficient information about what change might mean or simply because of inertia. There are also rebellious pre-contemplators who are motivated to avoid change and maintain the status quo. This may because of peer pressure or fear that change will make things even worse for them. There are resigned pre-contemplators who have given up hope that change is possible. They are demoralized and lack the energy to make changes. There are also rationalizing pre-contemplators who either do not see the problem, or who view the problem as a problem for someone else but not for them. When working with groups of mandated clients, the worker should carefully assess whether group members are reluctant, rebellious, resigned, or rationalizing pre-contemplators. Reluctant pre-contemplators may simply need information or a heightened sense of the consequences of their actions to move to the next stage of change. Rebellious pre-contemplators actively resist change because of peer pressure or feeling that their lifestyle is the better alternative. Resigned pre-contemplators are those who have tried and failed. They lack the motivation and the feelings of self-efficacy to do anything about their situation. Rationalizing pre-contemplators are those that blame others for their problems. Although each of these group members may respond to somewhat different approaches, there are some common strategies that the worker can use to help all members of mandated groups begin to make changes.

In order to determine where members are at on the continuum of change, the worker can start by asking members about how they feel about attending the group and what they hope to get out of it. By reflective and skillful listening the worker seeks to understand members' feelings without being judgmental, critical, or blaming (Miller & Rollnick, 2002). Rooney and Chovanec (2004) point out that in the early stages of the group the members may express their hostility at the worker. The worker should not be put off by this but instead may want to make statements early in the group that acknowledge the members' feelings about being pressured or coerced to attend, and their wary noncommittal approach to the group. The worker should also look for non-verbal signs about the members' motivation. Peer pressure, despair, hopelessness, and other factors that hold members back from even contemplating change may not come out directly, but are often expressed in silence or rebelliousness. Workers who are aware of these non-verbal cues should acknowledge them, feeding them back to the members of the group, and letting them know that the worker is aware of their feelings. The worker should avoid arguing or disputing what members are saying verbally and non-verbally, and instead should roll with the resistance, acknowledging it and letting the members know that they are at best ambivalent about their participation and at worst unwilling participants in the change process (Miller & Rollnick, 2002).

After acknowledging the resistance to change, the worker has to figure out what can motivate members to engage in the work of the group. There is no easy way to accomplish this and for each member the motivation may come from different sources. Miller and Rollnick (2002) suggest trying to develop a discrepancy between members' current behaviors and their long-term personal goals. The problem in some groups is that members have not thought about their long-range goals, or their long-range goals have become distorted by dysfunctional home lives and impoverished neighborhood environments. Poverty, despair, abuse, and neglect are often the root causes of these problems. Peer pressure, repeated failure, a lack of self-efficacy, or other issues may work against developing the discrepancy between current dysfunctional behavior patterns and the positive long-range goals that the worker is seeking to help members achieve. When this is the case, the worker should acknowledge these issues with empathy and concern. The worker should show a genuine concern for members' long-term well-being and realistically mention some of the consequences of continuing on the same path of dysfunctional behavior. Members may not buy into the worker's view, so a portion of the group's time may need to be spent on acknowledging these feelings and asking members to discuss their own world view and to describe where they think their current patterns of behavior will lead. Although at first members may rage against persons, situations, or systems that are unfair, gradually the worker can reframe the discussion into how they can negotiate the system and get what they need to live better lives. This type of discussion can heighten the discrepancy between the members' current behavior and what they want to achieve for themselves in the future.

Gradually, the worker sets expectations for the group but at the same time tries to maximize choice and minimize demand, helping the members themselves come up with what they would like to do in the group (Welo, 2001). Rooney (1992) points out that it is helpful to provide some choice and to point out what is and is not mandated. By pointing out the choices that the members have, the worker identifies what choices members have within these choices, and lets members know that it is in their own best interest to use their time in the group to accomplish something of value to themselves. Members have to be able to see that change is not only possible, but within their ability to reach. At some point during this process, it can be helpful for the worker to bring a guest speaker to the group with whom the members can identify. By relating his or her story about being a mandated client and overcoming obstacles to change, the speaker may help members see a path out of their current situation and open possibilities that the members may not have contemplated. The worker may also have some members in the group further along on the change continuum those who are actively contemplating change, or who are willing to take some action. The worker can help these members become a catalyst for the other members of the group who are still in the pre-contemplation stage, helping those in the contemplation or action stage to talk about their motivation for change and what steps they are willing to take toward change, and encouraging and praising them for their efforts.

Those who work with involuntary and mandated clients should recognize that change does not come easily or without setbacks. Working with involuntary clients is one of the most difficult challenges a worker can face, but seeing members becoming motivated to make changes is also one of the most rewarding experiences a worker can have. The worker should keep in mind that change has to come from within each member and that the worker's role is to foster a group climate where members can feel comfortable enough to talk about and begin to attain their aspirations for themselves. External incentives such as getting a driving license back, getting out of therapeutic community sooner, or reduced probation time will not lead to change over the long-term unless the members can see a better future for themselves, and develop the feelings of self-efficacy that are necessary for them to become self-motivated. The worker can be ready by being empathic about the difficulties the members' face but at the same time offering the encouragement and the resources that are needed to help motivate members to make a better life for themselves. For more about working with mandated clients see Goldstein (2001); Miller and Rollnick, (2002); Rooney (1992); Rooney and Chovanec (2004); and Welo (2001) and Chapter 9 of this text.

Anticipating Obstacles

In the beginning stage of group work, it is important for workers to help members anticipate the obstacles they may encounter as they work on specific goals and objectives. It is useful to ask members to describe the obstacles they foresee in accomplishing individual and group goals. Sometimes it is useful to encourage members to engage in a time-projection program activity. In this exercise, members are asked to imagine what it will be like for them at the end of the group when they have accomplished their goals. Members can be encouraged to discuss how changes brought about in the group are likely to be received by those around them and to focus on what might prevent accomplishments in the group from being implemented in settings outside the group. As members share potential impediments to long-term, meaningful change, the worker can facilitate a discussion about overcoming the impediments.

Experience suggests that when members and the leader are aware of potential obstacles, they can often plan ways to overcome them before the middle stage of the group. Chapter 9 describes a variety of methods that can be used during the middle stage of a group to help members overcome obstacles to accomplishing specific goals.

SUMMARY

Although all aspects of group work are important for the successful functioning of a group, the initial stage sets the tone for the group's future development. In the beginning stage, the worker's central task is to ensure that a group develops patterns of relating and patterns of task accomplishment that facilitate functioning as the group moves toward its middle stage of development.

To accomplish this, workers should focus on achieving certain objectives in the beginning stage of task and treatment groups. These include (1) introducing members of the group; (2) clarifying the purpose and function of the group as it is perceived by the worker, the members, and the sponsoring organization; (3) clarifying confidentiality issues; (4) helping members feel a part of the group; (5) guiding the development of the group; (6) balancing task and socioemotional aspects of the group process; (7) setting goals; (8) contracting for work; (9) facilitating members' motivation and ability to work in the group; (10) addressing ambivalence and resistance; and (11) anticipating obstacles.

Workers who are able to help their groups achieve these objectives in the initial stage will find themselves in a good position to help the group make a smooth transition to the middle stage of development. Any objectives that are not achieved early in the group's development will have to be reconsidered later as the group and its members encounter difficulties accomplishing agreed-on goals.

● CASE EXAMPLE

At first, Drew felt enthusiastic about being assigned to lead a group called "the Lunch Bunch." His enthusiasm was tempered when his field instructor told him that it would be composed of 10 fourth- and fifth-grade boys who were suspended from the school lunchroom because of acting-out behavior. The purposes of the group were to help members learn acceptable ways of dealing with their peers and to reintegrate each member into the main lunchroom milieu.

In addition to having no control over the composition of the group, Drew was concerned about what might happen when all of the "offending parties" would come together for the first session. He interviewed each of the members assigned to the group to introduce himself, to learn about their expectations, and to begin to orient them to the group's purposes and goals. During the interviews he learned that various members were suspended from the lunchroom because they fought with other students

and expressed their anger in inappropriate ways such as yelling, cursing, and throwing food. Most of the youngsters he met seemed to act appropriately during the initial interview and appeared enthusiastic about meeting with the Lunch Bunch.

On the day of the first session, Drew came prepared. In addition to a written agenda, name tags, art supplies, and some CDs for music, he brought chocolate chip cookies, hoping that after members ate their lunch, dessert would be an incentive for them to act appropriately until the group ended. As members entered, most seemed to know each other from classes. Drew chose to help members introduce themselves by playing a version of "Top Secret" in which each member wrote down something about himself that others would not ordinarily know. He read what each boy had written, and they had fun trying to figure out who had written each statement. Drew felt that this activity was moderately successful because it helped the members get involved with the group right away.

Next, Drew made an opening statement about the purpose of the group. He was careful to word the statement of purpose so that the boys could understand it and so that it gave them some guidance about what would happen in the group. He noted that the group's purpose was "to work together to learn safer ways of handling yourselves in the lunchroom, and to have fun while learning." Two of the members stated that they thought the group was like detention and was punishment for their behavior. Drew clarified that it was true that their behavior had gotten them referred to the group, but that the group was not punishment. He noted that both he and the members could plan some of the activities, and these would take into account what members wanted to do during group sessions. The boys seemed skeptical about this, so Drew asked for more discussion. He clarified that his role was to help them explore how to act with each other and to help them plan for activities in the group.

One of the most difficult discussions that took place early in the first session concerned confidentiality. One member wanted to know if Drew was going to tell the principal or his parents about what he might say or do in the group. Drew recognized that many of the boys frequently interacted with each other in settings outside the group, and this could easily compromise any promises of confidentiality. In addition, Drew was responsible for reporting the progress of members to his field instructor and, ultimately, to the school principal. Drew mentioned these two issues to the members and suggested a few ground rules about confidentiality that the group might discuss at their next meeting. He suggested that it would be appropriate for members to discuss aspects of his participation with his parents, but members should not refer to group members by name. He emphasized that under no circumstances should members talk to other students about what went on inside the group. Finally, Drew said that he had to report on each member's progress to his field instructor, but that he would try to share what he would say with each boy individually before he discussed it with his field instructor.

After this, the group started to work on other rules for how the group should operate. During the first session, they agreed that they should all be good listeners, should wait their turn before speaking, and should try to help each other. Drew was satisfied that, in the time allotted, the group seemed to be making some progress on formulating a beginning contract. He suggested that members might think of other rules for the group and could bring these up in the next meeting.

Drew recognized that the time allotted for this first session was running out and he wanted to provide the members with a fun experience before they left to return to their classes. During the remaining time, they played some music from Drew's collection. Drew asked members what they felt after listening to each song. This discussion was difficult for some of the members because they were not familiar with some of Drew's musical selections. Drew suggested that members could bring in some of their favorite music for the next session. The members received this news with enthusiasm. Drew said that when a member brought in a favorite musical selection, his responsibility would be to ask other members to identify what they felt after listening to it. Chocolate chip cookies for dessert tempered this early "demand for work."

Assessment

Because of the complexity of human behavior and group dynamics, assessment is one of the most challenging aspects of group work practice. The worker makes assessments to understand particular practice situations and to plan effective interventions. For a complete and thorough assessment, the group worker considers (1) individual group members, (2) the group as a whole, and (3) the group's environment. Workers begin their assessments during the planning stage and continue to assess and reassess the group's work until the group ends.

Although assessments are made in all stages of a group's life, the process dominates a worker's time in the beginning phase of group work. It is at this time that the worker is most actively engaged in understanding the functioning of the group and its members.

DEFINITION OF ASSESSMENT

Siporin (1975) has stated, "assessment is both a process and a product upon which the helping process is based" (p. 219). As a process, assessment involves gathering, organizing, and making judgments about information. As a product, assessment is a verbal or written statement of the functioning of the group and its members, which is useful in the development of intervention plans.

In this text, the term *assessment* rather than *diagnosis* is used because assessment is more compatible with a generalist approach to social group work practice. *Diagnosis* is a term borrowed from medicine. It refers to the identification of disease processes within an individual. In contrast, a thorough generalist assessment focuses on both the strengths and the problems encountered by individual group members and the group as a whole and carefully considers the effect of the larger social environment on the group and its members. This text also takes a holistic perspective, focusing on the biological, psychological, social, cultural, spiritual, and environmental functioning of the members of the group.

As with other aspects of social group work practice, assessment varies according to the type of group being conducted. In a treatment group, for example, the worker frequently focuses assessments on the problems experienced by individual members, but a task group leader's assessment is often focused on the ability of members to contribute to the group's productivity.

Despite differences in focus, there are many commonalities in the assessments made by workers leading different types of groups. For example, in both task and treatment groups, most workers assess the strengths and weaknesses of the group as a whole, the members, and the external environment in which the group and its members function. Commonalities also can be found in the assessment of different groups that are at the same stage of development. For example, in the beginning stage, workers make a systematic assessment of the functioning of the group and its members. During the middle stage, workers test the validity of their initial assessments and modify their intervention plans on the basis of the success of early interventions. In the ending stage of the group, the worker makes an assessment of the functioning of the group and its members to highlight accomplishments, to focus attention on areas that still need work, and to ensure that achievements accomplished during the group will be maintained after the group ends.

Relationship to Individual Assessment

Most readers are familiar with generalist social work practice approaches that rely on systems theory and take a holistic approach to assessment (Johnson, 2004; Kirst-Ashman & Hull, 1999). Using a generalist approach, group workers are supposed to assess individual members, the group as a whole, and the group in relation to its environment. In practice, however, there is a tendency for group workers to focus on individual members rather than on the processes of group interaction or the group in relation to its environment. This may be because many group workers were originally trained as caseworkers and have more experience working with individuals than with groups. Also, some workers do not have any formal education in group work. Data from analyses of the content and style of group leaders confirm the lack of focus on group dynamics (Hill, 1965; Toseland, Rossiter, Peak, & Hill, 1990). For example, Hill found that, on average, leaders spent less than 5 percent of their time on matters pertaining to dynamics of the group as a whole.

We strongly recommend that group workers be especially vigilant about spending time during each group meeting to discuss group processes. This can often be accomplished by making a conscious effort to point out processes in the here-and-now of group interaction. Sometimes, however, stopping the action to identify, clarify, or discuss group processes can be disruptive to the content being discussed. An effective alternative is to reserve a few minutes at the end of each group meeting for the worker and members to comment on and discuss the group processes. For example, a member might state that there seemed to be much member-to-member communication during the group meeting, that the discussion included only a few members, or that members did not seem to be considering the points of view of others. Similarly, the worker might comment on the norms developing in the group or the roles that members were playing. The members can then be encouraged to discuss what changes, if any, they would like to make in the group dynamics during future meetings.

If a separate time is set aside for discussing group process at the end of a meeting, care should be taken not to use the time to discuss content. It is easy to slip into discussions of content when group processes are being discussed. For example, during a discussion of group interaction patterns, two members might note that the entire session was spent focused on one member's problem. Another member might say, "John talked a lot because he is having a lot of problems with his wife." The worker should point out that the issue is not John's problem with his wife, but whether the group wants to spend an entire session focused on one member's concern. The worker can then guide the group to a discussion of the pros and cons of focusing on one member for an entire session.

With the exception of social action groups and coalitions, workers often fail to pay much attention to the group's broader environment. Periodically throughout the life of a group, workers and members should take time to describe and discuss their perceptions of the relationship of the group to the sponsoring organization and to the larger community that sanctions the group's work.

Overall, assessment in group work is more complex than assessment in practice with individuals. In addition to assessing the functioning of individual group members, assessment in group work also means examining the processes that take place in the group as a whole and the support and opposition the group as a whole is likely to encounter in the larger social environment.

THE ASSESSMENT PROCESS

Fisher (1978) has aptly described assessment as a funneling process. In the early stages, the worker is confronted with amorphous and sketchy data about the group and its members. Initially, the worker fills in gaps by collecting missing data. As information is collected, the worker begins to sort through it and organize it systematically. The group members should be involved as much as possible in collecting and analyzing the data. This will help them to formulate goals and decide on targets for intervention.

Gradually, the assessment process narrows as data are collected and organized and judgments are made about how to intervene in, cope with, or alleviate a problem. In a group for people getting a divorce, for example, the worker asked members to describe their feelings about their spouses. Information gathered from this preliminary assessment leads the worker to a further assessment of members' feelings of loss and anger toward their spouses.

● **CASE EXAMPLE** *A Group of People Getting Divorced*

Seeing that the members found it difficult to talk about how hard it was for them to deal with feelings about their spouses, the worker decided to do a group go-round, asking each member in turn to talk about their predominant feelings toward their spouse. Once the group go-round was completed, the worker helped the members to talk about the feelings that they shared in common and how they were dealing with them. Members began to realize that they were not alone with the feelings they were having. They then began to talk about some ways to cope with their feelings and move beyond them. For extra support, members decided to exchange telephone numbers so that they could talk about their emotional reactions between group meetings.

How Much Information?

Several issues arise when workers assess the functioning of the group and its members. One of the most basic issues is how much information to collect. Although it is often recommended that workers collect as much information as possible (psychosocial histories for members of treatment groups or extensive information-gathering efforts in task groups), increasing information beyond a certain point may not lead to more effective goal achievement. Also, workers are sometimes confronted with urgent situations that preclude extensive data collection. In these situations, workers should be guided by goals formulated during the planning and the beginning stages of group work. Workers also should be as clear as possible about the relevance of the information being collected. Extensive data collection that has little relation to the group's goals is a violation of members' right to privacy and of dubious value for accomplishing group and individual member goals.

No matter how much information is collected, workers should suspend their judgments about a problematic situation until they have reflected on all the data they have time to collect. A widespread and potentially damaging mistake of novice workers occurs when they make judgments and offer suggestions concerning intervention strategies before they fully understand a problem or have found out what the member has already done about it. When making premature suggestions, the novice is often confronted by a group member who says, "I tried that and it didn't work." The result is that the worker is at a loss as to how to proceed, and the member's faith in the worker's ability to help is shaken.

Some helpful principles to guide workers in their data-collection efforts follow.

Principles of Data Collection

- Use more than one mode of data collection whenever possible.
- Distinguish between the problem, concern, or task about which information is being collected and the source of the information.
- Obtain relevant samples of data from several sources.
- Structure data collection so that relevant information can be obtained quickly and efficiently.
- Develop a system that will not place overwhelming demands on persons who are collecting information or on persons who are asked for information.
- Avoid biasing data despite the selectivity and subjectivity that are inherent parts of any effort at data collection and assessment.
- Involve all group members in the assessment process so that multiple viewpoints can help overcome limitations of the worker's subjectivity.
- Discuss assessment data with a coleader or a supervisor between meetings.

Diagnostic Labels

Another issue that often arises when one makes assessments of the members of treatment groups is the use of diagnostic classification systems and labels. Diagnostic classification systems can be helpful in making differential assessments and arriving at effective treatment plans for group members. Classification systems such as the *Diagnostic and Statistical Manual of Mental Disorders* (DSM) are used in many mental health settings for assessment, intervention, and reimbursement purposes (American Psychiatric Association, 2000). Previous versions of the DSM were criticized as unreliable and irrelevant in relation to the selection of intervention procedures (Hersen & Bellack, 1976). However, the latest version (DSM-IV-TR) appears to overcome many of the earlier problems.

Diagnostic labels can carry social stigma. Members of a group may be at risk for harmful stereotyping when diagnostic labels are used indiscriminately. Also, members may start to behave in ways that are consistent with the labels ascribed to them (Kirk & Kutchins, 1999). Therefore, group work practitioners should be wary of the indiscriminate use of diagnostic labels in mental health and other settings. Although an in-depth examination of the applications of the DSM to group treatment is beyond the scope of this text, the following case example may help illustrate its usefulness.

● **CASE EXAMPLE**   *The Diagnostic and Statistical Manual (DSM)*

A 71-year-old man was misdiagnosed as having an organic brain syndrome. The diagnosis was based solely on the symptoms of confusion and disorientation that he exhibited. Based on that diagnosis it was recommended that the man participate in a reality orientation group and an activity group designed for persons with Alzheimer's disease and other dementias. However, a more extensive assessment using criteria from the DSM revealed that the person was actually suffering from major depression compounded by isolation and malnutrition. Given this diagnosis, a quite different form of group treatment was recommended after the person's malnutrition had been treated. For example, the person was encouraged to attend a therapy group for people suffering from problems of depression and he was encouraged to expand personal friendship networks by becoming involved in an activity group at a senior center and at a social group at a church.

Assessment Focus

A third issue that often arises in making an assessment is how to focus data-collection efforts. Workers should avoid becoming locked into one assessment focus. Premature allegiance to a particular view of a situation can result in ignoring important data or attempting to fit all data into a particular conceptualization of the situation.

Kottler (2001) points out that almost all mental health professionals use the DSM in their work, even if they do not subscribe to the underlying assumptions of the medical model when people are labeled with diagnoses using the DSM. They do so for billing purposes and because the DSM enables group workers to communicate with others using a common language and also to be held accountable for clinical decisions based on assessing and intervening with individual members of a group. However, Kottler (2001) also points out that there are other assessment approaches that are valuable. For example, in a developmental assessment process the worker is looking not for pathology or problems but rather for the current developmental functioning of a group member and where it places them in relationship to others at a given age or life situation. Thus in a developmental assessment, the leader is looking at whether a person has reached an appropriate developmental level for their age, and whether they are ready to move to and take on the tasks associated with the next developmental stage in their lives.

Kottler (2001) points out that behavioral assessments can be useful because they do not label pathology or what is normative during a particular developmental stage but rather what specific maladaptive behaviors need to be changed. Two other assessment models should also be kept in mind by leaders in the early stages of group work. One is to make a careful assessment of members' strengths and resiliency. Taking this kind of empowerment approach takes the focus off of members' pathology and maladaptive behaviors and instead clearly focuses it on members' existing coping skills and what they bring to a situation to help them overcome the issues and problems they may face. Also, it is important to keep in mind a systemic assessment of situations, focusing on the context of problems and issues that group members face and what the larger environment contributes to these problems. Therefore, although the DSM is widely used as a diagnostic tool, group workers should keep in mind that other assessment approaches are equally valid and may be more helpful than simply labeling a person with a particular disorder.

In focusing their assessments, workers should be guided by the unique needs and particular circumstances of each member and by the purposes of the group. In one group, for example, it may be important to focus on members' family situations, but in another group, it may be more beneficial to assess members' problem-solving skills. In other words, the focus of assessment should change with the changing needs of the group and its members.

To make an accurate assessment, workers should strive for objectivity. Although all observations contain some subjectivity, it is important to separate subjective impressions and opinions from more objective observations of behavior and events. Inferences should be based on logic and evidence.

It can also be helpful to share observations and inferences with group members. They can confirm the validity of the worker's observations and inferences and provide an alternative perspective. It is also helpful to check the validity of subjective inferences with supervisors. Obtaining alternative perspectives in this manner can help the worker make assessments and formulate intervention plans.

ASSESSING THE FUNCTIONING OF GROUP MEMBERS

During the assessment process, the worker should consider the current functioning of the members and, whenever possible, also examine members' functioning from a developmental perspective. A developmental perspective can help the worker assess whether a member's current functioning manifests itself in a transitory, acute pattern of behavior or a long-term, chronic pattern of behavior. It also helps the worker gain a greater understanding of the meaning of symptoms and their intensity, duration, and scope. Overall, assessments are more likely to be accurate and complete if the developmental context in which members' problems have developed are considered.

Workers should also assess how the personal characteristics of each member interact with their functional abilities. Personal characteristics such as racial and cultural identity, gender, and age have an important influence on how members interact with their one another in the group. For example, in working with groups of Native Americans, the worker should be aware of the cultural norm of withholding opinions about other people because of deep respect for the privacy of others and a tradition of noninterference (Good Tracks, 1973). When assessing members' behaviors and characteristics in a culturally sensitive way, a characteristic such as noninterference is viewed as a strength rather than as a limitation.

When making an assessment, workers should examine three broad aspects of members' functioning:

1. The intrapersonal life of the member
2. The interpersonal interactions of the member
3. The environment in which the member functions

In assessing members' intrapersonal lives, workers rely on their own observations, members' self-reports, and collateral reports. To examine members' intrapersonal functioning, the worker may focus on members' perceived health status; psychological and emotional well-being; and their cognition, beliefs, motivations, and expectations.

When assessing interpersonal functioning, workers focus on members' social skills, the extent and quality of their social support networks, and their role performance. The group provides a natural laboratory for the worker to observe the interpersonal functioning of each member, but it is also helpful to inquire about a member's interpersonal interactions with family and close friends because these relationships often have a significant effect on the member.

Workers should also examine the environmental context in which members function. Questions such as "Is the environment supportive or does it hinder members' ability to work on group and individual goals?" and "What resources can members draw on from their environment to help them achieve their goals?" are often pertinent.

In task groups, workers will also find it useful to assess the intrapersonal, interpersonal, and environmental functioning of members, but with a different focus. For example, leaders of task groups generally do not make in-depth assessments of members' physical, psychological, or emotional states. However, they are likely to examine a member's motivation for attending and the member's expectations about accomplishing the work of the group. Similarly, a task group leader would be unlikely to assess the extent to which members' families support their work in the group. The leader is more likely to consider what effect a controversial committee report might have on members' day-to-day interactions with their colleagues or on their interaction with the line staff they supervise.

Methods for Assessing Group Members

A variety of methods exists to help workers assess the functioning of group members. Among the most commonly used methods for assessing functioning are (1) members' self-observations, (2) worker observations, (3) reports by others who have seen the member function outside the group, and (4) standardized assessment instruments.

Self-Observation

Self-observation refers to members' examination and assessment of their own behavior. Usually, members simply recall and describe their own behavior, then examine and reflect on it with the help of the worker and other group members. Woods and Hollis (1990) referred to this process as "exploration-description-ventilation" (p. 115) and as "reflective discussion of the person-situation configuration" (pp. 124–134).

Retrospective self-observation and self-reflection are often helpful in developing insight about one's behavior, identifying patterns of behavior, and examining the effect of the environment. However, members' recollections may not be accurate; for a variety of reasons, recollections may be incomplete, vague, or distorted. Therefore, other methods of self-observation, such as self-monitoring, have been developed.

Because these methods are more intrusive and require more effort on the part of the member than simply recalling and reflecting on past behavior, workers should be sure that members are motivated to try the methods and have sufficient resources to implement them successfully. Workers should be aware that self-monitoring methods often presume members to be action oriented, insightful, and sensitive; thus, the methods may not be useful for all members.

SELF-MONITORING.   Rather than relying on memory of past events, members may examine their own behavior outside the group in a prospective and systematic fashion by collecting data on the frequency, intensity, and duration of a particular behavior and its antecedents and consequences. This process is often referred to as *self-monitoring*. An assessment of a particular behavior and its antecedents and consequences can be useful in determining how particular problematic behaviors are maintained.

Awareness of behavior patterns is a prerequisite for changing behavior. For example, an assessment of the antecedents of the anxiety that a member experiences in social situations may reveal that the statements the member tells himself about his lack of anything interesting to say trigger his anxiety.

Some evidence indicates that self-monitoring can be reactive; that is, the act of self-monitoring may by itself increase desired behaviors and decrease undesired behaviors (Stuart, 1977; Thoresen & Mahoney, 1974). However, self-monitoring can also have therapeutic and empowering benefits by heightening members' awareness of their current behavior patterns (Kopp, 1993).

To begin self-monitoring, the worker should be sure that members are motivated to examine their own behavior and to record it. Then the worker should help members decide exactly what they are going to monitor. It is often helpful to have members monitor behaviors they would like to increase as well as behaviors they would like to decrease. This process can help members to replace problematic behaviors with desired ones, rather than only reducing problematic behaviors.

In deciding what to monitor, workers should help members determine what is feasible and realistic, given their life circumstances. Members often want to collect data about several problematic behaviors at the same time. However, members are rarely able to follow through on such ambitious plans. Therefore, initially, members should be encouraged to develop realistic plans that they can readily accomplish. Later, they may wish to develop more ambitious monitoring plans.

In deciding on a realistic plan, it should be clear where, when, and under what conditions a particular behavior will be monitored. For example, it is unrealistic for a single parent with four children to expect to monitor the behavior of one child just before dinner or in the morning when the children are preparing for school. However, there may be time during the afternoon or evening when the parent can observe the child's behavior for a short period without being interrupted.

In most groups, members make a mental note of what they have observed between meetings, and they share their observations with other members during the next group meeting. Because it is sometimes difficult for members to accurately recall the data they have monitored, methods for recording self-monitored data have been developed. These methods include charts, logs, diaries, problem cards, and self-anchored rating scales.

Charting.   Some members find it useful to record monitored data on a chart because it provides an organized, visual display of the information. A chart allows members to see trends in the data—that is, whether a behavior is increasing or decreasing. It also may serve as a reminder for members to perform tasks that they agreed to complete between meetings. For an example of charting, see the following case example.

● **CASE EXAMPLE** *Charting*

During the early sessions of an assertiveness training group for single parents, members were encouraged to discuss examples of their behavior they would classify as unassertive. Members identified instances of how difficult it was for them to be assertive in work and social situations. The group worker asked members to chart their behavior outside of the group, concentrating on recording the frequency of their nonassertive behavior. Members charted incidents each day, for two weeks. After that, the worker helped members to review their "problem" behaviors and convert these into "positive" goal statements, leading to the establishment of individual goals for members.

Workers should help members be creative in designing charts. For example, in helping a parent develop a monitoring chart that will be shared with a young child, the worker can suggest using smiley faces, stars, or hearts instead of check marks to signify that a behavior was performed correctly.

The format of a chart depends on the method used to collect self-monitoring data. The simplest format uses a tally to measure the frequency of a behavior. More complicated formats are sometimes used to get an accurate assessment of the frequency of a behavior without having to count each occurrence. A chart divided into a number of time intervals can be used to count behaviors. For example, members can count the number of occurrences of a behavior in 10-minute intervals between 6 P.M. and 7 P.M. every evening. Charts can also be made that allow a member to record whether a behavior occurred at particular intervals during a designated period, such as at the beginning of every 30-minute time interval. For further discussion of methods to chart self-monitored data, see Bloom, Fisher, and Orme (2003) or Thoresen and Mahoney (1974).

Members sometimes fail to follow through on charting self-monitored behaviors. For some, charting may require too much organization. Others find it inconvenient to monitor and record their behavior immediately after it occurs. Members sometimes prefer one of the methods described in the following sections.

Logs and Diaries.   Logs and diaries are often less accurate than monitoring charts because members rely on their memory of events to record behaviors at some convenient time *after* they occur rather than *as* they occur. However, because of their convenience, members sometimes prefer keeping a log or diary to keeping a chart.

Logs and diaries require members to record events in a descriptive fashion and can be a valuable source of qualitative data for the worker to gain valuable insights into the world of each member. Logs and diaries can also be used to help the worker understand other data reported in quantitative self-observations. To avoid logs and diaries that become too idiosyncratic, the worker can give members a clear indication of what data they are to record. For example, a worker may ask members to record problematic situations and their immediate cognitive, affective, and behavioral responses to situations. For examples of logs and diaries and more information about how to use them, see Bloom and colleagues (2003).

Problem Card.   A variation on logs and diaries is the problem card (Rose, 1981). Group members are asked to fill in one or more problem cards between meetings. On each card, the member is asked to describe briefly a problem experienced between sessions that is relevant to the group's theme. The member is also asked to choose from within the group a judge or rater who is willing to assess the member's progress. At intervals throughout the group's life, the judges are asked to rate group members' progress in ameliorating problematic behavior. Because of the evaluation component, the problem card procedure can be used for both assessments and evaluations.

Self-Anchored Rating Scales.   Members can also record their observations by using a self-anchored rating scale. This is a measurement device made by the worker and a group member specifically to record data about a problematic behavior that has been identified as the target of an intervention. To develop a self-anchored rating scale, the worker helps a group member identify behaviors, feelings, and thoughts that are associated with various levels of the problematic behavior. For example, in developing a scale to measure depression, a member suggests that severe depression occurs when he has suicidal thoughts and does not eat or sleep. Moderate depression occurs when he has thoughts that he is not a good father or husband, when he has little appetite and eats only one meal a day, and when he falls asleep only after lying awake for a long time. The member suggests that he is not depressed when he has a good appetite, can sleep well, and has thoughts that he is a good father and husband. An example of a self-anchored scale to rate depression is shown in Figure 8.1 For further information about developing self-anchored rating scales, see Bloom and colleagues (2003).

Worker Observation

Workers can assess the functioning of group members by observing them during meetings. In most practice situations, workers rely on naturalistic observations. However, specific activities such as simulations and program activities to assess members' functioning in a particular area can also be used.

NATURALISTIC OBSERVATION.   As demonstrated in the following case example, workers can learn a great deal about members by observing their behavior in the group. Given free interaction within the group, members often display behaviors similar to behaviors exhibited outside the group. By scanning the group, the worker can stay aware of the reactions of all group members. The worker observes a member behaving in a certain manner, for example, and makes a mental note. Further observation, over time, helps the worker identify the member's behavior patterns and typical coping styles.

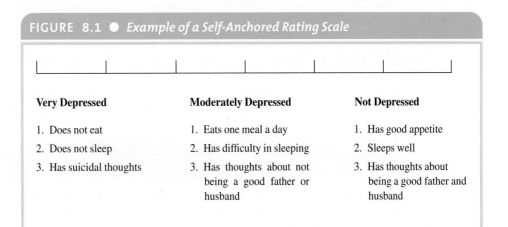

FIGURE 8.1 ● *Example of a Self-Anchored Rating Scale*

Very Depressed	Moderately Depressed	Not Depressed
1. Does not eat	1. Eats one meal a day	1. Has good appetite
2. Does not sleep	2. Has difficulty in sleeping	2. Sleeps well
3. Has suicidal thoughts	3. Has thoughts about not being a good father or husband	3. Has thoughts about being a good father and husband

---

● **CASE EXAMPLE** *Naturalistic Observation*

The leader of a group to teach employment skills to teens spent the initial sessions of the group observing how members demonstrated interpersonal skills. Using these naturalistic observations, the worker was able to point out the interpersonal strengths of each member and how these could be used during the job seeking process. The leader also asked members to give each other feedback, concentrating on identifying positive interpersonal skills that could be useful. Using these assessment techniques, members were able to identify their strengths and work on skills that needed strengthening. Later in the group, the leader asked members to practice these skills by assigning role playing exercises that simulated the employment interview situation.

As the group develops, members can be asked to describe their behavior. This feedback can be used to determine whether members' self-perceptions are consistent with the worker's observations. The worker may also solicit other members' observations and reactions. The process of formulating an assessment on the basis of observations and perceptions of more than one individual is often referred to as *triangulation*. Triangulation can lead to assessments that are more accurate than assessments made by a single individual.

Although naturalistic observation offers the worker an opportunity to observe members' behavior in an unobtrusive fashion, its chief limitation is that group interaction may not offer the right opportunities to assess pertinent aspects of a member's behavior. For example, in a parenting skills group, a parent may describe how she sets limits on her child's behavior, but group interaction does not provide the worker with an opportunity to view the parent actually setting limits.

In addition, experience suggests that members may not always give accurate or sufficiently detailed accounts of their behavior. When the worker can actually observe the member engaging in a behavior such as limit setting, for example, the worker may find that the member does not set limits in the way that is stated. For example, a member may appear angrier or more threatening than her self-report would indicate. Therefore, the worker may find other methods useful when observing members' behavior.

ROLE PLAYING.   Role playing, sociodrama, and psychodrama are as important for assessment as for intervention. They allow the worker and the other members of the group to observe a member acting out a situation. Role-play methods are described in detail in Chapter 13.

SIMULATIONS.   Simulations assess members' functioning in specific, predetermined role-play situations. The worker asks for one or more volunteers to simulate a specific, real life situation. Simulations are developed by workers to teach particular skills. The member whose behavior is being assessed is asked to respond to the situation enacted by the volunteers as they would if they were confronted with the situation in their everyday lives.

● **CASE EXAMPLE** *Creating a Simulated Situation in an Assertiveness Training Group*

In an assertion training group, three members are asked to volunteer to role play standing in a line at a grocery store. The member whose behavior is being assessed is asked to stand at the end of the line. Then, another volunteer is asked to try to get ahead of the member who is in line when he is looking at a magazine in a rack next to the checkout counter. The worker and the other members observe how the member handles the situation both verbally and non-verbally and give the member feedback. The situation can be role played again with the same member or with additional members for additional practice using the improved strategies.

Simulations can be developed for many other situations. For example, in a parenting group, a simulation may involve having two members play the role of siblings in an argument about who gets to play with a toy truck. The parent whose behavior is being assessed is asked to act as she would if such a situation occurred in her home and the other members of the group can give their feedback about the way the parent handled the situation, and alternative ways of responding.

Assessments of a member's behavior during a simulation can be made by all group members. Scales to rate a member's response can be developed specifically for the objectives and goals of a particular group. For example, in an assertiveness training group in which all group members are trying to reduce their anxiety and improve their responses, ratings may focus on (1) the anxiety level that a member demonstrates while making a response, and (2) the effectiveness of a response in asserting the member's rights in the situation.

Simulations have been developed for many different populations. New simulations can be developed by using the model described by Goldfried and D'Zurilla (1969). This model includes (1) analyzing a problematic situation and developing several realistic situations that members are likely to confront in their daily lives, (2) enumerating possible responses to these situations, (3) evaluating the responses in terms of their efficacy in handling the problematic situation, (4) developing a measurement format, and (5) evaluating the measure's reliability and validity. Workers can use this model to create simulations that address the needs of the populations with whom they work.

Simulations have the potential limitation that group members know they are acting rather than performing in real-life situations. In most cases, however, members appear to forget that they are acting and perform as they would in real life.

PROGRAM ACTIVITIES.   Many different types of program activities can be used to assess the functioning of group members. The selection of appropriate activities depends on the type of group the worker is leading. In children's groups, the worker can have members participate in play activities and games. For example, the game Charades can be used to assess how members act out particular situations. Games requiring cooperation can be used to assess the extent to which members are able to negotiate differences.

In adolescent groups, a party, a meal, or a sports activity can often help the worker make an assessment of members' social skills and their level of social development. In adult groups containing moderately or severely impaired members, preparing a meal together or going on an outing can help the worker assess daily living skills. Program activities should be age-appropriate and should give members the opportunity to demonstrate behaviors that they would like to improve through their participation in a group.

When using role plays and program activities to assess members' behavior, it is important to keep in mind the influence of cultural heritage on members' performances. Role playing may not be a readily accepted form of group participation. For example, Lewis and Ho (1975) suggest that in group work with Native Americans, the use of certain techniques (e.g., role plays) "are highly insensitive to the cultural orientation of Native Americans," and that Native Americans may "consider such group behavior to be false; it looks and sounds real but lacks genuineness, depth and real commitment" (p. 381). At the same time, the use of other program activities can be a particularly effective means of assessing members of culturally diverse groups (Delgado, 1983). For example, Ashby, Gilchrist, and Miramontez (1987) reported the usefulness of cultural activities in reaching sexually abused Native American adolescents. For more information about using program materials in groups, see the section on program activities in Chapter 9 and Appendix G.

Reports by Others

In addition to members' self-observations and workers' observations, leaders often rely on the reports of people who are familiar with members' behavior outside the group. When considering data reported by others, the worker should assess its reliability and validity, which can vary considerably from person to person and from one report to another. For example, some data may be based on rumors, assumptions, or the statements of unidentified third parties; other data may come from direct observations. Obviously, the worker should place less confidence in rumors than in direct observations.

The worker should also consider the relationship of the person reporting the data to the member about whom data have been collected. Is the person reporting the data interested in the well-being of the group member or is the person motivated by ill feeling, personal gain, or rivalry? By examining a person's motivation for reporting data about a group member, the worker is in a better position to assess any potential bias in a report.

When a worker has an ongoing relationship with individuals who regularly report data about group members' behavior, such as mental health therapy aides, child care workers, and teachers, it is often worth the effort to help these individuals use reliable and valid data-collection systems. For example, a therapy group leader can offer to help a mental health therapy aide develop a chart to monitor the behavior of a group member at meals or during recreational activities. Similarly, a school social worker can offer an elementary school teacher assistance in using the Achenbach (1997) checklist, which is a standardized instrument to measure children's social behavior. In this way, the worker can build a relationship with persons who have daily contact with group members and ensure that accurate data are reported about members' behaviors outside the group.

Standardized Instruments

A fourth way that workers can assess the functioning of group members is by using standardized assessment instruments. Some instruments require lengthy personal interviews, but others are brief, paper-and-pencil measures known as *rapid assessment instruments*. The Beck Depression Inventory (BDI), for example, is a 21-item scale that assesses the presence and severity of depression. Levitt and Reid (1981) and Toseland and Reid (1985) found that rapid assessment instruments such as the BDI can be used by clinical social workers who have little training or previous experience in test administration.

Rapid assessment instruments can be used in many ways in a group. For example, some members of an outpatient psychiatric group can be asked to spend a few minutes filling out the BDI during a group meeting or at home between meetings. Other members might be asked to fill out the Stait Trait Anxiety Inventory (Spielberger, Gorsuch, Lushene,

Vagg, & Jacobs, 1983) or other instruments that assess the particular symptoms individual group members are experiencing.

Despite the usefulness of standardized assessment instruments for understanding the problems and concerns experienced by group members, it should be kept in mind that these instruments may not be appropriate for use with all populations. For example, when administered to members of specific sociocultural groups or to developmentally disabled persons, such instruments may not be valid or reliable. In fact, they may give the worker a distorted impression of members' strengths. Thus, when considering use of a standardized measure with a particular group of individuals, workers should check whether the description of the instrument includes information about its use with particular populations. If no information is available, workers should select another measure that has been found to be valid for use with the population of interest. A measure suspected of being culturally biased should never be used because even if caution is exercised in interpreting the results, others who have access to the results may draw erroneous conclusions.

Because rapid assessment instruments are focused on particular problem areas, the type of assessment instrument selected depends on the group's focus. Fisher and Corcoran (2007) present a wide variety of rapid assessment instruments for use with children, adults couples, and families in a two-volume set. These volumes are a good desk reference for clinicians because they contain a wide variety of measures that can be used in many different situations. Walls, Werner, Bacon, and Zane (1977) also briefly describe more than 200 behavior checklists that can also be used in assessing the problematic behaviors of children and adults. There are also texts that describe measures for specific populations. For example, Kane and Kane (1981) describe measures for assessing older adults; Ollendick and Hersen (1984) and Marsh and Terdal (1997) describe methods for assessing children. For additional information about available standardized assessment instruments, see Kramer and Conoley (1992); Cone and Hawkins (1977); Hersen and Bellack (1976); Rauch (1993); and Robinson and Shaver (1973).

ASSESSING THE FUNCTIONING OF THE GROUP AS A WHOLE

Methods for assessing the group as a whole have been given less attention in the group work literature than have methods for assessing individual members (Fuhriman & Burlingame, 1994). In 1970, Klein proposed a schema for diagnosing and correcting group problems, and more recently, Fuhriman and Packard (1986) reviewed 26 ways of measuring group processes. Delucia-Waack (1997) also reviewed process and outcomes measures to encourage practitioners to evaluate their work with groups. The many different conceptualizations of group development mentioned in Chapter 3 are also attempts at assessing normal group functioning. In recent years, however, the group work literature has tended to emphasize assessing and treating the problems of individual group members within the group context and has de-emphasized methods to assess the functioning of the group as a whole. When assessing the group as a whole, the worker can focus on group processes, or the productivity of the group. Measures for assessing the productivity of certain types of groups, such as teams, have been developed (see, e.g., Heinemann & Zeiss, 2002). These measures, however, are specific to certain types of groups and are not useful to individuals who do not lead these types of groups.

The focus in this chapter is on assessing group-as-a-whole processes. Assessments of these processes can be used to improve social group work practice with many different types of treatment and task groups. When assessing group-as-a-whole processes, the worker should be guided by the four major areas of group dynamics mentioned in Chapter 3. These are the group's:

1. Communication and interaction patterns
2. Cohesion
3. Social integration and influence dynamics
4. Group culture

Communication and interaction patterns are established early in the group. Therefore, the worker should be especially concerned about these patterns as they develop during the beginning stage. A careful assessment of communication patterns can alert the worker to potential problems and prevent them from becoming established as a routine part of group functioning. It can also help facilitate member-to-member communication and disclosure of important information that may be helpful in attaining group or individual member goals.

At the beginning of a group, too many member-to-leader interactions and too few member-to-member interactions may be of concern (Toseland, Krebs, & Vahsen, 1978). In newly formed groups, there is a natural tendency for members to look to the worker for direction. The worker may feel gratified by this and encourage it. Unfortunately, this pattern may undermine the mutual aid and group problem solving that occur when members direct their communication to everyone in the group rather than exclusively to the worker.

Other communication patterns that may also alert the worker to potential problems can develop in a group. For example, one member may attempt to dominate group discussion and thus prevent other members from interacting. Another potential problem is a lack of communication by a member. Although it is not unusual for some members to communicate less frequently than others, the worker should be aware of the potential for isolation when a member says little or nothing during the beginning stage of the group.

It is also important for a worker to understand what attracts members to the group. The worker should assess the group's attraction for its members to maintain and increase these forces and help the group become a cohesive unit in working toward group and individual goals.

The initial attraction of a group for its members may come from a variety of sources. In treatment groups, for example, attraction may come from members' hopes that the group will help them solve their problems, reduce their emotional distress, or teach them to perform new or more effective roles in their everyday lives. In task groups, it may come from the status or prestige associated with membership, the importance of the task on which the group is working, or a rare chance to share ideas with colleagues.

When workers assess group cohesion, they sometimes find that its development has not progressed satisfactorily. There are many indications that the group is not attractive to one or more of its members. Indicators include apathy or hostility toward group goals, the failure of members to listen to one another, and the growth of allegiances to other reference groups. By observing these indicators, the worker can gain much information about the attraction of the group for its members. Group cohesion can be measured by using a sociometric scale, the semantic differential, the Systematic Multiple Level Observation of Groups (SYMLOG) method, or by using scales specifically designed to measure group cohesiveness (Budman et al., 1987, 1993; Seashore, 1954). Some measures are described later in this chapter.

Workers should also assess the norms, roles, and status hierarchies that develop in newly formed groups. The norms that develop are extremely important because they define acceptable and unacceptable behavior in a group. Schopler and Galinsky (1981) found that norms have an important influence on members' satisfaction with their group experiences. Both members and observers indicated that inappropriate norms were more important than were cohesion, roles, goals, leadership, composition, or extragroup relationships in negative group experiences. Workers should help members modify norms that detract from individual and group goals and promote and protect norms that are beneficial for goal achievement.

Members' roles also begin to develop early in the group. According to Levine (1979), initial role taking in a group is a tentative process and may not reflect the roles members will occupy later in the group. Members try out roles and often vacillate among them, such as the socioemotional leader, task leader, dominator, and so on. During this stage of the group, the worker can point out the functional and dysfunctional characteristics of the roles to members and help the members develop role behaviors that will facilitate the group's functioning and their own functioning in the group.

Several typologies of role behavior have been developed to help workers assess member roles. Benne and Sheats (1948), for example, have classified roles into three broad categories: (1) group task roles that are related to helping the group decide on, select, or carry out particular tasks; (2) group building and maintenance roles that help the group function harmoniously; and (3) individual roles that are related to individual members' goals. Examples of each type of role follow.

Typology of Role Behaviors (Benne & Sheats, 1948)

Group Task Roles
- Instructor, opinion seeker, information giver, elaborator, energizer, evaluator, procedural technician, recorder

Group Building and Maintenance Roles
- Encourager, harmonizer, compromiser, gatekeeper, expediter, standard setter, group observer, follower

Individual Roles
- Aggressor, blocker, recognition seeker, confessor, dominator, help seeker

Focusing on problematic roles, Shulman (1999) has identified the scapegoat, deviant member, gatekeeper, internal leader, defensive member, quiet member, and the talkative member as challenging roles that members frequently take on in groups. Most roles are not difficult for the worker to identify. The scapegoat, for example, receives much negative attention and criticism from the group because the member is blamed for a host of defects and problems. According to Shulman (1999), members attack the portion of a scapegoat's behavior that they least like about themselves. Although Shulman and others (Garland & Kolodny, 1967) mention that scapegoating is common, our experience suggests that scapegoating is relatively rare in adult groups. Scapegoating is more likely to occur in children's groups, but appropriate program activities, structured and timed to consider the developmental abilities and concentration of different groups of children, can reduce or eliminate it.

In the case of a scapegoat, the worker may want to point out the pattern of interaction to the group without taking sides (Shulman, 1999). In doing so, the worker should be aware that sometimes groups use scapegoats to avoid talking about difficult, emotionally charged issues that may be catalyzed by the scapegoat's behavior. This pattern could be pointed out to the group, and the group could be asked to address the difficult, emotionally charged issue directly. At the same time, the scapegoat's behavior may be deviant and annoying to the average person and the group's negative interactions with the scapegoat may simply be an effort to get the individual to stop the behavior. In this situation, the worker may want to help the group consider more appropriate ways to help the member change the behavior. In more extreme cases, the worker may want to consider whether the member is appropriate for the group, or whether the member could be helped to change the annoying behavior with feedback and encouragement from the group. The scapegoat's behavior may also represent an inappropriate way to get attention. In this situation, the worker can help the scapegoat to lead an activity or in some other way get attention for prosocial rather than antisocial behavior. Malekoff (1997) suggests that it is also helpful to humanize scapegoats by helping members to understand them more fully, to help the group understand their struggle to fit in, and the reasons why they behave in a fashion that elicits negative feedback from the group.

When one or more members of a group assume dysfunctional roles, it is often a signal that the group as a whole is not functioning at an optimal level. For example, when an assessment reveals that a member is functioning as a gatekeeper, that is, one who does not allow the group to discuss sensitive issues, the worker should help the group as a whole examine how to change its overall functioning rather than focus on the member who has assumed the dysfunctional role. The gatekeeper, for example, prevents the group as a whole from discussing difficult issues. A quiet member may signal difficulties in the communication and interaction patterns established in the group as a whole. It is rare that a problematic group role is an expression of one individual rather than of group dysfunction. Guidelines that workers can use to help the group change dysfunctional member roles are presented in the following list.

Helping Members with Dysfunctional Role Behaviors

- Keep in mind that all behaviors have meaning.
- Point the behavior out to the group in a tentative fashion.
- Ask the member displaying the behavior to describe his or her own perception of it.
- Ask the other group members to describe how they experience the member's behavior.
- Identify feelings and points of view expressed by all members about the behavior.
- Ask the member displaying the behavior to consider the perceptions of other members.

- Help all members to consider their reactions to the behavior and whether they wish to change the way they interact with others about it.
- Work with all members to change role behaviors so that they help the group to function effectively.

As shown above, the first step in helping groups to change dysfunctional member roles is to be aware that all behavior is meaningful and purposeful. Workers should consider what the member who is playing a dysfunctional role is trying to accomplish by behaving in such a fashion. For example, is the member attempting to gain attention or acceptance? Is the member fearful of what others may think? Pointing out and describing the member's behavior in a tentative manner helps all group members to be aware of the behavior and to think about the meaning of it. Asking a member who displays a dysfunctional behavior to describe how they perceive it enables the other members of the group to understand and empathize with the member's situation.

The next step, helping members to consider their reactions to the behavior and to consider whether they wish to change the way they interact about it, allows members the opportunity to think about the impact of the behavior on the whole group and their role in sustaining or changing it. In this way, the whole group begins to own and take responsibility for doing something about the behavior instead of leaving responsibility for the behavior with only the one member identified as playing a dysfunctional role. At this point, the group is often ready to talk together about role behaviors and how to change them in order to facilitate goal attainment. The worker can help by guiding the group to focus on group processes and goal attainment strategies.

The steps presented previously are intended as a general guide that workers can use to address dysfunctional role behaviors. These steps, however, have to be adapted sensitively when working with members with specific dysfunction role behaviors. For example, monopolizers may acknowledge their behavior, but may still not be able to change it. Therefore, when helping members who talk too much to change their behavior, it may be necessary to place time limits on communication by all group members, or to seek one or more volunteers who will prompt the talkative member when he or she exceeds time limits. It may also be necessary for the worker to take an active stance, reminding talkative members that they have been talking for a while, that they should consider giving others a turn to talk, or asking members to hold onto a thought for a later group discussion. In contrast, when working with quiet members it is important to find out if there is something about the group that is impeding their communication or if they tend not to talk much in groups. Experience suggests that most quiet members are good listeners who prefer to listen rather than to talk. Singling quiet members out by soliciting their opinions or pointing out their silence can make them uncomfortable. Instead, to ensure full participation from quiet members, workers can use go-rounds, program activities, or they can assign specific task roles that provide opportunities and encourage quiet members to participate.

Gatekeepers and rescuers are other common dysfunctional group roles that should be addressed sensitively. Gatekeepers and rescuers intervene when emotionally charged issues are raised in the group. They may change the subject, divert attention, make light of an issue, or become overly solicitous. These behaviors prevent discussion of emotionally sensitive issues that could make the work of the group more relevant and meaningful, because sensitive but important issues that members are confronting would be addressed. Gatekeepers and rescuers are often unaware that they are playing these roles. Workers can help by having all group members identify the fears they have about discussing particular emotionally charged issues. Gatekeeping and rescuing behaviors can then be viewed as attempts to avoid these feared discussions. The worker helps members to confront their fears while simultaneously ensuring that the group is a safe and supportive place where meaningful but emotionally charged issues can be openly discussed and addressed.

● **CASE EXAMPLE**   *A Gatekeeper in an Anger Management Group*

In an anger management group, members began to talk about their own backgrounds. When the topic of childhood physical and sexual abuse came up on two occasions, one member of the group, Fred, kept changing the topic by talking about his own recent experiences of abusive behavior toward his wife. The second time this occurred the group leader mentioned that it was good that Fred was talking about his experiences with his wife and showing some empathy toward her. At the same time, the leader pointed out that childhood sexual abuse was an emotionally charged but important topic that should be talked about in the group, and that it might be relevant to what some members were experiencing regarding their own anger and abusive behavior. Therefore, the leader asked the members who had brought up the topic of sexual abuse to talk about their experiences, and invited other members of the group to share their reactions and experiences. In this way, without explicitly mentioning that Fred was a gatekeeper who was not allowing the group to talk about an emotionally charged topic, the leader enabled group members to begin a discussion of an important issue they might not otherwise have had the opportunity to discuss.

The status of individual group members and the power that the leader and other group members have at their disposal also affect the development of social integration and influence dynamics within the group. For example, although high-status members are likely to adhere to group norms and procedures, they are also much more likely to influence the development of a group than are low-status members. Members in the middle of the status hierarchy are likely to strive for greater status within the group by adhering to group norms and upholding the status quo (Forsyth, 2006). Low-status members are less likely to conform to group norms than either high-status or middle-status members (Forsyth, 2006). An accurate assessment of the status hierarchy in the group can help workers understand and anticipate the actions and reactions of members when the worker intervenes in the group.

An accurate assessment of the power bases that the worker and the members have at their disposal can be important in the beginning stages of group work. Workers who understand the limits of their influence over group members are able to use their power effectively and avoid trying to use it when it will be ineffective. An accurate assessment of the sources of members' power can also help the worker in planning strategies for intervening in the group as a whole and for helping members to form a mutual-aid network of shared resources within the group.

A fourth area that workers should assess when examining the functioning of the group as a whole is the group's culture. Ideas, beliefs, values, and feelings held in common by group members have a profound effect on the therapeutic benefits that can be achieved in the group. Just as some societal cultures promote the public expression of emotion and others do not, groups develop cultures that value certain ways of behaving.

In the beginning stage, the worker should examine the culture that is developing in a group. Does the culture help the group and its members achieve their goals? Because group culture develops more slowly than the other group dynamics, the worker's initial assessment of a group's culture should be viewed as a tentative indication about how the culture may develop. It is difficult to change a group's culture after it is well established, so the worker may wish to share initial impressions with members early. For example, in a group in which a worker observes that a negative, unsupportive culture is developing, it may be helpful to point out in the first or second meeting that most members' communications are problem oriented rather than growth oriented or that few supportive comments are made within the group. Methods to modify or change a group's culture are described in Chapter 9.

A number of methods to assess the group's culture have been developed. Some methods, such as the Hill Interaction Matrix and SYMLOG, were designed to assess a variety of types of groups along several different dimensions; others, such as the Group Atmosphere Scale (Silbergeld, Koenig, Manderscheid, Meeker, & Hornung, 1975), were designed to assess only the psychosocial environment of therapy groups. More information about the Group Atmosphere Scale is presented in Chapter 13.

Methods for Assessing the Group as a Whole

In most practice situations, workers reflect on group functioning between meetings and rely on their own subjective observations to assess the functioning of the group as a whole. But it also can be beneficial to involve the group as a whole in a more structured assessment. In addition to helping members become aware of and involved in improving the group's functioning, using one or more of the structured assessment methods described in the following pages can help confirm or disprove a worker's subjective impressions of group functioning.

There is no measure of group processes that is perfect for all situations. Therefore, it is important to examine measures carefully, thinking about which group-as-a-whole processes are of greatest interest and which measure is most likely to capture what is occurring in a particular group. Fuhriman and colleagues' (Fuhriman & Barlow, 1994; Fuhriman & Packard, 1986; see also Delucia-Waack, 1997) reviews of group process measures are a helpful starting point.

Measuring Communication and Interaction

There are many ways to measure the meanings that underlie communications in the group. One widely used measure is the semantic differential. Using this method, members are asked to rate the meaning of an object or person on a series of seven-point bipolar attitude scales, such as good/bad, valuable/worthless, and so on. Three dimensions of attitudes that can be assessed by the semantic differential are individual group members' (1) evaluation; (2) perceptions of potency; and (3) perceptions of the activity of objects, concepts, or people being rated (Osgood, Suci, & Tannenbaum, 1957). An example of a semantic differential scale is shown in Figure 8.2.

By having members use the semantic differential to rate their fellow group participants, the worker can begin to understand how members perceive one another. For example, using the activity scale, group members may rate one member as being particularly active and another member as being particularly inactive. Similarly, the scales can be used to obtain members' attitudes about specific concepts that may be relevant to group functioning, such

FIGURE 8.2 ● Example of a Semantic Differential Scale

INSTRUCTIONS: On each of the scales below please place a check mark in the space that best describes how you feel about _____.

	7 Extremely	6 Quite	5 Slightly	4 Neither or In-between	3 Slightly	2 Quite	1 Extremely		
1. Large	___	___	___	___	___	___	___	Small	(Potent)
2. Worthless	___	___	___	___	___	___	___	Valuable	(Evaluative)
3. Fast	___	___	___	___	___	___	___	Slow	(Active)
4. Cold	___	___	___	___	___	___	___	Hot	(Active)
5. Happy	___	___	___	___	___	___	___	Sad	(Evaluative)
6. Weak	___	___	___	___	___	___	___	Strong	(Potent)
7. Good	___	___	___	___	___	___	___	Bad	(Evaluative)
8. Tense	___	___	___	___	___	___	___	Relaxed	(Active)
9. Tough	___	___	___	___	___	___	___	Soft	(Potent)
10. Active	___	___	___	___	___	___	___	Passive	(Active)
11. Heavy	___	___	___	___	___	___	___	Light	(Potent)
12. Fair	___	___	___	___	___	___	___	Unfair	(Evaluative)

A = ___ + ___ + ___ + ___ = ___
      3   4   8   10

P = ___ + ___ + ___ + ___ = ___

E = ___ + ___ + ___ + ___ = ___

as self-disclosure, communication, and leadership. The method can also be used to assess members' attitudes and perceptions about presenting problems or the group's task.

Sometimes the worker may be less interested in the meaning of members' communications than in the distribution of communication within the group. An observer can use a chart such as the one shown in Figure 8.3 to record member-to-member and member-to-leader interactions.

To avoid observer fatigue, a sampling procedure may be used instead of continuous recording. Types of sampling procedures include:

- Frequency recording—every time a behavior occurs it is recorded, for example, every communication in the group is recorded
- Interval recording—behavior is recorded for a specified interval of time, for example, the first two minutes of every five-minute time interval
- Time sample recording—behavior is recorded at a particular time, such as every 30 seconds

For ease of rating and to avoid the intrusiveness of live action ratings, group interaction can be videotaped or audiotaped, and observations can be made by replaying the tapes.

Measuring Interpersonal Attraction and Cohesion

Sociometry is a widely used method to measure interpersonal attraction. Originally developed by Moreno in the 1930s (Moreno, 1934), *sociometry* refers to the measurement of social preferences, that is, the strengths of members' preference or rejection of each other.

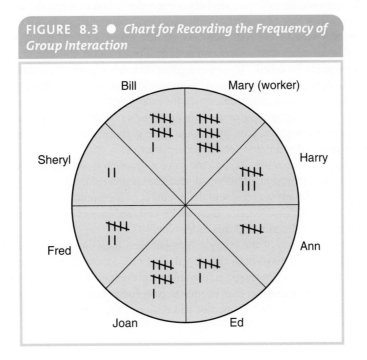

FIGURE 8.3 ● *Chart for Recording the Frequency of Group Interaction*

Sociometric measures are obtained by asking about each member's preference for interacting with other members in relation to a particular activity (Crano & Brewer, 1973; Selltiz, Wrightsman, & Cook, 1976). They can also be obtained by having observers rate members' preferences for one another. Patterns of choices can differ significantly, depending on the activity on which members' preferences are being evaluated (Jennings, 1950). For example, in relation to the activity "playing together," a member of a children's group expressed great willingness to play with a particular member, but in relation to the activity "working on a project together," the member expressed less willingness to interact with the same member.

Sociometric ratings can be made concerning any activity of interest to a worker. For example, a worker may want to assess members' preferences for other members in relation to socializing between group meetings or choosing a partner to complete a task. An additional example follows.

● **CASE EXAMPLE** *Using Sociometric Ratings*

During the assessment phase of a discharge planning group for teens in a residential treatment facility, the group worker administered a sociometric measurement to understand the patterns of member attraction for each other. Members were asked to identify, in order of preference, which members they would be most interested in seeing after discharge. Using the data from this assessment, the worker constructed a sociogram and "paired" members who indicated mutual attraction, creating a buddy system for work on tasks associated with individual member and group goals. The worker also used the data to identify members who were rated as less popular than most, allowing her to give special attention to these members during group sessions.

To obtain sociometric ratings, members are usually asked to write the names of the other members on one side of a sheet of paper next to a preference scale, for example, 1 = most preferred to 5 = least preferred. Members are then asked to rate everyone in the group except themselves in relation to a particular activity. For example, children in a residential treatment center might be asked, "If we were going on a day trip together, who would you like to sit next to during the bus trip?" and "Who would be your second choice?"

An index of preferences can be calculated for each member by dividing the total score a member receives from all group members by the highest possible score the member could receive. Members of attractive, cohesive groups have higher mean preference scores than do members of groups that are less cohesive and attractive.

Another way of presenting sociometric data is through a sociogram. As shown in Figure 8.4, solid lines represent attraction, dotted lines represent indifference, broken lines represent repulsion, and arrows represent the direction of preferences that are not reciprocal. For research purposes, sociometric data can be analyzed by more complicated methods such as multidimensional scaling (Gazda & Mobley, 1981).

Several other measures of the relationships between individual group members, and of overall group cohesion have been developed. Cox (1973), for example, developed the Group Therapy Interaction Chronogram, a graphic representation of interactions and relationships among group members that is similar to a sociogram but more complex. For assessments of the psychometric properties and utility of the Chronogram, see Fuhriman and Packard (1986) and Reder (1978).

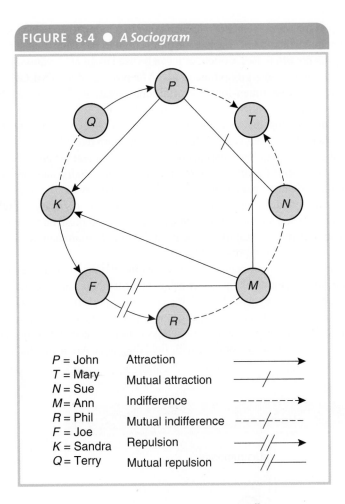

FIGURE 8.4 ● *A Sociogram*

P = John   Attraction
T = Mary   Mutual attraction
N = Sue
M = Ann   Indifference
R = Phil   Mutual indifference
F = Joe
K = Sandra   Repulsion
Q = Terry   Mutual repulsion

To measure cohesion, Seashore (1954) suggests assessing the degree to which members (1) perceive themselves to be a part of the group; (2) prefer to remain in the group rather than to leave it; and (3) perceive their group to be better than other groups with respect to the way members get along together, the way they help each other, and the way they stick together. More recently, Budman and colleagues (1987, 1993) developed the Harvard Community Health Plan Group Cohesiveness Scale, which can be used by trained clinical raters viewing half-hour, videotaped segments of psychotherapy groups. The Group Environment Scale has also been adopted recently to examine cohesion in teams and other task groups (Carless & DePaola, 2000).

Measuring Social Controls and Group Culture

The most fully developed method for assessing norms, roles, and other dimensions of a group as a whole is Bales' SYMLOG (Bales, 1980; Bales, Cohen, & Williamson, 1979). SYMLOG can be used as a self-report measure or as an observational measure.

As a self-report measure, members rate each other in relation to 26 behavioral descriptors, such as "dominant, talks a lot." Each descriptor is used to rate each member on a three-point scale from 0 = not often, to 2 = often, or it can be used as an observational measure in which independent raters assess group functioning. The product of a SYMLOG analysis of group functioning is a three-dimensional pictorial representation of group members' relationships to one another; it is called a SYMLOG field diagram.

In addition to assessing the functioning of groups, SYMLOG is useful in training novice group workers. Figure 8.5 is a SYMLOG field diagram made by Sharon, a member of an educational group for students learning how to lead treatment groups. The horizontal axis of Figure 8.5 represents the dimension friendly versus unfriendly, and the vertical axis represents the dimension instrumental versus emotionally expressive. The third dimension, dominant versus submissive, is represented by the size of the circles. Larger circles represent greater dominance and smaller circles represent greater submissiveness. For example, in Figure 8.5, Sharon perceives that Ann is the most dominant group member and Ed is the most friendly and emotionally expressive member.

Members rate all other members and themselves in relation to the three-dimensional SYMLOG space. In addition to rating overt behaviors, members can rate their values by evaluating which behavior they would avoid, reject, wish to perform, and think they ought to perform (see circles marked "avoid," "reject," "wish," and "ought" in Figure 8.5).

SYMLOG field diagrams can be used for assessment in a variety of ways. One of the most basic ways is for members to compare their field diagrams. Are members' perceptions

FIGURE 8.5 ● *Sharon's SYMLOG Diagram of the Group*

of the relationships among group members similar? Do individual members place themselves in the same position that other members place them?

A composite of group field diagrams can be made from the field diagrams of individual members. The composite can be used to analyze the functioning of the group as a whole. For example, who are the most dominant group members? Which members are included in the dominant subgroup (in Bales' terminology, "dominant triangle" as illustrated in Figure 8.5)? Which members are similar (spatially close) and which members appear to be dissimilar (spatially distant)? Who is the task (instrumental) leader and who is the socioemotional (emotionally expressive) leader? In this way, the SYMLOG procedure can be used to help members gain an understanding of how they are perceived within the group.

Particular roles of individual group members can also be identified. For example, Figure 8.5 shows Bill isolated in the unfriendly, instrumental quadrant of the field diagram. Is he an isolate or perhaps a scapegoat? Several more complicated and more sophisticated ways of interpreting field diagrams have been developed. For a detailed discussion of these methods, see Bales, Cohen, and Williamson (1979) and Bales (1980).

The SYMLOG method has two major limitations. First, the method is complex and takes time to learn before it can be used effectively. A more serious limitation is that a SYMLOG self-study takes about three hours to complete. Although this amount of time may be warranted for a team that functions together on a daily basis over a long period of time, it may not be justifiable for a short-term treatment group.

Other Methods of Assessing the Group as a Whole

Several other methods, including the Hemphill Index of Group Dimensions (Hemphill, 1956), the Hill Interaction Matrix (Hill, 1965, 1977), and the Group Rating Scale (Cooper, 1977), have been developed to rate dimensions of the group as a whole. For example, the Hill Interaction Matrix employs a 16-cell matrix to assess the content and style of group interaction. It has been used in a large number of published and unpublished studies to assess therapeutic processes in a wide range of therapy and support groups (Toseland, Rossiter, Peak, & Hill, 1990). Because these measures are used frequently to evaluate the functioning of a group, they are described in greater detail in Chapter 13.

ASSESSING THE GROUP'S ENVIRONMENT

The worker's assessment of the environment's influence on the functioning of the entire group should be distinguished from the assessment of environmental factors that affect individual group members. In both cases, however, the environment in which group members and the group as a whole function has an important effect on group work practice.

When assessing the influence of the environment on the group, the worker focuses on the following levels.

Levels of Assessment

- The organization that sponsors and sanctions the group
- The interorganizational environment
- The community environment

The emphasis on the influence of the environment is a distinctive aspect of social work practice and is not found to any great extent in the writings of group workers from other professional disciplines (Corey & Corey, 2006; Yalom, 1995).

Assessing the Sponsoring Organization

When assessing the influence on the group of the sponsoring organization, the worker examines how the group's purposes are influenced by the agency, what resources are allocated for the group's efforts, what status the worker has in relation to others who work for the agency, and how the agency's attitudes about service delivery influence the group work endeavor. Taken together, these factors can have a profound influence on the way the group functions.

As Garvin (1997) points out, an organization always has a purpose for sanctioning a group work effort. An organization's purpose may be stated explicitly or may be implied in the overall program objectives. The organization administration's purpose for encouraging the development of a group may not correspond to the worker's or the group members' ideas about a group's purpose. The extent to which the organization, the worker, and the group members can agree on a common purpose for the group will determine, in part, the extent to which the group will receive the support it needs to function effectively and the extent to which the group experience will be judged as beneficial by all concerned.

It is helpful for the worker to clarify the organization's purpose for sponsoring the group. A written group proposal, such as the one described in Chapter 6, can clarify the worker's intentions and provide the organization's administration with an opportunity to react to a written document.

During the process of clarifying the organization's purposes for the group, the worker can help shape the purposes proposed for the group. For example, a nursing home administrator may decide to sponsor a group to help the residents "fit in better" with the nursing home's schedule of bathing, feeding, and housekeeping. The worker could help the nursing home staff and residents reformulate the group's purpose by considering the needs of both the group members and the organization. For example, the purpose of the group might be changed to have residents and staff work together to find a way to accomplish all the personal care tasks in the staff's busy schedules while at the same time accommodating residents' needs for autonomy and individual preference.

An organization can also influence a group by its allocation of resources. As mentioned in Chapter 6, the worker should identify as early as possible the resources the group will need to function effectively. Once this is done, the worker can assess the likelihood that the organization will be able to allocate sufficient resources and can plan the best strategy to obtain any that may be needed. The worker's assessment may also include the extent to which resources, for example, a meeting room or some refreshments, can be obtained from alternative sponsors.

The worker's status in the sponsoring organization can also influence the group. If a worker is a low-status member of the sponsoring organization, there may be difficulty in obtaining resources for the group, in convincing the sponsor that the endeavor is a good use of his or her time, or in demonstrating that the group's purposes are consistent with the overall objectives of the organization. In this situation, the worker may want to consult with trusted colleagues who can give the worker some feedback about the feasibility of the proposed group. The worker might also ask these colleagues for their support for the development of the new group service.

The attitudes and practices of the sponsoring organization with regard to service delivery can have an important influence on the group work endeavor. The worker should assess whether the organization stresses individual or group work services. For example, in some organizations, the stated commitment to teamwork is not matched by the resources and reward structure to support effective team functioning (Goodman, 1986; Hackman, 1990; Katzenbach & Smith, 1993). Where individual services are given priority, the worker may have to spend considerable time developing the rationale for the group and convincing the organization it is important to undertake such an endeavor (Hasenfeld, 1985).

The organization's policies regarding recruitment and intake of potential members also can affect a group. The worker should assess whether the clients are receiving services voluntarily or whether they have been mandated to attend the group. Mandated clients are likely to be hostile or apathetic about becoming members of the group. It is also helpful to gather information about the extent to which individuals are prepared by intake workers to receive group work services.

The organization's commitment to a particular service technology, such as practice theories, ideologies, and intervention techniques, may also influence the group work endeavor. For example, if the organization is committed to a long-term psychodynamic treatment model, it may oppose the development of a short-term, behaviorally oriented group. When the service technology planned for a particular group runs counter to an organization's preferred service technology, the worker should develop a convincing rationale for the particular service technology that is planned. For a treatment group, the rationale might include the effectiveness and efficiency of a particular method for treating a particular problem. In the case of a task group, the rationale might include the effectiveness or efficiency of a particular method for generating ideas or making decisions about alternative proposals.

● **CASE EXAMPLE**   *A Psycho-Educational Group for Caregivers of Dementia*

In a family service agency that relied primarily on a long-term psychodynamic treatment model including long-term groups, a worker proposed a six-week psycho-educational group for caregivers of persons with dementia. In proposing the group at a staff meeting, the worker pointed out that many of the clients coming to the agency were elderly and that a number had talked about their problems with dealing with spouses who were forgetful, or who had been diagnosed with some form of dementia. The worker suggested that she research best practice models, and come up with a short-term group that focused on education about memory loss and dementia, community resources for care of the person with dementia, and support for the caregiver. The worker pointed out that the group could start out as a short-term, six-week, weekly meeting group. Then, if members were interested, or if more short-term groups were formed, a longer-term support and mutual aid group could be started with members who wanted to continue in a group. This latter group would be more in keeping with the family agency's traditional approach to its long-term group programs.

To help ensure continued organizational support for the group, workers should take every opportunity to describe the group's progress to clinical supervisors and other administrative staff. This tactic provides an opportunity for the worker to mention the helpfulness of organizational support and any additional resources that are needed. For example, a worker leading a parenting group could discuss the progress made by members and the importance of transportation to and from group meetings but also note that problems in attendance could be reduced if the agency provided child-care services during group meetings. In the following chapters, guidelines are presented for choosing interventions and for formulating treatment plans on the basis of the needs of members and of the group as a whole.

Assessing the Interorganizational Environment

When assessing the group's environment, it is important for the worker to pay attention to anything happening in other organizations that may be relevant to the group. The worker can make an assessment of the interorganizational environment by asking several questions: Are other organizations offering similar groups? Do workers in other organizations perceive needs similar to those that formed the basis for the worker's own group? Do other organizations offer services or programs that may be useful to members of the group? Would any benefit be gained by linking with groups in other organizations to lobby for changes in social service benefits?

Unless the worker or others in the organization are already familiar with what is being offered by all other organizations in the community, the worker's primary task in making an interorganizational assessment is to contact other organizations to let them know about the group offering. In addition to generating referrals and making other organizations aware of the group, the assessment may uncover needless duplication of service or, conversely, a widespread need that is not being met or is being met by uncoordinated individual efforts within separate organizations.

The following case example illustrates the importance of interorganizational assessments in group work.

● **CASE EXAMPLE**   *Making Interorganizational Assessments*

An executive director of a small organization decided to do an interorganizational assessment after problems encountered in serving homeless people had been raised several times in monthly staff meetings. The director discovered a lack of sufficient space in shelters and a general lack of community interest in the welfare of the homeless. The worker called a meeting of professionals from several organizations to see what could be done. The interorganizational group contacted a local planning organization. In cooperation with the planning organization, the interorganizational group sought federal, state, local, and private funding to address the needs of the homeless. After much work, a social service program for the homeless was founded with a combination of federal, state, and local funding, and a new community shelter was opened.

Assessing the Community Environment

The worker should also assess the effect of the community environment on the group, the extent of support for the group from other community groups, and the community as a whole. When assessing the effect of the community on a group, the worker should focus on the attitude of the community concerning the problems or issues being addressed by the group. Within Hispanic and African American communities, for example, support groups for people with Alzheimer's disease are difficult to organize because of the stigma attached to the disease. These communities also attach great significance to handling such matters privately through family caregiving (Ramos, Jones, & Toseland, 2005).

In treatment groups, if the problem is one that violates basic community values, members of the group are likely to be stigmatized. Lack of community acceptance and the resulting stigma attached to the problem may have other consequences, such as discouraging potential members from reaching out for help. It may also increase the level of confidentiality of group meetings and may affect procedures used to recruit new members. For example, because of the stigma attached to persons who abuse their children, Parents Anonymous groups generally have confidential meetings, and the recruitment process occurs on a first-name basis to protect members from people who may be more interested in finding out their identities than in attending meetings. Similar recruitment procedures are used in other professionally led and self-help groups that deal with socially stigmatized problems, such as spousal abuse, alcoholism, and compulsive gambling.

The worker should also make an assessment of the support for the group from other community groups and the community as a whole. For example, ministers, priests, and rabbis might be receptive to a group for abusive or neglecting parents, alcoholics, or spouse abusers. The worker can get referrals from these sources or obtain a meeting room such as a church basement. Similarly, a worker in a family service agency may find that several community groups—a women's civic organization, a battered women's shelter, a victim's compensation board, a council of churches, and a dispute resolution center—would welcome the development of a support group program for domestic violence victims. Workers who assess support from community groups are often in a better position to obtain new funding for a proposed group work service. This is demonstrated in the following case example.

● **CASE EXAMPLE** *Assessing the Community Environment*

In a rural county, a community coalition formed to assess the need for a shelter for runaway and homeless youth. Members of county social service organizations, local church leaders, and educators from a local social work program met to discuss the need and to examine whether the community would support a shelter. Coalition members initially divided into separate work groups concentrating on collecting data on the extent of the problem. One subgroup met with the local police department to determine how many reports of runaway children were filed each year. Another subgroup conducted individual interviews with community leaders to determine if they would support a shelter. A third subgroup conducted a focus group with residents of the neighborhood that was a potential site for the shelter. A fourth subgroup explored state and national data about homeless and runaway youth. While all these subgroups collected important data establishing need, the coalition discovered that neighborhood residents were very strongly against the idea of a shelter, especially one that would be located in their neighborhood. The coalition reassessed the idea of establishing a shelter and decided to more fully explore how they could involve neighborhood residents in planning for the needs of this population.

Group workers interested in building social action groups and coalitions need to be good at finding out the problems that are important to individuals in a community, which individuals have the capacity to make a change in a particular problem, and which individuals have the capacity to prevent or delay change. Information may be gathered from persons affected by the problem and those who have the capacity to affect it through a variety of means, such as (1) focused individual interviews, (2) focus groups, (3) community needs assessments, and (4) state and national survey data and reports.

The importance of unsolicited and unfocused information gathered while interacting with and forming alliances with community members, community leaders, politicians, and community activists should not be overlooked. It is essential for group workers who are interested in building social action groups and coalitions to get to know a community. To understand competing factions, uncover hidden problems, and form alliances often takes a considerable amount of time and commitment. Still, when the intent is to mobilize social action groups and coalitions, there is no substitute for taking the time necessary to get to know a community and to establish trusting relationships with as many different representatives of the community as possible.

A worker's assessment of the community environment may lead to a coalition of community forces to resolve a concern. According to Rubin and Rubin (2007), in assessing a community there may be a systematic gathering of information by people who are affected by a problem and who want to solve it. There may also be a fact-gathering endeavor to learn about the problem, a mobilization effort to become involved with the problem, and a capacity-building effort to solve the problem. For example, a community assessment may indicate that police officers have been asked increasingly to handle family disturbances. With the cooperation of the police force and local community leaders, a community organization might decide to reach out to persons experiencing family disturbances. In addition to casework service, these efforts could result in the development of several treatment groups, such as a couples communication group, a parenting group, and a recreational group for adolescents. It also might result in a task force of community leaders to work on issues of concern to families in the community.

LINKING ASSESSMENT TO INTERVENTION

In preparation for the middle stage of treatment groups, discussed in Chapter 9, workers should consider how they will use their assessment data to plan effective interventions. Few texts in group work or casework practice have addressed the way assessments are linked to intervention methods and treatment plans. This may, in part, account for findings from practice studies suggesting there is little correlation between workers' assessments or diagnoses and the interventions that are selected (Mullen, 1969; Stuart, 1970). Without guidelines about the interventions that are most appropriate for particular problems, workers will rely on interventions with which they are most familiar, regardless of their assessment of the group or its members.

Figure 8.6 illustrates a framework for developing treatment plans that result from an assessment of the individual group member, the group as a whole, and the group environment. Because problems are often multidimensional, several different interventions may be selected to become part of a comprehensive treatment plan. For example, in a couples group, the worker and each member may select specific interventions to meet individual needs. One member decides to use a cognitive restructuring intervention to help her stop getting defensive when confronted by her husband. As part of his treatment plan, another member decides to join Alcoholics Anonymous. At the same time, the worker helps the first member change her interaction patterns in the group and helps the second member stop avoiding confrontation in the group.

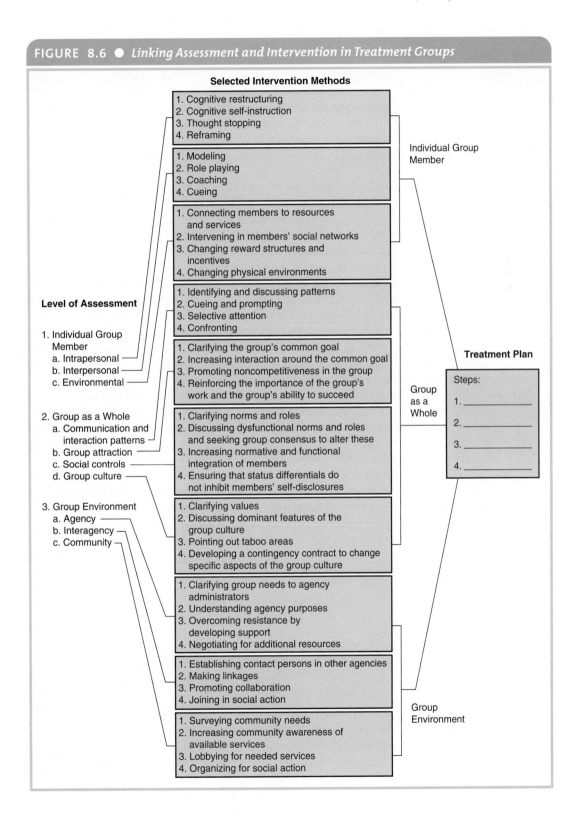

FIGURE 8.6 ● *Linking Assessment and Intervention in Treatment Groups*

SUMMARY

This chapter has suggested that the worker assess three areas of the functioning of individual group members, four areas of the functioning of the group as a whole, and three areas of the environment in which the group functions. Chapters 9 through 12 describe a variety of interventions that the worker can use when assessment indicates an intervention is warranted.

This chapter examines in detail the process of assessment. Although assessments are made throughout all stages of a group's development, they are often concentrated in the latter portions of the beginning stage and the initial portions of the middle stage. This is the time when the worker and the group members are planning intervention strategies to achieve the goals they have agreed on in the planning and beginning stages of the group.

In making assessments, the worker examines the functioning of individual group members, the group as a whole, and the group's environment. When assessing individual members, the worker examines intrapersonal, interpersonal, and environmental areas of each member's functioning. In addition, the worker examines each member's functioning in relation to what the member can contribute to the group, what needs the member brings to the group, and what intervention plans are most likely to be successful in helping the member alleviate concerns and problems. A number of methods that can be used separately or in combination for assessing the functioning of individual members are presented in this chapter.

To assess the group as a whole, the worker focuses on the four areas of group dynamics described in Chapter 3. These are (1) interaction and communication patterns; (2) the attraction of the group for its members; (3) social integration and influence dynamics such as roles, norms, and status hierarchies; and (4) the group's culture. Several methods for assessing the group as a whole are described.

Because group work practice occurs within the context of a larger service delivery system, it is important to consider the effect of the group's environment on its functioning. To make a thorough assessment of the group's environment, it is suggested that the worker assess the sponsoring organization, the interorganizational environment, and the larger community environment in which the group functions. After explaining the potential effects of each of these aspects of the environment on the group, the chapter describes the linkage between assessment and intervention.

● CASE EXAMPLE

Jody conducted a Banana Splits group for fourth graders whose parents were in the process of separating or divorcing. The group had been meeting for four weeks. Its purpose was to help the children discuss their concerns about their changing family situation and to assist them in finding support from each other. The beginning phase of the group was going well. Members were becoming more comfortable with Jody and with each other. They seemed to be opening up a little more about their concerns. Jody used a number of program materials to help members get to know each other and identify their feelings.

As she conducted the group, Jody recognized that she was beginning to gather information about each of the members and about how the group was working as a unit. She was also learning a good deal about how important it was to work with others in the group's environment, such as teachers, guidance counselors, and school administrators. It was time to take some of this information and prepare a more formal assessment that would be useful for her future work with the members of the group. Also, she wanted to become more systematic in her understanding of the dynamics in the group as a whole because she recognized that the group's environment played an important part in the success of the group process. She designed several methods for collecting additional data to help her begin the formal assessment process.

She began by assessing the needs of the individual members of the group. The membership was fairly homogeneous—all the students were fourth graders and came from the same school district. Yet, she noted that members had very different home situations that could affect how they were coping with their changing family situations. She used several sources to collect data about how students were coping with their family situations. First, she contacted the parents of each child. She asked each parent to fill out a short rating scale on the child that identified eating, sleeping, and study habits while the child was at home. Second, she asked each child's teacher to write a paragraph that described the child's behavior in the classroom. Specifically, she asked each teacher to comment on his or her observations of the child's social interaction, school performance, and overall mood in the classroom. Third, Jody recorded her own observations of each child during group sessions, carefully documenting her observations by using excerpts from the child's dialogue in the group. She also recorded the major concerns that surfaced for each member during group sessions.

She organized this information in individual files for each member and added to the information as the group progressed. As she collected more data, Jody synthesized them and wrote a summary assessment of each member's situation that included information about the home environment, adjustment to the separation process, class behavior, connections to other members in the group, socialization patterns at school, and grades. She planned to use this information to work with each member in formulating individual goals to be worked on during later group sessions.

Although Jody observed that the group seemed to be progressing well, she decided to assess more formally how the group was functioning. She began by taking careful notes on the patterns of communication and interaction between members. She noticed that the group had several small cliques that had formed, and she wondered if this dynamic was reinforced by interaction among subgroup members that took place outside of the group. She administered a short sociometric exercise to the members to more fully assess interaction within the group. On further investigation, she learned that subgroups seemed to form based on how classes were organized for the fourth grade students at the school. She also learned through observation that many members were communicating more to her than to other members. As a group goal for future meetings she planned to promote member-to-member communication by encouraging students to talk to each other rather than to her. One way Jody assessed the group's cohesion was by asking members to end each meeting with a comment about what they liked or didn't like about the group that day. She noted that many members made positive comments. She also noted that the members were becoming more independent and responsible for deciding things in the group, and she felt that the group's culture was developing adequately for this stage of the process.

Jody also took a good deal of time planning for this group, especially by preparing the organizational environment. She felt it was a good time to reassess aspects of the group's environment, particularly in relation to how the group was being perceived by teachers, administrators, and parents. She designed a short evaluation instrument and sent it to these constituencies, asking for their perceptions and feedback about the Banana Splits group. In addition, she interviewed the principal to share information about the group and to assess how important the group was to members of the school. On interviewing the principal, Jody learned that the school board was interested in replicating Jody's group with students in other classes. To avoid behavior problems and school violence that might occur if family problems were not addressed, the board currently seemed to favor early intervention and increased services to children whose parents were separating or divorcing. As a goal, Jody planned to make a presentation to the school board about expanding group work services to students experiencing turbulent family environments.

part **IV** The Middle Stage

chapter **9**

Treatment Groups: Foundation Methods

chapter **10**

Treatment Groups: Specialized Methods

chapter **11**

Task Groups: Foundation Methods

chapter **12**

Task Groups: Specialized Methods

Treatment Groups: Foundation Methods

During the middle stage, groups are focused on accomplishing the objectives, goals, and tasks developed earlier in the life of the group. It is assumed that by the middle stage, workers have already discussed the group's purposes; developed a group contract concerning confidentiality, attendance, and number of sessions; and developed individual contracts with particular treatment goals for each member. It is also assumed that the group as a whole has developed an initial set of dynamic processes, including a pattern of communication and interaction; a beginning level of interpersonal attraction and group cohesion, norms, roles, and other social control mechanisms; and a group culture. The primary task of the worker during the middle stage is to help members accomplish the goals they have contracted to achieve.

MIDDLE-STAGE SKILLS

The middle stage of treatment groups is characterized by an initial period of testing, conflict, and adjustment as members work out their relationships with one another and the larger group. Contracts are negotiated and renegotiated, members establish their positions in relation to one another, and the group develops a niche within the sponsoring organization.

The testing, conflict, and adjustment that occur in the group are signs that members are becoming comfortable enough to assert their own needs and their own vision of the group. During this period, members demonstrate their independence and abilities to engage in leadership activities. They may question the purposes and goals of the group or the methods that have been proposed to accomplish them. They may also express contrary opinions and concerns about group processes or their interactions with the leader or certain members. In the beginning stage, members are often glad to have the worker structure the group, but testing and conflict often signify that members are vying for ownership of the group (Henry, 1992).

In most circumstances, acknowledging members' issues and concerns, giving a nondefensive response, and fostering a group discussion about how to handle the concern is all that is needed to help the group continue to function in a smooth and satisfying manner. In some situations, however, conflicts may escalate. In these situations, the conflict resolution skills and strategies presented in Chapters 4 and 11 can be quite useful in helping to satisfy members' needs while accomplishing group goals.

Although some elements of testing and conflict will continue to emerge as a normal part of the life of a group, after an initial period of adjustment, the main focus of the middle stage turns to goal achievement. Members work together to achieve the goals expressed in the contracts they have made with the group's leader, other group members, and the group as a whole. During the middle stage, the worker makes modifications to these contracts based on an assessment of the group's development, the changing needs of members, and the changing demands of the social environment in which the group functions.

Although every group has a unique developmental pattern that calls for different leadership skills, workers are often expected to perform six broad activities during the middle stage of all treatment groups. These activities include the following:

1. Preparing for group meetings
2. Structuring the group's work
3. Involving and empowering group members
4. Helping members to achieve goals
5. Working with reluctant and resistant group members
6. Monitoring and evaluating the group's progress

Preparing for Group Meetings

During the middle stage, the worker should continuously assess the needs of the group and its members and plan to meet identified needs in subsequent meetings. The cycle of assessment, modification, and reassessment is the method by which the leader ensures continued progress toward contract goals.

In structured, time-limited groups, the worker spends a considerable amount of time between meetings preparing the agenda for the next group meeting. For example, for the fourth session of an educational group for prospective foster parents, a worker prepared (1) material on helping children develop values, (2) a handout on value clarification, (3) an exercise to illustrate some concepts about helping children develop their own value system, and (4) questions that helped to organize the group's discussion of values. In preparing for the meeting, the worker tried to select material that would lead to a stimulating and interesting discussion. In addition, the worker estimated the time needed to complete each of these educational components and discussed this with members during the initial part of the meeting.

Less structured, process-oriented groups also require preparation. This is illustrated in the following case example.

● **CASE EXAMPLE** *Preparing for Group Meetings*

A worker leading a group for residents of an adolescent treatment center prepared for the next meeting according to her assessment of the efficacy of the previous group meetings and the current functioning of each group member assessed during weekly treatment review meetings. The worker decided to focus the next meeting on helping members to improve how they expressed anger. When preparing for the group, the worker gathered examples of how anger had been expressed in the past by residents of the treatment center. She used these examples to prepare role-play exercises designed to improve members' expression of anger. During the next meeting, some of the role plays were enacted. The worker modeled appropriate ways of expressing anger and helped members to practice the new methods. Then, she encouraged the group to discuss factors that facilitated and hindered the use of these methods in real life situations.

Preparation is also required when workers use program materials to achieve group goals. Middleman (1980) points out that the use of program materials has had an important place in the history of group work. *Program materials* are activities, games, and exercises designed to provide fun, interesting experiences for members while achieving particular goals. Workers sometimes make the mistake of thinking that program activities such as arts and crafts or preparing for a dance are not appropriate group work activities because they are not focused solely on therapeutic verbal interactions. However, when carefully selected, program activities can be very therapeutic.

Program activities provide a medium through which the functioning of members can be assessed in areas such as interpersonal skills, ability to perform daily living activities, motor coordination, attention span, and ability to work cooperatively. Program activities can also be used as a part of specific treatment interventions. In addition to achieving specific goals such as improving skills in interpersonal functioning, leadership, problem solving, and activities of daily living, program activities help build group cohesion, prosocial group norms, and a group culture that fosters continued member participation. Program activities can also be used to make the group more attractive for its members. For example, in a children's group, the worker may place a program activity, such as charades, between group discussions to maintain members' interest.

Choosing appropriate program activities requires a careful assessment of the needs of group members. Characteristics of members should be matched with the characteristics of potential program activities. Vinter (1985b) has developed a scheme for rating program activities on their prescriptiveness, control, movement, rewards, competence, and interaction. Similarly, Middleman (1982) has attempted to point out some of the particular benefits of more than one hundred program activities, and Henry (1992) has attempted to categorize program activities that are especially useful for members at different stages of a group's development.

Because of the great number of possible program activities for children, adolescents, adults, and the elderly, workers should keep a resource file of catalogued activities to draw on as they are called on to work with different types of groups. Such a resource file can be an asset in selecting specific program activities during the life of a group. Appendix G lists a variety of sources for program activities that can be used in groups for children, adolescents, and older adults.

Figure 9.1 presents a procedure for evaluating program activities for specific group needs. Selection should be made on the basis of (1) the objectives of the program activity; (2) the purposes and goals of the group; (3) the facilities, resources, and time available for the activity; (4) the characteristics of the group members; and (5) the characteristics of particular program activities.

The procedure suggested in Figure 9.1 can be used to help workers select program activities for any type of treatment group. For example, when choosing activities for an inpatient group whose purpose is to help prepare members for community living, the worker

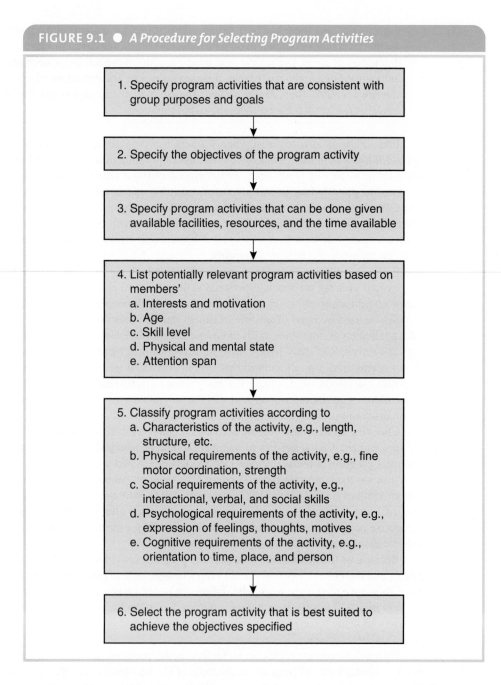

FIGURE 9.1 ● *A Procedure for Selecting Program Activities*

1. Specify program activities that are consistent with group purposes and goals

2. Specify the objectives of the program activity

3. Specify program activities that can be done given available facilities, resources, and the time available

4. List potentially relevant program activities based on members'
   a. Interests and motivation
   b. Age
   c. Skill level
   d. Physical and mental state
   e. Attention span

5. Classify program activities according to
   a. Characteristics of the activity, e.g., length, structure, etc.
   b. Physical requirements of the activity, e.g., fine motor coordination, strength
   c. Social requirements of the activity, e.g., interactional, verbal, and social skills
   d. Psychological requirements of the activity, e.g., expression of feelings, thoughts, motives
   e. Cognitive requirements of the activity, e.g., orientation to time, place, and person

6. Select the program activity that is best suited to achieve the objectives specified

should consider activities that stimulate members' interest in the outside world. In addition to the group's purpose and the objectives of particular program activities, the worker should consider the other factors shown in Figure 9.1. For example, an inpatient group meets in an occupational therapy room equipped with kitchen facilities, tables, blackboards, arts and crafts, and toys. All members are more than 70 years old and have poor physical and mental health. Their interests include gardening, nature, travel, and cooking.

The worker selects a program activity that stimulates members both physically and socially to prepare them for living in a community residence.

Using Figure 9.1 as a guide, the worker ruled out activities such as a discussion of current events and selected an activity in which each member helped prepare a meal to be shared by all. Afterward, the worker reconvened the group around the meal and asked members to share their feelings. Questions such as "Did the activity remind you of when you lived at home?" and "How do you feel about living on your own and having to prepare meals?" were used to stimulate a therapeutic discussion based on the program activity.

The therapeutic benefit of any program activity depends on how the activity is used by the worker. Activities provide little benefit if careful attention is not given to making sure they are directed toward therapeutic purposes. In the example above, the program activity of preparing the meal stimulated the sensory awareness of members. During the activity, the worker encouraged social interaction. At the end of the meal, a discussion of the thoughts, feelings, and behaviors that members experienced during the activity was used to stimulate members' interest and desire to return to the community.

To prepare for meetings, workers should also review recordings of previous meetings and data from other monitoring devices. Making effective use of feedback about the progress of a group is essential during the middle stage. The worker can use observations collected in summary recordings, for example, as the basis for determining that the interaction pattern of the previously described inpatient group should be changed to encourage participation from several members who have not been active in group discussions. In another case, data about members' satisfaction with the previous meeting of a single-parent support group suggested that information about educational opportunities for adult students should be included in future meetings.

Preparation for the next group meeting may also include visualizing how the meeting should be conducted and, if necessary, rehearsing intervention procedures or techniques. This strategy is particularly important when a worker is using a new or unfamiliar procedure or exercise.

In recent years, an increased awareness of the benefits of clear contracts and specific goal statements has highlighted the need for careful preparation between meetings. For example, Rose (1989) has suggested that specific written agendas be distributed at the beginning of each meeting. Such agendas are appropriate for structured, short-term groups that are focused on a single concern or problem. Other treatment groups may have broader concerns that are not easily anticipated or addressed by a written agenda for each meeting. However, regardless of whether a written agenda is used, workers should be sufficiently prepared so they are clear about their objectives for each meeting and their plans for achieving the objectives.

Structuring the Group's Work

Structuring the work of treatment groups has been recognized as a necessary ingredient of social work treatment for many years (Perlman, 1970). Recently, managed care has given greater impetus to short-term structured approaches to group work (Bauer & McBride, 2003; Bieling, McCabe, & Antony, 2006; Blay et al., 2002; MacKenzie, 1995; Murphy, DeBernardo, & Shoemaker, 1998; Passi, 1998; Schreiber, 2002). *Structure* refers to the use of planned, systematic, time-limited interventions and program activities. Highly structured interventions rely on the guidance and direction of the worker, but less structured approaches encourage members to take full responsibility for the purpose, goals, and interventions used in the group.

In general, structure encourages the rapid learning of new responses. Therefore, one advantage of structured groups is that they provide an efficient means for members to learn new skills. The appeal of the Minnesota Couples Communication Program (Miller, Nunnally, & Wackman, 1972), Parent Effectiveness Training (Gordon, 1975), Positive Peer Culture (Vorrath & Brendtro, 1985), Systematic Training for Effective Parenting (Dinkmeyer & McKay, 1990), and similar approaches testifies to the popularity of structured group programming for certain types of problems.

Structure is essential in multicomponent treatment programs, sometimes referred to as *psychoeducational* groups. For example, an assertion-training group may include a brief lecture and group discussion about what it means to be assertive, followed by role playing, modeling, rehearsal, reinforcement, and cognitive interventions—all activities are designed to help members practice becoming more assertive. As the number of treatment components grows, the need for careful structuring of the entire intervention program increases.

During the middle stage of treatment groups, the worker can perform a variety of activities to structure the group's work. Some of these activities are listed here.

Structuring the Group's Work

- Inform members about beginning and ending the group on time
- Give attention to apportioning time for ending meetings
- Set agendas: verbal or written
- Establish and maintain orderly communication and interaction patterns
- Help members progress toward their goals
- Attend to transitions between group activities
- Focus on multilevel interventions: individual, group, and environment

One of the most basic activities is to let members know that each meeting will begin and end on time. Except for the first meeting, openings should not be delayed in anticipation of late members. Starting meetings late only reinforces members' future tardiness.

The worker should also structure the end of a meeting to summarize and conclude interactions rather than to begin new agenda items. New items should not be introduced near the end of a session. Sometimes a group member will wait until the end of the meeting to disclose an important piece of information or to voice an important concern. Because these "doorknob" communications (Shulman, 1999) cannot be dealt with adequately in the short time remaining, the worker should ask the member to hold the new material until the next meeting. If the member's concerns cannot wait until the next group meeting, the worker may want to schedule an individual meeting.

One of the best ways for a worker to structure a group's time is by setting agendas. Whether verbal or written, a clear agenda helps focus attention on what will be covered during the meeting and makes members aware of how much time is available for exercises, role plays, presentations, and discussions. When preparing and presenting agendas, workers should encourage members to share their ideas about what direction the group should take.

The worker also can structure a group by establishing and maintaining orderly communication and interaction patterns. The structure of the interaction process should give all members an opportunity to participate. Some members, however, may receive more attention in one meeting and less in others. For example, in a remedial group in which members have individualized treatment contracts, the worker may decide to focus on one member at a time to help each one work on the personal treatment contract for an extended period. In other situations, such as an educational group, the worker may decide to present didactic material and then encourage all members to discuss the material. The worker may decide to structure the discussion so that each member is encouraged to participate and no member is allowed to talk for longer than several minutes at one time. In either case, the worker will have made a planned effort to structure the group's use of communication and interaction patterns.

The worker structures a group's communication and interaction patterns by helping the group determine how much time should be spent on a particular issue or problem and by guiding members' participation in role plays, exercises, and other group activities. In these efforts, the worker balances the socioemotional needs of individual members and the needs of the group as a whole to accomplish specific goals. The worker also should strive to foster members' initiative and leadership but should prevent the group from being dominated by a single individual or a subgroup.

Sometimes workers are reluctant to assert themselves, for example, by guiding the group from a discussion of one issue to another or directing role plays or program activities. Workers should be aware, however, that group members expect them to provide guidance and leadership, particularly when the group is having trouble staying focused on its stated objectives. Workers are expected to use their professional knowledge and skills to guide members' progress toward the goals that have been set without dominating or suppressing members' initiatives. When the worker is unsure about whether the group needs more time to work on an issue or an exercise, he or she can ask members a direct question about their needs.

When guiding group activities, the worker should ensure that the transition from one activity to another is as smooth as possible. This can be done by summarizing what has been said, recommending how the group might pursue unresolved issues, and suggesting that the group move on to remaining issues.

Time is an important factor in structuring the work of a group. Time-limited, structured group work methods have been shown to be effective for children, adolescents, and adults experiencing a variety of problems (Bauer & McBride, 2003; Bieling, McCabe, & Antony, 2006; McKay & Paleg, 1992; Rose, 1998; Shapiro, Peltz, & Bernadett-Shapiro, 1998). Despite the evidence for the effectiveness of time-limited approaches to group work, some needs are clearly better served in long-term groups. For example, the popularity of self-help groups indicates that they provide important support through life transitions and life crises (Powell, 1987; White & Madara, 1998). It may also be preferable to address other needs in groups that do not emphasize a time-limited structured format. For example, when members seek help in changing established personality characteristics, long-term rather than short-term group treatment approaches are often recommended (Frances, Clarkin, & Perry, 1984; Seligman, 1998).

Focusing is another way to structure the work of a group. In any treatment group, the focus of an intervention, sometimes referred to as the level of an intervention, can be either the individual member, the group itself, or the group's external environment. The focus of the group should change with the changing needs of the group. An example taken from work with a group of men who assaulted their partners is presented in the following case.

● **CASE EXAMPLE**   *Focusing on Different Intervention Levels*

A worker leading a group for men who abused their wives made an assessment that the group was failing to encourage members to express their feelings of anger, and this problem was inhibiting the group from achieving its goal of preventing further domestic violence. The worker decided to select the group as the target of an intervention designed to help members talk about their feelings. He had each member express two feelings about being a member of the group. Other exercises used in later group sessions helped members learn to identify their feelings of anger and to intervene before they escalated into violent outbursts. At the end of the first exercise, the group leader changed the focus of the group and concentrated on helping members work on individual treatment plans. In a subsequent group meeting, the leader again suggested a change in focus by asking group members if they would like to invite their partners to a meeting. The leader explained that this could help members appreciate the devastating effect that domestic violence had on their partners. By suggesting changes of focus, the leader helped the group to obtain new perspectives on problems and to tackle problems in multidimensional ways that add variety to the type of work that is done in the group.

For more information about groups for men who batter see Aldarondo and Mederos (2002); Browne, Saunders, and Staecker (1997); Dutton and Sonkin (2003); Edleson and Tolman (1992); Fall, Howard, and Ford (1999); Gondolf (1997; 2002); Hanson, 2002; and Saunders (1996; 2002).

Degree of Structure

Reviews of the effectiveness of group interventions (Budman et al., 1994; MacKenzie, 1990) indicate that structured interventions are effective in helping clients to achieve treatment goals. MacKenzie (1994), for example, indicates that early group structure has a variety of beneficial effects on group processes and outcomes, such as reducing members' fears and anxieties, promoting members' involvement and self-disclosure, and increasing group cohesion and positive feelings about the group.

Considerable controversy exists, however, about how *much* structure is useful for treatment groups. It has been argued, for example, that substantial structure may not be beneficial because it prevents members from exercising their own initiative (Glassman & Kates, 1990). Too much structure may decrease members' commitment to the group because they may feel structure has been imposed on them rather than selected by them to help them achieve their own self-monitored goals. Lieberman, Yalom, and Miles (1973) found that structured exercises did not facilitate group development or successful outcomes in the groups they observed.

Although much available evidence indicates that structured, short-term interventions are at least as effective as less structured, longer-term interventions (Budman et al., 1994; MacKenzie, 1990, 1994), highly structured interventions may be more appropriate for some problems than for others. For example, although a highly structured, multicomponent group treatment program was found to be more effective than a less structured program for helping older people increase their social skills (Toseland & Rose, 1978), a less structured, process-oriented approach that was focused on facilitating group members' determination of their own purposes and goals was found to be more effective than a structured approach in developing mutual support groups for older people (Toseland, Sherman, & Bliven, 1981).

Similarly, short-term, highly structured approaches may not be best for clients who are mandated to attend group treatment. These clients take time to develop relationships and to build trust in workers' efforts to help them. On the other hand, clients who are in crisis may need less time to build relationships with the worker and other members and therefore can profit from short-term treatment.

The nature of clients' problems and needs should be carefully considered when deciding how to structure a group. For example, work with antisocial adolescents, clients in residential treatment centers, severely impaired psychiatric patients, and street gangs often occurs in long-term groups. These groups focus on specific, narrowly defined concerns and objectives only in the context of broader, long-term objectives and goals. For example, a short-term goal for a group of psychiatric inpatients might be for the patients to learn specific social skills. This goal may be accomplished in a short-term social skills group. However, the long-term goal for each member—to live independently in the community—may best be accomplished through a program that includes a series of short-term groups focused on specific skills and a long-term group integrating what is learned in the brief, focused groups.

● **CASE EXAMPLE** *A Group of Parents of Children With Down Syndrome*

In forming a group for parents of children with Down's syndrome, the worker decided to use a semi-structured approach to group meetings. A portion of each meeting was devoted to an educational topic related to some aspect of Down's syndrome, such as variations in developmental delays, physical, occupational, and speech therapy resources that might prove helpful, and helping parents and their children to deal with other's reactions to Down's syndrome. After the brief educational portion of the group, plenty of time was left for parents to share and discuss their mutual concerns and their diverse efforts at being effective parents and advocates for their disabled children. In this way, a structured educational portion of the group meeting was combined with an unstructured portion.

Although it is important to carefully plan meetings, it is also important to recognize that at times it may be desirable or even necessary to abandon the agenda temporarily. Interpersonal interactions provide many opportunities for workers and members to achieve group goals. For example, it is better to use spontaneous opportunities during group interaction to teach appropriate assertiveness skills, than to teach concepts in a structured module that does not draw on actual group experiences. Similarly, it may also be necessary to temporarily abandon the group agenda when a member is in crisis, or an important point is raised by one or more members that should be addressed immediately. The "art" of effective group leadership is to identify opportunities to use group processes and content to help the group and its members achieve agreed on goals. Agendas and structure are tools to help groups function effectively, but they should not be adhered to rigidly. Effective workers use their judgment, their clinical experience, and their knowledge of human behavior to intervene at appropriate times during group meetings to help the group and its members to achieve goals.

Involving and Empowering Group Members

Another important activity in the work stage of treatment groups is to help members become fully involved in the work of the group. The ultimate goal of this process is to empower members so they can take charge of their lives both inside and outside the group. Workers who are insecure about their position often make the mistake of being overly directive or even manipulative. Instead of doing their utmost to help members take as much responsibility as they are able to for the direction of the group, insecure workers often think they have to be in control at all times. This view is often counterproductive and leads members to become rebellious or passive-aggressive.

An important first step in the process of involving and empowering group members is for workers to show their belief in members' strengths. Statements that express confidence in members' motivation and tenacity, point out their abilities, and describe their previous accomplishments help to foster members' resolve to accomplish particular goals.

Expressing belief in members' strengths does not mean that the worker should be unrealistic and ignore impediments to goal achievement. Thus, a second step in the process of empowering group members is to acknowledge the difficulties and obstacles they encounter as they attempt to reach particular goals and objectives. It is also important to recognize their efforts to overcome obstacles. Statements such as "Ann, I really admire that you're not giving up—that you continue to confront this difficult issue with your daughter" or "Expressing yourself about this painful issue really shows your courage, Charlie" affirm and validate members' efforts to take charge of their own lives, even when the work is difficult.

A third way to empower group members is to help them know that they have a stake in the content and direction of the group. Statements such as "This is your group—what do you want to see happen in it?" help members overcome a tendency to expect the worker to take full responsibility for group content and process.

A fourth step to encourage involvement and empowerment is to praise members for reaching out to help each other. Statements such as "I really liked the way you shared how you felt about Ann's situation" or "This group is really making progress—it's wonderful to see how supportive you are of each other" demonstrate support of members' self-help efforts and foster the continued development of cohesion in the group as a whole. Another way to empower group members is to encourage them to try out new behaviors and actions both within and outside the group. Members should be encouraged to begin by taking small action steps and carefully observing the results. Members can then report the results of their efforts to the group. They should be encouraged to acknowledge each other's accomplishments and to support each other when obstacles are encountered.

Program activities can also be used to involve and empower group members. Activities should involve as many members as possible, and members should be encouraged to take leadership roles and support each other's efforts. Rigid adherence to particular ways of conducting program activities should be deemphasized in favor of members adapting activities to meet their needs.

Involving and empowering members does not mean that the worker stops providing guidance and direction. However, when guiding the group interaction, workers should solicit members input and feedback, as the following case example illustrates.

● **CASE EXAMPLE** *A Group Teaching Cognitive Behavioral Techniques to Combat Depression*

In a cognitive behavioral group for people experiencing depression, the group worker described the way members' internal dialogue sometimes led to increased depression. The worker mentioned such things as catastrophic thinking, either-or dichotomous thinking, and self-talk that inhibit positive thinking. One member of the group spoke up and said that she was not sure what the worker meant or how this contributed to her depression. The worker solicited feedback from other members of the group, some of whom seemed to understand the point the worker was trying to make but others who did not. The worker then said to the first member who spoke up that she was glad that she had mentioned that she was unclear about what was being said and that maybe they were moving a bit too fast. The worker then went back and talked about inner dialogues, getting members to volunteer about what they say to themselves when they are in situations they are not feeling good about. The worker then used some of these internal dialogues to point out examples of catastrophic thinking, either-or dichotomous thinking, and other self-statements that added to members' feelings of depression.

Helping Members Achieve Their Goals

During the middle stage of the group, it is important for workers to concentrate on helping members achieve the goals they have agreed to accomplish. Contracting for treatment goals is an evolving process. A tentative agreement or contract is usually discussed while interviewing potential members during the planning stage of a group. The contract is reaffirmed and made more concrete and specific during the beginning stage of the group as members interact with one another for the first time. Although much of a treatment group's work during the middle stage is devoted to carrying out contracts developed during the beginning stage of the group, contracts continue to evolve as the group progresses during the middle stage.

Secondary contracts can be developed to refine initial contracts. For example, a member of a group for recently separated people might contract to reduce her angry feelings and violent outbursts toward her former spouse when he picks up their children. A secondary contract might involve the member in discussing her feelings of anger with another member outside the group and reporting back to the group what she has learned about how to handle angry feelings. A variety of different secondary contracts could be used to help the member achieve the goals specified in her primary contract. Thus, secondary contracts evolve as group members progress toward their treatment goals.

Although a portion of a treatment group's work should be devoted to maintaining a group's optimal functioning, most of an effective group's time during the middle stage should be focused on helping members achieve their goals. This can be accomplished by helping members (1) maintain their awareness of their goals, (2) develop specific treatment plans, (3) overcome obstacles to members' work on treatment plans, and (4) carry out treatment plans.

Awareness of Goals

The first step in helping members to achieve their goals is to maintain their awareness of the goals they identified and agreed to work on in earlier group meetings. It is a good practice to begin each meeting with a very brief review of what occurred during the previous meeting and then to review the goals that each member is working toward achieving. A brief go-round or check-in serves to keep members focused on their goals and lets members know that there is an expectation that they should be working toward specific goals. It also gives members a chance to talk about their accomplishments or any obstacles that they encountered that they might like to work on during the meeting.

Workers should not assume that members continue to be aware of these goals as the group progresses. Reconfirming members' commitment to the goals they decided to achieve in earlier meetings serves several purposes. It lets members know the worker remains interested in their progress. It checks for a continued mutual understanding of the contract. It helps ensure that the worker and members remain focused on the same issues. Confirming goals helps avoid confusion and promotes members' organized and systematic efforts to work on contracts. Periodically confirming goals also gives the worker an opportunity to check whether any changes need to be made in the contract, and it gives members a chance to share their feelings and thoughts about what has been accomplished and what remains to be done. For example, the contract for a group of parents waiting to adopt children might include attending group meetings on (1) child development, (2) legal proceedings for adoption, (3) special issues and concerns of adopted children, and (4) supportive resources and services available for adoptive parents and their children. During each meeting the worker might ask members whether the content of the meeting was useful. Members can be given the opportunity to express their reactions to what has occurred and to make suggestions for improving future meetings or continuing the meetings as originally planned.

Maintaining members' awareness of and commitment to contract goals is essential in treatment groups that focus their work on individual contracts. At times, the worker may spend a considerable amount of time helping one member work toward a particular goal. For example, in a group for alcoholics, the worker might spend 30 minutes working with one member in relation to a secondary contract to help the member improve his methods of expressing anger. As a result, during the two-hour group meeting, only three or four members may have an opportunity to work intensively on their treatment goals. When this occurs, it is particularly important to generalize work with an individual to other members so that everyone feels involved in the group as the following case illustrates.

● **CASE EXAMPLE** *An Anger Management Group*

One member, John, just spent some time talking about his struggles with anger. He said that he finds it useful to take a time out when he feels anger overwhelming him, taking a walk around the block or just getting out of the room for a few minutes. The leader asked to hear from others about this. He asked others to talk about their struggles with keeping their anger under control. How do they deal with anger? Several members spoke up and the leader made connections between the similarities and differences in the ways members coped. For example, one member said that he took several deep breaths and told himself not to respond; another member said he also tried to get out of the situation but found it difficult to get away because his wife would pursue him into another room. Other members had experienced similar problems with trying to take a time out when a situation was getting explosive and this lead to a productive discussion about making some rules ahead of time with spouses or others about getting them to back off and allow for space during confrontations. One member mentioned that he had tried this but that his spouse said that they then never got back to talking about the situation that led to the anger. The worker asked if this came up for other members and one member said that he made an agreement with his wife that he would come back and talk about the situation without prompting after he had calmed down, but that it might not happen for a couple of hours or even until the next day. He said that when his wife realized that he would follow through and talk about the situation after he calmed down their heated arguments had decreased substantially.

If extensive time is spent with only a few members during one meeting, the worker should spend a brief period of time checking on other members' progress. Members who did not have an extensive opportunity to participate in a meeting should be encouraged to participate more during the next meeting. This strategy helps prevent repeated and prolonged attention to a few members and reduces the possibility that some members will avoid working on their contracts.

During the middle stage, the worker should also help members to develop a process for reviewing their treatment goals and contracts. Although the review process may be idiosyncratic to the needs of a particular group, the worker should avoid haphazard or constantly changing review procedures. Without a clearly defined process that all members can expect, there is the danger that some members' progress will be carefully monitored but that of others will not. When monitoring is haphazard, members who are assertive and highly involved are more likely to be monitored, but members who are less assertive and those who are resistant will not receive the attention they require. One method that is widely used is to facilitate a brief go-round during the beginning of a meeting or after the education a portion of a meeting in which all members, in turn, spend a few minutes describing their goal, what they accomplished since the last meeting, and what they plan to accomplish before the next meeting.

With unsystematic monitoring procedures, tasks that are to be completed between meetings might not receive proper follow-up. There is nothing more frustrating and disconcerting for members than to complete a task between meetings and then not be given the opportunity to report the results during the next meeting. In addition to creating an ambiguous demand for work, failure to follow up on tasks often gives members the impression that the worker is disorganized and that there is little continuity from one meeting to the next.

Once a systematic procedure for monitoring is established, the worker rarely needs to remind members to report their progress to the group. The expectation of weekly progress reports helps maintain members' motivation to work toward contract goals between sessions and reduces the need to remind members of their contract agreements. It also helps members gain a sense of independence and accomplishment as they assume responsibility for reporting their own progress.

Developing Treatment Plans

A second way to help members achieve contract goals is by facilitating the development of specific, goal-oriented treatment plans. When all members are working on the same contract goal, the worker develops and implements plans with the group as a whole. For example, in a weight-loss group, a medical social worker might help members prepare a method for monitoring their daily caloric intake, present material on good nutrition, and introduce methods for modifying eating habits. The worker might then help individual members discuss their special needs and help them modify what has been presented to fit their specific circumstances.

When helping a member develop and implement an individual treatment plan, the worker should enlist the support of all group members, as illustrated in the following case example. The worker should use every available opportunity to make connections among members, to point out parallel issues and concerns among members' situations, and to encourage all members to participate. As members become involved as helpers, the group's cohesion increases and members feel satisfied that they have something to contribute. Known as the *helper-therapy principle* (Lieberman & Borman, 1979), this strategy works in such a way that members who help others often benefit as much as those who are helped.

● **CASE EXAMPLE** *Developing a Treatment Plan*

In an outpatient psychotherapy group, information gathered by a member who experienced depression suggested that negative, self-deprecating thoughts and self-statements were maintaining his depression. The negative thoughts and self-statements persisted despite the member's adequate performance in job- and family-related responsibilities. As a result of this information, the worker helped the member develop a treatment plan that would assist the member to replace negative thoughts and self-deprecating comments with realistic thoughts and self-statements about his abilities, accomplishments, and positive qualities. The member contracted with the group to make a list of positive self-statements to be repeated each time an obtrusive, negative self-statement occurred. Secondary contracts included having the member ask other group members to describe how they perceived him during the interactions of the group and having the member get positive feedback from other significant persons in his life.

Before deciding on a treatment plan, the worker helps members explore and gather facts about their situations. A guided group discussion on the specifics of a situation, the alternatives that have been tried, and the possibilities that have not been explored is often sufficient to help members develop intervention plans. Sometimes, however, members try to grab at potential solutions without exploring alternatives, particularly when members are experiencing a great deal of stress or psychic pain from their problems. The worker should encourage members to explore alternatives thoroughly before deciding on an action plan.

An exploration of the situation may reveal a need for additional information. The member, with or without the help of the worker, might be asked to spend time between sessions gathering data. The process of members monitoring their own behavior and gathering additional facts about their situation is essential to the development of effective treatment plans.

Sometimes exploration of the problem may not immediately lead to a clear plan of action. The worker should help members consider alternatives before deciding on a final plan of action. Because of their professional training and knowledge, workers are often the primary generators of alternative intervention plans. Although the intervention plan that is selected may have been originally generated by the worker or another group member, members should be encouraged to refine alternatives and select the most appropriate plans for their own needs. When this occurs, they will not experience a plan as imposed by someone else. Members who experience their action plans as self-selected are more likely to follow through on them.

A treatment plan can be quite complex. It may involve a sequence of actions suggested by different members of the group. These different sequences of actions occur simultaneously. A complex plan should be divided into a series of discrete steps that are defined as clearly and specifically as possible. For example, to become more assertive, a member might (1) clarify the difference between aggressiveness and assertiveness through group discussion and reading a book on assertiveness, (2) decide in what situations to become more assertive, (3) practice being more assertive in the group during role plays and group discussion, (4) practice being assertive outside the group with family members or a friend, and (5) practice being assertive in a real-life situation.

Ideally, each step of the treatment plan should specify (1) who, (2) does what, (3) when, (4) where, (5) how often, and (6) under what conditions. It is especially important to be clear and specific when there are several people responsible for different aspects of a comprehensive treatment plan. Treatment plans often require the involvement of the worker, the client, other agency personnel, and the client's family. The effective worker should make sure that all persons who are a part of the treatment plan are clear about their roles, their responsibilities, and their expected contributions.

In some groups, all work is completed during meetings, but it is often helpful to encourage members to complete tasks between meetings. Many different tasks can be developed to help accomplish treatment plans between meetings. According to Wells (1994), there are (1) observational or monitoring tasks to gather information or to increase awareness of behaviors, emotions, or beliefs; (2) experiential tasks to arouse emotion and to challenge beliefs or attitudes; and (3) incremental change tasks to stimulate change step by step. Other types of tasks include mental or cognitive tasks to help group members change cognition and belief systems and paradoxical or two-sided tasks that result in changes no matter how they are carried out. For example, the treatment plan of a nonassertive group member includes the paradoxical task of having the member assert her right in a situation in which she would normally remain passive. If the member does the task, she is learning to be more assertive. If she does not do it, she is showing that she can assert herself in reference to her treatment plan.

Tasks can be individual, reciprocal, or shared (Tolson, Reid, & Garvin, 1994). For example, an individual task for a member in a smoking-cessation group may be to keep a log of the number of cigarettes smoked each day. Workers may also agree to perform individual tasks. A worker in a rural county welfare agency, for example, might agree to find out whether there are any transportation services available to enable teenage parents to attend a parenting skills group.

In a reciprocal task, if one person does something, another person will also do something. For example, if a member of an adolescent group does his assigned chore in his community residence each day for one week, the worker will help the member to obtain a pass to see his parents the next weekend.

A third type of task is shared by two or more people. For example, members of the group may form a buddy system (Rose, 1989), in which each member is expected to remind the buddy to work on a specific task between group meetings.

In developing treatment plans and specific tasks, the worker should proceed by making sure that members are able to carry out each step successfully. It is especially important for members to have a successful experience in carrying out the first task they agree to accomplish. If they are successful with their first task, they are much more likely to successfully complete a second task.

● **CASE EXAMPLE** *A Parenting Group Task*

In a parenting group each member was asked to develop a chart with the days of the week. The worker passed out cardboard paper and each member made a chart following an example the worker presented. Each member was then asked to choose a problem that they wanted to work on with their children. After going around the group and identifying a problem, each member was then asked to turn the problem into a positive behavior. For example, instead of grabbing for a toy from a sister or brother, asking nicely for the toy, or saying "please" when they wanted something from their parent. The parents were then given gold stars to put on their charts, and asked to use the chart at home during the next week between meetings to see if it made a positive difference in their children's behavior. The leader talked about when the chart would be used, such as one hour before dinner, and the importance of not taking away any gold stars that were obtained if the child failed to use the positive behavior. The parents talked about whether they should give their child a prize if they got a certain number of gold stars during any day that the chart was being used. They discussed the number of gold stars needed to obtain a prize and they. They each decided on a healthy snack that they could offer to their children as a prize for getting the designated number of gold stars.

Successfully completing an initial task gives members a sense that their goals are reachable. It also helps build self-confidence, feelings of self-efficacy, and a sense of control and mastery over the problem the member is attempting to alleviate. As members begin to feel self-confident, they are more likely to persist in their attempts at solving problems and concerns and are therefore more likely to be successful than when feelings of inadequacy limit their attempts to solve problems (Bandura, 1977). In this way, feelings of self-efficacy are reinforced and enhanced, which in turn can result in more effective and persistent problem solving in the future.

In developing treatment plans, the worker should assess a member's competencies and work with the member to plan an initial task that can be accomplished without an extraordinary amount of effort. Novice workers often develop treatment plans that are unrealistic. Members may agree to a treatment plan to please a worker or another group member, only to find that they are not prepared to undertake the tasks contained in the plan. It is also helpful to ensure that tasks are paced appropriately so that they become progressively more difficult as the member gains confidence and skill.

The worker can intervene to reduce the possibility that a member might have considerable difficulty in completing a task. Simulations, role plays, and other exercises can be performed in the group before the member tries the task at home, in the community, or in any other less hospitable environment. Rose (1989) suggests that members can be prepared for unreceptive or hostile environments by simulating these conditions in the group. One of the advantages of group treatment is that members can practice with other members of the group before they attempt to perform a task in the natural environment. Acting out roles also helps members become more aware of their own roles in a situation. An entire treatment method known as *psychodrama* is based on the benefits of acting out life experiences with others (Blatner, 1996).

Members should be encouraged to tackle one task at a time. In treatment planning, it is surprising to find how many clients with multiple problems suggest working on several different problems and their resulting tasks simultaneously. Although members often have good intentions in the group session, when they return home they may have less motivation to follow through on the multiple tasks they have agreed to accomplish. It is better to start with one or two carefully planned tasks than to encourage a member to work on a variety of tasks simultaneously. When a member has completed the initial tasks, he or she can take on more difficult ones. If a member does not perform a task satisfactorily, the worker should help the member to view this as a learning experience rather than as a failure. A task that can be completed on the basis of the information and feedback gained from the initial experience can then be planned.

At the end of a session, the worker should ask members to review the tasks that were agreed on during the session. It is not uncommon for members or the worker to forget tasks that were agreed to one or two hours earlier in the midst of an active and interesting group session. A review can eliminate confusion, misconceptions, or discrepancies about specific tasks. At this time, members should also be encouraged to remind each other of any tasks or portions of tasks that have not been mentioned. This process ensures that everyone leaves the group with a clear notion of what has to be done before the next meeting. A recording form such as that shown in Figure 9.2 can be used to help the worker and the group members keep track of the tasks they have agreed to complete.

Overcoming Obstacles to Members' Work

It is important to help members to work on their treatment goals when they encounter obstacles. Members need help to work on their goals because making changes in habituated behavior patterns can be difficult. For example, a member of a psychotherapy group who has contracted to stop drinking alcohol might begin drinking again after only two days of

---

FIGURE 9.2 ● *A Group Task Recording Form*

Date: _____

Session #: _____

Group: _____

Member's Name	Task	When	Where	How Often	Under What Circumstances

abstinence. In a different group, a member who has contracted to become independent of her parents might make excuses about why she has not had time to explore alternative living arrangements.

In both cases, members encountered obstacles to achieving their goals. First, the worker should check with the member to find out whether he or she acknowledges encountering an obstacle. Shulman (1999) suggests that the worker should also make a clear and specific "demand for work." The initial demand for work is a gentle reminder to the member that the worker and the other group members are interested in helping that member achieve personal goals. The demand for work should be accompanied by an offer to help the member overcome any obstacles to goal achievement.

With a member's agreement, the worker can encourage the member to explore what has been happening to prevent or block work on a particular treatment goal. The worker can also involve the group as a whole by having members participate in the analysis of the factors that may be inhibiting a member's goal achievement. This technique can help both the member who is having difficulty following through on a treatment contract and other members, who can practice overcoming ambivalence and resistance in their own change efforts.

Obstacles interfering with members' abilities to work toward treatment goals may be the result of an inappropriate contract. A careful analysis of the contract may indicate that it was poorly designed and should be renegotiated. A contract can be inappropriate for several reasons.

Problems with Contracts

- Goals in the contract are vaguely defined or too global to be achieved.
- Goals are too difficult to achieve at the current stage of treatment.
- The worker and the member focused on long-term goals rather than on more immediate, short-term goals that have a higher probability of being accomplished in a shorter period of time.
- There is a misunderstanding between the member and the worker about the nature of specific contract goals.
- Inappropriate goals were set without careful assessment of the member's situation.
- Changing problems and situations necessitate modifications in the treatment goals developed for a contract made earlier in the group's development.

For all these reasons, helping members work toward treatment goals often means helping them clarify, redefine, or renegotiate contracts.

Working toward goals also involves increasing members' motivation to take action to overcome the obstacles they have encountered. If a member agrees that action is important, the worker's task is to help the member believe that change is possible. Many group members are willing to act but refuse to do so because they do not believe in their own ability to change their situation. In such cases, self-instructional training (Meichenbaum, 1977), described in Chapter 10, may be useful in increasing a member's willingness to attempt a new behavior. It can also be helpful to ask other members to share their experiences regarding behavior change. They often serve as convincing role models who inspire and motivate reluctant members.

When the lack of motivation is severe, the worker should consider renegotiating a contract, focusing the new contract on helping the member increase motivation to work on a specific issue or concern rather than to work on the concern itself. Such a contract may involve helping the member examine factors that affect motivation to work on a particular goal and to examine any potential consequences of not working toward the goal.

When helping members overcome obstacles, workers should not ask "why" questions. Group members often do not have the answers to "why" questions, and if they do, the explanation may attribute causes to incorrect sources, which further complicates the problem. Instead, the worker should ask members "how" or "what" questions that encourage members to describe cognitive, affective, behavioral, or environmental circumstances that may be diminishing their ability to work on treatment goals.

"How" questions and "what" questions keep members focused on current behaviors that lead to or exacerbate existing problems. For example, the worker might ask, "What occurred just before you became angry?" or "How did you feel when _____ happened?" Such questions tend to elicit actual behavior and events, but "why" questions, if they can be answered at all, tend to elicit the opinion or judgments of members on the basis of their interpretations of information. Thus, "how" questions are more likely than are "why" questions to elicit information that will help members make active behavior changes and achieve their treatment goals.

The final step is to help members decide what actions to take to overcome obstacles and renew their progress toward treatment goals. In making the plan, the worker helps members to get support for their efforts from as many sources as possible. This is demonstrated in the following case example.

● **CASE EXAMPLE** *Overcoming Obstacles to Members' Work*

In an alcoholism treatment group, the worker asked a member who had relapsed to go around the group and promise the other group members that he would not drink until the next group meeting. Members were encouraged to support the member, who emphasized that slips might occur for any member, and that temporary relapses should not be viewed as insurmountable relapses. By making replies such as "I admire your determination to work on this problem," group members' responses to the member displayed their support and empathy. Group members also helped by suggesting that the member think of cognitive self-statements that would support his sobriety and by suggesting strategies for home environment modification such as removing all remaining alcohol from his house—a suggestion that the member had resisted before the relapse. The worker asked several members to give the member a call during the week to help him follow through on his verbal commitment. To enlist the help of his family and friends, the worker asked the member for permission to contact family and friends and to gain their support and encouragement for the member's decision not to drink. To provide continued support during evening hours, the member was referred to an Alcoholics Anonymous group. In this way, the member received support from a variety of sources within and outside the group.

In summary, helping members work toward treatment goals is an important activity for any worker who plans to lead effective treatment groups. All treatment groups require effort from members if they are to be successful in achieving their goals. The worker's task is to help members mobilize their resources and maximize their use of the group to help them accomplish their goals. The worker should be constantly vigilant and point out inertia, ambivalence, and other psychological, social, and environmental barriers that block members' progress in the group. Because inertia, ambivalence, and reluctance to change are common even among highly motivated clients, the strategies and techniques on working with reluctant and resistant group members, presented later in this chapter, may also be useful in helping members to work on their treatment plans.

Helping Members Carry Out Treatment Plans

Workers can use five intervention roles to help members carry out their treatment plans. These roles are (1) enabler, (2) broker, (3) mediator, (4) advocate, and (5) educator. Although other roles have been identified as appropriate for helping members carry out their treatment plans, these five roles are the most important and most frequently assumed by workers leading various types of treatment groups. These roles are summarized in the following list.

Treatment Plan Intervention Roles

- *Enabler:* Helps members utilize their own resources and strengths; encourages members to share their thoughts with the group; supports a culture of mutual aid among members
- *Broker:* Identifies community resources that may help members carry out their treatment plans; connects members with these resources
- *Mediator:* Resolves disputes, conflicts, or opposing views within the group or between a member and some other person or organization; takes a neutral stand and helps members arrive at a settlement or agreement that is mutually acceptable
- *Advocate:* Represents members' interests and needs; helps members obtain services and resources
- *Educator:* Presents new information to help resolve members' concerns; demonstrates and models new behaviors; leads role plays, simulations, and in vivo activities to help members practice new or different ways of behaving in problematic situations

Working with Reluctant and Resistant Group Members during the Middle Phase

We have already described working with involuntary members during the beginning phase of group development. When working with involuntary group members during the middle phase, it should be kept in mind that members always have the right to refuse to participate. It is important, however, for the worker to point out the consequences of refusal, and to clarify nonnegotiable aspects of participation if involuntary members choose to participate in the group. Nonnegotiable aspects may include rules about attendance and participation, such as coming on time and not coming to the group intoxicated or high on drugs. It is also important to clarify members' rights and choices. The worker should attempt to maximize members' freedoms within the constraints of the legal and nonlegal pressures they are experiencing to be in the group and to change behaviors.

Behroozi (1992) points out that not all involuntary group members are alike. Individuals in involuntary groups resist goal setting for many reasons. Some perceive their problems to be too embarrassing to work on them in a group. Some are angry that they have been considered incapable of handling their own problems. Some view themselves as failures or as incompetent and consequently find their personal problems too daunting to tackle. Some deny problems because to admit them would throw their view of themselves into chaos.

One of the first tasks of the worker, therefore, is to develop a nonjudgmental, accepting, and safe group environment in which members can feel free to express their own views of their problems, as illustrated in the following case. As members express their views, it is important for the worker to assess members' motivation for being in the group and to identify how the group can be helpful to them (Rooney, 1992).

● **CASE EXAMPLE**   *Creating a Safe Environment*

Several members of a nursing home resident council were reluctant to participate in discussions about problems they were having in relation to their institutional environment. Some of the members were concerned that the group facilitator, who was also the staff social worker, would represent the viewpoints of the organization and its administration. In addition, this was the first formal group experience for several members and they seemed to be anxious when they tried to share their views. The facilitator also knew that other members had been criticized by staff members for complaining about their care. The worker commented on her observations of members' reluctance to talk about their perceptions of care in the home and encouraged members to listen carefully to each others' suggestions. The worker modeled this skill by using strong active listening skills and by using positive body language when responding to members' comments. In addition, the worker encouraged members to develop a policy on confidentiality of group discussions about problems encountered in the nursing home. The worker also clarified her role of instructed advocate in which she was responsible for helping council members bring their suggestions for change to the administrative officers of the organization. After the worker modeled nonjudgmental behaviors, members became more involved in sharing their ideas for change.

As members express their views, it is helpful to adopt a position that maximizes members' sense of control and expertise. Acknowledging that members can help the leader understand what it is like to be in their shoes and that members are in the best position to help themselves demonstrates respect and can do much to help the worker join with members in their fledgling attempts to express and work on their concerns.

It is also essential to acknowledge members' feelings and reactions to being in the group during the middle phase when the work gets harder and members are being asked to make changes in their lifestyles. Authentic and direct communication helps members to express their feelings rather than hide them. Sometimes, paradoxical interventions can be combined with authentic and direct communication to help members to express and begin to deal with their feelings of resistance (Milgram & Rubin, 1992). For example, the worker might state that he or she is aware that the members were ordered to attend the group or face more severe consequences and that they are not interested in what the group has to offer. This can sometimes have a paradoxical result in that often one or more members react by talking about how the group might be helpful.

The worker should try to uncover the feelings and thoughts that underlie members' resistant behavior. For example, are members scared or hurt? Are they trying to control the situation or to avoid confronting issues that they experience as too difficult to face? Kottler

(1992) points out that, once the underlying meaning of resistant behavior has been figured out, the worker is in a much better position to offer therapeutic assistance.

Engaging in collaborative problem solving can also be helpful when working with reluctant or resistant clients (Trotter, 1999). Collaborative problem solving involves soliciting members' views and definitions of their problems, helping them to develop modest but highly achievable goals that they are motivated to work on, and working with members to develop strategies to achieve these goals. It is important that the goals that are developed are the members', not the worker's (Trotter, 1999).

Dramatizing naturally occurring consequences also works well with some members who are reluctant to work on problems (Edelwich & Brodsky, 1992). The worker should avoid talking about abstract consequences and, instead, focus on the natural consequences that have occurred because members failed to confront their problems. For example, the worker might say, "You almost lost your license for driving while you were drunk. What would you do if they took away your license? How would you get to work? In what other ways would not being able to drive affect you?"

The worker should avoid moralizing or blaming. Problem behaviors should be discussed in a direct, factual way. Whenever possible, members should be asked to describe in their own words the negative consequences that have resulted from problem behaviors. For example, the worker might divulge what members' blood-alcohol levels were at the time of their arrests for driving while intoxicated and ask them to describe what consequences they have had as a result of the arrest.

Workers should encourage resistant members to make "I" statements. Instead of allowing members to project blame onto someone else, "I" statements help members take responsibility for their feelings, thoughts, and actions.

Confrontation is sometimes necessary to help members overcome their resistance (Kottler, 1992). It is better for members to confront each other, rather than for the leader to confront members (Edelwich & Brodsky, 1992; Milgram & Rubin, 1992). The latter approach can lead members to coalesce against the leader. Also, because members' confrontations are based on members' experiences, their confrontations are often more powerful than workers' confrontations.

The leader should strive to build a group culture that encourages confrontation of members' motivation to work in the group. However, because resistant members avoid taking responsibility for their actions, it is unrealistic to expect them to confront each other initially. The worker must first model constructive confrontation.

According to Edelwich and Brodsky (1992), constructive confrontations should be (1) solicited rather than imposed, (2) done gently and with caring, (3) descriptive rather than evaluative, (4) specific and concrete, (5) presented in an atmosphere of trust, and (6) timed so that the member is able to hear and experience the full effect of the interaction. Constructive confrontations should include a descriptive statement, an "I" statement, and a reference to natural consequences (Edelwich & Brodsky, 1992). For example, the worker might say, "You say that you didn't do anything and you can't understand why you're being singled out. But if I had been caught driving with a blood alcohol level as high as yours, I would have been given the same choice as you: lose my license or come here. And if I kept avoiding the consequences of my behavior, I'd have problems on the job, at home, and with the law—as you are having."

To build a group culture in which confrontation of resistance and avoidance of problems is normative among members, rather than solely emanating from the leader to members, it can be helpful to include former members or members with greater longevity in the group. Members who have already confronted and grappled with their own resistance can discuss their initial reluctance to participate in the group and how the group enabled them to work through their resistance and confront their problems. For example, it is helpful to have more experienced members talk about how avoiding problems does not help and how facing up to problems is the first step to doing something about them.

To create empathy and to help members take responsibility for their actions, as Rooney (1992) points out, it can also be helpful to invite victims to group meetings. These individuals can talk about the experience of victimization and its impact on them.

Even though constructive confrontations can help overcome members' resistance to working in the group, it is important to remember that reluctant and resistant members will continue to experience obstacles to goal achievement as they attempt to develop and implement treatment plans. These obstacles can reduce their motivation, which makes them reluctant to continue to work to accomplish specific goals. Reid (1992), for example, points out that beliefs about change and obstacles encountered in the external environment reduce members' motivation to engage in tasks to resolve particular problems. Methods designed to help members change their beliefs and to make the external environment more responsive are described in Chapter 10.

Although all the tactics mentioned can be helpful when working with resistant clients, the most important thing the worker can do is maintain a therapeutic stance. In a wonderful book on working with difficult clients, Kottler (1992) points out that it is essential for workers to avoid personalizing oppositional behavior. Also, one must avoid retaliating, threatening, and levying punitive sanctions. Instead, the worker should be patient and compassionate, keep a sense of humor, and avoid feeling omnipotent, that is, believing that one can help anyone, all the time.

Monitoring and Evaluating the Group's Progress

Monitoring and evaluating progress provides feedback for workers and members, which is useful in developing, modifying, and changing treatment plans. It also is helpful in maintaining the functioning of the group as a whole. Monitoring and evaluating are important ongoing processes that should occur throughout the life of a group.

One of the most common methods of obtaining feedback from members during the middle stage of a group's development is to give members a session evaluation form (such as that shown in Chapter 13, Figure 13.3) at the end of each group session. Although the format of session evaluation questions (closed-ended, Likert-type questions and open-ended questions) remains fairly standard from group to group, the content of questions varies. Changing the content of questions provides workers with the specific information they need about a particular group's work.

How frequently should session evaluation forms be administered? In some groups, they can be used at the end of each session. Workers who are not familiar with using session evaluation forms sometimes wonder how they will be received by members, but brief forms that take only a few minutes to fill out are not a burden for members to complete. In fact, members often enjoy the chance to let the worker know what they like and dislike about the group.

In other groups, workers may prefer to evaluate the group's progress after every second or third session. The exact frequency of monitoring and evaluating ultimately depends on the need for ongoing feedback about the group's development. Verbal evaluations are often used as a substitute for written evaluations, but anonymous written evaluations may offer better feedback because they can offer a measure of confidentiality not available through verbal evaluations.

Other frequently used methods of monitoring and evaluating include having members self-monitor their behaviors and having others who are familiar with members' concerns (such as other workers or family members) report progress to the worker. These and other monitoring and evaluation methods are described in Chapters 8 and 13. The actual methods used for obtaining feedback are, however, not as important as whether the feedback is systematically solicited, collected, and acted on. Obtaining feedback allows workers to fine-tune a group as it progresses through the middle stage. It also is a signal to members that their opinions are valued and that their ideas and concerns will be analyzed and acted on. For these reasons, monitoring and evaluating a group's progress is an essential worker activity during the middle stage of group development.

SUMMARY

The middle stage of treatment groups is the period in which members focus on the goals they have contracted to achieve in the group. This chapter focuses on six foundation activities that all workers perform while leading treatment groups during their middle stage. The section about preparing for group meetings includes a discussion of how to select program activities. The section on structuring the group's work includes a discussion of the optimal amount of structure to meet members' needs. The section about involving and empowering group members includes building on members' strengths and their commitment to the group as a whole. The section on helping members achieve contract goals includes techniques for (1) keeping members aware of goals they have contracted for, (2) developing treatment plans, (3) overcoming obstacles to members' work on treatment plans, and (4) helping members carry out their treatment plans. The section about working with reluctant and resistant group members includes a discussion of constructive uses of confrontation. The chapter concludes with the foundation activity of monitoring and evaluating the group's progress.

● CASE EXAMPLE

As Jim planned for the middle stage of his group for men who were physically abusive to their partners, he grew increasingly concerned about how he was going to help overcome their resistance to participating in the group. As a condition of their probation, members were mandated to attend a 10-session group that had both an educational and a rehabilitative focus. Jim's responsibility was to conduct the group and write individual progress reports for the probation department.

During the initial two meetings, members spent a great deal of time objecting to being mandated to attend the group. Several members noted that although the probation department required them to be there, they felt little obligation to participate in discussions. Others stated that they were thinking of dropping out. Jim knew that these statements represented initial resistance to being mandated for treatment. Jim also recognized that these members, who once exercised control over their relationships through violence, were now in a position of being controlled through the legal process. Because domestic violence often involves power and control, the involuntary status of the membership was particularly difficult for members to accept.

During the first session, Jim allowed members to express their feelings and to ventilate. He also pointed out their ambivalence about dealing with the problems that had caused their situation. He hoped that by doing this he could overcome some of the initial resistance and help members accept the purpose of the group. Although this helped somewhat, several members continued to demonstrate verbal and nonverbal expressions of resentment and anger about being required to attend the group. However, Jim asked members to talk about what the consequences of nonattendance might be. This discussion helped reinforce and make more vivid members' recognition that, if they chose not to attend, they would have their probation revoked and be jailed. Through discussing possible consequences, members seemed to become more resigned to their attendance, although they continued to show some resentment about having to discuss what they considered to be private matters.

During the second session, Jim helped some members to overcome resistance by reframing their situations. Jim assured the members that they had rights and choices about attending the group. He suggested that although they were ordered by the court to attend, they had also actively chosen to obey this mandate. He gave them positive feedback for making this choice, and suggested that now that they had made this decision, they might as well decide to make the best possible use of the group. By avoiding threats, moralizing, and blaming, Jim secured the initial participation of the members.

As the group entered the middle stage, Jim sensed that the men were beginning to accept their involuntary status as members. However, when he suggested that members begin to discuss what individual goals they might want to accomplish in the group, he was again met with silence and nonverbal communications that suggested to him that members were not willing to move into the middle (i.e., work) phase of the group. A few members eventually noted that they felt that they could handle their problems by themselves and were reluctant to discuss their personal situations with other members. Jim stated that sometimes he thought that, as a man, he was expected always to be in control of his feelings and be competent enough to handle his own problems. He asked members if they sometimes felt this way too. One member agreed that this seemed to be true for him, and then several other members nodded in agreement. This led to some meaningful discussion about role expectations but did not seem to help members identify individual goals for changing their feelings and behaviors.

By modeling nonjudgmental and accepting behavior, Jim helped members talk briefly about their relationships with their partners. Jim noted that most of the members verbalized a strong need for having power and control in their relationships with their partners. He wondered out loud whether members were reluctant to have their assumptions about relationships challenged. He acknowledged members' feelings and beliefs, but at the same time, he challenged members to rethink how they viewed their relationships. He speculated that this might be one of the reasons that members were unwilling to discuss individual goals for themselves. Although some members still blamed their partners for the violence, for the most part, they responded well to Jim's honest and authentic confrontations.

Jim used two techniques that gradually helped members respond to his demand for work. First, he gave members a copy of the "Power and Control Wheel," which illustrates how domestic violence centers around power and control. He discussed some of the theoretical aspects of the cycle of domestic violence. It took some discussion for members to understand the point of view expressed in this material, but Jim could see that it was sinking in. Second, he discussed how he had helped members of other groups like this to have more satisfying relationships with their partners. He noted that success and better relationships were both possibilities if members committed themselves to working hard in the group. He again assured members that he would be supportive of their efforts, but that they needed to take the first step by thinking about their individual goals. The introduction of new information that challenged members' beliefs, accompanied by the instillation of hope, eventually overcame members' resistance to moving into deeper aspects of their problems. By the end of the fourth session, members had developed individual goals they could work on for the rest of the group sessions. In later sessions, resistance re-emerged again. For example, some members had great dif-

ficulty accepting that they needed to change some of their thoughts and behaviors. Other members had difficulty at work or in other environments that contributed to their resistance to investing themselves in change efforts.

The sessions were difficult ones because of the different types and levels of resistance in the group. Nevertheless, Jim's understanding about involuntary group members and about resistance within the group helped him to avoid taking the resistance he encountered personally. Jim continued to struggle, however, both with his own strong feelings about violence and working with men who had dysfunctional beliefs about relationships and with the group's constant testing of his ability to be accepting and nonjudgmental. He discussed these feelings, and how he was handling them, with his supervisor.

chapter 10

Treatment Groups: Specialized Methods

This chapter focuses on specialized intervention methods for individual group members, the group as a whole, and the group's external environment. Even though this chapter sequentially presents interventions at the three levels, in actual practice, interventions at one level often affect other levels. As the group unfolds, the skilled worker moves easily among all the levels by combining interventions for the individual member, the group as a whole, and the group's environment to help members reach their treatment goals.

INTERVENING WITH GROUP MEMBERS

When intervening with individual group members, the worker may select from:

- Intrapersonal interventions that focus on members' cognition and affects, that is, their thoughts, beliefs, values, feelings, sensations, and emotions
- Interpersonal interventions that focus on members' relationships with others within and outside the group
- Environmental interventions that seek to change or modify the psychosocial and physical space in which members function

Intrapersonal interventions are particularly appropriate when an assessment has determined that a member's bio-psychosocial development may have helped to contribute to dysfunctional or irrational belief systems. Interpersonal interventions are particularly useful when an assessment has determined that members need further development of their skills in relating to others. Environmental interventions are particularly useful when an assessment determines that a member lacks material resources to ameliorate a problem or when the environment is impeding a member's ability to accomplish a goal.

Intrapersonal Interventions

Since the beginnings of group work practice, workers with psychodynamic orientations have focused most interventions in treatment groups on the intrapersonal aspects of group members' behavior. In recent years, there has also been a growing interest in techniques to intervene in the covert, intrapersonal lives of group members using cognitive and cognitive-behavioral approaches to practice (Beck, 1995; Bieling, McCabe, & Antony, 2006; Dobson, 2001; Heimberg & Becker, 2002; Klosko & Sanderson, 1998; Rathus & Sanderson, 1999; Reinecke, Dattilio, & Freeman, 2003; Rose, 1998; Segal, Williams, & Teasdale, 2002; Smucker, Dancu, & Foa, 1999; Wright, Basco, & Thase, 2006). These approaches to practice have been found to be efficacious in clinical trials and hence fit in with the recent focus in social work on evidence-based practice approaches.

Before using specific techniques, group workers should be aware of the overall process of helping members make intrapersonal changes. This process includes helping members to:

- Identify and discriminate among thoughts, feelings, and behaviors
- Recognize associations between specific thoughts, feelings, and behaviors
- Analyze the rationality of thoughts and beliefs
- Change distorted or irrational thoughts and beliefs

Identifying and Discriminating

The first step in any intrapersonal intervention is to help members accurately identify thoughts, feelings, and behaviors and to discriminate among them. Some members have great difficulty putting their subjective thoughts and feelings into words. But without clearly identifying a member's thoughts and feelings for the rest of the group, it is not possible to help members cope with or change these covert processes.

In helping members identify and discriminate behavior from thoughts and feelings, members should be encouraged to describe their behavior in specific, observable terms as if a camera were taking a picture of the event and the member were a bystander observing the behavior. Sometimes, members have a difficult time describing feelings. It is common for group members to respond to a question about what they are feeling with a description of a behavior or a thought. This response is particularly true of men, who are taught as they are growing up that expressing feelings is a feminine, not masculine, trait. This is illustrated in the following case.

● **CASE EXAMPLE** *Describing Feelings*

In response to a question about what he was feeling, an obviously angry group member stated, "I'm not feeling anything." When the worker responded that people are always feeling something, no matter how slight, the member said, "I'm feeling that your interpretation of my behavior is not correct." This statement was, of course, a thought, not a feeling. The statement also reflected the difficulty this member had in acknowledging this feeling. The worker had several choices at this point. The worker could wait for other members to talk about how they experienced the member's behavior or ask the group how they perceived the member. Then, the worker could lead the group in a discussion about how feelings are expressed and how they are perceived. The worker could also help the member to comment on and integrate the feedback he received from the group and become more aware of how he is perceived by others.

To help members who have difficulty discriminating feelings from thoughts, the worker can have the member get feedback from the group. In the previously described situation, for example, the member went around the group and asked the other members how they perceived he was feeling. Responses expressing that he appeared to be angry gradually indicated to the member that he was not in touch with his feelings. Sometimes it is necessary to have members practice discriminating thoughts from feelings in several situations inside and outside the group before they are able to identify and separate them correctly.

Recognizing Associations

The second step in intrapersonal interventions is to help members recognize that there is an association among thoughts, feelings, and behaviors. For example, if a man thinks someone is deliberately following him as he walks home one evening, he is likely to feel apprehensive and to behave accordingly. He may look over his shoulder or walk on the well-lighted side of a street. Similarly, if a woman thinks she is not skillful at a particular task, she is likely to feel incompetent and is less likely to continue to work on the task if she encounters difficulty than if she thinks that she can perform the task adequately.

For members to alter associations among thoughts, feelings, and behaviors, they must be aware of their existence. Awareness can be accomplished through a self-monitoring process. Members are asked to monitor particular thoughts and the feelings and behaviors that occur immediately following them. The group helps members look for patterns of association among particular thoughts, feelings, and behaviors. Sometimes members may clearly remember specific thoughts and their associated feelings and behaviors, and it may not be necessary to spend time monitoring them before reporting them to the group. This is often the case with automatic thoughts that constantly recur to members (Beck, 1995; Beck & Freeman, 1990; Freeman, Pretzer, Fleming, & Simons, 2004; Smucker et al., 1999).

Data about thoughts, feelings, and behaviors collected either prospectively or retrospectively should be discussed in the group. Such a discussion usually reveals that specific thoughts are exacerbating or maintaining unwanted feeling states and behavior patterns. For example, an anxious group member may find that her thoughts are focused on her "inability to do anything right" and that she would not be able to complete her work assignments on time. By discussing her thoughts in the group, she became aware that the thoughts led to her fears and her anxiety about her performance on the job and, in turn, tended to distract her from her work, which led her to feel more anxious. Both consequences were reinforcing her beliefs that she would not be able to complete her assignments, that she could not do anything right, and that she was a failure.

The previous example suggests that thoughts lead to feelings and behavior, but it is also possible that particular cues or signals can lead to thoughts, which can, in turn, lead to feelings and behavior. For example, a cue for an anxiety-producing thought might be the approach of a person of the opposite sex in a singles bar. The approach signals the person who begins to think anxiety-producing thoughts, such as "I hope he doesn't come over here" and "I won't know what to say." The thoughts can then lead to feelings of anxiety and to avoidance behavior. Such a sequence of events can become habituated, and thus a particular cue or even the thought of the particular cue can lead to the entire sequence of dysfunctional thoughts, feelings, and behaviors.

The second step in the process of intrapersonal interventions, therefore, also includes helping members become aware of internal cues, such as muscle tension or butterflies in the stomach, and external cues, such as the approach of a person, that trigger a sequence of events. In long-term treatment focused on personality change, workers may want to help members gain insight into the historical determinants of the cues. Once members are aware of the cues that trigger an association between thoughts, feelings, and behavior, they are ready to move to the next step in the process.

Analyzing the Rationality of Thoughts and Beliefs

The third step in intrapersonal intervention is to help members analyze the rationality of the thoughts and beliefs that maintain or exacerbate dysfunctional feelings and behavior patterns. Epictetus wrote in *The Enchiridion:* "Men are not disturbed by things but by the views taken of them." According to many cognitive psychologists, dysfunctional and irrational thoughts and beliefs arise from erroneous or misleading interpretations of events (Ellis, 1962; Freeman, Pretzer, Fleming, & Simons, 2004; Klosko & Sanderson, 1998; Mahoney, 1974; Meichenbaum, 1977; Stern & Drummond, 1991). Group members may engage in the faulty thinking patterns and cognitive distortions.

Cognitive Distortions

- Overgeneralize from an event
- Selectively focus on portions of an event
- Take too much responsibility for events that are beyond their control
- Think of the worst possible consequence of future events
- Engage in either-or dichotomous thinking
- Assume that because certain events have led to particular consequences in the past they will automatically lead to the same consequences if they occur in the future

Sometimes corrective information and feedback are sufficient to change thoughts and beliefs based on incomplete or incorrect information. For example, some teenage girls believe that they will not become pregnant if they have sexual intercourse only once or twice. With proper information, however, beliefs about the result of sexual activity can be changed.

Ellis (1962) and others (Beck, 1995; Leahy, 1996; Sheldon, 1995; Smucker et al., 1999; Stern & Drummond, 1991; Yost, Beutler, Corbishley, & Allender, 1985) have suggested that faulty interpretations occur because of irrational beliefs and ideas people have about the way things should operate in their world. For example, members may believe that they must be thoroughly "competent, adequate, and achieving in all possible respects if they are to consider themselves worthwhile" (Ellis, p. 63). Ellis lists 11 common irrational ideas that affect members' interpretations of events. These beliefs are usually based on absolutist thinking, rather than on well-reasoned, logical interpretations or elaborations from factual evidence. Words such as *should, ought,* and *must* are cues to the existence of absolutist thinking, which may lead to irrational or erroneous interpretations of events. For example, a group member might believe that to consider himself worthwhile he must be competent in all possible respects. When his performance falls short of his unrealistically high standards, he becomes depressed.

From a psychodynamic point of view, the worker may also want to explore with the members how what they learned from their families of origin contribute to their current thoughts and beliefs about themselves (Rutan & Stone, 2001). In this framework, thoughts and beliefs are shaped early in life by relationships with the mother, father, and other primary caretakers. The worker's role is to help group members explore how these early relationships affect their current functioning. The insight gained from this exploration can then be used by group members to examine current coping strategies. This, in turn, can lead to a reduction in coping strategies that are no longer effective and to new coping skills that are more responsive to the current situation.

Changing Thoughts, Beliefs, and Feeling States

The fourth step in intrapersonal interventions is to help members change irrational or distorted thoughts, beliefs, and associated feeling states. Several techniques that have been developed for this purpose are listed here along with a brief description of their use in group treatment.

COGNITIVE RESTRUCTURING.   *Cognitive restructuring* is a term first used by Mahoney (1974) to refer to a group of techniques such as rational emotive therapy and misattribution therapy. These techniques are designed to expose faulty logic in group members' thought patterns and to help them replace the irrational thought processes with logical, rational patterns of thought. Yost, Beutler, Corbishley, and Allender (1985), for example, report using cognitive restructuring techniques effectively when working with groups of depressed older adults.

Mahoney (1995a, 1995b) has pointed out that belief systems are formed through the course of development as individuals interact with their social environment. Thus, beliefs may not be "faulty" or "irrational" but constructed from the unique social experiences and the processing of these experiences that continually occurs within each individual. Smucker and colleagues (1999), for example, describe how childhood trauma experiences can affect adult survivors. Group work can help members become more aware of the factors that shape and maintain belief systems and how these factors might be modified through new experiences within and outside the group. For example, Bauer and McBride (2003) help members who suffer from manic depressive illness to identify the thoughts, feelings, and behaviors they experience while being depressed. This helps members to become more self-aware. These feelings, thoughts, and behaviors can then be used to develop a Personal Depression Profile. In subsequent sessions, a personal care plan and illness management skills can be developed based on this profile.

The worker can help members change belief systems by pursuing the activities listed here.

Changing Belief Systems

- Have members examine the experiences on which thoughts and beliefs are based
- Help members examine the way past experiences were construed
- Help members consider the impact of their construction of experiences in their current lives
- Help members get feedback from others in the group about alternative ways of construing and responding to experiences
- Practice new ways of responding both cognitively and behaviorally that will enhance members' current coping abilities

Through a combination of group discussion, analysis, and action, members help each other gain insight into their attributions concerning previous events and the effects of their construction of events on their current lives. Cognition and behaviors that result from the attributions are replaced with thoughts, beliefs, and behaviors that are more functional for coping with events in their current lives. Smucker and colleagues (1999) refer to this as *imagery rescripting and reprocessing.*

COGNITIVE SELF-INSTRUCTION.   Cognitive self-instruction refers to helping members use internal dialogues and covert self-statements for solving problems and coping with difficult life events. Children and adults can use the technique to replace dysfunctional internal dialogues with self-statements that help them to solve a problem. For example, instead of a member's saying to herself, "I can't do this," she can learn to say, "I'll try to do it the best I can" or "I'll bet my answer is as good or better than anyone else's," and "First I'll examine all the data and then I'll think of the possible solutions."

Also referred to as stress inoculation training (Meichenbaum & Fitzpatrick, 1993), cognitive self-instructions can be used to prepare for a particular situation or to help a member perform effectively during a situation. For example, to prepare for a situation, a member might say, "When I talk to Sally, I'll tell her directly that I can't do it. If she tries to persuade me, I'll just repeat that I've decided not to do it." While in a particular situation, a member might say, "I'm in control" or "I can do this."

It has been found by D'Zurilla and Goldfried (1971) and Meichenbaum (1977) that internal dialogues are important mediators of effective problem solving. Poor problem solvers tend to repeat dysfunctional self-statements, which make them give up more quickly and get blocked more easily in problem-solving efforts than persons whose self-statements encourage active problem-solving efforts. Research evidence and clinical experience confirms that this procedure is an effective intrapersonal intervention for members who engage in dysfunctional internal dialogues (Beck, 1995; Leahy, 1996; Sheldon, 1995).

THOUGHT STOPPING.   Some group members have difficulty controlling maladaptive or self-defeating thoughts and internal dialogues. The thought-stopping technique is a way to help members reduce these thoughts (Davis, Eshelman, & McKay, 2000). While the member is concentrating on a thought, the worker suddenly and emphatically says, "Stop." This procedure is repeated several times. The member gradually begins to think "Stop" and to remember the worker's voice saying "Stop" whenever the obtrusive thought occurs. Variations of the technique include having members pinch themselves when obtrusive thoughts occur, having them replace obtrusive thoughts with covert dialogues and images that are not self-defeating, and having members meditate on a particular scene or phrase when obtrusive thoughts occur.

REFRAMING.   Reframing is a cognitive technique used to help group members see situations or problems from another point of view. It means "to change the conceptual and/or emotional setting or viewpoint in relation to which the situation is experienced and to place it in another frame which fits the facts of the same concrete situation equally well or even better, and thereby changes its entire meaning" (Watzlawick, Weakland, & Fisch, 1974, p. 95).

For example, a member who complains that he is afraid to ask a coworker to dinner might be helped to reframe the situation as one in which he is sparing himself and his coworker from possible romantic entanglements that may interfere with job performance. In another case, a single parent who is angry at her former husband for encouraging their child to fight back when teased may be helped to reframe the situation as one in which her former husband is helping the child develop and maintain a male identity.

Once a member experiences a problem from a new perspective, the positive aspects of the situation are highlighted and the negative aspects of the situation have a better chance of being changed. The woman, for example, may then thank her former husband for staying involved with their child and suggest some other ways that the husband might help the child, such as how to settle disputes without fighting. The male group member may develop a platonic friendship with his coworker.

Reframing can also be used to help a member experience a problem or concern as an asset (Yost et al., 1985). For example, in a situation in which a member's spouse does not want to have sexual relations, the problem can be viewed as a helpful sign that something is wrong in their relationship.

VISUALIZATION AND COGNITIVE IMAGERY TECHNIQUES. Everyone daydreams, has memories of certain places, people, and things. Visualization encourages group members to focus on a particular image that is relaxing for them. For example, group members might be asked to imagine themselves on a beach, sitting on a bench near a pond, or in a park. When visualizing the scene, members are asked to try to get all their senses involved. For example, members are asked to visualize their favorite beach, the boats, trees, and the cloud formations. They are asked to feel the sunlight hitting their body, to hear the sound of the waves, and to smell and taste the salt air and the other aromas they remember. As members are visualizing the scene they are asked to say things to themselves that reduce tension such as "The sun feels good and I am feeling at peace with myself and the world around me." When using visualization in a group, workers should guide the group through a particular visualization. Have the group members sit in a relaxing position and close their eyes. Set the scene and gradually add details. If workers have access to an audiotape with sounds from the scene, such as waves, breezes blowing, and so forth, they can use it to enhance the experience. Workers can also ask group members to do their own visualization, asking them to add imagery, sound, color, smell, and tastes as they go along. Once the visualization is complete, workers can do a group go-round asking members what scene they imagined, why they find it especially relaxing, and how they might use visualization at home between sessions.

Flooding and implosion are two other cognitive imagery techniques used to extinguish excessive and unproductive reactions to feared or anxiety-provoking events (Masters, Burish, Hollon, & Rimm, 1987; Shipley & Boudewyns, 1980). In *Implosion,* the member is asked to imagine the most extreme version of a feared event or stimulus within the protected environment of the group. Thus, if a group member experiences anxiety when thinking about asking someone for a date, the member would be asked to imagine that person saying no and making a disparaging remark such as "I wouldn't go out with someone like you" or "You're not sophisticated enough for me." Because the member will not experience any horrible consequences from such a rebuff, he or she will overcome the fear associated with the possible consequences of asking for a date. Members often react to this technique with comments such as "That wasn't so bad" or "I didn't like the reaction I received, but I learned that I could live with it. I won't be so afraid of the consequences the next time."

Flooding is a procedure similar to implosion except that the member is asked to imagine the actual feared event rather than an extreme or exaggerated version of it. Feedback from other group members can be used to help the member see that although reactions may, at times, be unpleasant, they can be handled without great difficulty. The member learns how others cope with unpleasant reactions and develops personal methods for coping.

Research evidence on flooding and implosion suggests that in vivo exposure to the situation or event is more successful than imagined exposure (Masters et al., 1987). In group treatment, a role-play exercise may be used to expose a member to the feared situation. When the member practices handling the situation in the group, the member can then be assigned the task of experiencing the situation outside the group. Because duration of exposure is also associated with treatment outcome, the member should be encouraged to practice coping with the situation several times inside and outside the group.

A variety of other cognitive imagery techniques can be used effectively in groups. Kottler (1992) suggests that rational imagery can be used effectively to help members challenge irrational beliefs and assumptions and to act effectively in anxiety-producing situations. For example, in a group for agoraphobics, members could be asked to imagine themselves walking in a beautiful outdoor setting on a sunny, autumn day.

When using imagery techniques, the worker should ensure that members remain in a relaxed state and that they are able to imagine the situation vividly. Members should be instructed to signal the worker immediately if their anxiety increases or if the cognitive image they are visualizing fades. To help produce vivid imagery, the worker should recite a richly detailed image while members are in a relaxed state with their eyes closed.

Deep Breathing

One of the simplest yet most effective strategies for reducing tension is deep breathing. Although deep breathing can be done almost anywhere and in any position, Davis, Eshelman, and McKay (2000) recommend that members do it while sitting or lying down with their feet slightly apart. The basic procedure starts with members inhaling slowly and deeply through the nose and exhaling through the mouth. The idea is to take long slow breaths focusing on the air as it goes into the member's nose, fills up the abdomen, and then as it is released again through the nose. Members are asked to meditate on their breath going slowly in and out as they become more relaxed. They are asked to repeat the deep breathing about 5 times. Members can combine deep breathing with words. For example, each time members take in a breath they can say "I am" and when they exhale "relaxing." There are many alternatives to this simple deep breathing procedure. For example, Davis, Eshelman, and McKay (2000) suggest an alternative breathing procedure where members sit in a comfortable position and rest the index and second finger of their right hand on their forehead and close their right nostril with their thumb. After inhaling through their left nostril, members are asked to close their left nostril with their ring finger and open their right nostril by removing their thumb and exhale through their right nostril. Next, they are asked to inhale through their right nostril, close their right nostril with their thumb, and open their left nostril. Then, they are asked to exhale through their left nostril and then inhale through their left nostril. Members are asked to repeat the procedure several times and encouraged to practice it at home.

Davis, Eshelman, and McKay (2000) also give instructions for breath retraining or controlled breathing to avoid panic breathing. People who panic often gasp for breath, holding on to it, and then follow it with shallow breathing or hyperventilation. To avoid this, they suggest, at the first sign of nervousness or panic, members should exhale first and then breathe in and exhale through their nose. When members exhale they should make sure their exhalation is longer than their inhalation. One way to ensure this is to count to three while inhaling slowly, and then count to four while exhaling. Members can slow their breathing even further by counting to four while inhaling and counting to five while exhaling. While counting members are encouraged to focus on their breath going in and out. Gradually they may also want to say while inhaling "I am" and while exhaling "relaxing."

When done in a group setting, deep breathing can be practiced by the whole group. Following the practice, a group go-round can be used so that each person can talk about how it felt for them, and where and when they might use it in between sessions. Workers may find that some members say that they have used deep breathing before and found it helpful. Workers can encourage members to discuss these experiences by asking these members if they count breaths, say anything to themselves, or do any other variation on the technique.

PROGRESSIVE MUSCLE RELAXATION.   This technique combines cognitive instructions with physical activities to relieve stress and help group members overcome anxiety. The premise is that muscle tension is related to anxiety and stress. Helping members reduce muscle tension, therefore, helps relieve anxiety.

With members seated in comfortable chairs or reclining on the floor, the worker explains the entire procedure to them. Members should be as comfortable as possible throughout the procedure. In a calm, hypnotic voice, the worker (or an audiotaped voice) repeats the relaxation instructions, which include tensing and relaxing each major muscle group in the body. For example, the worker might say, "Stretch your arms out next to you [or on your lap, if seated]. Make a fist with both hands as hard as you can. Feel the tension and tightness in your hands. Keep your hands clenched [10 seconds]. Now relax. Just let your hands rest against the floor [or on your lap, if seated]. Notice how the tension and tightness are leaving your hands. Notice how the feelings of tension are being replaced by warm feelings of relaxation and comfort. Notice how your hands feel now compared with when you were tensing them."

Each muscle group is tensed and relaxed in this manner. Instructions for the entire relaxation procedure are not given here, but they are available in several excellent sources (Bernstein, Borkovek, & Hazlett-Stevens, 2000; Davis, Eshelman, & McKay, 2000; Lazarus, 2000; Payne, 2000). Audio and videotape cassettes are also available from many sources (see, for example, Cambridge Educational, 2000; Weber & Friedman, 2000; Yee, 1999).

Although progressive muscle relaxation is most often conducted in individual treatment, it can be used effectively in group treatment (Rose, 1989). The major drawback in using this technique in group treatment is that it requires cooperation from every member. One member who distracts the group can ruin the effect of the procedure for everyone else. Sometimes the distraction may be unintentional, such as when a member falls asleep and begins to snore. In other situations, the distraction may be intentional. For example, a member who is not motivated may laugh or joke during the first tension-release cycle and thereby distract other group members.

To use relaxation effectively, the entire procedure should be explained before beginning. To reduce intentional distractions, members should have the opportunity to voice any questions or any reluctance about using the procedure before beginning. To reduce unintentional distractions, members should be given a signal to let the group leader know if they are having a problem. For example, a member might not be able to relax or, in rare cases, may become more tense. The member can signal the worker and the worker can give that member individual attention.

The relaxing nature of the procedure, dim lights, and comfortable position sometimes causes members to fall asleep. However, the regular breathing or snoring of a sleeping member can be distracting to other group members. Such unintentional distractions can be reduced if the worker explains that sleeping members will be awakened by a touch on the hand or arm.

Other relaxation procedures can be used as a substitute for progressive muscle relaxation. Some workers prefer meditation, bioenergetics, hypnosis, rolfing (deep muscle massage), jogging, or yoga. Although each procedure was developed from differing theoretical orientations, they all can achieve a similar result: a relaxed group member.

SYSTEMATIC DESENSITIZATION.   The technique of systematic desensitization can be particularly effective for treatment groups composed of members with phobias. With this technique, the worker helps members construct a hierarchy of situations or scenes that are feared. Starting with the least feared situations and progressing to the most feared situation, members are asked to imagine each situation while they are in a state of deep relaxation induced by progressive muscle relaxation.

A hierarchy of situations should consist of at least 10 scenes in which the member experiences gradually increasing levels of anxiety. For example, a hierarchy for a member who has been too fearful to date consists of (1) thinking about a prospective dating partner, (2) considering asking that person for a date, (3) planning where to go on the date, (4) planning how to ask the person for a date, (5) approaching the person to ask for a date, (6) starting a conversation, (7) asking the person for a date, (8) driving to the person's house, (9) walking up to the person's home, and (10) going out with the person.

Depending on the extent and the intensity of the anxiety, hierarchies may contain many more scenes. Scenes should not jump too quickly from a low to a high level of anxiety. For very fearful members, it is often necessary to construct hierarchies with as many as 20 or 30 scenes.

Once the members are helped to construct their own hierarchies (even if each member has the same phobia, individual hierarchies differ), the progressive muscle relaxation technique is used to induce a state of relaxation. The members are then asked to imagine the first scene on their hierarchy as if they were actually involved in it for about 10 seconds. If members experience anxiety, they are instructed to signal by raising a finger. Members experiencing anxiety are told to stop imagining the scene and helped to return to their former state of relaxation. When they are fully relaxed, they can imagine the scene again.

At this point, desensitization proceeds at the pace of the slowest group member unless some provision is made for members to complete their hierarchies at their own pace. One method to overcome this problem is to have members work in pairs to help each other work through the hierarchy each has developed (Rose, 1989). The worker should not allow members to work on their hierarchies for more than 30 minutes because the desensitization procedure is quite demanding, both in terms of continuously visualizing scenes and in remaining in a deeply relaxed state. If members do not complete their hierarchies during one meeting, they can begin the next meeting with the next to last scene they completed successfully in the previous meeting.

Interpersonal Interventions

Group work is an especially appropriate modality for dealing with interpersonal problems. Used effectively, the group can become a natural laboratory for examining and improving the relationships members have with one another. Unlike individual treatment, a group offers members the opportunity to demonstrate their interpersonal skills and to receive feedback from a variety of people. Members can serve as models of particular interpersonal skills and can play various roles in situations acted out in the group.

Interpersonal behaviors can be learned indirectly by listening to others describe how to behave in a situation. But behaviors are more effectively learned (1) vicariously, by watching what other people do or say, and (2) directly, by repeating and practicing new behaviors. When learned directly, a new behavior is usually performed on a trial-and-error basis until it is performed appropriately.

Learning a new behavior by hearing it described is often imprecise and is fraught with potential misinterpretation. Therefore, behavior is most adequately taught by having a member watch someone else perform it correctly and having the member practice the new behavior in a role-play exercise.

Many workers tend to allow the group to spend too much time discussing how to behave without actually helping members practice new behaviors, perhaps because of the contrived nature of role-play situations, the initial resistance of some members to role playing, and the extra instructions and direction the worker must provide to make role play successful. The learning that occurs from watching a model and rehearsing a new behavior, compared with merely talking about how to perform a new behavior, suggests that both modeling and role-play techniques should be used more frequently by workers helping members learn new or improved interpersonal behaviors.

Learning by Observing Models

Several factors affect the extent to which behaviors are learned by observing others (Bandura, 1977). Workers should understand the process underlying observational learning so that they can use modeling to help members solve interpersonal problems and learn new interpersonal skills.

Figure 10.1 illustrates the major components of observational learning. Performance of the modeled behavior depends on:

- The level of attention or awareness of the observer
- The extent to which the observer retains what is seen
- The observer's abilities to perform the observed behavior
- The extent to which the observer is motivated to perform the behavior

The attention of a member who observes a model is important because, although behavior may be learned without one's awareness, attention is always selective and is greatly facilitated by focusing on what is being observed. The worker can help focus awareness by calling members' attention to particular aspects of a model's behavior. For example, a member who is learning to be more assertive may be asked to pay particular attention to the facial expressions, body positions, and voice tones of a member who is modeling an assertive response. Attentional processes are also enhanced by the attractiveness of the model. For example, a member is more likely to pay attention to a group member who is held in high regard than to a member who has low status in the group. Members are also likely to be more attentive to models who are similar to themselves. Thus, workers should try to match the characteristics of models to the members who are observing them.

Retentional processes are also important in learning an observed behavior. In addition to developing images of the behavior that can be easily retrieved from a member's memory,

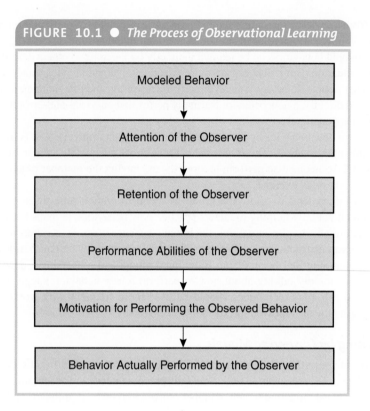

FIGURE 10.1 ● *The Process of Observational Learning*

Modeled Behavior

Attention of the Observer

Retention of the Observer

Performance Abilities of the Observer

Motivation for Performing the Observed Behavior

Behavior Actually Performed by the Observer

retention is often facilitated if the model explains the covert and overt processes he or she goes through before performing a behavior. Explanations help the member develop a cognitive structure in which to organize perceptual images. As can be seen in the following case, explaining general principles also provides an organizing framework that the member can use in different situations encountered in the future.

● **CASE EXAMPLE** *Learning New Behaviors*

When modeling an assertive behavior, a worker helped members to understand how internal monologues and dialogues can facilitate an assertive response. For example, she explained that she makes self-statements such as "I have a right to tell the person . . ." She explained that those kinds of self-statements encourage assertiveness, and that self-statements that focus on why an assertive response should not be made contribute to a lack of assertiveness. The worker also explained general principles that she keeps in mind when responding to situations that require an assertive response. For example, she explained that she makes direct statements, explaining her needs or perceptions and making a clear statement or a request of the person with whom she is interacting. The members of the group were then encouraged to describe situations where they would like to be more assertive and to practice these and other strategies contributed by all members of the group.

The member's ability to perform the modeled response is a critical component of observational learning. The member may pay careful attention to the way a model performs a behavior and retain details of the performance but may not be able to respond in a similar fashion. The best way to ensure that a member is able to perform a behavior correctly is to have the member perform the behavior in the group and receive feedback about the performance. If it is available, videotape feedback of the member's performance can also be effective in teaching new interpersonal behaviors.

Group members may know how to behave in interpersonal situations but may not be motivated to do so. What factors increase motivation? According to Bandura (1977), behaviors are more likely to occur if the observer sees others being rewarded for similar performances. Conversely, if an observer sees others being sanctioned for a given behavior, the observer is less likely to behave in a way that may result in similar sanctions.

A member, however, may not have to observe someone being sanctioned to not perform a new behavior. New behaviors are often difficult to perform until they are well learned. Difficulties associated with learning a new behavior, along with the absence of strong incentives, are frequently a sufficient disincentive for members considering performing new behaviors. Therefore, observational learning is selective. In daily living, for example, we often do not repeat a new behavior that we see performed by someone else.

To ensure that group members learn new behaviors by observing the worker or other members, several factors should be present. Members' attention should be carefully focused on how the behavior is being performed. Members should be helped to retain cognitive images of observed behavior by developing a set of organizing principles—a cognitive framework—that explains why a model responded in a particular manner. To build their capacity to respond, members should practice responses and receive feedback about the quality of their performances. Members' motivation for performing observed behaviors can be increased by demonstrating to them that the incentives sufficiently outweigh the disincentives for performing a particular behavior.

Learning by Role Playing

Role playing is an enactment of a social role in an imagined social situation. Role playing can be used for (1) assessment, (2) simulation, (3) understanding, (4) decision making, or (5) behavior change (Etcheverry, Siporin, & Toseland, 1987). Role playing is a powerful tool for any of these purposes. As shown in Table 10.1, role-playing techniques increase members' awareness and understanding of their interpersonal skills and produce behavior changes by providing members with corrective feedback and the opportunity to practice improved responses in the sheltered environment of the group.

Role-playing techniques can be structured, semi-structured, or unstructured. Structured procedures use predetermined scripts or vignettes developed by the leader, and members act out prescribed roles believed to be important by the leader. For example, in an assertiveness training program group members may be asked to role play a number of common situations requiring assertive responses, such as dealing with someone who has cut into a line, returning damaged merchandise, or turning down a request to borrow an item. Structured role plays are not spontaneous, but they have the advantage of ensuring that the worker is ready with an effective response.

Semi-structured role plays have some structure but they also enable the worker and the members to be spontaneous. During psychodrama, for example, there is a warm-up period followed by the action, and then a period for closure. Within this structure, there is plenty

TABLE 10.1 ● *Uses of Unstructured Role-Play Procedures*

Procedure	Awareness/Understanding	Behavior Change
A. *Primary Role-Play Procedures*		
1. Own role	Demonstrates and clarifies members' behavior, their role in interpersonal interactions, and their concerns and problems Facilitates members' insight into their own feelings, thoughts, and behaviors Identifies situational cues to facilitate differential responses Identifies members' problems and concerns	Allows members to practice new behaviors Reduces members' performance anxiety Prepares members for obstacles and setbacks
2. Role reversal	Stimulates empathy for another person whose role is being enacted by the protagonist Increases members' awareness of cognitive and affective aspects of other people Objectifies and clarifies the situational context of members' own behaviors	Encourages spontaneity and participation Facilitates changes in members' expectations of others Facilitates change in members' behavior Improves empathic skills
3. Autodrama/ monodrama/ chairing	Same as for own role and role-reversal procedures Identifies and clarifies members' own feelings at deeper levels than own role or role-reversal procedures Increases members' awareness of their own self-talk	Same as for own role and role-reversal procedures Facilitates learning of adaptive self-talk Enables changes on deeper, more complex levels than own role or role-reversal procedures
4. Sculpting/ choreography (Action sociogram)	Stimulates members' awareness and discussion of their own behavior and the group's interaction patterns	Facilitates changes in members' attitudes, behaviors, and interaction patterns
B. *Supportive Role-Play Procedures*		
1. On-the-spot interview	Identifies and clarifies members' thoughts and feelings while they are in a role Connects thinking and feeling to behaviors in a role	Provides practice in self-awareness and self-talk
2. Soliloquy	Same as on-the-spot interview procedure but less structured	Same as on-the-spot interview procedure
3. Doubting	Helps members verbalize and express covert thoughts, feelings, and behaviors Same as on-the-spot interview procedure Identifies new behaviors for acquisition	Same as on-the-spot interview procedure Gives permission and support for members' owning their own thoughts, feelings, and behaviors Facilitates expression of feelings Promotes members' skill in using feelings as cues for appropriate responses Allows members to practice their self-expression skills

TABLE 10.1 ● *Continued*		
4. Mirror	Promotes members' knowledge of the consequences of their own behavior on others Enables self-confrontation	Provides members the opportunity to practice new behaviors Enables feedback and reinforcement when learning new behaviors
5. Sharing	Universalizes members' experiences Models self-disclosure	Provides support and confirmation of members' experiences, abilities, etc. Facilitates learning of self-disclosure skills

of freedom for the worker and the group members to shape the content. Some psychodrama techniques such as the "magic shop" employ structure and spontaneity at the same time (Verhofstadt-Deneve, 2000). The basic structure in the "magic shop" is that members who volunteer to participate have to buy psychological qualities or characteristics that they feel they lack. The types of qualities that are bought, and the type of payment made to purchase the qualities, are unique to the members engaged in the role play, but the group can profit from a discussion of the choices no matter what choices members make.

Unstructured role-play procedures are listed in Table 10.1. The procedures are developmental and open ended to allow spontaneous, emerging processes of learning and problem solving. Unstructured role-play procedures can be further divided into primary and secondary procedures. Primary role-play procedures can be used alone to accomplish particular purposes; secondary procedures are used in conjunction with primary procedures to extend their effect and widen their scope (Etcheverry et al., 1987).

Primary Role-Play Procedures

OWN ROLE.   In the own-role procedure, a member uses his or her experiences and plays the protagonist. Other roles are played by the worker or other group members, who may represent people, feeling states, thoughts, or objects. The own-role technique is particularly useful in assessing a member's interpersonal skills because it allows the worker and other group members to observe how the protagonist acts in a particular situation. The own-role procedure is also helpful as a means for members to practice new behaviors. Supportive procedures such as the soliloquy, on-the-spot interview, or doubling can be used to increase a member's awareness of behavior while performing the role of protagonist.

ROLE REVERSAL.   In role reversal, a group member acts as the protagonist by taking on the role of another person. For example, a husband may act in the role of his spouse. The procedure enables a member to experience a situation from another's point of view. Role reversal is particularly useful for teaching empathy, especially if it is used with doubling or soliloquy. It helps to clarify situations and to increase members' self-awareness. It also increases the spontaneity, flexibility, and openness of the member playing the protagonist's role. Variations of this procedure include substitute role playing (playing a symbolic, substitute role) and role distance (playing an emotionally distant role).

AUTODRAMA, MONODRAMA, AND CHAIRING.   A procedure in which a group member plays multiple roles is variously called autodrama, monodrama, and chairing

(Blatner, 1996). The multiple roles represent the different ways members view themselves or the different ways others view a member. The procedure is usually conducted using one or more empty chairs, each representing a role, a character part, or a personality aspect. The member switches from one chair to another in changing roles. When occupying each chair, the person initiates and maintains a dialogue with the other chairs, which represent other aspects of the person's self.

The technique is particularly useful in helping members become aware of the various roles they play and their effects on each other. It is also useful in helping members assess internal dialogues and self-talk, such as irrational beliefs and devaluating self-statements. Therefore, the procedure can be used effectively in cooperation with cognitive restructuring procedures to practice adaptive self-statements and self-instructions that aid effective problem solving. Self-role and double chairing are other names for this procedure.

SCULPTING AND CHOREOGRAPHY.   Also called action sociogram, variations of the sculpting and choreography technique are psychodrama and sociodrama (Blatner, 1996; Moreno, 1946). In this procedure, a member, as protagonist, is directed to sculpt or position himself or herself and other group members in a drama that represents a symbolic or real situation in the member's life. The protagonist explains each person's role, and the worker directs the action, which can last for an extended period of time.

The dramatic enactment is designed to expose intense feelings and conflicts in a member's life and thus it can be used as an assessment device by the worker. Another benefit of the technique is that it immerses the whole group in intense participatory involvement leading to in-depth self-disclosure and enactment of crucial concerns and issues. In addition to the self-awareness this technique produces, the procedure helps the protagonist understand the importance of others in personal life situations. Although there is little empirical evidence for the efficacy of the technique, clinical reports and experience suggest that the cathartic experience and heightened awareness that result from participating in a dramatic enactment can lead to changes in members' thoughts, feelings, behaviors, attitudes, and interaction patterns.

The psychodrama variation of the technique focuses on the internal, psychological status of the actors. The sociodrama variation emphasizes the social and environmental aspects of the protagonist's situation. For an excellent, in-depth explanation of these procedures, see Blatner (1996).

Supplementary Role-Play Procedures

ON-THE-SPOT INTERVIEW.   On-the-spot interviewing involves stopping the role-play action before it is finished and interviewing one or more actors. The worker asks specific, detailed questions designed to elicit particular thoughts and feelings at that point in the role play. The procedure is designed to increase a member's awareness of cognitive, affective, and behavioral aspects of a role performance. It identifies self-statements and self-talk that are dysfunctional and self-devaluating. It also teaches self-observation and enhances self-awareness.

SOLILOQUY.   The soliloquy procedure involves stopping the role-play action and asking an actor to disclose what he or she is thinking or feeling. Unlike the on-the-spot interview, in which the actor is asked specific, closed-ended questions, soliloquy questions are open ended and encourage the member to engage in a monologue that discloses in-depth thoughts and feelings. The procedure is particularly useful for increasing a member's self-awareness.

DOUBLING.   The doubling procedure uses a group member to act as the alter ego or inner voice of the protagonist. To emphasize identification with the protagonist, the double is required to speak in the first person, for example, saying, "I feel . . ." or "I think . . ." Variations on the procedure are the "divided double" and the "multiple double." In the divided double, the alter ego speaks for different parts of the protagonist's inner self. The multiple double calls for two or more actors to speak for different aspects of the protagonist's self. To validate the truth of a double's statements in offering inferences, interpretations, or alternative reactions, the protagonist is sometimes asked to repeat and accept or reject the double's statements.

The doubling procedure can serve several important functions. It helps make role plays more dramatic and produces more in-depth experiences. It facilitates understanding and self-awareness of the protagonist's behavior. In addition to fostering insight, it gives permission for the protagonist to acknowledge repressed or taboo thoughts and feelings. It also increases the emotional sensitivity and self-expression of the protagonist. The procedure is often used in conjunction with own-role, chairing, and sculpting procedures.

MIRROR.   In the mirror procedure, a group member reenacts a role-played performance for the protagonist. Other members can verify the accuracy of the replay. The procedure may also be used in an exaggerated, amplified, and stereotypical manner to emphasize particular aspects of the protagonist's behavior.

The procedure is useful as a confrontational technique to help the protagonist gain awareness of behavior. It is an excellent substitute for videotape feedback when videotape equipment is unavailable. The procedure is particularly useful in conjunction with modeling, coaching, and prompting to provide feedback to a member attempting to learn a new behavior. It is also a way of involving other group members in a member's situation to facilitate their empathy and their skills in self-expression.

SHARING.   The sharing procedure is often used at the close of role-play action. Group members give members who have role-played feedback about their performances. The procedure is designed to provide supportive feedback to the member who risked himself or herself in revealing a difficult situation by acting as the protagonist in the role play. It also enables members to share their own reactions and feelings to the role play.

Environmental Interventions

Environmental interventions help members to modify or change the psychosocial and physical situations in which they live. Environmental interventions consist of:

- Connecting members to concrete resources
- Expanding members' social networks
- Modifying the contingencies that result when members perform desired behaviors
- Planning physical environments to facilitate members' goal achievement

Connecting Members to Concrete Resource

To connect clients to concrete resources, the worker first identifies the member's need and then assesses the member's ability and motivation to follow through and obtain the resource. For a highly motivated, well-functioning group member, the worker may be able to act as a broker to identify a contact person at the appropriate resource and give the member general information about what to expect when contacting the resource. The worker verifies that the member has obtained the needed resource at the next group session.

In some treatment groups, such as those composed of severely disabled psychiatric patients or older people with dementia, workers may have to take additional steps to ensure that members obtain the resources they need. For example, it may take some time to prepare members for a referral because of their lack of motivation or their failure to recognize their need for services. It may also be necessary to contact family members or guardians to help prepare them for a referral. In addition, medical disabilities may limit or prevent members from contacting resources without assistance. Transportation may have to be arranged and the worker, an aide, or a volunteer may have to accompany the member to the resource. It may also be necessary to teach members the skills necessary to obtain a needed resource. For example, an unemployed group member might need to learn interviewing and resume-writing skills before beginning a job search. Some of the steps for making an effective referral for impaired group members are presented below.

Making Referrals on Behalf of Group Members with Severe Disabilities

- Thoroughly prepare the member for the referral. Review the reasons for the referral, how it is expected to help the member, and how it will help members to achieve individual and group goals.

- Whenever possible, involve family and other support system members in both the referral decision and the choice of the referral source.

- Carefully consider the member's ability to get to and engage the referral source.

- Arrange for escort services, transportation, or other resources that will ensure that the member reaches the referral source.

- Help the member with the skills and the support systems necessary to obtain and utilize the referral source.

- Check to see that the member has reached the referral source and that it is meeting the member's needs.

- Help family members and others in the member's support system to become advocates and brokers for the member, helping the member to obtain needed resources while maintaining and respecting the member's ability to participate in decision making about obtaining and using a referral.

Expanding Members' Social Networks

Another type of environmental intervention consists of helping socially isolated members expand their social networks by gaining needed support from others (Forse & Degenne, 1999). The first step in expanding a member's social network is to analyze the member's current social relationships. Figure 10.2 illustrates the social network of Tom, a socially isolated member of a support group for people who have recently separated. The diagram indicates that Tom has only two active social relationships. Tom's other network relationships are inactive. He no longer plays with the softball team; he no longer sees Jean or Bob, with whom he used to be friendly; and because his brother lives nearly 1,000 miles away, they rarely see one another.

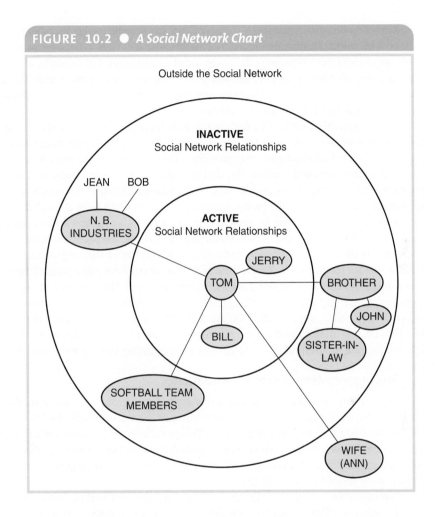

FIGURE 10.2 ● *A Social Network Chart*

Outside the Social Network

INACTIVE
Social Network Relationships

JEAN   BOB

N. B.
INDUSTRIES

ACTIVE
Social Network Relationships

JERRY

TOM   BROTHER

JOHN

BILL   SISTER-IN-LAW

SOFTBALL TEAM
MEMBERS

WIFE
(ANN)

Diagramming a member's social network on a flip chart or blackboard can stimulate group discussion about ways to expand the network. This is illustrated in the following case example.

● **CASE EXAMPLE** *Diagramming a Member's Social Network*

After examining the chart shown in Figure 10.2, several group members suggested that Tom renew former network relationships that lapsed after his marriage. To do this, Tom rejoined the softball team and renewed his friendships with Jean and Bob. Tom was also encouraged to join Parents Without Partners, a self-help group that sponsors many social, recreational, and educational events in his community. In a subsequent group meeting Tom reported making several new friends in this organization and that he had also begun dating someone that he met during a dinner sponsored by the organization. He also mentioned that he had become friendly with several members of the softball team and that one person invited him to join a bowling league.

Analyzing one group member's social network can stimulate other members to consider their own networks. Examining Figure 10.2 might cause members to become aware that they could also benefit from expanding their own social relationships. For example, after confirming that group members wanted to become more involved with one another, the worker suggested that members exchange telephone numbers and choose one person to call during the week. By scheduling one meeting at a member's home and supporting members' suggestions that they get together informally after the meeting, the worker encouraged the members to form a supportive social network for one another. As the members began to meet regularly, it became apparent that child care responsibilities limited many of the members' abilities to socialize, so members with children decided to help each other with child care, thereby freeing each other to engage in social activities. Thus, through a worker's intervention efforts and the mutual-aid properties of the group, members' social networks were expanded.

Another strategy that can be used to expand members' social networks is to ask them during the first group meeting if they would like to exchange telephone numbers and e-mail addresses. If all members give their permission, and if between-meeting contact is not contraindicated for therapeutic reasons, a list of telephone numbers and e-mail addresses of all group members can be shared during the second meeting. The worker can also facilitate members' contacting each other between meetings by helping members to choose a partner who they will call or e-mail during the week. Clinical experience suggests that, for this to be effective, it is often helpful for the pair to pick a time to call and who will make the call. It is also helpful to briefly discuss the calls or e-mails during subsequent group meetings.

Contingency Management Procedures

So that members can maintain their successes between group sessions, it is often necessary to modify or change the rewards and punishments they receive for behaving in ways that are not consistent with their treatment goals. This procedure is sometimes called *contingency management* because the rewards or punishments that are contingent on the performance of a behavior are modified to increase or decrease the probability that a behavior will be performed in the future (Sheldon, 1995).

Contingencies that increase the probability that a member will perform a behavior are called *reinforcers*. Typical positive reinforcers include social rewards that are verbal, such as praise, and nonverbal, such as a smile, a pat on the back, and similar signs of approval. Positive reinforcers also include tangible rewards such as money and food.

Negative reinforcers also increase behaviors. But unlike positive reinforcers that increase behavior through rewards, negative reinforcers increase behavior by giving someone attention or some other reward for doing something that is inappropriate. To decrease unwanted behaviors, the worker can either ignore the behavior, or can administer some kind of sanction or punishment. Often, inappropriate behaviors will extinguish themselves if they are simply ignored or not reinforced. This works when the member in question is seeking attention for an inappropriate behavior. However, it will not work if the inappropriate behavior is self-reinforcing. Then, the worker may have to apply a sanction. Social disapproval or denial of a tangible reward can then be used to try to distinguish an unwanted behavior. For example, a member of an inpatient group for people suffering from severe and persistent mental disorders may loose the privilege to go to a "movie night" with other residents because he did not follow group rules about confidentiality. Workers, however, should emphasize the use of positive reinforcers that members enjoy receiving rather than sanctions that are unpleasant and often result in deleterious side effects such as anger. In addition to causing anger and resentment, sanctions such as taking "movie night" away do not address the problem (why the breach of confidentiality occurred, for example) and they do not reinforce those behaviors that would avoid future breaches of confidentiality.

In general, workers should encourage the use of positive reinforcers to encourage therapeutic behaviors and inattention, ignoring, or other extinction procedures to discourage behaviors that do not help the group reach agreed upon goals. Often, it is sufficient to reward a desired behavior and ignore an undesirable behavior. Although positive reinforcers are preferred whenever possible, in some circumstances punishments may be imposed for failure to comply with group rules. For example, the members of a children's group decided together that those who came late to group meetings would clean up after snacks were served.

Rose (1998) points out that the undesirable side effects of punishment procedures are avoided when members impose their own punishments, sometimes referred to as *response costs*. Thus, punishment procedures should not be imposed unilaterally by the worker. The group as a whole should decide on a policy, that is, the type of punishment (social disapproval or removal from the group) and the circumstances in which sanctions will be applied. The resulting policy should be applied uniformly.

The worker should help the group develop realistic rules that are not too restrictive. Sometimes members develop unrealistically harsh rules to govern behavior in the group. William Golding's novel, *Lord of the Flies,* is a literary example of how groups can decide on rules for behavior and punishments that are too severe. It is common for members of children's groups, for example, to develop group rules that, left unchallenged, lead to severe punishment. For example, in one group, members decided that anyone caught laughing should be thrown out of the group. In such cases, the worker should intervene and help the group develop less severe sanctions for misbehavior.

When using contingency management procedures, the worker should begin by helping members identify the rewards and punishments they receive for performing desired and undesired behaviors. Contingencies are identified by monitoring the consequences resulting from the performance of a particular behavior. If contingencies do not act to increase desired behavior and decrease undesired behavior, the worker can help the member modify them. Sometimes members may be able to administer their own rewards. For example, members may be encouraged to praise themselves for performing a certain behavior—to take themselves out for a good meal or buy a new piece of clothing. Such self-reinforcement procedures have been shown to be effective in helping members control their own behaviors and feel better about themselves (Yost et al., 1985). Behaviors are also frequently self-reinforcing, so that changes in behavior are sustained by the approval of others, improved feelings about oneself, and so forth.

It can be helpful to involve other group members or significant others in members' lives in modifying the contingent rewards and punishments members receive for performing desired and undesired behaviors. Family members and friends can help provide an environment that promotes therapeutic goals. For example, a wife or husband may compliment the spouse for positive changes. A mother or father may praise their daughter for helping her little brother with his homework.

To formalize an agreement about what behaviors to reinforce, a verbal or written contingency contract can be developed. The following list specifies the points that should be covered in these contracts.

What Contingency Contracts Should Specify

- What specific behaviors will be performed
- Who will perform the behaviors
- How the behaviors will be reinforced
- Who will administer the reinforcement

For example, the father of an adolescent group member may agree to take his son on a fishing trip if his son agrees to attend classes without misbehaving for two weeks. Although developing a written contingency contract may strike some individuals as too rigid or formal, it should be recognized that written agreements have the advantage of avoiding confusion later when individuals may have different recollections of the nature of an agreement.

There are many different types of contingency contracts. As mentioned, members may administer their own rewards and punishments in self-administered contingency contracts. Contracts may be made between the group member and significant others, between two group members, or between all group members and the worker. Contracts may also be reciprocal; that is, parties to the contract reward each other for performing desired behaviors. Reciprocal contracts are particularly useful in couples' groups because spouses can reinforce each other for performing desired behaviors.

By using contingency management procedures, the worker helps members perform desired behaviors by changing the environmental consequences that result when a behavior is performed. Too often, workers intervene effectively in the group to help members reach desired goals but fail to pay attention to what will happen when members try to perform desired behaviors outside the group. Contingency management procedures are a useful way to extend therapeutic interventions beyond the boundaries of group sessions. Yost and colleagues (1985), for example, described how contingency management procedures can be used to help group members who are depressed to engage in pleasurable activities that help to reduce depression.

Some individuals react negatively to contingency contracts because they perceive them as manipulative, artificial, or as relying exclusively on extrinsic rather than intrinsic motivation. It is important to remember that contingency contracts are *voluntary* and *explicit* agreements between two or more parties. Coercive, exploitative, and underhanded attempts to control behavior have no place in the design or the execution of contingency contracts. It is true that contingency contracts specify artificial arrangements of rewards and punishments, but they should be prepared with consideration of the naturally occurring consequences that will sustain the behavior over the long term. For example, in the situation described previously, although the father will not be able to take his son on a fishing trip each time the son behaves well for a two-week period in school, it is anticipated that by behaving well, the son will stop receiving negative feedback from teachers, administrators, and peers and will start enjoying school. Therefore, the artificial arrangement of contingencies will be replaced with naturally occurring contingencies such as praise from the teacher and good report cards. The extrinsic rewards for behaving well will be replaced, over the long term, by intrinsic rewards such as feeling competent, well liked, or self-confident.

Modifying Physical Environments

Helping members modify their physical environments is another type of environmental intervention. Although often given little consideration, the physical environment has a profound effect on the problems and concerns that members experience. Environmental stimuli can make it easier or more difficult for a member to accomplish treatment goals. For example, members of a weight-loss group find that it is more difficult to lose weight if their refrigerators are stocked with fattening foods than if their refrigerators contain only those items that are a part of the diet that members agreed on. Similarly, it is difficult for a member of an inpatient psychotherapy group who is about to be discharged to learn independent living skills in an institutional environment that does not allow the person to cook, clean, or shop.

To the extent possible, workers should help members modify physical environments so they promote goal achievement. In general, physical environments should give members the opportunity to practice the skills they are learning in the group. Members who are learning skills for independent living, for example, should have the opportunity to practice as many of the skills as feasible in the institutional setting in which they live. Physical environments should reduce barriers that are likely to impede a member's attempts to accomplish a goal. For example, a member who is attempting to stop drinking should remove all alcohol from his or her home.

Environmental interventions should be proactive as well as reactive; that is, in addition to ensuring that an environment does not provide unwanted stimuli, the worker should help members modify environments so that they encourage goal-directed behavior. A member who is attempting to lose weight may, for example, place a calorie chart on his refrigerator door to help him plan meals. A member of a parenting group may place a monitoring chart in her child's room. Each time the child behaves correctly, gold stars are placed on the chart. When a certain number of stars accumulate, they can be redeemed for a trip to the zoo or extra play time with Mom or Dad. In both cases, modifications of the environment stimulate efforts toward goal achievement.

In inpatient settings, environmental modifications can include a restructuring of the entire milieu. Wright, Thase, Beck, and Ludgate (1993), for example, describe how cognitive therapy with inpatients can be enhanced by developing a cognitive milieu that permeates the entire residential unit.

INTERVENING IN THE GROUP AS A WHOLE

Workers select the group as a whole as the focus of interventions when they decide that the group process should be altered to help members achieve their goals. In this way, the group becomes the means as well as the context of treatment. As discussed in Chapter 3, four areas are critical to the effective functioning of any group: (1) communication and interaction patterns, (2) cohesion, (3) social integration, and (4) culture. These are the primary areas in which the worker intervenes when selecting the group as a whole as the focus of interventions.

Because most group dynamics have developed before the middle stage begins, the worker's task during this stage is to maintain and enhance dynamics that are contributing to the group's success and intervene to change dynamics that are interfering with the group's development. Experienced workers realize the power that group dynamics have in leading to successful group outcomes. In comparing 10 different methods of leading encounter groups, Lieberman, Yalom, and Miles (1973) found that "group characteristics" such as norms, cohesiveness, and climate had an important effect both on members' satisfaction with their experience in different groups and on the overall outcomes achieved by the groups. Similarly, in a study comparing methods of working with antisocial boys in groups, Feldman, Caplinger, and Wodarski (1983) also found that group dynamics had a powerful mediating effect on outcome, regardless of the type of treatment modality used. In the following sections, some suggestions are made about how group dynamics can be modified to achieve therapeutic purposes.

Changing Communication and Interaction Patterns

The worker may intervene to change the frequency, duration, distribution, or content of the communication and interaction patterns occurring in a treatment group. The frequency of interactions a member initiates in a group is important because it is difficult, if not impossible, to assess and treat a member who remains relatively silent throughout the group. Members must actively participate if they are to benefit from group treatment.

Shulman (1999) points out that what silent members really fear is being confronted with their silence. Therefore, it is more helpful to prompt such members to speak with statements such as, "What do you think about what _____ is saying?" or "You have some experience with this _____, what do you think?" rather than to confront the members with data that suggest they are not participating frequently enough.

Another way to increase participation is to praise members when they add to the group's discussion. Positive comments such as "That was really helpful" or "I see that you understand what _____ is saying" can be used to show quiet group members that their contributions are valued. Positive reinforcement procedures have been demonstrated to be effective in several studies that have examined methods to increase members' participation in groups (Rose, 1989). Other techniques to increase the frequency of communication include asking members to lead the group discussion on a certain topic and going around the group and eliciting members' thoughts and comments on a particular topic, so that those who tend to be silent do not feel singled out.

Workers also may wish to change the duration of a member's communications in the group. This is particularly true for very talkative members who dominate the group's discussions. Sometimes simply pointing out that other members of the group need time to participate is sufficient to limit a talkative member's communications. For others, it is necessary to develop a contingency contract in which members agree to ignore the talkative member when the member talks for more than a specified length of time. Alternatives to this procedure include interrupting the member after he or she talks for a certain amount of time as well as reminding the member with a nonverbal cue that he or she is talking too much.

Workers may also want to change the distribution of communication and interaction patterns. Ideally, each member of the group should have an opportunity to participate. Although some group members may be more involved in a particular discussion than other members, communications should be distributed fairly evenly among all members over the course of several meetings. Workers should prevent situations in which they are doing most of the communicating or situations in which members direct most of their comments to the worker rather than to each other. Workers may also want to intervene when members of subgroups interact primarily with one another rather than with everyone.

As in efforts to change the frequency and duration of members' communication patterns, the most successful interventions for changing the distribution of communication patterns include cues to help members remain aware of their inappropriate communications, accompanied by prompts and positive reinforcement to help them change these patterns. For example, Toseland and colleagues (1978) reported that an intervention consisting of cues, verbal prompts, and reinforcement was successful in reducing the number of member-to-leader communications and increasing the number of member-to-member communications in a parenting skills group.

The content of the messages sent and received in the group is just as important as the frequency, duration, and distribution of group members' communications. Workers should be particularly concerned about the task orientation and the tone of the messages communicated in the group. Workers should intervene when most communications are not task relevant or when they are excessively negative.

Of course, some group discussion will not be task relevant. Joking, small talk, and interesting but irrelevant stories often make the group more attractive. Members have a need to express their own identity in the group. However, task-irrelevant discussions should not be allowed to take much of the group's time. Members come to treatment groups for particular purposes, and too much irrelevant conversation interferes with their ability to achieve goals, which ultimately leads to their dissatisfaction with the group.

Usually, it is sufficient to point out excessive digressions to the group and call the group's attention back to the session's agenda and the goals that should have been briefly mentioned at the beginning of the meeting. In some cases, however, such intervention may not be sufficient to help the group return to a task-centered discussion. The group's digression may signify a test or a challenge to the worker's authority, dissatisfaction with the content outlined in the session agenda, or an indication that group members are too fearful or anxious to discuss a particular topic. In such cases, it is helpful for the worker to point out a personal hypothesis about the reasons for the group's digression. Through discussion and feedback, the worker can help members to decide on how best to renew their focus on the group's goals. This process may make members aware that they are avoiding a difficult issue that they need to discuss. In other cases, it may lead to changes in the worker's style or the session's agenda.

Workers should also be concerned about the tone of the messages conveyed in the group. Frequent put-downs; excessive negative comments without suggestions for improvement; and infrequent occurrences of supportive, warm, or reinforcing comments make the group unattractive for its members. To change the tone of messages being communicated in the group, workers can act as models by making supportive comments whenever possible. Workers can also show their disapproval of negative comments by ignoring them or by suggesting that the member who makes the negative comment accompany it with a positive comment. Exercises designed to help members give positive feedback can also be helpful. For example, a worker might say, "I've noticed we make a lot of comments about what a person does wrong during our role plays. How about for the next role play, each member will identify at least one thing that the person does well."

Changing the Group's Attraction for Its Members

There is a consensus in group work literature (see Chapter 3) that cohesiveness and interpersonal attraction have many beneficial effects on group functioning. Group cohesion is built in a warm, caring, and empathic group environment. The worker can foster the development of this type of environment by actively listening to members, validating their experiences, and affirming their attempts to cope with the situations confronting them. By modeling genuine concern and interest in each member's experiences, the leader encourages members to tune in to each other's needs and to reach out in supportive, mutually helping interactions.

Cohesion and interpersonal attraction can also be stimulated by acknowledging members' efforts to support each other and by praising members for their active and constructive participation in the group. Thus, in addition to modeling concern and interest, the leader should take an active stance in guiding the group to increased cohesion and intimacy. Appropriate self-disclosures and revelations that deepen the group experience and make it more meaningful and more profound should be encouraged. Similarly, gentle and caring confrontations that encourage members to get in touch with their strengths or realize overlooked possibilities and alternative perspectives should be invited.

Physical arrangements can also make a difference in building group cohesion. Groups tend to be more cohesive and attractive when they are relatively small and there is plenty of interaction that is distributed fairly evenly throughout the group. In small groups in which there is considerable interaction, members have the feeling that their ideas are being heard and considered; in large groups and groups with poorly distributed communication patterns, members who are not a part of the "inner circle" of decision makers often feel that their ideas and suggestions are not being given sufficient attention. Suggestions for redistributing communication patterns can also be helpful to make a group more attractive.

Simple creature comforts can also make a difference in the attractiveness of the group. Refreshments such as coffee and doughnuts can be offered, and socializing over coffee during a break in a long session or immediately after a short session helps reduce the exclusive problem focus of groups and allows members to get to know each other as ordinary people rather than as clients. In addition, for some group members, refreshments and snacks can be strong incentives for participating in a group, particularly for children and psychiatric inpatients because their access to snacks is often limited.

Other ways to increase the attractiveness of a group include dispensing rewards such as a weekend pass as an incentive for participation in a group, planning interesting program activities and outings for the agenda of future group meetings, encouraging members to select topics for group discussion, and ensuring that members continue to make progress toward their treatment goals.

As the group becomes more cohesive, some members may fear becoming overly dependent on the group. The leader should encourage members to talk about these feelings and ease their concerns by indicating that such feelings are commonly experienced in groups when cohesion and intimacy increase. Acknowledging the support and security that the group provides and also acknowledging members' efforts to maintain their autonomy and their ability to function independently can help allay members' fears.

Fears about becoming overly dependent sometimes have their roots in problems with members' ability to develop intimate relationships. Intimacy implies vulnerability. When members disclose personal, emotionally charged issues that they may not have been able to talk about with others, they are exposing their vulnerability to the group. Members may have had previous unsatisfactory experiences in revealing emotionally charged issues to persons with whom they felt intimate. Thus, it is natural for members to feel ambivalent about sharing personal issues with the group. It is helpful for the leader to point this out so that all members of the group will be more likely to respond in a sensitive and caring way to fledgling attempts to self-disclose personal issues. Leaders should also make clear that they will protect members by blocking critical, insensitive comments and by encouraging supportive and caring interactions. The following case example illustrates this point.

● **CASE EXAMPLE** *Supporting Members' Self Disclosures*

In a support group for recently widowed persons, a member who had not talked a great deal broke her silence by stating that she felt that her situation was very different from the situations described by other members. Another member of the group asked her what she meant. She stated that unlike the other members of the group, "she was relieved that her husband had died, and she did not miss him." A member of the group jumped in and said that that was a terrible thing to say. The worker, sensing that this could stop the member from disclosing anything else, asked the gentleman who had responded to the woman who had made the disclosure to hold off in making a judgment about the statement until the member could elaborate and fully explain what she meant. The member then went on to say that this was a second marriage for her. She had had a very difficult relationship with her second husband, including much verbal abuse, and during his long illness he was "miserable to be with." She also said that he suffered during his long illness with throat cancer, and that "no one should go through that much pain, not even him." The worker asked other members if they had any similar feelings. One woman said that her husband died from complications related to Alzheimer's disease, and that for many years he was "not himself." She said that she also felt a sense of relief when he died, but felt guilty about saying that. She thanked the original member for self-disclosing her feelings, because it made it easier for her to self-disclose. The group member who had originally responded negatively then jumped in stating that he was wrong, and that if her husband "was miserable anyway," that it was probably good that "the Lord decided to take him." Other members then stepped in to talk about how difficult it was to care for their spouses before they died. For example, one member picked up the angry feelings expressed by the person who first self-disclosed by stating, "It was really hard not to lose my temper. I lost it all the time. I felt guilty about that, I still do."

There are times when a worker does not want to increase a group's cohesion. For example, cohesion should not be increased in groups in which antitherapeutic norms have been established. Research by Feldman, Caplinger, and Wodarski (1983), for example, found that in groups composed solely of antisocial boys, *interpersonal integration,* defined as the reciprocal liking of the boys in a group for one another, was negatively associated with treatment outcomes. In these groups, cohesion apparently resulted in peer pressure to conform to antitherapeutic group norms. Thus, antisocial behaviors were reinforced rather than extinguished by group treatment.

Using Social Integration Dynamics Effectively

When it is present, social integration can enhance the functioning of the group as a whole, but when it is absent it can lead to the demise of the group. Social integration is promoted through norms, roles, and status hierarchies. These group dynamics can be viewed both as social controls and as methods of enhancing the integration of individual group members and the cohesion of the group as a whole. Without social controls, group interaction would become chaotic and unpredictable, and the group would soon cease functioning. But in groups in which social controls are too strong, members soon feel restricted and coerced. They tend to rebel against the control or refuse to attend future meetings. Instead of achieving social integration, members feel devalued and lack commitment to the group and to each other.

Workers who command the admiration and respect of group members encourage norms, roles, and status hierarchies that foster the interpersonal integration of each member into the life of the group. Personal characteristics such as an empathic and warm demeanor; a sense of humor; sensitivity; insight; and the ability to remain calm, collected, and professional in diffi-cult situations encourage members to follow the worker's guidance and leadership. Similarly, specialized knowledge and the judicious use of wisdom gained from personal and profes-sional experience help to increase the potency of the worker. Potent workers are self-confident but able to admit mistakes. They lead by example, not by applying social sanctions or by attempting to control, dominate, or manipulate the group. They tend to ignore rather than to sanction deviant behavior exhibited by group members, preferring instead to acknowledge and praise positive contributions and to set a tone and an atmosphere that encourage members to support and uplift one another. These are the characteristics of transformational leaders previously discussed in Chapter 4.

During the middle stage of treatment groups, the effective worker helps the group develop norms, roles, and status hierarchies that integrate members' activities for goal achievement. Both normative integration (members' acceptance of group norms) and func-tional integration (members' assuming roles and activities that contribute to the group's work) are positively associated with beneficial group outcomes (Feldman, Caplinger, & Wodarski, 1983). One step that can help members to become normatively and functionally integrated into a group is to prevent domination of the group by one or more members who have a great deal of social power and who do not use it for therapeutic purposes. It has been found, for example, that socially dominant members in groups for youth with antisocial behavior problems often tend to ignore or subvert therapeutic group norms and resist efforts to promote prosocial behavior change (Feldman et al., 1983).

When facilitating normative integration, potent workers help members adhere to thera-peutic group norms and change norms that are interfering with the group accomplishing its goals. For example, in a group that has developed a norm that members are not to be ver-bally abusive with one another, a member who becomes verbally abusive may be asked to leave the group until he or she can regain control.

In other cases, the worker may encourage and protect members who are deviating from antitherapeutic group norms. For example, a worker supports and encourages a member of a couples' group who begins to describe problems in the couple's sexual relations, a topic that has not been previously discussed by group members. In another group, the worker encour-ages a member to talk about the scapegoating of a member who is intensely disliked by other group members.

Workers should also help members become functionally integrated in the group. As mentioned in Chapter 8, some members take on deviant group roles such as the "group jester" or the "isolate." It is the worker's responsibility either to help the member assume a more functional role or to help the group modify its processes to find a useful role for the member. For example, the jester might be encouraged to take on a more functional role, such as expressing feelings and concerns about a particular problem.

Changing Group Culture

Another aspect of group dynamics that workers should consider during the middle stage of treatment groups is the culture that has developed in the group. Does the culture help the group achieve its goals? If not, one way to change the group's culture is to challenge commonly accepted beliefs and ideas held by members. This is illustrated in the following case.

● **CASE EXAMPLE** *Changing Group Culture*

In a group of abusive parents, the worker wanted to change a group culture that discouraged the expression of intense emotions and feelings. First, the worker pointed out that feelings were rarely expressed during group sessions. Next, the worker invited the group to discuss this observation. Several members indicated that they were afraid they might lose control of their actions if they showed these feelings. The worker suggested a series of role-play exercises designed to help the members gradually express more intense emotions. During these exercises, members learned that they could express feelings without losing control. As the group progressed, members acknowledged that allowing feelings to become pent up until they exploded was much less healthful for themselves and their families than learning to express feelings before they built up. The worker then helped the group to discuss tension and how it builds in the body. This was followed by a discussion about what coping mechanisms members used to deal with stress and what other coping strategies might be adopted.

Another way workers can change the existing group culture is to point out its dominant features and areas that appear to be taboo or not able to be discussed. When this is done, members often indicate that they had wanted to discuss taboo areas in previous group meetings but feared the group would not be receptive. These members can then be encouraged to express their thoughts and feelings on the taboo subject. In other instances, role-play exercises can be used to stimulate the group's consideration of an area that was formerly taboo.

A third way to change the culture established in a group is for the worker to develop a contingency contract with members. This procedure was used successfully in working with adolescents in a group home. The contract specified that if a member was supportive and helpful to other members who disclosed personal problems and concerns during three of five group meetings each week, the member would have access to special rewards such as a trip to a sports event or tickets to a movie. The contract helped change the group culture from one in which members were ridiculed for expressing personal issues to one in which members supported and encouraged personal disclosures.

A similar procedure was used in a children's group. Peer pressure had created an environment in which members were teased for participating in role play and program activities. The worker developed a contingency contract using a point system. Points accumulated for participating in role plays could be used at the end of the group meeting to obtain special refreshments, games, or small toys. The incentive system was effective in encouraging the children to participate in role-play exercises designed to teach them problem-solving skills.

CHANGING THE GROUP ENVIRONMENT

The material resources provided for group work services, the types of clients eligible for services, and the service technologies and ideologies endorsed by the agency all have a bearing on the services the group worker offers. Group services are also influenced by interagency linkages and by the community's response to the problems and concerns of persons who seek group treatment. In this section, suggestions are made about ways to:

- Increase social service agency support for group work services
- Develop links to interagency networks
- Increase community awareness of social problems that could be treated through group work services

Increasing Agency Support for Group Work Services

Before intervening to increase support for group work services, workers must first have a thorough understanding of their agencies. Like people, agencies have unique histories that influence their continued growth and development. It is often helpful to trace the development of clinical services within an agency to learn about the changes and innovations that have taken place over time. This process can help the worker understand the rationale for current clinical services, the agency's responsiveness to proposals for change, and the ways in which previous proposals for change were incorporated into the agency's structure.

A historical perspective helps the worker avoid making a proposal for increased support for group work services on the basis of a rationale that has been rejected in the past. It also helps to give the worker an understanding of the long-term development of the agency, an understanding that is likely to be shared by administrators whose support for innovations in clinical programming is essential.

Before proposing an increase in support for group work services, the worker should have a sound grasp of the current needs and future development plans of the agency. A proposal for group work services should be structured in such a way that it clearly shows how new or increased services will meet the current needs and future developments anticipated by the agency's administrators and board members. The proposal should emphasize the distinct advantages of group work services. For example, it may be possible to show that treatment groups are a cost-effective alternative to individual treatment services (see the cost-benefit analysis example in Chapter 14). Because most agencies want to get the most out of their resources by serving as many clients as possible for as little cost as possible, group treatment services may be an attractive alternative to individual treatment services.

A well-developed proposal itself is not enough to guarantee that an agency will increase its support for group work services. Workers also should know how to proceed within their agencies to get proposed changes accepted. Workers should be aware of several organizational factors that help to predict the degree of resistance that can be expected to a change proposal. These factors include:

- The extent of the proposed change
- The value orientation and decision-making style of the administrator responsible for deciding whether to accept the proposal
- The administrative distance between the practitioner and the decision maker
- The agency's investment in the status quo

The worker can, for example, expect greater resistance to a proposal for a basic change in the agency's services, such as a change from individual treatment to group treatment in all clinical programs, than to a modest proposal for group services to a specific client group.

The rationale for a proposal is also important in terms of the resistance it will encounter. An administrator who is concerned about saving money will probably be less inclined to accept a proposal that requires new funding than a proposal that is expected to reduce costs. Whenever possible, workers should try to present multiple rationales for group work services. For example, the worker might cite relevant research about the type of group being proposed, suggest how desired individual and group outcomes might be achieved, and describe how the group work service may reduce agency costs or increase reimbursement for clinical services.

The more levels of approval—that is, the further a proposal must go from the originator to final administrative approval—the greater the likelihood of resistance. If a group worker's proposal requires approval from administrators who are at a much higher level in the bureaucratic structure, the worker will have to elicit the support of supervisors who can argue for the proposal when it reaches higher levels of review. Even with support from supervisors, proposals are more likely to be altered the higher they go in the bureaucracy.

Resistance may also be encountered if the worker is proposing changes that reverse or negate program components or services that have received substantial support in the past. Agencies are not likely to abandon funded commitments in favor of a new proposal unless the proposal can be proved to be quite exceptional.

Once the worker has anticipated the resistance a proposal may encounter, support to overcome this resistance can be developed. Brager and Holloway (1978) suggest involving resistant coworkers in the proposal's development. Because they have had a hand in shaping the proposal, initially reluctant coworkers can usually be counted on for support in later negotiations. It is especially important to allow administrators who will be deciding whether to accept the proposal and persons who will be responsible for carrying out the proposal to have input into its development. During its development, a proposal may be revised several times to gain the support of critics who have reservations about the proposed changes. By the time it is ready for final consideration, the proposal is likely to have gone through several levels of review in which important participants have become sensitized to its benefits and their own questions or concerns have been addressed.

During each stage of review, it is important for the worker to provide evidence for the effectiveness of the proposed group. Providing information about successful group programs in similar organizations is one way to accomplish this. Information about successful group programs that are similar to the proposed group can be obtained through personal and professional contacts with government and nongovernment organizations, literature reviews, conferences, listservs, trade journals and similar sources, and by searching the Internet.

Links with Interagency Networks

Interventions in a group's environment include establishing links between agencies. Interagency links can be established by identifying and contacting workers in other agencies who work with similar populations or deal with similar social service problems. After informal telephone discussions are initiated, a planning meeting should be scheduled.

Interagency links can have several benefits. When other agencies are aware of particular types of group services offered by an agency, they may refer clients for treatment. For example, if a worker at a community agency is aware that a battered women's shelter offers support groups for women, the worker can refer women who would otherwise not receive services to this agency.

Agency networks help identify needs for particular services. In a meeting of workers from several agencies, for example, it became apparent to a group worker from a family service agency that no services existed for treating men who battered their wives. After carefully documenting the need in other agencies, a group work service was established for this population by the family service agency.

Interagency networks also help avoid duplication of services. Competition between agencies can be avoided by preventing the development of duplicate services existing elsewhere in the community and by facilitating the development of services when gaps in service delivery exist. Workers who cultivate interagency links can share the knowledge and practice experience they have gained from working with specific client groups and learn from the experiences of group workers in other agencies. In this way, knowledge can be pooled and mistakes made by one worker can be avoided by others.

Interagency networks are useful in lobbying for new group work services. For example, in a meeting of workers from a number of community agencies, it became apparent that additional services were needed to prevent criminal activity among unemployed youths. Although no worker was able to do anything about this problem alone, together they put enough pressure on the city's youth services program to obtain funding for a half-time group worker for the local community center.

Increasing Community Awareness

Ultimately, group work services depend on the support of local community residents. Residents' awareness of the social problems that exist in their communities and their belief that group work services can help maintain adequate social functioning and alleviate social problems are essential. Group workers have a responsibility to bring community problems to the attention of local officials and civic organizations and to make them aware of how group work services can help to alleviate their problems.

A variety of methods can be used to raise a community's awareness of social problems and increase its commitment to group work services. Needs assessments (see Chapter 14) are especially effective for documenting the need for additional services. Agency statistics about the number of clients not served because of a lack of resources or a lack of available services can also be useful. To call attention to community problems, workers can testify at legislative hearings, they can become members of local planning bodies, or they can help to elect local officials who are supportive of the community's social service needs. Only through such efforts will group work services remain available to persons who need them.

A group worker's skills can also be used to organize clients so that they can lobby on their own behalf for needed services. For example, an outpatient group in a community mental health center in a poor urban area was composed entirely of women who were receiving Aid to Families with Dependent Children (AFDC) benefits. It became apparent that many of the women's problems were tied to the subsistence-level benefits they received as well as to the environmental conditions in which they lived. The worker informed the women of a national welfare rights coalition and helped them form a local rights group. Although this effort did not make a tremendous or immediate change in their life circumstances, it did give the women a constructive way to voice their complaints and lobby for changes in their community. It helped them to overcome what Seligman (1975) called "learned helplessness."

SUMMARY

This chapter focuses on specialized intervention methods that can be used during the middle stage of treatment groups. The methods are commonly used to intervene at the level of (1) the group member, (2) the group as a whole, and (3) the environment in which the group functions. Interventions at the level of the group member can be subdivided into those that deal with (1) intrapersonal, (2) interpersonal, and (3) environmental concerns. Interventions in the group as a whole can be subdivided into those that focus on (1) communication and interaction patterns, (2) attraction for its members, (3) social integration, and (4) culture.

The chapter concludes with an examination of interventions to change the environment in which a group functions, an important, but often neglected, area of group work practice. Discussion of interventions in this portion of the chapter includes ways to (1) increase agency support for group work services, (2) develop links to interagency networks, and (3) increase community awareness of social service problems that can be alleviated by group treatment.

● CASE EXAMPLE

Diana instituted several groups as part of the Mental Health Association's Assertive Community Treatment Program. The mission of this program was to actively reach out to persons who lived in the community and experienced a variety of severe and persistent mental health problems, particularly schizophrenia. Employment, with accompanying case management and family support counseling, was strongly associated with successful treatment outcomes.

One of Diana's groups was aimed at empowering members by helping them build the interpersonal and problem-solving skills necessary for successfully finding and keeping employment. The group also served as a support system for members as they attempted to find and keep jobs in the community. The members of the group were adult men and women who lived in either the association's community residences or at home with their families.

The group had been together for several weeks. Members had worked through the beginning stage of group development, despite a difficult "storming" period during which several members had expressed some discomfort with the level of disclosure in the group. Following this, Diana was successful in helping each member

articulate and set individual goals to work on during the group. Diana encouraged them to help each other and the group as a whole to achieve the goals they had agreed to accomplish.

Diana guided the group in its middle phase by introducing some structure into meetings. She divided work done during group meetings into two time periods. During the first part of the meeting members engaged in structured role plays and program activities aimed at increasing their readiness for seeking employment. These activities helped members learn new skills that would help them do job searches and make initial contacts with employers. They also practiced interpersonal skills by doing mock employment interviews with each other. After each interview, members gave and received feedback from each other and from Diana. They also learned to use modeling and rehearsal to develop better interviewing skills. During the second part of the meeting members had open discussion time, when they could share their successes and concerns about securing and maintaining employment. During this part of the group session members were able to provide mutual aid and support to each other. Diana found that structuring the time during sessions and using exercises and role plays were helpful for reinforcing job readiness skills. These activities also bolstered members' confidence in the effectiveness of the group.

Diana gave individual attention and encouragement to members and expressed her belief in their strengths and capacities, helping members feel validated as individuals and as members. Getting members involved in the group also meant helping them to feel they had a stake in the work of the group. For example, she would ask the group as a whole to plan activities they thought would be helpful. She also encouraged them to fully participate in these activities, and to try new experiences in the protective environment of the group.

Diana also helped remind members of their individual goals by utilizing individual contracts between members and the group. For example, one of the members mentioned that she had difficulties in working with older persons in her previous work environment. As part of her individual contract, this member agreed to talk to three older persons in her neighborhood and report back to the group about her experiences. Another member who had a history of being late for previous jobs was asked to keep track of when he woke up and to make notes about his morning routine. These notes were used during group problem solving to make suggestions about how this member could become more organized and punctual.

As each session began, Diana had a brief check-in period during which members reviewed what they had done between sessions and reported on any homework they had to complete from the previous session. She asked members to talk about how they were progressing in meeting their individual goals. She also discussed and demonstrated ways for them to monitor their progress. She used effective modeling skills to show members how to give each other positive reinforcement when they made progress on their goals.

Work with the group was not always easy. Diana found herself helping members deal with setbacks that stemmed from interpersonal difficulties. Some of these obstacles to achieving goals were related to difficulties members had in forming mutually supportive relationships. Diana helped the group discuss how best to achieve good social relationships with others. She also helped members to see how some of their social behaviors might interfere with their job search efforts. Discussion with members about these issues proved useful in helping her to design role plays and rehearsals to build members' social and interpersonal skills.

chapter 11

Task Groups:
Foundation Methods

This chapter focuses on the foundation skills, procedures, and methods used in task groups during their middle stage. After a brief discussion of the importance of task groups in social service and health agencies, the first section of the chapter describes nine activities that workers commonly engage in during the middle stage of task group development.

The second section of this chapter describes a six-step model for effective problem solving in groups. The model includes a discussion of the practice skills workers use during each step of the process.

THE UBIQUITOUS TASK GROUP

It has been said that U.S. citizens are involved in committees and other task groups more than any other people (Tropman, 1996). Participation in the decisions that affect their lives is characteristic of a democratic society. Every day millions of meetings take place throughout the United States. Social service agencies could not function without committees, treatment conferences, teams, boards, and other work groups.

Social workers and other helping professionals are often called on to chair committees, teams, and other task groups. For example, social workers are frequently designated team leaders in interdisciplinary health-care settings because social work functions include coordination, case management, and concern for the bio-psychosocial-cultural functioning of the whole person. Workers also are asked to staff task groups (Tropman, 1996). In general, the staff person plays a supportive role in helping the group clarify its goals and carry out its work. Acting under the direction of the task group's leader, the staff person reports directly to the group. The duties and roles of a staff person are quite varied and can include serving as a resource person, consultant, enabler, analyst, implementer, tactician, catalyst, and technical adviser. Despite the importance and widespread use of task groups in social service agencies, with a few notable exceptions (Brill, 1976; Ephross & Vassil, 2005; Fatout & Rose, 1995; Toseland & Ephross, 1987; Tropman, 1996), the human services have paid little attention to how task groups work.

Although task groups can be useful, they can be a source of frustration for their participants when they function ineffectively. For example, Napier and Gershenfeld (1993) describe the "incredible meeting trap" in which little is accomplished and members leave feeling frustrated by the group process. Meetings that are not well run are boring and unsatisfying. They suffer from a lack of participation and corrective feedback from members from who easily lose interest.

Although task group meetings are often seen as a chore to be endured by members for the good of the organization,[1] well-run meetings can be a positive experience. They help draw people together by creating effective teamwork in which ideas are shared, feelings are expressed, and support is developed for group members and for the decisions made by the group. There are few experiences in the workplace to equal the sense of cohesion, commitment, and satisfaction that members feel when their ideas have been heard, appreciated, and used in resolving a difficult issue and arriving at a decision. The next sections of this chapter describe methods that can help workers lead task groups effectively.

LEADING TASK GROUPS

Although workers perform many similar activities in task and treatment groups during the middle stage, there is a greater emphasis on certain activities because of the differing foci of task and treatment groups. Task groups, for example, are more concerned than are treatment groups with creating new ideas, developing plans and programs, solving problems that are external to the group, and making decisions about the organizational environment.

To lead task groups effectively during their middle stage, it is important to stay focused on the purposes and functions that the group is expected to accomplish. In his classic text on leading task groups, Maier (1963) suggests that the primary purposes of task groups are problem solving and decision making. Although problem solving and decision making are important, several other objectives of task groups have been identified in the literature (Napier & Gershenfeld, 1993; Scheidel & Crowell, 1979). These objectives may include keeping members informed and involved, empowering members, and monitoring and supervising their performance.

● **CASE EXAMPLE**   *A Home Health-Care Team*

In a community health-care team serving homebound older people, home health-care aides met with their supervisor every two weeks to discuss the situations of the frail older people with whom they were working. The meetings were also used to discuss psychological, social, medical, and other community services the aides might use to help maintain the independent function of those with whom they were working. Because the workers spent so much time away from the office, the team meetings also had the secondary objective of helping the workers to get to know each other and to identify with the organization with which they were working.

---

[1]See the film *Meeting in Progress,* Round Table Films, 113N. San Vincente Blvd., Beverly Hills, CA 90211, for a vivid example of task group members who are ready to end a meeting as soon as a decision is reached.

To accomplish these objectives during the middle stage of task groups, workers are called on to help with a variety of activities including the following:

- Preparing for group meetings
- Sharing information, thoughts, and feelings about concerns and issues facing the group
- Involving members and helping them feel committed to the group and the agency in which they work
- Facilitating fact finding about issues and concerns facing the group
- Dealing with conflict
- Making effective decisions
- Understanding the political ramifications of the group
- Monitoring and evaluating the work of the group
- Problem solving

Preparing for Group Meetings

During Meetings

At the beginning of a meeting, the worker is responsible for several tasks. The worker begins by introducing new members and distributing handouts not included with the material distributed before the meeting. Before working on agenda items, the worker should make a brief opening statement about the purpose of the meeting. In this statement, the worker may want to call members' attention to previous meetings and to the mandate of the group as a way to indicate that the meeting will undertake a necessary and important function related to the overall objectives of the group. Making members aware of the overall objectives of the group and the salience of particular agenda items to be considered that day is important for maintaining members' interest and willingness to work during the meeting.

The worker should seek members' approval of written minutes that were distributed before the meeting and request that members raise any questions, changes, or amendments they would like to enter into the minutes. After the minutes are approved, the worker should make announcements and call on group members to make designated reports. Reports should be brief and to the point. Members should verbally summarize written reports that have been circulated with the agenda rather than reading them verbatim because reading lengthy reports can be boring and result in loss of interest and attention of other members.

During the middle portion of the meeting, the worker's task is to help the group follow its agenda. Whatever the purpose of a specific meeting, the middle portion is the time when the group accomplishes much of its most difficult work. To avoid getting stuck on one item of business in meetings that have extensive agendas, details of particular items should be worked out before the meeting. If this is not possible, Tropman (1996) suggests that the group should agree "in principle" on overall objectives and goals about a particular task and then charge a subcommittee or an individual group member with working out the details and bringing them back to the group later.

The worker should model the behavior that is expected of all members. A worker who shows respect, interest, integrity, and responsibility will convey these feelings to members.

By encouraging equitable participation, the expression of minority-group opinions, and an appreciation of all sincere contributions to the group's work, the worker sets a positive example for group members to follow.

The worker should act more as a servant of the interests of the group as a whole than as a master who imposes his or her will on the group. By demonstrating that the good of the group as a whole is foremost when conducting the group's business, the worker gains the respect of members. Authority, control, and discipline should be used only to reduce threats to the group's effective functioning, not to impose the worker's wishes on the group. As members perceive that the worker is committed to accomplishing the group's common objective, the worker will gain the cooperation and the admiration of group members.

The worker should ensure that the pace of the meeting leaves enough time to accomplish the items specified in the agenda. Workers should not rush through important decisions because they are pressed for time at the end of a meeting. Members also become frustrated when they are expected to present or discuss ideas but have no time to do so because the group has spent too much time on earlier agenda items. Part of the responsibility of an effective worker in preparing for a meeting is making sure that the number of agenda items is manageable. Items sometimes take longer to discuss than anticipated, so it is good practice to plan extra time into an agenda. When too many agenda items are submitted for a meeting, the worker should rank the items for importance. Items that are assigned a low priority should be postponed to a later meeting.

Before adjourning, the worker should carry out several actions. These are summarized in the following list.

Ending a Session

- Summarize the meeting's accomplishments
- Praise members for their efforts
- Identify issues and agenda items that need further attention
- Mention where the meeting has placed the group in terms of its overall schedule
- Mention major topics for the next group meeting
- Summarize as clearly as possible the tasks that members agreed to accomplish before the next meeting

These strategies help to clarify responsibilities, reduce confusion, and increase the probability that members will complete assignments that were agreed to during earlier portions of the group's discussion.

Between Meetings

Two major tasks to accomplish between meetings are (1) seeing that decisions and tasks decided on at the previous meetings are carried out, and (2) preparing for the next meeting. The worker can do the first task by reading the minutes of previous meetings. Properly kept minutes include summaries of actions taken, tasks that were assigned, and the time frame for reporting back to the group. It is also helpful for the worker to make brief notes during a meeting or soon after the meeting ends about any decisions made that need to be followed up before the next meeting.

In seeing that the decisions agreed on by the group are carried out between meetings, Tropman (1996) suggests that a worker ensure that members work on and complete reports and other assignments that are necessary for the next group meeting. This does not mean that the worker takes over these tasks, but rather encourages and facilitates the progress of members assigned to carry out particular tasks. For example, the worker might meet with subcommittees of the larger group to provide information or guidance as they carry out their functions.

Between meetings, the worker should also develop and maintain close contacts with administrative staff, governing bodies, and other constituencies that may be affected by the group's work. As the spokesperson for the group, the worker should keep in mind that he or she represents the group's public image. A worker should express the officially accepted opinions of the committee, not personal views. The worker should not enter into private agreements or commit to decisions or positions that have not been discussed and accepted by the group. In all but emergency situations, the worker should convene the group and consult with it before making decisions. The only exception is when the group, the agency, or a regulatory body has empowered the worker to act independently without first consulting with the group.

The second major task of the worker between meetings is to prepare for the next group meeting. When there is a written agenda for each meeting, the worker or the member designated as the group's secretary should send a memo to each group member soon after a meeting to request agenda items well ahead of the next meeting. This process allows enough time for the agenda and background or position papers to be completed and sent to members so they can be read before the next meeting. Meeting agendas should be established to facilitate discussion. One effective framework is illustrated in the following meeting agenda outline.

Meeting Agenda Outline

- Examine and approve (with any corrections) brief, relevant minutes from the last meeting
- Make information announcements
- Vote to include special agenda items
- Work on less controversial, easier items
- Work on difficult items
- Break
- Work on "for discussion only" items
- Consider any special agenda items if there is sufficient time
- Summarize
- Adjourn

In preparing for the next meeting, the worker should also organize opening remarks and administrative summaries to be presented. Special care should be taken in preparing for meetings that do not have a written agenda. In such instances, the worker should be clear about how to direct the meeting, what tasks the group will work on, and what goals are to be achieved.

Part of the worker's responsibility in preparing for a meeting is assessing the group's functioning. Questions such as "What is the group's relationship with its outside environment?"

"Has the group been functioning smoothly?" "What norms, roles, and interaction patterns have developed in the group?" can stimulate the worker to consider how best to prepare for the next meeting.

In many task groups, the worker acts as both the leader and staff person. However, if a separate staff person is available to a task group, that person can prepare background reports and memos that analyze the group's options, develop resources, set up the meeting arrangements, and attend to other group needs.

Sharing Information

Another important activity of the leader during the middle stage is to help members share information, thoughts, and feelings with one another. For example, medical social workers from different community hospitals organize into an informal support group. Once each month, the leader and the group meet to share information about their work and new techniques for working with people in medical settings.

Teams, committees, delegate councils, and boards use group meetings as a means for members to share their concerns, their experiences, their perspectives, and their expertise. This is an important activity because, as a result of highly differentiated work roles, contact among workers in many agencies is infrequent. Job assignments such as individual treatment sessions and home visits limit opportunities for communication among workers.

Social issues and problems often affect several agencies, and task groups can bring workers from different agencies together. A group meeting is a convenient way for them to share unique viewpoints and differing perspectives on issues, problems, or concerns they face in their own agencies. By providing a forum for sharing knowledge and resources, interagency task groups encourage cooperative and coordinated problem solving.

Open communication and unimpeded sharing of information are prerequisites for task groups to accomplish their objectives. Vinokur-Kaplan (1995) suggests that effective communication within the group and between the group and the organization are key elements of effective teamwork. Empirical findings regarding group productivity and group process confirm that how information is communicated and used in a group has an important effect on the quality and the quantity of a group's productivity (Forsyth, 2006).

The first step in aiding effective communication and sharing information is to ensure that all members have a clear understanding of the topic being discussed and the task facing the group. To stimulate all members' participation in the discussion, the topic must be relevant. If members have little interest in the topic and no stake in the outcome, there is little reason for them to participate. In many groups, members become bored, disinterested, and dissatisfied because they do not understand the importance of a particular topic. The leader should help each member see the relevance and importance of issues as they are brought before the group. When it is clear that a discussion topic is relevant to only a few members of a task group, the worker should consider forming a subgroup to meet separately from the larger group and have the subgroup provide a brief report of its deliberations and recommendations at a later meeting of the entire group.

To focus interest, promote task-relevant discussions, and reduce confusion among members, it is often helpful to develop clear procedural steps such as the six-step, problem-solving model presented later in the chapter. Summarizing and focusing skills can also help the group remain on task. Summarizing can be used to check understanding, to review previously discussed subjects, to go back to items that were not fully discussed, to help separate a problem or issue into several parts, and to bring members' attention to a particularly important aspect of the discussion.

Focusing can be accomplished by suggesting that the group discuss one issue at a time, by pointing out that the group has digressed from the discussion topic, and by making task-relevant statements. Effective workers often have self-imposed rules limiting their communications early in group meetings to allow members the maximum opportunity to participate in the discussion. Often, a few brief summaries and comments that focus the discussion are all that is needed by the worker early in the group's work.

Another method of establishing open communication channels and promoting information sharing among all group members is to ensure equitable participation in the group. According to Huber (1980), equitable participation "is the level of participation that is in keeping with the individual's information, knowledge, or other contribution to the group's effort" (p. 185).

The worker can help the group develop a standard of fairness in participation by encouraging the development of rules for participation. Members may agree to keep their comments brief, be attentive to the communication of others when they are speaking, and encourage silent members to participate. The worker can help members follow the rules that are established. This can be accomplished by inviting the participation of other members and asking for feedback about the proposal. The worker can also interrupt long monologues by asking members to summarize their comments briefly or suggesting that members give others a chance to reply.

In some cases it is helpful to structure the discussion by using a round robin procedure or the rules of parliamentary procedure. This is illustrated in the following case example.

● **CASE EXAMPLE** *The Round Robin Procedure*

In a round robin procedure, each group member is asked to present one idea or one piece of information. Going around the group, members take turns presenting one idea. This procedure is continued and each member takes as many turns as needed to share all their ideas with the group. Members who do not have additional ideas simply pass their turn. The round robin is completed when all members have shared all their ideas.

The round robin procedure has several advantages over unstructured, interactive communication procedures. All members have an equal opportunity to participate. Because only one idea is presented at a time, the procedure avoids the boredom that often results when one member enumerates several ideas one after another. By continuing to go around the group until all ideas are heard and by asking members to pass if they do not have any new information to present, a norm is established for sharing as many ideas as possible.

In large task groups, however, round robin procedures are often too time-consuming. Unless the group is divided into subgroups, the procedure is not useful. To facilitate equitable participation in large groups, the worker should consider using parliamentary procedures (Gulley, 1968; Maier, 1963; Scheidel & Crowell, 1979) following *The New Robert's Rules of Order* (Robert, 1983). These procedures, which have been developed over the past 600 years in meetings in business, industry, and political bodies in Britain and the United States, provide for orderly and structured participation in large group meetings.

Group workers should be aware that parliamentary procedures are subject to manipulation by members who are familiar with their complexities. By trading favors for votes before a meeting and calling for votes with few members present, parliamentary procedures can be used to subvert majority rule. Despite these disadvantages, *Robert's Rules of Order* can be helpful in ensuring equitable participation in large meetings. A brief description of parliamentary procedures is included in Chapter 12.

Enhancing Involvement and Commitment

A third important activity during the work stage of task groups is to help members feel that they are a vital part of their agency and the task groups that it sponsors. Because much of any organization's work is done by individuals, there is a danger that staff can become isolated and alienated from an organization. Task groups provide support for their members and a sense of belonging that reduces alienation. For example, a worker in an outreach program for the frail elderly spends much time working with the frail elders who comprise the caseload. Monthly team meetings with other outreach workers provide support and recognition for the worker who is faced with the difficult, often emotionally charged, task of working with frail older adults.

Helping members become involved through their participation in a task group benefits both the organization and its employees. Task groups provide an organized means of developing, implementing, and getting employees to follow policies, procedures, and goals of the agency. They allow employees an opportunity to influence the policies and procedures developed by the agency, which, in turn, helps to make the agency responsive to the needs of its workers. Task groups also help to organize, coordinate, and channel employees' input by clearly delineating how a task group fits into the overall structure of an agency—to whom the group reports and what authority and power the group has to develop or change agency policies. Employees' input can be organized and channeled appropriately.

Several steps can be taken to help task group members feel their input is vital to the agency's sound functioning.

Helping Members to Feel Involved

- Workers should help members understand the importance of the group's work, its relationship to the agency's purpose, and how the group fits into the agency's administrative structure

- Assign members specific roles in the group

- Invite members' input into the agenda and the decision-making process of the group

- Encourage members to participate in the decision-making process of the group

To help members feel involved, state the purpose of the group and explain how the group fits into the agency's administrative and decision-making structure. Clarify the duties, responsibilities, authority, and power that result from membership in the group. When assigning roles, encourage members to work with one another to accomplish group tasks. This helps members feel that they are a part of a collective effort that is of vital importance to effective agency functioning. Members can be invited to develop and submit agenda items for future group meetings. Circulating the agenda and any background papers before a meeting can help members prepare their thoughts and concerns before a meeting. It also increases the chances that they will participate and share their thoughts about the agenda items during the meeting. It has been shown that that the greater a member's effort in preparing for the group, the more likely the member is to stay involved and committed to the work of the group (Kiesler, 1978). Therefore, asking members to prepare for the meeting by reading background papers, collecting information, preparing reports, and submitting agenda items tends to increase involvement and commitment to the group and the larger organization. Shared decision making has also been shown to increase motivation, and the acceptance and understanding of decisions. It has also been shown to increase information available for decision making, and helps in processing complex information (Forsyth, 2006).

Despite the advantages of keeping members involved in decision making there are some potential disadvantages to giving members decision-making authority. According to Huber (1980), the disadvantages are (1) the great amount of personnel time spent in group decision making, (2) the tendency for groups to produce decisions that are not acceptable to management, (3) expectations that future decisions will also be made through group participation, (4) the tendency for groups to take longer than individuals to reach decisions, and (5) the possibility that group decision making could cause conflict among group members who may have to work together every day. Thus, the decision to delegate decision making to groups should be made only after carefully considering both its advantages and disadvantages in a particular situation. When the advantages of group decision making are questionable, it is possible to have the group make recommendations but leave the final decision to one person. This approach, however, should be used cautiously because most experts recommend consensus building and shared decision making as the preferred method for leading task groups (Frosyth, 2006; Susskind & Cruikshank, 2006). The following case example illustrates how a task group team in a psychiatric setting handled one problem they were facing.

● **CASE EXAMPLE** *Problem Solving in a Psychiatric Team*

The leader of psychiatric team in an inpatient setting for adolescents noticed that the team had trouble discussing problems about the way it functioned with teenagers who were aggressive or violent. Instead of singling out any members who had recently dealt with patients who had become aggressive, the team leader reframed the problem as one shared by all members of the team. The leader mentioned that all members of the team would benefit from coming up with new ways to handle these adolescents. After an extensive discussion, new rules for handling aggressive and violent outbursts were decided upon. The team also came up with the idea of having an in-service training by someone who specialized in dealing with problems of aggressive and violent adolescents.

Developing Information

A fourth activity of the worker during the middle stage of task groups is to help members generate information and develop creative alternatives for responding to difficult issues and problems facing the group. Although task groups are often thought to be particularly effective for sharing information and developing creative ideas, the available evidence suggests that ordinary interactive group discussions inhibit rather than increase the disclosure of information, ideas, and creative solutions (Hare, Blumberg, Davies, & Kent, 1995).

There are many reasons that group processes may inhibit information sharing and the development of creative ideas.

Group Factors that Inhibit Ideas and Creativity

- Status-conscious group members feel intimidated by members with higher status. Lower-status members tend to share less information and avoid making suggestions that offend higher-status members.
- Norms and social pressures for conformity tend to limit the expression of new and creative ideas.
- Groups have the advantage of the variety of opinions and knowledge offered by all members, but group members may censor controversial opinions.
- Covert judgments are often made but not expressed openly in groups. Members, therefore, become concerned about the effects their self-disclosures will have on future interactions with group members.
- Interacting groups tend to reach premature solutions without considering all available evidence.

The worker can help in several ways to improve group members' opportunities to present new ideas, combine information, and generate creative solutions in interactive groups. First, the worker must clearly indicate to all members that their input is welcome, which means that the worker must be able to address the members' concerns about sanctions that may result from expressing sensitive or controversial ideas in the group. If the worker cannot guarantee freedom from sanctions, he or she should try to be as clear as possible about the boundaries of the discussion. For example, it might be possible for committee members to discuss new policies regarding service delivery, but it might not be acceptable for them to criticize existing supervisory staff who have to follow current policy guidelines. When sanctions are possible from individuals outside the group, the worker can encourage the group to consider keeping their discussions confidential. If lower-status members fear reprisals from higher-status members, the worker can discuss the use of sanctions with higher-status members before the group meeting and gain their cooperation in refraining from applying them. The worker can also suggest that higher-status and lower-status members discuss this issue in the group.

Feedback can both help and hinder the group's development of information and creative solutions. It is commonly thought that all feedback is useful because it helps group members detect and correct errors in information processing, but this is not true in all circumstances. In the early phase of developing information and forming creative solutions, evaluative feedback can have the effect of suppressing further suggestions (Forsyth, 2006). Members fear their ideas may be evaluated negatively and that this will reflect on their competence and their status in the organization. Under these circumstances, few members risk making suggestions, giving opinions, or volunteering information that will not be readily accepted. To encourage free discussion, creative ideas, and new insights about a problem or issue, the worker should ask members to refrain from evaluating ideas early in the group's discussion.

Several other steps can also be taken to help the group develop information and creative ideas to solve a problem.

Developing Information and Creative Ideas

- Encourage the group to develop norms that promote free discussion of ideas
- Point out group pressures that inhibit members' free discussion

- Model an open exchange of ideas by presenting creative, controversial, and thought-provoking ideas
- Encourage members to continue to share unique ideas by praising those who present innovative suggestions
- Encourage lower-status members, who often find it difficult to present their ideas, to share their ideas as early as possible in the group's discussion
- Help the group separate information and idea-generating steps from decision-making steps

When these suggestions are implemented, interacting groups can develop more creative solutions than they would under ordinary conditions.

Dealing with Conflict

It is unlikely that all members of a task group will immediately agree on all aspects of the work of the group. Thus, it is important for workers to realize that conflicts occur even in effective task groups (Forsyth, 2006; Napier & Gershenfeld, 1993). Conflicts often emerge at the end of the beginning stage or beginning of the work stage of the group. Earlier in the life of a group, members are just getting to know one another and are less likely to express conflicting viewpoints.

Although some view all conflict as a problem that should be prevented or resolved (Smith & Berg, 1997), a distinction can be made between what has been called instrumental, substantive, or task conflict and what has been called affective, social, process, or relationship conflict (Guetzkow & Gyr, 1954; Wittman, 1991; Jehn & Chatman, 2000). *Task conflict* is based on members' differing opinions about ideas, information, and facts presented during the task group's work. This type of conflict is often helpful to the development of the group because it stimulates healthy dialogue, the development of solutions that encompass different points of view, and the careful analysis of proposed solutions.

Relationship conflict is based on the emotional and interpersonal relationships among members within and outside of the group. This type of conflict is rarely helpful to the development of the group. In general, relationship conflict is more difficult to resolve than task conflict because it is resistant to persuasive reasoning.

Certain personality characteristics have also been associated with productive and non-productive conflict. For example, a win-win orientation is often associated with productive conflict, whereas zero-sum orientation is often associated with nonproductive conflict (Jehn & Chatman, 2000; Wall & Nolan, 1987). Similarly, rigidity is associated with conflict escalation, and flexibility is associated with the ability to change perceptions and to accommodate differing points of view (Wall & Nolan, 1987).

Timely intervention into group processes can often help to defuse conflicts. For example, the worker leading a treatment conference in a mental health center might notice that a subgroup of members is not participating as expected. The worker comments on this and discovers that subgroup members are quiet because they disagree with the opinions of a vocal, controlling member. The worker helps the subgroup and the individual member resolve their differences by pointing out the conflict and helping the members confront it. The worker also acts as a mediator to help the subgroup and the member negotiate differences.

Some workers have difficulty dealing with conflict. They avoid, ignore, or minimize it, hoping it will go away. These strategies are generally counterproductive. Avoiding conflict rarely leads to satisfying and meaningful dialogue about the issues facing the group. Most often, when conflicts are avoided, members get the message that they should not express their true feelings and that an honest sharing of information and opinions should be sacrificed so that the group can function "harmoniously." When conflicts are ignored, they sometimes smolder until a particular interaction or event causes them to intensify and erupt. At other times, conflicts subside, but one or more group members are left feeling they have lost the battle. Neither outcome is desirable.

How can the worker handle conflict in a productive and satisfying manner? Substantive and affective conflicts can be reduced by the following procedures.

Suggestions for Handling Conflict in the Group

- View conflict as a natural and helpful part of group development.
- Help members recognize the conflict.
- Encourage group norms of openness and respect for others' viewpoints.
- Encourage group members to suspend judgment until they have listened to the entire group discussion.
- Encourage members to view issues in new ways, to understand situations from other members' vantage points, and to be flexible in their own views of a situation.
- Help members avoid focusing on personality conflicts or personal differences. Instead, help members express the facts and preferences underlying their alternative viewpoints and opinions.
- Emphasize factors that promote consensus in the group discussion.
- Develop information and facts about the situation and seek expert judgments to help resolve conflicting information.
- Follow orderly, preplanned steps for considering alternatives and deciding on solutions.
- Use decision criteria that are mutually agreed on by group members.
- Clarify and summarize the discussion frequently so that all members have a similar understanding of what is being discussed and the decision criteria that will be used.
- Be sensitive to members' personal concerns and needs in developing solutions and arriving at a decision.
- Remain neutral in the conflict and ask questions that seek clarification whenever possible.

In the classic text *Getting to Yes,* Fisher, Ury, and Patton (1997) suggest that the worker should help members (1) separate the person from the issue or problem being addressed, (2) focus on interests or attributes of the problem rather than on members' positions on the issue, (3) generate a variety of possible options before deciding what to do, and (4) insist that the decision about how to proceed be based on some objective standard.

Probably the single most important step in dealing with conflicts in a group is to help members view disagreements as opportunities to gather information and to share views and opinions, rather than as personal attacks or as threats to authority or position. Cooperative processes involve recognizing the legitimacy of others' interests (Ephross & Vassil, 2005). Thus, it is important for the leader to welcome differing viewpoints and to encourage the members to do the same. Also, it is helpful to (1) ask members to elaborate on the thinking that led to their viewpoints, (2) suggest that other members listen carefully and ask questions before they react, and (3) highlight points of consensus and mutual interest as they arise. Another step in dealing with conflict involves helping members to avoid turning conflicts into personal attacks. The worker should ask members to keep their comments focused on the issues rather than on members' personal characteristics and should encourage members to make "I" statements and to avoid "you" statements that attack other members or subscribe motives to their behavior. The worker should not react to outbursts and should not encourage members to defend their positions. Instead, the worker should help members in a conflict describe their interests, values, fears, and their goals or objectives. This is illustrated in the following case.

● **CASE EXAMPLE** *Handling Conflicts*

Consider the following two ways of handling a conflict. In the first version, a member of a committee defends his position opposing the development and implementation of a new program by saying, "I don't want my staff to take on this proposed new program because they are already overworked. We were asked just last month to take on more work. I just don't think it is fair to ask us again. What about Joe's department [referring to another member of the committee who is not present]? Why can't Joe and his staff handle this? Joe's not that busy!" In the second version, the member defends his position by using "I" statements. "My interests are in ensuring that the workers in my department don't get so overloaded with work that quality and morale goes down. I appreciate your faith in my department, but I fear that my already overworked staff will become overwhelmed. My objective is to ensure that the workers in my department don't get so burned out that they just throw up their hands and stop trying to do a quality job." The first type of response could be viewed as a personal attack on Joe, who is likely to learn about the member's comments and become angry. The second monologue using "I" statements avoids personalizing the issue. Notice that the second statement lends itself to further discussion and negotiation. For example, the leader might ask the member to describe the workload of his department and how it has changed over the past year. If the workload has increased and concerns about an overload are warranted, the leader might facilitate a discussion among group members about options for getting the work accomplished.

Another useful procedure for dealing with conflict is to help members look beyond their particular positions on an issue and to understand what others hope to accomplish. The worker should encourage members who are having a conflict to state their concerns and their priorities as concretely as possible, but discourage them from defending their positions. Instead, the worker can encourage members to ask questions of each other and to put themselves in each other's positions. The worker should point out shared interests and mutual gains. For example, the worker might point out that all department heads have a stake in ensuring that the members of one department do not become so overloaded that they cannot do a good job. The following case example points out how this can be accomplished.

● **CASE EXAMPLE** *Conflict Resolution*

In the committee where the member is worried about a work overload, the leader might say, "Jim, I understand your concern for your people. They have been working hard. We are all worried about it. Everyone here, and many others, have a stake in your group not getting bogged down, because without the programming your group is doing, none of the other groups could complete their assignments. Let's go around the group and see if we can get some suggestions and ideas about how we could get this new work accomplished without just expecting Joe's group to do it all. I will give you a minute or two to think about it, I will start with the first idea, and then we can go around the group starting with Tom to get everybody's ideas. Okay?"

The worker can help members to reach consensus by agreeing in principle to mutually acceptable goals. As many solutions as possible for achieving the goals should be generated. For example, the committee members might agree that Joe's group should not be asked to take on all the new work, and that the work should be divided up and given to several departments to complete, but first, the worker should ask members to express their preferences for particular options. If a single option is not preferred by all parties, the worker should negotiate a solution by combining options that include some gains and some sacrifices on the part of all parties to the conflict.

Making Effective Decisions

Facilitators of task groups are often called on to help members make effective decisions. For example, a board president helps the board of directors decide whether to expand their agency's geographical service area. A community organizer helps a neighborhood association decide whether to establish a neighborhood watch group to address the crime rate in the community. The leader of an executive council helps the group determine who will be promoted within the organization.

Although groups are often used to make decisions, evidence about their effectiveness is mixed. Groups are better than individuals at influencing opinions and obtaining commitments from members (Kelley & Thibaut, 1969; Lewin, 1948). Napier (1967) found that groups are better at integrating complex perceptual and intellectual tasks because members can rely on one another for assistance. However, for other types of problems, groups may not be any more effective than individuals, and sometimes may be less efficient than individuals working alone (Forsyth, 2006). In summarizing the literature that has compared the problem-solving activities of task groups with the activities of individuals, Hare and colleagues (1995) drew the following conclusions.

Problem Solving: Groups versus Individuals

- Groups are superior to individuals in solving manual problems such as puzzles, particularly when the problem can be subdivided so that each person can use personal expertise to work on a problem component. The superiority of groups has been less consistently documented when the task to be accomplished is of a more intellectual nature, such as a logic problem.
- Although groups are better than the average individual, they are not better than the best individual. Therefore, a group of novices may perform worse than one expert.
- Groups have the advantage of the variety of opinions and knowledge offered by the members, but group members may censor controversial opinions.

- Part of the superiority of group problem solving results from the pooling of individual judgments to converge on a group norm. For some problems, similar accuracy may be achieved by averaging the decisions of noninteracting individuals.

- When groups solve intellectual tasks, members' rational, information-processing orientation may be impeded by socioemotional concerns.

- Because task groups require members to deliberate until they reach a decision, the decisions made in task groups may be more costly than decisions made by one or more individuals working alone.

To improve group decision making, workers should help members avoid the phenomenon known as *group think,* which is mentioned in earlier chapters (Janis, 1972). Group think occurs when group contagion takes over and members fail to express their own thoughts and feelings. Instead, they go along with the predominant sentiment of the group. This phenomenon has been recognized for years. For example, more than 90 years ago, LeBon (1910) referred to *group mind,* a state in which members allow an emotion generated from their participation in a group to dominate their intellectual powers. Similarly, more than 80 years ago, Freud (1922) wrote about the power that the group has over an individual's ego. *Group think* continues to be an important topic in the literature (see, e.g., Flippen, 1999; Forsyth, 2006; Paulus, 2000; Turner & Pratkanis, 1998). For example, the concept of *group think* has been used to compare the coercive power and the malevolent authority of cults and gangs (Knox, 1999b). Also, a videotape has also been made to illustrate group decision making and the processes which inhibit creativity and foster "group think" (Katten & Janis, 2000).

Before 1960, it was generally thought that problem-solving groups make more conservative decisions than do individuals. Experiments by Stoner (1968) and Ziller (1957), however, indicated that groups make riskier decisions than individuals. Stoner (1968) called this phenomenon the *risky shift.* As evidence began to accumulate, it became clear that the shift may be toward greater or lesser risk. Riskier decisions are made when a group's members approve of risk taking (Teger & Pruitt, 1967; Wallach & Wing, 1968), when persuasive information is presented (Ebbesen & Bowers, 1974), when the responsibility for the decision is shared among group members (Myers & Arenson, 1972; Zajonc, Wolosin, & Wolosin, 1972), or when the leader approves of a risky decision (Myers & Arenson, 1972). On the other hand, risk taking is discouraged in some groups, and members are rewarded for developing conservative solutions (Stoner, 1968).

Several steps can be taken to help members avoid group think and risky shifts. Norms and a group climate that encourages free and open discussion of ideas tend to discourage conformity and to decrease group think. Procedures that clarify how a group will use information and arrive at a decision also tend to reduce conformity. An example, shown in the following case, illustrates this point.

● **CASE EXAMPLE** *Avoiding "Group Think"*

In a family service agency, the personnel committee was charged with the hiring of a new clinical supervisor. Many applications were received for the position, and a cursory review suggested that many appeared to be well qualified. However, some of the members of the committee favored one particular applicant and other members started to agree, mentioning the skills of this person. The leader cautioned the group against deciding before giving all candidates careful consideration. In order to avoid deciding on one applicant before carefully considering all others, the leader of the personnel committee suggested that the group come up with a set of decision criteria that they could apply evenly to all candidates. The leader indicated that these decision criteria should include all the factors that the members of the committee felt were important for the new clinician to possess. The committee came up with criteria that included clinical and supervisory experience, ability to speak Spanish, and familiarity with the type of psychotropic medications typically used by clients of family service agencies.

To arrive at a final group decision, a procedure for choosing among alternatives is needed. Most groups make their final decisions using consensus, compromise, or majority rule. In certain situations, each procedure can result in quite different decisions. To avoid the suspicion that a particular decision-making procedure is being chosen to influence a decision about a particular issue, a method of choosing among alternatives should be agreed on as early as possible in a task group's deliberations.

Consensus is often considered the ideal way to select among alternatives because all group members commit themselves to the decision. When reviewing conditions for effective work with groups, Susskind and Cruikshank (2006) suggest that helping a group achieve consensus reduces conflict within the group and makes the group more effective. Consensus does not, however, necessarily imply agreement on the part of all group members. Napier and Gershenfeld (1993) point out that consensus requires that individuals be willing to go along with the group's predominant view and carry it out in good faith.

Although other decision-making procedures are quicker, reaching consensus often brings considerable support for a decision because members are more likely to cooperate in implementing decisions that they have thoroughly discussed and agreed on. Consensus is sometimes difficult to achieve in groups. It can be time-consuming and tension-provoking because each alternative must be discussed thoroughly along with dissenting viewpoints. Also, there is the danger that members will acquiesce and decision quality will be sacrificed to arrive at a solution that is acceptable to all group members (Napier & Gershenfeld, 1993). Nevertheless, reaching consensus rather than deciding by majority rule builds group cohesion and member satisfaction.

When issues are controversial and there is much dissenting opinion, it is often possible to reach consensus by modifying original proposals. To develop amendments to proposals that are acceptable to all group members, the discussion of each alternative should focus on the reasoning behind members' objections to the alternative. This process helps all group members identify the acceptable and unacceptable parts of each alternative. After a discussion of all the alternatives, the acceptable parts of several alternatives can often be combined into one solution that is acceptable to most, if not all, members.

Majority rule is a frequently used procedure to decide between alternatives in task groups because it is less time-consuming than consensus or compromise procedures, and when the vote is done by secret ballot, it protects the confidentiality of members. Majority rule is an excellent procedure for deciding routine and relatively minor questions. However, because a significant minority may not agree with the final outcome, majority rule is a less appealing procedure when the issue is important and when the support and cooperation of the entire group are needed for successful implementation. For important decisions, a two-thirds majority vote is an alternative to simple majority rule. A two-thirds majority vote ensures at least substantial support for a decision made by the group.

Understanding Task Groups' Political Ramifications

Although much of this chapter and the next are focused on problem solving and decision making, task groups also have political functions that are frequently overlooked or ignored by group workers because they are uncomfortable with the notion of behaving in a political fashion. Levinson and Klerman (1973) recognized this stance when they said the cultivation of power is viewed by many professions, including social work, "as vulgar, as a sign of character defect, as something an upstanding professional would not be interested in or stoop to engage in" (p. 66). Yet, politics are an important part of the dynamics that govern the functioning of task groups during the middle stage.

An essential step in becoming more aware of the political functions of task groups is to develop an orientation that views political behavior as an essential ingredient of all task groups. Gummer (1987) points out that rather than viewing political behavior as symptomatic of a character defect, it may be better viewed "as the quest of the mature personality for the resources needed to affect increasingly larger areas of one's world" (p. 36).

Gummer suggests that task groups should be analyzed and understood in terms of how they are used to exercise and enhance the power of the members who participate in them. Although the overt exercise of power is generally frowned on in our society, there are many symbolic ways that task groups help managers exercise their power and position within an organization. In a power-oriented analysis of task groups, Gummer (1987) focused on four elements: (1) the physical setting, (2) membership, (3) the agenda, and (4) procedural rules.

In regard to the physical setting, Gummer suggested considering the symbolic meaning of the meeting location. For example, is the meeting taking place in a neutral place, or in a place that is "owned" by the leader or a particular member? Is the meeting taking place in a symbolic setting such as an outreach office or a new building to symbolize the importance of the setting? Gummer also suggested analyzing the symbolism attached to how the meeting room is arranged. For example, does the setting promote work or comfort? Are chairs set up around a table with paper, pencils, overhead projectors, and other work-oriented aids? Or is the setting filled with couches, soft chairs, food, and other items that convey a relaxed, informal atmosphere?

Who is invited to participate in a meeting is also important from a political perspective. Participation in meetings is the organizational equivalent of enfranchisement. Gummer (1987) stated "whether an organization is run along autocratic, oligarchic, or democratic lines, whatever rights members are entitled to are accorded by their inclusion in certain organizational groups. Conversely, limits on one's organizational position are established by exclusion from certain groups" (p. 30).

Determining who can participate is an important source of power because it "organizes into attention" the interests and positions associated with the included individuals (Forester, 1981). For example, the character of a task group might be changed when consumers are included on advisory boards. Similarly, the substantive deliberations of a committee examining staffing ratios and workloads is likely to change when both nonprofessional and professional staff are included in the meetings.

Meeting agendas can also be used for political purposes. Bachrach and Baratz (1962) suggested that power can be exercised by confining the scope of decision making to relatively safe issues. The ordering of items on the agenda may also be used for political purposes. For example, the leader or certain members may take a long time to discuss several trivial issues at the beginning of a meeting as a way to leave little time to work on issues that they would rather not address. Similarly, how agenda items are presented often has political ramifications. Gummer (1987) suggests that politically oriented individuals who want certain items tabled, defeated, or changed encourage their proponents to present their issues in the broadest terms possible so that the specifics of the issue are not discussed, and thus the specifics become confused or obfuscated by a general discussion of the philosophical principles of the organization. Conversely, items that these members would like to see acted on and accepted by the group are presented as specifically and noncontroversially as possible.

Procedures governing how the group conducts its business can also be developed with political purposes in mind. In democratic organizations it is expected that, at a minimum, procedural rules should (1) provide task group members with sufficient time to deliberate the issues the group is charged to address and (2) provide for adequate representation of minority opinions. However, procedural rules can be manipulated by politically minded individuals. For example, important decisions may be deferred to the executive committee of a board rather than taken up during a full board meeting. Similarly, the membership of a nominating subcommittee or a finance subcommittee may be stacked to favor the wishes of the board chairperson or a certain subgroup of powerful members.

Monitoring and Evaluating

The worker is also often called on to help task groups to monitor and evaluate their efforts. Monitoring by the group leader should focus on both group processes and group outcomes. The leader monitors group processes to ensure that they are leading to a satisfying experience for group members while at the same time facilitating the group's work. The duel focus on members' satisfaction and goal accomplishment has long been identified as an effective means of working with task groups (Bales, 1954, 1955). It continues to be an important focus for the leadership of task groups in contemporary society.

Task groups may monitor and evaluate their own performance or be called on to monitor and evaluate other systems. For example, an outpatient mental health team may monitor and evaluate its own performance by reviewing recidivism data on all former clients at three-month, progress-review meetings (Vinokur-Kaplan, 1995).

Task groups may also monitor and evaluate the functioning of other entities. For example, boards of social service agencies are responsible for monitoring and evaluating the functioning of the entire agency. Because boards are ultimately responsible and legally liable for the proper conduct of social service agencies, monitoring and evaluating functions are a critical component of an effective board's work (Blackmon & Holland, 2000; Chait, Holland, & Taylor, 1993; Hughes, Lakey, & Bobowick, 2000; Wolf, 1990).

For effective monitoring and evaluation during the middle stage, task groups must be clear about their mandate from the agency and the ethical, moral, and legal obligations as expressed by regulatory agencies, professional societies, legislative bodies, and the larger society. Sometimes these items are clearly specified in the bylaws of the sponsoring organization. Often, however, it is the responsibility of the task group to develop a set of standards, rules, or guidelines that can be used to monitor and evaluate performance. An example presented in the following case illustrates this function of a board.

● **CASE EXAMPLE** *Development of an Institutional Research Review Board*

A large, private social service agency decided to encourage evaluations of several of its service programs. To ensure that the research would serve a useful purpose, protect the rights and the confidentiality of their clients, and meet state and federal rules and regulations, an institutional research review board was formed. The first meeting of this group focused on reviewing the procedures of similar review boards at other agencies and examining state and federal regulations. The group then prepared guidelines governing its own operation and guidelines for researchers to use when preparing proposals to be reviewed by the board. The guidelines were, in turn, modified and ratified by the executive staff and the board of the social service agency.

To fulfill their monitoring and evaluating functions adequately, task groups develop feedback mechanisms to help them obtain information about the results of a decision and take corrective actions when necessary (Nadler, 1979). The type of feedback useful to a task group depends greatly on the group's mandate and the monitoring and evaluating required in the particular situation. A board, for example, may require periodic reports from the agency director, the director of clinical services, the agency executive, and the coordinator of volunteer services. In addition, the board may review program statistics, quarterly financial statements from a certified accountant, and reports from funding sources about the performance of the agency. In other cases, a task group may use formal data-gathering procedures to perform its monitoring and evaluation functions. A discussion of these methods is presented in Chapter 14.

Problem Solving

Problem solving has been given more consideration in the group work literature than any other function of task groups. Task groups spend much time performing other functions, but problem solving is often seen as a task group's major function. The next section describes a generic, six-step, problem-solving model that can be used effectively in a variety of task groups.

A MODEL FOR EFFECTIVE PROBLEM SOLVING

The effectiveness of problem-solving efforts depends on the extent to which an optimal solution is developed and implemented. Effective problem solving involves six steps:

1. Identifying a problem
2. Developing goals
3. Collecting data
4. Developing plans
5. Selecting the best plan
6. Implementing the plan

FIGURE 11.1 ● *The Problem-Solving Process in Task Groups*

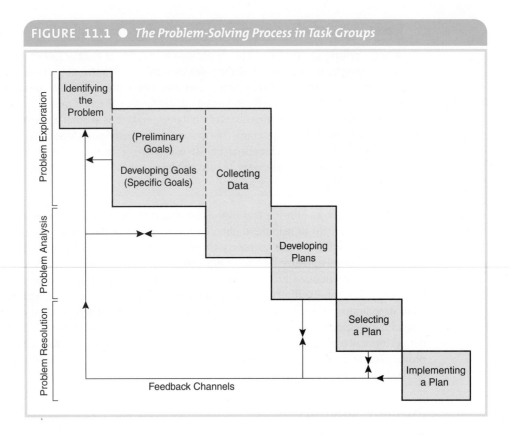

As shown in Figure 11.1, the steps are not discrete. In practice, they tend to overlap. For example, preliminary goals are often discussed during problem identification, and goals are modified and refined as data collection continues.

Problem-solving processes are used repeatedly by groups as they conduct their business. A task group may have to use two or more cycles of a problem-solving process to accomplish a single task. The process is represented in Figure 11.2.

● CASE EXAMPLE *Problem Solving*

An adult protective services team spends three meetings developing a plan for emergency evening coverage for all clients on team members' caseloads. The plan is then implemented for three months on a trial basis. After the trial period, the team may reconsider aspects of the plan. Using the problem-solving process a second time, the team decides on a modified version of the plan that includes greater cooperation with police and emergency health and mental health providers in the county.

Identifying a Problem

How a problem is identified and defined is crucial to effective problem solving. It affects what data will be collected, who will work on the problem, what alternatives will be

FIGURE 11.2 ● *Two Cycles of a Problem-Solving Process*

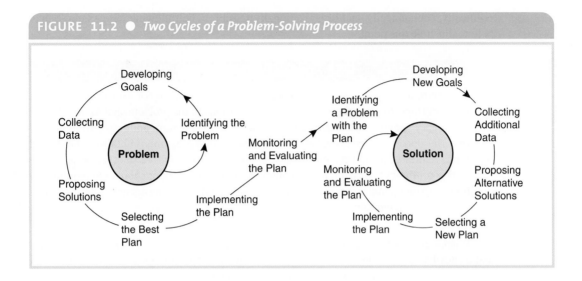

considered, and who will be affected by the problem's resolution. When they are first identified, problems are often unclear and muddled. For example, the staff of a social service agency perceives a problem in serving a large group of Mexican Americans who live in the area. The problem could be defined in several ways, including (1) not having Spanish-speaking workers, (2) not conducting any outreach efforts to this population, (3) having a poor public image with Mexican Americans in the community, (4) not having the financial resources to develop programs, and (5) providing the wrong services to meet the needs of the population.

Several steps can be taken to help a group define a problem to promote problem solving. These include (1) clarify the boundaries of the problem, (2) seek out members' perceptions of the problem and their expectations about how it will be solved, (3) develop a problem-solving orientation, (4) define a solvable problem, and (5) specify the problem as clearly as possible.

Clarifying Boundaries

The first issue that confronts workers and members as they define the boundaries of a problem is how to handle large problems that may have several interrelated components. One method of handling a large problem is to partialize it. Partializing problems gives members a sense of direction and helps them to avoid feelings of being overwhelmed by the enormity of the problem.

As problems are partialized, they should have clear boundaries. Boundaries refer to the extent and scope of a problem or issue facing the group. Defining clear boundaries helps problem solvers focus and clarify their thoughts and suggestions about a problem, which leads to more effective solutions (D'Zurilla & Goldfried, 1971).

When setting boundaries, workers are in a delicate position. On the one hand, they do not want to hamper the group's creative problem-solving ability. The worker wants the group to consider all the relevant options for problem resolution. On the other hand, the worker is often in a better position than is any other group member to recognize what is politically, economically, and organizationally feasible. The following case example may help to illustrate this point.

● **CASE EXAMPLE** *Setting Boundaries*

In a community group working on ways to increase services for Mexican Americans, the worker informs members that potential solutions to the problem should not commit the agency sponsoring the group to new services that require additional funding this year. The worker goes on to explain how funding for new programs is obtained and that all funds requested for the current fiscal year are already committed to other projects. The worker continues to explain that although the proposed solutions should not require new funds, the group might consider making recommendations to the agency's administrative staff about seeking additional funding during the next fiscal year.

Whenever possible, the boundaries of the problem-solving process should be as broad and as flexible as possible so as not to stifle creative problem solutions. The worker should point out members' freedom within the boundaries and the importance of accomplishing the task within specified limits. The group should be given a convincing rationale for limiting the scope of a problem and the scope of the efforts used to resolve it. Without guidelines, the group may arrive at a solution that is unacceptable to persons who must implement it. Members who spend their time and energy developing a solution that is not feasible will feel frustrated and disappointed when they realize their recommended solution was not implemented.

Members' Perceptions and Experiences

Members' perceptions of problematic situations and their expectations about how the situations should be resolved determine the way the members approach a problem. If the members of a group are to be satisfied with the group's problem-solving process and committed to the solution that is reached, the members' views about problems facing the group must be respected. There is no better way to show respect than to solicit their views and ensure that they are given a fair hearing by all members. Failure to clarify members' expectations and perceptions about a problem often leads to difficulties later in the group's problem-solving process. Hidden agendas can develop, in part, because unclarified expectations are acted on by members. An open discussion often causes a modification of members' perceptions and expectations and forms the basis for mutually agreed-on goals.

Careful consideration of the views of individual group members does not mean that every opinion or bit of information should be treated as equally correct or important. Although there is a tendency to associate equality of ideas with equal treatment of group members, the concepts should not be confused. Members should be treated equitably in the group process, but the importance of their contribution changes as the work of the group changes.

Problem-Solving Orientation

During the process of identifying a problem it is important for the worker to help members develop a problem-solving orientation (D'Zurilla & Goldfried, 1971). Such an orientation includes (1) minimizing irrational beliefs about problematic situations, (2) recognizing and being willing to work on problems as they occur, and (3) inhibiting tendencies to respond prematurely on the first impulse or do nothing. Irrational beliefs about "how the world should be" can inhibit members from recognizing problematic situations and can also interfere with problem resolution (Ellis, 1962). Members should be guided to use evidence, logic, and sound reasoning as they identify and define a problematic situation (Barker, 1979; Gouran, 1982; Harnack & Fest, 1964; Stattler & Miller, 1968).

An effective problem-solving orientation includes recognizing problems that need attention and being willing to work on them. It is sometimes difficult for task groups to confront and work on problems facing them. For example, a team in a psychiatric hospital may avoid discussing problems in its own functioning for fear that the discussion will be viewed as an attack on individual members. In this case, the team leader should facilitate the development of a group climate that encourages problems to be viewed as shared concerns whose resolution will benefit all team members.

In developing a problem-solving orientation within the group, it is important to help members reduce their tendency to make immediate and automatic responses. Frequently, members suggest solutions without carefully considering the problem. It has been found that less effective problem solvers are impulsive, impatient, and quick to give up (Bloom & Broder, 1950). Therefore the workers should encourage members to stop to think about the problem, collect data, and analyze alternative solutions before deciding what to do.

There should be sufficient time during a meeting agenda to grapple with difficult problems. According to Tropman (1996), difficult items should be placed in the middle third of the agenda. At this point, members are at the peak of their (1) psychological focus, (2) physiological awareness, (3) attention, and (4) attendance. Easier items should be placed earlier in the agenda. Because they require less energy, items for discussion only can be placed at the end, when members have little energy for problem solving.

Defining a Solvable Problem

Groups are sometimes blocked in their problem-solving ability because they fail to frame the problem correctly (Maier, 1963). Group members may fail to identify the correct actors, the correct systems, or the correct obstacles that constitute the problem situation. In the early stages of problem solving, the group should be tentative and flexible with its problem definition so that the definition can be modified when new data are collected.

The worker can use several techniques to improve the group's ability to define a solvable problem. Maier (1963) suggests that, whenever possible, problems should be stated in institutional rather than personal terms. For instance, in the example presented earlier, a definition that attributed the problem of lack of services for Mexican Americans to an inept director of clinical services would have alienated the director of clinical services and thus have made the problem more difficult to solve. However, identifying the problem as a lack of service hours for Mexican Americans would have opened possibilities for modifying service delivery patterns. Similarly, defining the problem as a lack of knowledge and expertise about Mexican American clients would have suggested that the committee consider assessing members' willingness to learn more about the Mexican American population.

To help the group obtain a new perspective on a problem, the worker can use the reframing technique described in Chapter 10 and illustrated in the following example.

● **CASE EXAMPLE** *Reframing*

Some of the members of the committee considering services for Mexican Americans are not convinced that services for this population are lacking. The worker asked members to imagine going to an agency where no one speaks English and where all workers and most clients have different cultural backgrounds from their own. The exercise encouraged skeptical members to reconsider their stand on the question of whether something should be done to improve services for Mexican Americans.

Reframing may also be done by focusing on the positive aspects of a problem. For example, a problem that is experienced as anxiety provoking may be reframed as one that motivates the group to improve a situation. In these ways, members' motivation to solve problems can be increased.

Specifying the Problem

Having a clearly defined and mutually understood problem is essential if members are to work effectively together. When problems are first expressed in a meeting, they are often stated as partially formulated concerns. For example, a committee member might say, "I get a sense that some of our staff may be having difficulty with the new record-keeping system." Many terms in this statement are vaguely defined. Terms such as "get a sense," "some of our staff," and "difficulty" can have different meanings for each member of the group.

As concerns are raised by members, the worker should help them clarify vague or ambiguous terms. The statement in the previous paragraph, for example, could be clarified to indicate that three members of the community team and one member of the day treatment team expressed concerns that the new record-keeping forms took too long to fill out. Further, the phrase "took too long to fill out" should be clarified so that it becomes clear what it is the group is being asked to consider. For example, "took too long to fill out" could mean "cannot complete the case record in the 15 minutes allocated for that purpose," or could mean "being asked to collect data that are not needed to work with clients." Sometimes members of the task group may find that they cannot specify the problem further without collecting additional information.

After the group has clarified the problem, the worker should summarize it in a clear, brief statement. Ideally, the problem should be defined in objective terms that have similar meanings for all members. Objective terms with clear, observable referents help members arrive at a common understanding of the situation. When summarizing, the worker should restate the boundaries of the problem and the group's authority and responsibility so that members have a clear idea of their role in resolving the problem.

● CASE EXAMPLE Specifying a Problem

The worker stated that it had come to her attention that several members expressed having a hard time with the new record-keeping system that had recently become required. She asked for members to provide as specific feedback as possible about the record-keeping system. Several members gave their opinions. However, because the worker wanted to get everyone's feedback she went around the group and asked members to state their experiences with the new system. She wrote the comments on an easel so that all members could see the different and similar comments she wrote on the paper. After all the members had a chance to give their opinions, the worker noted that she was not in a position to change the new record-keeping system by herself, but that she would take all the comments that had been written down and share them with her supervisor. She promised to report the extent of concern expressed by the members and report back to the group the next time they met. At the next meeting, the worker reported that the supervisor was going to bring the concerns of the group to the executive committee, and that the supervisor had asked her to come to the meeting and also to invite one member of the staff to attend. The group then spent time deciding on which member would represent them at the executive committee meeting, and listed a number of points about the new record-keeping system that the representative could make at the meeting.

Developing Goals

The second step in the problem-solving process is goal setting. Goal setting does not occur only once in the problem-solving process. Tentative goals are formulated soon after the problem has been identified and aid in data collection because they help shape the scope of the information to be collected. Goals are often modified and specified as information is accumulated. Initial goals may sometimes be abandoned entirely, with new goals developed on the basis of the data accumulated. Through a process of exploration and negotiation, the worker and the members share their perspectives about the goals the group should achieve relative to a particular problem. The emphasis should be on formulating goals that are mutually acceptable.

Goal statements should be as clear and specific as possible. Desired changes in problem situations should be stated as objective tasks. For example, goals to increase services to the Mexican Americans mentioned in a previous example might include (1) providing eight hours of training for each outreach worker during the next six months, (2) increasing the number of Mexican Americans served by the agency from an average of three per month to 15 per month by the next fiscal year, (3) translating program brochures into Spanish within three months, and (4) printing 400 bilingual Spanish-English brochures at the beginning of the next fiscal year. Each goal is specific and easily understood.

Group workers can use several other principles for developing effective goals. These are presented in the following list.

Principles for Developing Goals

- Goals should be directed at the mutual concerns of all members.
- Goals should be consistent with the group's mandate, its overall objectives, and the values that have been agreed on by the group as a whole.
- Goals should be attractive enough to gain the commitment, cooperation, and investment of all group members.
- Goals should be realistic and attainable through the resources available to the group and its members.
- Goals should be time limited.
- The goal-setting process should set a supportive, encouraging climate for goal attainment.

At the end of the goal-setting process, members should be clear about the tasks they must perform to achieve the goals. It is important for the worker to summarize the goals that have been decided on by the group and to review each member's role in their achievement. This process avoids misunderstandings about who is responsible for what during a specified time period. Members should be clear about the time frame for accomplishing goals and about the mechanisms for reporting their achievements to the group.

Collecting Data

Data collection is the third step in the problem-solving process. Groups sometimes arrive at hasty, ill-conceived solutions because they rush to implement initial ideas without carefully exploring the situation, the obstacles to problem resolution, and the ramifications of a proposed solution. Data collection is concerned with the generation of ideas. This process should be kept separate from analyzing facts and making decisions because analysis and evaluation tend to inhibit idea generation.

The group should have as much information as possible about the problem as it analyzes data and prepares alternative solutions. Knowing the history of the problem helps the group develop a longitudinal perspective on the problem's development and course. Comparing the state of affairs before and after a problem has occurred can often point to potential causes and possible solutions. While gathering data about the history of the problem, the group should become familiar with previous attempts to solve it. This information can help the group avoid repeating past failures.

Conditions that can help to create a group climate that encourages members to share information and views about a problem include the following:

Principles for Sharing Information

- Maintain the group's openness to speculation
- Encourage an open search for all pertinent data
- Encourage all group members to present their ideas
- Demonstrate genuine appreciation for differences
- Refrain from evaluation
- Express communications non-judgmentally, genuinely, without the intent of controlling others, and as an equal rather than a superior contribution

Facilitating this type of communication in a group increases problem exploration and contributes to high-quality solutions. However, members occasionally can become stuck in the ways they explore and review a problem. To develop new approaches, members should be encouraged to (1) view problems flexibly, (2) expand the way information is collected and combined, (3) recognize and fill gaps in available information, (4) generate new ideas by viewing situations from alternative perspectives, and (5) use both lateral and vertical thinking processes.

Vertical thinking processes are often associated with rational problem-solving strategies. *Vertical thinking* relies on inductive and deductive reasoning. Evidence and reason are used in a logical fashion until a solution is reached. Solutions are grounded in facts that are built one on another in an orderly, systematic, and linear fashion.

Lateral thinking processes are particularly useful when vertical thinking processes have not yielded a creative solution. Lateral thinking helps free ideas that have been blocked by stale, routine ways of conceptualizing a problem and its potential solutions. Instead of relying on an orderly, linear combination of facts, *lateral thinking* is characterized by the use of analogies, metaphors, similarities, contrasts, and paradoxes. Seemingly disparate facts, thoughts, and ideas are put together in new and creative ways. Analogies, for example, help bring out similarities between objects or situations that were previously considered to be different. For example, solutions found to be helpful in analogous situations might be tried by group members in their current problem-solving situation. For further information about the lateral thinking process, see De Bono (1968, 1971, 1972).

Developing Plans

Data collection encourages divergent thinking processes, but preparing plans for problem resolution encourages convergent thinking processes (Scheidel & Crowell, 1979). The worker calls on members to organize, analyze, and synthesize facts, ideas, and perspectives generated during problem exploration. Displaying the data for all members to see can be helpful. It is difficult for members to keep a large amount of information in mind as they attempt to develop alternative solutions. Displaying information on newsprint or a blackboard helps to ensure that all members are aware of the full range of information shared during a discussion. Ordering and clarifying the information generated by the group can also be helpful. Useful techniques for doing this are presented in the following list.

Handling Information Generated by the Group

- Separate relevant from irrelevant facts
- Combine similar facts
- Identify discrepancies
- Look for patterns across different facts
- Rank facts from most important to least important

During the process of organizing data, members should be encouraged to discuss the logic behind their reasoning. Members should be encouraged to give each other a chance to explain why they see things the way they do, rather than to defend their own choices. Defending choices often entrenches group members' opinions, whereas a discussion of how members think information should be used often brings out commonalities and similarities in their views of the situation.

Before making a decision, members should be encouraged to develop as many alternative solutions as possible. Because critical and evaluative comments tend to inhibit the production of creative ideas, workers should caution members not to criticize each other's solutions as they are presented.

Selecting the Best Plan

After all members have presented their alternatives, the group should review each one. The review serves several purposes. It helps ensure that all members understand each alternative. Misunderstandings at this point can cause conflict and reduce the chances for achieving closure in the problem-solving process. When reviewing each alternative, members can be encouraged to discuss how they would overcome obstacles and challenges likely to be encountered if the alternative were implemented. Members should be encouraged to consider the overall likelihood that a plan will resolve the problem in a manner that is valued by all group members. For this purpose, it is helpful for members to develop criteria that can be used to judge each plan. Rational methods based on multiattribute utility analysis (see Chapter 12) have been developed to help members develop decision criteria. Although much has been written about these methods (Baron, 1994; Clemen, 1996; Watson & Buede, 1987), they have not been widely applied in the human services. (For exceptions, see Dalgleish, 1988; Milter & Rohrbaugh, 1988; and Toseland, Rivas, & Chapman, 1984.) Sometimes groups rely on decision criteria developed by experts as illustrated in the following example.

● **CASE EXAMPLE**   *Decision Criteria for Solving a Problem*

A task group formed by the U.S. Department of Health and Human Service was charged with distributing funds for health maintenance organizations in medically underserved areas. By using panels of experts, the committee developed four criteria for deciding among programs that applied for funds in medically underserved areas. These criteria included (1) the number of physicians per 1,000 people, (2) the percentage of families in the area with less that $12,000 annual family income, (3) the infant mortality rate in the area, and (4) the percentage of the area's population over age 65. The panel then went on to select 50 programs from the ones submitted best fit the criteria.

In most situations, groups rely on the expertise of their own members to develop decision criteria. This is frequently done by having members rate the advantages and the disadvantages of each alternative. Alternatives may be combined or modified to maximize advantages and minimize disadvantages. As members decide among alternatives, they should keep in mind the group's mandate, its goals, and the ideal situation they would like to see result if the problem were resolved successfully. Members may also want to consider other factors, such as the benefits and costs of implementing alternative solutions, the comfort and ease with which particular solutions are likely to be implemented, and the political ramifications of alternative solutions. The most effective solution to a problem may not be the most desirable solution if it is too costly or if it is likely to offend, inconvenience, or otherwise upset persons who will be asked to implement it.

Implementing the Plan

Excellent decisions can be worthless if they are not implemented properly. Effective problem solving requires that a task group actively oversee the implementation of its plan.

Input from persons who will be influential in implementing the plan should be solicited as early as possible in the problem-solving process. Once a solution is decided on, members should begin to gain support for it from constituencies outside the group. Members should seek the support of persons who will be accountable for the decision and with authority to implement it. For example, the committee that decided to improve outreach efforts to Mexican Americans by training staff and publicizing agency programs in the community sought the cooperation of the board of directors, the agency's executive director, the directors of programs responsible for implementing staff training and publicity campaigns, all the direct service staff who were going to be involved in the program, and the leaders of the Mexican American community.

When seeking the support of others, members may have to educate people about the value of a new approach to a problem. Motivating people to cooperate with the implementation of a decision is not an easy task. Persuasion, lobbying, and other tactics may be necessary to gain support for the proposed solution (Rothman, Erlich, & Tropman, 1995).

Once the receptivity of persons responsible for implementing the decision is ensured, the group can begin to organize and supervise the plan's implementation. With a large plan, a division of labor is often helpful—each member may be assigned specific responsibilities. There may also be a need for training to educate persons who will implement the plan.

It is often helpful to delineate steps in the implementation sequence and to develop a time line. Objectives can be specified for each step, and the group can obtain periodic feedback about implementation progress. Feedback channels should be established to keep the group apprised of the solution's utility in terms of its expected outcome. Feedback can be used to overcome obstacles, stabilize change, and meet the challenges of a continually changing environment.

Implementing the proposed solution also includes identifying, contacting, and utilizing available resources. A heterogeneous group can be advantageous in this process because of the resources a diverse membership brings to the group. It is also important to prepare members for opposition. Obstacles may include inertia, passive resistance, or active attempts to block implementation of a proposed solution. Chapter 9 contains information on how to overcome inertia and resistance.

SUMMARY

This chapter focuses on the foundation skills, procedures, and methods needed to work effectively with task groups. Task groups have an important place in all human service organizations. Each day, meetings take place that have an important effect on what services are provided and how they are delivered. Social workers and other helping professionals are frequently called on to chair or staff committees, teams, and other task groups. When meetings are well run, members become a satisfied and cohesive team committed to achieving its objectives. Poorly run meetings, however, often lead to boredom and frustration.

During the work stage of task groups, the worker often is called on to engage in the following activities: (1) preparing for group meetings, (2) helping members share information, (3) helping all members get involved in the work of the group, (4) helping members develop ideas and information, (5) dealing with conflict, (6) helping members make effective decisions, (7) understanding the political ramifications of task groups, (8) monitoring and evaluating, and (9) problem solving.

Problem solving is probably the single most important function of task groups. The chapter concludes with a six-step, problem-solving model: (1) identifying a problem, (2) developing goals, (3) collecting data, (4) developing plans, (5) selecting the best plan, and (6) implementing the plan. In practice, these steps overlap and they are interconnected by feedback channels. Task groups repeat variations of problem-solving processes during the life of the group as they perform their functions and work on the tasks that confront them.

● CASE EXAMPLE

Lola's supervisor reviewed her accomplishments as a group leader in preparation for her annual review. Two years ago Lola was assigned to chair the organization's long-range planning committee. Lola felt she had been an active group leader. Lola lived in a rural part of West Virginia called Blair County. She worked for Join Together, an outreach and community development organization. The organization's long-range planning committee was composed of representatives from all levels of the organization, including administration, client services, program development, and finance. Over the course of her tenure as leader, the group had achieved a high level of functioning. Lola's supervisor identified several activities and skills that helped the group to function effectively and achieve its purpose.

Lola spent a good deal of time preparing for group meetings. In addition to reviewing and monitoring the work of the subcommittees, she researched issues for future meetings, prepared an agenda, and made numerous personal contacts with group members. Lola hoped that her level of activity between meetings served as a model for all members. After evaluating the amount of work done by members outside of meetings, Lola's supervisor concluded that her modeling behavior had helped to establish a group norm of hard work.

One of the most impressive aspects of the group meetings was the sharing of information that occurred among members. Lola encouraged all members to keep the group updated on existing programs and ideas for new services. Between meetings Lola shared important information with all members of the committee. At the beginning of each meeting, members shared updates and suggestions with each other. Lola's supervisor noted to herself that through this process, the group had achieved a high level of communication and interaction. Members were familiar and comfortable with the roles they played in the group. Her assessment was that these factors fostered group cohesiveness and raised the productivity of group members.

Lola also helped the group develop a clear structure for the monthly meetings. She helped establish clear procedures for developing information, solving problems, and making decisions. She encouraged members to participate actively during meetings by modeling good member skills such as listening, asking good questions, and giving support. She also helped members feel that their feedback and recommendations were taken seriously by the organization. Lola worked carefully with the administrators to ensure that group deliberations would be influential on the future directions of organizational policy and programs. Group members felt empowered by this knowledge.

Lola's organizational skills helped the group adopt a clear structure for solving problems and making decisions. She helped the group decide on a standard format for problem solving. For example, when faced with having to decide how to find funding for a new volunteer outreach program in the local school, the group followed the steps of identifying the problem, setting goals, collecting data, developing plans, and selecting and implementing the plan. The group learned and relied on this format in many of its problem-solving discussions. During decision-making activities, Lola suggested clear guidelines about how to proceed. These were discussed, modified, and adopted by the group. She encouraged the group to develop decision criteria and procedures before making important decisions. Although this took some time, Lola's organizational skills helped the group decision-making process become easier and more systematic. Lola was also good at helping the group build consensus by finding common interests and points of agreement. Consensus building helped members be more committed to the group decision.

Lola spent time monitoring and evaluating the group. She devoted a regular portion of each meeting agenda to discussions of members' efforts and their effectiveness. She also developed a survey form to obtain members' feedback about her leadership skills and for gathering suggestions about how the group could be improved. Lola shared the results of the survey with members and incorporated members' suggestions into the work of the group.

The long-range planning committee had some history of disagreements and conflicts. Several of the members had strong personalities. Others felt that their departments should have more control over the projects chosen for future funding and implementation. Lola's greatest difficulty was her ability to deal with the conflicts that arose in the group. Her supervisor noted that she seemed uncomfortable with conflict in the group. She suggested that Lola listen carefully to both sides of discussions and remain neutral in the face of pressure to agree with one side or the other. Lola helped the group recognize that some disagreements about issues were healthy

for group discussions. Lola's supervisor suggested that she help the group differentiate these substantive conflicts from affective conflicts, in which members personalized conflicts with other members. At different times, Lola helped the group resolve both types of conflicts. Still, she worked hard to more fully develop her skills of listening, mediating, negotiating, and compromising.

As Lola's supervisor reflected on the group's accomplishments, she noted that Lola had guided the group by providing it with many of the elements it needed to function effectively. Lola felt a sense of pride in knowing that she had used her talents and skills to guide the development of an effective task group. Through her efforts, the group identified several service needs and helped to implement programs for persons living in rural West Virginia.

chapter 12

Task Groups: Specialized Methods

This chapter describes specialized methods for helping organizational and community groups accomplish their goals during the middle stage. The first section is divided into two parts describing methods for helping small and large organizational groups accomplish their objectives. The second section describes specialized methods for helping community groups accomplish their objectives. A brief introduction of each method is followed by a description of the procedures necessary to implement the method, its recommended uses, and evidence about its effectiveness.

SMALL ORGANIZATIONAL GROUPS

Brainstorming

Brainstorming is probably the best known of the specialized methods presented in this chapter. The primary purpose of brainstorming is to increase the number of ideas generated by members. Elements of brainstorming, such as suspending judgment of ideas, have long been recognized as effective techniques, but Osborn (1963) was the first to develop a systematic set of rules for generating creative ideas, which he called *brainstorming*.

During brainstorming, total effort is directed toward creative thinking rather than to analytical or evaluative thinking. Analytical and evaluative thinking can reduce ability to generate creative ideas. Members are concerned about their status in a group, and if they expect critical judgments about their thoughts and ideas, they are not likely to express them. Analytical and evaluative thinking can also serve as a social control mechanism. Members who continue to present ideas that are viewed critically are likely to be sanctioned. Members may also screen out potentially creative, but controversial, ideas before they are ever expressed. By attempting to reduce analytical and evaluative thinking, brainstorming encourages free disclosure of ideas.

Some rules for managing the group's interaction during brainstorming follow.

Procedures for Brainstorming

- *Freewheeling* is welcomed. Members are encouraged to express all their ideas, no matter what they are. Members should not hold back on ideas that might be considered wild, repetitious, or obvious.

- Criticism is ruled out. Members are asked to withhold analyses, judgments, and evaluations about any ideas presented during the idea-generating process. Members should not try to defend or explain their ideas.

- Quantity is wanted. According to Osborn (1963) and Clark (1958), the more ideas suggested in the allotted time, the better the quality of ideas. Quality occurs by itself if enough ideas are generated.

- Combining, rearranging, and improving ideas are encouraged. Often called *hitchhiking,* this technique calls on group members to build on ideas that have already been expressed. Members can combine or modify ideas and suggest how other members' ideas can be improved.

Procedures

Brainstorming can be conducted in any size of group, although large groups may inhibit idea generation and reduce a member's ability to participate in the allotted time. Because brainstorming encourages the generation of creative and unique ideas, a heterogeneous membership representing many points of view facilitates the process. The procedure can be conducted in a short period of time (15 minutes), but longer meetings may produce more quality ideas because ideas presented in the last third of a group's meeting are often of a higher quality than ideas produced during the first two thirds of the meeting (Stattler & Miller, 1968).

At the beginning of the meeting, the worker explains the problem to be brainstormed and the four basic rules of brainstorming. A warm-up period of 10 to 15 minutes can be used to familiarize members with the procedure and to help them learn to express and hear ideas without criticizing them. During this time, the worker can model appropriate behavior and make some suggestions about procedures such as lateral thinking that may increase creativity. Even when some members of the group have used brainstorming procedures previously, the warm-up time gives all members an opportunity to prepare to change routine patterns of analyzing and evaluating ideas. It also allows them to become acclimated to freewheeling idea generation.

During the brainstorming procedure, the leader or coleader writes the members' ideas on a flip chart or a blackboard. Having a coleader record ideas is particularly helpful during warm-up sessions because it is difficult for the leader to train members, record ideas, and model appropriate behavior at the same time. Ideas should be recorded by using the words of the speaker as much as possible. Key words should be abstracted so suggestions fit on a sheet of newsprint or a blackboard.

The interaction pattern in the group should encourage the free flow of ideas. Members should be asked to offer one idea at a time and to allow everyone to have a turn presenting ideas. Occasionally, it is necessary to limit talkative members by encouraging members who have not contributed extensively to express their ideas. In large groups (more than 15 members), it has been recommended that members raise their hands before they begin to speak (Scheidel & Crowell, 1979). This procedure also makes it easier to record ideas because they can be clarified more quickly when the recorder's attention is focused on the speaker.

Sometimes groups run out of ideas or repeat similar ideas without pursuing new or alternative thinking patterns. At this point, instead of closing a session, the worker should read ideas from the list to stimulate thinking, focus the group's attention on unexplored areas of the problem, or pick out one or two ideas around which the group may want to generate additional ideas. Throughout the process, the worker should (1) express interest in the ideas as they are presented, (2) urge members to continue to produce creative ideas, and (3) help the group elaborate on ideas that have already been presented.

The worker should not try to have the group evaluate ideas immediately after the brainstorming procedure. Waiting a day or longer allows members to think of new ideas to add to the list and allows time for them to return to an analytical way of evaluating ideas. Once the meeting has ended, the worker should ensure that members are not blamed or sanctioned for the ideas they have expressed. If they are, brainstorming will not succeed in future meetings.

Uses

Brainstorming procedures are useful under certain conditions. Brainstorming should be done in groups that have already defined a problem. In many respects, brainstorming can be used as a substitute for the methods described in the Developing Plans section of the problem-solving model described in Chapter 11. Brainstorming procedures are particularly appropriate if the problem the group is working on is specific and limited in range (Scheidel & Crowell, 1979). It has been shown that the quality of solutions improves in groups that have been instructed to focus on specifically defined problems rather than on broadly defined problems (Davis, Manske, & Train, 1966). Parnes (1967) suggests using *limited critical thinking* rather than *free associating* as recommended by Osborn (1963). This process ensures that group members focus their ideas by making them relevant to a specific situation being examined by the group.

Brainstorming can be used in groups to accomplish organizational goals as shown in the following case.

● CASE EXAMPLE *Brainstorming in an Organizational Setting*

When a board of directors of a social service organization began a search for a new executive director, the board president decided to involve line staff in the hiring process. The president convened a diverse group of staff members to brainstorm ideas about what qualities a new executive director should demonstrate. Members of the brainstorming group were encouraged to think of as many positive qualities as they could, and each was asked to contribute creative ideas. The board president, acting as a group leader, prepared a list of ideal qualities or attributes the staff contributed and presented the list to the board of directors for consideration during the search for the new executive director.

Brainstorming methods are useful when the group wants to generate as many ideas as possible. Brainstorming, therefore, should not be used when the group faces a technical problem that requires systematic, organized thinking. Implicit in the brainstorming approach is the notion that the problem can have many solutions (Scheidel & Crowell, 1979). In many situations, groups confront problems that can be solved several ways, but sometimes problems have only one right answer. In these situations, brainstorming is not appropriate. Other rational, structured problem-solving methods such as social judgment analysis or the nominal group technique are more likely to help a group produce the best solution (Toseland & Rivas, 1984). There is also some recent research that suggests that extended brainstorming sessions may not be necessary because producing fewer options may actually result in better and more consistent decisions than producing many options (Johnson & Raab, 2003).

Effectiveness

Most evidence for the effectiveness of brainstorming is based on anecdotal accounts of its use in business meetings (Clark, 1958; Osborn, 1963), but the method has been investigated through empirical research (Bayless, 1967; Maltzman, Simon, Raskin, & Licht, 1960; Taylor, Berry, & Block, 1958). Although the Taylor study is often cited to disclaim the effectiveness of brainstorming, the study did not compare brainstorming and nonbrainstorming conditions. Taylor, Berry, and Block (1958) found that brainstorming produced better results when it was done by individuals working alone than by individuals in a group. Findings from the study suggest that nominal group brainstorming is better than interacting group brainstorming but do not suggest whether group brainstorming is better than a group meeting without brainstorming.

Other studies show that when brainstorming is used in a group context, the results are positive (Bayless, 1967; Maltzman et al., 1960). Groups that use brainstorming produce more ideas of a higher quality than groups that do not use this approach (D'Zurilla & Gold-fried, 1971). Nominal brainstorming, in which members generate as many ideas as possible without interacting, may be even more effective than brainstorming in interactive groups. In a more recent study, it was found that members of brainstorming groups were more satisfied, felt their groups used a more effective process, and felt they communicated more effectively than members of groups who were not trained in the procedure (Kramer, Kuo, & Dailey, 1997). These important outcomes have been neglected in previous research on brainstorming. Thus, brainstorming may have some positive unintended consequences that are unrelated to the goal of generating more and higher-quality ideas.

Brainstorming generates ideas from a wide base because it encourages all group members to participate fully. The method also tends to establish members' commitment to the idea that is ultimately decided on because members have helped shape the idea that is selected. Napier and Gershenfeld (1993) have listed other benefits of brainstorming in groups as illustrated below.

Benefits of Brainstorming

- Dependence on a single authority figure is reduced.
- Open sharing of ideas is encouraged.
- Members of highly competitive groups can feel safe.
- A maximum output of ideas occurs in a short period of time.
- Members' ideas are posted immediately for everyone to see.
- Ideas are generated internally rather than imposed from outside the group, which increases the feeling of accountability.
- Brainstorming is enjoyable and self-stimulating.

Despite its benefits, brainstorming is not without drawbacks. It is not easy to achieve an atmosphere in which ideas are generated freely. Brainstorming can initially cause discomfort to members who are not used to freely sharing their ideas (Collaros & Anderson, 1969; Hammond & Goldman, 1961; Vroom, Grant, & Cotton, 1969). The brainstorming procedure breaks norms that ordinarily protect members from making suggestions that may result in overt or covert sanctions (Bouchard, 1972b).

Other factors also may reduce the efficacy of brainstorming procedures. For example, although the warm-up period is essential for optimal performance during brainstorming, warm-ups require time, which may not be available. Inertia may also interfere with brainstorming because the technique requires a change from ordinary group procedures. The worker may not feel justified in imposing the procedure on reluctant or skeptical members who are unaware of its benefits. Although brainstorming has many potentially beneficial effects, if it is to be used effectively, members must be made aware of its usefulness and workers must apply it correctly.

Variations on Brainstorming

Reverse Brainstorming

First proposed by Richards (1974), reverse brainstorming is a procedure that can be used to list the negative consequences of actions quickly and thoroughly. Group members are asked, "What might go wrong with this idea?" Reverse brainstorming is useful after a variety of ideas have been generated. Members should first use a scanning procedure, such as the one suggested by Etzioni (1968), to reduce a long list of ideas to several alternatives. Members then brainstorm about the consequences of carrying out each alternative. When the group is aware of potential obstacles to solving the problem, the worker then can ask members to suggest ideas for overcoming the obstacles.

Trigger Groups

The trigger group procedure uses the findings of Taylor, Berry, and Block (1958) and Dunnette, Campbell, and Joastad (1963), who discovered that brainstorming is more effective when it is done by individuals working alone than by individuals interacting in groups. In a trigger group, each individual works alone for 5 to 10 minutes to develop a list of ideas and suggestions (Richards, 1974). Members then read their lists to the group. The group takes about 10 minutes to clarify, add to, or combine ideas that each member has presented. As in brainstorming, suggestions are made without criticism. After all members have presented their ideas, the group decides together on criteria for evaluating the ideas. Ideas are then screened by the group, one at a time, to arrive at a single solution to a problem.

This approach allows members to work independently to develop ideas without verbal or nonverbal evaluative comments from other group members. Also, as each member reads, it focuses the attention of the entire group on the ideas of one individual, which gives members a feeling that their ideas are heard, understood, and carefully examined. It gives each member an opportunity to receive constructive comments from all group members. Trigger groups are best when conducted with five to eight members because the time necessary to develop ideas, to brainstorm, and to critically evaluate each individual's ideas can be prohibitive in larger groups.

Synectics

Synectics is a method for generating creative ideas during problem solving. *Synectics* is a Greek word that means the joining of different and seemingly irrelevant elements. Gordon (1961) developed synectics after years of exploring methods to increase creativity. Prince (1970) added to Gordon's ideas and expanded the method for use in group problem solving.

A synectics meeting lasts about three hours and includes five to eight members with diverse interests and experiences. Much of the meeting follows an ordinary problem-solving sequence. A problem is introduced by the worker, and members are encouraged to present their ideas about it. To avoid coercion and intimidation, the worker should not be someone with influence or power over other group members. The worker also should have a neutral view of the problem. A major goal of synectics is to develop a climate of trust in which all ideas are valued. During the preliminary discussion, the problem is clarified and specified. The worker's job is to help members reframe the problem by separating it from its usual context, help members present unique ideas without criticism, and help the group refrain from making premature decisions.

As the problem-solving process continues, the worker may notice that members are making predictable, noncreative responses to a problem. At a timely point during this discussion, the worker can suggest that the group go on an excursion (Napier & Gershenfeld, 1993). An *excursion* is a method of using analogies to stimulate new ideas. For members who have not participated in synectics meetings before, the worker should begin with a direct analogy that is easy to develop. See the following list for examples of different types of analogies.

Using Analogies in Brainstorming

- Direct analogy—"What is there about this problem that's like what is often found in nature?"
- Personal analogy—"How would you feel if you were this problem?"
- Symbolic analogy—"What object or thing do you associate with this problem?"
- Fantasy analogy—"Imagine that you could control time; how would you use time to help resolve this problem?"

Such questions can help members develop creative ideas about a problem (Gordon, 1961).

Synectics is an interesting alternative to rational problem-solving approaches, such as social judgment analysis. Although there have been several anecdotal accounts of the effectiveness of synectics (Prince, 1970), only one study confirms assertions that groups using this method develop more creative ideas than they would if they used ordinary problem solving or brainstorming (Bouchard, 1972a). In recent years, however, there has been additional research on various idea generating techniques, including those that are similar to ones first suggested by synectics (Smith, 1998).

Focus Groups

Focus groups are designed to collect in-depth, qualitative information about a particular service or topic of interest to the managers of an organization. The emphasis is on facilitating members' discussion of a subject until viewpoints are fully understood and points of agreement and disagreement become clear. The strength of focus groups is their ability to explore topics and generate hypotheses through the explicit use of group interaction (Morgan, 1997). They are also used to clarify and enrich data collected during surveys or other research methods. Focus groups are often associated with marketing research in which they are used to solicit opinions and reactions to new or existing products. However, within the social sciences, they were used as early as World War II to examine the effectiveness of wartime propaganda (Merton & Kendall, 1946). Since that time, focus groups have been used by health and social service organizations as a qualitative research method to collect information about a variety of topics, but especially to assess clients' satisfaction and opinions about particular services.

Procedures

Focus group meetings consist of a semistructured group interview and discussion with 6 to 12 group members. Meetings typically last one to two hours. The worker's task is to gently direct the group to discuss items of interest to the sponsor of the group, probe superficial answers, and encourage the group to move on when a particular topic appears to be exhausted.

Aaker, Kunar, and Day (2001) have presented four key elements to the success of a focus group: (1) planning a specific agenda, (2) recruiting and screening appropriate participants, (3) effective moderation during meetings, and (4) clear and detailed analysis and interpretation of the results. Planning the agenda begins by carefully considering the purpose for the group and the topics to be covered. Because focus groups are meant to encourage in-depth discussion, it is important to maintain the focus by not exploring too many topics. Next, the worker should develop a series of relevant questions for which responses are sought. From these questions, a discussion guide is prepared. The guide is an outline that helps ensure that specific issues are covered. The discussion guide should proceed in a logical order from general to specific areas of inquiry. Although all topics should be covered, the guide is not meant to be a rigid template for the conduct of group meetings. If a question does not generate useful, nonrepetitive information, the facilitator should move on to the next question or probe. Similarly, new or interesting ideas that emerge from the interaction between members should be pursued.

Careful screening of participants is crucial to the success of a focus group. Focus group participants should be interested in and have opinions about the topic to be discussed. They should have enough characteristics in common so that they will feel comfortable interacting. To get a broad, in-depth understanding of a subject, it is important to select individuals with a wide range of experience and diverse opinions. Because individuals who have participated in previous focus groups may dominate the discussion, they are generally excluded from participation. Also, it is preferable to recruit individuals who do not know one another. Relatives, friends, and neighbors tend to talk to each other rather than to the whole group, and, because of the presence of individuals they know, they are sometimes less open about their true opinions.

Because positive, freewheeling group interaction can help reticent participants express in-depth opinions and discuss all aspects of a particular topic, effective leadership is essential in focus groups. Leaders should be familiar with the topic to be discussed and sensitive to the verbal and nonverbal cues given off by participants. Aaker, Kunar, and Day (2001) suggest that focus group leaders should have the ability to (1) establish rapport quickly, (2) listen carefully to each member's opinions, (3) demonstrate a genuine interest in each member's views, (4) avoid jargon and sophisticated terminology that may turn off members, (5) flexibly implement the discussion guide, (6) sense when a topic is exhausted or when it is becoming threatening, (7) know what topic to introduce to maintain a smooth flow of the discussion, and (8) facilitate group dynamics that encourage the full participation of all members and avoid domination by talkative members.

Focus groups often yield a wealth of disparate comments and opinions. To prepare reports and to do qualitative analyses of the data derived from a focus group meeting, it is useful to have an audiotape or videotape of group meetings. Reports of focus group meetings should capture the diverse opinions that are expressed as well as any consensus that is achieved. It is also useful to categorize members' comments in a manner that relates the comments to the specific hypotheses or questions that the focus group was intended to address.

Uses

Focus groups can be used for many purposes (Kinnear & Taylor, 1996). Major purposes are listed here.

Uses of Focus Groups

- Generating hypotheses about the way individuals think or behave that may be tested quantitatively at a later point
- Obtaining in-depth information about a topic
- Generating or evaluating impressions and opinions about the services an organization offers or plans to offer
- Overcoming reticence to obtaining personal views and opinions
- Generating information to help develop client-satisfaction questionnaires and other types of questionnaires
- Providing in-depth analysis and interpretation of previously collected data and the findings of previously reported studies

Focus groups are particularly well suited for gathering in-depth data about the attitudes and cognition of participants (Edmunds, 1999; Morgan, 1997). This is illustrated in the following case.

● CASE EXAMPLE *Using a Focus Group in the Community*

The director of a community mental health clinic was concerned about her agency's ability to reach out and effectively serve Native Americans. During a weekly executive committee meeting, it was decided to recruit a focus group of Native American community leaders to explore community perceptions of the mental health center and its services. Following a carefully planned agenda and using a structured interview guide, the group leader helped the focus group members to identify and elaborate on their perceptions of the agency and its strengths and weaknesses in serving Native Americans. The group leader prepared a written report summarizing the focus group findings for the executive committee. The information that was gained from the focus group meeting spurred the executive committee to plan a larger needs assessment project. The goal of this project was to develop recommendations to the executive committee and to the board of directors of the agency for improvements in service delivery to Native Americans in the agency's catchment area.

Although the information derived from focus groups is excellent for developing hypotheses and for exploring issues in-depth, caution should be exercised when using the information as the sole basis for making important decisions affecting large groups of individuals. Because a limited number of participants can be included in focus groups, the data derived may not be as representative of a larger population as data derived from a well-designed survey.

Effectiveness

Many data about the effectiveness of focus groups are based on case examples and anecdotal data (Dillon, Madden, & Firtle, 1994). According to Kinnear and Taylor (1996), compared with other procedures for soliciting attitudes and cognition, focus groups have the following advantages: (1) synergism, resulting from interacting group members who produce a wider range of information, insight, and ideas than do individuals who are interviewed alone; (2) snowballing, resulting from group members' stimulating each other to share their ideas and opinions and express their feelings; (3) security, resulting from having others express similar opinions and feelings; and (4) speed, resulting from interviewing several individuals together.

Swenson, Griswold, and Kleiber (1992) indicate that focus groups can have a positive effect on participants. For example, 67 percent of the participants of the focus groups in their study reported continuing to think about the topics raised in the meetings, 67 percent reported that the discussion during the groups affected their thinking, and about 27 percent reported discussing and following up on the issues raised in the focus groups after the meetings had ended. In contrast, Fern (1982) found that individual interviews produced more ideas than did focus groups. Byers and Wilcox (1991) and Lederman (1989) found that focus groups were not suitable to many types of data collection but did generate rich qualitative data and hypotheses for future exploration.

Most experts agree that the effectiveness of focus groups depends heavily on the moderator's ability to facilitate the discussion. As with any group, the effectiveness of a focus group can be limited by group think, domination by a talkative member, and a host of other problems with group dynamics described in earlier chapters. Goebert and Rosenthal (2002) state that there are other limitations of focus groups such as respondents being prone to exaggeration, over-analysis and a tendency toward conservative, familiar ideas. The interpretation of data from focus groups can also present problems because the small sample of individuals makes it unclear whether the opinions expressed are representative. Also, it can be difficult to interpret sharp discrepancies in group members' views of a particular situation.

Despite these limitations, with adequate preparation and a skillful moderator, focus groups can provide an effective and efficient method for collecting in-depth, qualitative data about the thoughts and opinions of consumers of health and social services. For more information about conducting focus groups, see Krueger (1998b; Krueger & Casey, 2000) or Goebert and Rosenthal (2002), and for more information about using focus groups as a qualitative research method, see Morgan (1997) or Edmunds (1999).

Nominal Group Technique

The nominal group technique (NGT) is different from traditional interacting approaches to solving problems in task groups. The technique was developed in the late 1960s by Andre Delbecq and Andrew Van de Ven as they studied program planning groups in social service agencies and the operation of committees and other idea-aggregating and decision-making groups in business and industry (Delbecq, Van de Ven, & Gustafson, 1986). Since its development, the technique has been used extensively in health, social service, industrial, educational, and governmental agencies as an aid to planning and managing programs (Anderson, 2000; Gill, 1991).

Procedures

An NGT meeting should have six to nine group members. Larger groups should be separated into two or more smaller groups. Because participants are required to write and because ideas are presented on a flip chart, group members should be seated around a U-shaped table. A flip chart with newsprint should be placed at the open end of the U. Supplies that are needed include a flip chart, a felt-tip pen, a roll of tape, index cards, worksheets, and pencils. A summary of NGT procedures follows.

Procedures for Using NGT

- Develop a clear statement of the problem
- Round robin recording of ideas generated by group members
- Hitchhiking: generating new ideas from ideas already listed
- Serial discussion to clarify ideas
- Preliminary ordering of ideas by importance
- Choosing highest priority ideas and ranking in order of priority
- Discussion of ranked ideas

Before an NGT meeting, the worker should develop a clear statement of the problem. According to Delbecq, Van de Ven, and Gustafson (1986), the agency is responsible for deciding on the group's purpose and the problem to be addressed before the meeting. At the beginning of the group, the worker states the purpose of the meeting. Then the worker hands out lined paper with the problem statement written at the top, reads the problem statement, and asks all members to take five minutes to list their ideas or responses to the problem. Ideas and responses should be written in brief phrases, without verbal or nonverbal communication with other group members. To give the members some notion of what types of responses are being asked for, workers may want to prepare some sample ideas or responses as models. While group members are working, the leader also writes ideas in silence and ensures that members of the group do not interact with one another.

The next step is a round robin recording of ideas generated by each group member. The ideas are listed on a flip chart that is visible to all group members. The worker asks one member for an idea, writes it on the flip chart, and then goes around the group by asking each person in turn for one idea. Members are encouraged to *hitchhike,* that is, use ideas already on the chart to stimulate their thinking and add on their worksheets ideas that they did not think of during the silent period. When a member has no new ideas, the member passes and allows the next group member to present an idea until everyone is finished.

The ideas should be recorded as rapidly as possible in members' own words. During the round robin, members should not critique, elaborate on, or defend ideas. Completed sheets from a flip chart should be taped to a flat surface in view of all group members.

The third step is a serial discussion to clarify the ideas that have been presented. Items from the flip chart are taken in order and discussed for two or three minutes. Each member who expressed an idea is encouraged to explain briefly the evidence and the logic used in arriving at it. At this point, members are free to express their agreement or disagreement with the idea and to discuss its relative importance. Although evaluative comments are welcome, the group should not be allowed to focus on any one idea for a long period of time or to get into a debate over the merits of a particular idea.

The fourth step is a preliminary ordering of the importance of the ideas that have been listed. Each member is asked to work independently in selecting from the list a predetermined number of the ideas with the highest priority. The number of items selected varies, depending on the length of the list, but should include about one quarter to one half the original ideas. Members write their choices on index cards and hand them to the worker. The number of votes that each idea receives from all members is recorded next to the item. This process helps individual members obtain feedback about ideas that are highly regarded by their fellow members.

Each member is then asked to choose five highest-priority ideas from the narrowed-down list. The members rank the ideas on a scale of 5 = highest priority to 1 = lowest priority. The idea and its rank order are then placed on an index card. One index card is used for each idea. The cards are collected and the rank orders are tallied by writing them next to their corresponding ideas on the flip chart. After all ranks have been tallied, the mean rank for each idea is determined by adding the numbers (ranks) next to each item and dividing by the number of group members.

Delbecq, Van de Ven, and Gustafson (1986) suggest that the group may want to discuss the ranks when (1) there are large discrepancies among members' rating patterns or (2) items that are obviously rated too high or low (in the leader's opinion) appear when the items are tallied. These writers claim the resulting discussion and second vote often increase the judgmental accuracy of the group. It is usually the worker or a powerful group member who calls aspects of preliminary votes into question, but this action may be viewed by less powerful group members as a way to manipulate the group process. Therefore, it is recommended that before beginning NGT, the group as a whole should decide under what circumstances a second vote will be taken.

Uses

The NGT technique was created to "increase rationality, creativity, and participation in problem-solving meetings associated with program planning" (Delbecq et al., 1986, p. 1). It is designed to prevent group processes that inhibit interaction (Van de Ven & Delbecq, 1971). These inhibiting influences are presented in the following list.

Factors Inhibiting Group Interaction

- The pursuit of a single thought pattern for a long time period
- Members' relying on other group members to do the work, i.e., social loafing

- Covert judgments which may or may not be expressed
- Status hierarchies and differentials preventing participation by low status members
- Group pressure for conformity, such as members' participating only to the extent that they feel equally competent to other members
- Dominant or talkative group members
- Reaching quick decisions without fully exploring the problem by information gathering and fact finding

By combining the positive aspects of noninteracting nominal groups and interacting problem-solving groups, Delbecq, Van de Ven, and Gustafson (1986) developed NGT. According to Van de Ven and Delbecq (1971), NGT has several benefits.

Benefits of NGT

- Stimulates activity through the presence of others and by everyone's working in silence
- Avoids evaluative comments when the problem dimensions are being formed
- Provides members an opportunity to search their own thought processes
- Avoids dominance by strong personalities
- Prevents premature decision making
- Encourages all members to participate
- Allows minority opinions to be expressed
- Tolerates conflicting and incompatible ideas that are written in silence before they are presented to the entire group
- Eliminates hidden agendas
- Gains members' cooperation in achieving a solution
- Structures the process so that members feel obligated to work on the problem

The NGT method can be used to create a long list of ideas or alternative solutions to a problem. Scheidel and Crowell (1979) suggest that it produces more ideas than any other idea-generating and problem-solving techniques they reviewed. It can also be used as a consensus-building technique because each group member is given an equal opportunity to express ideas and participate in reaching a decision. By structuring the interaction, NGT reduces the domination of a few members and makes full use of the creative capabilities and pooled wisdom of all group members. This, in turn, helps to ensure a broad base of support for any decision made by the group. A brief example of NGT is presented in the following case.

● **CASE EXAMPLE** *Nominal Group Technique*

A multiservice community agency was facing a physical crisis. The executive council charged with tightening and balancing the budget by the board of directors decided to use NGT to generate ideas for saving money. The executive director lead the council in this effort by first asking that each member work alone and write down creative ideas for saving money in the budget. In round robin fashion, each member was then asked to present one idea at a time to the group until all ideas were presented and recorded on a flip chart. Next, the executive director led the group in very brief discussions of the pros and cons of each suggested savings method. Then, she asked each member to independently rank each item in order of its value to the savings effort. These rankings were then used during a brief group discussion that focused on eliminating ideas that were not rated highly ranked by any member. Also during the discussion, whenever possible, similar money savings ideas were combined. Then, the members were asked to rank the five highest-priority suggestions. These ideas were studied more closely for their impact on the budget by the management of the agency. During the next board meeting, these and other recommendations were presented to the board for approval as part of the overall plan to balance the budget and restore the agency to fiscal health.

Effectiveness

The NGT procedure is based on social science findings about task groups that have been accumulated over decades of research. Each step is designed to make use of these findings. Delbecq, Van de Ven, and Gustafson (1986) reported that research findings indicate several procedures that increase judgmental accuracy in decision making.

Procedures to Increase Judgment Accuracy

- Having members make independent judgments
- Expressing judgments mathematically by ranking or rating items
- Using the arithmetic mean of independent judgments to form the group's decision
- Having members make decisions anonymously
- Using feedback about preliminary judgments for final voting

The NGT technique uses these research findings in its decision-making step by taking the mean rating of independent rank-order judgments that have been placed on anonymous index cards. Similarly, scientific evidence is the basis for each step in the NGT procedure. Reliance on scientific evidence in developing NGT has apparently worked. Overall, the empirical evidence supports contentions that NGT is more effective than interacting group methods for idea generation, problem solving, and consensus building (Toseland, Rivas, & Chapman, 1984; Van de Ven, 1974), and members are more satisfied with their participation in NGT groups than in untrained groups (Kramer, Kuo, & Dailey, 1997).

However, NGT does have drawbacks. The method is cumbersome. It takes a considerable amount of time (at least one and one half hours), which may not be available to a task group that must complete its work in a short time, especially for routine decisions that may not require the precision afforded by this method. Also, the worker should be familiar with the method and equipped with the necessary supplies to conduct an NGT meeting.

A seemingly inconsequential, though often important, drawback of NGT is that the group process is highly structured, which some members may find unpleasant. One study found that members of NGT groups were less satisfied than members of less structured groups using a problem-solving approach (Toseland et al., 1984). Initially members may be suspicious that they are being manipulated. Aspects of NGT tend to exacerbate rather than quell these fears. For example, having the worker rather than group members define the problem, and having the worker or a powerful group member influence voting procedures by calling for a second vote may feel constricting or even manipulative to members who are used to more freedom during problem solving and decision making. Despite these drawbacks, NGT groups have been found to be more satisfying to members than groups in which no structure is provided (Kramer et al., 1997), and the procedure can help task groups generate ideas and solve difficult problems more effectively than in groups where no training is provided.

In recent years, computers have been increasingly used to enhance brainstorming in groups. Rather than write ideas on paper as in NGT, group members are seated in a computer-supported meeting room with their own computer keyboards and screens. Participants enter their ideas with their keyboards (often anonymously) and can see what others are writing simultaneously on their screens. Evidence suggests that such computer support can significantly increase the creativity of a group in comparison to a traditional NGT process (Jessup & Valacich, 1993; Valacich, Dennis, & Connolly, 1994). With greater access to the Internet and the World Wide Web, groups are beginning to engage in brainstorming from their individual workplaces using electronic meeting support tools available on local area or wide area networks. For example, the group leader might ask a question through e-mail and ask participants to reply electronically with all their ideas (Schuman & Rohrbaugh, 1996).

Multiattribute Utility Analysis

Although NGT structures the method used in problem-solving groups to maximize beneficial group dynamics, multiattribute utility (MAU) analysis focuses on the content of the interactions in a group. An MAU method structures the group only to the extent that participants are given a method for using information about a problem. An MAU model uses decision rules to specify the relationships between attributes of a problem. The decision rules are used to increase the utility of decisions made by task groups.

Procedures

A group's use of an MAU model may begin by having each member work alone, either in individual meetings between each member and the worker or in a nominal group meeting in which all members work separately on instructions given by the worker. During this time, the problem and its alternative solutions are explained to members. For example, members are informed that their group has been appointed to decide among applicants for the position of assistant program director. The worker helps group members clarify their thinking about the problem. Specifically, the worker helps each member determine the attributes that are thought to be relevant to making a decision. For example, a member might decide that the attributes she considers important for the position of assistant program director include (1) amount of supervisory experience, (2) amount of clinical experience, (3) level of management skills, and (4) extent that the candidate likes to develop new and innovative service programs. Alternatively, the attributes might be developed through a brainstorming or NGT process.

The worker also helps each member specify the levels of each attribute by specifying minimal criteria for the solution, any constraints on the solution, and the functional form of each attribute. For example, members might decide that minimal criteria for the assistant program director's position include three years of supervisory experience and five years of clinical experience. The members also decide that the candidate must have an MSW or an MPA degree.

The utility function of an attribute specifies the attribute's functional relationship to the overall solution—that is, how levels of an attribute are related to the utility of choice of a particular solution. Figure 12.1 gives one member's utility functions for the four attributes mentioned previously. The utility functions indicate that as the amount of supervisory experience increases, satisfaction with the candidate (the utility of choosing a particular candidate) increases until the candidate has more than 10 years of experience, at which time the member's satisfaction with the candidate declines. At this point, the member thinks a candidate may have too much supervisory experience for the position.

For the clinical experience attribute, a similar utility function occurs, except that satisfaction with a candidate increases until the candidate has more than 15 years of clinical experience. For the management skills attribute, a straight linear relationship exists, which suggests that the higher the score on a management skills test and interview, the higher the satisfaction with the candidate. In the case of developing innovative programs, a curvilinear relationship is present; that is, candidates who are either low or high on this attribute are less preferred than candidates who have moderate inclination to develop new programs.

Figure 12.1 also shows the weight that a group member gave to each attribute. Weights can be assigned by dividing 100 points among all attributes in a manner that reflects the relative importance of each in proportion to the others. In Figure 12.1, the management skills attribute is assigned a weight of 40, making it four times as important as clinical experience, which has been assigned a weight of 10.

The procedure of establishing minimal criteria, constraints, and attributes with their weights and functional forms is the basis of a member's decision rule—that is, how a group member will use information about a problem to make a judgment. Members develop their own decision rules. When all members have completed this task, they share their decision rules with each other. It is helpful for the worker to post each member's decision rules side by side on a flip chart or blackboard so that all members can see how their decision rules compare.

The next step in an MAU process is to have members discuss the logic behind their decision rules. During this unstructured discussion, the only rule is to focus on the reasoning behind the choice of attributes, weights, and functional forms (Edwards, 1977; Huber, 1980). For example, members should not discuss individual candidates for the position, but would be encouraged to discuss why a member gave management skills four times the weight of clinical experience when considering candidates for this particular job.

Members discuss the decision rules until they agree on a common group rule that satisfies all members. Consensus is usually not difficult to reach because members find it easier to agree on how information will be used than on specific alternatives. Once a group decision rule has been decided, it is a routine procedure to see how each alternative is ranked on the basis of the decision rule. First, alternatives that do not meet the criteria or the constraints set up by the decision rule are eliminated. The next step is to calculate each alternative's score on the decision rule. Each score is multiplied by that attribute's weight, and the total score is summed across each attribute. A total score on each alternative is calculated. The alternative (in this case, a candidate) that is rated the highest based on the decision rule is the one selected by the group as its final decision.

FIGURE 12.1 ● *A Group Member's Decision Rules for Choosing among Applicants for Assistant Program Director*

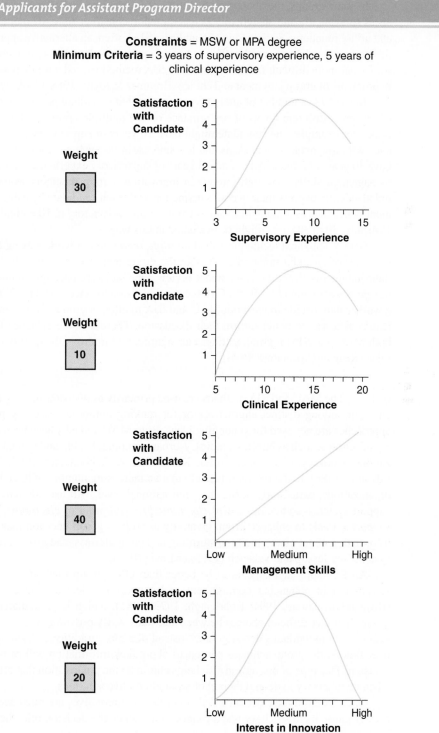

An Alternative Approach

In some groups, members may feel uncomfortable when asked to express their preferences so explicitly and analytically as is required to construct an MAU model with weights and utility functions. Social judgment analysis (SJA) offers an alternative approach for identifying members' decision rules. The SJA technique can be less demanding on the group but somewhat more difficult for the worker. The SJA method is used with increasing frequency in problems of group judgment and choice (Brehmer & Joyce, 1988; Cooksey, 1996).

To use SJA, a number of alternatives (often called *cases*) are presented to a group. The cases depict different levels of performance on the multiple criteria (often called *cues*) at issue. For example, one candidate might have 10 years of supervisory and clinical experience with low management skills and low interest in innovation. Another candidate might have 20 years of clinical experience, 3 years of supervisory experience, a moderate level of management skills, and high interest in innovation. Group members would be asked to independently express their overall satisfaction with each candidate by using a single judgment scale, such as a rating that ranges from 0 = not satisfactory to 10 = highly satisfactory. Typically, 20 to 30 cases might be evaluated in this way.

With a statistical technique called *multiple regression,* a worker using SJA can compute the weights and function forms that the group members appear to be using to make their judgments about the cases under review. One software package commonly used for this purpose is called POLICY PC (Executive Decision Services, Albany, NY). Sometimes a worker may decide to use both MAU and SJA to allow a group to compare and contrast results as a way to better inform their discussion. There is some evidence that the use of both MAU and SJA in group settings can significantly improve the quality of group judgment (Reagan-Cirinicione, 1994).

USES.   The MAU and SJA methods are used primarily as decision-making techniques for choosing among distinct alternatives or for ranking numerous cases by priority. These approaches are not used for generating ideas. Both MAU and SJA have been used in a variety of settings, such as business, industry, urban planning, health, and mental health organizations (Cooksey, 1996; Kleindorfer, Kunreuther, & Schoemaker, 1993; Winterfeldt & Edwards, 1986). In the future, it is likely that an increasing number of large human service organizations, particularly at the state and national level, will use computer-based group support systems, sometimes called *electronic brainstorming* or *electronic group decision support systems* to enhance group creativity as well as group decision making. For more information about electronic brainstorming and computer-assisted group decision support systems see Jessup and Valacich (1993) or Levi (2007).

An SJA approach appears to be better than other group methods in achieving consensus and in enhancing commitment and support for decisions made by the group (Reagan-Cirinicione, 1994; Rohrbaugh, 1979, 1981), which is particularly important in groups that face difficult choices between alternatives. By providing for a thorough discussion of each individual's decision rules instead of a more traditional discussion of alternative choices, the group achieves consensus about how information will be used to make a decision. This type of discussion also helps eliminate the polarization that often takes place when members try to defend their choices of alternative solutions.

Once the group decides on a decision rule, all alternatives are rated according to that rule. Because members have had a chance to influence the decision rule, the choice that is made by the group reflects the input of all members and, therefore, is likely to have the cooperation and commitment of all members when it is implemented.

Effectiveness

The SJA approach is the most rational and technical method discussed in this chapter for leading task groups. It attempts to order and systematize information by assigning each piece of information a weight and a functional relationship to the overall decision. Empirical evidence about this approach (Edwards, 1977; Harmon & Rohrbaugh, 1990; Huber, 1980; Rohrbaugh, 1979, 1981) suggests that it can be helpful as an analytical tool in making decisions based on the information available in a problematic situation. Rohrbaugh (1979, 1981) also found that SJA is more effective than both interacting group methods and NGT in developing group consensus and commitment to a decision, and research by Toseland, Rivas, and Chapman (1984) suggests that SJA is better than NGT or problem solving in producing consistent, high-quality decisions. Still, inspirational leadership is essential for the effective use of SJA and other computer-assisted group decision support systems (Sosik, Avolio, & Kahai, 1998).

The primary drawback to SJA is that it is a complicated method limited to making decisions between clear, established alternatives. When decisions between clearly delineated alternatives are crucial and consensus is important, SJA should be considered the method of choice for problem-solving groups. However, SJA should be used only by a trained worker who has both conceptual and practical experience in developing decision rules. In addition, SJA is not useful for generating ideas or alternative solutions but can be used after alternatives have been developed by other methods (Rohrbaugh, 1984).

Quality Circles, Quality Improvement Teams, and Self-Managed Work Teams

Although quality circles (QCs) and quality improvement teams (QITs) are associated with business and industry, they are now used widely in social service mental health and health organizations (Al-Assaf & Schmele, 1997; Gummer & McCallion, 1995; Schmidt & Finnigan, 1993; Sluyter & Mukherjee, 1993). Quality circles are small groups of line employees from the same department who get together voluntarily, elect a leader, and identify and solve problems they have in completing their work assignments. In the United States, the idea behind QCs is to encourage line workers to get together and use both their brains and their hands to produce a quality product (Robson, 1988). Management intent, however, was not only to improve quality but also to prevent workers from becoming alienated from the process and place of their work.

The use of QITs is a newer concept that has evolved from total quality management (TQM). In contrast to QCs, QITs frequently consist of employees from different organizational levels and a variety of departments or functions within the organization. Members are often selected by management, and membership on the team is required. Also, the project the team works on is often selected, and almost always approved, by management (Berry, 1991).

There are frequent misconceptions about the origins of quality circles and their original purposes. Although they are often associated with Japanese business (see, e.g., Ho, 1999), the U.S. quality control expert W. E. Deming taught statistical quality control techniques and the value of cooperation to workers during World War II (Walton, 1990). The concept was not received well in the United States. However, after World War II, Japanese business became increasingly interested in statistical quality control and found Deming's ideas appealing. Later, when his ideas were reintroduced in the United States during the 1970s, less emphasis was placed on statistical quality control and more emphasis was placed on the socioemotional and participatory aspects of QCs (Cole & Tachiki, 1983; Seely & Sween, 1983). Today, however, QCs and QITs are encouraged to rely on data from statistical quality control procedures (Costin, 1999; Glassop, 2002; Lawler, Mohrman, Albers, & Benson, 2001).

Procedures

An organization generally has a coordinator for all QC activities. This individual's role is to ensure that (1) training is provided, (2) there is coverage when facilitators are sick or take personal leave, and (3) each circle has a way of communicating suggestions about problem solving to top-level management.

Each QC consists of six to eight employees who meet for about one hour each week to identify and solve problems facing their department or work group. A facilitator is selected by the membership. Often this individual is a mid-level manager who serves as the link between the QC and upper management. To ensure that QCs run smoothly and effectively, facilitators should be trained in group dynamics and leadership skills. During meetings, the facilitator uses group dynamics, problem solving, brainstorming, and other procedures to facilitate an in-depth discussion and analysis of the topic or issue being addressed by the group.

There are few specific procedures for the operation of QCs. Rather, QCs operate on the basis of core principles, illustrated in the following list.

Quality Circle Core Principles

- Commitment from top-level management to the process
- A commitment to providing training for staff in QC, problem-solving, and statistical control procedures
- Voluntary membership in QC groups
- A focus on problems identified by workers rather than by management
- The selection of leadership and the ownership of the QC process by line staff
- A focus on data-based problem solving
- A focus on solving problems in ways that benefit both line workers and management

According to Kinlaw (1992), QITs use the following steps for quality improvement: (1) understanding the opportunity or problem, (2) defining the specific target for improvement, (3) designing strategies to reach the target, (4) designing data-acquiring strategies, (5) designing a process to use the data, and (6) determining how the project will be managed. Quality circles are often used for idea generation and for improving the work environment, but QITs emphasize systematic, data-based, problem-solving strategies for improving the quality of services delivered by an organization.

Uses

The primary purpose of QCs and QITs is to improve the quality of the service or product delivered to consumers. Thus, QCs and QITs are two ways for management and line staff to demonstrate their commitment to delivering health and social services in the most effective manner. For example, in a multiservice agency serving developmentally disabled adults, staff members may become increasingly aware that clients often have multiple service providers and that problems arise in the coordination of service plans. In QIT meetings, staff would decide to review a selected number of cases to obtain data about the number of providers and how services are currently coordinated. The QIT group would use these data as the basis for recommendations about the design of a new case management system.

In addition, QCs and QITs have several other benefits. They encourage workers to solve problems that interfere with job satisfaction and their performance, and they help workers gain a greater sense of control and autonomy. In turn, workers may have more sense of responsibility and commitment to their work.

Effectiveness

Many writers have claimed that QCs improve productivity, quality, and employee attitudes. For example, Goldstein (1985) suggests that in addition to quality improvements, QCs have been reported to have

> *increased productivity, raised level of morale, increased employee motivation, improved communication, changed the emphasis from fire fighting to prevention, enhanced the commitment to job and organization, reduced reliance on authority to get things done, reduced costs, reduced delivery times, developed people, trained leaders and supervisors, introduced an orientation toward learning, enhanced the coordination of work, and reduced vertical and horizontal demarcations over ownership of problems. (p. 514)*

Despite these assertions, findings about the effectiveness of QCs and QITs are equivocal. Although some studies have found a strong correlation between participatory management systems and the quality and quantity of the work produced, other studies have found little correlation (Gummer, 1988; Gummer & McCallion, 1995). In reviews of studies of QC performance, Adam (1991) and Barrick and Alexander (1987) found that most studies revealed that quality circle programs resulted in improved quality and efficiency of services and the reduction of production costs and unpleasant working conditions. However, with some noticeable exceptions (Marks, Mirvis, Hackett, & Grady, 1986), QCs were not effective in improving employees' attitudes or in reducing staff turnover, absenteeism, or tardiness. Overall, therefore, Adam (1991) tentatively concluded that QCs are effective in improving services but are not effective in improving worker attitudes and morale.

Despite positive findings about the improved efficiency of services, Lawler and Mohrman (1985) report that managers' initial enthusiasm for quality circles is often dampened when they try to document savings. To avoid QCs and QITs becoming fads that end after initial enthusiasm wanes, Lawler and Mohrman (1985) suggest the approaches might best be viewed as part of a larger organizational effort to move toward a more participatory management system.

Also, for QCs and QITs to have a lasting effect on an organization, there must be a commitment to them from all levels of management and they must be compatible with the organization's work culture (Gummer & McCallion, 1995). For example, in a study of the use of QCs in state government, Denhardt, Pyle, and Bluedorn (1987) concluded that, in many departments, employees had never been asked to consider how their work processes might be improved. Smith and Doeing (1985) point out that, in contrast to U.S. managers, Japanese managers often take a longer-term perspective on the development of employees. Thus, making a meaningful shift to participatory management styles that include QCs or QITs is a slow process that takes long-term and concerted commitment at all levels of an organization.

LARGE ORGANIZATIONAL GROUPS

Parliamentary Procedure

Parliamentary procedure is a framework for guiding decision making and problem solving in large task groups. It has been developed over time in many different settings to meet the needs of a variety of task groups. Although there are some commonly accepted rules, there is no single body of laws that is universally accepted as parliamentary procedure.

Parliamentary procedure originated in 1321 in the English Parliament as a set of rules called *modus tenedia Parlia-mentarium* (Gray, 1964). From these roots, Thomas Jefferson developed a *Manual of Parliamentary Practice* in 1801 for use in Congress, and in 1845, Luther Cushing formulated a manual for use in lay, as well as legislative, assemblies (Robert, 1983). *Robert's Rules of Order* was initially published in 1876 and has had many subsequent revisions and printings. Today, *The New Robert's Rules of Order* is the set of parliamentary procedures most frequently followed by task groups.

Procedures

In parliamentary meetings, the activity of the group is determined by motions brought by group members.

Classes of Motions in Parliamentary Procedures

- *Privileged motions* deal with the agenda of the group meeting as a whole. They do not have a relationship with the business before the group and include motions such as adjournment and recess.

- *Incidental motions* are concerned with procedural questions relating to issues *on the floor.* Some examples are a *point of order* and a *point of information.*

- *Subsidiary motions* assist in the handling and disposal of motions on the floor. Motions to table, postpone, or amend are subsidiary motions.

- *Main motions* introduce the central, substantive issues for group consideration. There can be no pending motions when a main motion is proposed. Examples of main motions are reconsideration of an issue previously disposed of and resuming consideration of a tabled motion.

All motions made from the floor follow procedures governing the introduction of that type of motion. It is the chairperson's job to ensure that the rules and procedures are followed. Although the chairperson is supposed to remain neutral during group deliberations, the person can influence the group's work in a variety of ways. Group members must be recognized by the chair before they can make a motion. The chairperson rules on questions of procedure that arise during a meeting and also organizes the meeting by ordering the agenda items and specifying the amount of time available to discuss each item.

Robert's Rules of Order provides a method for prioritizing motions during parliamentary meetings. Table 12.1 shows the priority that each motion takes during a meeting. Although main motions contain the essential business of the parliamentary meeting, they receive the lowest priority because privileged motions govern how all agenda items are

TABLE 12.1 ● *Procedures for Acting on Motions during a Parliamentary Meeting*

Type of Motion	Priority of the Motion	Can the Speaker Be Interrupted?	Does the Motion Need a Second?	Is the Motion Debatable?	Can the Motion Be Amended?	Vote Needed to Adopt the Motion
Privileged Motions						
Set the time of adjournment	1	N	Y	N	Y	Majority
Call for adjournment	2	N	Y	N	N	Majority
Call for recess	3	N	Y	N	Y	Majority
Question of privilege	4	Y	N	N	N	Chair's decision
Call for prescheduled items of business	5	Y	N	N	N	No vote
Incidental Motions						
Point of order	6	Y	N	N	N	Chair's decision
Request for information	6	Y	N	N	N	No vote
Call for a revote	6	N	N	N	N	No vote
Appeal the chair's decision	6	Y	Y	N	N	Majority
Object to consideration of a motion	6	Y	N	N	N	2/3
Call to suspend the rules	6	N	Y	N	N	2/3
Request to withdraw a motion	6	Y	Y	N	N	Majority
Subsidiary Motions						
Table a motion	7	N	Y	N	N	Majority
Call for immediate vote	8	N	Y	N	N	2/3
Limit/extend debate	9	N	Y	N	N	2/3
Postpone the motion	10	N	Y	Y	Y	Majority
Refer the motion to a subcommittee	11	N	Y	Y	Y	Majority

(continued)

TABLE 12.1 ● *Continued*

Type of Motion	Priority of the Motion	Can the Speaker Be Interrupted?	Does the Motion Need a Second?	Is the Motion Debatable?	Can the Motion Be Amended?	Vote Needed to Adopt the Motion
Amend the motion	12	N	Y	Y	Y	Majority
Postpone the motion indefinitely	13	N	Y	Y	N	Majority
Main Motions						
General main motion	14	N	Y	Y	Y	Majority
Reconsider a motion already voted on	14	Y	Y	Y	Y	2/3
Rescind a motion under consideration	14	N	Y	Y	Y	2/3
Resume consideration of a tabled motion	14	N	Y	N	N	Majority
Set a special order of business	14	N	Y	Y	Y	2/3

considered, and incidental and subsidiary motions are always made in reference to a main motion. Therefore, these motions are given a higher priority than main motions. For further information about parliamentary meetings, see *Robert's Rules of Order* (Robert, 1983).

Uses

Parliamentary procedure is often used in large groups because it provides a well-defined structure to guide group process. The rules of parliamentary procedure help ensure a high level of order and efficiency in task group meetings when many agenda items are discussed. Order and efficiency are achieved through rules that demand consideration of one issue at a time. The rules prescribe the way in which issues are brought before the group, processed by the group, and disposed of by the group. In a meeting of a delegate council composed of representatives from many social service agencies, for example, parliamentary procedure can be used to lend order to how representatives interact. Thus, with many members representing the diverse interests of several agencies, meetings are run in a formal manner, and members are generally guaranteed a structured means by which they can bring their interests, motions, and agenda items to the large group.

Parliamentary procedure is especially useful for considering well-developed agenda items that need some discussion and debate and a relatively speedy decision by an entire task group (Gulley, 1968). Parliamentary procedure is of limited value, however, when a problem or issue facing the group has not been clearly defined, when sufficient data have not been gathered about the problem, or when alternative solutions have not been explored and developed for consideration during decision making. Thus, these procedures should not be used as a substitute for problem solving done by subcommittees of the larger task group.

Effectiveness

The long history of using parliamentary procedure in important decision-making bodies throughout the Western world testifies to its usefulness in providing a structure for task group meetings. By limiting and focusing the deliberations of a task group to one solution at a time, discussion and debate are facilitated, and motions are dealt with expeditiously. Clearly specified rules lead to an orderly and systematic consideration of each agenda item. Rules that remain consistent throughout the life of a group assure members that there is an established order that they can rely on for fair and equitable treatment when sensitive or controversial issues are presented.

Parliamentary procedure also protects the rights of the minority. For example, it takes only two members to introduce a main motion, one to state the motion and another to second the motion. Some motions can be made by a single member. Every group member is given an equal opportunity to participate. Majority rights are also protected because a quorum is needed to conduct a meeting, and majority rule is relied on for all decisions.

Parliamentary meetings have several disadvantages. Meetings are subject to manipulation by members who are familiar with parliamentary procedures. Members who are less familiar with the procedures may be reluctant to speak or be unsure of when or how to raise an objection to a motion. Another limitation is that private deals may be made outside a meeting to gain a member's support for an agenda item in a forthcoming meeting. Private deals circumvent the intent of parliamentary procedure, which is based on openly debating the merits of a proposal. They also tend to enforce the will of powerful members who offer attractive incentives to members who support their positions on particular agenda items.

Parliamentary meetings have other limitations. The procedure encourages debate, which can lead to polarization of members' opinions. Also, members often try to defend their positions rather than understand the logic behind opposing viewpoints. Perhaps the most important limitation of parliamentary procedure is that it is not well suited for problem solving, especially when the problem is complex, muddled, or not fully understood. A large task group using parliamentary procedure does not usually attain the level of interaction, the depth of communication, or the flexibility necessary to explore alternative solutions that may be necessary to resolve difficult problems. Large task groups should conduct most problem-solving efforts in subcommittees that report back to the larger group. The larger group can then debate the merits of a proposed solution and reach a decision based on majority rule.

Phillips' 66

Phillips' 66 was developed to facilitate discussion in large groups (Phillips, 1948). Originally, Phillips' 66 referred to a technique of dividing a large group or audience into groups of six and having each group spend six minutes formulating one question for the speaker. The method has been expanded to include many different ways to facilitate communication in large groups. For example, Maier and Zerfoss (1952) suggest using multiple role-playing strategies for training staff in large groups. Members of the larger group are asked to form smaller groups and role-play the same or similar situations. Each group designates a recorder, who reports a summary of group members' experiences when the large group reconvenes.

Other variations have also been developed. Bradford and Corey (1951) have suggested organizing audience listening teams in which each team is asked to listen to, discuss, and report back to the larger group about an aspect of the speaker's presentation. They have also suggested selecting individuals from the audience to serve on an *audience representational panel* to react to the speaker. All these techniques are modifications and expansions of the basic principles of Phillips' 66.

Procedures

Phillips' 66 should be used only after clear instructions are given to members about what they will be doing during the procedure, especially because once the large group has broken down into smaller groups, the sudden change from the structure and control of a large group meeting can cause confusion. If the groups are not clear about their direction, they may flounder or begin to work on something other than what was assigned by the leader.

To reduce the chances for confusion, the worker should ensure that each group is clear about the problem or task it is facing. Problem statements, tasks, and goals should be specific. When they are broad and nonspecific, the small groups have to spend time refining them, which may lead to work that is quite different from what the worker had intended. Members should also be clear about their assignments. They should understand what subgroup they belong to, what the group is supposed to do, what should be contained in the recorder's report, how much time they have, and where and when the subgroup is supposed to meet.

The size of the subgroups and the amount of time each subgroup spends together depend on the situation. The original design for Phillips' 66, six-member groups meeting for six minutes, may be appropriate in some situations but not in others. Generally, at least 20 to 30 minutes are required for a large group to break down into smaller groups and accomplish any meaningful work. Subgroups should be separated so members can hear each other and conduct their work. However, in a large meeting room, it is not necessary to ask members to talk quietly. The noise and activity of other groups can be contagious and thus spur all groups to work harder (Maier, 1963).

In very large meetings, having each subgroup report back to the larger group may be monotonous and time-consuming. Alternatives include limiting the reporting time to a few minutes for each subgroup, having each subgroup report on a portion of the discussion, and having each subgroup prepare a brief written report that can be shared after the meeting.

Phillips' 66 can be combined with a procedure known as *idea writing* (Moore, 1994). When participants break into small groups, each member can be given a sheet of paper with a triggering question or item to which the member should respond in writing. After approximately five minutes, members place their sheets in the center of the group. Each member then selects another member's sheet and responds in writing for approximately five to ten minutes to the initial idea prepared by the first member. This process is repeated until all members have prepared written responses on every idea sheet. Members may react by writing what they like and dislike about the previous ideas and reactions and can offer suggestions for improvement. After this process is completed, members find their original sheets and read their ideas and other members' reactions to it. The members of the small group then discuss the ideas that emerge from the written interaction, and the group facilitator summarizes the discussion on a flip chart. When the larger group reconvenes, the small-group facilitator can use information on the flip chart to present a summary of the small group's ideas.

Another way to use Phillips' 66 is to have each of the smaller groups who have worked on ideas on a flip chart, tear off their pages and tape them to the walls around the room. Then members of the larger group can go around the outer circle where the pages are taped to the wall and select their top two or three favorite ideas, by placing a tally mark on the flip chart sheet of their choice. Then, when the group reconvenes, the marks can be tallied and the larger group can decide to work on one or more of the ideas on the flip charts that have been given the most favorable ratings by members of the larger group.

Uses

Although most problem-solving activities take place in small task groups, occasionally there is a need for large groups, such as members of a social agency or a delegate assembly, to engage in problem-solving discussions. Parliamentary procedure, in which the chair must recognize individual speakers from the floor, is not designed for large problem-solving discussions. It is designed for debating the merits of proposals and voting on alternatives that are already well developed. Phillips' 66 can be used as an alternative method for problem solving in large task groups. For example, during an in-service training program covering management skills, the group trainer asks the large group to divide into smaller groups and answer the question "What makes a good manager?" Members of the small groups work to develop a short list of answers to the question within a limited period of time. When the large group reconvenes, each group reports its answers, and the material is used by the trainer in the didactic presentation and in group discussion following the presentation.

Although Maier (1963) suggests that a skillful, self-confident worker can conduct large problem-solving discussions by using techniques such as summarizing and posting alternatives, the obstacles to large-group interaction tend to make such discussions difficult. For example, it can be difficult to hold the attention of all members when individual members are speaking. It is also difficult to encourage shy members to express themselves, particularly if they have minority opinions.

Using Phillips' 66, the worker can involve all members in a group discussion. The small size of the groups makes it easier for shy members to express themselves. Also, members can choose to participate in groups that are focused on topics of particular interest to them. Reporting ideas generated by subgroups back to the larger assembly ensures that input from all members is considered in the problem-solving process. Overall, Phillips' 66 is a useful method that overcomes the limitations of parliamentary procedure when large groups are called on to solve problems.

Effectiveness

Phillips' 66 is a practical, commonsense procedure for facilitating discussion and problem solving in large groups. Its effective use has been reported in a variety of sources (Gulley, 1968; Maier, 1963; Stattler & Miller, 1968). When applied correctly, Phillips' 66 can be used in a variety of situations. However, poor planning, confused or nonspecific instructions, or a muddled explanation of the goals of the procedure can turn a large task group meeting into disorganization and chaos.

METHODS FOR WORKING WITH COMMUNITY GROUPS

Work with community groups such as social action groups, coalitions, and delegate councils involves many of the methods and skills described throughout this text. For example, community groups frequently use brainstorming and other problem-solving methods to generate ideas and address issues during meetings. Work with community groups is distinguished from other forms of group work practice by special emphasis on the following: (1) mobilizing individuals to engage in collective action, (2) building the capacity of the group and its members to effect community change, and (3) planning and organizing social action strategies. The remainder of this chapter focuses on these three aspects of practice with community groups.

Mobilization Strategies

Whether working with social action groups, coalitions, or delegate councils, a primary task of the worker is to mobilize individual members to action. The worker is a catalyst to stimulate interest in community problems and motivate members to work together. When engaging in mobilization efforts, the worker identifies and works with several constituencies, including the individuals who are experiencing the problem, community leaders, informal and formal community groups and organizations, and larger social institutions. For example, to mobilize a coalition to prevent domestic violence, a worker meets with victims of domestic violence, women's groups, the staff of domestic violence shelters, dispute resolution centers, police departments, family courts, and departments of social services, as well as with ministers, priests, rabbis, and local politicians.

An important initial step in any mobilization effort is to become familiar with the perceptions of community members about the issues the community group will attempt to address. It is often helpful to begin by meeting with civic and religious leaders and with community activists. These individuals can provide a helpful overview of the community's past responses to the issue and to similar issues. However, it is also essential to meet with as many community residents as possible.

Kahn (1991) notes that person-to-person contact with community residents helps build community groups and organizations in which each member feels valued. When meeting with community residents, the worker should avoid telling residents why they should be concerned about a particular issue or problem. A more effective strategy is to ask them to describe their problems and concerns and validate and affirm the issues they raise by mentioning how their views are consistent with views of other community residents. In this way, community residents begin to get a sense that it is their issues, not the worker's issues, that will be addressed through collective action.

As the worker becomes familiar with the community, the worker should identify individuals, community groups, and organizations that might be willing to help with mobilization efforts. To determine the extent to which individuals, groups, and organizations can help, the worker should evaluate their positions within the power structure of the community. The worker should then consider how forming a partnership with particular individuals and groups may help or hinder mobilization efforts. Often, the worker decides to form partnerships with a wide range of individuals, community leaders, and organizations.

However, the worker should also be careful about involving individuals or organizations who do not share compatible goals or who have such a negative reputation in the community that they might damage the group's effort.

Mobilization involves consciousness raising. Working with individual citizens, community leaders, and formal and informal organizations, the worker attempts to bring a single issue or a group of related issues to greater public awareness. Consciousness raising may be done in several ways.

Strategies for Raising Public Awareness

- Meeting with community residents
- Making presentations to civic and religious organizations
- Testifying at public hearings
- Publicizing the issue through local newspapers, radio or television stations, and websites
- Demonstrating, picketing, and boycotting

The goal of consciousness-raising efforts is to encourage community members to gain a renewed sense of individual and community pride and to join forces to improve their community.

Mobilization to action involves helping members understand the power of collective action against injustices and inequities. Helping individuals vent their frustration and anger by public declarations and acting against those causing the problem (Rubin & Rubin, 2007) can sometimes resolve individual problems. However, individual actions are easily ignored, dismissed, or punished by persons in power. Therefore, the goal of the worker should be to help individuals understand the value of pooling their efforts so they can exert sufficient influence to effect change.

One way to accomplish this goal is to highlight the incentives for collective action. Individuals become actively involved in a community group if they think they have something to gain, if they think they can contribute, and if they believe in the goals of the group. According to Rubin and Rubin (2007), the worker can use a variety of material incentives such as improved income or better housing, solidarity incentives such as the enjoyment of belonging to the group, and expressive incentives such as the excitement and satisfaction of articulating opinions and values.

Mobilization to action also involves *bootstrapping,* that is, engaging in action projects that build interest and commitment in a community (Rubin & Rubin, 2007). A good way to begin bootstrapping is to identify a project or activity that is relatively easy and leads to an immediate success. For example, a social action group, a coalition, or even a delegate council might sponsor a community forum to which they invite local politicians and the news media. Similarly, a "community education day" might be planned at a shopping mall, a "teach-in" might be scheduled at a school, or a rally might be organized in a public square. Later, when members have experienced the initial successful completion of a project, they can be encouraged to tackle larger projects, such as a community survey or an extensive lobbying effort, that require more effort and resources.

Capacity-Building Strategies

Capacity building means helping community groups develop the ability and the resources to successfully tackle one issue or a set of issues. Community development and other forms of community work are a form of capacity building. They facilitate the formation of groups of involved citizens in private, voluntary, and public settings for the purpose of social action (Benjamin, Bessant, & Watts, 1997; Drysdale & Purcell, 1999).

The worker plays the role of coordinator in helping members gather data and build resources. A first step in capacity building is to help group members become as knowledgeable as possible about the issues they are addressing. Workers should facilitate exchanges of information among members about the issues facing the group and about ways to accomplish particular objectives.

In many instances, the worker and the members will not have enough information about a problem. In these situations, the worker should encourage the group to gather data before proceeding. Original data can be gathered through community surveys or focused interviews with key informants. The worker might also help members gain access to public records and reports. For example, in helping to organize a neighborhood association, (1) city building department files could be used to gather data on building-code violations, (2) police department records could be used to collect data on the number and type of crimes in a particular neighborhood, (3) the county clerk's office could be used to gather data on property ownership, and (4) the department of public welfare or the local community development agency could be used to obtain estimates of poverty rates or the homeless population.

A second step in capacity building involves helping the group become familiar with the structures within a community that can aid change efforts. It is important to identify individuals with the power to bring about needed changes within a community and determine to whom these individuals report. The worker also can help the group identify and contact religious and civic organizations that may be interested in joining forces to work on a particular issue, analyze the strengths and weaknesses of opponents to change, or decide what tactics might be used to change opponents' minds. For example, would a landlord be most vulnerable to a rent strike, to moral pressure from a church group, or to having housing code violations strictly enforced?

A third step is to help the group learn how to influence local government. The worker can help group members identify policy makers and bureaucrats who might support group efforts to have existing laws enforced or introduce new legislation to address a particular issue. The worker can help the group develop a clear position on the issues with as much supporting documentation as available. To the extent possible, the group might form a partnership with legislators and bureaucrats so they can collaborate on the change effort. Rubin and Rubin (2007) note that legislators are receptive to ideas that make them look active, creative, and effective. The worker can help legislators and bureaucrats place the issue on the agenda by testifying at public hearings and by using lobbying efforts.

A fourth step in capacity building is to help the group make an inventory of its existing resources and identify resources needed to accomplish particular goals. In this way, members are empowered to use their own resources to help them tackle the problems they are facing as a community. For example, the group may find it needs legal advice. Can a lawyer be identified who would be willing to work with the group? Similarly, the group may want to publish a fact sheet or a brochure for a lobbying effort. Can a business or community organization that would be willing to help the group design or print the brochure be identified? An important role of the worker is to help the group locate resources to accomplish its objectives. For more information about capacity building through the formation of coalitions see Lawson, Bronstein, McCallion, Ryan, and Fish (2003), and Mattessich, Murray-Close, and Monsey (2001).

Social Action Strategies

According to Harrison and Ward (1999), social action has two central characteristics. First, it promotes the capacity of all people to take action to improve their situation. Second, this action is based on open participation, where people working collectively in groups explore underlying social issues and take action to alleviate problems. Self-management and empowerment are essential ingredients. There is no victim blaming or focus on deficits. Instead, workers facilitate members' skills, helping them to take action for themselves. Social action is based on the idea that the people who are most affected by a problem are in the best position to articulate their experiences and to define and implement solutions (Benjamin et al., 1997).

A variety of social action strategies can be used to help community groups accomplish their objectives during the middle stage. The techniques include political action strategies, legal strategies, and direct action strategies (Rubin & Rubin, 2007). Many forms of political activity are available to community groups, such as those that follow.

Community Group Political Activity

- Organizing voter registration drives
- Nominating and working on the campaigns of public officials
- Developing and supporting referendums, propositions, and other grass-roots efforts to bypass legislators and get proposals directly on the ballot
- Lobbying and advocating positions
- Participating in public hearings
- Monitoring compliance with laws by bureaucratic and regulatory agencies

Although political action strategies are designed to get persons in power to pay attention to the goals of a community group, legal action strategies are designed to force politicians and bureaucrats to take action on issues supported by a community group or a coalition of community groups. Political action strategies can have sweeping and binding effects, but they are often expensive and time-consuming. Sometimes, the threat of legal action by a single counsel on retainer can create some action. More often, however, legal action requires a professional staff, a large budget, and a great deal of patience. Although coalitions of community groups and community groups affiliated with national organizations can use legal strategies effectively, political action strategies and direct action strategies are often preferred.

Direct action strategies include rallies, demonstrations, marches, picketing, sit-ins, vigils, blockades, boycotts, slowdowns, strikes, and many other forms of nonviolent and violent protest. Direct action strategies allow members to ventilate frustration and anger, but they can be counterproductive. Negative publicity, fines, physical injury, and time lost at work are just a few of the possible consequences. Thus, direct action strategies should not be undertaken without careful thought and preparation, and then only if it is clear that safer political and legal strategies are unlikely to achieve the desired objective. It is also important to keep in mind that the threat of direct action is often as terrifying as the action itself. Therefore, if a community group is serious about engaging in a direct action strategy, it is often wise to publicize the group's intent and the specific steps that an opponent can take to avoid the action.

In his text, *Rules For Radicals,* Alinsky (1971) developed a number of pragmatic rules for choosing among different action strategies. For example, he suggested picking a direct action strategy that enjoys wide support among members. He also suggested picking a strategy that emphasizes the weaknesses of the opponent. Thus, a rally that gets widespread news coverage might be particularly effective against an opponent concerned about negative publicity, but an economic boycott might be more effective against a corporation under pressure from shareholders to increase profits.

When selecting a social action strategy, there is a generally accepted protocol that should be adhered to when carrying out work with community groups. Less intrusive and more cooperative strategies should be tried before disruptive or conflict-oriented strategies are engaged. Collaboration and negotiation strategies should be employed before conflict strategies. Collaboration means that in attempting to effect some change in a target system, the worker tries to convince the target system that change is in the best interests of all involved. In negotiation, the worker and the target system both give and receive something in the process of change. The process of bargaining involves a good faith quid pro quo arrangement and assumes that each party will make some change desired by the other.

Should collaboration and negotiation fail to achieve a desired change, the group may be forced to engage in conflict strategies. In any case, the worker should always help group members use each of the three strategies in a constructive and an ethical fashion. The worker should carefully guard against a group choosing conflict as an initial strategy because of the perception that the strategy will result in change more quickly or because members wish to carry out personal retribution.

SUMMARY

A variety of methods have been developed in industry, business administration, and human service organizations to help task groups accomplish their goals during the middle stage. This chapter examines some of the most widely used methods: (1) brainstorming, (2) reverse brainstorming, (3) trigger groups, (4) synectics, (5) focus groups, (6) the nominal group technique, (7) social judgment analysis, (8) quality circles, and (9) quality improvement teams. The chapter also includes descriptions of methods such as parliamentary procedure and Phillips' 66 that can be used to lead large task groups.

The second section of the chapter describes specialized methods for helping community groups accomplish their objectives during the middle stage. This section focuses on three methods for helping community groups achieve their objectives: (1) mobilizing individuals to engage in collective action, (2) building the capacity of the group and its members to effect community change, and (3) social action strategies.

● CASE EXAMPLE

Funding sources for the AIDS Outreach Association were so impressed with Nora's research and documentation that they approved a budget allocation for hiring four people to fill newly created case management positions. Because of the importance of this new initiative, Nora wanted to have input from all constituencies within the organization. Therefore, she formed an ad hoc committee composed of supervisors, program directors, and two consumers to assist in the recruitment and selection procedures and processes.

During the first meeting of the committee, Nora discussed the development and implementation of the purpose of the group and its charge. She noted that the group would be responsible for deciding what skills would best fit the position and for rating and ranking job candidates. During this first session, the group discussed the tasks, activities, and services that case managers would be providing to consumers. The first session ended with a list of potential duties that could be assigned to the new employees.

One week later, Nora convened the group for the second time. The group members tried to design a procedure for screening candidates but were unable to focus on what criteria would guide the selection process. There were lots of ideas, but the group could not seem to keep track of them. Nora suggested that the group take a short break. When group members returned, Nora placed a flip chart at the head of the table. She suggested that members use brainstorming techniques to generate ideas about the skills and attributes needed for the job. She explained that in brainstorming, members should develop as many ideas as possible without evaluating the importance of the ideas. In other words, members were asked to come up with as many ideas as possible and not to critique any ideas until the idea-generation phase of the process was complete. As each member contributed an idea it was recorded on the flip chart. At the end of the brainstorming

session, Nora took all the criteria that had been listed and rearranged them into a comprehensive list. She was amazed at the number of criteria the group had generated.

Armed with many creative ideas for how to rate candidates, the group now faced the task of reducing the list to the most important set of criteria. Nora suggested that the group use elements of the nominal group technique (NGT) to identify important criteria. She guided the group members in a review of the list of criteria, and she asked members to write their top choices on a piece of paper, ranking their choices from highest to lowest. During this process members were asked to refrain from discussing their choices with each other. Next, Nora asked members to present their highest-ranked ideas in round robin fashion, going around the group until all members had contributed their choices for the five highest criteria. Nora used this list to sort criteria into categories. She then asked members to take turns discussing their choices with the rest of the group. Following the discussion, Nora asked members to vote on a consolidated list of criteria by assigning values to their top five choices within each category. After this was done, Nora tallied up the numerical ratings and listed the top five criteria as determined by the vote of each group member. These included amount of experience working with persons with AIDS, knowledge about AIDS, knowledge of the service system, interpersonal skills, and potential for developing new programs. The group agreed that these would be the criteria that they would use to screen and rank job applicants. They ended the group meeting by developing a position description using the criteria and directed Nora to advertise the position in two local newspapers.

Some weeks later, Nora convened the group to discuss their next task. Since the last meeting, the positions had been advertised and a number of applications had been sent to the organization. The group's next task was to screen the candidates and to rate them according to the criteria the group had established.

At first, members rushed into the task of discussing individual candidates without establishing ground rules for how to proceed. Nora suggested that the group use a more organized approach to the process, namely, multiattribute utility (MAU) analysis. This required the group to review and specify the criteria they had previously decided on to rank candidates, to specify minimum and optimum levels of qualifications for the job, and to systematically rate candidates according to the decision criteria. Although some members were skeptical in the beginning of this procedure, they soon found that using this method enabled them to more systematically review each job candidate. At the close of this procedure, members were able to rank the top candidates for the open positions. To ensure that consensus about the ranking of the top candidates was achieved, a final round of discussion followed the group's ranking process. The committee ended its work by presenting the chief executive officer of the AIDS Outreach Association with a ranked list of candidates to be interviewed for the new positions.

part **V** The Ending Stage

chapter 13
Ending the Group's Work

chapter 14
Evaluation

chapter 15
Case Examples

Ending the Group's Work

The ending stage, a critical part of group work practice, has been given increasing attention in the literature.[1] The skills workers use in the ending stage determine, in part, the success of the entire group experience. In this stage, workers and members form their lasting impressions of the group. An otherwise satisfying and effective group can be ruined by a worker who is not skillful at ending the group's work.

During the ending stage, the group's work is consolidated. In task groups, the decisions, reports, recommendations, and other products of the group as a whole are completed, and consideration is given to how the results of the work can best be implemented. In treatment groups, the changes made by individual group members are stabilized, and plans are made for maintaining these gains after the group ends. In groups in which members' self-disclosure has been high, it is necessary to help members work through their feelings about terminating their relationships with the worker and with each other. It is also a time when workers confront their own feelings regarding ending their work with a particular group. This chapter examines the tasks and skills involved in ending individual group meetings and ending the work of the group as a whole.

FACTORS THAT INFLUENCE GROUP ENDINGS

Endings vary depending on whether a group has an open or closed membership policy. In closed groups, unless there are unplanned terminations, all members end at the same time. In these groups, the worker can help all members to deal with common issues and feelings that arise as the group draws to a close. Open groups present a more difficult challenge for the worker. Some members may be experiencing reactions to termination, but others may experience reactions common to the beginning stage of the group. In open groups, the worker should individualize work with each member. However, because each member will eventually experience disengagement from the group, the worker can use the reactions of members who are terminating to help members who will experience similar reactions in the future.

---

[1] See, for example, the *International Journal of Group Psychotherapy* (1995) 46(1), which is mainly devoted to the process of termination.

Endings also vary according to the attraction of the group for its members. In groups that members find attractive, endings may not be viewed as a positive event. Conversely, if group meetings are viewed as something to be endured, news of the last meeting may be received with relief.

In addition, endings vary depending on whether the group is a treatment group or a task group. In many therapy groups and support groups, for example, members reveal intimate details of their personal lives. They let down their defenses and become vulnerable as they share concerns and issues that are important to them. In these types of groups, mutual aid and support develop as members deepen relationships with one another and the worker. They come to trust each other and to rely on the therapeutic advice and suggestions given by the worker and fellow group members. Thus, endings for such groups can have a significant impact on members.

THE PROCESS OF ENDING

In therapy, support, and growth groups, termination may be accompanied by strong emotional reactions. However, in educational and socialization groups, termination rarely results in the expression of strong emotional reactions.

Terminating the relationships that may have influenced the members of treatment groups is quite different from terminating the relationships formed in task groups. In task groups, members' self-disclosure is generally at a relatively low level. Because the focus of these groups is on a product, such as a report or the development of a plan of action, members often look forward to the end of a group with a sense of accomplishment or with relief that their work is finished. Because they have not let down their defenses or shared their personal concerns to any great extent, there is rarely an intense emotional reaction to ending. Also, members of task groups may work together again on other committees, teams, or councils. Therefore, the endings of task groups do not have the same sense of finality as do endings of treatment groups.

In the task group literature, with the notable exception of Keyton (1993), the focus is on the skills the leader uses to end individual group meetings rather than on how the leader ends the entire group experience (Tropman, 1996). This focus contrasts sharply with treatment group literature, which generally focuses on ending work with the group rather than ending work in a particular meeting.

PLANNED AND UNPLANNED TERMINATION

At the beginning of closed, time-limited groups, workers and members decide how many times the group will meet. Northen (1969) points out, "Ideally, termination occurs when a person or a group no longer needs the professional services" (p. 223). Fortune and colleagues (Fortune, 1985; Fortune, Pearlingi, & Rochelle, 1991) found that few social workers considered terminating with a client unless they considered that their work together had been successful. The most important criteria for termination were improved coping in the environment, improved intrapsychic functioning, the client's wish to terminate, meeting initial goals, and changes in therapeutic content (Fortune et al., 1991).

Member Termination

Sometimes members stop attending before the planned ending date. Unplanned termination of membership is a relatively common experience. Review studies have found unplanned termination rates of about 30 percent (Connelly & Piper, 1984; Connelly, Piper, DeCarufel, & Debbane, 1986). Unplanned termination varies with the length of the group. For example, unplanned termination rates of 5 percent to 20 percent have been reported for short-term, structured, psychoeducational groups in outpatient settings (Budman, Simeone, Reilly, & Demby, 1994; Labrecque, Peak, & Toseland, 1992; Toseland, 1995; Toseland, Labrecque, Goebel, & Whitney, 1992). In contrast, Fieldsteel (1996) reported unplanned termination rates of 28 percent to 78 percent in psychoanalytic group therapy.

In treatment groups in which participation is voluntary, a reduction in membership sometimes occurs after the first or second meeting of a group. After the initial drop, groups often develop a stable core of members who continue until the group ends.

When leading groups, workers sometimes find themselves asking rhetorically, "What have I done to cause members to fail to return to the group?" In follow-up contacts with members who terminated prematurely, many workers find they did not cause premature termination.

● **CASE EXAMPLE** *Premature Termination*

In a group for separated and divorced persons, three people did not return to the second group meeting. When they were contacted, it was found that one person lived 40 miles from where the group met and, after driving home on foggy rural roads after the first group meeting, had decided not to return. Another member's job had unexpectedly changed and required the person to be at work during the group's meeting times. It was learned from the third person's employer that one of his children had experienced a serious accident. The member called two weeks later to explain that "I have been running between the hospital and my responsibilities to the other two [children]."

There is also empirical data that indicates that workers may not be responsible for some unplanned terminations. For example, when evaluating a smoking-cessation group treatment program, it was found that members left treatment prematurely for a variety of reasons (Toseland, Kabat, & Kemp, 1983). Several were dissatisfied with their group or their group's leader, but others left for reasons unrelated to their treatment experience. Although it is commonly assumed that dropouts are treatment failures, in evaluating eight smoking-cessation groups, it was found that one of seven dropouts left treatment prematurely because he had stopped smoking and believed he no longer needed treatment. Another dropout quit smoking before a follow-up evaluation. Thus, it is important to realize that unplanned termination of members may be the result of their lack of interest or motivation, particular life circumstances, or other factors beyond the control of the worker that have little or nothing to do with a worker's leadership skills. Toseland and colleagues (1997), for example, found that attendance at group meetings by older adults in nursing homes was greatly affected by their health status.

Yalom (1995) lists nine factors that may cause group members to drop out of treatment prematurely. Yalom points out that some members leave because of faulty selection processes and others are the result of flawed therapeutic technique (Yalom, 1995). These factors are presented in the following list.

Factors Leading to Termination

- External factors, such as scheduling conflicts and changes in geographical location
- Group deviancy, such as being the richest group member, the only unmarried member, and the like
- Problems in developing intimate relationships
- Fear of emotional contagion
- Inability to share the worker's time
- Complications arising from concurrent individual and group therapy
- Early provocateurs
- Inadequate orientation to therapy
- Complications arising from subgrouping

Workers should not, however, assume that members' decisions to terminate prematurely have nothing to do with the group's process or its leadership. Sometimes members drop out as a result of their dissatisfaction with the group or its leader. For example, in therapy and growth-oriented groups in which confrontation is used as a therapeutic technique, members occasionally become so angry when confronted with an emotionally charged issue that they threaten to terminate. To prevent premature termination, MacKenzie (1994) suggests use of a careful pregroup screening interview to select members who have the capacity to benefit from the group. It is not always possible, however, to screen out members whose defensiveness, anger, and impulsivity may cause them to abruptly leave a group. Therefore, some workers also specify in the initial contract that members must give two weeks' notice before leaving the group so that members have a chance to rethink their decisions.

Pregroup training has also been found to be an effective way to prevent premature dropouts from therapy groups (Bednar & Kaul, 1994; Kaul & Bednar, 1994). For example, Piper, Debbane, Bienvenu, and Garant (1982) found a reduction of 13 percent to 30 percent in the dropout rate attributed to the successful management of anxiety and the development of interpersonal bonds that resulted from a pregroup training program. Many other studies have been conducted over the past twenty years about the benefits of pregroup training. Overall, the studies indicate that pregroup training works by reducing the ambiguity and uncertainty in beginning group meetings. For a summary of these studies, and the findings from them, see Kaul and Bednar (1994).

When workers take the time to explore members' reasons for terminating, the data gathered can help reduce premature terminations in subsequent groups. Sometimes, for example, workers learn that arranging for child care while the group is in session helps reduce the number of dropouts. Arranging transportation to and from the group may also help. At other times, workers may find that there are ways they can improve their own skills to prevent members from dropping out of the group. For example, they may learn to be more gentle or tentative when they use confrontation methods.

Occasionally, an entire group may end prematurely. Just as there are many reasons for the premature termination of individuals, there are also many reasons for the premature termination of groups. A group that begins with a small number of members may lose several members and thus be unable to continue functioning effectively (Hartford, 1971). Groups may not receive sufficient support from their sponsoring agencies to continue functioning, or groups may be unable or unwilling to respond to external pressure to change their functioning.

Groups may also end prematurely as a result of internal dysfunction. For example, communication and interaction patterns may be maldistributed and cause subgrouping, scapegoating, or domination by a few members. The group may lack sufficient attraction for its members and, therefore, may fail to coalesce or function as a cohesive unit. Social controls such as norms, roles, status hierarchies, and power may cause severe tension and conflict when some members rebel against the control of the worker or other members. Lack of appropriate social controls may cause chaos or an aimless drift that eventually leads to dissolution of the group as a whole. Members may also have great difficulty deciding on common values, preferences, ways of working together, or other aspects of the group's culture.

Whenever workers confront the possibility that a group may end prematurely, they should carefully examine the factors that are contributing to the problem. It is often possible to trace a group's dysfunction back to the planning stage. Careful examination of the factors that contributed to a group's demise can help workers avoid such pitfalls in future groups.

Worker Termination

Although rarely mentioned in the literature, there are times when workers have to terminate their work with a group. Probably the most common reason for worker termination is that students leave at the end of their field placements, but change of employment or shifting job responsibilities also lead to worker termination. In a study of two groups in which workers terminated their participation, Long, Pendleton, and Winter (1988) found that the termination of the worker led to testing of the new worker and to a reorganization of the group's processes and structures.

Several steps can be taken to reduce the disruption that can be caused by worker termination in an ongoing group.

Steps to Reduce Disruption

- Group members should be told as early as possible when termination will occur.
- The reasons for termination should be shared with the group, and members should be encouraged to discuss their feelings frankly.
- Unfinished business should be completed.
- The new worker should be introduced to the group and, if possible, colead the group for a while with the terminating worker.

ENDING GROUP MEETINGS

Scheidel and Crowell (1979) list four generic worker tasks in ending group meetings: (1) closing the group's work, (2) arranging another meeting, (3) preparing a summary or report of the group's work, and (4) planning future group actions. In preparing to close, the worker should help the group keep to its agenda. The worker should ensure that all items of business and all members' concerns are given sufficient attention, but the group should not be allowed to spend too much time discussing one item of business or one member's concerns. To move the group along, the worker can do the following:

- Keep members focused on the topic of discussion
- Limit the time that each member has to discuss an issue
- Summarize what has been said
- Obtain closure on each issue or concern as it is discussed

In closing the group's work, the worker should avoid bringing up new issues, concerns, or items of business. According to Birnbaum and Cicchetti (2000), when conducting treatment groups, the ending of a session is a good time to engage in a process of reflection. This process entails (1) focusing on the session, (2) looking back on what transpired to see what it meant for members, (3) analyzing the significance of what occurred, and (4) examining what members can take away from the discussion and put into practice in their own lives. It is also a good time to identify unfinished work and to think about work that should be accomplished in future sessions (Birnbaum & Cicchetti, 2000). A discussion of what was accomplished and what needs to be done in future sessions lends continuity to the group. Enabling members to have a role in setting the agenda for future sessions and to give feedback about the group experience empowers them (Birnbaum, Mason, & Cicchetti, 2002). It provides an opportunity for members to express their satisfaction and sense of accomplishment with what occurred in the meeting, as well as any concerns they have about how the group is functioning. Birnbaum and Cicchetti (2000) point out that it is helpful for group leaders to invite members to raise discrepant points of view during ending discussions. Leaders who solicit discrepant viewpoints and feelings about how the group is going can help group members to express and resolve conflicts before they can become inflamed. At the same time, soliciting different points of view can help members to discuss group processes as well as the content of group meetings. In this way, members of the group take increasing responsibility for both the content and the process of future group meetings.

Despite efforts to structure the agenda to ensure that there is enough time to discuss important issues at the end of a meeting, Shulman (1999) points out that members occasionally raise "doorknob" issues just before ending. If consideration of these issues can be postponed, they are best handled during the next meeting when they can be given fuller consideration. When discussion of an important issue cannot be postponed, the worker should ask group members whether they prefer to continue the discussion for a brief period. If not, the issue may be taken up outside the group by the worker and any interested members.

In closing the group's work, the worker should also help members to resolve any remaining conflicts. Resolving conflicts helps members to work in harmony for the decisions reached by the group as a whole. In addition, the worker may want to discuss the strengths and weaknesses of the working relationship that has developed among members during the group meeting, particularly if the group will work together in the future.

During the ending minutes, the worker should help the group plan for future meetings. When considering whether to meet again, it is helpful to review and summarize the group's work. A summary of the group's activities during the meeting clarifies issues that have been resolved and points out issues that remain unresolved. A clear summary of the group's progress is a prerequisite for arranging another meeting. Summaries also remind members of the activities or tasks they have agreed to work on between meetings and help the worker become aware of items that should be included in the agenda for the next meeting.

If a group has completed action on a particular task, the final minutes can also be used to ensure that all members understand and agree to the oral or written information that will be presented at the conclusion of a group's work. Some task forces may prepare extensive written reports of their findings and conclusions. In these groups, it is not productive to prepare the report during the group meeting. The closing minutes can be used to formulate and highlight the major conclusions to be enumerated in the report, to assign members responsibility for preparing major sections of the report, and to develop a mechanism for obtaining approval from members before disseminating the report.

The endings of group meetings can also be used to plan future group actions. However, because planning action steps is time-consuming, plans are usually developed during the middle of a group meeting. At the ending of a meeting, plans are summarized, and members select (or are assigned) tasks to carry out.

The worker should help members maintain their motivation, commitment, and responsibility to implement and carry out the tasks they have agreed to complete between meetings. To help members maintain their motivation, the worker should praise members for their work in the group and for their willingness to commit themselves to tasks outside the meeting. The worker may also want to mention any benefits that will accrue to members for maintaining their commitment to the plans and activities they have agreed to complete.

ENDING THE GROUP AS A WHOLE

A variety of tasks are associated with ending a group as a whole:

- Learning from members
- Maintaining and generalizing change efforts
- Reducing group attraction and promoting the independent functioning of individual members
- Helping members deal with their feelings about ending
- Planning for the future
- Making referrals
- Evaluating the work of the group

With the exception of evaluating the work of the group, which is discussed in Chapter 14, the remaining portion of this chapter examines each ending task and the skills and techniques the worker can use to facilitate the effective ending of a group. Many of these tasks may be carried out simultaneously. The specific order in which each task is completed depends on the specific group the worker is leading.

Learning from Members

In the last session of a group, in addition to any formal evaluation procedures, workers should give members a chance to describe what it was like for them to be in the group. One way to do this is s final group go-round where each member gets a chance to say what they enjoyed about the group, what they learned, and how they will use what they learned in the future. Members should also be encouraged to talk about what they think could be improved in future groups. It is also helpful for all members to have a discussion of what they learned from one another, and to give individual members a chance to give some final feedback to others who they would especially like to thank for their contributions to the group. Workers can make a statement about what they learned from individual members, and what individual members contributed to the group. Workers should also give positive but realistic feedback about what each member accomplished and what each member should remember about their resiliency and strengths, and how they can use them in the future to work on any issues that arise after the group ends. If there are no follow-up group sessions planned, it can also be useful to schedule individual follow-up meetings with members a month or two after the group ends to get additional feedback from them about the group experience, to praise them for any changes in their lives that they have started or sustained, and to help them with any problems or issues that may have arisen since the last group meeting.

Maintaining and Generalizing Change Efforts

After treatment plans have been developed and carried out, workers should ensure that the changes that have been achieved are maintained and generalized to other important aspects of members' lives. Evaluations of results of therapeutic interventions suggest that positive changes are often difficult to maintain over time. For example, in an evaluation of two different group intervention programs for caregivers of the frail elderly, it was found that some of the positive changes found immediately after group intervention were not sustained at one year (Labrecque, Peak, & Toseland, 1992; Toseland, 1990).

Positive changes are even harder to maintain in group treatment programs that are focused on individuals with addictive disorders. For example, in an evaluation of a group treatment program for smokers, it was found that although more than 60 percent of members who attended the program initially stopped smoking, the cessation rate had dropped to 36 percent after three months (Toseland, Kabat, & Kemp, 1983). Results obtained for a variety of other addictive disorders, such as narcotics use, alcohol use, and overeating, show similarly high relapse rates (Chiauzzi, 1991; Marlatt, 1996; Marlatt & Barrett, 1994; Vaillant, 1995). Maintenance is also difficult to achieve in working with antisocial group members such as juvenile delinquents and in working with group members who have severe psychological disorders.

Both novice and experienced workers often mistakenly believe that changes in specific behaviors can be taken as a sign of generalized improvement in a member's level of functioning. These workers do little to ensure that specific behavior changes generalize to related, but untreated, behaviors. Results of a variety of different treatment programs have shown, however, that therapeutic changes occurring in specific behaviors do not always generalize to similar behaviors performed by a member in other contexts (Masters, Burish, Hollon, & Rimm, 1987). For example, an unassertive group member may learn to be assertive in a particular situation but may continue to be nonassertive in other situations.

Similarly, a parent may learn how to reduce a child's temper tantrums, but this success may not affect the parent's ability to help the child play cooperatively with other children.

Although some people seek group treatment only for changes in specific behaviors, most people enter group treatment with the expectation that there will be a generalized improvement in their life situations. Therefore, it is important for workers to help members generalize changes achieved in specific behaviors and performed in particular situations to related behaviors performed in other contexts.

With the notable exception of Rose (1989, 1998), little has been written about these topics in group work. Almost all the theoretical and clinical work on maintenance and generalization of change has come from the literature on behavior modification and learning theory. The literature suggests several things workers can do to help members maintain and generalize the changes they have achieved.

Maintaining and Generalizing Changes

- Helping members work on relevant situations
- Helping members develop confidence in their abilities
- Using a variety of different situations and settings in helping members learn new behaviors
- Using a variety of naturally occurring consequences
- Extending treatment through follow-up sessions
- Preventing setbacks in an unsympathetic environment
- Helping members solve problems independently by providing a framework for organizing data and solving problems that can be used in many different situations

Relevant Situations

To achieve long-lasting changes that will generalize to similar situations in members' lives, the concerns and issues worked on in the group should be a relevant and realistic sample of concerns and issues experienced by members in their daily lives. Sometimes members become distracted by issues that are not central to their concerns, a possible sign that the members are avoiding difficult issues and the changes they necessitate. The worker can help by drawing members' attention back to the central concerns that brought them together as a group.

In other cases, the situations discussed may be highly specific and individual. Although it is important to be as specific and concrete as possible when developing treatment plans, it is also important to ensure that situations that are relevant to all group members are included in the group's work so that members are prepared for situations they are likely to encounter in the future.

Although group meetings should provide a protected environment in which members receive support, encouragement, and understanding, the group should also be a place in which members can get honest feedback about how their behavior is likely to be seen outside the group. Members should be encouraged to try out new behaviors in the group, but they should not be misled into thinking they will receive the same level of support and encouragement for trying new behaviors outside the group. In short, although the group should provide a supportive and caring atmosphere in which to work, the group should help members to understand, cope with, and prepare for reactions likely to be experienced outside the group.

Helping Members Develop Confidence

Many treatment groups spend much time discussing members' problems and concerns as well as their inappropriate ways of handling situations. Although ventilating thoughts and feelings may be therapeutic, Lee (2001) points out that too much time in treatment is often spent on the negative aspects of members' problems and not enough time is spent empowering members and building their self-confidence. Lee suggests that emphasis on negative thoughts, feelings, and experiences reinforces the members' tendency to continue to express these problems outside the group.

As the group progresses, workers should encourage members to focus on adaptive alternatives to the problematic situations they are experiencing. If members dwell on poor performances and inhibiting thoughts in the group, they are less likely to feel confident about their abilities to cope with or resolve the problems they experience in their daily lives. Although it is not possible or desirable to avoid discussions of problems in treatment groups, workers should help members become more aware of their own abilities. Members should be encouraged to use their abilities and their resources to resolve the problematic situations that they encounter as they prepare for leaving the group. Program activities, role plays, and exercises are particularly useful in helping members to become more aware of their strengths and to build confidence in their ability to solve problems. This process, in turn, will help members gain confidence in their abilities to continue to function adaptively after they leave the group.

● **CASE EXAMPLE**   *An Adolescent Group*

A worker in a day treatment program asked members of her group to think about a situation when they were scared or anxious about their performance, but when they actually got into the situation it worked out well. The worker then asked each member, in turn, to describe the situation and what happened. After each member shared, the worker asked the group what they had learned from these experiences and how they could use them in the future to develop confidence in their abilities to get through difficult situations.

Using a Variety of Situations and Settings

Another aspect of maintaining and generalizing change is preparing members for different situations that may interfere with their abilities to maintain the changes they have made. Although preparations for maintaining changes are emphasized during ending-stage meetings, such activities should be given attention throughout members' participation in a group. Issues and concerns brought to group treatment are rarely, if ever, confined to one situation or setting in a member's life. A member who experiences communication difficulties, for example, often experiences them in many situations with different people. Therefore, it is helpful in treatment groups to have members practice responses with different members in a variety of situations. Because of the availability of group members who will respond differently from one another, group treatment is ideally suited for this purpose. Bandura's research (1977) confirms that the use of multiple models (group members) promotes generalization of treatment effects.

Easier situations should be role-played before more difficult situations. What constitutes an easy or a difficult situation varies from person to person, so the worker should assess each person's needs when developing a hierarchy of situations to work on in the group. Once a member demonstrates the ability to handle a variety of situations in the group, the member should be encouraged to get additional practice by trying new ways of behaving between meetings.

Program activities can also be used to simulate situations that may be encountered outside the group. For example, children referred to a group because they have difficulty playing with classmates can be encouraged to participate in team sports in which cooperative play is essential; long-term psychiatric patients may be encouraged to prepare and participate in a group dinner as a way of practicing skills that will help them when they are placed in a community residence.

Using Naturally Occurring Consequences

Although it is often difficult to make changes initially, changes are maintained and generalized by the resulting positive consequences. For example, although losing weight is initially uncomfortable, loss soon results in positive compliments from peers and feeling better about oneself. To maintain and generalize behavior changes, the worker should help group members experience the positive consequences of changes as soon as possible and maintain the positive consequences for as long as possible.

One method is to help members focus on positive rather than negative consequences.

● **CASE EXAMPLE** *An End Smoking Group*

Once members have decided to stop smoking they should be encouraged to seek out the reactions of family members and friends about their decision. Members might talk with these individuals and think to themselves about the benefits of quitting. They might talk and think about: (1) the savings that they will accrue related to the cost of not buying cigarettes, (2) their breath will no longer smell like stale cigarettes, (3) their clothes, their home and their car will no longer smell like cigarette smoke, (4) food will taste better, (5) they will have increased lung capacity and greater vitality and endurance while walking and climbing stairs, (6) they will no longer live in smoke-filled rooms with the dangers of second-hand smoke, and (7) they may feel better and live longer. Members should be encouraged to replace urges to smoke with thoughts of the previously mentioned soon-to-be expected positive effects of smoking. With members' permission, the worker can also contact significant others in members' lives and ask them to continue to reinforce the ex-smoker's resolve not to smoke after the group ends. The worker can also discuss with members the possibility of setbacks and relapse and how to return to being a non-smoker.

Another way to enhance naturally occurring contingencies is to help members modify environmental consequences so that behavior change is more readily maintained and generalized. For example, a buddy system may be established so that group members receive positive feedback for changes between group sessions. Group members may be asked to modify friendship patterns, social activities, or their home environment in ways that provide positive consequences for changes they have made through their efforts in the group. By enhancing and highlighting naturally occurring positive consequences and by reducing negative consequences, initial changes can be maintained and generalized.

Follow-Up Sessions

Another way to help ensure that treatment results are maintained and generalized is to provide members the opportunity to meet together for follow-up sessions after the completion of a formal group treatment program. For example, a time-limited, outpatient psychotherapy group might meet for 12 weekly sessions and then for six follow-up sessions at one-month intervals. After this time, two quarterly meetings during the rest of the year might complete the treatment contract.

Follow-up sessions reinforce members' commitment to maintaining changes. They remind members of the changes that have taken place in their lives since they began treatment. Members can share similar experiences about their difficulties in maintaining changes and trying to generalize changes to new situations and new life experiences.

Follow-up sessions are generally not used to introduce members to new material. Instead, they are used as an opportunity for members to share their experiences since the previous meeting. Members should be encouraged to discuss new problem situations they have encountered and to describe how they have handled these situations. The emphasis should be on helping members identify the coping skills they have developed to maintain changes achieved during treatment.

Follow-up sessions are particularly helpful for members who have difficulty maintaining treatment gains. Members can discuss the circumstances surrounding particular relapses and consult the group worker and other members about how to best handle these occurrences. The additional support provided by follow-up sessions is often sufficient to help members overcome brief relapses that might otherwise turn into treatment failures.

The popularity of self-help groups can, in part, be attributed to the flexible, open-ended, long-term membership that is encouraged in many of these groups. Self-help groups often have a small group of members who regularly attend meetings, along with many other members who attend as needed (Toseland & Hacker, 1982). For self-help group participants who have attended sessions regularly in the past, occasional attendance at future meetings can maintain treatment gains and gradually reduce dependency on the group.

Preventing Setbacks in Unsympathetic Environments

Even when careful attention has been given to the environment that a member faces outside the group, the support, trust, and sharing found in well-functioning treatment groups is rarely duplicated in the members' home or community environments. Members should be prepared to face possible setbacks in the unsympathetic environment they are likely to experience outside the group. Rose (1989) suggests that the experiences of the worker in leading previous groups, as well as the experiences of former group members, are useful in developing vignettes that describe realistic and typical situations group members are likely to encounter outside the group. During the final few group sessions, members should discuss how to respond to such situations and practice responses with one another by using modeling, role play, rehearsal, and coaching.

Because members are likely to experience situations that threaten their treatment gains soon after changes are initiated, members should be encouraged to describe such situations in the group sessions. In this way, all group members become exposed to a variety of situations and reactions to changes, and they can learn to handle reactions before the situations occur in their own lives. Meichenbaum (1977), for example, reported that a stress inoculation treatment program in which members were taught to anticipate negative reactions and ways to cope with the reactions was effective in helping members maintain treatment gains.

Members may encounter difficult situations any time of the day or night. Because the group worker may not be available to members at those times, the worker should inform members about how to contact on-call workers, emergency hot lines, and other 24-hour services.

The difficulty of maintaining changes among members with drug, alcohol, and other addictive behavior problems suggests a need for intensive and extensive treatment. One way to augment group treatment with a professional worker is to link members to self-help groups. Alcoholics Anonymous groups, for example, often meet each evening, or at least several times each week, and can provide members with an alternative to spending their evenings in a neighborhood bar or drinking alone at home. These groups also encourage recovering alcoholics to form close relationships with new members, which provides new members with models of sobriety and encourages the development of a network of supportive relationships. Similarly, organizations such as Recovery, Inc., Parents without Partners, Parents Anonymous, and Gamblers Anonymous help members with other types of problems and concerns to become involved with a network of people to whom they can turn at particularly difficult times.

Members of task groups can also benefit from preparing for an unsympathetic environment. Plans, reports, and other products of a task group's work may encounter resistance as they are considered by others outside the group. Resistance is especially likely when the products of a task group are controversial or have negative implications for a particular program, an entire organization, or a social service delivery system. Also, resistance is more likely to be encountered when proposals must go through several levels of review before they are approved (Brager & Holloway, 1978). Therefore, it is important for task group members to anticipate resistance to implementing the group's work and to plan strategies to counteract the resistance.

Helping Members Solve Problems Independentlys

No matter how many different situations are discussed and practiced within a group, it is not possible to cover the full range of situations that members may experience outside a group. Therefore, during the group, members should learn how to solve their own problems independently. This gradually lessens the need for continued treatment. Teaching problem-solving skills should begin as early as possible in the group experience and be given particular emphasis in the last few meetings.

Throughout the group treatment process, workers can support independent functioning by building members' confidence in their existing coping skills and by helping members develop and rely on new coping skills. Workers should also teach members the principles underlying the intervention methods used in the group. Workers sometimes fail to teach members the underlying therapeutic principles of an intervention because they think professional knowledge should not be shared with clients, that group members may not be able to understand therapeutic principles, or that members may misuse the information they receive. Most group members who enter treatment voluntarily are eager to learn more about ways to cope with their concerns. For example, having members of an assertion-training group read *Your Perfect Right* (Alberti & Emmons, 2001), having members of a parent-training group read *Parents Are Teachers* (Becker, 1971), or having members of a weight-loss group read *Slim Chance in a Fat World* (Stuart & Davis, 1972) helps them to learn basic principles that they can use as they encounter situations not discussed in the group.

Some treatment approaches, such as Eric Berne's *transactional analysis* (Berne, 1961) and Albert Ellis' *rational-emotive therapy* (Ellis, 1962, 1992), encourage workers to help members understand the basic principles underlying their treatment approaches. Workers who use other treatment approaches should also consider spending time teaching members the basic principles underlying therapeutic interventions. When teaching members, workers should translate technical terms into jargon-free explanations, especially if members use English as a second language.

Having members summarize what they have learned in the group and deduce general principles from the summaries are other effective ways to help members see how principles can be applied to other situations. For example, in summarizing what they have learned, members of a couples' group became aware of general principles regarding communication, such as maintaining eye contact to show that they are listening, summarizing core content of messages to ensure understanding, and using "I" messages to communicate their feelings and thoughts.

Reducing Group Attraction

In addition to helping members maintain and generalize the changes they have made in a group, the ending stage should help members become less dependent on the group. This goal can be achieved by helping members rely on their own skills and resources as well as on sources of support outside the group. Planning for termination should begin with workers' awareness of their own feelings about terminating with individual members and with the group as a whole. Particularly in support groups and therapy groups, it is not uncommon for workers to become emotionally attached to individual members or to the group as a whole. Workers should be careful not to foster dependence. They should carefully assess whether they are being overly protective of members or covertly or overtly undermining members' efforts to function without the group. Supervision can be useful in helping workers examine their feelings about terminating.

To ensure that members are prepared for ending, it is good practice to begin discussions of termination at least four sessions before the planned termination date. Members should be fully involved in planning for termination. Program activities can be used effectively at the end of a group to help members prepare for termination (Henry, 1992; Mayadas & Glasser, 1981; Wayne & Avery, 1979). Workers should describe the ideas they have about program activities for ending the group, solicit members' feedback, and ask for additional suggestions. Appropriate program activities for ending a group include the following principles.

Principles for Program Activities

- Demonstrate or encourage reflection about the skills members have learned in the group
- Encourage members to express their feelings about the group and each other
- Focus on future activities
- Encourage participation in activities outside of the group

For example, getting together for a dinner is a program activity that is commonly used at the ending of a group. Planning for a dinner encourages both individual and group-oriented participation. During the dinner, members often discuss the things they have learned in the group, their feelings about ending, and their plans for the future.

Endings are often marked by ceremonies. Program activities, such as having a party or a potluck dinner, awarding certificates of merit, or having each member say or write something special about other members, can be viewed as ceremonies that signify the end of the group. Barlow, Blythe, and Edmonds (1999) have developed a series of exercises that can be done in the last meetings of a group. These include exercises that are focused on ending the group on a positive note, celebrating the ending of a group, summarizing progress, reflecting on what has been accomplished, and thinking about the future. Used creatively, ceremonies can also help to maintain and generalize changes made by members. One example of the creative use of ceremonies and program activities is illustrated in the following case.

● **CASE EXAMPLE** *Maintaining Changes*

In the next-to-last session of a weight-loss group, members were asked to write themselves two letters, each containing (1) their feelings about being overweight, (2) how good it felt to be losing weight, and (3) a reiteration of their commitment to continue losing weight. The self-addressed letters were mailed by the worker after the group had ended at three-week intervals as a reminder to members of their commitment to losing weight and maintaining weight losses. In the last session of the group, the worker arranged for members to meet at a local restaurant and participate in cooking a meal that reinforced useful nutritional knowledge members had learned from participating in the group. During the dinner, members were asked to evaluate the overall group and discuss how they would modify their eating behaviors in the future.

Group attraction can be reduced in other ways. Members can be encouraged to summarize their accomplishments and discuss why they no longer need the group. Meetings can be scheduled less frequently or for shorter periods of time to reduce the importance of the group for members. Workers can encourage members to become involved in outside activities that compete with the group for members' time and energy. Such activities also can support members and help them maintain changes.

Feelings about Ending

The feelings that members and workers have about ending are related to the relationships that have developed in the group. Feelings about ending are also affected by whether the group is planned to be time limited or open ended, how long the group meets, the nature of the group's work (e.g., primarily task or socioemotional), the intensity of the relationships that develop among members, and the extent to which the ending is associated with a sense of progress, achievement, or graduation (Germain & Gitterman, 1996). After examining reactions to termination, Fortune and colleagues (Fortune, 1987; Fortune, Pearlingi, & Rochelle, 1992) concluded that the strongest reactions were positive affect, positive flight to constructive outside activities, and objective evaluations of treatment goals and processes.

Many positive feelings can result from a skillfully facilitated group ending.

Positive Feelings About Ending

- A feeling of empowerment and potency as members realize they are capable of accomplishing goals
- A feeling of independence resulting from being in greater control of their own lives
- A sense of satisfaction and pride in successfully completing the group experience

- A feeling of usefulness resulting from helping other members during group interaction
- A feeling of confidence that problems can be coped with or solved

At the same time, however, members may experience negative feelings about the ending of a group. A common reaction is denial (Levine, 1979). Not wanting to show that they will miss the worker or others in the group, members sometimes ignore workers' attempts to prepare them for ending by changing the topic of discussion or by indicating that they are looking forward to ending. Other common reactions are feelings of disappointment, powerlessness, abandonment, or rejection (Brabender & Fallon, 1996). Members may act out these feelings by becoming angry or hostile. In other cases, they may engage in regressive behavior that exhibits the symptoms or problems they had when they first entered the group (Malekoff, 1997). Other reactions include emotional or psychological clinging to the worker, acting out, and devaluing the group experience or the skill of the worker (Levinson, 1977; Malekoff, 1997).

More often, members simply wish they could continue with the warm, supportive relationships they have found in the group. Therefore, they may experience a sense of loss and accompanying sadness at the ending of the group. Members may also question their ability to maintain changes without the help of the group.

As mentioned earlier, workers are not immune to reactions to ending a group. In a study of practitioners' reactions to termination of individual treatment, Fortune, Pearlingi, and Rochelle (1992) report that practitioners have strong reactions to termination. Some of these reactions follow.

Reactions to Termination

- Pride and accomplishment in the client's success
- Pride in their own therapeutic skill
- A renewed sense of therapeutic process
- Sadness, sense of loss, or ambivalence about no longer working with the client
- Doubt or disappointment about the client's progress or ability to function independently
- A re-experiencing of their own losses
- Relief, doubt, or guilt about their therapeutic effectiveness

Workers should be aware of their own reactions to ending to fully appreciate the difficulties that members may be experiencing. If workers are not aware of their own feelings, they may withdraw emotionally or they may encourage the dependence of members and prolong treatment beyond what is needed. Workers also may want to share their reactions as a way of helping members identify and express their own feelings and reactions.

It is helpful to begin termination several meetings before the end of the group. As members begin to react to ending, the worker can point out that conflicting or ambivalent feelings during this stage are common. Members should be encouraged to discuss their conflicting and ambivalent feelings.

Workers can help members with their negative emotional and behavioral reactions to ending by developing increased awareness of the connection between their feelings and behaviors and the termination process. It is also helpful to encourage members to discuss the coping abilities and other gains they have achieved as a result of being in the group. The worker can prepare members for ending by clarifying what the role of the worker and the sponsoring agency will be in helping members maintain gains after the group ends.

Planning for the Future

In time-limited groups, some members may wish to contract for additional services. When considering new services, the worker should help members clarify (1) their continuing needs, (2) the goals they hope to achieve, (3) the duration of the new service period, and (4) any appropriate modifications of the original contract. Recontracting should occur when there is a clear need for additional services and when members are highly motivated to achieve additional goals or to continue work on original goals that they have only partially completed. Occasionally, all members of a group may express interest in continuing to meet. In such cases, the worker may recontract for additional meetings with all members or may encourage members to meet on their own without the worker.

When workers encourage members to continue to meet on their own, they are participating in the development of a self-help group. The worker helps groups continue to meet by developing natural leadership and by helping with any resources that may be needed (Toseland & Coppola, 1985). Rather than total independence, many new self-help groups prefer continuing contact, guidance, and leadership from the worker until the new group has been firmly established. Many existing self-help groups have been started by professional workers in this manner (Toseland & Hacker, 1982). The worker can continue to assist self-help groups after they have developed by (1) providing material support to maintain the group, (2) referring clients to the group, and (3) acting as a consultant to the group.

In rare instances, the members of a group may wish to continue meeting because they are unable to terminate the group in a positive and responsible fashion. The group may develop a culture that supports members' dependency rather than preparing them for independent functioning in the environment outside the group. When this occurs, the worker should explore the situation with the group and, in a supportive manner, help the members end the group experience by using activities as discussed in this chapter. Klein (1972) has referred to this process as a worker's skill in letting go of the group.

Sometimes the ending of a group may result in no further contact with members. However, workers are rarely sure that members will not need services in the future. Changing life situations, new crises, or relapses may cause members to seek help again. The worker should discuss how members can seek additional services if they are needed. In some agencies, the worker may explain that he or she has an open-door policy, so that members who need additional services can contact the worker directly. In other agencies, the policy may be for former clients to apply for services in the same manner that new clients apply. Taking this step clarifies the position of the worker and the agency with regard to how members can obtain any additional services that may be needed.

The worker should plan for the future with each member. Plans should include the support systems and resources that will be available after the group ends. Workers should also encourage members to use their own skills, resources, and strengths to meet their needs by expressing confidence in members' abilities, encouraging them to try new skills outside the group, and repeating successful skill-building activities and role plays so members develop feelings of mastery and self-confidence.

In some situations, preparation for the future may involve planning with others for continuing treatment for members. For example, in preparing for the ending of the children's group, the worker should contact the children's parents to review each child's progress and to plan for additional services. In groups in which members are participating in other agency services such as individual counseling, the worker should contact the member's case manager or primary worker to evaluate the member's progress in the group and to plan for additional services. Similarly, in residential and inpatient settings, the ending of a group may not signify the end of service. The worker should meet with other staff, perhaps in a case conference or team meeting, to report progress and to plan for the future needs of members.

Members who prematurely terminate from groups should not be forgotten when plans for future service needs are made. Without follow-up contact, dropouts may feel abandoned. Their failure to continue with a particular group may signify to them that their situation is hopeless. Therefore, dropouts from treatment should be contacted whenever possible. One of the primary objectives of a follow-up contact is to motivate persons who terminate prematurely to seek further treatment if it is needed. The worker can inquire about difficulties the former members may be having in continuing to attend group meetings, and may suggest ways to overcome these impediments. During this process, the worker should identify any needs that former group members have for continuing service and refer them to appropriate resources and services.

Making Referrals

During the ending stage of group work, workers frequently connect members to other services or resources. In some cases, members may be transferred to workers in the same agency. In other cases, referrals may be made to workers in other agencies.

A referral should be made only after the worker and the member have appraised the member's need for additional services or resources. If the member is motivated to seek additional services, the referral can proceed. If the member is not motivated to seek additional services, but the worker's assessment suggests that additional services may be beneficial, the worker should proceed by helping the member explore reasons for resistance.

Whenever possible, the member should be helped to use informal, natural helping systems. If these types of systems are unavailable or are judged to be inadequate, the member should be referred to professional helping resources. Before making a referral, the worker should discuss the reasons for the referral with the member and answer any questions the member has. It is often helpful to find out whether the member has had any prior contact with the referral source or has heard anything about the source. Members' impressions and previous experiences with particular referral sources can be influential in determining whether members will follow through and use the resources to which they are referred.

In preparing to make effective referrals, workers should become familiar with available community resources. They should also get to know a particular contact person in frequently used referral sources. It is also helpful to be familiar with basic information about referral sources to share with members who are being referred, such as information about eligibility requirements, the waiting time for service, the business hours of the agency, and the type of service provided. Such information will prepare the member for what to expect when contacting the referral source and will avoid members' developing expectations that will not be met. Because it may be difficult for workers to be familiar with all community resources that are available in an area, agencies should maintain up-to-date files with basic information about such resources and services.

When making a referral, the worker should write the name of the agency, the contact person, and the agency's address on a card to give to the member. In some cases, referral sources may have forms that have to be filled out before a member can be seen. Often, release forms need to be signed by the member so that information in a member's file can be sent to the referral source. Information should never be sent without a signed release form from the member. Because many people never reach the resources or services to which they were referred (Craig, Huffine, & Brooks, 1974; Weissman, 1976), it is helpful for the worker to use the following referral principles.

Referral Principles

- Call the contact person while the member is with the leader
- Emphasize that the member is expected at the referral source
- Provide instructions for getting to the referral source
- Assist with transportation if necessary
- Check to make sure that disabilities or other obstacles do not prevent a successful referral
- Check to ensure that the member reached the referral source and received the needed information or services

Members also should be instructed to contact the worker if they fail to get what they need from the referral sources. Members who are severely impaired may need help in getting to referral sources. The worker, a volunteer, or a case aide may have to accompany the member during the first visit. A referral may fail for a number of reasons.

Failure of Referrals

- The referral source has had a change in policy; for example, eligibility requirements may have become more stringent.
- The member lacks motivation or desire.
- The member lacks the skill necessary to obtain the needed resources.
- The worker has given the member incorrect information or insufficient help to contact the referral source.

Follow-up contacts allow workers to assess why members did not obtain needed services or resources. They also allow workers to plan with members about how to obtain needed resources and services in the future.

SUMMARY

The ending stage is a critical time in the life of a group. During the ending stage, the work of the group is consolidated and lasting impressions are made about the efficacy of the entire group experience. Endings can either be planned or unplanned. Unfortunately, in many voluntary groups, unplanned terminations are fairly common. This chapter makes suggestions about how to facilitate planned endings and what to do when members terminate before the planned ending of a group.

Procedures for facilitating endings vary, depending on the type of group being led. In task groups and treatment groups in which members have not been encouraged to self-disclose or form supportive relationships, endings are less emotionally charged than are endings in groups in which considerable self-disclosure has taken place and in which members depend on one another for help with their personal concerns and problems. Other variations in group endings depend on whether the group has an open or closed membership policy, is short-term or long-term, and is attractive or unattractive to its members.

Major tasks in ending a meeting of a group include (1) closing the work, (2) arranging another meeting, (3) preparing a summary or a report of the group's work, and (4) planning for future group actions. Major tasks in ending the group as a whole include (1) maintaining and generalizing change efforts, (2) evaluating the work of the group, (3) reducing group attraction and promoting independent member functioning, (4) helping members with their feelings about ending, (5) planning for the future, and (6) making effective referrals. This chapter examines the skills and strategies needed to carry out each of these tasks.

● CASE EXAMPLE

As the facilitator of a staff support group for hospice workers, Carla was familiar with the needs of the group members. She had been hired two years ago to conduct weekly sessions of the group so that the staff could have an opportunity to discuss their feelings and the stress associated with working with the terminally ill. But Carla faced a new challenge when Nick, the new executive director, informed her that the group would have to be discontinued because of cost constraints. Although Nick had insisted that she give the group only one week's notice before it ended, Carla had been able to negotiate for three more group sessions.

Carla pondered the group's situation and wondered how the members would take the news. As hospice workers, the group members faced endings with their clients every day. Now, the group members would have to deal with the ending of the group and the dissolution of an important support system. Although group members had achieved high levels of cohesiveness and mutual aid in the group, Carla feared that ending the group would detrimentally affect staff morale and the quality of their work.

Carla outlined some of the goals she hoped to accomplish in the next three sessions. She wanted to present the news about discontinuing the group in as positive a way as possible.

Members would need time to adjust to the idea of ending the group, so she planned on telling the group during the next meeting. She also wanted to help members maintain some of the gains they had accomplished through the group, particularly those that helped them deal with the stress of their work. At the same time, she wanted to help members reduce their reliance on the group for formal support and find sources of support outside of the group. Finally, she hoped that the members would be able to spend time evaluating the effectiveness of the group. These were formidable goals for the group's last sessions.

The ending of the group was announced at the next meeting. Carla took a supportive but matter-of-fact approach to making the announcement. Despite her own feelings about the actions of the new executive director, she refrained from blaming him for ending the group. By doing this she hoped to redirect some of the members' energies into accomplishing as much as they could in the next three sessions. However, members spent a good deal of time expressing strong feelings about ending the group. Several were angry and others expressed a sense of sadness and loss. Some members wondered how they would be able to deal with the stress of their jobs without the support of the group. Carla allowed a good deal of time for members to ventilate.

As members came to accept the ending of the group, Carla made some suggestions about how to proceed. She challenged group members to discuss how the group had helped them. Despite some early resistance, members were able to discuss the benefits they had obtained by participating in the group. Several were quite articulate about how, as a result of their group participation, they had accomplished personal changes that helped them deal with the emotional impact of their work. Carla used the discussions to encourage members to maintain these changes after the group ended. She then suggested that members come to the next group session prepared to discuss how they could get personal and emotional support from sources outside the group. Members accepted this homework assignment and the session ended.

During the next session, members began by revisiting their reactions to the ending of the group. Members expressed feelings of anger, loss, grief, and frustration. Carla again allowed them time to ventilate and work through these feelings. She pointed out that in a symbolic way, the ending of the group would mirror the dying, death, and grief process so familiar to the members in their everyday work at the hospice. She observed that members needed time to work through their own sense of loss over ending the group.

Later in the session, Carla reviewed each member's suggestions about how to find support outside of the group. As a result of this discussion, the group decided to develop a buddy system in place of the weekly group. Relying on this system, members could systematically exchange feelings and experiences related to their work. Carla suggested that the support system would allow members to become more independent from the group and more focused on other sources of support. She emphasized that the development of the buddy system demonstrated members' ability to create a new way to obtain support. Then, as the meeting ended, she reviewed and reinforced some of the capacities and skills members had demonstrated during previous group sessions when describing how they coped with emotionally challenging patient care situations.

Carla was totally surprised by the group's last meeting. She had expected that the beginning of the last session would be somber because of the strong emotional bonds among members and the feelings they had expressed about ending. On her arrival, however, she was greeted with a chocolate cake, refreshments, and a nicely wrapped present from the group. Members expressed their gratitude to Carla for her strong leadership and support. Carla gratefully accepted the members' comments and asked if the group could finish its formal discussions and then move on to its party.

Members mentioned that they were more resigned to ending the group. They expressed fewer feelings of anger and more feelings of sadness during this last session. Members also discussed their favorite memories of the group and how the group had benefited them. Finally, Carla asked members to evaluate the effectiveness of the group by completing a short questionnaire with open-ended questions. After completing the questionnaire, members discussed plans for the future. Although the last session went well, it was a bittersweet experience.

chapter 14

Evaluation

Evaluation is the process of obtaining information about the effects of a single intervention or the effect of the total group experience. Workers can use informal or formal measures to obtain such information. In conducting an informal evaluation, a worker might ask the members of a group to evaluate how the group is progressing. To complete a formal evaluation, a worker might collect information systematically using preplanned measurement devices before, during, or after the group has met. In either case, the worker uses the information to evaluate the group. This chapter explores many ways to obtain information about a group and guides the worker in deciding what evaluation methods will be most useful in various situations.

THE PRACTITIONER'S DILEMMA

Increasingly in social work and allied disciplines, there has been a push toward accountability and empirically validated practice. Workers have been urged to become practitioner-researchers to improve their work as they practice (Thomas, 1990). The push for evaluating practice has occurred even though group workers sometimes fail to keep adequate records, let alone perform systematic evaluations of their practice.

The dilemma for many practicing group workers is that other demands of practice seem to be more pressing than evaluations, which require valuable time and energy. Further, many practitioners find it difficult to understand the logic of evaluation methods or their day-to-day usefulness. It has been proposed that practitioners (1) leave research to researchers, (2) become consumers of research, and (3) concentrate on developing experience and expertise as group leaders (Trotzer, 1999). However, Trotzer and most others urge group workers to evaluate their own practice whenever possible. Recently, the focus has been on developing evidence-based practice guidelines that describe the most effective interventions for particular problems (Howard & Jenson, 2003; Roberts & Yeager, 2004; Rosen & Proctor, 2003). For example, practice guidelines for the treatment of depression indicate that the most effective method for treating it is a combination of pharmacotherapy and psychotherapy (American Psychiatric Association, 2002).

The push toward accountability and empirically validated group work practice has made a difference. In a review of the literature in 1986, Feldman (1986) found that compared with a review completed 20 years before (Silverman, 1966), the number of research studies had more than doubled. However, Feldman noted that the number of research studies was still small and that much needed to be done before group workers could claim that their practice is well grounded in scientific research and evidenced-based practice. There is hope that this will occur because a more recent review of some selected journals by Gant (2004) has shown that social work group research has continued to expand, and research reviews in an edited book by Wheelan (2005) that contains group research from a variety of disciplines suggests that evidenced-based group work practice is increasing. For reviews of the history of group research, see the special issue of *Group Dynamics, Theory, Research and Practice* edited by Forsyth (2000), Barlow, Burlingame, and Fuhriman (2000), Forsyth and Burnette (2005), and Wheelan (2005).

WHY EVALUATE? THE GROUP WORKER'S VIEW

When evaluating their work with a particular group, workers should consider the resources they have available for conducting an evaluation. For example, it is important to assess the encouragement they will receive from their agency for evaluating their own practice. It is also important to consider the time they have available for an evaluation. Matching resources and available time with an appropriate method for evaluating their practice is essential.

Reasons for Conducting Evaluations

Workers' reasons for wanting information about a group depend on how they believe they can use the information. Some of the benefits of evaluation for group workers are presented here.

Benefits of Evaluations

- Evaluations can satisfy workers' curiosity and professional concerns about the effects of specific interventions they perform while working with a group.
- Information from evaluations can help workers improve their leadership skills.
- Evaluations can demonstrate the usefulness of a specific group or a specific group work method to an agency, a funding source, or society.
- Workers can assess the progress of group members and see whether the group is accomplishing agreed-on purposes.
- Evaluations allow group members and others who may be affected to express their satisfactions and dissatisfactions with a group.
- Workers can gather knowledge that can be shared with others who are using group methods for similar purposes and in similar situations.
- Workers can systematize and make overt the covert hypothesis-generating and hypothesis-testing processes they routinely engage in as they practice.
- Evaluations can examine the cost-effectiveness of group work services.

Organizational Encouragement and Support

To evaluate their practice with a group, workers should begin by assessing the willingness of the organization for whom they work to provide the resources to conduct an evaluation. Some organizations do little or nothing to encourage evaluations and may even penalize the worker for attempting one. Agency norms, peer pressure, or administrative directions may suggest to workers that other tasks are more important than evaluating their practice. In other cases, high caseloads may inhibit workers' abilities to evaluate their practice.

Without active encouragement by an organization's administrators, workers are left to rely on their own motivations for evaluating their work with a group. Organizations can increase workers' opportunities for evaluation by including evaluation tasks as a part of workers' practice responsibilities, by providing the time for evaluations, and by encouraging workers to discuss evaluations during regularly scheduled staff meetings. Rather than requiring workers to fill out forms and records that they do not use and often do not see again after administrative processing, organizations can instead help by developing and implementing information systems that can be used by workers to evaluate their practice. A well-designed information and evaluation system can provide feedback for group work practitioners as well as for agency administrators.

Time Considerations

Workers should consider how much time they have available to conduct an evaluation. Most workers collect some information about the groups they lead, and this information can often be the basis for an evaluation if it is collected appropriately. Little additional time is needed for evaluation beyond the time necessary to make modifications in the original data-collection system.

In other situations, workers may want information that is not routinely collected. They should estimate the amount of time it will take them to collect, process, and analyze the additional information. They can then compare the time needed for the evaluation with the time they have available and decide whether the evaluation is feasible.

When workers have valid reasons for evaluating their practice, they may be able to persuade their organization to allow them sufficient time to conduct the evaluation, particularly when a worker is developing a new, innovative program to achieve the goals the organization has set as a priority for service delivery.

Selecting an Evaluation Method

After determining how much time is available for an evaluation, workers should consider how to match their information needs and available time to an appropriate evaluation method. This chapter reviews the major types of evaluations. Each evaluation method is discussed in terms of its strengths and weaknesses, time requirements, and flexibility.

Workers must also decide what data-collection instruments they will use in conjunction with a particular evaluation method. The major types of data-collection instruments used by group workers follow.

Data Collection Instruments

- Progress notes
- Self-reports or personal interview data from workers, members, and observers

- Questionnaires
- Analysis of reports or other products of a group's work
- Review of audiotapes and videotapes of group meetings
- Observational coding schemes
- Role play or in vivo performance tests
- Reliable and valid scales

These data-collection instruments can be used with any of the major types of evaluation methods. Some measures, however, are frequently associated with one type of evaluation. For example, progress notes are often used in monitoring evaluation methods; reliable and valid scales are more frequently used in effectiveness and efficiency evaluations. As each type of evaluation method is reviewed, the methods of collecting data that are often associated with each method are described.

EVALUATION METHODS

Workers can use four broad types of evaluation methods to obtain data: evaluations for (1) planning a group, (2) monitoring a group, (3) developing a group, and (4) testing the effectiveness and efficiency of group outcomes. Workers can use any of the evaluation methods to obtain information about the process or the outcome of a group. Process evaluations focus on the interaction in a group; properties of a group such as cohesion, norms, roles, and communication patterns; how the group is being conducted; or other aspects of the functioning of a group. Outcome evaluations focus on the products or tasks achieved by individual members or the group as a whole.

Regardless of the type of evaluation employed or whether the evaluation focuses on processes or outcomes, workers should be able to use evaluations to receive feedback about their practice. Instead of viewing practice evaluations as useless administrative requirements, workers should see them as a way to help them become more effective, and as a way to develop new knowledge that can be shared with other group workers.

EVALUATIONS FOR PLANNING A GROUP

Evaluations used for planning a group are seldom mentioned in the group work literature. This section discusses two important evaluation methods for planning: (1) obtaining program information, technical data, and materials for specific groups that the worker is planning to lead and (2) conducting needs assessments to determine the feasibility of organizing a proposed group.

Obtaining Program Information

The worker can often benefit from information about methods previously used in working with similar groups. Workers may be able to obtain some information from colleagues or from workers in other agencies in which similar groups have been conducted. Workers may also find it useful to utilize the sources listed here.

Ways to Obtain Program Information

- Examine records from previous groups that focused on similar concerns
- Attend workshops and conferences where group workers share recent developments in the field
- Review relevant journals[1] and books using computerized or manual search procedures
- Read the minutes of previous group meetings
- Read the bylaws of the sponsoring organization
- Read any operating procedures that may exist from previous meetings of the task group
- Be clear about the charges and responsibilities of the group
- Obtain information about how similar objectives and goals were accomplished in other organizations and by other task groups
- Attend meetings of groups working on similar concerns

Library literature searches have been made much easier and much less time-consuming in recent years by the availability of online CD-ROM computerized databases. Two databases that are particularly relevant to social group workers are Social Work Abstracts Plus and PSYCLIT (psychology). Also, group workers in health settings may find MEDLINE (medicine) useful; group workers in school settings may find ERIC (education) useful; and group workers in forensic settings may find NCJRS (National Criminal Justice Reference Service) useful. There are also specialized bibliographies that can be helpful in developing new group work services. For example, John Ramey (1999) has prepared a comprehensive bibliography of social groups, which is updated periodically and can be found at the Association For the Advancement of Social Work With Groups website, www.aaswg.org.

Needs Assessment

Workers might also find it useful to have some information about potential members of a proposed group as illustrated in the following case. This information might include (1) potential members' willingness to attend the group, (2) their motivations for attending, and (3) their capabilities for helping the group achieve its purposes. In treatment groups, workers may want to conduct a needs assessment by asking other workers whether clients with whom they work might be appropriate for the group or whether workers have received requests for a particular group service they have been unable to meet.

---

[1]Some of the most important journals that focus on specific groups and specific group work methods are *The Group, Group and Organization Management, International Journal of Group Psychotherapy, Journal for Specialists in Group Work, Small Group Research,* and *Social Work with Groups.*

● **CASE EXAMPLE** *Evaluating the Need for a Group*

In order to assess the need for a support group for teen parents, the worker began by consulting existing research from several government organizations, including the local Department of Health and the state Department of Children and Family Services. Data suggested that the incidence and prevalence of teen parenting was particularly high in the local community. The worker also conducted "key informant" interviews with community leaders and executive directors of several local social service organizations. Information obtained during the interviews confirmed the results found in the initial analysis of existing data. In addition, several interviewees suggested that they would be interested in referring potential members to the group; the worker sent them copies of a survey designed to obtain information about the number of potential referrals to the group and any other information about the interests and motivation of potential members.

Data from community needs assessments designed for multiple purposes can be useful in obtaining information about potential group members. Contacting people or organizations in the community may also provide access to potential members. When workers have identified the clients, they can contact them directly by a personal interview, a telephone call, or a letter. Toseland (1981) has described methods of reaching out to clients in more detail.

In some task groups, membership may result from elections, appointments, or the person's position in an organization. A planning evaluation can familiarize a worker with rules and regulations governing a task group's composition and operation. Planning evaluations can also help a worker collect information and assess the potential contributions that members can make in helping the group achieve its objectives (Rothman, 1974). For more information about conducting planning evaluations, see Rossi, Freeman, and Lipsey (1999).

EVALUATIONS FOR MONITORING A GROUP

Monitoring refers to keeping track of the progress of group members and group processes. Monitoring is discussed in Chapter 8 as an assessment device, but it can also be used to evaluate group work practice. Monitoring methods have received more attention in the group work literature than has any other type of evaluation method. Monitoring is the least demanding and most flexible of the evaluation procedures described in this chapter. It can be useful for obtaining information for process or outcome evaluations.

Monitoring Methods

The first step in the monitoring process is to decide what information to collect. For example, persons who work with remedial groups designed for clients with psychological disorders may be interested in monitoring changes in individual members over the course of the group on the five axes presented in the *Diagnostic and Statistical Manual of Mental*

Disorders (American Psychiatric Association, 2000). A worker asked to lead an interdepartmental committee of a large public welfare agency may be interested in monitoring the extent to which individual committee members complete assigned tasks.

Whatever information group workers decide to collect, they must be clear about how they define it so it can be monitored with appropriate measures. Concepts that are ambiguous, obscure, or unspecified cannot be measured accurately.

The next step in monitoring is to decide how the needed information will be collected. Data can be collected by administering questionnaires; asking for verbal feedback about the group; or by recording information about the group through written records, tape recordings, or video recordings of group sessions.

In treatment groups, members may be asked to record information about their own behavior or the behavior of other group members. Self-monitoring methods include (1) counting discrete behaviors; (2) keeping a checklist, a log, or a diary of events that occur before, during, and after a behavior or a task that is being monitored; and (3) recording ratings of feeling states on self-anchored rating scales. These types of monitoring methods are described in Chapter 8 because they are often used for assessment. As illustrated in the following sections, in the monitoring process, collecting data can be the task of the worker or of the group members.

Monitoring by the Group Worker

One of the easiest methods of monitoring a group's progress is to record the activities that occur during or after each meeting. This form of record keeping involves writing or dictating notes after a meeting (Wilson, 1980). The worker may use a process-recording method of monitoring or a summary-recording method. Process recordings are narrative, step-by-step descriptions of a group's development. Wilson and Ryland (1949) noted that process recordings can help a worker analyze the interactions that occur during a group meeting. However, process recordings are time-consuming and, therefore, are rarely used by experienced group workers. They are, however, useful in the training and supervision of beginning group workers because they provide rich detail and give trainees an opportunity to reflect on what occurs during group meetings.

Summary recording is less time-consuming, more selective, and more focused than process recording. Summary recording focuses on critical incidents that occur in a group and involves using a series of open-ended questions. The questions are most frequently used for monitoring a group's progress after each group session, although they may be used at less frequent intervals during a group's development. Figure 14.1 is an example of a summary recording form used to record a meeting of a family life education group for foster parents.

When using either summary or process recordings, it is important for the worker to record the information as soon as possible after the meeting so that events are remembered as accurately as possible. The meaning of the open-ended summary-recording questions should be as clear as possible so that workers' recordings are consistent from group to group. Ambiguous questions open to several interpretations should be avoided. The amount of time required for summary recordings depends on the number of questions to which the worker responds and the amount of analysis each question requires. The next case provides an example of how a group recording form can be employed.

FIGURE 14.1 ● *Group Recording Form*

Group name: _____   Beginning date: _____

Worker's name: _____   Termination date: _____

Session number: _____   Date of session: _____

Members present: _____

_____

_____

_____

Members absent: _____

_____

_____

Purpose of the group: _____

_____

Goals for this meeting: _____

_____

_____

Activities to meet these goals: _____

_____

_____

_____

Worker's analysis of the meeting _____

_____

_____

_____

_____

Plan for future meetings: _____

_____

_____

_____

_____

The open-ended questions of summary-recording devices sometimes fail to focus or define the recorded information sufficiently, especially when the worker wants similar information about all clients. Summary-recording devices are usually not designed to connect the group worker's activities to specific goals and outcomes.

● **CASE EXAMPLE** *Audiotape Evaluations*

In a family life education group for foster parents, the worker wanted to systematically analyze whether the group was achieving its goals. Using a group recording form after each meeting, she spent time writing down the goals of the group, the activities to accomplish the goals, and the quality of the interaction. She also recorded her analysis of how well the group worked toward achieving its overall purpose (see Figure 14.1). After several group sessions, she reviewed the completed weekly recordings in order to obtain a summary of how well the group was achieving its purpose. Based on her weekly analyses of meetings, the worker concluded that although members appeared to achieve a high degree of learning about family life, they failed to create significant supportive relationships with each other. Based on these conclusions, the worker increased program activities that provided members with opportunities to develop closer and more supportive relationships.

Recording systems such as the problem-oriented record (Kane, 1974), have been designed to overcome this problem. In the problem-oriented record-keeping system, problems to be worked on by the group are clearly defined, goals are established, and data are collected and recorded in relation to each specified problem. The system enables workers to show how group work interventions designed to accomplish a certain goal are connected to a specific assessment of the problem.

In task groups, the minutes of a meeting serve as the record of the group's business. They are often the official record of the proceedings of a group. Minutes are prepared from notes taken during the meeting by a person designated by the worker or elected by the group's membership. A staff person, the secretary of the group, or another person may take notes regularly. Sometimes, members rotate the task. The minutes of each meeting are usually distributed to members before the next meeting and are approved by members, with any revisions, during the first part of the next meeting.

Workers may also want to use audiotape or videotape recorders to obtain information about a group. Recordings have the advantage of providing an accurate, unedited record of the meeting. In remedial groups, audiotapes provide immediate feedback about members' verbal behavior. Members may want to replay a segment of the tape if there is a discrepancy about what was said during some portion of the meeting.

● **CASE EXAMPLE** *Audiotapes to Improve Coleadership*

Bonnie and Fred decided to audiotape a new employment skills group they were coleading in a day treatment program for persons recently discharged from inpatient mental health settings. With the members' permission, they taped the meetings; they then listened to the tapes between meetings to identify ways they might improve their leadership of future group meetings.

In educational and other groups, videotapes can be used to demonstrate appropriate behavior and critique inappropriate behavior. Videotaping is especially useful during program activities, such as role playing, that are designed to increase skills or change behavior patterns. Video feedback helps members review their behavior during role-play practices to discuss alternative ways of behaving. For example, members of an assertion training group might watch videotapes of themselves in a situation requiring an assertive response. They may analyze voice tone, facial expressions, body posture, and the verbal interactions that occurred. Audiotapes and videotapes provide the worker with a permanent record that can be shared with the group, with supervisors, or in educational workshops.

There are some disadvantages to taping a group. A recording's absolute quality makes it difficult for members to make statements off the record, which may inhibit the development of trust in the group. The worker may not find it necessary or even desirable to have the level of detail provided by a tape. The worker may have to spend too much time reviewing irrelevant portions of a tape to find information that could have been obtained quickly if brief, summary recordings had been used instead. However, if a worker is interested in monitoring the group's interaction patterns in a thorough and precise fashion or if an entire transcript of the group session is needed, audio or videotapes are ideal.

Sometimes it is desirable to use specialized coding systems to obtain reliable and valid data from tape-recorded group sessions, particularly when the worker wishes to obtain a detailed and accurate picture of group processes for research. Coding systems can be used by one or more raters of the tapes to determine the frequency and content of a group's interactions. Coding systems described by Bales (1950), Bales, Cohen, and Williamson (1979), Budman et al. (1987), Hill (1977), and Rose (1989) are examples of methods that can be used to analyze specific group interactions. Other coding systems are described in comprehensive reviews of group process instruments prepared by Fuhriman and colleagues (Fuhriman & Barlow, 1994; Fuhriman & Packard, 1986).

Monitoring by Group Members

The most common use of monitoring by group members occurs in treatment groups in which individual members keep a record of their behavior between group meetings and report back on the behaviors during the next meeting. An illustration of the steps in the self-monitoring procedure appears in Figure 14.2. During this procedure, the worker and the group members together decide (1) what data to collect, (2) when to collect the data, (3) how much data to collect, (4) how to collect the data, and (5) when the information collected by members should be analyzed by the group. As these questions are discussed and answered, the worker reviews each member's monitoring plan.

Members can also monitor a group's progress at the end of each meeting or at intervals during the life of the group. Members may use a short questionnaire devised for this purpose or they can discuss the group's performance orally with the worker. Monitoring of this type encourages members to provide periodic feedback that can be used by workers to improve their practice throughout the life cycle of a group.

Group members also benefit from self-monitoring procedures. Members can share ideas about the group's performance and how it might be improved, which gives them a sense of control and influence over the group's progress and increases their identification with the group's purposes. Also, members who believe their ideas are valued, respected, and listened to are more likely to feel satisfied with their participation in the group. See, for example, the following case example.

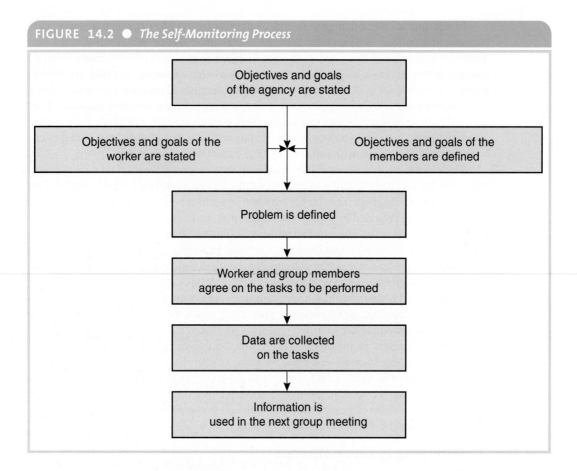

FIGURE 14.2 ● *The Self-Monitoring Process*

● CASE EXAMPLE *Monitoring the Progress of a Single Parent's Group*

In an educational group for single parents, the worker asked each member to complete a session evaluation form during the last five minutes of each meeting. The form was composed of short, closed-ended questions using a Likert scale, as well as open-ended questions designed to obtain qualitative data about member satisfaction with the group meetings (see Figure 14.3). At several intervals during the life of the group, the worker did a quantitative analysis of members' ratings on the level of helpfulness of information obtained from the group sessions as well as members' satisfaction with the group and with its leader. These data indicated a steady positive progression in how members valued the information they received and how they rated the group and the leader. Data collected about what members liked most and least about each session suggested that members particularly disliked some of the guest speakers brought in by the leader and preferred sessions where they could practice child management skills.

Verbal evaluations of a group's performance do not provide a permanent record. An evaluation form consisting of closed-ended, fixed-category responses and open-ended items can be used if the worker, group members, or the agency wants written feedback about

---

FIGURE 14.3 ● *Session Evaluation Form*

Was the information presented about child development helpful to you in understanding your child's behavior?

4	3	2	1
Very Helpful	Somewhat Helpful	A Little Helpful	Not at All Helpful

What information did you find most helpful? _____

_____

_____

Rate the effectiveness of the leader in this group session.

4	3	2	1
Very Helpful	Somewhat Helpful	A Little Helpful	Not at All Helpful

What did you find most helpful about the group during this session? _____

_____

_____

What did you find least helpful about the group? _____

_____

_____

Overall, rate your satisfaction with today's group meeting.

4	3	2	1
Very Helpful	Somewhat Helpful	A Little Helpful	Not at All Helpful

Additional comments: _____

_____

_____

---

the group. Figure 14.3 shows a session evaluation form developed by a worker leading a group for single parents. The form contains several easily understood closed- and open-ended questions. The closed-ended questions are Likert-type scales that require respondents to record their opinions on an ordered scale. Because the same scale values are used for all group members, responses made by each member can be compared with one another. Open-ended items are designed to allow each member to reply uniquely; responses may vary considerably from member to member. An alternative session evaluation form to the one shown in Figure 14.3 can be found in Rose (1998).

In task groups, members often make oral reports of their progress. Although the reports are often not considered to be evaluation devices, they are an important means by which the worker and the members monitor the group's work. At the completion of a task group, minutes, documents, final reports, and other products that result from the group's efforts can also be used to evaluate the success of the group.

In treatment groups, an important indicator of the group's performance is the completion of contracts that individual members make with the group or the worker about tasks to be done during the week to resolve a problem or change a particular behavior. Another indicator is the completion of between-session tasks. Rose (1989) calls the completion of between-session tasks the "products of group interaction." He suggests that the rate of completion of tasks is an important indicator of the success of the group.

EVALUATIONS FOR DEVELOPING A GROUP

A third method of evaluating group work practice, developmental evaluation, is useful for the worker who is interested in preparing new group work programs, developing new group work methods, or improving existing group programs. Developmental research, as it has been called by Thomas (1978), is similar to research and development in business and industry. It allows practicing group workers to create and test new group work programs.

The process of developmental evaluation includes developing, testing, evaluating, modifying, and re-evaluating intervention methods as new groups are offered. Developmental evaluations are especially appealing for workers who offer the same or similar group programs repeatedly because the evaluations require workers to evaluate group programs in a sequential manner. A developmental evaluation occurs as successive group programs are offered.

Unlike monitoring evaluations, which are relatively easy for group workers to conduct, developmental evaluations are rather complex. They require careful thought, planning, and design by the worker. The steps for conducting a developmental evaluation are presented in the following list.

Steps in a Developmental Evaluation

- Identifying a need or problem
- Gathering and analyzing relevant data
- Developing a new group program or method
- Evaluating the new program or method
- Modifying the program or method on the basis of the data obtained

As shown in Figure 14.4, the process may be conducted several times as new group programs are offered and evaluated by the worker. Although developmental research requires careful thought as well as time and energy, it yields improvements in programs and methods that can make group work practice more effective and more satisfying.

In developing and evaluating a new group program or a new group method, the worker can select from a variety of research designs, depending on the type of program or method being developed and the context in which the evaluation will occur. Single-system methods and case study methods are particularly useful for developmental evaluations. Although

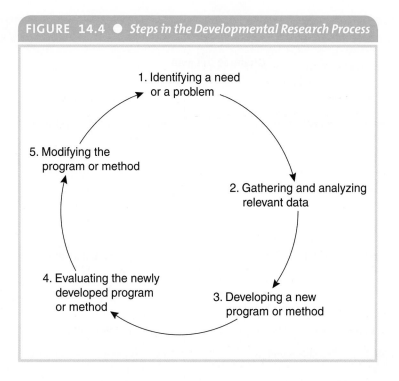

FIGURE 14.4 ● *Steps in the Developmental Research Process*

1. Identifying a need or a problem

2. Gathering and analyzing relevant data

3. Developing a new program or method

4. Evaluating the newly developed program or method

5. Modifying the program or method

quasi-experimental design methods are also frequently used in developmental research, in this chapter the methods are described in relation to effectiveness and efficiency evaluations because they are also frequently used in evaluations of group outcomes. For a more thorough discussion of the issues involved in choosing an appropriate method for developmental research, see Bailey-Dempsey and Reid (1996), Fortune and Reid (1998), Kirk and Reid (2002), Rothman and Tumblin (1994), and Thomas and Rothman (1994).

Single-System Methods

Single-system methods (often called single-subject designs) have been developed to evaluate data collected over time from a single system such as a group. The data obtained by using single-system designs may include information about a single group member or the group as a whole. Single-system methods compare baseline data to data collected when an intervention is made in the group. The baseline period occurs before the intervention period. Data collected during the preintervention or baseline periods are intended to represent the functioning of the group as a whole or a group member on a particular variable. After the baseline period, an intervention occurs, which may cause a change in the data collected during the baseline period.

As shown in Figure 14.5, a change in level or in slope of the data collected may occur after the intervention. Observations before and after the intervention are compared to see how the change has affected what the group worker is measuring. For example, after

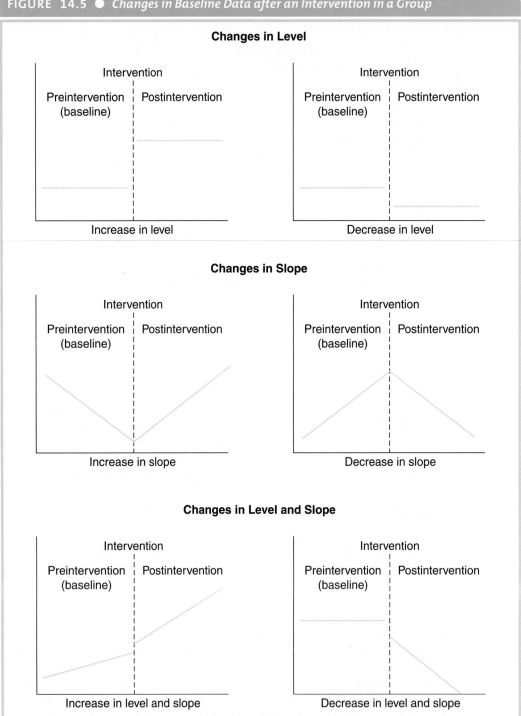

FIGURE 14.5 ● *Changes in Baseline Data after an Intervention in a Group*

collecting baseline data and finding that members of a group were talking almost exclusively to the worker rather than to each other, the worker may intervene by discussing the issue with the group, prompting members to talk with one another more frequently, and praising them when they initiate conversation with one another.

After the intervention, communications between members and the worker decrease, and communications between members increase. Figure 14.6 graphs the results of such an intervention. The single-system method illustrated in Figure 14.6 is often called an *AB design,* in which A is the baseline period before intervention and B is the postintervention, data-collection period.

Various single-system designs are multiple baseline, withdrawal, reversal, and changing criterion. These types of single-system designs are more complicated to apply for the practicing group worker than is the AB baseline-intervention design, but they are also more effective than the AB design in reliably evaluating practice outcomes. They are especially useful when workers have the time, energy, interest, and resources to test the efficacy of a new or alternative intervention to improve practice with future groups working on similar problems. For additional information about single-system methods, see Bloom, Fisher, and Orme (2003).

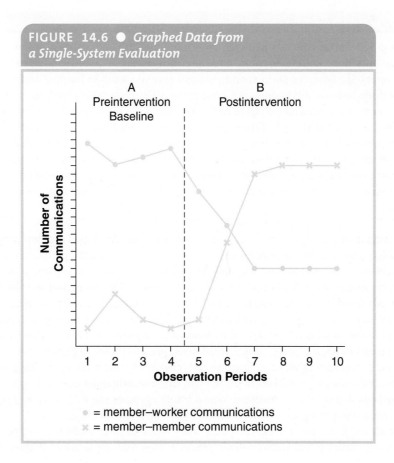

FIGURE 14.6 ● *Graphed Data from a Single-System Evaluation*

Case Study Methods

Case studies rely on precise descriptions, accurate observations, and detailed analyses of a single example or case. Case studies were developed by researchers interested in qualitative research methods. Because group workers are accustomed to keeping records and analyzing their work in detail, these methods may have more appeal for some group workers than the quantitatively oriented, single-system research methods.

As with single-system methods, case study methods are based on intensive analysis of a single case. Therefore, the data collected may not be as internally or externally valid as data collected using classic control-group designs. Nevertheless, the strengths of case studies are that they can provide a clear, detailed, vivid description of the processes and procedures of a group in action, and they are often more feasible to apply in practice settings than in control-group designs.

Case study methods include participant and nonparticipant observation (Marshall & Rossman, 1999; Padgett, 1998; Patton, 2000), case comparison methods (Butler, Davis, & Kukkonen, 1979), ethnographic methods (Scheneul, Lecompte, Borgatti, & Nastasi, 1998), and focus group interviews (Greenbaum, 1998; Krueger & Casey, 2000; Morgan, 1997). The following example illustrates the use of case study methods.

● **CASE EXAMPLE** *Using Case Study Methods*

A group worker who was planning on leading a health and wellness group for cardiac patients found it useful to "sit in" on several other wellness groups conducted in the community. She obtained permission to observe several groups in hospital and nonhospital settings and was able to videotape some of these. Using case study methods to analyze the content of the video recordings as well as her own notes made from observing each group, she concluded that most of the groups not only provided important education information, but also provided a strong sense of "universality" among members, that is, helping members to understand that they were not unique or alone in experiencing particular problems. She also concluded that members provided a strong component of mutual aid to each other in these groups. She used this information to develop a new group in her own setting.

Using a case comparison method, a worker who has developed a group program for alcoholics may want to compare the program with similar programs, perhaps those offered by Alcoholics Anonymous and a county alcoholism program. A comparison of the three programs along prespecified dimensions created by the worker to answer specific information needs could lead to innovations in the worker's program. The worker may also want to conduct focus group interviews with individuals who have participated in each program to determine the most- and least-valued features of each program. These features could then be evaluated for their efficacy, as described in the process shown in Figure 14.4.

Group workers might also want to use case study methods in working with task groups. For example, a worker might want to use nonparticipant observation to compare the methods that other day-treatment mental health agencies use when reviewing clients in treatment-team meetings.

Both single-system methods and case study methods offer workers the opportunity to continually develop and improve their practice. Rigorous application of these methods requires that workers spend time designing and implementing evaluation methods and collecting data that are not routinely available. The worker must decide whether the extra effort spent in organizing and carrying out a developmental evaluation is worth the new or improved programs that may result.

EVALUATIONS FOR DETERMINING EFFECTIVENESS AND EFFICIENCY

Effectiveness evaluations focus on the extent to which a group accomplishes its objectives. They give workers the opportunity to gain objective feedback about the helpfulness of the methods being used and the outcomes achieved. Efficiency evaluations compare the benefits of a group program with its cost. They attempt to place a monetary value on the outcomes of a group and to compare this cost with the costs incurred by conducting a group.

Effectiveness and efficiency evaluations rely on experimental and quasi-experimental designs, reliable and valid measures, and statistical procedures to determine the significance of an intervention on the outcome of task or treatment groups. Compared with the other types of evaluations mentioned in this chapter, effectiveness and efficiency evaluations are less flexible, more technically complex, and more difficult to conduct. Because of the nature of the methods employed and the precision and rigor necessary to apply them, a flexible and cooperative setting is needed to conduct effectiveness and efficiency evaluations. The sponsoring agency must be willing to supply the needed resources and the technical assistance necessary for conducting such evaluations.

One method for evaluating outcomes that is less difficult to apply than many other effectiveness evaluation methods is called *goal attainment scaling* (Kiresuk & Sherman, 1968). Using this method, the worker can obtain information about the achievement of goals by individual group members or the group as a whole. An example of goal attainment scaling is shown in Figure 14.7.

Members and the group leader can work together to develop outcome measures for each scale level. For example, a group may decide that the most unfavorable outcome for the problem of depression is suicide. Similarly, the group may decide that the most favorable outcome for loss of appetite is to eat three meals a day and to snack between meals. After work on the problem areas is completed, goal attainment can be measured by using the scales that have been developed for each problem area. In the example in Figure 14.7, goal attainment is indicated by a box around the actual outcome. For the problem of anxiety, the outcome was one self-rated occurrence of feeling anxious each day. This outcome was given a score of 4.

As shown in Figure 14.7, it is possible to weight each scale differentially so that attaining more important goals receives greater emphasis in the overall evaluation than does attaining less important goals. Thus, the goal attainment score of 4 obtained for the problem of anxiety is multiplied by its weight of 5 to yield a goal attainment score of 20. Even though the goal attainment score on the problem area of depression is a 3, after it is multiplied by its weight (25), the weighted goal attainment score for the problem of depression (75) is much greater than that obtained on the problem of anxiety (20). Goal attainment scores on each scale can be added together to form a composite score for individual or group goal attainment.

FIGURE 14.7 ● *Example of Goal Attainment Scaling*

Scale Levels	Problem Areas		
	Anxiety	**Depression**	**Loss of Appetite**
1. Most unfavorable expected outcome	Four or more self-rated occurrences of feeling anxious each day	Suicide	Refuses to eat any daily meals
2. Less than expected outcome	Three self-rated occurrences of feeling anxious each day	One or more attempts at suicide	Eats one meal each day
3. Expected outcome	Two self-rated occurrences of feeling anxious each day	No attempt at suicide, discusses feelings of depression	Eats two meal each day
4. More than expected outcome	One self-rated occurrence of feeling anxious each day	No attempt at suicide, discusses possible causes of depression	Eat three meals each day
5. Most favorable expected outcome	No self-rated occurrence of feeling anxious each day	No attempts at suicide, identifies two causes for depression	Eats three meals a day and snacks between meals
Weight	5	25	5
Goal Attainment Score	4	3	3
Weighted Goal Attainment Score	20	75	15

Statistical procedures have been developed to compare goal attainment scores across individual group members and across groups (Garwick, 1974). Although goal attainment scaling has received some methodological criticism (Seaberg & Gillespie, 1977), the procedure remains an important tool for group workers to consider when conducting effectiveness evaluations.

A variation on goal attainment scaling that has been used successfully in several studies of the effectiveness of group treatment is the pressing problem index (Toseland, Labrecque, Goebel, & Whitney, 1992; Toseland, et al., 2001; Toseland, McCallion, Smith, & Banks, 2004). During the intake interview, potential group members are asked to describe several problems they would like to work on in the group. These problems, plus any other problems known to commonly affect the individuals targeted for the intervention, are listed in an inventory of pressing problems. Before meeting and again at the end of the group, participants are asked to rate the stress caused by each pressing problem and their efficacy in coping with the problem. Change in stress and efficacy in coping with the pressing problems are assessed by adding up the responses to all pressing problems at each time of measurement.

Effectiveness evaluations rely on experimental and quasi-experimental designs to determine whether a group accomplishes its objectives. A true experimental design employs random assignment of participants to treatment and control groups. It compares the treatment and control groups on specific outcome variables to measure differences between treatment and control group subjects. In *quasi-experimental designs,* participants cannot be randomly assigned to treatment and control groups. It is often difficult to assign subjects randomly to treatment and control groups in practice settings. Therefore, quasi-experimental designs are often used in effectiveness evaluations even though they are subject to possible biases because nonrandomly assigned subjects are more likely to be non-equivalent on important variables that may affect the outcome variables being measured.

It is especially difficult to conduct adequate effectiveness evaluations in group research projects. To do valid statistical analyses of data from experimental designs, the observations or measures on each unit of analysis must be independent. Researchers testing the effectiveness of group treatment sometimes assume that individual group members are the unit of analysis. However, individual members are not independent of one another in a group setting because they are affected by other members of the group. For example, while members are taking a questionnaire, a lawn mower might go past the window and disturb all members of the group. Members' scores are not totally independent of one another; that is, the lawn mower affects all members in a similar manner. One way to overcome this problem is to ensure that all evaluation instruments are given to group members on a one-to-one basis outside of the group meeting.

The requirement for independent observations is also violated by researchers interested in group-level phenomena such as cohesion and leadership. Glisson (1986) has pointed out that some statistical procedures such as analysis of variance (ANOVA) are not robust to this violation, which can lead to serious overestimates of the effectiveness of group procedures (Eisenhart, 1972). Because there must be a relatively large number of units of analysis to obtain valid statistical comparisons of a group-level phenomenon, effectiveness evaluations of group work practice require that a relatively large number of groups be conducted. Evaluating large numbers of groups is often difficult to do in practice settings because of the limitations on resources, group participants, and competent group leaders. For these reasons, alternatives to using the group as the unit of analysis have been proposed (Bonito, 2002; Brower, Arndt, & Ketterhagen, 2004; Burlingame, Kircher, & Honts, 1994; Magen, 2004).

Efficiency evaluations can be complex and time-consuming, but they can also be useful to persons who want to assess whether their programs are cost-effective. For example, a nonprofit health agency employs a group worker to conduct a smoking-cessation group program. The worker conducts an effectiveness evaluation and finds that 60 percent of the group members become nonsmokers after the group program. The worker also collects data about the costs of the program and the costs to employers who have employees who smoke. These data provide the basis for the worker's efficiency evaluation.

Figure 14.8 shows the worker's calculations and illustrates that at a success rate of 50 percent, the smoking-cessation group program saves the employer $220 each year, beginning one year after the program ends. Savings to the employer last for as long as the employee remains with the company as a nonsmoker. Because the smoking-cessation program has a success rate of 60 percent, employers who have long-term employees are likely to save more than $220 each year for each employee who participates in the smoking-cessation program. This information would be helpful to the nonprofit health agency in motivating large employers whose workers' average length of employment exceeds one year to offer smoking-cessation group programs to their employees.

A description of the methodology for effectiveness evaluations can be found in Babbie (2007) or Rossi, Freeman, and Lipsey (1999), and a description of efficiency evaluations can be found in Drummond, Stoddart, and Torrance (1987), Gold, Siegel, Russell, and

FIGURE 14.8 ● *An Efficiency Evaluation of a Group Program for Smoking Cessation*

Costs of Smoking to the Employer per Employee per Year*

Insurance:

Health	5220.00
Fire	10.00
Workers' Compensation and other accidents	40.00
Life and disability	30.00

Other:

Productivity	166.00
Absenteeism	100.00
Smoking effects on nonsmokers	110.00
Total cost of smoking	$660.00

Per Employee Cost of the Smoking-Cessation Program	
Smoking-cessation program	$120.00
Employee time to complete the program	100.00
Total Cost for Each Employee	$220.00

Total Cost of Achieving One Nonsmoker	
(based on a projected success rate of 50%)	$440.00

Savings to Employers	
Total cost of smoking	$660.00
Total cost of the smoking-cessation program	−440.00
	$220.00

*Cost figures taken from Marvin Kristein, "How Much Can Business Expect to Earn from Smoking Cessation," presented at the Conference of the National Interagency Council on Smoking and Health, Chicago, Illinois, January 9, 1980.

Weinstein (1996), Levin and McEwan (2001), or Nas (1996). Group workers should have a basic understanding of these methods to be able to assess the efficacy of their own practice and to be able to critically evaluate methodologies used in published reports about the effectiveness and efficiency of group work methods and group programs.

EVALUATION MEASURES

The four broad types of evaluation methods provide a framework that workers can use to collect information for planning, monitoring, developing, or assessing the efficacy or efficiency of their practice with a group. In applying these methods, workers can choose from a variety of measures to collect the necessary information for an effective evaluation.

Numerous measures have been developed for evaluating group work practice; some specifically focus on properties of the group as a whole, and others may be useful to the worker in evaluating changes in members of specific groups. Decisions about which measures to use depend on (1) the objectives of the evaluation, (2) properties of the measures being considered for use, (3) the form in which the data will be collected, and (4) what constructs will be measured.

Choosing Measures

The first and most essential step in choosing appropriate measures is to decide on the objectives of the evaluation. Clarifying the information that is needed, what the information collected will be used for, and who will use the information can help the worker choose the appropriate measures for the evaluation. For example, if the worker is interested in obtaining feedback from members about their satisfaction with a particular group, the worker may be less concerned about the reliability and validity of a measure than about the difficulties members might experience in providing the information. The worker may also be concerned about members' reactions to the evaluation and the time needed to administer it, particularly if the worker has a limited amount of group time available for conducting an evaluation.

The worker should be familiar with two properties of measures that govern the quality of the data to be collected. *Reliability* refers to the extent to which an instrument measures the same phenomenon in the same way each time the measure is used. A reliable measure is consistent. When measuring the same variable, it yields the same score each time it is administered. *Validity* refers to the extent to which a data-collection instrument measures what it purports to measure. A valid measure is one that yields a true or actual representation of the variable being measured. The ideal situation is for a group worker to use a reliable and valid measure that has already been constructed. When such measures exist, they are generally superior to measures developed quickly by the worker without regard to reliability or validity.

Constructing reliable and valid measures takes a considerable amount of time. Workers should decide what level of measurement precision and objectivity is needed when deciding how much time to spend constructing and validating a measure. For additional information about constructing reliable and valid measures, see Hopkins (1998), Nunnally (1994), or Sax (1996).

Another consideration in choosing appropriate evaluation measures is to decide what form of data collection would be most useful to the group worker and most convenient for group members. Data can be collected by interviewing members, by written response to a questionnaire, or by audio or video recordings. The data-collection form that will be most helpful to the worker depends on how the data will be used and the extent to which group members are willing and able to cooperate with the data-collection procedures used. In evaluating group work with children, older people, and disabled people, for example, audiotaped responses can often overcome any difficulties the individuals might have in making written responses.

Finally, the worker must decide how a particular property or concept will be measured. For example, after deciding that the objective of an evaluation is to test the effectiveness of a particular group, the worker must decide whether information is sought about changes in the behavior, cognition, or the affect of individual group members. In task groups, the worker may want to measure both the extent to which a group completes its tasks and the quality and the quantity of the products or tasks achieved.

When one conducts evaluations, it is often helpful to have multiple measures of the property being measured. When measuring the effectiveness of a group program for drug abusers, for example, the worker might want to measure reductions in drug intake, changes in self-concept, and changes in beliefs about the effects of drug abuse. Multiple measures, such as blood tests, attitude scales, and a questionnaire concerning information about drug use, might be useful in assessing the group's effectiveness in helping members become drug free.

Types of Measures

A wide variety of reliable and valid measures are available for group workers to use when they are evaluating interventions with specific groups (Fisher & Corcoran, 2007; Kramer & Conoley, 1992; Robinson & Shaver, 1973). These sources include self-report measures, observational measures, and measures of the products of group interaction. In the description of each type of measure, the text indicates particular measures that have often been used in evaluations of group work.

Self-Report Measures

Perhaps the most widely used evaluation measures are written and oral self-reports, in which group members are asked to respond to questions about a particular phenomenon. Although they may focus on any phenomenon, self-report measures are particularly useful in measuring intrapersonal phenomena such as beliefs or attitudes, which cannot be measured directly by observational measures. Group workers can also construct their own self-report measures for specialized situations in which no published self-report measures exist. However, it is difficult to construct a reliable and valid self-report measure. Fortunately, a variety of published self-report measures are available, including measures of anxiety, depression, assertiveness, self-concept, and locus of control. Five published measures that may be of particular interest to group workers are the Group Atmosphere Scale (Silbergeld, Koenig, Manderscheid, Meeker, & Hornung, 1975), Hemphill's Index of Group Dimensions (Hemphill, 1956), the Hill Interaction Matrix (Hill, 1977), Yalom's Curative Factors Scale (Lieberman, Yalom, & Miles, 1973; Stone, Lewis, & Beck, 1994) and the Therapeutic Factors Inventory (Lese & MacNair-Semands, 2000).

The Group Atmosphere Scale (GAS) was designed to measure the psychosocial environment of therapy groups. It consists of 12 subscales: (1) aggression, (2) submission, (3) autonomy, (4) order, (5) affiliation, (6) involvement, (7) insight, (8) practicality, (9) spontaneity, (10) support, (11) variety, and (12) clarity. Each subscale contains 10 true-false items. The GAS has been assessed to have acceptable reliability and validity (Silbergeld et al., 1975).

Hemphill's Index of Group Dimensions measures 13 properties of groups: (1) autonomy, (2) control, (3) flexibility, (4) hedonic tone, (5) homogeneity, (6) intimacy, (7) participation, (8) permeability, (9) polarization, (10) potency, (11) stability, (12) stratification, and (13) viscidity. The measure consists of 150 items to which group members respond on a five-point scale from definitely true to mostly false.

The Hill Interaction Matrix (HIM-A, HIM-B, HIM-G) is a self-report measure in which a group leader, a group member, or an observer responds to 72 items about group process. The measure is designed to discriminate between types of group interactions on two dimensions: the content discussed and the level and type of work occurring in the group.

Yalom's Curative Factors Scale is a widely used, 14-item measure that assesses 12 therapeutic dimensions in treatment groups: (1) altruism, (2) catharsis, (3) cohesiveness, (4) existentiality, (5) family re-enactment, (6) guidance, (7) hope, (8) identification, (9) interpersonal input, (10) interpersonal output, (11) self-understanding, and (12) universality. Stone, Lewis, and Beck (1994) have reported some psychometric properties of the instrument.

The Therapeutic Factors Inventory is a 99-item scale that measures Yalom's (1995) therapeutic factors. It contains 11 subscales that measure (1) altruism, (2) catharsis, (3) cohesiveness, (4) corrective enactment of the primary family group, (5) development of socializing techniques, (6) existential factors, (7) imitative behavior, (8) imparting information, (9) instillation of hope, (10) interpersonal learning, and (11) universality. The scale has good reliability, but validity testing is needed (Lese & MacNair-Semands, 2000).

The Group Environment Scale (GES) is another instrument for measuring group conditions (Moos, 1986). The GES is a 90-item true-false measure that consists of three domains: relationship, personal growth, and system maintenance/system change. The relationship domain measures cohesion, leader support, and expressiveness. The personal growth domain measures independence, leader support, and expressiveness. The system maintenance/system change domain measures order and organization, leader control, and innovation. Data are provided on the reliability and validity of the scale which has been used with 148 task and treatment groups (Moos, 1986).

Macgowan (2000) has also developed the Groupwork Engagement Measure (GEM), which is conceptualized as measuring seven dimensions: (1) attendance, (2) contributing, (3) relating to the worker, (4) relating to members, (5) contracting, (6) working on one's own problems, and (7) working on others' problems (Macgowan & Levenson, 2003). The GEM has 37 items scored on five-point scales from 1("rarely or none of the time") to 5 ("most or all of the time"). The psychometric properties of the GEM have been established in several studies (Macgowan, 1997, 2000; Macgowan & Levenson, 2003; Macgowan & Newman, 2005).

Observational Measures

Unlike self-report measures that rely on the accuracy of a respondent's memory, observational measures use independent, objective observers to collect data as they occur or as they are replayed from video or audio recordings. Although observational measures are less susceptible to biases and distortions than are self-report measures, observational measures are used less frequently than self-report measures because they require the availability of one or more trained observers to collect the data. The observers code discrete group interactions into categories that are mutually exclusive and exhaustive; that is, during each observation period, only one observation is recorded and it can be recorded in only one category.

The most well-known observational measure for groups is called Bales' Interaction Process Analysis (Bales, 1950). This observational index consists of 12 categories. Interactions are coded by assigning each person a number. For example, when an interaction occurs from member 1 to member 4 or from member 3 to member 1, the interaction is marked 1-4 or 3-1 in the appropriate category. With well-trained observers, Bales' Interaction Process Analysis can be a useful tool for the evaluation of group interactions.

More recently, Bales (1980) and Bales, Cohen, and Williamson (1979) have developed a measure called Systematic Multiple Level Observation of Groups (SYMLOG). As explained in Chapter 8, SYMLOG is a method for analyzing the overt and covert behaviors of group members. With SYMLOG, a three-dimensional graphic presentation or field diagram of the interaction of group members is made. Through the field diagram, group members can analyze the way they interact with one another to improve the ability of the group to accomplish its tasks. An example of the use of SYMLOG for assessing group functioning can be found in Chapter 8. As an evaluation tool, SYMLOG can be used to measure several variables affecting both the socioemotional and the task aspects of members' behavior in groups.

Other observational measures have also been used for evaluating changes in a group over time. For example, Moreno's (1934) scales of sociometric choice and sociometric preference, described more fully in Chapter 8, assess relationships among members of a group by having each member rank other members on certain dimensions such as their preference for working with other group members or their liking for other group members.

Products of Group Interaction

A worker may be able to measure the products of group interaction in a simple and straightforward manner. In task groups, products of the group's work are often tangible. For example, a team may develop a written document that governs how services will be delivered to clients. The work of a delegate council may be evaluated by the number of agenda items it acts on during its monthly meeting. In both instances, group products can be used for purposes of evaluation. In treatment groups, products of group interaction may also be useful measures. Rose (1989) suggests that measurable products of group interaction include behavior change, the number of between-meeting tasks generated at a group meeting, and the number of tasks actually completed.

Evaluation measures from which workers can choose when evaluating their practice with a group range from measures consisting of a few open-ended questions made by a worker who wants to get some feedback from group members to sophisticated observational measures requiring highly trained observers. Workers develop or select measures in relation to the evaluation design they are going to use and, ultimately, in relation to the information they hope to obtain. Although selecting appropriate measures and implementing effective evaluations is time-consuming for the practicing group worker, it is often well worth the effort because it may result in improved service and in new and innovative group programs.

SUMMARY

Evaluation is the method by which practitioners obtain information and feedback about their work with a group. In the current age of accountability and fiscal constraints by which difficult program choices are made, evaluation methodologies are useful tools for practitioners. This chapter discusses some reasons that group workers may choose to use evaluation methods in their practice.

Practitioners are often faced with a dilemma when considering whether to evaluate their practice. They must decide whether the demands of serving clients are compatible with developing and conducting evaluations. This chapter describes the strengths and weaknesses of a number of evaluation methods that may be used in differing practice situations and settings.

Four broad types of evaluation methods are evaluations for (1) planning a group, (2) monitoring a group, (3) developing a group, and (4) testing the effectiveness and efficiency of a group. These methods are used with a variety of evaluation measures to help practitioners develop, test, and implement more effective group work methods. Evaluation methods can also be combined with knowledge accumulated from practice experiences (sometimes referred to as *practice wisdom*) to improve the methods used by group workers to meet a variety of needs in diverse practice settings.

● CASE EXAMPLE

Despite telling his group work students always to monitor and evaluate their practice with groups, Bob knew that they would be caught in the classic practitioner's dilemma. The demands of service delivery would make it difficult for them to spend the time and resources needed to formally evaluate their work with groups. He was surprised, however, when a former student returned with good news about research funding and a request for help. Maureen had been awarded a demonstration grant of $5,000 to develop an evaluation of her violence reduction group. In addition, the state's education department suggested that if her research project was successful, Maureen could apply for a much larger grant to implement and evaluate additional groups. She hoped that Bob could give her some helpful ideas for a research design.

Maureen's violence reduction group was aimed at sensitizing elementary students to the types of violence in their school environment and helping them find nonviolent ways of behaving. It had an educational component that consisted of a series of standardized lessons about violence. In addition, it had a growth component in which members learned new ways of handling themselves when confronted with anger from their peers.

Based on her conversations with Bob, Maureen decided to use the Achenbacl Child Behavior Checklist (Achenbacl, 1991) in her evaluation because it had been found to be a reliable and valid measure of children's behavior by researchers who had examined its psychometric properties. Although there is both a parent and a teacher version of the Achenback Child Behavior

Checklist, she decided to use only the parent form because she was concerned that teachers were too busy to spend the time to fill out the form for each student involved in the project. Instead, she designed a short questionnaire aimed at collecting feedback from teachers about students' behaviors in the classroom.

Maureen decided to use a partial-crossover control group design to evaluate the impact of the group. She would start a new group from the waiting list and use some of the students who were still on the waiting list as a control group. In a partial-crossover design, after the intervention is conducted with the experimental group, the control group is then offered the intervention.

Although the design would provide good information about the effectiveness of the group, it posed several ethical issues. First, Maureen had to secure written permission from the parents of the children who would participate in both the experimental and control groups. Second, Maureen had to discuss and justify the use of the waiting list as a control group with the children's parents and with school administrators. Confidentiality and voluntary participation were also issues. As a result of her discussions with students, parents, and administrators, Maureen secured permission to proceed with the research.

To help ensure the equivalence of the experimental and control groups, Maureen randomly assigned students on the waiting list to either of the two groups. When the groups were composed, she asked the parents of children in both groups to fill out the behavior checklist. This measurement served as a pretest for both the experimental and control groups and provided important baseline information. She triangulated these data with information obtained from teachers who filled out the short questionnaire she had developed. Maureen then conducted the violence reduction sessions with the experimental group. At the end of the group, she again administered the Achenback checklist to parents of children in the experimental and control groups and again collected data from teachers. She then compared the pretest and posttest results for both groups. Students in the experimental group achieved positive movement on their checklist scores whereas scores for the control group members did not change significantly. Using the control group scores as a second pretest, Maureen then ran the violence reduction group for the members of the control group. Posttest scores for this crossover group were significantly higher than their pretest scores.

The parents of students who participated in Maureen's violence reduction groups reported fewer incidents of acting out behavior of a violent nature, especially related to school. In addition, teachers reported that students who participated in the violence reduction groups had more control over their feelings of anger and used more positive measures for mediating their personal disputes in the classroom.

Maureen spent a good deal of time preparing a final report on her research project. She made sure to document both the results of her findings as well as the nature of the intervention that took place within the violence reduction groups. School administrators were pleased at the outcome of her evaluation efforts. With a sense of pride and gratefulness, Maureen sent a copy of the final report to her former research teacher with a note of thanks for helping her with the project. She later learned that her research report was the highlight of the state education department's review panel's deliberations on funding new initiatives aimed at reducing violence in schools.

chapter 15

Case Examples

Although case examples are useful in the teaching and learning of group work practice, there is a dearth of examples illustrating practice with treatment and task groups. This chapter presents two case examples. The first example, a caregiver support group, illustrates work with a treatment group. The second example, a community coalition helping people with AIDS, illustrates work with a task group.

A CAREGIVER SUPPORT GROUP

The case example selected to illustrate practice with treatment groups describes a support group for family members who are providing care for frail elderly relatives. It illustrates the blending of supportive, educational, and psychotherapeutic interventions in a single group. It also illustrates a blending of a relatively structured group format with relatively unstructured follow-up meetings.

The leader of the group is a professional social worker who has had extensive clinical experience working with individuals and family members with chronic disabilities. The group met for eight weekly two-hour sessions and then decided to continue to meet monthly. During the first eight meetings, the group agreed to use a structured approach that included support, education, coping skills, and problem solving. Monthly follow-up meetings were less structured, with members reporting in turn what had transpired since the last meeting and seeking support and assistance as needed.

The Support Component

Although specific time was set aside during each meeting for the educational, problem-solving, and coping-skills components, support interventions were used throughout each group meeting. Supportive interventions included (1) ventilation of stressful experiences in an understanding and supportive environment, (2) validation and confirmation of similar caregiving experiences, (3) affirmation of members' abilities to cope with their situations, (4) praise for providing high-quality care, (5) support and understanding during difficult situations, (6) hopefulness about the future, and (7) mutual aid. The worker took the lead in modeling supportive interventions and encouraged members to be supportive of each other.

The Educational Component

The educational component occurred during the first 30 to 40 minutes of each of the initial eight meetings. A different topic was covered each week:

- Session 1 provided an introduction to the support group.
- Session 2 focused on caregivers' emotions and feelings.
- Session 3 focused on care receivers' reactions to illness.
- Session 4 focused on how caregivers could take care of themselves but still do positive things with their frail parent.
- Session 5 focused on communication between the caregiver and care receiver and between the caregiver and other family members.
- Session 6 focused on community resources.
- Session 7 focused on medical needs, pharmacology issues, and the nursing home placement process.
- Session 8 focused on home management techniques and strategies and on resources for environmental modifications including specialized home-care appliances and devices.

After a brief presentation by the leader or a guest speaker, members were encouraged to ask questions, share information, and discuss issues related to the weekly topic presented by the leader.

The Coping-Skills Component

This part of the program was conceptually linked to Lazarus and Folkman's (1984) model of stress and coping based on Stress Inoculation Training (SIT), developed by Meichenbaum and colleagues (Meichenbaum, 1977, 1985; Meichenbaum & Cameron, 1983). SIT involves multiple strategies such as didactic teaching, relaxation training, cognitive restructuring, self-monitoring, and self-instruction. Instead of teaching a single stress-management technique, the leader introduced members to several techniques and encouraged members to use the techniques that worked best for them. Although the leader's goal was to cover specific coping skills during each meeting, the contents of the coping-skills component were incorporated flexibly into the first eight sessions according to the needs of the members and the pressing problems members expressed during discussions in the educational component and during the problem-solving component (Everly, 1989).

Session 1 of the coping-skills component was focused on assuring caregivers that their reactions to their family members' health problems were normal. The session also focused on acquainting members with the concepts of stress, appraisal, and coping (Lazarus & Folkman, 1984). At the end of the session, members were given the opportunity to discuss their reactions to their family members' illness, their illness-related appraisals, and the coping strategies they had been using to deal with their reactions.

Session 2 focused on helping members identify and label their emotional and bodily coping responses to their family members' physical and mental condition and to their role as a caregiver. The leader reinforced effective coping skills and encouraged members to work toward changing ineffective coping skills. As in previous successful group intervention programs for caregivers of the chronically ill (McCallion, Toseland, & Diehl, 1994; Toseland & Rossiter, 1989), members were encouraged to recognize their own specific emotional and bodily reactions to stress and to identify situations that provoked stress and characteristic coping responses. They were also taught to better recognize early signs of stress and their typical cognitive appraisals and coping reactions. To facilitate the learning process, members were asked to keep a diary between group meetings to record the stressors they experienced during the week and their cognitive and behavioral responses to the stressors. Practice in recognizing stressors and identifying typical appraisals and coping reactions continued during the remaining sessions.

During sessions 3 and 4, two relaxation techniques were introduced and practiced by members as a means to creatively counteract the negative effects of strain associated with caregiving and to cope with other, unavoidable life stresses. First, a deep breathing technique was introduced and practiced (Toseland, Labrecque, Goebel, & Whitney, 1992). The technique, which is easily learned, provided members with an effective strategy to moderate their typical reactions to stress by interrupting their habituated responses and slowing down their cognitive processes, thereby increasing the likelihood that more planned and effective coping reactions could be chosen.

Second, progressive muscle relaxation (Jacobson, 1978) was introduced and practiced. Members were given an audiotape containing muscle relaxation instructions and encouraged to practice at home between sessions. The tape contained two sets of instructions, a complete, 45-minute set of instructions on side 1, and, for individuals who had mastered side 1, a shorter version of the same instructions on side 2. Members' experiences with the relaxation tape were reviewed during subsequent sessions.

Sessions 5 through 8 focused on cognitive restructuring strategies, including self-talk, perspective taking, and cognitive self-instruction strategies (Meichenbaum, 1985; Meichenbaum & Cameron, 1983). Building on exercises presented in session 2, members were taught how to use early stress cues as signals to activate more effective appraisals and coping strategies. In particular, members were taught how to use the method of inner dialogue (coping self-talk) to plan coping reactions that were more effective and gratifying for them. Members were asked to identify their typical and preferred coping self-talk phrases and to reflect on the usefulness of the phrases.

In addition, members were introduced to the concept of coping imagery and asked to identify coping images they preferred. Between meetings, members were asked to continue to note stressful events in their diaries and also record what self-talk and cognitive imagery strategies they had used to cope with stressful events. Entries in their diaries were discussed during each meeting. During session 8, members' use of cognitive restructuring strategies was reviewed, and potential problems were addressed.

The Problem-Solving Component

A problem-solving model similar to the one described in Chapter 11 was introduced during session 1 as a device to help members move beyond ventilation of experiences and emotional reactions to using methods for improving their coping skills. Each week, members were encouraged to take turns working on their individual concerns by using the problem-solving model, which was displayed on two flip charts for easy viewing. Frequently, the problem-solving component was combined with the coping-skills component. Sometimes, members learned a new skill and then practiced it on a pressing problem that they were experiencing. At other times, members shared a problem they were having and the group leader or another member suggested a coping skill that might help.

It should be noted that because the members of the caregiver support group had a tremendous need to ventilate pent-up emotions and to share their experiences and concerns with each other, the problem-solving model was not always carried out in a linear, step-by-step fashion. Still, by using the model, the leader was able to help all members address at least one pressing problem during the eight-week group, and many members addressed several problems.

Session 1

During the first session, members shared information about themselves. The leader, Mrs. S, spoke first. She modeled the level of self-disclosure she hoped members would engage in when they introduced themselves. She described her professional experience, her own caregiving experience, some positive experiences she had in previous caregiver groups, and what she hoped would be some beneficial outcomes of participating in the support group. Next, she asked members to introduce themselves one by one. They shared the following information about themselves and the person for whom they were caring:

Mrs. Z: Mrs. Z has four children and is 54 years old. Because she married late in life, two of her four children are teenagers and living at home. Mrs. Z's mother, age 81, lives alone, has diabetes, is extremely overweight, has been widowed twice, and is depressed. Although married and working full time, Mrs. Z still manages to see her mother almost every day. She does her mother's shopping and supervises her mother's medication.

Mrs. B: Mrs. B is a 61-year-old widow with one child who lives in another state. Mrs. B cares for her mother-in-law, age 86, who came to live in Mrs. B's home seven years ago after suffering a stroke. Three years ago, Mrs. B's husband died. Since his death, her mother-in-law, who is a diabetic, has been totally dependent on Mrs. B and is home alone all day while Mrs. B works as a legal secretary.

Mrs. A: Mrs. A is caring for her bedridden mother, who has heart disease and Parkinson's disease and has lived with Mrs. A and her husband for five years. Mrs. A's mother has also been recently diagnosed with cancer. An aide comes in three times a week for four hours a day, but the remaining burden of care is left to Mrs. A.

Miss G: Miss G is 28 and works part-time as a clerk in a neighborhood store. Miss G's 76-year-old mother, a fiercely independent woman, lived alone until she suffered a stroke six months before the first group meeting. She now lives next door to Miss G in a duplex that Miss G bought with her mother's help.

Mrs. H: Mrs. H's father, age 87, has lived with her for 10 years. Mrs. H is an only child, divorced, with no children. Her father has a heart condition, arthritis, wears a hearing aid, and is argumentative.

Mrs. L: Mrs. L's mother, age 83, has Alzheimer's disease and diabetes. Mrs. L's husband resents his mother-in-law's presence and would like Mrs. L to place her mother in a nursing home.

Miss O: Miss O has been taking care of her mother for 13 years since her father died. Her mother, age 74, lives next door. Miss O's own health is poor because of arthritis and open heart surgery three years ago.

Mrs. M: Mrs. M's mother, age 77, lived alone until four years ago when she had a series of strokes. Her physician did not think she should be home alone when released from the hospital. She has since been living with Mrs. M.

Mrs. T: Mrs. T is a 36-year-old married woman with three children, ages 4, 7, and 12. Mrs. T had planned to go back to work when her youngest child entered first grade, but she is not sure that she can manage this now because her mother has come to live with the family. Mrs. T is caring for her 71-year-old mother, who is suffering from manic depression and high blood pressure. Mrs. T's mother has been in the United States for 45 years and has lived with Mrs. T since being released from a state psychiatric institution three-and-a-half years ago. Mrs. T's mother had worked as a house cleaner but is now retired. She has had mental health problems for many years and has been in and out of the psychiatric units of local hospitals. She takes medication to control her psychiatric symptoms and her high blood pressure.

Notice that all members of the group are women and that all are caring for parents or parents-in-law. Having done some research before leading her first caregiver group, the leader, Mrs. S, was aware that the two most common groups of caregivers of the frail elderly are spouses and adult children. In a previous group that Mrs. S conducted for caregivers, she found that adult child caregivers had concerns and issues that were different from issues of spouse caregivers. For example, she found that adult children were more concerned about the effect of caregiving on their relationships with their spouses and their own children. They were also more concerned about work-related issues and about the responsibilities and duties of a child to a parent.

Mrs. S also found that women and men react differently to caregiving and have different concerns and issues. She observed, for example, that women were less comfortable discussing their relationships with their husbands and in discussing their roles as wives, mothers, and caregivers when men were present in the group. She also realized that many daughters-in-law shared the same concerns as daughters. Therefore, Mrs. S decided to limit participation in this particular group to daughters and daughters-in-law.

After the introductions, norms for group participation were discussed and agreed to by all members. Emphasis was placed on the confidential nature of the group discussions. Because problem solving was a major focus of the group, the eight-step problem-solving model was presented in some detail by Mrs. S. She also tried to incorporate problem solving into each of the weekly educational topics. For example, when the group discussed feelings that caregivers typically experienced, the focus was not only on group sharing of emotions such as anger or guilt, but also on problem-solving techniques that could help members to cope better with these feelings outside the group.

Session 2

By the second session, members were beginning to feel comfortable with each other. Cohesion and trust were beginning to build. The following dialogue occurred during the problem-solving component of the session:

Mrs. T: My husband really has a hard time dealing with my mother. I can understand his feelings. She is hard to live with. But I'm caught in the middle—I'm the only daughter she has.

Mrs. L: I know what you mean. You know, my mother has Alzheimer's disease. In the past two years it's gotten a lot worse. My husband says it's about time that I think about putting Mom in a nursing home. I do think about it, but I just can't bring myself to do it.

Mrs. T: [looking at Mrs. S] What should I do? I feel like I'm trapped.

Mrs. S: Both of you are in a difficult situation. [She looks at Mrs. T.] Is there one thing that your mother does that is particularly bothersome?

Mrs. T: [pause] When Mom refuses to take her medication, her mood swings really get out of hand. At that point, even I have trouble with her.

Mrs. S: Is there any pattern to your mom's refusal to take her medication?

Mrs. T: It seems she does it when we try to get away. We have a summer camp on Lake Jones. [pause] We've been going up there on weekends for years. It's only been the past few years when Mom has gotten so frail that going to camp has become a real problem. We have a neighbor that we met at church look after her when we go now, but I think she resents us leaving her alone.

Mrs. S asks Mrs. T to elaborate on her relationship with her mother. After gathering additional information, several possible solutions to the problem are suggested by members.

Mrs. L: Why don't you take her when you go?

Mrs. T: We've tried that. The trip is too much for her. She gets exhausted. Besides, she really doesn't like it up there. You know, it's a pretty primitive camp. TV and radio reception aren't very good, and the place is small—only three rooms. That's the way they were built years ago.

Mrs. H: Maybe you could put the medication in her favorite beverage and leave it for her in individual containers in the refrigerator.

Mrs. T: I don't think that will work. My mother insists on taking her own medication.

Miss G: How about using that respite service up at St. Peter's (hospital)? We used it, and it was good. They could give her medications.

Mrs. T: Mother would never go for that.

Mrs. S: Remember about step 2 of the problem-solving model [pointing to the flip chart and turning to Mrs. T]. Don't judge the solutions before hearing what everyone has to say. Okay?

Mrs. T: Oh, right. I forgot.

Miss G: What does her psychiatrist say? Why don't you ask him what to do?

Mrs. M: What about having a home health aide come in when you're gone?

Mrs. S: Anybody else have any suggestions?

Miss O: You have a brother, don't you?

Mrs. T: Yes, I do.

Miss O: Does he live in town?

Mrs. T: Yes, he does. We've always been close.

Miss O: What about asking him to take your mother, or to sit with her when you want to go away?

Mrs. S: Anybody else? [She scans the group for suggestions.] Okay, then, let me go over what has been suggested.

Mrs. S recaps the suggestions. Mrs. T says that asking the psychiatrist is the suggestion she is most comfortable with. Mrs. T describes what she will ask the psychiatrist, and the group helps her figure out how she will respond if he does not address her questions appropriately. Mrs. S suggests that Mrs. T role-play the situation, but Mrs. T is reluctant. Mrs. S models a response with Mrs. Z playing the psychiatrist. The group laughs as Mrs. Z pretends she has a Viennese accent and introduces herself as Dr. Freud. Next, Mrs. T practices her response. At the end of the role play, Mrs. T also says she might ask her brother to help out. She explains that she has not wanted to trouble him because "he is very busy with his own family." She also explains that he has offered to help out in the past. During subsequent sessions, Mrs. S tries to reinforce problem-solving skills and to focus group discussion in that direction.

The following dialogue, which occurred at the end of the group meeting, illustrates how Mrs. S tries to help group members become more aware of group processes, and how she encourages members' input.

Mrs. S: Gee, I don't know where the time goes, but we're almost out of time. As you know, I like to spend a few minutes at the end of each meeting talking about what I've observed and getting some feedback from you. I noticed today that you are really becoming comfortable with each other. I like the way you're connecting with each other, the way you share with each other and support each other.

Miss G: You mean you can't get a word in! [laughter from the group]

Mrs. S: It's good to see. What about the rest of you? What are your feelings about the group? [She scans the group.]

Mrs. T: So far, it's been great. I really look forward to coming.

Miss O: I wish I had joined a group a long time ago. It's really helping me to see how others are managing.

Mrs. A: I really like it, too. If I had one suggestion, I guess it would be that I'd like to get a little more specific information.

Mrs. S: Specific information?

Mrs. A: Well, my mother's doctor really didn't tell me much about what I should expect. I mean, I'd like to find out more about Parkinson's disease.

Mrs. S: I see. I won't be able to get too specific during meetings because of all the different problems you're coping with. [She scans the group.] But what I can do is to identify resources where you can find out more information. How would that be?

Mrs. A: I'd really appreciate that.

Mrs. L: If it's possible, I'd like to find out more about Alzheimer's disease.

Mrs. S: Okay, on the way out write down what illnesses, or what things you'd like more information about. During the week, I'll do a little investigating and see if I can't find out where you can get more information.

Session 3

The following dialogue from the third session illustrates how the coping-skills component was implemented.

Mrs. B: I feel really sorry for my mother-in-law. I have to work and she's home alone all day. She really misses Tom [her son]. She keeps saying she can't understand why he died and she's still alive. She says she wants to die.

Mrs. S: That's really hard.

Mrs. B: The thing is, there's nothing I can do. She just keeps repeating the same things. Sometimes, you know, I get really frustrated. Then I feel guilty because I know she can't help it.

Mrs. S: What's the feeling like?

Mrs. B: I can feel myself getting tense just before I get home. I think I'm anticipating hearing her say how much she misses Tom and that she wishes she was with him. Sometimes, I feel like pulling out of the driveway and not walking in. But I know that's not realistic.

Mrs. S: What about the deep breathing exercise we just practiced? Do you think that might help calm you down? You could practice that while you're still out in the car before you come in.

Mrs. B: Yes, I could try that. I'll try anything at this point. Sometimes, my stomach really starts to churn when I start driving down my street. Maybe if I take a few deep breaths and remind myself that I'm doing the best I can for her, then it won't get to me so much.

Miss G: Yeah, I know that when Mother drives me crazy it helps me to disappear into another room for a few minutes. Anything that will get me to stop and think before I snap at her might help. Maybe the deep breathing will help me not to lose it—if you know what I mean.

Mrs. H: I sure do. Sometimes, I could strangle my father. You know, it's funny. I would never say that in front of anybody else. They'd think I was a terrible person, a terrible daughter.

Miss O: I think we all feel like that sometimes. [Several group members nod.] How can you help it! I love her [Miss O's mother], but sometimes it just gets to me, it's so constant.

Mrs. S: [looking at Miss G, Mrs. H, and Miss O] It's a real struggle but you can really be proud of how much you are doing. Well, maybe the deep breathing will help. Try it and let me know what you think next week. Okay?

During session 3, a brief sample of dialogue also illustrates how the support component of the group has a positive effect.

Mrs. L: I feel better than I did before coming here. The situation hasn't become any easier, but I've begun thinking about various alternatives [for her mother]. You [looking at Mrs. S and then around the group] really understand what I'm going through deciding if it's time to put her in a home. I think that somehow that has given me the courage to really begin to explore options. I feel like I'm not an awful person.

Mrs. Z and others: Of course you're not! You've done so much for her, more than what a lot of others would have done. But, sometimes it's time. It may be better for her and for you.

Mrs. L: Before I came here I really felt like I was going crazy. Like I was the only one in this kind of a situation. But I'm not. Some of you have it a lot worse than me.

Miss O: Jean [Mrs. L], I just wanted you to know that you're an inspiration to me. Sometimes, when I'm down and I think about giving up, I think of you. I'm sure whatever you decide about your mom, it will be for the best.

Mrs. L: I hope so, I'm trying to do what's right.

Mrs. Z: We're all trying our best, it's just so hard!

Session 4

The following dialogue, taken from a discussion after the educational component of session 4, illustrates that it is possible for more than one member of a group to derive benefit from the discussion of a particular topic.

Mrs. H: Does anybody feel that their parent is manipulative in their caregiving situation?

Mrs. A: I think manipulation gains advantage.

Mrs. S: I don't understand quite what you mean. Why don't you give us an example?

Mrs. H: When my father says he really doesn't feel good, I think he is really telling me that I shouldn't go out and leave him [alone]. I feel like my life is out of my control—that I'm being manipulated by him. If I leave him, and something happens while I'm out, I'd feel terribly guilty for not being there. But when I stay home, I really resent having to give up my plans, my life.

Mrs. S: Maybe he needs to be reassured that he's still as important to you as you are to him.

Mrs. T: You know the need to be reassured could explain my mother's behavior, too.

Mrs. S: Do you see a connection between your mother's medication problem and feeling manipulated?

Mrs. T: Well, yes, when she doesn't take her medicine she becomes the center of attention.

It's almost like she believes it will distract us from going to our camp without her on weekends.

Mrs. H: Your mother won't take her pills just to feel that you still love her and will not abandon her?

Mrs. T: It sounds like that could be, don't you think so? [She looks at Mrs. S.]

Mrs. S: [scanning the group] What do you think?

Mrs. L: Even if it's true, what can she do about it?

Mrs. Z: You know, I've found it helps to let them know you know they are manipulating you. Sometimes if you lay your cards on the table, you can be in a better position to prevent the manipulation.

Mrs. B: That's fine, but it's not easy to do. My mother-in-law would just say I was overreacting.

Miss O: You have to remember that you have rights, too. You have to stand up for yourself. Remember the topic for today's meeting, taking care of yourself.

Mrs. S asks Mrs. T if she has any other thoughts. Mrs. T brings up her worries about vacation plans for the upcoming summer season.

Mrs. T: If my husband and I can't handle her intrusion into our weekend trips, what would she do if we tried to go on a longer vacation? I thought I was going to go back to work now that my children are getting older. But even having company over is a problem. Mental illness is not like physical illness. I can't even take a short vacation without worrying. How will I ever be able to go back to work?

The group members respond with empathy. They agree that mental illness is potentially more embarrassing because of the unpredictable nature of some psychiatric symptoms.

Mrs. T: And you know, I'm darn tired of hearing, "I don't know how you do it" from family and friends. I'm not looking for meaningless praise.

Mrs. B: I know exactly what you mean. Occasionally, I'd like to hear an offer of help, rather than being praised for what I'm doing all by myself!

Miss G: What's the use? I have four brothers and they expect me to do everything. It's always been that way. When I complain to my mother, all she does is stick up for them. She makes excuses for them. She says they are busy with their own families, that if they could help out they would. But, what about me? What about my life? Don't I deserve a break?

Mrs. S: It's frustrating, isn't it?

Miss G: It sure is. But at least I can share some of my feelings here. Before, I had no one I could talk to.

Mrs. T: It does help to talk about it. My husband commented the other day that the group meetings seem to help me have a little more patience with the children and with my mother.

Mrs. S: [scanning the group] I'm glad to hear you're getting something out of the group. You deserve it. And I'm glad you're here for each other. There's nothing like sharing and giving and getting ideas and suggestions from each other. [Members nod and there is a pause.] Well, what about a break? When we come back, I'll go over a strategy that may help you cope with your frustration, and then during problem solving we can think of ways that may help us get family more involved.

Miss G: Sounds good to me.

Mrs. B: Me too.

Session 6

The original group contract was for members to meet for eight weekly sessions (no monthly follow-up meetings), so during session 6, Mrs. S brings up the issue of group termination. She mentions that another group she conducted had continued to meet. She also mentions that group members could be a resource for each other by keeping in regular phone contact, which leads to a general discussion by group members about the benefits of the support group.

Miss O: On the way over here tonight I was worrying about what I would do when the group ended. You know, friends don't really understand. They mean well, but unless they are doing it too, they just don't know what it's like to be tied down like this and not know when it's going to end. Sometimes, I think my mother will go on forever and I will die first.

Mrs. Z: You're right, how many friends can you discuss the differences between Depends and Attends [different brands of adult diapers], which ones to use, and what store has the best prices?

Mrs. M: Yeah, even if you have a good friend, you might drive her away if you talk about what's really on your mind. Can you tell your friend you think about what it would be like if your mother died? Your friend will think you're a monster and tell you that you should be grateful your mother is still alive. I don't know what I would do without the group.

Mrs. T: You know, ever since I started coming here I've been more patient with my mother. I think it's because I know I can let it all out here. I really look forward to coming here because I know you all understand what I'm going through.

Mrs. S: I take it, then, from all your comments that you're not sure if you want to end. Why don't you all give it some thought? We'll discuss this again next week. Okay?

Session 7

During the problem-solving component, Mrs. T admits to still feeling manipulated.

Mrs. T: I'm playing her game, playing into her hands, and I can't take it anymore. I finally got a chance to speak to Dr. L about my mother's medication. He mentioned an apartment where they have staff 24 hours a day, run by the county mental health center. I think he called it the Supportive Living Program.

Mrs. S: How do you feel about the suggestion from the doctor?

Mrs. T: Terrible. I can't even bring myself to dial the phone numbers to find out more about it. I want to, but I feel like I'd be abandoning her.

Mrs. Z and Mrs. H both say that even if she feels uncomfortable considering this move, Mrs. T has still come a long way since session 1. However, other members confront Mrs. T and remind her it takes two to continue the manipulative pattern.

Mrs. B: Nobody can manipulate you unless you let them.

Mrs. M: That's right, it takes two, you know. You must be letting her do this to you or she wouldn't be able to do it.

Mrs. B: By not going [on weekends] you give your mother a tremendous sense of power and control.

Mrs. T: But even her psychiatrist says he never dealt with someone like her before.

Mrs. M: Do you find that reassuring?

Mrs. T: Yeah, wouldn't you?

Mrs. S: I think that the other members of the group are trying to point out that you are the one who is responsible for your own happiness, not Anna [Mrs. T's mother]. They are trying to convey that it's up to you to take control of this situation, and that you can do it.

Mrs. T: I know I have to do it, I have to do something.

Member-to-member confrontation in the context of mutual aid and mutual support helps members to gain new perspectives and become motivated to handle problems in new ways.
During the seventh session the following dialogue occurred:

Mrs. T: I have some good news. I finally got up the courage to ask my brother. He spoke to his wife and they agreed to team up and help out. They said they would take care of Mom anytime we went away, as long as we let them know in advance, and that's not a problem. Jack [her husband] was real happy about that, so he hasn't bothered me one bit about Mom being in our house recently. In fact, he's been a big help lately.

Mrs. S: That's wonderful. [Other members nod and there is a pause.]

Mrs. L: I've been thinking maybe it's time to find a place [nursing home] for Mom. But, every time I do, I get to feeling so guilty.

Mrs. S: [speaking to Mrs. L and the entire group] Remember the self-talk coping skills we learned earlier; part of guilt is what you tell yourself.

Mrs. Z: Give yourself credit for time served, look at what you have done, and have tried to do already. That's what I do, that and read the Bible.

Mrs. S: [speaking to the entire group] Mrs. Z says positive things to herself and reads the Bible. What about the rest of you? What things have you found that help you cope?

During the seventh group meeting, the members also decided to continue to meet once a month and to stay in contact with each other by telephone between meetings.

A Follow-Up Session

During a follow-up meeting almost one year after the eight weekly group meetings, Mrs. L reported the following news.

Mrs. L: As some of you already know, Mom is now at Eaton Park [a skilled nursing facility]. She took a turn for the worse about a month ago. She had to be sent to St. Peter's [hospital] for over a week. I didn't know what to do [pause] about taking her back. I mean, I still wanted her home. I know that's what she would have wanted. But she was so bad she didn't even recognize me anymore. I thought about what you had said to me [during the meetings], how I shouldn't feel guilty when it was time to have her go to a home, how much I had done for her over the years. It meant a lot to me.

Mrs. S: You've meant a lot to us.

Mrs. L: I just couldn't keep taking care of her. I had to watch her every minute, afraid she'd walk out of the house and get lost—or worse, burn down the house or something. I had lunch with Beatrice [Mrs. M] while my mother was in the hospital, and Mary and Sarah [Mrs. W and Mrs. Z] called. That helped give me the courage to go ahead with what I had to do. You know, without the support of the group, I think I would have fallen apart.

A COMMUNITY COALITION

This case example describes a group work effort to bring together representatives of several community service agencies to help establish a community residence for people with AIDS. The case was selected because it portrays how the group worker plans and implements a strategy for community change by using a range of group work skills during several sessions of the group. The case also illustrates that members of coalitions have varied special interests and political concerns that require the worker to assess and intervene both within the group and within larger systems outside the group, such as the community.

The group worker, Ms. C, is an experienced social worker employed by the United Services Association (USA), a small, multiservice agency in River Falls, a city of about 250,000. River Falls has a well-developed social service system, several hospitals and health facilities, and a number of community residences for the mentally ill and the developmentally disabled. However, there are no community residences for people with AIDS, perhaps because the AIDS crisis has never been fully acknowledged by community residents and leaders.

The chief executive of USA asked Ms. C to compose a group to help the agency establish a community residence for people with AIDS. The executive had recently been contacted by representatives of two local hospitals. They urged him to involve the agency in community residence programming for people with AIDS. The hospitals were receiving more AIDS cases, but few had discharge-planning options for patients who no longer required hospitalization but who were unable to return home.

The state had recently announced funding for community residences for people with AIDS, and the executive director had completed the agency's grant application for the project. The agency expected a response to its application in about two months. Meanwhile, the executive director thought the coalition group could begin to discuss how they could assist in establishing the residence and its services. The cooperative effort of the agency representatives was an important factor in establishing the community residence because the agency would provide a wider resource base in support of such an effort and might help overcome the anticipated negative reaction to the residence from members and leaders of this conservative community.

The Planning Stage

Several planning considerations needed resolution before the coalition could be established:

- Ms. C was assured of the support of the USA organization in planning for and financing the new residence, but she was concerned about how other social service agencies would perceive the organization's intentions. In establishing other community residences for the developmentally disabled, the agency had encountered resistance from other agencies, which USA assessed as "turf issues." It would be necessary to involve these agencies early in the planning effort to help avoid similar resistance.

- However, Ms. C noted that she had several important contacts in local social service and community organizations and that these people could probably be counted on to support the plan and work together.

- Ms. C decided to identify potential members and assess their organizations' willingness to align with the purpose of the coalition (planning and supporting the community residence). In addition, she would need to assess potential differences of opinion and inform potential coalition-group members about how the coalition could help USA in its efforts.

- In recruiting for the coalition, a diverse group of members representing a variety of service issues relevant to people with AIDS would be sought. Ms. C would seek coalition members who displayed a homogeneity of attitude about support for people with AIDS and who had heterogenous talents and resources that were needed for the group to achieve its purpose.

- Although the coalition could start out as a small group, it would probably be necessary to add members as other agencies important to the project were identified. Thus, the coalition would function as an open group.

- Because of the potential for interagency turf issues and because of the likelihood of community resistance to the proposed residence, the coalition would need to meet in a neutral community setting. The setting would also have to accommodate larger numbers of community people when public testimony and discussion were sought by the coalition.

It was arranged for meetings to take place every other week in the meeting room of the local Episcopal church. The church had adequate space, and outreach workers from the church's volunteer service committee had a strong history of serving people with AIDS in River Falls. Ms. C made a list of potential members, visited several of them, and telephoned others. Briefly orienting the potential members to the purpose of the group, she was able to secure promises of weekly attendance from the following people, who would represent their organizations:

The Rev. and Mrs. W: Codirectors, River Falls Episcopal Street Ministry

Mr. S: Manager, River Falls City Housing Authority

Ms. P: Director, The Fallsview Homeless Shelter

Mr. L: Outreach worker, The Gay and Lesbian Community Center

The Rev. G: Pastor, Our Lady Star of the Sea, Roman Catholic Church

Mr. A: AIDS educator, AIDS Council of River Falls

Dr. J: Chief of staff, River Falls General Hospital

Mrs. B: Social worker, St. Mary's Hospital of River Falls

Mr. Z: Support group coordinator, Families of PWA

Ms. T: Director of social services, River County

Mr. R: Professor of social work, River College

The Beginning Stage

Ms. C arranged a mutually agreeable time for all potential members to meet in the Episcopal church's meeting room. Before the first session, she reviewed the purpose of the coalition as she envisioned it. To help members fully identify with the goals of the group, she prepared a short statement that included recognition that the members might want to discuss the group's purpose in the early sessions.

> *The purpose of this group is to discuss the need for community residence planning for people with AIDS in River Falls. The USA organization is prepared to sponsor a community residence for people with AIDS and is interested in securing planning assistance and support from this coalition. Of particular importance is how to secure community acceptance for this new type of community residence. As a group, I think it would be really helpful for us to discuss how we might attempt to gain community acceptance and support for the residence.*

The First Session

Members arrived on time and appeared to be enthusiastic. Ms. C noted that members greeted each other eagerly and broke into groups of two or three to discuss topics of mutual interest and exchange small talk. For several members who knew each other from telephone conversations or who had heard of each other before, this was their first face-to-face contact, so the mood of the group took on a festive tone. Ms. C called the group to order, and members gathered chairs in a circle. The following dialogue occurred:

Ms. C: I want to thank all of you for coming today. I noticed that several of you have finally seen faces of people you have only known from the telephone. This is a great way to start this group, and it suggests that we need to find other ways of getting together more often. [She pauses.] As I discussed with each of you, the USA organization is interested in exploring the possibility of starting a community residence for persons with AIDS. I have been asked to convene a coalition group of experts in this work to assist in this project. Your initial reaction to our proposal has been quite positive, and the next step is for us to meet and discuss the project. I am distributing a statement that I envision as a beginning purpose for this group. [She hands out a copy of the statement of purpose.] I would appreciate it if you would take a minute and read this. [Members read silently.] Having read the statement, perhaps this would be a good time to introduce ourselves. Would each of you introduce yourself, and give the group some feedback about the statement of purpose?

The Rev. W: I'll start, since it is our pleasure to host all of you today in our community meeting room. My wife and I have long been supporters of services to people with AIDS, and we have a special program in our street ministry that offers support and emergency assistance to people with AIDS and their families. We see the need for housing for these folks, and we are pleased to offer any support we can.

Mr. S: I agree. The Housing Authority supports the idea of community residences for people with AIDS, although I would add that many of our elected officials would rather see them treated in larger facilities in other communities. There is a housing shortage in River Falls, and I don't see it getting any better. I would suggest that we proceed carefully so we can overcome some of the stereotypes about people with AIDS and convince other community leaders that this project is a worthy one.

Ms. P: I believe there are several people with AIDS residing on a temporary basis in our homeless shelter. We have been offering shelter to several people who are in the process of testing and treatment for AIDS, but we can offer little help other than our shelter, which is not particularly well equipped for dealing with people with health problems such as AIDS. Our organization recognizes the need for a more specialized facility, but we are skeptical about whether such a residence would be accepted in any of River Falls' neighborhoods.

Mr. L: The Gay and Lesbian Community Center has offered some support to people with AIDS, but we are not equipped for dealing with some of their difficult health concerns. It would seem to us that any community residence for people with AIDS should have a strong health or medical services orientation. We see the major issue here as overcoming the strong homophobic reaction of community leaders and residents, even though many persons with AIDS are heterosexual.

Mr. A: The AIDS Council is prepared to contract with the USA organization to provide health and medical services for residents of the proposed residence. We also think we can be valuable in educating the public about AIDS, as this is part of our mission. Any proposal such as this would need to have a strong component of community education; this is the only way to overcome the usual resistance to dealing with AIDS.

The Rev. G: It is a shame that our community has such narrow ideas about people with AIDS. I agree with what has been said so far. I can't speak for our parish, but our priests recognize the need to minister to people with AIDS—we need assistance in learning more about how to be helpful. This is why I am here.

Dr. J: The River Falls General Hospital has been seeing more patients who have been diagnosed as HIV-positive, and has been treating increasing numbers of people with serious opportunistic infections related to AIDS. Some of these people remain in the hospital for extended periods, but when they are ready to be discharged, they find that they have no place to go. Many lose their housing because they can't afford to keep up mortgage or rent payments. Many also lose their jobs, and, as you know, this means they lose their health insurance. It is a very difficult situation, and I'm not sure that the County Social Services Department is doing its share to help these people.

Mrs. B: Our experience in the social services department of St. Mary's Hospital is very similar. I agree with Dr. J.

Ms. T: I don't think that last statement is an accurate one. The county has emergency funds to help people with some of the costs for temporary housing, but we are not equipped to serve the increasing numbers of homeless people in this county. I'm not sure that the hospitals are taking enough responsibility in these matters.

Mr. Z: The support groups we run for families of people with AIDS have many similar themes. We think a community residence would assist people in transition from hospital to more permanent housing. In some cases, people with AIDS will never return to a place they call home.

Mr. R: I am here because River College, particularly the social work program, is interested in lending support and perhaps student assistance to this effort to plan for people with AIDS. Last semester, my students and I did a preliminary needs assessment in cooperation with the Department of Health, and what we found may surprise you. I brought copies of our report today and I will gladly discuss our findings with this group.

Ms. C noted that all members had spoken and contributed their organization's initial reaction to the USA proposal. Although there appeared to be support expressed for the idea of a community residence, she noted tension between the director of the County Social Services Department and representatives of the local hospitals. She decided not to address the tension at this time. Instead, she decided to summarize some of the major points of the previous discussion.

Ms. C: I appreciate your candid comments. Several themes have emerged; let me try to summarize them. The problem of housing for people with AIDS seems to be verified based on most of your comments. Another important issue identified by some of you is the potential reaction of community residents to housing for individuals who are HIV-positive. Several of you commented on local reaction, in general, to the AIDS crisis. In addition, some of you suggested services for people with AIDS, as well as health and medical services and the need for community education about AIDS. How does that summary sound to you? Is it a fair portrayal of our first conversation together?

The summary of the initial comments helped the group review some of the overt agendas of the individual members and their agencies. Ms. C thought it important to let the group know that the USA organization was in the process of applying for state funding and was prepared to take action on establishing the community residence within the next few months if funding were received. The agency also wanted to make it clear at the first eting that it would be the actual service provider, with autonomy and control over the operation of the residence. Ms. C stated the USA's agenda and solicited feedback from the group:

Ms. C: I need to speak briefly on behalf of my own agency. My executive has asked me to make clear our intentions to carry out this project. Although we intend to do most of the work of establishing funding, finding a location, and applying for housing permits and other regulatory requirements, we need your help in two ways. First, we recognize the collective expertise in this room today. We hope to use many of the services your organizations offer. We may contract for services with some of you and ask others for guidance in this effort to provide services to people with AIDS. Second, we recognize that there is potential for a great deal of community resistance to this project. We hope that you will assist us in challenging potential resistance and help us mediate conflicts that could occur. I'd like to get some feedback from you about our intentions and how we can cooperate in this important endeavor.

Dr. J: I appreciate your openness, and I think my organization can support your intentions.

Mr. Z: I'm not sure how I can help, but perhaps we can find that out as we go along.

Ms. C: Thank you. Are there other comments from members? [She scans the group.]

Mr. R: I have discussed the need for community residence programming with students at River College and they are interested in helping. Could a student representative of the Social Work Club attend our meetings?

Ms. C: How would everyone feel about that? [Members nod in agreement.]

The Rev. W: It looks to me as if most of us here think this is a good idea. It also appears that most of us support the idea of USA taking the lead in this project.

Ms. C: Can I ask if there are concerns about the project that any of you have?

Ms. T: I personally support this project. However, I think it's important to recognize that many of our local leaders and politicians in River Falls might not feel the same way. They may also think the Department of Social Services should not be involved. Since our funding is somewhat controlled by our community leaders, our agency may have some difficulty in participating.

The Rev. W: I appreciate what you are saying, and you might count on some of us talking to our politicians about the project if you think it will help.

Mr. L: We can't forget politics here. Many of our political leaders are not in favor of services that make them or their constituents uncomfortable.

Ms. C: Can you elaborate on this for us?

Mr. L: I just think there is a lot of resistance to acknowledging that our community has a problem with AIDS. I think we should start discussing this and how we can overcome the resistance. [Members verbalize agreement.]

Ms. C: It is easy to see, from all of your reactions to [Mr. L's] comment, that you think River Falls should acknowledge the AIDS crisis. This seems to be a recurring theme in our discussions so far. Do others want to comment on this?

Ms. P: I would suggest that this group concentrate on helping the community learn about AIDS. This would allow the USA to do what it does best—namely, work on establishing community residences.

Mr. L: This seems reasonable.

The Rev. G: You're suggesting we establish some sort of educational effort to get information about AIDS to the community?

Ms. P: Yes, that's a possibility. If the public could see us working together to do this, they might take this information more seriously.

Mr. L: Then perhaps community residence programming might go more smoothly.

Ms. P: Exactly!

This interaction demonstrates how group discussion helped the group come to a fuller understanding of the group's purpose. Although Ms. C stated the general purpose for the group (assisting in establishment of a community residence), the group started to define and modify the purpose through its initial discussions. Ms. C realized that modifying the group purpose was an important step to building group cohesion and was necessary before the group could be productive.

In the next interaction, Ms. C probed the group for potential obstacles to group consensus on purpose, including differences of opinion about the work of the group. She recognized that groups often mask their differences in the beginning stage and that the illusion of unanimity among members can hide obstacles to productive work.

Ms. C: Most of us appear to be in favor of helping the community accept the AIDS crisis, but I wonder if we all mean the same thing? How do you think the group might approach this task of community education?

Mr. S: I hope this doesn't mean that we want to have a demonstration or picket the city offices! I could lose my job.

Ms. C: Could you elaborate on that?

Mr. S: Well, you might have read last week in the papers, there was an organization called ACT-UP demonstrating at the Center City Commissioner's office. They were trying to get the attention of some local politicians and were hoping to get them to appropriate money for support of persons with AIDS. They made the commissioner and themselves look bad.

Mr. L: ACT-UP demonstrations are only one way to educate the public, but sometimes that type of strategy is necessary.

Mr. S: I can't be part of anything like that. I'm a city employee!

Mr. L: I can understand that; maybe there are other ways you can contribute.

Mr. Z: Most of the members of our support group for families do not agree with ACT-UP's philosophy and tactics. Many of our members have a need for anonymity and confidentiality. I doubt they would support that kind of experience.

Ms. C: Perhaps we need to consider some ideas about how to go about our task. Planning a demonstration or using conflict as a strategy are only two ways to approach our task; let's discuss other ways.

Two members expressed their mutual concern about how the group would achieve its goals. Although Ms. C encountered potential obstacles to the group working together, she recognized that the concerns were part of a normally functioning group in its beginning stage. She facilitated work on how the group would achieve its goals. During the first session, the group agreed to consider possible strategies for carrying out a community education project to help USA in its efforts to establish a community residence.

The Second Session

The second session focused on the content of the planned educational presentation—how group members could gather general information about AIDS and specific information about its prevalence in River Falls. The group decided to divide into two subcommittees, one to collect resources such as videotapes, written material, and names of possible speakers, and the other to collect specific information on how many cases of AIDS have been diagnosed in River

Falls. Each member volunteered for a particular subcommittee depending on what expertise was needed. Each subcommittee was to bring its information back to the next meeting.

The Third Session

In the third session, each subcommittee presented its findings, and the session was educational for all. Discussions centered on how the group would use the findings to teach members of the community about AIDS. The group discussed how to design the educational effort. Ms. C led the group in a brainstorming exercise to generate as many ideas as possible about how to teach members of the community about AIDS. The group then had a freewheeling discussion of all options, and members were asked to rank their top three choices. The choices with the most votes were listed on a flip chart, and members were again asked to discuss the top few choices. Although the group was asked to vote one more time to choose the best options, it decided to try to reach consensus without a formal vote. The following dialogue took place:

Mr. R: It appears that we have a few good ideas about how to inform the public about AIDS. I prefer a general educational meeting, open to the public.

Ms. C: [scanning the group] What are other members' preferences?

Mrs. B: I have been impressed with the work done by Mr. A and the AIDS Council. I wonder if the council would take major responsibility for presenting a program open to the public?

Mr. R: I was wondering the same thing. It seems this type of educational program should be done by experts, who have the most up-to-date information.

Mr. A: Our agency would be glad to take the lead.

Ms. C: How would other members feel about that?

Ms. P: This seems like a logical choice. Still, we should be involved in the effort to provide support and to suggest that we are all in this together.

Mr. R: I suggest we all be available to be discussion leaders, perhaps divide into smaller groups to discuss questions.

Ms. P: I agree. We need to be part of all of the strategies to get this information to the public. Let's decide where and when.

Ms. C: I just want to make sure that we are all in agreement. Can I ask all of you if an open educational presentation is your first choice? [All members indicate their support.] Then we have reached consensus on this issue.

The Middle Stage

The group met for its fourth and fifth sessions to plan the details of the educational meeting with the public. Room and space arrangements were made, refreshments were purchased, and members of the group took responsibility for advertising and encouraging community leaders to attend. One day before the presentation, the local television news ran a story about the coalition and its work, which gave much-needed publicity to the educational effort. Despite a small group of community residents who expressed their opposition to the event, the presentation was well attended and well received, and community residents had opportunities to ask questions in small group discussions.

The coalition had a debriefing session at a local restaurant, and Ms. C announced that the community residence proposal had received the grant and the project was ready to proceed. The next step was to find a suitable location with room to house five to eight people with AIDS. She reported that a house had been found in a neighborhood near a hospital and that discussions were taking place between the owners of the house and the USA agency. Ms. C asked the group to convene again to discuss further planning for the project.

The Sixth Session

The sixth session of the group was supposed to focus on plans to open the community residence. The USA agency was taking the responsibility for many of the details involved in opening the residence, but the executive director wanted the group to help plan how some of the health, counseling, transportation, and other services could be provided.

However, as news of the proposed residence spread throughout the community, opposition to the chosen location began to grow. Community political leaders, responding to pressures from residents, threatened to pass zoning legislation that could exclude the USA from opening the residence in the chosen area. Ms. C convened the group to discuss the new development. After Ms. C's opening remarks, the group started a discussion of a newspaper feature story about local reaction to the idea of opening a community residence for people with AIDS and the threatened zoning change by the River Falls City Council.

Ms. C: As we all know, our plans for a community residence are well under way, and we need to consider what steps the group can take to make this residence a reality. But I have some bad news to announce. It now appears that some members of the River Falls City Council are opposing our efforts. I have been informed by my agency's director that soon the City Council will attempt to rezone the area we have chosen for the residence to prevent us from opening a multiple-resident dwelling. Our agency is prepared to go to court to prevent this, but I was wondering if the group had some suggestions for a different strategy?

Ms. P: I think the coalition can do several things. For one thing, we all know some of our City Council members—we could meet with them individually and try to persuade them to change their minds.

Ms. C: How do you suggest we go about that?

Ms. P: There are any number of ways, but I wonder if some of us could make individual appointments with some of them, perhaps to discuss the proposal and find out what their objections are.

The Rev. G: I agree. At least we could show up, identify ourselves, and ask for a public meeting or hearing to discuss the residence.

Ms. C: This strategy sounds very good. We have an important perspective to offer here. Any other ideas?

Dr. J: I can provide all of us with our latest figures on new cases of AIDS among River Falls residents. Some of this information might suggest that our City Council members need to start making plans for these people rather than ignore them.

Ms. C: I think we can all agree that we have more information than the council members do and that we need to get the information to them before they vote to rezone.

Mr. L: I think they would lose a case in court. They are clearly discriminating against people with AIDS, which is against federal and state antidiscrimination laws.

Mr. S: I share that opinion, but I wonder if an adversarial position is the first strategy we should use?

Mr. R: I'm afraid they're the ones taking the adversarial position. However, I'm in favor of working with them rather than against them.

Mr. S: I don't like this whole idea of going against the City Council. I have to remind you again that I am a city employee, and it would look pretty bad if I were involved in a group that supported a court action against the city.

Mr. L: I'm sorry to hear you say this, because I think eventually we will have to take sides here.

In addition to dealing with the crisis precipitated by the threatened actions of the City Council, Ms. C now faces conflict within the group. The opposing viewpoints of two of the members pose a threat to the cohesiveness of the group. The outside threat—the possible actions of the City Council—brought the group together, but the internal conflict threatens to split the group into opposing sides.

Ms. C: I think it is good that we are open and honest about our reactions here. I appreciate your position, Mr. S, and I wonder if others wish to comment on what you have said?

Mr. Z: I support taking the more conservative approach. As I mentioned before, many members of the support groups my agency sponsors wish to keep their anonymity, and others are not inclined to challenge their City Council members.

Mr. L: I respect what you are saying, but eventually, when things can't be worked out, we will have to challenge them. Perhaps we need to discuss this possibility.

Ms. C: The group seems to be struggling here. I suggest we discuss how we can work out our differences before they interfere with our important efforts to make the residence a reality. Each of you has a valid point. How can we come together on this?

Mrs. B: I think we should consider taking it one step at a time. I was always taught to consider collaboration before conflict. It seems to be more effective for some situations.

Mr. L: Our agency is often forced into conflict with public officials around their continuing homophobia. As you remember, the City Council recently failed to pass antidiscrimination legislation for gay men and lesbian women. I am becoming accustomed to having to fight for the rights of our organization's members.

Ms. C: And you think their opposition to the residence is a similar problem?

Mr. L: Well, no. I guess there are some similar issues here, but I think the City Council might respond positively if we contacted them and discussed the residence and the incidence of new cases of AIDS in our hospitals.

Ms. C: Do others feel the same way? [The group members appear to agree.] So if we agree that our first strategy should be talking and collaborating, can the group work together to accomplish this?

Mr. S: I have no problem with this. I just want us all to agree as a group before we try any other strategy.

Ms. C: You're suggesting that we discuss and reach a consensus on each strategy before we try it?

Mr. S: Yes, this will guarantee we all work together.

Mr. L: We should present a united front and work together whenever we can.

Ms. C: Can the group agree on a rule of consensus when deciding which strategies to employ? [The group orally indicates agreement.]

In this interaction, Ms. C attempted to mediate differences among the members. She remained neutral in the discussion, recognized the validity of opposing viewpoints, and used the resources of the group to support a solution. In addition, Ms. C recognized the necessity of processing group dynamics with the members when the group appeared to be struggling, which had the eventual effect of helping members agree on the rule of consensus that became a norm for the group's future deliberations.

The Seventh Session

The strategy of meeting individually with City Council members was successful. Members divided into subgroups of three and met with council members to share information and make recommendations. The concerted effort of the coalition helped persuade the council to support the project. Two members of the council who were particularly supportive of the community residence were invited to join the group and help implement the project.

The following excerpt is from a group discussion on how to obtain some of the necessary support services for the community residence. Ms. C told the group members they could help USA by suggesting how services could be arranged and financed. The climate of the group was positive because the group had resolved the crisis posed by the threat of rezoning and had added new members who supported the purpose of the group.

Ms. C: I wanted to let you know that progress is being made on the community residence. We have a signed contract with the seller, and we are planning renovations. Our time line is about ten weeks. We have also begun to identify potential staff for the residence. Do any of you have suggestions about how to find additional staff who might be interested in working in the residence?

The Rev. G: I wanted to know if volunteers would be used. Some of our parishioners are interested in donating items, cooking meals, being companions.

Mr. R: I'm proud of the fact that some of our social work students are interested in volunteering to work at the residence.

Ms. C: The USA organization briefly discussed the use of volunteers, but we didn't reach any conclusions. Are other members in touch with possible sources of volunteers?

Mr. A: The AIDS Council has a Buddy Program—a volunteer is paired with a person with AIDS. We could also provide volunteers to help with shopping and transportation and to provide companionship.

Mrs. W: Our church has a volunteer committee, and if some group members could make a short presentation to them, they might be helpful in providing volunteers.

Ms. C: Are there any suggestions about how to proceed on the volunteer possibility?

Mr. R: I would be glad to take responsibility for studying the volunteer idea, talking to those of you who are interested in helping provide volunteers. Would that be agreeable? [Mr. R looks around at the other members.]

Ms. C: It looks like we have a lot of support for this idea. [She looks at Mr. R.] Can you form a subcommittee and get back to us at our next meeting?

Mr. R: Sounds good!

Ms. C: Any other ideas about staffing?

Ms. P: We have several applications for employment in our shelter, and we don't have any openings right now.

Ms. C: I don't think we could have access to applications without violating confidentiality and informed consent, could we?

Ms. P: No problem. If you develop a short employment announcement, we can send it to people whose applications we have. Just don't read it to any of our current staff. [The group laughs.]

Ms. C: I promise!

This excerpt illustrates how the members developed a system of mutual aid during the middle stage of the group's development. Frequent intervention on the part of the group leader was not as necessary as it was in earlier sessions when the group processes included organizing, norm development, and conflict resolution. Members took more responsibility for the business of the group by playing important leadership and task accomplishment roles.

The work of the group continued, which supported the eventual opening of the USA community residence for people with AIDS. Several members of the coalition helped develop a service plan for the residence. The AIDS Council provided educational services for families of the residents. Visiting social workers from the two hospitals were assigned to the residence as part of the discharge planning process for some of the residents. A volunteer program was initiated with the cooperation of several agencies, and oversight of the program was assigned to Mr. Z, the support group coordinator of the Families of People with AIDS organization. Eventually, the coalition changed its focus from providing support for the community residence to carrying out a community needs assessment for further community residences for people with AIDS.

The Ending Stage

The coalition continued to meet during the implementation phase of the new community residence. The residence had a waiting list of many potential residents, and this troubled the coalition. The following excerpt illustrates how the coalition agreed to change its focus and reformulate its goals.

Ms. C: It has been over a year since we started this group. I think we have accomplished quite a bit. This might be a good time to evaluate what we have done as a group. How do you feel about this?

Mr. Z: It seems to me we have achieved our initial goals. I think there is more work to be done in establishing other community residences.

Dr. J: I think we have learned a lot about community residence programming. We have helped educate the community about AIDS, and we have gained support from some important community leaders. We should continue to meet and think about what other tasks we can accomplish.

Ms. C: Do other members feel this way?

Mr. R: I agree. It might be possible for the group to continue but change its focus slightly.

Ms. T: What do you have in mind?

Mr. R: I have been doing some research on the number of new cases of AIDS treated at the local hospitals. I am concerned that the residence only serves a few people, and many more need this service. Perhaps we should study this problem and try to come up with some recommendations to solve it.

Ms. C: I agree with your observations. Would other members be interested in continuing?

Mrs. B: I would be very interested in continuing, especially if we can develop some additional resources for people with AIDS. At the hospital, we are very concerned about developing new discharge planning options.

Ms. C: I notice that many of you appear receptive to the idea of continuing the group. If we agree to continue meeting, we should reformulate our goals. Perhaps we can brainstorm for a while and try to develop some new ideas.

Mr. A: This is a good strategy. We have worked well together and accomplished a lot. I think we should discuss this further.

In it sending stage, the group attempted to evaluate its effectiveness in accomplishing its goals. Although the community residence was operational, and other important tasks had been accomplished by the group, several members identified additional possible tasks. Members felt that it was important to continue the work of the group by doing further research on the needs of people with AIDS in River Falls.

SUMMARY

This chapter presents two cases that illustrate group work practice in a treatment group and a task group. The first case deals with a support group for family members who are providing care for frail elderly relatives. The case illustrates four different components of the group: support, education, developing coping skills, and problem solving. The dialogue concentrates on how members support each other and how they solve problems by developing a system of mutual aid.

The second case illustrates a coalition of community organizations who work together to open a community residence for people with AIDS. The case illustrates how task groups are used in the community and how members with different interests and approaches can work together to accomplish the group's goals.

The two case examples do not necessarily illustrate the ideal processes or outcomes for such groups. The examples were developed to help readers improve their abilities to analyze group work and to apply group work theory to practice situations. It is hoped that the case examples will encourage readers to develop and analyze their own case material.

Guidelines for Ethics

American Group Psychotherapy
Association, Inc.[1]

INTRODUCTION

The American Group Psychotherapy Association is a multi-disciplinary, membership organization dedicated to advancing knowledge, research, and training in group psychotherapy and other group interventions to benefit the client/patient population. The National Registry of Certified Group Psychotherapists advances group psychotherapy by certifying group psychotherapists according to nationally accepted criteria, and promotes these practitioners and principles to other mental health professionals, employers, insurers, educators, and clients for the purpose of maintaining the highest standards for group psychotherapy practice and quality care. Membership in AGPA and/or inclusion in the National Registry requires adherence to standards of ethical practice as outlined by state licensing boards and/or designated national professional organizations, whichever was applicable in establishing clinical credentials. Those who do not belong to a professional group having a published standard of ethics must follow the principles of ethics established by the American Psychological Association.

Ethical complaints about individuals who are members of AGPA and/or listed in the Registry should be directed to the state licensing board or, in the absence of a state license, to the designated primary professional organization of the individual. Should an ethical complaint be received regarding an individual who is a member of AGPA and/or listed in the Registry whose state does not have licensure and who does not belong to a primary professional organization, the complainant will be directed to the state or federal legal system to file his or her complaint.

In the event of the revocation, suspension or voluntary relinquishment of a clinical license to practice or membership/certification in the designated national professional

[1]Reprinted with the permission of the American Group Psychotherapy Association, Inc., 25 East 21st Street, 6th Floor, New York, NY 10010, Telephone: (212) 477-2677.

organization, membership in AGPA and/or inclusion in the Registry will be revoked. In the event an individual referred to the governmental agencies or courts of law is found guilty, his or her AGPA membership and/or his or her inclusion in the Registry will be revoked. It is the responsibility of the individual to inform AGPA and/or the Registry of any revocation, suspension or voluntary relinquishment of licensure or membership/certification, whichever was used to verify clinical credentials for inclusion in the Registry.

GUIDELINES OF GROUP PSYCHOTHERAPY PRACTICE

The following guidelines of group psychotherapy practice shall serve as models for group therapists' ethical behavior.

Responsibility to Patient/Client

1. The group psychotherapist provides services with respect for the dignity and uniqueness of each patient/client as well as the rights and autonomy of the individual patient/client.

   1.1 The group psychotherapist shall provide the potential group patient/client with information about the nature of group psychotherapy and apprise him or her of the risks, rights and obligations as a member of a therapy group.

   1.2. The group psychotherapist shall encourage the patient/client's participation in group psychotherapy only so long as it is appropriate to the patient/client's needs.

   1.3 The group psychotherapist shall not practice or condone any form of discrimination on the basis of race, color, sex, sexual orientation, age, religion, national origin or physical handicap, except that this guideline shall not prohibit group therapy practice with population specific or problem specific groups.

2. The group psychotherapist safeguards the patient/client's right to privacy by judiciously protecting information of a confidential nature.

   2.1 The group shall agree that the patient/client as well as the psychotherapist shall protect the identity of its members.

   2.2 The group therapist is knowledgeable about the limits of privileged communication as they apply to group therapy and informs group members of those limits.

   2.3 The group psychotherapist shall not use identifiable information about the group or its members for teaching purposes, publication or professional presentations unless permission has been obtained and all measures have been taken to preserve patient/client anonymity.

   2.4 Except where required by law, the group psychotherapist shall share information about the group members with others only after obtaining appropriate patient/client consent. Specific permission must be requested to permit conferring with the referring therapist or with the individual therapist where the patient/client is in conjoint therapy.

2.5 When clinical examination suggests that a patient/client may be dangerous to himself/herself or others, it is the group psychotherapist's ethical and legal obligation to take appropriate steps in order to be responsible to society in general, as well as the patient/client.

3. The group psychotherapist acts to safeguard the patient/client and the public from the incompetent, unethical, illegal practice of any group psychotherapist.

3.1 The group psychotherapist must be aware of her/his own individual competencies, and when the needs of the patient/client are beyond the competencies of the psychotherapist, consultation must be sought from other qualified professionals or other appropriate sources.

3.2 The group psychotherapist shall not use her/his professional relationship to advance personal or business interests.

3.3 Sexual intimacy with patients/clients is unethical.

3.4 The group psychotherapist shall protect the patient/client and the public from misinformation and misrepresentation. She/he shall not use false or misleading advertising regarding her/his qualifications or skills as a group psychotherapist.

Professional Standards

The group psychotherapist shall maintain the integrity of the practice of group psychotherapy.

1. It is the personal responsibility of the group psychotherapist to maintain competence in the practice of group psychotherapy through formal educational activities and informal learning experiences.

2. The group psychotherapist has a responsibility to contribute to the ongoing development of the body of knowledge pertaining to group psychotherapy whether involved as an investigator, participant or user of research results.

3. The group psychotherapist shall accept the obligation to attempt to inform and alert other group psychotherapists who are violating ethical principles or to bring those violations to the attention of appropriate professional authorities.

(Revised, February 2002)

Ethical Guidelines for Group Counselors[1]

Association for Specialists in Group Work[2]

ETHICAL GUIDELINES

1. **Orientation and Providing Information:** Group counselors adequately prepare prospective or new group members by providing as much information about the existing or proposed group as necessary.

2. **Screening of Members:** The group counselor screens prospective group members (when appropriate to their theoretical orientation). Insofar as possible, the counselor selects group members whose needs and goals are compatible with the goals of the group, who will not impede the group process, and whose well-being will not be jeopardized by the group experience. An orientation to the group (i.e., ASGW Ethical Guideline #1) is included during the screening process.

3. **Confidentiality:** Group counselors protect members by defining clearly what confidentiality means, why it is important, and the difficulties involved in enforcement.

4. **Voluntary/Involuntary Participation:** Group counselors inform members whether participation is voluntary or involuntary.

5. **Leaving a Group:** Provisions are made to assist a group member to terminate in an effective way.

---

[1]Reprinted From Journal for Specialists in Group Work. 15, 119–226. © (1989) The American Counseling Association. Reprinted with Permission. No Further reproduction without written permission from the American Counseling Association

[2]These guidelines were approved by the Association for Specialists in Group Work (ASGW) Executive Board, June 1, 1989.

6. **Coercion and Pressure:** Group counselors protect member rights against physical threats, intimidation, coercion, and undue peer pressure insofar as is reasonably possible.

7. **Imposing Counselor Values:** Group counselors develop an awareness of their own values and needs and the potential effect they have on the interventions likely to be made.

8. **Equitable Treatment:** Group counselors make every reasonable effort to treat each member individually and equally.

9. **Dual Relationships:** Group counselors avoid dual relationships with group members that might impair their objectivity and professional judgment, as well as those which are likely to compromise a group member's ability to participate fully in the group.

10. **Use of Techniques:** Group counselors do not attempt any technique unless trained in its use or under supervision by a counselor familiar with the intervention.

11. **Goal Development:** Group counselors make every effort to assist members in developing their personal goals.

12. **Consultation:** Group counselors develop and explain policies about between-session consultation to group members.

13. **Termination from the Group:** Depending upon the purpose of participation in the group, counselors promote termination of members from the group in the most efficient period of time.

14. **Evaluation and Follow-Up:** Group counselors make every attempt to engage in ongoing assessment and to design follow-up procedures for their groups.

15. **Referrals:** If the needs of a particular member cannot be met within the type of group being offered, the group counselor suggests other appropriate professional referrals.

16. **Professional Development:** Group counselors recognize that professional growth is a continuous, ongoing, developmental process throughout their career.

Standards for Social Work Practice with Groups[1]

Association for the Advancement of Social Work with Groups, Inc., an International Professional Organization (AASWG)

PURPOSE

These standards represent the perspective of the Association for the Advancement of Social Work with Groups, Inc., on the value and knowledge and skill base essential for professionally sound and effective social work practice with groups and are intended to serve as a guide to social work practice with groups.

INTRODUCTION

The Standards focus on central distinguishing concepts of social work with groups and highlight the unique perspective that social group workers bring to practice. By design, the standards are general rather than specific, and descriptive rather than prescriptive. They are applicable to the wide range of groups encountered by social group workers in a variety of practice settings. These groups include, among others, treatment, support, psycho-educational,

[1]Reprinted with the permission of AASWG.

task, and community action groups. The Standards draw heavily on the Code of Ethics from the National Association of Social Work (United States), group theory from the social sciences, knowledge of individuals and the environment, the historical roots of social group work practice, current practice with groups, and practice research. Thus, they are based on practice wisdom, theories of group work practice, and empirical evidence. They emphasize the understanding and use of group processes and the ways members help one another to accomplish the purposes of the group. The role of the worker, as articulated in the standards reflects the values of the social work profession generally as well as the unique features associated with social work with groups.

Overview of the standards

Various comprehensive perspectives of social work practice provide a broad underpinning of the values and knowledge bases of social group workers' practice. Values and types of knowledge that have particular relevance for group work practice are addressed in Section I. Sections II through IV identify the required knowledge and major worker tasks and skills in each of the phases of group work practice, from planning to ending. These sections are structured around the understanding, also, that groups change and evolve over time, thus requiring changes in the worker's tasks and responsibilities. For example, certain worker actions enable group members to start to work together in a new groups; other actions enable members who have already developed relationships to engage in work to achieve the purpose of the group. Thus, as the groups develops, the nature of the workers' responsibilities will change.

The stages and the associated tasks described in these standards are guides for practice. They represent the wisdom that has been acquired from practice, theory, and research. However, each group is unique, and practitioners must apply these standards in terms of their appropriateness for each group and its particular members.

Section V examines ethical considerations for social group work practice.

SECTION I
CORE VALUES AND KNOWLEDGE

The group worker should understand the history of group work and the evolving visions of group workers as they faced the challenges posed by each historical era. During this evolution, the following values emerged as the ones that are essential to the practice of group work.

A. Core Values

1. Respect for persons and their autonomy.

In view of the equality of persons, people are to be treated with respect and dignity. In group deliberations no one person should be more privileged in a group than other persons, not a worker, a group member, nor the agency director. In a group this occurs when a worker helps each member to appreciate the contributions of the other members so that everyone's ideas are heard and considered. This principle is stated while recognizing that the worker, by virtue of his or her position in the agency and his or her expertise, is likely to have a great deal of influence. This requires the worker to use his or her influence prudently and transparently.

A major implication of this principle is a respect for and a high value placed on diversity in all of its dimensions such as culture, ethnicity, gender, sexual orientation, physical and mental abilities, and age.

2. The creation of a socially just society.

The group offers an opportunity to live and practice the democratic principles of equality and autonomy, and the worker should use his/her knowledge and skills to further this. The worker should be mindful of the quest for a society that is just and democratically organized, one that ensures that the basic human needs of all its members are met. This value is presented to the group whenever this is appropriate and reinforced when members articulate it.

B.   Core Knowledge

There are special areas of knowledge that enable group workers to more ably serve the group. This includes knowledge of the history and mission of our profession as it impacts group work with poor people, minorities, and other disenfranchised people. Understanding when group work is the practice of choice is important. The skills needed to carry out the professional mission emerge from our values and knowledge and requires specialized education.

1. Knowledge of Individuals

   a. The nature of individual human growth and behavior, utilizing a bio-psycho-social perspective and a "person in environment" view. The forces impacting the person and the group are important factors in group work assessment and intervention. This includes viewing the member in the context of the group and of the community.

   b. The familial, social, political, and cultural contexts that influence members' social identities, interactional styles, concerns, opportunities and the attainment of their potentials.

   c. The capacity of members to help one another and to change.

   d. The capacity of members to contribute to social change in the community beyond the group.

   e. Competency-based assessment.

   f. The group worker places an emphasis on members' strengths, in addition to their concerns. The worker also must understand protective and risk factors that affect individuals' need for services and their ability to act.

   g. The worker has an appreciation and understanding of such differences as those due to culture, ethnicity, gender, age, physical and mental abilitiesy, and sexual orientation among members and between members and him/ herself that may influence practice.

2. Knowledge of groups and small group behavior

   a. The worker understands that the group is an entity separate and distinct from the individual members. The group has its own dynamics, culture, and other social conditions.

b. The worker understands that the group consists of multiple helping relationships, so that members can help one another to achieve individual goals and pursue group goals. This is often referred to as "mutual aid."

c. The democratic process in groups occurs as the members evolve a sense of "ownership" of the group in which each member's contribution to the group is solicited and valued.

d. The group can develop in such a way that members, individually and collectively, are empowered to act on their own behalf as well as on behalf of the group.

e. Groups can develop goals that members are committed to pursuing. These goals may be for either individual member growth, group development, and/or social change.

f. Group members as well as the group as-as-a-whole can seek changes in the social environment.

g. The phases of group development influence change throughout the life of the group.

h. Group processes and structures encompass all transactions that occur within the group and gives meaningfulness to the life of the group. These consist of such conditions as roles, norms, communications, the expression of affect, and the nature of interaction patterns. These shape and influence individual member behavior as well as the development of the group and also determine whether and how the group will accomplish its purposes. The members can come to understand how group processes and structures shape and influence both individual member behavior as well as the development of the group.

i. Groups are formed for different purposes and goals, (e.g., education problem solving, task accomplishment, personal change, social action) and this influences what the worker does and how the group accomplishes its goals, as well as the nature of the contract between the worker and members, among the members, and between the group and the sponsoring organization.

3. Knowledge of the function of the group worker.

a. The worker promotes individual and group autonomy.

b. The worker helps the group members to select means of achieving individual and group purposes.

c. The worker's assessments and interventions are characterized by flexibility, sensitivity, and creativity.

d. The worker should have a clear understanding of the stages of group development and the related group character, members' behaviors and tasks, and worker tasks and skills that are specific to each stage.

e. Practice should be based on currently available knowledge and research and represent contemporary practice principles.

f. The worker has responsibility for ongoing monitoring and evaluation of the success of the group in accomplishing its objectives through personal observation, as well as collecting information in order to assess outcomes and processes. The worker seeks the involvement of the members in the process of evaluation. Specifically this means that members should be involved in evaluation of outcomes throughout the life of the group. Workers should systematically evaluate the achievement of goals. The worker should be knowledgeable about methods of evaluation of group work and ways of measuring or otherwise determining accomplishment of group and individual goals. The worker should use all available evidence regarding effectiveness of particular interventions for different kinds of groups.

g. The worker should maintain appropriate records of group processes and outcomes and ensure the confidentiality of these.

h. The worker should have a commitment to supporting research on group work and to disseminating knowledge about effective practices through professional meetings, education, and scholarship.

i. The worker adheres to professional, ethical, and legal requirements generally associated with social work practice as well as those specifically associated with social work with groups. The worker seeks to prevent any action in the group that may harm any member.

j. Workers should have a commitment to engage in reflective practice in which they assess their own practice and seek supervision and/or consultation in order to enhance their practice.

SECTION II
PRE-GROUP PHASE: PLANNING, RECRUITMENT, AND NEW GROUP FORMATION

A. **Tasks and skills**

1. The worker should identify aspirations and needs of potential group members as perceived by members, worker, and agency.

2. The worker should obtain organizational support for and affirmation of the group.

3. The worker should select the group type, structure, processes, and size that will be appropriate ones for attaining the purposes of the group.

4. The worker should reach out to and recruit potential group members.

5. The worker should obtain consent from potential members and relevant others as required by ethical guidelines and organizational requirements.

6. The worker should clarify potential group members' goals and expectations of the group work service and use this information to assess prospective members' potential investments in the pursuit of group goals. The worker should help members specify these goals in terms that can lead to the determination of their attainment.

7. The worker should establish an appropriate meeting place and meeting time that will be conducive to members' comfort, safety, and access to the group.

8. The worker should prepare members for the group in ways that are appropriate. This will differ depending on the extent to which the group is intended to attain

individual goals or to accomplish task purposes in the agency and community. The worker should be empathic in identifying members' feelings and reactions to joining the group.

9. The worker should know how to select members for the group in relationship to principles of group composition although this principle may not apply to some task groups in which other bodies determine the group's membership.

10. The worker should develop a clear statement of group purpose that reflects member needs and agency mission and goals. This is often done cooperatively with the group members.

11. The worker should consider potential contextual, environmental, and societal impacts on the group.

12. The worker, as appropriate, should explain group purposes and processes to non-members such as other agency personnel, relevant community entities, and parents or referring agencies in the case of groups promoting individual change.

13. The worker should consider issues of group content as well as the use of activities, supplies needed, and resources.

14. The worker should identify methods that will be used to track group progress (e.g., group progress notes, formal and informal evaluations).

15. After each session, the worker should debrief and plan with the co-facilitator (if there is one) and arrange for consultation and/or supervision on a regular basis. If there is a co-facilitator, they should consider together the implications of their similarities and differences with respect to such issues as approaches, styles, and communication.

B. Required Knowledge

1. Organizational mission and function and how these influence the nature and development of the group work service.

2. Social and institutional barriers which may impact on the development of group work service.

3. How to assess the impact on the group of the community and agency context.

4. Issues associated with group composition (e.g., gender, education, socio-economic status, previous group experience, occupation, race, ethnicity, age, and presenting problems).

5. The influence of cultural factors on potential members' lives and their ways of engaging in group interactions and relationships with others, the agency, and the worker.

6. The importance of diversity in relationship to how a group attains its goals.

7. The theoretical approaches utilized by group workers and how to select the ones most appropriate and effective for the proposed group.

8. Issues associated with group structure (e.g., group size, length of sessions, duration of group, meeting place, open or closed to new members, resources, and supplies, and transportation).

9. The impact of human development/life cycle factors on potential members' needs and abilities and group goals.

10. Types of groups such as task groups, treatment groups, psycho-educational groups, socio-recreational groups, and their applicability to individual, organizational, and community needs.

11. Issues related to group content such as discussion processes, and purposeful use of activities and simulations. Such issues include how these kinds of content are affected by stage of group development, capacities of members, and the purposes of the group.

12. Contracting procedures including the identification and clarification of group purpose and behavioral standards and norms needed to actualize group goals as determined by potential members, the worker, and the agency.

13. Recruitment procedures such as community outreach and referral processes.

14. How to identify and develop resources required for group functioning.

15. Group monitoring and evaluation procedures (e.g., group progress notes, pretest-posttest measures, questionnaires) to track worker interventions, group progress, and the group work service.

16. The importance of consultation and supervision in enhancing the quality of group work service.

SECTION III
GROUP WORK IN THE BEGINNING PHASE

A. Tasks and Skills

1. Task: Establishing a Beginning Contract

The worker and members collaboratively develop a beginning contract for work that identifies tasks to be accomplished, goals to be achieved, and the process by which the work is to occur. The worker identifies the community's and/or agency's stakes in the group, the group purpose and process, and clarifies worker and member role. Confidentiality and limits thereof are clearly identified. The worker assists members in identifying and clarifying individual goals and group goals. The worker helps the members to link individual goals with group purposes. The worker invites full participation of all members and solicits member feedback on the progress of the group. The worker employs special skills in working with mandated members and understands the impact on group dynamics of member's mandated status.

2. Task: Cultivating Group Cohesion

The worker establishes rapport with individual members and the group as a whole. The worker also aids the group members in establishing relationships with one another so as to promote group cohesion. The worker highlights member commonalities, links members to one another and encourages direct member to member communication.

3. Task: Shaping Norms of Participation

The worker seeks to aid the group in establishing norms for participation that promote safety and trust; facilitate a culture of work, and cultivate mutual aid. The worker is active in modeling these norms and instructing members when needed about productive group participation. The worker appreciates the impact of various psychological, socio-cultural, and environmental forces on these norms. The worker promotes group exploration of non-productive norms when these arise. The worker demonstrates respect for socio-cultural differences; promotes autonomy and self-determination; and encourages member empowerment.

B. Required Knowledge

1. An understanding of the dynamic interaction between the community, agency, group, and individual members of the group with which he/she is working.

2. The relevant theories and evidence based practices regarding the developmental, psychosocial, and clinical needs of the group members and how this informs beginnings.

3. The group type and technology being employed and the ways such may impact group functioning in the beginning stage.

4. The characteristics and needs of the beginning stage of group development and the related skills. Knowledge is needed regarding such variations as working with mandated members; replacing a previous worker; and receiving new members into an on-going group.

SECTION IV
GROUP WORK IN THE MIDDLE PHASE

A. Group tasks and worker skills/actions:

1. Task: Assist group to make progress on individual and group goals. When group goals are a major focus, as in task and community groups, the worker encourages individual members to use their skills in pursuit of group goals.

Skills/actions:

a. Reinforce connection between individual concerns/needs and group goals.
b. Offer programmatic ideas and activities that support group purpose and assist in helping members achieve individual and group goals.
c. Assess progress towards individual and group goals.
d. Identify difficulties and obstacles that interfere with the group and its members' abilities to reach their goals.

e. If obstacles are related to the specific needs of an individual member, when appropriate offer individual time, outside of group.

f. Ensure that group has attended to any special needs of individual members, (e.g. physical, cognitive, language, or cultural needs).

g. Assist members to engage in problem solving, in making choices and decisions, and in evaluating potential outcomes of decisions.

h. Summarize sessions with the group.

i. Plan next steps with the group.

j. Re-contract with members, if needed, to assist in achieving individual and group goals.

2. Task: Attend to group dynamics/processes.

Skills/actions:

a. Support members to develop a system of mutual aid.

b. Clarify and interpret communication patterns among members, between members and worker and between the group and systems outside the group.

c. Model and encourage honest communication and feedback among members and between members and workers.

d. Review group values and norms.

e. Assist members to identify and articulate feelings.

f. Assist members to perceive verbal and non-verbal communication.

g. Help members mediate conflict within the group.

h. Assist members to make connections with other group members that may continue after the group ends, if this is appropriate.

i. Use tools of empowerment to assist members to develop "ownership" of the group.

Tasks:

1. Assist members to identify and access resources from inside and outside the group.

2. Includes knowledge, skills and other resources of group worker, group members and sources outside the group.

3. Ensure that workers are using the best possible practice techniques in facilitating the group.

Skills/actions:

1. Uses group approaches appropriate to the populations served and the tasks undertaken as demonstrated in the literature, worker and agency experience, and other sources of professional knowledge.

2. Uses record keeping techniques to monitor leadership skills and group process.

3. Accesses and uses supervision.

B. Required Knowledge

1. Group dynamics.

2. Role theory and its application to members' relationships with one another and the worker.

3. Communication theory and its application to verbal and non-verbal interactions within the group and between the group and others external to the group.

4. Problem-solving processes in groups.

5. Conflict resolution in groups.

6. Organizational theories.

7. Community theories.

8. Developmental theories.

9. Evaluation theories and methods.

10. The impact of diversity: class, race, gender, sexual orientation, and ability status.

11. Knowledge about the group's relations with its environment.

12. Specific knowledge of issue being addressed in the group.

13. Awareness of self.

SECTION V
GROUP WORK IN THE ENDING PHASE

A. **Tasks and Skills**

1. Prepare members for the group's ending in advance.

2. In a direct practice group help members identify gains they have made and changes that have resulted from their participation in the group. In a task group, members may discuss what they have learned from this experience that will be useful to them in other task groups. This involves a consideration of how achieving group goals will contribute to the functioning of the organization and/or community.

3. Discuss the impact of the group on systems outside of the group (e.g., family, organization, community).

4. Discuss the movement the group has made over time.

5. Identify and discuss direct and indirect signs of members' reactions to ending.

6. Share worker's feelings about ending with the group.

7. Assist members in sharing their feelings about ending with one another and with the worker.

8. Systematically evaluate the achievement of individual and group goals. Routine and systematic evaluation of the group experience could/should occur over time rather than in the ending stage alone.

9. Help members make connections with other agencies and programs as appropriate.

10. Assist members in applying new knowledge and skills to their daily lives.

11. Encourage members to give feedback to the worker on the worker's role and actions in the group.

12. Help members apply new knowledge and skills to their activities outside of the group.

13. Prepare record material about the group for the agency, for individual members, and for referrals as needed.

B. Required Knowledge

1. Group dynamics related to endings. These will be different depending on the type of group (e.g., long term, short term, open ended, single session). There are also special issues when a member or worker ends? but parts of the group continue or there is a new worker.

2. Formal and informal resources which maintain and enhance members' growth.

3. Influence of past losses and separation in lives of members and the worker on endings.

4. Agency policies related to worker maintaining connections following ending of a group or member service.

5. Various forms of evaluation, formal and informal and of evaluation measures, both qualitative and quantitative.

SECTION VI
ETHICAL CONSIDERATIONS

National and/or regional social work organizations typically have codes of ethics to which social workers must adhere. For example, social group workers in the United States of America are expected to be knowledgeable about and responsive to the ethical mandates of the social work profession, as explicated in the National Association of Social Workers (NASW) Code of Ethics. While the entire code is important, there are items with particular relevance to social group work.

Similarly, Canadian social workers must follow the Canadian Association of Social Workers Code of Ethics (2005). The expectation of AASWG is that social workers will respect the code of ethics relevant to their locations of practice wherever in the world that may be as long as it is respectful of all persons.

Other social work ethical guides exist and may be more relevant for specific countries. Each needs to be considered in the context of work with groups and may call for some modifications or additions that reflect the unique situations of group work.

A. Elements of Ethical Practice in Social Group Work.

1. Knowledge of and use of best practices that reflect the state of the art and knowledge and research evidence regarding social work with groups.

2. A basic discussion with prospective members of informed consent and an explanation of what group work offers and requires of the members individually and as a group.

3. Maximizing member choice and minimizing coercive processes by members or worker to the extent possible. Emphasizing member self-determination and empowerment of the group.

4. Discussion of the importance, limits, and implications of privacy and confidentiality with the members.

5. Helping the group maintain the purposes for which it was formed, allowing for changes as mutually agreed upon.

6. Each member is given the help s/he requires within the parameters of the group's purpose, including individual meetings when appropriate.

7. Clarifying the decision making process.

8. Clarifying how members may be chosen for or excluded from the group.

9. Maintaining group records and storing them in a secure location.

B. Ethical Issues in the use of new techniques.
As new techniques are used, such as those based on electronic communications, workers should pay attention to ethical issues, practice skills, and knowledge and evaluation of these techniques. The following is a general statement with reference to electronic communications:

Increasingly, practice with groups of all kinds is being done by utilizing technologies such as computer and telephone facilities, and professional associations are assessing both effectiveness and ethical issues.

Issues such as member interaction, decision-making, group structure, mutual aid, and, particularly, confidentiality are of vital concern.

Worker competency may require new skills and knowledge, not only in technology use, but also in communication techniques.

Clearly these technologies are likely to be extremely valuable for all persons seeking resources, as well as for the profession's ability to share information about practice including emerging approaches. In the meantime workers contemplating their use should consider the appropriate codes of ethics as a guides and document all of their processes related to such work.

NOTES

1. The terms "social group work", "social work with groups" and "group work" are used interchangeably in these Standards.
2. In the NASW Code current at the time of approval of these Standards these sections include the Preamble and Ethical Principles 1.01, 1.02, 1.05 1.06, 1.07, 2.06, 3.02, 3.07, 3.09, and 4.01.

REFERENCES

National Association of Social Workers. (approved 1996, revised 1999) Code of Ethics for Social Workers, Washington, DC: NASW.

Canadian Association of Social Workers/Association canadienne des travailleuses sociaux (2005) Code of Ethics, Ottawa. CASW/ACTS.

January 2006, first printing

July 2006, second printing

jhr.

Films and Videotapes

Blue Sky Productions. (1997). *Discovering community: A future search as a spring-board for action in Santa Cruz County.* Blue Sky Productions, 39201 Schoolcraft Road, Suite B-12, Livonia, MI 48150.

Len Brown. *Problem Solving.* Rutgers University, School of Social Work, 536 George Street, New Brunswick, NJ 08903.

Len Brown. *Termination.* Rutgers University, School of Social Work, 536 George Street, New Brunswick, NJ 08903.

M. R. Carroll. *Group Work: Leading in the Here and Now.* American Counseling Association, 5999 Stevenson Avenue, Alexandria, VA 22304-3300.

Tom Casciato. *Circle of Recovery, with Bill Moyers.* Circle of Recovery, Box 2284, South Burlington, VT 05407.

Center for Psychological Issues in the Nuclear Age. *Meetings That Lead to Action.* Center PINA, 475 Riverside Drive, New York, NY 10115.

Gerald Corey, Marianne Schneider Corey, & Robert Haynes. (2000). *Evolution of a Group.* Pacific Grove, Cal: Brooks Cole Wadsworth.

Edmund S. Muskie Institute of Public Affairs. *Mattering . . . A Journey with Rural Youth.* The Clearinghouse, Muskie School, PO Box 15010, University of Southern Maine, Portland, ME 04112.

Naomi Feil. *Looking for Yesterday.* Edward Feil Productions, 4614 Prospect Avenue, Cleveland, OH 44103.

Naomi Feil. *The More We Get Together: How to Form a Validation Group.* Edward Feil Productions, 4614 Prospect Avenue, Cleveland, OH 44103.

Mel Goldstein. *Reflections on Group Work: The Video Curriculum to Teach Social Group Work.* School of Social Work, State University of New York at Stony Brook, Health Sciences Center, Stony Brook, NY 11794.

Mary Goulding. *Brief therapy-redecision model.* The Milton H. Erickson Foundation, 3606 North 24th Street, Phoenix, AZ 85016.

Mary Goulding. *One-session group therapy with six clients from the audience.* The Milton H. Erickson Foundation, 3606 North 24th Street, Phoenix, AZ 85016.

Insight Media. *Groups and Group Dynamics.* Insight Media, 121 West 85th Street, New York, NY 10024.

Institute for Mental Health Initiatives. (2000). *Learning to manage anger: The RETHINK workout for teens.* Research Press, P.O. Box 9177, Champaign, IL. 61826.

International University College. *Group dynamics in the electronic environment.* Jones Digital Century. Englewood Company, 9697 East Mineral Avenue, Englewood, CA 80112.

Sandra Janoff, Allan Kobernick & Yvonne Agazarian. *Systems-centered psychotherapy—module II—discussion around shame in a shamed group.* Blue Sky Productions, 39201 Schoolcraft Road, Suite B-12, Livonia, MI 48150.

Paul Kadis & Vernessa Gipson. *Dealing with anger: Givin' it, takin' it, workin' it out.* Research Press, P.O. Box 9177, Champaign, IL 61826.

Steven Katten & Irving Janis. *Groupthink.* CRM Learning, 2215 Faraday Avenue, Carlsbad, CA 92008.

Allen Kobernick. *Self-differentiation: A day with John and Joyce Weir.* Blue Sky Productions, 39201 Schoolcraft Road, Suite B-12, Livonia, MI 48150.

William Lauzon. *Staff Groups: Wellness in the Workplace.* Office of Television and Radio, Building 4048–Kilmeer, Rutgers University, New Brunswick, NJ 08903.

Walter Lifton. *Just Like a Family.* University Film Service, University at Albany, State University of New York, 1400 Washington Avenue, Albany, NY 12222.

Marsha Linehan. *Understanding borderline personality disorder: The dialectical approach.* Guilford Press, 72 Spring Street, New York, NY 10012.

Andrew Malekoff. *A Sense of Alienation or Belonging: Building Bridges through Group Involvement.* Institute for Group Work with Children & Youth, 480 Old Westbury Road, Roslyn Heights, NY 11577-2215, Attn: Jane Yazdpour.

Edward Mason. *Chrysalis '86: The Development of a Therapeutic Group.* Penn State AudioVisual Services, 1127 Fox Hill Road, University Park, PA 16803.

Vivian Nelson & Bill Roller. *The promise of group therapy: A live to tape demonstration of a time-limited group.* Jossey Bass, 989 Market Street, San Francisco, CA 94103-1741.

Robert Pasick. *Men in Therapy: Men's Issues and Group Treatment.* AGC United Learning, Menninger Video Productions, 1560 Sherman Avenue, Suite 100, Evanston, IL 60201.

William Piper. *Helping People Adapt to Loss: A Short-Term Group Therapy Approach.* Guilford Publications, Catalog #2498, 72 Spring Street, New York, NY 10012.

Public Broadcasting Video. *Frontline: The Color of Your Skin.* PBS Video, 1320 Braddock Place, Alexandria, VA 22314. No. Fron-9211K. (This is not a film about group work, but a film showing group dynamics at the U.S. Army's Defense Equal Opportunity Management Institute. This film can be used to discuss sensitivity training or race relations in groups.)

Research Press. *Skills & techniques for group counseling with youth.* Research Press, Dept. 23W, P.O. Box 9177, Champaign, IL 61822.

Sheldon Rose. *The Best of the Children's Groups.* School of Social Work, University of Wisconsin–Madison, 425 Henry Mall, Madison, WI 53706.

Sheldon Rose. *Common Problems in Parent Training Groups.* School of Social Work, University of Wisconsin–Madison, 425 Henry Mall, Madison, WI 53706.

Sheldon Rose. *The Golden Eagles.* School of Social Work, University of Wisconsin–Madison, 425 Henry Mall, Madison, WI 53706.

Sheldon Rose. *Problem Solving in Groups.* School of Social Work, University of Wisconsin–Madison, 425 Henry Mall, Madison, WI 53706.

Round Table Films. *Meeting in Progress.* Round Table Films, 113 North San Vincente Boulevard, Beverly Hills, CA 90211.

Saul Scheidlinger & Cary Sandberg. *Reunion with the Mother of Abandonment: A Group Fantasy.* Insight Media, 121 West 85th Street, New York, NY 10024.

Lawrence Shulman. *Skills of Helping: Leading a First Group Session.* Instructional Communication Center, McGill University, Montreal, Quebec, Canada H3A 2K6.

Lawrence Shulman. *Skills of Helping: The Married Couples Group.* Instructional Communication Center, McGill University, Montreal, Quebec, Canada H3A 2K6.

Rosemary Snead. *Skills and Techniques for Group Counselling with Youth.* Research Press, 2612 North Mattis Avenue, Champaign, IL 61821.

David Spiegel & Pat Fobair. *Supportive-Expressive Group Therapy for People with Cancer and Their Families.* Center for Media and Independent Learning, University of California Extension, 2000 Center Street, 4th Floor, Berkeley, CA 94704.

David Spiegel & Pat Fobair. *Tape I, The Process of Forming a Support Group and Detoxifying Death; Tape II, Taking Time and Fortifying Families; Tape III, Dealing with Doctors and Controlling Pain through Self-Hypnosis; Tape IV, A Model Session.* Center for Media and Independent Learning, University of California Extension, 2000 Center Street, 4th Floor, Berkeley, CA 94704.

Roberta Starzecpyzl. *Shooting Stars.* Dragon Rising Productions, P. O. Box 629, Village Station, New York, NY 10014.

Irving Yalom. *Understanding Group Psychotherapy.* Center for Media and Independent Learning, University of California Extension, 2000 Center Street, 4th Floor, Berkeley, CA 94704.

Irving Yalom. *Understanding group psychotherapy: Volume II. Inpatient group psychotherapy. Tape A: Orientation and agenda formation. Tape B: Agenda filling and summary.* Brooks/Cole Publishing Company, 511 Forest Lodge Road, Pacific Grove, CA 93950.

Irving Yalom. *Inpatients.* Center for Media and Independent Learning, University of California Extension, 2000 Center Street, 4th Floor, Berkeley, CA 94704.

Irving Yalom. *Outpatients.* Center for Media and Independent Learning, University of California Extension, 2000 Center Street, 4th Floor, Berkeley, CA 94704.

Irving Yalom. *Yalom: An interview.* Center For Media and Independent Learning, University of California Extension, 2000 Center Street, 4th Floor, Berkeley, CA 94704.

OTHER FILM RESOURCES

Interviews of Saul Bernstein, Giesela Konopka, Helen Northen, Helen Phillips, Mary Lou Sommers, and Gertrude Wilson as well as other films are available in VHS format from David Klaassen, Social Welfare History Archives, University of Minnesota, 1012 Walter Library, 117 Pleasant Street, SE, Minneapolis, MN 55455.

Group Announcements

SUPPORT GROUP FOR NEW PARENTS

You are invited to join a support group of parents who have children ages 6 months to 2 years. The group will discuss concerns identified by its members including such possible issues as infant care, sharing household responsibilities, disciplining your child, toilet training, and child-care resources.

Sponsor

Greenwich Community Mental Health Center
49 Cambridge Avenue
Greenwich, NY
(212) 246-2468

Group Leaders

George Oxley, ACSW, clinic director
Marybeth Carol, BSW, clinic social worker

Membership

Open to all parents with children from ages 6 months to 2 years

Dates and Times

March–April–May, Thursday evenings from 7:30 to 9:30 P.M.

Child Care

Parents are encouraged to bring their children to the center. Child care will be available from human service interns of Hudson Center Community College.

Cost

Enrollment fee for the three-month group, total $90.00 per couple, payable monthly
For further information, call Mr. Oxley or Ms. Carol at (212) 246-2468.

YOUTH CENTER INTEREST MEETING

The residents of the Johnsonville, Pittstown, and Valley Falls area are invited to discuss the proposed establishment of a youth center for these communities. Issues to be discussed include cost of service, fundraising, need for service, and support for such a service.

Sponsor

Rensselaer Council of Community Services

Meeting Place

Johnsonville Firehouse

Date and Time

Thursday, March 25, from 7 to 9 P.M.

Further Information

Call Jim Kesser, ACSW
(212) 241-2412

Refreshments will be served.

Outline for a Group Proposal

Treatment/Task

Abstract

Short statement summarizing major points of
group

Purpose

Brief statement of purpose
How the group will conduct its work
Job description of the worker

Agency Sponsorship

Agency name and mission
Agency resources (physical facilities, financial,
staff)
Geographic and demographic data on agency

Membership

Specific population for the group
Why population was chosen

Recruitment

Methods to be used

Composition

Criteria for member inclusion/exclusion
Size, open or closed group, demographic
characteristics

Orientation

Specific procedures to be used

Contract

Number, frequency, length, and time of meeting

Environment

Physical arrangements (room, space, materials)
Financial arrangements (budget, expense,
income)
Special arrangements (child care, transportation)

An Example of a Treatment Group Proposal

ADOLESCENT DISCHARGE GROUP

The Children's Refuge Home

Abstract

This is a proposal for a social skills training group for adolescents who are about to be released into the community from the children's refuge home.

Purpose

The group will discuss what each member expects to be doing on release to the community. The group will reinforce social learning that has taken place during the residential placement and will help members learn new social skills that will be needed to successfully relate to parents, siblings, teachers, and employers. Role playing, behavior rehearsal modeling, and reinforcement will be employed as methods of teaching social skills.

Agency Sponsorship

The Children's Refuge Home, a residential treatment facility for delinquent youth, serves teenage boys who cannot live at home because of law-breaking activities. About 200 boys reside here in 15 cottages. The agency has a 200-acre campus with an on-campus school. Staff ratio is about one staff member per four boys; direct-care staff include child care workers, social workers, nursing staff, psychologists, psychiatrists, and clergy.

Membership

Approximately 10 boys are released to the community each month. The discharge group will be composed from a population of boys for whom discharge is planned within the next three months.

Recruitment

Because this group represents a new service for the institution, members will be recruited by asking cottage parents for volunteers from their respective cottages. An announcement will be printed and delivered to the senior cottage parents for all cottages. In addition, teachers and social workers will be contacted to suggest possible candidates for the group.

Composition

The group will be composed of six to eight boys from 12 to 14 years old who anticipate discharge from CRH within the next three months. In addition, this first group will include only children who will be returning to natural parents or relatives rather than to foster care or group homes. The group will be closed and will not add new members because it is important that social skills be learned in a gradual and cumulative fashion.

Orientation

Each member will be interviewed by the leaders. During this interview, the members will view a videotape on group treatment for children, and the details of the tape will be discussed to demonstrate how group meetings will be conducted.

Environment

The ideal location for this group is the diagnostic classroom within the campus school. Proximity to videotaping equipment is necessary so group members can tape and view role plays. A small budget is required ($120) for proposed field trips, charts, and materials for listing skills and posting individual and group progress, and for refreshments after meetings. Additional expenses include two color videotapes ($60). Special arrangements will have to be made so that each member's afterschool recreation schedule is free for Monday afternoon meeting times.

An Example of a Task Group Proposal

TASK FORCE ON RESEARCH UTILIZATION IN PROBATION

Abstract

This is a proposal for establishing an interagency task force to study how research and research procedures are used in three county probation offices. The group will issue a report with recommendations for increasing research use in probation settings.

Purpose

This group will be formed to study the use of research in county probation offices. The group will meet to discuss the results of surveys taken on each probation office regarding the extent to which probation workers use published research to inform their practice and the extent to which they conduct research in conjunction with their practice. The group will be convened by Robert Rivas, ACSW, at Siena College.

Agency Sponsorship

The task force will be sponsored by the tri-county consortium of probation agencies. The Rockwell County agency will provide physical facilities for meetings. Financial costs will be shared by all county agencies.

Membership

Each county agency will nominate three representatives to attend meetings to ensure equal representation among agencies.

Recruitment

Mailings will be sent to all agency directors. Members of the tri-county association will be informed by an announcement in the newsletter. Each agency director will be requested by letter to appoint three representatives to the task force.

Composition

The task force will require that each agency appoint one representative from each of the following categories: probation administrator, probation supervisor (or senior officer), and probation officer. The task force will include nine representatives from agencies and two research consultants from local colleges. All members of the task force should have some knowledge about research methods. This will be a closed group, although interested people may attend specific meetings after obtaining permission from the group's leader.

Orientation

The group will be given several research reports to read to prepare for discussions. The group leader will contact each member individually to get ideas for composing an agenda.

Contract

The task force will meet once a month for six sessions. Meetings will last for three hours and will take place every fourth Monday of the month from 9 A.M. to noon. The group will be required to compose and issue a preliminary report on research use within one month after the final meeting.

Environment

The Rockwell County agency will provide the use of its staff meeting room, which is equipped with tables and blackboards, for the group's work. Copying facilities will be provided by Rockwell County, and each county will be billed for one third the expenses (limit $30.00 per county). About $100 will be required to prepare and distribute the task force's final report and recommendations (contributed by the county association). Agency directors for each county have been requested to provide travel allowance (25 cents a mile) for all travel in conjunction with the work of the task force.

Suggested Readings on Program Activities

PROGRAM ACTIVITIES FOR GROUPS OF CHILDREN AND ADOLESCENTS

Allen, J. S., & Klein, R. J. (1996). *Ready, set, relax: A research-based program of relaxation, learning, and self-esteem for children.* Watertown, WI: Inner Coaching.

Baker, J. E. (2003). *Social skills training for children and adolescents with Asperger syndrome and social communication problems.* Shawnee Mission, KS: Autism Asperger Publishing Co.

Borba, M., & Borba, C. (1993). *Self-esteem: A classroom affair.* (2nd ed.). San Francisco: Harper.

Carrell, S. (1993). *Group exercises for adolescents: A manual for therapists.* Newbury Park, CA: Sage Publications.

Cartlege, G., & Milbrun, J. F. (Eds.). (1980). *Teaching social skills to children.* Elmsford, NY: Pergamon Press.

Cheung, M. (2006). *Therapeutic games and grided imagery.* Chicago, Illinois: Lyceum Books.

Coucouvanis, J. (2005). *Super skills: A social skills group program for children with Asperger syndrome, high functioning autism, and related challenges.* Shawnee Mission, KS: Autism Asperger Publishing Co.

Duncan, T., & Gumaer, J. (1980). *Developmental group for children.* Springfield, IL: Charles C. Thomas.

Ehly, S., & Dustin, R. (1989). *Individual and group counseling in the schools.* New York: Guilford Press.

Ferrara, M. (1992). *Group counseling with juvenile delinquents: The limit and lead approach.* Newbury Park, CA: Sage Publications.

Goldstein, A. P., Sprakin, R. P., Gerhaw, N. J., & Klein, P. (1980). *Skill streaming the adolescent. A structured learning approach to teaching prosocial skills.* Champaign, IL: Research Press.

Hazel, J. S., Schumaker, J. B., Sherman, J. A., & Sheldon, J. (1999). *A social skills program for adolescents.* Champaign, IL: Research Press.

Jones, A. (1998). *104 activities that build: Self-esteem, teamwork, communication, anger management, self-discovery and coping skills.* Richland, WA: Rec Room Publishing.

Kaufman, G., & Lev, R. (1999). *Stick up for yourself: Every kid's guide to personal power and positive self-esteem.* Minneapolis, MN: Free Spirit.

Mandell, G., & Damon, L. (1989). *Group treatment for sexually abused children.* New York: Guilford Press.

Mannix, D. (1993). *Social skills activities for special children.* West Nyack, NY: The Center for Applied Research in Education.

McElherne, L. M. (1999). *Jumpstarters: Quick classroom activities that develop self-esteem, creativity and cooperation.* Minneapolis, MN: Free Spirit.

McGinnis, E., & Goldstein, A. P. (1984). *Skill streaming the elementary school child: A guide for teaching prosocial skills.* Champaign, IL: Research Press.

McGinnis, E., & Goldstein, A. P. (1990). *Skill streaming in early childhood.* Champaign, IL: Research Press.

Middleman, R. (1982). *The non-verbal method in working with groups: The use of activity in teaching, counseling, and therapy.* An enlarged edition. Hebron, CT: Practitioners Press.

Morganett, R. (1990). *Skills for living: Group counseling activities for young adolescents.* Champaign, IL: Research Press.

Norem-Hebeisen, A. A. (1976). *Exploring self-esteem.* New York: National Humanities Education Center.

Paulson, L., & van den Pol, R. (1998). *Good talking Words:* A social communication skills program *for preschool and kindergarden classes.* Longmont, CO: Sporis West.

Payne, L. M. (1997). *Just because I am: A child's book of inspiration.* Minneapolis, MN: Free Spirit.

Payne, L. M., & Rohling, C. (1997). *We can get along: A child's book of choices.* Minneapolis, MN: Free Spirit.

Pfeiffer, J. W., & Goodstein, L. (Eds.). (2001). *The annual: Developing human resources.* San Diego, CA: University Associates, Inc.

Pope, A. W., McHale, S. M., & Craighead, W. E. (1988). *Self-esteem enhancement with children and adolescents.* New York: Pergamon Press.

Rathjen, D. P., & Foreyt, J. P. (Eds.). (1980). *Social competence: Interventions for children and adults.* Elmsford, NY: Pergamon Press.

Rose, S. (1998). *Group psychotherapy with troubled youth: A cognitive behavioral approach.* Thousand Oaks, CA: Sage Publishing.

Rose, S., & Edleson, J. (1998). *Working with children and adolescents in groups.* San Francisco: Jossey-Bass.

Simons, L. (2000). *Taking "No" for an answer and other skills children need.* Seattle, WA: Parenting Press, Inc.

Smith, M. A. (1977). *A practical guide to value clarification.* La Jolla, CA: University Associates.

Stuecker, R. (2004). *Cultivating kindness in school: Activities that promote integrity, respect, and compassion in elementary and middle school students.* Champaign, IL: Research Press.

Teolis, B. (2002). *Ready-to-use conflict resolution activities for elementary students.* West Nyack, NY: Center for Applied Research in Education.

Wells, H. C., & Canfield, J. (1976). *One hundred ways to enhance self-concept in the classroom.* Englewood Cliffs, NJ: Prentice-Hall.

Whitehouse, E., & Pudney, W. (1996). *A volcano in my tummy: Helping children to handle anger. A resource book for parents, caregivers, and teachers.* Gabriola Island, BC: New Society.

PROGRAM ACTIVITIES FOR GROUPS OF OLDER PEOPLE

Beisgon, B. (1989). *Life enhancing activities for the mentally impaired elderly.* New York: Springer.

Birren, J., & Deutchman, D. (1991). *Guiding autobiography groups for older adults.* Baltimore: John Hopkins Press.

Booth, H. (1986). Dance/movement therapy. In I. Burnside (Ed.), *Working with the elderly: Group processes and techniques* (2nd ed., pp. 211–224). Boston: Jones and Bartlett.

Clark, P., & Osgood, N. J. (1985). *Seniors on stage: The impact of applied theater techniques on the elderly.* New York: Praeger.

Clements, C. (1994). *The arts/fitness quality of life activities program: Creative ideas for working with older adults in group settings.* Baltimore: Health Professions Press.

Dickey, H. (1987). *Intergenerational activities.* Buffalo, NY: Potentials Development for Health & Aging Services.

Fisher, P. (1989). *Creative movement for older adults.* New York: Human Sciences Press.

Flatten, K., Wilhite, B., & Reyes-Watson, E. (1988). *Exercise activities for the elderly.* New York: Springer.

Flatten, K., Wilhite, B., & Reyes-Watson, E. (1988). *Recreation activities for the elderly.* New York: Springer.

Foster, P. (Ed.). (1983). *Activities and the "well elderly."* New York: Haworth Press.

Fry, P. (1983). Structured and unstructured reminiscence training and depression among the elderly. *Clinical Gerontologist, 1*(13), 15–37.

Goodwin, D. (1982). *Activity Director's bag of tricks.* Chicago: Adams Press.

Helgeson, E., & Willis, S. (Eds.). (1987). *Handbook of group activities for impaired older adults.* New York: Haworth Press.

Hennessey, M. (1986). Music therapy. In I. Burnside (Ed.), *Working with the elderly: Group processes and techniques* (2nd ed., pp. 198– 210). Boston: Jones and Bartlett.

Houten, L. (1990). *Moving for life: Movement, art & music.* Buffalo, NY: Potentials Development for Health & Aging Services.

Hurley, O. (1996). *Safe therapeutic exercise for the frail elderly: An introduction* (2nd ed). Albany, NY: Center for the Study of Aging.

Ingersoll, B., & Goodman, L. (1983). A reminiscence group for institutionalized elderly. In M. Rosenbaum (Ed.), *Handbook of short-term therapy groups* (pp. 247–269). New York: McGraw-Hill.

Ingersoll, B., & Silverman, A. (1978). Comparative group psychotherapy for the aged. *The Gerontologist, 18*(2), 201–206.

Jacobs, R. (1987). Older women: Surviving and thriving. Milwaukee, WI: Family Service America.

Kamin, J. (1984). How older adults use books and the public library: A review of the literature. Occasional papers number 165 (ERIC Document Reproduction Service No. ED 247954).

Karras, B. (1994). *Say it with music: Music games and trivia.* Mt. Airy, MD: Eldersong Publications.

Killeffer, E., Bennett, R., & Gruen, G. (1985). *Handbook of innovative programs for the impaired elderly.* New York: Haworth Press.

King, K. (1982). Reminiscing psychotherapy with aging people. *Journal of Psychosocial Nursing and Mental Health Services, 20*(2), 21–25.

Lesser, J., Lazarus, L., Frankel, R., & Havasy, S. (1981). Reminiscence group therapy with psychotic geriatric in-patients. *The Gerontologist, 21*(3), 291–296.

Lewis, M., & Butler, R. (1974). Life review therapy: Putting memories to work in individual and group psychotherapy. *Geriatrics, 29*(11), 165–173.

Lowman, E. (1992). *Arts & crafts for the elderly.* New York: Springer.

McMorde, W., & Blom, S. (1979). Life review therapy: Psychotherapy for the elderly. *Perspectives In Psychiatric Care, 17*, 292–298.

Schlenger, G. (1988). *Come and sit by me: Discussion programs for activity specialists.* Owings Mills, MD: National Health Publishing.

Schulberg, C. (1986). *The music therapy sourcebook.* New York: Human Sciences Press.

Sherman, E. (1987). Reminiscence groups for the community elderly. *Gerontologist, 27*(5), 569–572.

Sherman, E. (1990). Experiential reminiscence and life review therapy. In G. Lietaer, J. Rombauts, & R. Van Balen (Eds.), *Client-centered and experiential psychotherapy in the nineties.* Leuven, Belgium: Leuven University Press.

Suchan, C. (1985). *Edible activities.* Buffalo, NY: Potentials Development for Health & Aging Services.

Thurman, J., & Piggins, C. (1996). *Drama activities with older adults: A handbook for leaders.* New York: Haworth Press.

Toseland, R. (1995). *Group work with the elderly and family caregivers.* New York: Springer.

Wilson, M. (1977). Enhancing the lives of aged in a retirement center through a program of reading. *Educational Gerontology, 4*(3), 245–251.

Wolcott, A. (1986). Art therapy: An experimental group. In I. Burnside (Ed.), *Working with the elderly: Group process and techniques* (pp. 292–310). North Scituate, MA: Duxbury Press.

Zgola, J. (1987). *Doing things: A guide to programming activities for persons with Alzheimer's disease and related disorders.* Baltimore: Johns Hopkins Press.

Bibliography

Aaker, D., Kunar, V., & Day, G. (2001). *Marketing research* (7th ed.). New York: John Wiley & Sons.

Abels, P. (1980). Instructed advocacy and community group work. In A. Alissi (Ed.), *Perspectives on social group work practice* (pp. 326–331). New York: The Free Press.

Abramson, J. (1983). A non-client-centered approach to program development in a medical setting. In H. Weissman, I. Epstein, & A. Savage (Eds.), *Agency-based social work* (pp. 178–187). Philadelphia: Temple University Press.

Abramson, J. (1989). Making teams work. *Social Work with Groups, 12*(4), 45–63.

Abramson, J. S. (2002). Interdisciplinary team practice. In A. R. Roberts & G. J. Greene (Eds.), *Social workers' desk reference* (pp. 44–50). Albany, NY: Oxford University Press.

Abramson, J. S., & Bronstein, L. R, (2004). Group process dynamics and skills in interdisciplinary teamwork. In C. D. Garvin, L. M. Gutierrez, & M. J. Galinsky (Eds.), *Handbook of social work with groups* (pp. 384–399). New York: The Guilford Press.

Achenbach, T. (1991). *Manual for the Child Behavior Checklist: 4–18 and 1991 Profile.* Burlington, VT: University Associates in Psychiatry.

Achenbach, T. (1997). *Child Behavior Checklist.* Burlington, VT: University Medical Education Associates.

Adam, E. (1991). Quality circle performance. *Journal of Management, 17*(1), 25–39.

Addams, J. (1909). *The spirit of youth and the city streets.* New York: Macmillan.

Addams, J. (1926). *Twenty years at Hull House.* New York: Macmillan.

Al-Assaf, A., & Schmele, J. (Eds.). (1997). *The textbook of total quality in healthcare.* Boca Raton, FL: St. Lucie Press.

Alberti, R., & Emmons, M. (2001). *Your perfect right* (8th ed.). San Luis Obispo, CA: Impact Press.

Aldarondo, E., & Mederos, F. (Eds.). (2002). *Programs for men who batter: Intervention and prevention strategies in a diverse society.* Kingston, NJ: Civic Research Institute.

Alemi, F., Mosavel, M., Stephens, R., Ghaderi, A., Krishnaswamy, J., & Thakkar, H. (1996). Electronic self-help and support groups. *Medical Care, 34,* OS32–OS44.

Alimo-Metcalfe, B., & Alban-Metcalfe, R. (2001). The development of a new transformational leadership questionnaire. *Journal of Occupational and Organizational Psychology, 74,* 1–27.

Alinsky, S. (1971). *Rules for radicals.* New York: Random House.

Alissi, A. (Ed.). (1980). *Perspectives on social group work practice.* New York: The Free Press.

Alissi, A. S. (2001). The social group work tradition: Toward social justice in a free society. *Social Group Work Foundation Occasional Papers,* 1–25.

Allport, F. (1924). *Social psychology.* Boston: Houghton Mifflin.

American Association of Group Workers. (1947). *Toward professional standards.* New York: Association Press.

American Psychiatric Association. (2000). *Diagnostic and statistical manual of mental disorders:DSM-IV-TR* (4th ed., text revision). Washington, DC: Author.

Anderson, B. F. T. (2000). The nominal group technique. *Quality Progress, 33*(2), 144.

Anderson, J. (1979). Social work practice with groups in the generic base of social work practice. *Social Work with Groups, 2*(4), 281–293.

Anderson, J. (1997). *Social work with groups: A process model.* New York: Longman.

Anderson, J., & Carter, R. W. (2003). *Diversity perspectives for social work practice: Constructivism and the constructivist framework.* Boston, MA: Allyn and Bacon.

Aponte, J., Rivers, R., & Wohl, R. (2000). *Psychological interventions and cultural diversity* (2nd ed.). Boston, MA: Allyn and Bacon.

Appleby, G., Colon, E., & Hamilton, J. (2001). *Diversity, oppression, and social functioning: Person-in-environment assessment and intervention.* Boston: Allyn and Bacon.

Aronson, H., & Overall, B. (1966). Therapeutic expectations of patients in two social classes. *Social Work, 11,* 35–41.

Asch, P. (1957). An experimental investigation of group influences. In Walter Reed Army Institute of Research, *Symposium on preventive and social psychiatry.* Washington, DC: Walter Reed Army Institute of Research.

Asch, S. (1952). *Social psychology.* Englewood Cliffs, NJ: Prentice Hall.

Asch, S. (1955). Opinions and social pressures. *Scientific American, 193*(5), 31–35.

Asch, S. (1957). *An experimental investigation of group influence.* Paper presented at the Symposium on Preventative and Social Psychiatry, Walter Reed Army Institute of Research, Washington, DC.

Ashby, M., Gilchrist, L., & Miramontez, A. (1987). Group treatment for sexually abused Indian adolescents. *Social Work with Groups, 10*(4), 21–32.

Asher-Svanum, H. (1991). *Psychoeducational groups for patients with schizophrenia.* Gaithersburg, MD: Aspen.

Association for the Advancement of Social Work with Groups. (1998). *Standards for social work practice with groups.* Akron, OH: AASWG.

Atieno Okech, J. E., & Kline, W. B. (2006). Competency concerns in group co-leader relationships. *The Journal for Specialists in Group Work, 31*(2), 165–180.

Atkinson, D., & Lowe, S. (1995). The role of ethnicity, cultural knowledge, and conventional techniques in counseling and psychotherapy. In J. Ponterotto, J. Casas, L. Suzuki, & C. Alexander (Eds.), *Handbook of multicultural counseling* (pp. 387–414). Thousand Oaks, CA: Sage.

Axelson, J. A. (1999). *Counseling and development in a multicultural society* (3rd ed.). Pacific Grove, CA: Brooks/Cole.

Bachrach, P., & Baratz, M. S. (1962). Two faces of power. *American Political Science Review, 56,* 947–952.

Back, K. (1951). Influence through social communication. *Journal of Abnormal and Social Psychology, 46,* 9–23.

Bailey, D., & Koney, K. M. (1996). Interorganizational community-based collaboratives: A strategic response to shape the social work agenda. *Social Work, 41,* 602–611.

Bailey-Dempsey, C., & Reid, W. J. (1996). Intervention design and development: A case study. *Research on Social Work Practice, 6*(2), 208–228.

Bales, R. (1950). *Interaction process analysis: A method for the study of small groups.* Reading, MA: Addison-Wesley.

Bales, R. (1954). In conference. *Harvard Business Review, 32,* 44–50.

Bales, R. (1955). How people interact in conference. *Scientific American, 192,* 31–35.

Bales, R. (1980). *SYMLOG: Case study kit.* New York: The Free Press.

Bales, R., Cohen, S., & Williamson, S. (1979). *SYMLOG: A system for the multiple level observations of groups.* New York: The Free Press.

Balgopal, P., & Vassil, T. (1983). *Groups in social work: An ecological perspective.* New York: Macmillan.

Bandura, A. (1977). *Social learning theory.* Englewood Cliffs, NJ: Prentice-Hall.

Bandura, A. A. (1995). *Exercise of personal and collective efficacy in changing societies.* New York: Cambridge University Press.

Bandura, A. A. (1997a). *Self efficacy: Exercise and control.* New York: Freeman.

Bandura, A. A. (1997b). *Self-efficacy in changing societies.* New York: Cambridge University Press.

Banker, R. D., Field, J. M., Schroeder, R. G., & Sinha, K. K. (1996). Impact of work teams on manufacturing performance: A longitudinal field study. *Academy of Management Journal, 39*(4), 867–890.

Barker, L. (1979). *Groups in process: An introduction to small group communication.* Englewood Cliffs, NJ: Prentice-Hall.

Barker, V., Abrams, J., Tiyaamornwong, V., Seibold, D., Duggan, A., Park, H., & Sebastian, M. (2000). New contexts for relational communications in groups. *Small Group Research, 31*(4), 470–503.

Barlow, C., Blythe, J., & Edmonds, M. (1999). *A handbook of interactive exercises for groups.* Boston: Allyn and Bacon.

Barlow, S. H., Burlingame, G. M., & Fuhriman, A. (2000). "Therapeutic application of groups: From Pratt's 'Thought control classes' to modern group psychotherapy." *Group Dynamics, Theory Research, and Practice 4*(1): 115–134.

Baron, J. (1994). *Thinking and deciding* (2nd ed.). New York: Cambridge University Press.

Barrick, M., & Alexander, R. (1987). A review of quality circle efficacy and the existence of positive-findings bias. *Personnel Psychology, 40,* 579–593.

Bass, B. M. (1985). *Leadership and performance beyond expectations.* New York: The Free Press.

Bass, B. M. (1998). *Transformational leadership: Industry, military, and educational impact.* Mahwah, NJ: Erlbaum.

Bass, B. M., & Avolio, B. J. (1990a). The implications of transactional and transformational leadership for individual, team, and organizational development. In R. W. Woodman & W. A. Passmore (Eds.), *Research in organizational change and development.* Greenwich, CT: JAI Press.

Bass, B. M., & Avolio, B. J. (1990b). *Manual for the multifactor leadership questionnaire.* Palo Alto, CA: Consulting Psychologists Press.

Bass, B. M., & Avolio, B. J. (1993). Transformational leadership: A response to critiques. In M. M. Chemers & R. Ayman (Eds.), *Leadership theory and research: Perspectives and directions.* San Diego, CA; Academic Press.

Bass, B. M., & Avolio, B. J. (1994). *Improving organizational effectiveness through transformational leadership.* Thousand Oaks, CA: Sage.

Bass, D., McClendon, M., Brennan, P., & McCarthy, C. (1998). The buffering effect of a computer support network on caregiver strain. *Journal of Aging and Health, 10*(1), 20–43.

Bauer, M. M., & McBride, L. (2003). *Structured group psychotherapy for bipolar disorder: The life goals program.* New York: Springer Publishing Company.

Baugh, S., & Graen, G. (1997). Effects of team gender and racial composition on perceptions of team performance in cross-functional teams. *Group & Organization Management, 22*(3), 366–383.

Bayless, O. (1967). An alternative pattern for problem solving discussion. *Journal of Communication, 17,* 188–197.

Beck, A., & Freeman, A. (1990). *Cognitive therapy of personality disorders.* New York: Guilford.

Beck, J. (1995). *Cognitive therapy: Basics and beyond.* New York: Guilford.

Becker, W. (1971). *Parents are teachers.* Champaign, IL: Research Press.

Bednar, K., & Kaul, T. (1994). Experimental group research: Can the cannon fire? In A. Bergen & S. Garfield (Eds.), *Handbook of psychotherapy and behavior change* (4th ed., pp. 631–663). New York: John Wiley & Sons.

Behroozi, C. S. (1992). A model for social work with involuntary applicants in groups. *Social Work with Groups, 15*(2/3), 223–238.

Bell, J. (1981). The small group perspective: Family group-therapy. In E. Tolson & W. Reid (Eds.), *Models of family treatment* (pp. 33–51). New York: Columbia University Press.

Benjamin, J. B., Bessant, J., & Watts, R. (1997). Working with groups in community work and social movements. In J. Benjamin, J. Bessant, & R. Watts, *Making groups work: Rethinking practice.* (pp. 165–188). Australia: Allen & Unwin Aust.

Benne, K., & Sheats, P. (1948). Functional roles of group members. *Journal of Social Issues, 4*(2), 41–49.

Berger, R. (1996). A comparative analysis of different methods of teaching group work. *Social Work with Groups, 19*(1), 79–89.

Bergeron, L. G., & Gray, B. (2003). Ethical dilemmas of reporting suspected elder abuse. *Social Work*, *48*(1), 96–105.

Berne, E. (1961). *Transactional analysis in psychotherapy.* New York: Ballantine Books.

Bernstein, D., & Borkovec, T. (1973). *Progressive relaxation training: A manual for the helping professions.* Champaign, IL: Research Press.

Bernstein, D. B., Borkovek, T., & Hazlett-Stevens, H. (2000). *New directions in progressive relaxation training: A guidebook for helping professionals.* Westport, CT: Praeger.

Berry, J. (1997). Individual and group relations in plural societies. In C. Granose & S. Oskamp (Eds.), *Cross-cultural work groups: An overview* (pp. 17–35). Thousand Oaks, CA: Sage Publications.

Berry, T. (1991). *Managing the total transformation.* New York: McGraw-Hill.

Bertcher, H. (1990). *Tell-a-group: How to set up and operate group work by telephone.* Unpublished manuscript, University of Michigan, School of Social Work, Ann Arbor.

Bertcher, H., & Maple, F. (1977). *Creating groups.* Newbury Park, CA: Sage.

Bertcher, H., & Maple, F. (1985). Elements and issues in group composition. In M. Sundel, P. Glasser, R. Sarri, & R. Vinter (Eds.), *Individual change through small groups* (2nd ed., pp. 180–203). New York: The Free Press.

Bieling, P. J., McCabe, R. E., & Antony, M. M. (2006), *Cognitive-behavioral therapy in groups.* New York: The Guilford Press.

Bion, W. (1991). *Experiences in groups and other papers.* London: Routledge.

Birnbaum, M. C., & Cicchetti, A. (2000). The power of purposeful sessional endings in each group encounter. *Social Work with Groups 23*(3), 37–52.

Birnbaum, M. M., Mason, S., & Cicchetti, A. (2002). Impact of purposeful sessional endings on both the group and the practitioner. *Social Work with Groups 25*(4), 3–19.

Blackmon, M., & Holland, T. (2000). *Measuring board effectiveness.* Washington, DC: BoardSource.

Blatner, H. (1996). *Acting-in: Practical applications of psychodramatic methods* (3rd ed.). New York: Springer.

Blau, P. (1964). *Exchange and power in social life.* New York: John Wiley & Sons.

Blay, S., Vel-Fucks, J., Barruzi, M., Di-Piertro, M., Gastal, F., Neto, A., DeSouza, M., Glausiusz, L., & Dewey, M. (2002). Effectiveness of time-limited psychotherapy for minor psychiatric disorders. *British Journal of Psychiatry, 180*(5), 416–422.

Blazer, D. (1978). Techniques for communicating with your elderly patient. *Geriatrics, 33*(11), 79–84.

Bloom, B., & Broder, L. (1950). *Problem-solving processes of college students.* Chicago: University of Chicago Press.

Bloom, M., Fisher, J., & Orme, J. (2003). *Evaluating practice: Guidelines for the accountable professional* (4th ed.). Boston: Allyn and Bacon.

Blouin, J., Schnarre, K., Carter, J., Blouin, A., Tener, L., Zuro, C., & Barlow, J. (1995). Factors affecting dropout rate from cognitive-behavioral group treatment for bulimia nervosa. *International Journal of Eating Disorders, 17,* 323–329.

Bonito, J. (2002). The analysis of participation in small groups: Methodological and conceptual issues related to interdependence. *Small Group Research, 33*(4), 412–438.

Borkovec, T. D., Hazlett-Stevens, H., & Diaz, M. L. (1999). The role of positive beliefs about worry in generalized anxiety disorder and its treatment. *Clinical Psychology & Psychotherapy, 6*(2), 126–139.

Bouchard, T. (1972a). A comparison of two group brainstorming procedures. *Journal of Applied Psychology, 56,* 418–421.

Bouchard, T. (1972b). Training, motivation and personality as determinants of the effectiveness of brainstorming groups and individuals. *Journal of Applied Psychology, 56,* 324–331.

Bowman, L. (1935). Dictatorship, democracy, and group work in America. In *Proceedings of the National Conference of Social Work* (p. 382). Chicago: University of Chicago Press.

Bowman, R., & Bowman, V. (1998). Life on the electronic frontier: The application of technology to group work. *Journal for Specialists in Group Work, 23*(4), 428–445.

Boyd, N. (1935). Group work experiments in state institutions in Illinois. In *Proceedings of the National Conference of Social Work* (p. 344). Chicago: University of Chicago Press.

Boyd, N. (1938). Play as a means of social adjustment. In J. Lieberman (Ed.), *New trends in group work* (pp. 210–220). New York: Association Press.

Brabender, V., & Fallon, A. (1996). Termination in inpatient groups. *International Journal of Group Psychotherapy, 46*(1), 81–99.

Brackett, J. (1895). The charity organization movement: Its tendency and its duty. In *Proceedings of the 22nd National Conference of Charities and Corrections.* Boston: G. H. Ellis.

Bradford, L., & Corey, S. (1951). Improving large group meetings. *Adult Education, 1,* 122–137.

Brager, G., & Holloway, A. (1978). *Changing human service organizations: Politics and practice.* New York: The Free Press.

Brehmer, B., & Joyce, C. (1988). *Human judgment: The SIT view.* New York: North-Holland.

Brekke, J. (1989). The use of orientation groups to engage hard-to-reach clients: Model, method and evaluation. *Social Work with Groups, 12*(2), 75–88.

Breton, M. (1994). On the meaning of empowerment and empowerment-oriented social work practice. *Social Work with Groups, 17*(3), 23–37.

Breton, M. (1995). The potential for social action in groups. *Social Work with Groups, 18*(2/3), 5–13.

Breton, M. (1999). The relevance of the structural approach to group work with immigrant and refugee women. *Social Work with Groups, 22*(2–3), 11–29.

Brilhart, J. (1974). *Effective group discussion* (2nd ed.). Dubuque, IA: William C. Brown.

Brill, N. (1976). *Team-work: Working together in the human services.* Philadelphia: J. B. Lippincott.

Brill, N. & Levine, J. (2005). *Working with people: The helping process* (8th ed.). Boston: Allyn and Bacon.

Brook, D., Gordon, C., & Meadow, H. (1998). Ethnicity, culture, and group psychotherapy. *Group, 22*(2), 53–80.

Brower, A. M., Arndt, R. G., & Ketterhagen, A. (2004). Very good solutions really do exist for group work research design problems. In C. D. Garvin, L. M. Gutierrez, & M. J. Galinsky (Eds.), *Handbook of social work with groups* (pp. 435–446). New York: The Guilford Press.

Brown, A., & Mistry, T. (1994). Group work with mixed membership groups: Issues of race and gender. *Social Work with Groups, 17*(3), 5–21.

Brown, B. M. (1995). A bill of rights for people with disabilities in group work. *Journal for Specialists in Group Work, 20,* 71–75.

Brown, L. (1991). *Groups for growth and change.* New York: Longman.

Browne, K., Saunders, D., & Staecker, K. (1997). Process-psychodynamic groups for men who batter. *Families in Society, 78,* 265–271.

Browning, L. (1977). Diagnosing teams in organizational settings. *Group and Organization Studies, 2*(2), 187–197.

Budman, S., Demby, A., Feldstein, M., Redondo, J., Scherz, B., Bennett, M., Koppenall, G., Daley, B., Hunter, M., & Ellis, J. (1987). Preliminary findings on a new instrument to measure cohesion in group psychotherapy. *International Journal of Group Psychotherapy, 37*(1), 75–94.

Budman, S., Simeone, P., Reilly, R., & Demby, A. (1994). Progress in short-term and time-limited group psychotherapy: Evidence and implications. In A. Fuhriman & G. M. Burlingame (Eds.), *Handbook of Group Psychotherapy* (pp. 319–339). New York: John Wiley & Sons.

Budman, S., Soldz, S., Demby, A., Davis, M., & Merry, J. (1993). What is cohesiveness? An empirical examination. *Small Group Research, 24*(2), 199–216.

Bufe, C., & DeNunzio, D. (1998). *Exercises for individual and group development.* Tucson, AZ: Sharp Press.

Burlingame, G., Kircher, J., & Honts, C. (1994). Analysis of variance versus bootstrap procedures for analyzing dependent observations in small group research. *Small Group Research, 25*(4), 486–501.

Burns, J. M. (1978). *Leadership.* New York: Harper & Row.

Burwell, N. (1998). Human diversity and empowerment. In H. W. Johnson, et al. (Eds.), *The social services: An introduction* (5th ed., pp. 357–370). Itasca, IL: Peacock Press.

Butler, H., Davis, I., & Kukkonen, R. (1979). The logic of case comparison. *Social Work Research and Abstracts, 15*(3), 3–11.

Byers, P. Y., & Wilcox, J. R. (1991, Winter). Focus groups: A qualitative opportunity for researchers. *The Journal of Business Communication, 28*(1), 63–77.

Cambridge Educational. (2000). *Stress management.* Charleston, WV: Cambridge Research Group.

Carless, S. D., & De Paola, C. (2000). The measurement of cohesion in work teams. *Small Group Research, 31*(1), 71–88.

Carletta, J., Garrod, S., & Fraser-Krauss, H. (1998). Placement of authority and communication patterns in workplace groups. *Small Group Research, 29*(5), 531–559.

Carron, A., & Spink, K. (1995). The group size-cohesion relationship in minimal groups. *Small Group Research, 26*(1), 86–105.

Cartwright, D. (1951). Achieving change in people. *Human Relations, 4,* 381–392.

Cartwright, D. (1968). The nature of group cohesiveness. In D. Cartwright & A. Zander (Eds.), *Group dynamics: Research and theory* (3rd ed., pp. 91–109). New York: Harper & Row.

Cartwright, D., & Zander, A. (Eds.). (1968). *Group dynamics: Research and theory* (3rd ed.). New York: Harper & Row.

Chait, R., Holland, T. P., & Taylor, B. E. (1993). *The effective board of trustees.* Phoenix, AZ: Oryx Press.

Chau, K. (1992). Needs assessment for group work with people of color: A conceptual formulation. *Social Work with Groups, 15*(2/3), 53–66.

Chemers, M. M. (2000). Leadership research and theory: A functional integration. *Group Dynamics: Theory, Research, and Practice, 4*(1), 27–43.

Chiauzzi, E. J. (1991). *Preventing relapse in the addictions: A biopsychosocial approach.* New York: Pergamon Press.

Clark, A. (1998). Reframing: A therapeutic technique in group counseling. *Journal for Specialists in Group Work, 23*(1), 66–73.

Clark, C. H. (1958). *Brainstorming.* New York: Doubleday.

Clemen, R. T. (1996). *Making hard decisions: An introduction to decision analysis* (2nd ed.). Belmont, CA: Duxbury Press.

Clifford, M. W. (1998). A short-term model of social group work with adults: Theory, practice, teaching, and evaluation. *Psychotherapy in Private Practice, 17*(2), 11–27.

Cohen, M. B., & Mullender, A. (1999). The personal in the political: Exploring the group work continuum from individual to social change goals. *Social Work with Groups, 22,* 13–31.

Cohen, S. G., & Bailey, D. E. (1997). What makes teams work: Group effectiveness research from the shop floor to the executive suite. *Journal of Management, 23*(3), 239–290.

Cole, R., & Tachiki, D. (1983, June). A look at U.S. and Japanese quality circles: Preliminary comparisons. *Quality Circles Journal, 6,* 10–16.

Collaros, R., & Anderson, L. (1969). Effects of perceived expertness upon creativity of members of brainstorming groups. *Journal of Applied Psychology, 53*(2), 159–164.

Commission on Accreditation. (2001). *Handbook of accreditation standards and procedures* (5th ed.). New York: Council on Social Work Education.

Cone, J., & Hawkins, R. (Eds.). (1977). *Behavioral assessment: New directions in clinical psychology.* New York: Brunner/Mazel.

Connelly, J. L., & Piper, W. (1984). *Pretraining behavior as a predictor of process and outcome in group psychotherapy.* Paper presented at the 15th Annual Meeting of the Society for Psychotherapy Research, Lake Louise, Alberta.

Connelly, J. L., Piper, W., DeCarufel, F., & Debbane, E. (1986). Premature termination in group psychotherapy: Pretherapy and early therapy predictors. *International Journal of Group Psychotherapy, 36*(1), 145–152.

Conrad, W., & Glenn, W. (1976). *The effective voluntary board of directors: What it is and how it works.* Chicago: Swallow Press.

Cooksey, R. W. (1996). *Judgment analysis: Theory methods and applications.* New York: Academic Press.

Cooley, D. (1909). *Social organization.* New York: Charles Scribner's Sons.

Cooper, C. (1977). Adverse and growthful effects of experimental learning groups: The role of the trainer, participant, and group characteristics. *Human Relations, 30,* 1103–1129.

Cooper, L. (1976). Co-therapy relationships in groups. *Small Group Behavior, 7*(4), 473–498.

Corey, M., & Corey, G. (2006). *Groups: Process and practice* (7th ed.). Pacific Grove, CA: Brooks/Cole.

Costin, H. (1999). *Strategies for quality improvement: TQM, reengineering, and ISO 9000.* Forth Worth, TX: Dryden Press.

Counselman, E. F. (1991). Leadership in a long-term leaderless women's group. *Small Group Research, 22,* 240–257.

Cox, E. (1988). Empowerment of the low income elderly through group work. *Social Work with Groups, 11*(4), 111–119.

Cox, E., & Parsons, R. (1994). *Empowerment-oriented social work practice with the elderly.* Pacific Grove, CA: Brooks/Cole.

Cox, M. (1973). The group therapy interaction chronogram. *British Journal of Social Work, 3,* 243–256.

Coyle, G. (1930). *Social process in organized groups.* New York: Richard Smith.

Coyle, G. (1935). Group work and social change. *Proceedings of the National Conference of Social Work* (p. 393). Chicago: University of Chicago Press.

Coyle, G. (1937). *Studies in group behavior.* New York: Harper & Row.

Coyle, G. (1938). Education for social action. In J. Lieberman (Ed.), *New Trends in Group Work* (pp. 1–14). New York: Association Press.

Craig, T., Huffine, C., & Brooks, M. (1974). Completion of referral to psychiatric services by inner-city residents. *Archives of General Psychiatry, 31*(3), 353–357.

Crano, W., & Brewer, M. (1973). *Principles of research in social psychology.* New York: McGraw-Hill.

D'Andrea, M. (2004). The impact of racial-cultural identity of group leaders and members: Theory and recommendations. In J. L. Delucia-Waack, D. A. Gerrity, C. R. Kalodner, & M. T. Riva (Eds.), *Group counseling and psychotherapy* (pp. 265–282). Thousand Oaks, CA: Sage Publications.

Dalgleish, L. I. (1988). Decision making in child abuse cases: Applications of social judgment theory and signal detection theory. In B. Brehmer & C. R. B. Joyce (Eds.), *Human judgment: The SJT view.* New York: North-Holland.

Davis, F., & Lohr, N. (1971). Special problems with the use of co-therapists in group psychotherapy. *International Journal of Group Psychotherapy, 21,* 143–158.

Davis, G., Manske, M., & Train, A. (1966). An instructional method of increasing originality. *Psychonomic Science, 6,* 73–74.

Davis, I. (1975). Advice-giving in parent counseling. *Social Casework, 56,* 343–347.

Davis, L., Galinsky, M., & Schopler, J. (1995). RAP: A framework for leadership of multiracial groups. *Social Work, 40*(2), 155–165.

Davis, L., & Proctor, E. (1989). *Race, gender and class: Guidelines for practice with individuals, families and groups.* Englewood Cliffs, NJ: Prentice-Hall.

Davis, L., Strube, M., & Cheng, L. (1995). Too many blacks, too many whites: Is there a racial balance? *Basic and Applied Social Psychology, 17*(1/2), 119–135.

Davis, L., & Toseland, R. (1987). Group versus individual decision making. *Social Work with Groups, 10*(2), 95–105.

Davis, M., Eshelman, E., & McKay, M. (2000). *The relaxation and stress reduction workbook* (5th ed.). Oakland, CA: New Harbinger.

De Bono, E. (1968). *New think: The use of lateral thinking in generation of new ideas.* New York: Basic Books.

De Bono, E. (1971). *Lateral thinking for management.* New York: American Management Associations.

De Bono, E. (1972). *Lateral thinking: Productivity step by step.* New York: Harper & Row.

Delbecq, A., Van de Ven, A., & Gustafson, D. (1986). *Group techniques for program planning: A guide to nominal group and delphi processes.* Middleton, WI: Green Briar Press.

Delgado, M. (1983). Activities and Hispanic groups. *Social Work with Groups, 6,* 85–96.

Delucia-Waack, J. (1997). Measuring the effectiveness of group work: A review and analysis of process and outcome measures. *Journal for Specialists in Group Work, 22,* 277–292.

Denhardt, R., Pyle, J., & Bluedorn, A. (1987). Implementing quality circles in state government. *Public Administrative Review, 47*(4), 304–309.

Devore, W., & Schlesinger, E. (1999). *Ethnic-sensitive social work practice* (5th ed.). Boston: Allyn and Bacon.

Diaz, T. (2002). Group work from an Asian Pacific Island perspective: Making connections between group worker ethnicity and practice. *Social Work with Groups, 25*(3), 43–60.

Dienesch, R. M., & Liden, R. C. (1986). Leader-member exchange model of leadership: A critique and further development. *Academy of Management Review, 11,* 618–634.

Dies, R. (1994). Therapist variables in group psychotherapy research. In A. Fuhriman & G. M. Burlingame (Eds.), *Handbook of Group Psychotherapy* (pp. 114–154), New York: John Wiley & Sons.

Diller, J. (1999). *Cultural diversity: A primer for the human services.* Belmont, CA: Wadsworth.

Dillon, W., Madden, T., & Firtle, N. (1994). *Marketing research in a marketing environment* (3rd ed.). Burr Ridge, IL: Irwin.

Dinges, N., & Cherry, D. (1995). Symptom expression and use of mental health services among ethnic minorities. In J. Aponte, R. Rivers, & J. Wohl (Eds.), *Psychological interventions and cultural diversity* (pp. 40–56). Boston: Allyn and Bacon.

Dinkmeyer, D., & McKay, G. (1990). *Systematic training for effective parenting* (Rev. ed.). New York: Random House.

Dion, K. L. (2000). Group cohesion: From "Field of forces" to multidimensional construct. *Group Dynamics: Theory, Research, and Practice, 4*(1), 7–26.

Dion, K., Miller, N., & Magnan, M. (1970). Cohesiveness and social responsibility as determinants of risk taking. *Proceedings of the American Psychological Association, 5*(1), 335–336.

Dluhy, M. (1990). *Building coalitions in the human services.* Newbury Park, CA: Sage.

Dobson, K. (2001). *Handbook of cognitive-behavioral therapies.* New York: Guildford Press.

Dodge, K., Gilroy F., & Fenzel, L. (1995). Requisite managment characteristics revisited: Two decades later. *Journal of Social Behavior and Personality, 10,* 253–264.

Dolgoff, R., & Skolnik, L. (1992). Ethical decision making, the NASW code of ethics and group work practice: Beginning explorations. *Social Work with Groups, 15*(4), 99–112.

Douglas, T. (1979). *Group process in social work: A theoretical synthesis.* New York: John Wiley & Sons.

Drum, D., & Knott, J. (1977). *Structured groups for facilitating development: Acquiring life skills, resolving life themes and making life transitions.* New York: Human Science Press.

Drummond, M., Stoddart, G., & Torrance, G. (1987). *Methods for the economic evaluation of health care programmes.* Oxford, UK: Oxford University Press.

Drysdale, J. P., & Purcell, R. (1999). Breaking the culture of silence: Groupwork and community development. *Groupwork, 11*(3), 71–87.

Dunnette, M., Campbell, J., & Joastad, K. (1963). The effect of group participation on brainstorming effectiveness for two industrial samples. *Journal of Applied Psychology, 47,* 30–37.

Dutton, D., & Sonkin, D. (Eds.). (2003). *Intimate violence: Contemporary treatment innovations.* Binghamton, NY: Haworth Press.

D'Zurilla, T., & Goldfried, M. (1971). Problem solving and behavior modification. *Journal of Abnormal Psychology, 78,* 107–126.

Earley, P. R., & Randel, A. (1997). Self and other: "Face" and work group dynamics. In C. Granrose & S. Oskamp (Eds.), *Cross-Cultural Work Groups: An Overview* (pp. 113–133). Thousand Oaks, CA: Sage Publications.

Early, B. (1992). Social work consultation with the work group of the school. *Social Work In Education, 14*(4), 207–214.

Ebbesen, E., & Bowers, R. (1974). Proportion of risky to conservative arguments in a group discussion and choice shift. *Journal of Personality and Social Psychology, 29,* 316–327.

Edelwich, J., & Brodsky, A. (1992). *Group counseling for the resistent client: A practical guide to group process.* New York: Lexington Books.

Edleson, J., & Syers, M. (1990). The relative effectiveness of group treatments for men who batter. *Social Work Research and Abstracts, 26,* 10–17.

Edleson, J., & Tolman, R. (1992). *Intervention for men who batter.* Newbury Park, CA: Sage.

Edmunds, H. (1999). *The focus group research handbook.* Chicago: NTC Business Books.

Edwards, W. (1977). How to use multiattribute utility measurement for social decision making. *IEEE Transactions on Systems, Man and Cybernetics, 7,* 326–340.

Egan, G. (2002). *The skilled helper* (7th ed.). Pacific Grove, CA: Brooks/Cole.

Eisenhart, C. (1972). The assumptions underlying the analysis of variance. In R. Kirk (Ed.), *Statistical issues* (pp. 226–240). Pacific Grove, CA: Brooks/Cole.

Elliott, H. (1928). *Process of group thinking.* New York: Association Press.

Ellis, A. (1962). *Reason and emotion in psychotherapy.* Secaucus, NJ: Lyle Stuart.

Ellis, A. (1992). Group rational-emotive and cognitive-behavior therapy. *International Journal of Group Psychotherapy, 42*(1), 63–82.

Empey, L., & Erikson, M. (1972). *The Provo experiment: Impact and death of an innovation.* Lexington, MA: Lexington Books.

Emrick, C. D., Lassen, C. L., & Edwards, M. T. (1977). Nonprofessional peers as therapeutic agents. In A. Gurman & A. Razin (Eds.), *Effective psychotherapy: A handbook of research* (pp. 120–161). New York: Pergamon Press.

Ephross, P. H., & Vassil, T. (in press). *Groups that work* (2nd ed.). New York: Columbia University Press.

Etcheverry, R., Siporin, M., & Toseland, R. (1987). The uses and abuses of role playing. In P. Glasser and N. Mayadas (Eds.), *Group workers at work: Theory and practice in the 1980s* (pp. 116–130). Lanham, MD: Littlefield, Adams & Company.

Etzioni, A. (1961). *A comparative analysis of complex organizations on power, involvement and their correlates.* New York: The Free Press.

Etzioni, A. (1968). *The active society: A theory of societal and political processes.* New York: The Free Press.

Evans, C., & Dion, K. (1991). Group cohesion and performance. *Small Group Research, 22*(2), 175–186.

Everly, G. S. (1989). *A clinical guide to the treatment of the human stress response.* New York: Plenum.

Ewalt, P., & Kutz, J. (1976). An examination of advice giving as a therapeutic intervention. *Smith College Studies in Social Work, 47,* 3–19.

Falck, H. (1988). *Social work: The membership perspective.* New York: Springer.

Fall, K., Howard, S., & Ford, J. (1999). *Alternatives to domestic violence: A homework manual for battering intervention groups.* Philadelphia: Taylor & Francis.

Fallon, A. (2006), Informed consent in the practice of group psychotherapy. *International Journal of Group Psychotherapy,* 56 (4), 431–454.

Fatout, M., & Rose, S. (1995). *Task groups in the social services.* Thousand Oaks, CA: Sage.

Feldman, R. (1986). Group work knowledge and research: A two-decade comparison. *Social Work with Groups, 9*(3), 7–14.

Feldman, R., Caplinger, T., & Wodarski, J. (1983). *The St. Louis conundrum: The effective treatment of antisocial youth.* Englewood Cliffs, NJ: Prentice-Hall.

Feldman, R., & Wodarski, J. (1975). *Contemporary approaches to group treatment: Traditional, behavior modification and group-centered.* San Francisco: Jossey-Bass.

Fern, E. (1982). The use of focus groups for idea generation: The effects of group size, acquaintance-ship, and moderator on response quantity and quality. *Journal of Marketing Research, 19,* 1–13.

Festinger, L. (1950). Informal social communication. *Psychological Review, 57,* 271–282.

Fieldsteel, N. D. (1996). The process of termination in long-term psychoanalytic group therapy. *International Journal of Group Psychotherapy, 46*(1), 25–39.

Finn, J. (1995). Computer-based self-help groups: A new resource to supplement support groups. In M. Galinsky & J. Schopler (Eds.), *Support groups: Current perspectives in theory and practice* (pp. 109–117). New York: Haworth.

Finn, J., & Lavitt, M. (1994). Computer-based self help groups for sexual abuse survivors. *Social Work with Groups, 17*(1/2), 21–46.

Fisher, J. (1978). *Effective casework practice: An eclectic approach.* New York: McGraw-Hill.

Fisher, J., & Corcoran, K. (2007). *Measures for clinical practice and research: A sourcebook* (4th ed.). (Vol. 1, Couples Families and Children & Vol. 2, Adults). New York: Oxford University Press.

Fisher, R., Ury, W., & Patton, B. (1997). *Getting to yes: Negotiating agreement without giving in* (2nd ed.). London: Arrow Business Books.

Flippen, A. (1999). Understanding group think from a self-regulatory perspective. *Small Group Research, 30*(2), 139–166.

Flores, M. (2000). *La familia Latina.* In M. Flores (Ed.), *Family therapy with Hispanics: Toward appreciating diversity.* Boston, MA: Allyn and Bacon.

Follett, M. P. (1926). *The new state: Group organization, the solution of popular government.* New York: Longmans, Green.

Forester, J. (1981). Questioning and organizing attention: Toward a critical theory of planning and administrative practice. *Administration and Society, 13*(2), 181–205.

Forse, M. D., & Degenne, A. (1999). *Introducing social networks.* London: Sage.

Forsyth, D. (2000). One hundred years of groups research: Introduction to the special issue. *Group Dynamics Theory, Research, and Practice, 4*(1), 3–6.

Forsyth, D. R. (2006). *Group dynamics (4th ed.).* Belmont, CA: Thomson Wadsworth.

Forsyth, D. R, & Burnette, J. L. (2005). The history of group research. In S. A. Wheelan (Ed), *The handbook of group research and practice* (pp. 3–18). Thousand Oaks, CA: Sage Publications Inc.

Forsyth, D., & Corazzini, J. (2000). Groups as change agents. In C. Snyder & R. Ingram (Eds.), *Handbook of psychological change: Psychotherapy processes & practices for the 21st century* (pp. 309–366). New York, NY: John Wiley & Sons, Inc.

Fortune, A. (1979). Communication in task-centered treatment. *Social Work, 24,* 390–397.

Fortune, A. (1985, December). Planning duration and termination of treatment. In A. Fortune (Ed.), *Social service review* (pp. 648–661). Chicago: University of Chicago Press.

Fortune, A. (1987). Grief only? Client and social worker reactions to termination. *Clinical Social Work Journal, 15*(2), 159–171.

Fortune, A., Pearlingi, B., & Rochelle, C. (1991, June). Criteria for terminating treatment. *Families in Society: The Journal of Contemporary Human Services, 72*(6), 366–370.

Fortune, A., Pearlingi, B., & Rochelle, C. (1992). Reactions to termination of individual treatment. *Social Work, 37*(2), 171–178.

Fortune, A., & Reid, W. J. (1998). *Research in social work* (3rd ed.). New York: Columbia University Press.

Frances, A., Clarkin, J., & Perry, S. (1984). *Differential therapeutics in psychiatry: The art and science of treatment selection.* New York: Brunner/Mazel.

Frank, J. (1961). *Persuasion and healing: A comparative study of psychotherapy.* New York: Schocken Books.

Freeman, A., Pretzer, J., Fleming, J., & Simons, K. (2004). *Clinical applications of cognitive therapy* (2nd ed.). New York: Plenum.

French, J., & Raven, B. (1959). The bases of social power. In D. Cartwright (Ed.), *Studies in social power.* Ann Arbor, MI: Institute for Research, University of Michigan.

Freud, S. (1922). *Group psychology and the analysis of the ego.* London: International Psychoanalytic Press.

Fuhriman, A., & Barlow, S. (1994). Interaction analysis: Instrumentation and issues. In A. Fuhriman G. M. Burlingame (Eds.), *Handbook of group psychotherapy* (pp. 191–222). New York: John Wiley & Sons.

Fuhriman, A., & Burlingame, G. (1994). Group psychotherapy: Research and practice. In A. Fuhriman & G. M. Burlingame (Eds.), *Handbook of group psychotherapy* (pp. 3–40). New York: John Wiley & Sons.

Fuhriman, A., & Packard, T. (1986). Group process instruments: Therapeutic themes and issues. *International Journal of Group Psychotherapy, 36*(3), 399–525.

Furman, R. (2005). *An introduction to group work practice. Student workbook for Toseland and Rivas.* Boston: Allyn and Bacon.

Galinsky, M., & Schopler, J. (1977). Warning: Groups may be dangerous. *Social Work, 22*(2), 89–94.

Galinsky, M., & Schopler, J. (1980). Structuring co-leadership in social work training. *Social Work with Groups, 3*(4), 51–63.

Galinsky, M., & Schopler, J. (1989). Developmental patterns in open-ended groups. *Social Work with Groups, 12*(2), 99–114.

Gant, L. M. (2004). Evaluation of group work. In C. D. Garvin, L. M. Gutierrez, & M. J. Galinsky (Eds.), *Handbook of social work with groups* (pp. 461–475). New York: The Guilford Press.

Garland, J., Jones, H., & Kolodny, R. (1976). A model of stages of group development in social work groups. In S. Bernstein (Ed.), *Explorations in group work* (pp. 17–71). Boston: Charles River Books.

Garland, J., & Kolodny, R. (1967). Characteristics and resolution of scapegoating. In *National Conference of Social Welfare, Social Work Practice* (pp. 198–219). New York: Columbia University Press.

Garvin, C. (1997). *Contemporary group work* (3rd ed.). Boston: Allyn and Bacon.

Garvin, C. (1998, October). *Potential impact of small group research on social group work practice.* Paper presented at the 20th Annual Symposium of the Association for the Advancement of Social Work with Groups, Miami, FL.

Garwick, G. (1974). *Guideline for goal attainment scaling.* Minneapolis: Program Evaluation Project.

Gazda, G., & Mobley, J. (1981). INDS-CAL multidimensional scaling. *Journal of Group Psychotherapy, Psychodrama and Sociometry, 34,* 54–72.

Gebhardt, L., & Meyers, R. (1995). Subgroup influence in decision-making groups: Examining consistency from a communication perspective. *Small Group Research, 26*(2), 147–168.

Gelles, R. (2002). Standards for programs for men who batter? Not yet. *Journal of Aggression, Maltreatment and Trauma, 5*(2), 11–20.

Gentry, M. (1987). Coalition formation and processes. *Social Work with Groups, 10*(3), 39–54.

Germain, C., & Gitterman, A. (1996). *The life model of social work practice* (2nd ed.). New York: Columbia University Press.

Getzel, G. (1998). Group work practice with gay men and lesbians. In G. P. Mallon (Ed.), *Foundations of social work practice with lesbian and gay persons* (pp. 131–144). New York: Harrington Park Press.

Gibb, C. (1969). Leadership. In G. Lindzey & E. Aronson (Eds.), *The handbook of social psychology* (2nd ed., pp. 205–273). Reading, MA: Addison-Wesley.

Gibbs, L., & Gambrill, E. (1998). *Critical thinking for social workers.* Thousand Oaks, CA: Pine Forge Press.

Gibson, A. (1999). *Project-based group work facilitator's manual: Young people, youth workers, & projects.* Bristol, PA: Jessica Kingsley Publications.

Gill, S. (1991). *Learning nominal group technique a leader's guide.* Brighton, CO: Brighton Books.

Giordano, J. (1973). *Ethnicity and mental health.* New York: Institute of Human Relations.

Gitterman, A., & Shulman, L. (Eds.). (2005). *Mutual aid groups, vulnerable populations, and the life cycle* (3rd ed.). New York: Columbia University Press.

Glassman, U., & Kates, L. (1990). *Group work: A humanistic approach.* Newbury Park, CA: Sage.

Glassop, L. (2002). The organizational benefit of teams. *Human Relations, 55*(2), 225.

Glisson, C. (1986). The group versus the individual as the unit of analysis in small group research. *Social Work with Groups, 9*(3), 15–30.

Glueckauf, R. L., & Ketterson, T. U. (2004). Telehealth interventions for individuals with chronic illness: Research review and implications for practice. *Professional Psychology: Research and Practice, 35, 615–627.*

Glueckauf, R. L., & Loomis, J. S. (2003). Alzheimer's caregiver support online: Lessons learned, initial findings and future directions, *NeuroRehabilitation, 18,* 135–146.

Glueckauf, R. L., Nickelson, D., Whitton, J., & Loomis, J. S. (2004). Telehealth and healthcare psychology: Current developments in telecommunications, regulatory practices, and research. In R. G. Frank, A, Baum, & J. L. Wallander (Eds.), *Handbook of clinical health psychology: Models and perspectives in health psychology* (Vol. 3, pp. 377–411). Washington, DC: American Psychological Association.

Glueckauf, R. L., Pickett, T. C., Ketterson, T. U, Loomis, J. S., & Rozensky, R. H. (2003). Preparation for the delivery of telehealth services: A self-study framework for expansion of practice. *Professional Psychology: Research and Practice, 34,* 159–163.

Goebert, B., & Rosenthal, H. (2002). *Beyond listening: Learning the language of focus groups.* New York: John Wiley.

Gold, M., Siegel, J., Russell, L., & Weinstein, M. (1996). *Cost-effectiveness in health and medicine.* New York: Oxford University Press.

Goldfried, M., & D'Zurilla, T. (1969). A behavioral-analytic model for assessing competence. In C. D. Spielberger (Ed.), *Current topics in clinical and community psychology* (Vol. 1, pp. 151–196). New York: Academic Press.

Goldstein, A. P. (2001). *Reducing resistance: Methods for enhancing openness to change.* Champaign, II: Research Press.

Goldstein, A., Keller, K., & Sechrest, L. (1966). *Psychotherapy and the psychology of behavior change.* New York: John Wiley & Sons.

Goldstein, H. (1983). Starting where the client is. *Social Casework, 64,* 267–275.

Goldstein, H. (1988). A cognitive-humanistic/social learning perspective on social group work practice. *Social Work with Groups, 11,* 9–32.

Goldstein, S. (1985). Organizational quality and quality circles. *Academy of Management Review, 10*(3), 504–517.

Gondolf, E. (1997). Batterer programs: What we know and need to know. *Journal of Interpersonal Violence, 12,* 83–98.

Gondolf, E. (2002). *Batterer intervention systems: Issues, outcomes, and recommendations.* Thousand Oaks, CA: Sage.

Goodman, P. (1986). *Designing effective work groups.* San Francisco: Jossey-Bass.

Good Tracks, J. (1973). Native-American noninterference. *Social Work, 18,* 30–34.

Gordon, T. (1975). *P.E.T.* New York: Plume Books.

Gordon, W. (1961). *Synectics: The development of creative capacity.* New York: Harper & Row.

Goto, S. (1997). Majority and minority perspectives on cross-cultural interactions. In C. Granrose & S. Oskamp (Eds.), *Cross-cultural work groups: An overview* (pp. 90–112). Thousand Oaks, CA: Sage Publications.

Gouran, D. (1982). *Making decisions in groups: Consequences and choices.* Glenview, IL: Scott Foresman.

Graen, G., & Schiemann, W. (1978). Leader-member agreement: A vertical dyad linkage approach. *Journal of Applied Psychology, 63,* 206–212.

Granrose, C. O., & Oskamp, S. (1997). *Cross-cultural work groups.* Thousand Oaks, CA: Sage, Publications.

Gray, G. (1964). Points of emphasis in teaching parliamentary procedure. *The Speech Teacher, 13,* 10–15.

Gray-Little, B., & Kaplan, D. (2000). Race and ethnicity in psychotherapy research. In C. R. Snyder & R. Ingram (Eds.), *Handbook of psychological change* (pp. 591–613). New York: John Wiley & Sons.

Grayson, E. (1993). *Short-term group counseling* (3rd ed.). Washington, DC: American Corrections Association.

Green, J. (1999). *Cultural awareness in the human services: A multi-ethnic approach* (3rd ed.). Boston: Allyn and Bacon.

Greenbaum, T. (1998). *The handbook for focus group research* (2nd ed., Rev.). Thousand Oaks, CA: Sage.

Gruenfeld, D. (Ed.). (1998). *Research on managing groups and teams, Vol. 1.* Stamford, CT: JAI Press.

Guetzkow, H., & Gyr, J. (1954). An analysis of conflict in decision-making groups. *Human Relations, 7,* 368–381.

Gulley, H. (1968). *Discussion, conference and group process* (2nd ed.). New York: Holt, Rinehart & Winston.

Gully, S., Devine, D., & Whitney, D. (1995). A meta-analysis of cohesion and performance: Effects of level of analysis and task interdependence. *Small Group Research, 26*(4), 497–520.

Gummer, B. (1987). Groups as substance and symbol: Group processes and organizational politics. *Social Work with Groups, 10*(2), 25–39.

Gummer, B. (1988). Post-industrial management: Teams, self-management, and the new interdependence. *Administration in Social Work, 12*(3), 117–132.

Gummer, B. (1991). A new managerial era: From hierarchical control to "collaborative individualism." *Administration in Social Work, 15*(3), 121–137.

Gummer, B. (1995). Go team go! The growing importance of teamwork in organizational life. *Administration in Social Work, 19*(4), 85–100.

Gummer, B., & McCallion, P. (Eds.). (1995). *Total quality management in the social services: Theory and practice.* Albany: State University of NY, University at Albany, School of Social Welfare, Professional Development Program of Rockefeller College.

Gutierrez, L., & Ortega, R. (1991). Developing methods to empower Latinos: The importance of groups. *Social Work with Groups, 14*(2), 23–43.

Hackman, J. R. (Ed.). (1990). *Groups that work (and those that don't).* San Francisco: Jossey-Bass.

Haas, L., Benedict, J., & Kobos, J. (1996). Psychotherapy by telephone: Risks and benefits for psychologists and consumers. *Professional Psychology: Research and Practice, 27*(2), 154–160.

Hackman, J. R. (2002). *Leading teams: Setting the stage for great performances.* Boston, MA: Harvard Business School Press.

Halpin, A. (1961). *Theory and research in administration.* New York: Macmillan.

Halstead, L. (1976). Team care in chronic illness: A critical review of the literature of the past 25 years. *Archives of Physical Medicine and Rehabilitation, 57,* 507–511.

Hammond, L., & Goldman, M. (1961). Competition and non-competition and its relationship to individuals' non-productivity. *Sociometry, 24,* 46–60.

Hanson, B. (2002). Interventions for batterers: Program approaches, program tensions. In A. Roberts (Ed.), *Handbook of domestic violence intervention strategies* (pp. 419–450). New York: Oxford.

Hare, A. P. (1976). *Handbook of small group research* (2nd ed.). New York: The Free Press.

Hare, A. P., Blumberg, H. H., Davies, M. F., & Kent, M. V. (1995). *Small group research: A handbook.* Norwood, NJ: Ablex.

Harmon, J., & Rohrbaugh, J. (1990). Social judgement analysis and small group decision making: Cognitive feedback effects on individual and collective performance. *Organizational Behavior and Human Decision Processes, 46,* 35–54.

Harnack, R., & Fest, T. (1964). *Group discussion: Theory and technique.* New York: Appleton-Century-Crofts.

Harrison, M. W., & Ward, D. (1999). Values as context: Groupwork and social action. *Groupwork, 11*(3), 89–103.

Hartford, M. (Ed.). (1964). *Papers toward a frame of reference for social group work.* New York: National Association of Social Workers.

Hartford, M. (1971). *Groups in social work.* New York: Columbia University Press.

Hasenfeld, Y. (1985). The organizational context of group work. In M. Sundel, P. Glasser, R. Sarri, & R. Vinter (Eds.), *Individual change through small groups* (2nd ed., pp. 294–309). New York: The Free Press.

Heap, K. (1979). *Process and action in work with groups.* Elmsford, NY: Pergamon Press.

Heimberg, R. B., & Becker, R. (2002). *Cognitive-behavioral group therapy for social phobia.* New York: Guilford Press.

Heinemann, G. Z., & Zeiss, A. (2002). *Team performance in health care: Assessment and development.* New York: Kluwer Academic/Plenum Publishers.

Hemphill, J. (1956). *Group dimensions: A manual for their measurement.* Columbus: Monographs of the Bureau of Business Research, Ohio State University.

Henry, S. (1992). *Group skills in social work: A four-dimensional approach* (2nd ed.). Itasca, IL: F. E. Peacock.

Hersen, M. & Bellack, A. (1976). *Behavioral assessment: A practical handbook.* Elmsford, NY: Pergamon Press.

Hersey, R., & Blanchard, K. (1977). *Management of organizational behavior: Utilizing human resources* (3rd ed.). Englewood Cliffs, NJ: Prentice-Hall.

Hersey, R., Blanchard, K., & Natemeyer, W. (1979). Situational leadership, perception and the impact of power. *Group and Organization Studies, 4*(4), 418–428.

Herzog, J. (1980). Communication between co-leaders: Fact or myth. *Social Work with Groups, 3*(4), 19–29.

Hill, W. (1965). *Hill interaction matrix* (Rev. ed.). Los Angeles: Youth Studies Center, University of Southern California.

Hill, W. (1977). Hill interaction matrix (HIM): The conceptual framework, derived rating scales, and an updated bibliography. *Small Group Behavior, 8*(3), 251–268.

Ho, S. (1999). *TQM, an integrated approach: Implementing total quality through Japanese 5-S and ISO 9000.* Hong Kong: Hong Kong Baptist University.

Hogan-Garcia, M. (1999). *The four skills of cultural diversity competence: A process for understanding and practice.* Belmont, CA: Wadsworth.

Homans, G. (1950). *The human group.* New York: Harcourt Brace Jovanovich.

Homans, G. (1961). *Social behavior: Its elementary forms.* New York: Harcourt Brace Jovanovich.

Hopkins, K. (1998). *Educational and psychological measurement and evaluation* (8th ed.). Boston: Allyn and Bacon.

Hopps, J., & Pinderhughes, E. (1999). *Group work with overwhelmed clients.* New York: The Free Press.

Horne, A., & Rosenthal, R. (1997). Research in group work: How did we get where we are? *Journal for Specialists in Group Work, 22*(4), 228–240.

Howard, M., & Jenson, J. (2003). Clinical guidelines and evidence-based practice in medicine, psychology and allied professions. In A. Rosen & K. Proctor (Eds.), *Developing practice guidelines for social work intervention: Issues, methods, and research agenda* (pp. 83–107). New York: Columbia University Press.

Howe, F. (2002). *Fund-raising and the nonprofit board member* (3rd ed.). Washington, DC: National Center for Nonprofit Boards.

Huber, G. (1980). *Managerial decision making.* Glenview, IL: Scott Foresman.

Hughes, S., Lakey, B., & Bobowick, M. (2000). *The board building cycle: Nine steps of finding, recruiting, and engaging nonprofit board members.* National Center for NonProfit Boards.

Hula, K. (1999). *Lobbying together: Interest group coalitions in legislative politics.* Washington, DC: Georgetown University Press.

Jackson, S, (1992). Team composition in organizational settings: Issues in managing an increasingly diverse workforce. In S. Worchel, W. Wood, & J. Simpson (Eds.), *Group process and productivity* (pp. 138–173). Newbury Park, CA: Sage.

Jacobsen, B., & Jacobsen, M. (1996). The young bears. In R. Rivas & G. Hull (Eds.), *Case studies in generalist practice* (pp. 14–21). Pacific Grove, CA: Brooks/Cole.

Jacobson, E. (1978). *You must relax.* New York: McGraw-Hill.

Janis, I. (1972). *Victims of group think.* Boston: Houghton Mifflin.

Janis, I. (1982). *Groupthink* (2nd ed.). Boston: Houghton Mifflin.

Janis, I., & Mann, L. (1977). *Decision making: A psychological analysis of conflict, choice and commitment.* New York: The Free Press.

Janssen, P. (1994). *Psychoanalytic therapy in the hospital setting.* London: Routledge.

Jehn, K. C., & Chatman, J. (2000). The influence of proportional and perceptual conflict composition on team performance. *The International Journal of Conflict Management, 11*(1), 56–73.

Jennings, H. (1947). Leadership and sociometric choice. *Sociometry* (10), 32–49.

Jennings, H. (1950). *Leadership and isolation* (2nd ed.). New York: Longman.

Jessup, L., & Valacich, J. (1993). Support group systems [Special issue]. *Small Group Research, 24,* 427–592.

Jette, A. (2001). Disability trends and transitions. In R. Binstock & L. George (Eds.), *Handbook of aging and the social sciences* (5th ed., pp. 94–116). San Diego, CA: Academic Press.

Johnson, D. W. (2003). *Reaching out: Interpersonal effectiveness and self-actualization* (8th ed.). Boston: Allyn and Bacon.

Johnson, J. (1975). *Doing field research.* New York: The Free Press.

Johnson, J., & Raab, M. (2003). Take the first: Option-generation and resulting choices. *Organizational Behavior and Human Decision Processes, 91,* 215–229.

Johnson, L. (2004). *Social work practice: A generalist approach* (8th ed.). Boston: Allyn and Bacon.

Johnson, S., & Bechler, C. (1998). Examining the relationship between listening effectiveness and leadership emergence: Perceptions, behaviors, and recall. *Small Group Research, 29*(4), 452–471.

Kadushin, A., & Kadushin, G. (1997). *The social work interview: A guide for human service professionals* (4th ed.). New York: Columbia University Press.

Kaduson, H. G., & Schaefer, C. E. (Eds.). (2000). *Short term play therapy with children.* New York: Guilford Press.

Kahn, S. (1991). *Organizing: A guide for grassroots leaders.* Silver Spring, MD: NASW.

Kane, R. (1974). Look to the record. *Social Work, 19,* 412–419.

Kane, R. (1975a). The interprofessional team as a small group. *Social Work in Health Care, 1*(1), 19–32.

Kane, R. (1975b). *Interprofessional teamwork.* Syracuse, NY: Syracuse University School of Social Work.

Kane, R., & Kane, P. (1981). *Assessing the elderly: A practical guide to measurement.* Lexington, MA: Lexington Books.

Karakowsky, L., & McBey, K. (2001). Do my contributions matter? The influence of imputed expertise of member involvement and self-evaluations in the work group. *Group Organization & Management, 26*(1), 70–92.

Kart, G., Metress, E., & Metress, J. (1978). *Aging and health.* Reading, MA: Addison-Wesley.

Kaslyn, M. (1999). Telephone group work: Challenges for practice. *Social Work with Groups, 22,* 63–77.

Katten, S., & Janis, I. (2000). *Victims of groupthink.* CRM Productions.

Katz, A. H., & Bender, E. I. (1987). *The strength in us: Self-help groups in the modern world.* Oakland, CA: Third Party Associates.

Katz, A. H., Hedrick, H., Isenberg, D., Thompson, L., Goodrich, T., & Kutscher, A. (Eds.). (1992). *Self-help: Concepts and applications.* Philadelphia: Charles Press.

Katzenbach, J., & Smith, D. (1993). *The wisdom of teams.* Boston: Harvard Business School Press.

Kaul, T., & Bednar, R. (1994). Pretraining and structure: Parallel lines yet to meet. In A. Fuhriman and G. M. Burlingame (Eds.), *Handbook of Group Psychotherapy* (pp. 155–188). New York: John Wiley & Sons.

Keith, R. (1991). The comprehensive treatment team in rehabilitation. *Archives of Physical Medicine and Rehabilitation, 72,* 269–274.

Kelleher, K., & Cross, T. (1990). *Teleconferencing: Linking people together electronically.* Norman: University of Oklahoma Press.

Keller, T., & Dansereau, F. (1995). Leadership and empowerment: A social exchange perspective. *Human Relations, 48*(2), 127–146.

Kelley, H., & Thibaut, J. (1969). Group problem solving. In G. Lindzey & E. Aronim (Eds.), *Handbook of social psychology* (2nd ed., pp. 1–101). Reading, MA: Addison-Wesley.

Kellner, M. H. (2001). *In control, a skill-building program for teaching young adolescents to manage anger.* Champaign, IL: Research Press.

Kephart, M. (1951). A quantitative analysis of intragroup relationships. *American Journal of Sociology, 60,* 544–549.

Keyton, J. (1993). Group termination: Completing the study of group development. *Small Group Research, 24*(1), 84–100.

Kiesler, S. (1978). *Interpersonal processes in groups and organizations.* Arlington Heights, VA: AHM.

Kim, B., Omizo, M., & D'Andrea, M. (1998). The effects of culturally consonant group counseling on the self-esteem and internal locus of control orientation among Native American adolescents. *Journal for Specialists in Group Work, 23*(2), 143–163.

Kinlaw, C. D. (1992). *Continuous improvement and measurement for total quality: A team-based approach.* San Diego, CA: Pfeiffer & Co.; Homewood, IL: Business One Irwin.

Kinnear, T., & Taylor, J. (1996). *Marketing research: An applied approach* (5th ed.). New York: McGraw-Hill.

Kiresuk, T., & Sherman, R. (1968). Goal attainment scaling: A general method for evaluating comprehensive community mental health programs. *Community Mental Health Journal, 4*(6), 443–453.

Kirk, S. A., & Kutchins, H. (1999). Making us crazy. *DSM: The psychiatric bible and the creation of mental disorders* (2nd ed.). London: Constable.

Kirk, S. R., & Reid, W. (2002). *Science and social work: A critical appraisal.* New York: Columbia Press.

Kirst-Ashman, K., & Hull, G. (1999). *Understanding generalist practice* (2nd ed.). Chicago: Nelson Hall.

Kivlighan, D. M., & Tarrant, J. M. (2001). Does group climate mediate the group leadership-group member outcome relationship? A test of Yalom's hypotheses about leadership priorities. *Group Dynamics: Theory, Research, and Practice, 5*(3), 220–234.

Klein, A. (1953). *Society, democracy and the group.* New York: Whiteside.

Klein, A. (1956). *Role playing.* New York: Associated Press.

Klein, A. (1970). *Social work through group process.* Albany: School of Social Welfare, State University of New York at Albany.

Klein, A. (1972). *Effective group work.* New York: Associated Press.

Klein, M. (1997). *The American street gang* (2nd ed.). Oxford, UK: Oxford University Press.

Klein, R. H., Bernard, H. S., & Singer, D. L. (Eds.). (2000). *Handbook of contemporary group psychotherapy: Contributions from object relations, self psychology, and social systems theories.* Madison, CT: International Universities Press.

Kleindorfer, P. R., Kunreuther, H. C., & Schoemaker, P. J. H. (1993). *Decision sciences: An integrative perspective.* New York: Cambridge University Press.

Klosko, J., & Sanderson, W. (1998). *Cognitive behavioral treatment of depression.* Northvale, NJ: Jason Aronson.

Knottnerus, J. (1994). Social exchange theory and social structure: A critical comparison of two traditions of inquiry. *Current Perspectives in Social Theory* (Suppl. 1), 29–48.

Knox, G. (1999a). *Achieving moral health.* New York: Crossroad Publishing Co.

Knox, G. (1999b). A comparison of cults and gangs: Dimensions of coercive power and malevolent authority. *Journal of Gang Research, 6*(4), 1–39.

Kolb, J. (1997). Are we still stereotyping leadership? A look at gender and other predictors of leader emergence. *Small Group Research, 28*(3), 370–393.

Kolodny, R. (1980). The dilemma of co-leadership. *Social Work with Groups, 3*(4), 31–34.

Konig, K. (1994). *Psychoanalytic group therapy.* Northvale, NY: Jason Aronson.

Konopka, G. (1949). *Therapeutic group work with children.* Minneapolis: University of Minnesota Press.

Konopka, G. (1954). *Group work in the institution.* New York: Association Press.

Konopka, G. (1983). *Social group work: A helping process* (3rd ed.). Englewood Cliffs, NJ: Prentice-Hall.

Kopp, J. (1993). Self-observation: An empowering strategy in assessment. In J. Rauch (Ed.), *Assessment: A sourcebook for social work practice* (pp. 255–268). Milwaukee, WI: Families International.

Koss-Chioino, J. (1995). Traditional and folk approaches among ethnic minorities. In J. Aponte, R. Rivers, & J. Wohl (Eds.), *Psychological interventions and cultural diversity* (pp. 145–163). Boston: Allyn and Bacon.

Kottler, J. (1992). *Compassionate therapy: Working with difficult clients.* San Francisco: Jossey-Bass.

Kottler, J. A. (2001). *Learning groupleadership: An experiential approach.* Needham Heights, MA: Allyn & Bacon.

Kramer, J., & Conoley, J. (1992). *Eleventh mental measurement yearbook.* Lincoln, NE: Buros Institute of Mental Measurements.

Kramer, M., Kuo, C., & Dailey, J. (1997). The impact of brainstorming techniques on subsequent group processes. *Small Group Research, 28*(2), 218–242.

Krueger, R. (1998a). *Analyzing and reporting focus group results.* Thousand Oaks, CA: Sage.

Krueger, R. (1998b). *Developing questions for focus groups.* Thousand Oaks, CA: Sage.

Krueger, R., & Casey, M. (2000). *Focus groups: A practical guide for applied research* (3rd ed.). Thousand Oaks, CA: Sage.

Kurtz, L. (1997). *Self-help and support groups: A handbook for practitioners.* Thousand Oaks, CA: Sage.

Kurtz, L. F. (2004). Support and self-help groups. In C. D. Garvin, L. M. Gutierrez, & M. J. Galinsky (Eds.), *Handbook of social work with groups* (pp. 139–159). New York; The Guilford Press.

Labrecque, M., Peak, T., & Toseland, R. (1992). Long-term effectiveness of a group program for caregivers of frail elderly veterans. *American Journal of Orthopsychiatry, 62*(4), 575–588.

Lakin, M. (1991). Some ethical issues in feminist-oriented therapeutic groups for women. *International Journal of Group Psychotherapy, 4,* 199–215.

Langelier, C. A. (2001). *Mood management: A cognitive-behavioral skills building program for adolescents: Leader's manual.* Thousand Oaks, CA: Sage Publications.

Lang, N. (1972). A broad range model of practice in the social work group. *Social Service Review, 46*(1), 76–84.

Lang, N. (1979a). A comparative examination of therapeutic uses of groups in social work and in adjacent human service professions: Part I—The literature from 1955–1968. *Social Work with Groups, 2*(2), 101–115.

Lang, N. (1979b). A comparative examination of the therapeutic uses of groups in social work and in adjacent human service professions: Part II—The literature from 1969–1978. *Social Work with Groups, 2*(3), 197–220.

Lasky, G. B., & Riva, M. T. (2006). Confidentiality and privileged communication in group psychotherapy. *International Journal of Group Psychotherapy, 56*(4), 455–476.

Lauffer, A. (1978). *Social planning at the community level.* Englewood Cliffs, NJ: Prentice-Hall.

Lawler, E., III, & Mohrman, S. (1985, Spring). Quality circles after the fad: There are benefits for managers and employees—and there are limitations. *Public Welfare, 43*(2), 37–44.

Lawler, E., Mohrman, E., Albers, S., & Benson, G. (2001). *Organizing for high performance organizations: Employee involvement, TQM, reengineering. and knowledge management in the Fortune 1000: The CEO report.* San Francisco: Jossey-Bass.

Lawson, H., Bronstein, L., McCallion, P., Ryan, D., & Fish, F. (2003). *Developing coalitions and collaborations: A resource guide for the 21st century.* Albany, NY: New York State Office for the Aging.

Lazarus, J. (2000). *Stress relief & relaxation techniques.* Oakland, CA: New Harbinger Publications.

Lazarus, R. S., & Folkman, S. (1984). *Stress, appraisal, and coping.* New York: Springer.

Lazell, E. W. (1921). The group treatment of dementia praecox. *Psychoanalytical Review, 8,* 168–179.

Leahy, R. (1996). *Cognitive therapy: Basic principles and applications.* Northvale, NJ: Jason Aronson.

LeBon, G. (1910). *The crowd: A study of the popular mind.* London: George Allen & Unwin Ltd.

Lederman, L. C. (1989). *Assessing educational effectiveness: The focus group interview as a technique for data collection.* Paper presented at the meeting of the Speech Communication Association, San Francisco.

Lee, J. (2001). The empowerment group: The heart of the empowerment approach and an antidote to injustice. In J. Parry (Ed.), *From prevention to wellness through group work* (2nd ed., pp. 290–320). New York, NY: Columbia Univ. Press.

Lese, K., & MacNair-Semands, R. (2000). The therapeutic factors inventory: Development of a scale. *Eastern Group Psychotherapy Society, 24*(4), 303–317.

Leszcz, M. (1992). The interpersonal approach to group psychotherapy. *International Journal of Group Psychotherapy, 42*(1), 37–62.

Levi, D. (2007), *Group dynamics for teams* (2nd ed.). Thousand Oaks, CA: Sage Publications.

Levin, H. M., & McEwan, P. (2001). *Cost-effectiveness analysis: Methods and applications.* Thousand Oaks, CA: Sage Publications, Inc.

Levine, B. (1979). *Group psychotherapy: Practice and development.* Englewood Cliffs, NJ: Prentice-Hall.

Levine, B. (1980). Co-leadership approach to learning group work. *Social Work with Groups, 3*(4), 35–38.

Levine, B., & Gallogly, V. (1985). *Group therapy with alcoholics: Outpatient and inpatient approaches.* Newbury Park, CA: Sage.

Levinson, D., & Klerman, G. (1973). The clinician-executive: Some problematic issues for the psychiatrist in mental health organizations. *Administration in Mental Health, 1*(1), 52–67.

Levinson, H. (1977). Termination of psychotherapy: Some salient issues. *Social Casework, 58*(8), 480–489.

Levitt, J., & Reid, W. (1981). Rapid assessment instruments for social work practice. *Social Work Research and Abstracts, 17*(1), 13–20.

Lewin, K. (1946). Behavior as a function of the total situation. In L. Carmichael (Ed.), *Manual of child psychology* (pp. 791–844). New York: John Wiley & Sons.

Lewin, K. (1947). Frontiers in group dynamics. *Human Relations, 1,* 2–38.

Lewin, K. (1948). *Resolving social conflict.* New York: Harper & Row.

Lewin, K. (1951). *Field theory in social science.* New York: Harper & Row.

Lewin, K., & Lippitt, R. (1938). An experimental approach to the study of autocracy and democracy: A preliminary note. *Sociometry, 1,* 292–300.

Lewin, K., Lippitt, R., & White, R. (1939). Patterns of aggressive behavior in experimentally created "social climates." *Journal of Social Psychology, 10,* 271–299.

Lewis, E., & Ford, B. (1990). The network utilization project: Incorporating traditional strengths of African-American families into group work practice. *Social Work with Groups, 13*(4), 7–22.

Lewis, H. (1982, October). Ethics in work with groups: The clients' interests. In N. Lang & C. Marshall (Chairs), *Patterns in the mosaic.* Symposium conducted at the Fourth Annual Meeting of Social Work with Groups, Toronto.

Lewis, R., & Ho, M. (1975). Social work with Native Americans. *Social Work, 20,* 379–382.

Lieberman, M. (1975). Groups for personal change: New and not-so-new forms. In D. Freedman & J. Dyrad (Eds.), *American handbook of psychiatry* (pp. 345–366). New York: Basic Books.

Lieberman, M., & Borman, L. (Eds.). (1979). *Self-help groups for coping with crisis.* San Francisco: Jossey-Bass.

Lieberman, M., Yalom, I., & Miles, M. (1973). *Encounter groups: First facts.* New York: Basic Books.

Lighthouse International, Inc. (1995). *The Lighthouse National Survey on vision loss: The experience, attitudes and knowledge of middle-aged and older Americans.* New York: The Lighthouse.

Likert, R. (1961). *New patterns of management.* New York: McGraw-Hill.

Likert, R. (1967). *The human organization.* New York: McGraw-Hill.

Lippitt, R. (1957). Group dynamics and the individual. *International Journal of Group Psychotherapy, 7*(10), 86–102.

Loewenberg, F., & Dolgoff, R. (1996). *Ethical decisions for social work practice* (5th ed.). Itasca, IL: Peacock Press.

Lonergan, E. C. (1989). *Group intervention* (3rd ed.). Northvale, NJ: Jason Aronson.

Long, K., Pendleton, L., & Winter, B. (1988). Effects of therapist termination on group processes. *International Journal of Group Psychotherapy, 38*(2), 211–223.

Lopez, J. (1991). Group work as a protective factor for immigrant youth. *Social Work with Groups, 14*(1), 29–42.

Luft, J. (1984). *Group processes* (3rd ed.). Palo Alto, CA: Mayfield.

Lum, D. (Ed.). (2003). *Culturally competent practice: A framework for understanding diverse groups and justice issues.* Sacramento, CA: Thomson, Brooks/Cole.

Lum, D. (2004). *Social work practice and people of color: A process-stage approach* (5th ed.). Belmont, CA: Brooks/Cole— Thomson Learning.

Lum, D. (Ed.). (2005). Cultural *competence, practice stages, and client systems.* Belmont, CA: Thomson Brooks/Cole.

Macgowan, M. J. (1997). A measure of engagement for social group work: The groupwork engagement measure (GEM). *Journal of Social Service Research, 23*(2), 17–37.

Macgowan, M. J. (2000). Evaluation of a measure of engagement for group work. *Research in Social Work Practice,* 10(3), 348–361.

Macgowen, M. J. (2000). A measure of engagement for social groupwork: The groupwork engagement measure (GEM). *Journal of Social Service Research, 23(2),* 17–37.

Macgowan, M. J., & Levenson, J. S. (2003). Psychometrics of the group engagement measure with male sex offenders. *Small Group Research, 34*(2), 155–160.

Macgowan, M. J., & Newman, F. (2005). Factor structure of the group engagement measure. *Social Work Research, 29* (2), 107–118.

Macgowan, M. J., & Pennell, J. (2001). Building social responsibility through family group conferencing. *Social Work with Groups, 24*(3-4), 67–87.

MacKenzie, K. R. (1990). *Introduction to time-limited group psychotherapy.* Washington, DC: American Psychiatric Press.

MacKenzie, K. R. (1994). Group development. In A. Fuhriman & G. M. Burlingame (Eds.), *Handbook of group psychotherapy* (pp. 223–268). New York: John Wiley & Sons.

MacKenzie, K. R. (Ed.). (1995). *Effective use of group therapy in managed care.* Washington, DC: American Psychiatric Press.

MacKenzie, K. R. (1996). Time-limited group psychotherapy. *International Journal of Group Psychotherapy, 46*(1), 41–60.

MacLennon, B. (1965). Co-therapy. *International Journal of Group Psychotherapy, 15,* 154–166.

Magen, R. (1999). *Recent contributions to empirical group work.* Thousand Oaks, CA: Sage Publications.

Magen, R. (2004). Measurement issues. In C. D. Garvin, L. M. Gutierrez, & M. J. Galinsky (Eds.), *Handbook of social work with groups* (pp. 447–460). New York: The Guilford Press.

Maguire, L. (1991). *Social support systems in practice: A generalist approach.* Silver Spring, MD: National Association of Social Workers Press.

Maheu, M., Whitten, P., & Allen, A. (2001). *E-Health, telehealth, and telemedicine: A guide to start-up and success.* San Francisco, CA: Jossey-Bass.

Mahoney, M. J. (1974). *Cognitive and behavior modification.* Cambridge, MA: Ballinger Books.

Mahoney, M. J. (Ed.). (1995a). *Cognitive and constructive psychotherapies: Theory, research and practice.* New York: Springer.

Mahoney, M. J. (Ed.). (1995b). *Constructive psychotherapy.* New York: Guilford.

Maier, N. (1963). *Problem-solving discussions and conferences: Leadership methods and skills.* New York: McGraw-Hill.

Maier, N., & Zerfoss, L. (1952). MRP: A technique for training large groups of supervisors and its potential use in social research. *Human Relations, 5,* 177–186.

Malekoff, A. (1997). *Group work with adolescents.* New York: Guilford Press.

Maloney, S. (1963). *Development of group work education in social work schools in U.S.* Unpublished doctoral dissertation, Case Western Reserve University, School of Applied Social Science, Cleveland.

Maltzman, I., Simon, S., Raskin, D., & Licht, L. (1960). Experimental studies in the training of originality. *Psychological Monographs, 74*(6), 23.

Marks, M., Mirvis, P., Hackett, E., & Grady, J. (1986). Employee participation in a quality circle program: Impact on quality of worklife, productivity, and absenteeism. *Journal of Applied Psychology, 71,* 61–69.

Marlatt, G. (1996). Taxonomy of high-risk situations for alcohol relapse: Evolution and development of a cognitive-behavioral model. *Addiction, 91* (supplement), S37–S49.

Marlatt, G., & Barrett, K. (1994). Relapse prevention. In M. Galanter & H. D. Kleber (Eds.), *The American Psychiatric Press textbook of substance abuse treatment* (pp. 285–299). Washington, DC: American Psychiatric Press.

Marsh, E., & Terdal, L. (Eds.). (1997). *Behavioral assessment of childhood disorders* (3rd ed.). New York: Guilford.

Marsh, L. C. (1931). Group treatment of the psychoses by the psychological equivalent of the revival. *Mental Hygiene, 15,* 328–349.

Marsh, L. C. (1933). An experiment in group treatment of patients at Worchester State hospital. *Mental Hygiene, 17,* 396–416.

Marsh, L. C. (1935). Group therapy and the psychiatric clinic. *Journal of Nervous & Mental Disorders, 82,* 381–393.

Marshall, C. R., & Rossman, G. (1999). *Designing qualitative research.* Thousand Oaks, CA: Sage Publications.

Marsiglia, F., Cross, S., & Mitchell-Enos, V. (1998). Culturally grounded group work with adolescent American Indian students. *Social Work with Groups, 21*(1), 89–102.

Martindale-Adams, J., Nichols, L., Burns, R., & Malone, C. (2002). Telephone support groups: A lifeline for isolated Alzheimer's disease caregivers. *Alzeimer's Care Quarterly, 3*(2), 181–189.

Masters, J., Burish, T., Hollon, S., & Rimm, D. (1987). *Behavior therapy: Techniques and empirical findings* (3rd ed.). San Diego, CA: Harcourt Brace Jovanovich.

Matsukawa, L. A. (2001). Group therapy with multiethnic minorities. In W. Tseng & J. Streltzer (Eds.), *Culture and psychotherapy: A guide to clinical practice.* Washington, DC: American Psychiatric Publishing Inc.

Mattessich, P., Murray-Close, M., & Monsey, B. (2001). *Collaboration: What makes it work?* Saint Paul, MN: Amherst H. Wilder Foundation.

Mayadas, N., & Glasser, P. (1981). Termination: A neglected aspect of social group work. *Social Work with Groups, 4*(2), 193–204.

Mayer, J., Soweid, R., Dabney, S., Brownson, C., Goodman, R., & Brownson, R. (1998). Practices of successful community coalitions: A multiple case study. *American Journal of Health Behavior, 22*(5), 368–369.

Mayer, J., & Timms, N. (1970). *The client speaks: Working class impressions of casework.* New York: Atherton Press.

Maznevski, M., & Peterson, M. (1997a). Societal values, social interpretation, and multinational teams. In C. Granrose & S. Oskemp (Eds.), *Cross-cultural work groups: An overview* (pp. 61–89). Thousand Oaks, CA: Sage Publications.

Maznevski, M., & Peterson, M. (1997b). Societal values, social interpretation and multi national executive realms. In C. Granrose & S. Oskamp (Eds.), *Cross cultural work groups* (pp. 61–89). New York: Sage.

McCallion, P., Toseland, R., & Diehl, M. (1994). Social work practice with caregivers of frail older adults. *Research on Social Work Practice, 4,* 64–68.

McCaskill, J. (1930). *Theory and practice of group work.* New York: Association Press.

McClane, W. (1991). The interaction of leader and member characteristics in the leader-member exchange model of leadership. *Small Group Research, 22,* 283–300.

McCorkle, L., Elias, A., Bixby, F. (1958). *The highfields story: An experimental project for youthful offenders.* New York: Holt.

McDougall, W. (1920). *The group mind.* New York: G. P. Putnam's Sons.

McFarlane, W. (2002). *Multifamily groups in the treatment of severe psychiatric disorders.* New York, NY: Guilford Press.

McGee, T., & Schuman, B. (1970). The nature of the co-therapy relationship. *International Journal of Group Psychotherapy, 20,* 25–36.

McGrath, J. (1984). *Groups: Interaction and performance.* Englewood Cliffs, NJ: Prentice-Hall.

McGrath, J. (1992). Time, interaction, and performance (TIP): A theory of groups. *Small Group Research, 22,* 147–174.

McGrath, J., Arrow, H., & Berdahl, J. (2000). The study of groups: Past, present, and future. *Personality and Social Psychology Review, 4*(1), 95–105.

McGrath, P., & Axelson, J. (1999). *Accessing awareness & developing knowledge: Foundations for skill in a multicultural society* (3rd ed.). Pacific Grove, CA: Brooks/Cole.

McKay, M., & Paleg, K. (Eds.). (1992). *Focal group psychotherapy.* Oakland, CA: New Harbinger.

McKenna, K. Y. A., & Bargh, J. (1999). Causes and consequences of social interaction on the Internet: A conceptual framework. *Media Psychology, 1,* 249–269.

McKenna, K. Y. A., & Bargh, J. (2000). Plan 9 from cyberspace: The implications of the Internet for personality and social psychology. *Personality and Social Psychology Review, 4*(1), 57–75.

McKenna, K. Y. A., & Green, A. S. (2002). Virtual group dynamics. *Group Dynamics: Theory, Research, and Practice, 6*(1), 116–127.

McKenna, K. Y. A., Green, A. S., & Gleason, M. E. J. (2002). Relationship formation on the Internet: What's the big attraction? *Journal of Social Issues, 58*(1), 9–31.

McLeod, P., Lobel, S., & Cox, T. (1996). Ethnic diversity and creativity in small groups. *Small Group Research, 27*(2), 248–264.

McRoberts, C., Burlingame, G. M., & Hoag, M. J. (1998). Comparative efficacy of individual and group psychotherapy: A meta-analytic perspective. *Group Dynamics, 2*(2), 101–117.

McRoy, R. (2003). Cultural competence with African Americans. In D. Lum (Ed.), *Culturally competent practice: A framework for understanding diverse groups and justice issues.* Sacramento, CA: Thomson, Brooks, Cole.

Meichenbaum, D. (1977). *Cognitive-behavior modification: An integrative approach.* New York: Plenum.

Meichenbaum, D. (1985). *Stress inoculation training.* New York: Plenum.

Meichenbaum, D., & Cameron, R. (1983). Stress inoculation training: Toward a general paradigm for training coping skills. In D. Meichenbaum & M. E. Jaremko (Eds.), *Stress reduction and prevention* (pp. 115–154). Norwell, MA: Plenum.

Meichenbaum, D., & Fitzpatrick, D. (1993). A constructivist narrative perspective on stress and coping: Stress inoculation applications. In L. Goldberger & S. Breznitz (Eds.), *Handbook of stress: Theoretical and clinical aspects* (2nd ed., pp. 706–723). New York: Free Press.

Merenda, D. (1997). *A practical guide to creating and managing community coalitions for drug abuse prevention.* Alexandria, VA: National Association of Partners in Education.

Merton, R., & Kendall, P. (1946). The focused interview. *American Journal of Sociology, 51,* 541–557.

Meyer, C. (Ed.). (1983). *Social work in the eco-systems perspective.* New York: Columbia University Press.

Meyer, C. (1988). The ecosystems perspective. In R. A. Dorfman (Ed.), *Paradigms of clinical social work* (pp. 275–294). New York: Brunner/Mazel.

Middleman, R. (1978). Returning group process to group work. *Social Work with Groups, 1*(1), 15–26.

Middleman, R. (1980). The use of program: Review and update. *Social Work with Groups, 3*(3), 5–23.

Middleman, R. (1982). *The non-verbal method in working with groups: The use of activity in teaching, counseling, and therapy* (Enlarged ed.). Hebron, CT: Practitioners Press.

Middleman, R., & Wood, G. (1990). Reviewing the past and present of group work and the challenge of the future. *Social Work with Groups, 13*(3), 3–20.

Milgram, D., & Rubin, J. (1992). Resisting resistance: Involuntary substance abuse group therapy. *Social Work with Groups, 15*(1), 95–110.

Milgram, S. (1974). *Obedience and authority.* New York: Harper and Row.

Miller, S., Nunnally, E., & Wackman, D. (1972). *The Minnesota couples communication program couples handbook.* Minneapolis: Minnesota Couples Communication Program.

Miller, W., & Rollnick, S. (Eds.). (2002). *Motivational interviewing: Preparing people for change.* New York: Guilford Press.

Mills, T. (1967). *The sociology of small groups.* Englewood Cliffs, NJ: Prentice-Hall.

Milter, R. G., & Rohrbaugh, J. (1988). Judgment analysis and decision conferencing for administrative review: A case study of innovative policy making in government. In R. L. Cardy, S. M. Puffer, & J. M. Newman (Eds.), *Advances in information processing in organizations* (pp. 245–262). Greenwich, CT: JAI Press.

Mistry, T., & Brown, A. (1997). *Race and groupwork.* London: Whiting & Birch.

Mizrahi, T., & Rosenthal, B. (1998, March). *Complexities of effective coalition-building: A study of leaders' strategies, struggles, and solutions.* Paper presented at the Annual Program Meeting of the Council on Social Work Education. Orlando, FL.

Mondros, J., & Wilson, S. (1994). *Organizing for power and empowerment.* New York: Columbia University Press.

Moore, C. (1994). *Group techniques for idea building.* Thousand Oaks, CA: Sage.

Moos, R. H. (1986). *Group environment scale manual* (2nd ed.). Palo Alto, CA: Consulting Psychologists Press.

Moreno, J. (1934). *Who shall survive?* Washington, DC: Nervous and Mental Diseases.

Moreno, J. (1946). *Psychodrama* (Vol. 1). Boston: Beacon Press.

Moreno, C. L., & Guido, M. (2005). Social work practice with Latino Americans. In L. Doman (Ed.), *Cultural competence, practice stages, and client systems* (pp. 88–111). Belmont, CA: Thomson Brooks/Cole.

Morgan, D. (1997). *Focus groups as qualitative research* (2nd ed.). Thousand Oaks, CA: Sage.

Moscovici, S. (1994). Three concepts: Minority, conflict, and behavioral styles. In S. Moscovici, M. Faina, & A. Maass (Eds.), *Minority influence* (pp. 235–251). Chicago: Nelson-Hall.

Moscovici, S. (1985). *The age of the crowd: A historical treatise on mass psychology.* Cambridge: Cambridge University Press.

Moscovici, S., & Lage, E. (1976). Studies in social influence: III. Majority versus minority influence in a group. *European Journal of Social Psychology, 6*(2), 149–174.

Moscovici, S., Lage, E., & Naffrechoux, M. (1969). Influence of a constant minority on the responses of a majority in a color perception task. *Sociometry, 32*(4), 365–380.

Mullen, B., & Cooper, C. (1994). The relationship between cohesiveness and performance: An integration. *Psychological Bulletin, 115*(2), 210–227.

Mullen, E. (1969). The relationship between diagnosis and treatment in casework. *Social Casework, 50,* 218–226.

Mullender, A., & Ward, D. (1991). *Self-directed groupwork: Users take action for empowerment.* London: Whitney & Birch.

Munzer, J., & Greenwald, H. (1957). Interaction process analysis of a therapy group. *International Journal of Group Psychotherapy, 7,* 175–190.

Murphy, M., DeBernardo, C., & Shoemaker, W. (1998). Impact of managed care on independent practice and professional ethics: A survey of independent practitioners. *Professional Psychology: Research and Practice, 29,* 43–51.

Myers, D., & Arenson, S. (1972). Enhancement of the dominant risk in group discussion. *Psychological Reports, 30,* 615–623.

Nadler, D. (1979). The effects of feedback on task group behavior: A review of the experimental research. *Organizational Behavior and Human Performance, 23,* 309–338.

Napier, H. (1967). Individual versus group learning: Note on task variable. *Psychological Reports, 23,* 757–758.

Napier, R., & Gershenfeld, M. (1993). *Groups: Theory and experience* (5th ed.). Boston: Houghton Mifflin.

Nas, T. (Ed.). (1996). *Cost-benefit analysis: Theory and application.* Thousand Oaks, CA: Sage Publications.

Newcomb, T. M. (1943). *Personality and social change.* New York: Dryden.

Newstetter, W. (1948). The social intergroup work process. *Proceedings of the National Conference of Social Work* (pp. 205–217). New York: Columbia University Press.

Newstetter, W., Feldstein, M. J., & Newcomb, T. M. (1938). *Group adjustment: A study in experimental sociology.* Cleveland, OH: School of Applied Social Sciences, Western Reserve University.

Nickelson, D. (2000), Telehealth, health care services, & health care policy: A plan for action in the new millennium. *New Jersey Psychologist, 50*(1), 24–27.

Nixon, H. (1979). *The small group.* Englewood Cliffs, NJ: Prentice-Hall.

Northen, H. (1969). *Social work with groups.* New York: Columbia University Press.

Northen, H. (1995). *Clinical social work* (2nd ed.). New York: Columbia University Press.

Nosko, A., & Breton, M. (1997–1998). Applying strengths, competence and empowerment model. *Groupwork, 10*(1), 55–69.

Nosko, A., & Wallace, R. (1997). Female/male co-leadership in group. *Social Work with Groups, 20*(2), 3–16.

Nunnally, J. C. (1994). *Psychometric theory* (3rd ed.). New York: McGraw-Hill.

Nye, J., & Forsyth, D. (1991). The effects of prototype based biases on leadership appraisals: A test of leadership categorization theory. *Small Group Research, 22,* 360–379.

Nystrom, N. M. (2005), Social work practice with lesbian, gay, bisexual, and transgender people. In L. Doman (Ed.), *Cultural competence, practice stages, and client systems* (pp. 203–229). Belmont, CA: Thomson Brooks/Cole.

Oei, T. K., & Kazmierczak, T. (1997). Factors associated with dropout in a group cognitive behaviour therapy for mood disorders. *Behavior Research and Therapy, 35,* 1025–1030.

Ollendick, T., & Hersen, M. (Eds.). (1984). *Child behavioral assessment.* Elmsford, NY: Pergamon Press.

Olmsted, M. (1959). *The small group.* New York: Random House.

Olsen, M. (1968). *The process of social organization.* New York: Holt, Rinehart & Winston.

Orasanu, J., Fischer, U., & Davison, J. (1997). Cross-cultural barriers to effective communication in aviation. In C. Granrose & S. Oskamp (Eds.), *Cross-cultural work groups: An overview* (pp. 134–162). Thousand Oaks, CA: Sage Publications.

Oravec, J. (2000). Online counseling and the Internet: Perspectives for mental health care supervision and education. *Journal of Mental Health, 9*(2), 121–135.

Osborn, A. (1963). *Applied imagination: Principles and procedures of creative problem solving* (3rd ed.). New York: Charles Scribner's Sons.

Osgood, C., Suci, C., & Tannenbaum, P. (1957). *The measurement of meaning.* Urbana, IL: University of Illinois Press.

Padgett, D. (1998). *Qualitative methods in social work research: Challenges and rewards.* New York: Sage Publications.

Papell, C. (1997). Thinking about thinking about group work: Thirty years later. *Social Work with Groups, 20*(4), 5–17.

Papell, C., & Rothman, B. (1962). Social group work models—possession and heritage. *Journal of Education for Social Work, 2,* 66–77.

Papell, C., & Rothman, B. (1980). Relating the mainstream model of social work with groups to group psychotherapy and the structured group approach. *Social Work with Groups, 3*(2), 5–23.

Parnes, S. (1967). *Creative behavior guidebook.* New York: Charles Scribner's Sons.

Parrillo, V. (2006). *Strangers to these shores: Race and ethnic relations in the United States* (8th ed.). Boston: Allyn and Bacon.

Parsons, R. (1991). Empowerment: Purpose and practice principle in social work. *Social Work with Groups, 14*(2), 7–21.

Parsons, T. (1951). *The social system.* New York: The Free Press.

Parsons, T., Bales, R., & Shils, E. (Eds.). (1953). *Working papers in the theory of action.* New York: The Free Press.

Passi, L. (1998). *A guide to creative group programming in the psychiatric day hospital.* New York: Haworth Press.

Patton, M. (2000). *Qualitative research and evaluation methods.* Thousand Oaks, CA: Sage Publications.

Paulus, P., Larey, T., & Dzindolet, M. (2000). *Creativity in groups and teams.* NJ: Lawrence Erlbaum Associates, Inc.

Payne, M. (2000). *Teamwork in multiprofessional care.* Chicago: Lyceum.

Pearson, V. (1991). Western theory, Eastern practice: Social group work in Hong Kong. *Social Work with Groups, 14*(2), 45–58.

Pepitone, A., & Reichling, G. (1955). Group cohesiveness and the expression of hostility. *Human Relations, 8,* 327–337.

Perlman, H. (1970). The problem-solving method in social casework. In R. Roberts & R. Nee (Eds.), *Theories of social casework* (pp. 129–180). Chicago: University of Chicago Press.

Pernell, R. (1986). Empowerment and social group work. In M. Parnes (Ed.), *Innovations in social group work* (pp. 107–118). New York: Haworth Press.

Pescosolido, A. T. (2001). Informal leaders and the development of group efficacy. *Small Group Research, 32*(1), 74–93.

Pescosolido, A. T. (2003). Group efficacy and group effectiveness: The effects of group efficacy over time on group performance and development. *Small Group Research, 34*(1), 20–42.

Peters, A. (1997). Themes in group work with lesbian and gay adolescents. *Social Work with Groups, 20*(2), 51–69.

Pfeiffer, J., & Goodstein, L. (Eds.). (1984–1996). *The annual: Developing human resources.* San Diego, CA: University Associates.

Phillips, J. (1948). Report on discussion 66. *Adult Education Journal, 7,* 181–182.

Phillips, L. R., Torres de Ardon, E., Komnenich, P., Killeen, M., & Rusinak, R. (2000). The Mexican American caregiving experience. *Hispanic Journal of Behavioral Sciences, 22*(3), 296–313.

Pillari, V. (2002). *Social work practice: Theories and skills.* Boston: Allyn and Bacon.

Pincus, A., & Minahan, A. (1973). *Social work practice: Model and method.* Itasca, IL: F. E. Peacock.

Pinderhughes, E. B. (1979). Teaching empathy in cross-cultural social work. *Social Work, 2*(4), 312–316.

Pinderhughes, E. B. (1995). Empowering diverse populations: Family practice in the 21st century. *Families in Society, 76,* 131–140.

Pinkus, H. (1968). *Casework techniques related to selected characteristics of clients and workers.* Unpublished doctoral dissertation, Columbia University, New York.

Piper, W. (1992). *Adaptation to loss through short-term group psychotherapy.* New York: Guilford.

Piper, W. (1994). Client variables. In A. Fuhriman & G. M. Burlingame (Eds.), *Handbook of group psychotherapy* (pp. 83–113). New York: John Wiley & Sons.

Piper, W., Debbane, E., Bienvenu, J., & Garant, J. (1982). A study of group pretraining for group psychotherapy. *International Journal of Group Psychotherapy, 32,* 309–325.

Piper, W., & Joyce, A. (1996). A consideration of factors influencing the utilization of time-limited, short-term group therapy. *International Journal of Group Psychotherapy, 46*(3), 311–329.

Piper, W., Ogrodniczuk, J., & Duncan, S. (2002). Psychodynamically oriented group therapy. In F. W. Kaslow (Editor In Chief) & J. J. Magnavita (Vol. Ed.), *Comprehensive handbook of psychotherapy. Volume 1: Psychodynamic/object relations* (pp. 457–479). New York: Wiley & Sons.

Postmes, T., Spears, R., & Lea, M. (1999). Social identity, normative content, and "deindividuation" in computer-mediated groups. In N. Ellemers, R. Spears, & B. Doosje (Eds.), *Social identity: Context, commitment, content* (pp. 164–183). Malden, MA: Blackwell Publishers.

Postmes, T., Spears, R., Sakhel, K., & de Groot, D. (2001). Social influence in computer-mediated communication: The effects of anonymity on group behavior. *Personality and Social Psychology Bulletin, 27*(10), 1243–1254.

Powell, T. (1987). *Self-help organizations and professional practice.* Silver Spring, MD: National Association of Social Workers Press.

Prapavessis, H., & Carron, A. (1997). Cohesion and work output. *Small Group Research, 28*(2), 294–301.

Prigmore, C. S. (1974). Use of the coalition in legislative action. *Social Work, 19*(1), 96–102.

Prince, G. (1970). *The practice of creativity.* New York: Harper & Row.

Prochaska, J., DiClimente, C., & Norcross, C. (1992). In search of how people change. *American Psychologist, 41*(4), 1102–1114.

Proctor, E., & Davis, L. (1994). The challenge of racial difference: Skills for clinical practice. *Social Work, 39,* 314–323.

Purdy, J. A., & Arguello, D. (1992). Hispanic familism in caretaking of older adults: Is it functional? *Journal of Gerontological Social Work, 19,* 29–43.

Putnam, R. D. (2000). *Bowling alone: The collapse and revival of American community.* New York: Simon & Schuster.

Putnam, R. D. (2001). *Bowling alone.* New York: Touchstone.

Ramey, J. H. (Ed.). (1999). *Bibliography on group work.* Akron, OH: Association for Advancement of Social Work with Groups.

Ramos, B., Jones, L., & Toseland R. (2005). Culturally competent social work practice with elderly of color. In D. Lum (Ed.), *Social work practice and people of color: A process stage approach.* Belmont, CA: Brooks Cole.

Rathus, J., & Sanderson, W. (1999). *Marital distress: Cognitive behavioral interventions for couples* (2nd ed.). Northvale, NJ: Jason Aronson.

Rauch, J. (Ed.). (1993). *Assessment: A sourcebook for social work practice.* Milwaukee, WI: Families International.

Reagan-Cirinicione, P. (1994). Improving the accuracy of group judgment: A process intervention combining group facilitation, social judgment analysis, and information technology. *Organizational Behavior and Human Decision Processes, 58,* 246–270.

Reamer, F. G. (1998). *Ethical standards in social work: A review of the NASW Code of Ethics.* Washington, DC: NASW Press.

Reamer, F. G. (2001). *The social work ethics audit: A risk-management tool.* Washington, DC: NASW Press.

Reder, P. (1978). An assessment of the group therapy interaction chronogram. *International Journal of Group Psychotherapy, 28,* 185–194.

Redl, F. (1942). Group emotion and leadership. *Psychiatry, 5,* 573–596.

Redl, F. (1944). Diagnostic group work. *American Journal of Orthopsychiatry, 14*(1), 53–67.

Reid, K. (1981). *From character building to social treatment: The history of the use of groups in social work.* Westport, CT: Greenwood Press.

Reid, K. (1997). *Social work practice with groups: A clinical perspective* (2nd ed.). Pacific Grove, CA: Brooks/Cole.

Reid, W. J. (1992). *Task strategies: An empirical approach to clinical social work.* New York: Columbia University Press.

Reid, W. J. (1997). Research on task-centered practice. *Social Work Research, 21*(3), 132–137.

Reid, W. J., & Shapiro, B. (1969). Client reactions to advice. *Social Service Review, 43,* 165–173.

Reinecke, M., Dattilio, M., & Freeman, A. (2003). *Cognitive therapy with children and adolescents.* New York: Guilford Press.

Rhode, R., & Stockton, R. (1992, Winter). The effect of structured feedback on goal attainment, attraction to the group, and satisfaction with the group in small group counseling. *Journal of Group Psychotherapy, Psychodrama, and Sociometry, 44*(4), 172–179.

Rice, C. (1987). *Inpatient group psychotherapy: A psychodynamic perspective.* New York: Macmillan.

Richards, T. (1974). *Problem solving through creative analysis.* New York: John Wiley & Sons.

Richmond, M. (1917). *Social diagnosis.* New York: Russell Sage Foundation.

Ricker, M., Nystul, M., & Waldo, M. (1999). Counselors' and clients' ethnic similarity and therapeutic alliance in time-limited outcomes of counseling. *Psychological Reports, 84,* 674–676.

Riess, H., & Dockray-Miller, M. (2002). *Integrative group treatment for bulimia nervosa.* New York: Columbia University Press.

Riessman, E., & Carroll, D. (1995). *Redefining self-help: Policy and practice.* San Francisco: Jossey-Bass.

Rittenhouse, J. (1997). Feminist principles in survivor's groups: Out-of-contact. *Journal for Specialists in Group Work, 22*(2), 111–119.

Rittner, B., & Nakanishi, M. (1993). Challenging stereotypes and cultural biases through small group process. *Social Work with Groups, 16*(4), 5–23.

Riva, M. T., Lippert, L., & Tackett, M. J. (2000). Selection practices of group leaders: A national survey. *Journal for Specialists in Group Work, 25*(2), 157–169.

Rivas, R., & Toseland, R. (1981). The student group leadership evaluation project: A study of group leadership skills. *Social Work with Groups, 4*(3/4), 159–175.

Roback, H., Moore, R., Bloch, F., & Shelton, M. (1996). Confidentiality in group psychotherapy: Empirical findings and the law. *International Journal of Group Psychotherapy, 46*(1), 117–135.

Roback, H., Ochoa, E., Bloch, F., & Purdon, S. (1992). Guarding confidentiality in clinical groups: The therapist's dilemma. *International Journal of Group Psychotherapy, 42*(1), 81–103.

Robert, H. (1983). *The new Robert's rules of order.* Glenview, IL: Scott Foresman.

Roberts, R., & Northen, H. (Eds.). (1976). *Theories of social work with groups.* New York: Columbia University Press.

Roberts, A. R., & Yeager, K. R. (Eds.) (2004). *Evidence-based practice manual: Research and outcome measures in health and human services.* New York: Oxford University Press.

Roberts, A. R., & Yeager, K. R. (Eds.) (2006), *Foundations of evidence-based social work practice.* New York: Oxford University Press.

Robinson, J., & Shaver, P. (Eds.). (1973). *Measures of social psychological attitude* (2nd ed.). Ann Arbor: University of Michigan Press.

Robson, M. (1988). *Quality circles: A practical guide* (2nd ed.). Aldershat, Hants, England: Gower.

Roethlisberger, F. (1941). *Management and morale.* Cambridge, MA: Harvard University Press.

Roethlisberger, F., & Dickson, W. (1939). *Management and the worker.* Cambridge, MA: Harvard University Press.

Roethlisberger, F., & Dickson, W. (1975). A fair day's work. In P. V. Crosbie (Ed.), *Interaction in small groups* (pp. 85–94). New York: Macmillan.

Roffman, R. (2004). Psychoeducational groups. In C. D. Garvin, L. M, Gutierrez, & M. J. Galinsky (Eds.), *Handbook of social work with groups* (pp. 160–175). New York; The Guilford Press.

Rohrbaugh, J. (1979). Improving the quality of group judgment: Social judgment analysis and the delphi technique. *Organizational Behavior and Human Performance, 24,* 73–92.

Rohrbaugh, J. (1981). Improving the quality of group judgment: Social judgment analysis and the nominal group technique. *Organizational Behavior and Human Performance, 26,* 272–288.

Rohrbaugh, J. (1984). Making decisions about staffing standards: An analytical approach to human resource planning in health administration. In L. Nigro (Ed.), *Decision making in the public sector* (pp. 93–116). New York: Marcel Dekker.

Rokeach, M. (1968). *Beliefs, attitudes and values: A theory of organization and change.* San Francisco: Jossey-Bass.

Roller, B., & Nelson, V. (Eds.). (1991). *The art of co-therapy: How therapists work together.* London: Guilford.

Rooney, R. (1992). *Strategies for work with involuntary clients.* New York: Columbia University Press.

Rooney, R. H., & Chovanec, M. (2004). Involuntary groups. In C. D. Garvin, L. M. Gutierrez, & M. J. Galinsky (Eds.), *Handbook of social work with groups* (pp. 212–226), New York: The Guilford Press.

Rose, S. (1981). Assessment in groups. *Social Work Research and Abstracts, 17*(1), 29–37.

Rose, S. (1989). *Working with adults in groups: A multi-method approach.* San Francisco: Jossey-Bass.

Rose, S. (1991). The development and practice of group treatment. In M. Hersen, A. Kazdin, & A. Bellack (Eds.), *Handbook of clinical psychology* (pp. 627–642). New York: Pergamon Press.

Rose, S. (1998). *Group therapy with troubled youth.* Newbury Park, CA: Sage.

Rose, S. D, (2004). Cognitive-behavioral group work. In C. D. Garvin, L. M. Gutierrez, & M. J. Galinsky (Eds.), *Handbook of social work with groups* (pp. 111–135). New York: The Guilford Press.

Rose, S., Cayner, J., & Edleson, J. (1977). Measuring interpersonal competence. *Social Work, 22*(2), 125–129.

Rose, S., & Edleson, J. (1987). *Working with children and adolescents in groups.* San Francisco: Jossey-Bass.

Rose, S., & Hanusa, D. (1980). *Parenting skill role play test.* Interpersonal skill training and research project, University of Wisconsin, Madison.

Rose, S., & LeCroy, C. (1991). Group treatment methods. In F. Kanfer & A. Goldstein (Eds.), *Helping people change* (4th ed., pp. 422–453). New York: Pergamon Press.

Rosen, A. & Proctor, E. (Eds.) (2003). *Practice Guidelines for Social Work Interventions: Issues, Methods, and research agenda.* N.Y.: Columbia University Press.

Rosenthal, L. (1978). *Behavioral analysis of social skills in adolescent girls.* Unpublished doctoral dissertation, University of Wisconsin, Madison.

Rossi, P., Freeman, H., & Lipsey, M. (1999). *Evaluation: A systematic approach.* Thousand Oaks, CA: Sage Publications.

Rossi, P., Freeman, H., & Wright, S. (1979). *Evaluation: A systematic approach.* Newbury Park, CA: Sage.

Rosswurm, M., Larrabee, J., &. Zhang, J. (2002). Training family caregivers of dependent elderly adults through on-site and telecommunications programs. *Journal of Gerontological Nursing, 28*(7), 27–38.

Rothman, J. (1974). *Planning and organizing for social change: Action principles for social science research.* New York: Columbia University Press.

Rothman, J., Erlich, J., & Tropman, J. (Eds.). (2007). *Strategies of community intervention* (5th ed.). Itasca, IL: F. E. Peacock.

Rothman, J., & Tumblin, A. (1994). Pilot testing and early development of a model of case management intervention. In J. Rothman & E. J. Thomas (Eds.), *Intervention research: Design and development for human service* (pp. 215–233). New York: Haworth Press.

Rounds, K., Galinsky, M., & Stevens, L. S. (1991, January). Linking people with AIDS in rural communities: The telephone group. *Social Work, 36,* 13–18.

Rubin, H., & Rubin, I. (2007). *Community organizing and development* (4th ed.). New York: Macmillan.

Rutan, J. (1992). Psychodynamic group psychotherapy. *International Journal of Group Psychotherapy, 42*(1), 19–36.

Rutan, J., & Stone, W. (2001). *Psychodynamic group psychotherapy* (3rd ed.). New York: Guilford.

Salazar, A. (1996). An analysis of the development and evolution of roles in the small group. *Small Group Research, 27*(4), 475–503.

Sanchez-Ayende, M. (1998). Middle-aged Puerto Rican women as primary caregivers to the elderly: A qualitative analysis of everyday dynamics. *Journal of Gerontological Social Work, 30*(1/2), 75–97.

Santhiveeran, J. (1998, October). *Virtual group meetings on the net: Implications for social work practice.* Paper presented at the meeting of the Association for the Advancement of Social Work with Groups, Miami, FL.

Sarri, R., & Galinsky, M. (1985). A conceptual framework for group development. In M. Sundel, P. Glasser, R. Sarri, & R. Vinter (Eds.), *Individual change through small groups* (2nd ed., pp. 70–86). New York: The Free Press.

Sarri, R., Galinsky, M., Glasser, P., Siegel, S., & Vinter, R. (1967). Diagnosis in group work. In R. D. Vinter (Ed.), *Readings in group work practice* (pp. 39–71). Ann Arbor, MI: Campus Publishing.

Saunders, D. (1996). Feminist-cognitive-behavioral and process-psychodynamic treatments for men who batter: Interaction of abuser traits and treatment models. *Violence and Victims, 11,* 394–414.

Saunders, D. (2002). Developing guidelines for domestic violence offender programs: What can we learn from related fields and current research? *Journal of Aggression, Maltreatment and Trauma, 5*(2), 235–248.

Sax, G. (1996). *Principles of educational and psychological measurement* (4th ed.). Belmont, CA: Wadsworth.

Schachter, S. (1959). *The psychology of affiliation.* Stanford, CA: Stanford University Press.

Scheidel, T., & Crowell, L. (1979). *Discussing and deciding: A deskbook for group leaders and members.* New York: Macmillan.

Scheneul, J., Lecompte, M., Borgatti, S., & Nastasi, B. (1998). *Enhanced ethnographic methods: Audiovisual techniques, focused group interviews, and elicitation techniques.* Thousand Oaks, CA: Altamira Press.

Schilder, P. (1937). The analysis of ideologies as a psychotherapeutic method, especially in group treatment. *American Journal of Psychiatry, 93,* 601–615.

Schiller, L. (1995). Stages of development in women's groups: A relational model. In R. Kurland & R. Salmon (Eds.), *Group work practice in a troubled society* (pp. 117–138). New York: Haworth Press.

Schiller, L. (1997). Rethinking stages of development in women's groups: Implications for practice. *Social Work with Groups, 20*(3), 3–19.

Schinke, S. P., & Rose, S. (1976). Interpersonal skill training in groups. *Journal of Counseling Psychology, 23,* 442–448.

Schlenoff, M., & Busa, S. (1981). Student and field instructor as group co-therapists. Equalizing an unequal relationship. *Journal of Education for Social Work, 17,* 29–35.

Schmidt, W. H., & Finnigan, J. P. (1993). *TQ manager: A practical guide for managing in a total quality organization.* San Francisco: Jossey-Bass.

Schmitt, M., Farrell, M., & Heinemann, G. (1988). Conceptual and methodological problems in studying the effects of interdisciplinary geriatric teams. *The Gerontologist, 28*(6), 753–763.

Scholtes, P., Joiner, B., & Streibel, B. (1996). *The team handbook.* Madison, WI: Oriel Incorporated.

Schopler, J. (1994). Interorganizational groups in human services: Environmental and interpersonal relationships. *Journal of Community Practice, 1*(3), 7–27.

Schopler, J., Abell, M., & Galinsky, M. (1998). Technology-based groups: A review and conceptual framework for practice. *Social Work, 43*(3), 254–267.

Schopler, J., & Galinsky, M. (1981). When groups go wrong. *Social Work, 26*(5), 424–429.

Schopler, J., & Galinsky, M. (1984). Meeting practice needs: Conceptualizing the open-ended group. *Social Work with Groups, 7*(2), 3–21.

Schopler, J., & Galinsky, M. (1990). Can open-ended groups move beyond beginnings? *Small Group Research, 21*(4), 435–449.

Schopler, J., Abell, M., & Galinsky, M. (1998). Technology-based groups: A review and conceptual framework for practice. *Social Work, 43*(3), 254–267.

Schopler, J., Galinsky, M., & Abell, M. (1997). Creating community through telephone and computer groups: Theoretical and practice perspectives. *Social Work with Groups, 20*(4), 19–34.

Schreiber, B. (2002). Brief-term group psychotherapy with late adolescents. *Southern-African Journal of Child and Adolescent-Mental Health, 14*(1), 50–56.

Schriver, J. (1998). *Human behavior and the social environment* (2nd ed.). Boston: Allyn and Bacon.

Schuman, S., & Rohrbaugh, J. (1996, June). Meet me in cyberspace. *Government Technology, 9,* 32–34.

Schwartz, W. (1966). Discussion of three papers on the group method with clients, foster families, and adoptive families. *Child Welfare, 45*(10), 571–575.

Schwartz, W. (1971). On the use of groups in social work practice. In W. Schwartz & S. Zalba (Eds.), *The practice of group work* (pp. 3–24). New York: Columbia University Press.

Schwartz, W. (1976). Between client and system: The mediating function. In R. Roberts & H. Northen (Eds.), *Theories of social work with groups* (pp. 171–197). New York: Columbia University Press.

Schwartz, W. (1981, April). *The group work tradition and social work practice.* Paper presented at Rutgers University, School of Social Work, New Brunswick.

Seaberg, J., & Gillespie, D. (1977). Goal attainment scaling: A critique. *Social Work Research and Abstracts, 13*(2), 4–9.

Seashore, S. (1954). *Group cohesiveness in the industrial work group.* Ann Arbor: University of Michigan Press.

Seely, H., & Sween, J. (1983, March). Critical components of successful U.S. quality circles. *Quality Circles Journal, 6,* 14–17.

Segal, Z., Williams, M., & Teasdale, J. (2002). *Mindfulness-based cognitive therapy for depression.* New York: Guildford Press.

Seligman, L. (1998). *Selecting effective treatments* (2nd ed.). San Francisco: Jossey-Bass.

Seligman, M. (1975). *Helplessness: On depression, development, and death.* San Francisco: W. H. Freeman.

Selltiz, C., Wrightsman, L., & Cook, S. (1976). *Research methods in social relations* (3rd ed.). New York: Holt, Rinehart & Winston.

Sexton, T., & Whiston, S. (1994). The status of the counseling relationship: An empirical review, theoretical implications, and research directions. *Counseling Psychologist, 22*(1), 6–77.

Shapiro, J., Peltz, L., & Bernadett-Shapiro, S. (1998). *Brief group treatment for therapists and counselors.* Florence, KY: Wadsworth.

Shaw, C. (1930). *The jack roller.* Chicago: University of Chicago Press.

Shaw, M. (1964). Communication networks. In L. Berkowitz (Ed.), *Advances in experimental social psychology* (Vol. 1, pp. 111–149). New York: Academic Press.

Shaw, M. (1976). *Group dynamics: The psychology of small group behavior.* New York: McGraw-Hill.

Sheldon, B. (1995). *Cognitive-behavioural therapy: Research, practice and philosophy.* London: Routledge.

Shepard, C. (1964). *Small groups: Some sociological perspectives.* San Francisco: Chandler.

Sherif, M. (1936). *The psychology of social norms.* New York: Harper & Row.

Sherif, M. (1956). Experiments in group conflict. *Scientific American, 195,* 54–58.

Sherif, M., & Sherif, C. (1953). *Groups in harmony and tension: An introduction of studies in group relations.* New York: Harper & Row.

Sherif, M., White, J., & Harvey, O. (1955). Status in experimentally produced groups. *American Journal of Sociology, 60,* 370–379.

Shils, E. (1950). Primary groups in the American army. In R. Merton & P. Lazarsfeld (Eds.), *Continuities in social research* (pp. 16–39). New York: The Free Press.

Shimanoff, S., & Jenkins, M. (1991). Leadership and gender: Challenging assumptions and recognizing resources. In R. Cathcart & L. Samovar (Eds.), *Small group communication: A reader* (6th ed., pp. 504–522). Dubuque, IA: William C. Brown.

Shipley, R., & Boudewyns, P. (1980). Flooding and implosive therapy: Are they harmful? *Behavior Therapy, 11*(4), 503–508.

Shulman, L. (1978). A study of practice skills. *Social Work, 23*(4), 274–280.

Shulman, L. (1999). *The skills of helping individuals, families and groups* (4th ed.). Itasca, IL: F. E. Peacock.

Shuster, H. D. (1990). *Teaming for quality improvement: A process for innovation and consensus.* Englewood Cliffs, NJ: Prentice-Hall.

Siegel, J., Dubrovsky, V., Kiesler, S., & McGuire, T. (1986). Group processes in computer-mediated communication. *Organizational Behavior and Human Decision Processes, 37*(2), 157–187.

Silbergeld, S., Koenig, G., Manderscheid, R., Meeker, B., & Hornung, C. (1975). Assessment of environment-therapy systems: The group atmosphere scale. *Journal of Consulting and Clinical Psychology, 43*(4), 460–469.

Silver, W. B., & Bufiano, K. (1996). The impact of group efficacy and group goals on group task performance. *Small Group Research, 27*(3), 345–472.

Silverman, M. (1966). Knowledge in social group work: A review of the literature. *Social Work, 11*(3), 56–62.

Siporin, M. (1975). *Introduction to social work practice.* New York: Macmillan.

Siporin, M. (1980). Ecological system theory in social work. *Journal of Sociology and Social Work, 7,* 507–532.

Slavson, S. R. (1939a). *Character education in a democracy.* New York: Association Press.

Slavson, S. R. (1939b). Democratic leadership in education. *The Group, 2,*1–2.

Slavson, S. R. (1940). Group psychotherapy. *Mental Hygiene, 24,* 36–49.

Slavson, S. R. (1945). *Creative group education.* New York: Association Press.

Slavson, S. R. (1946). *Recreation and the total personality.* New York: Association Press.

Sluyter, G., & Mukherjee, A. (1993). *Total quality management for mental health and mental retardation.* Annandale, VA: National Association of Private Residential Resources.

Smith, A. (1935). Group play in a hospital environment. *Proceedings of the National Conference of Social Work* (pp. 372–373). Chicago: University of Chicago Press.

Smith, G. (1998). Idea-generation techniques: A formulary of active ingredients. *Journal of Creative Behavior, 32*(2), 107–133.

Smith, H., & Doeing, C. (1985, Spring). Japanese management: A model for social work administration? *Administration in Social Work, 9*(1), 1–11.

Smith, K. K., & Berg, D. N. (1997). *Paradoxes of group life.* San Francisco: Jossey-Bass.

Smith, M. (1977). *Value clarification.* La Jolla, CA: University Associates.

Smith, M., Tobin, S., & Toseland, R. (1992). Therapeutic processes in professional and peer counseling of family caregivers of frail elderly. *Social Work, 37*(4), 345–351.

Smith, P. (1978). Group work as a process of social influence. In N. McCaughan (Ed.), *Group work: Learning and practice* (pp. 36–57). London: George Allen & Unwin.

Smith, T., & Toseland, R. (2006). The evaluation of a telephone caregiver support group intervention. *The Gerontologist, 46*(5), 620–629.

Smokowski, P. R., Rose, S. D., Todar, K., & Reardon, K. (1999). Post-group casualty-status, group events and leader behavior: An early look into the dynamics of damaging group experiences. *Research on Social Work Practice, 9*(5), 555–574.

Smokowski, P. R., Galinsky, M., & Harlow, K. (2001). Using technologies in groupwork Part II: Technology-based groups. *Groupwork, 13*(1), 6–22.

Smokowski, P. R., Rose, S. D., & Bacallao, M. L. (2001). Damaging experiences in therapeutic groups: How vulnerable consumers become group casualties. *Small Group Research, 32*(2), 223–251.

Smucker, M., Dancu, C., & Foa, E. (1999). *Cognitive behavioral treatment for adult survivors of childhood trauma: Imagery rescripting and reprocessing.* Northvale, NJ: Jason Aronson.

Sosik, J., Avolio, B., & Kahai, S. (1998). Inspiring group creativity: Comparing anonymous and identified electronic brainstorming. *Small Group Research, 29*(1), 3–31.

Sosik, J., & Jung, D. (2002). Work group characteristics and performance in collectivistic and individualistic cultures. *Journal of Social Psychology, 142*(1), 5–23.

Spielberger, C., Gorsuch, R., Lushene, R., Vagg, P., & Jacobs, G. (1983). *Manual for the stait-trait anxiety inventory.* Palo Alto, CA: Consulting Psychologists Press.

Spink, K., & Carron, A. (1994). Group cohesion effects in exercise classes. *Small Group Research, 25*(1), 26–42.

Spitz, H. I., & Spitz, S. T. (1999). *Group psychotherapy.* Philadelphia, PA: Brunner/Mazel.

Staples, L. H. (2004). Social action groups. In C. D. Garvin, L. M. Gutierrez, & M. J, Galinsky (Eds.), *Handbook of social work with groups* (pp. 344–383). New York: The Guilford Press.

Starak, Y. (1981). Co-leadership: A new look at sharing group work. *Social Work with Groups, 4*(3/4), 145–157.

Stattler, W., & Miller, N. (1968). *Discussion and conference* (2nd ed.). Englewood Cliffs, NJ: Prentice-Hall.

Steckler, N., & Fondas, N. (1995). Building team leader effectiveness: A diagnostic tool. *Organizational Dynamics, 23*(3), 20–35.

Stern, L., Rothman, B., & Nakanishi, M. (1993). The telephone group: Accessing group service to the homebound. *Social Work with Groups, 16*(½), 203–215.

Steinberg, D. M. (1997). *The mutual-aid approach to working with groups: Helping people help each other.* Northvale, NJ: Jason Aronson.

Stern, R., & Drummond, L. (1991). *Practice of behavioural and cognitive psychotherapy.* New York: Cambridge University Press.

Stewart, D. W., & Shamdasani, P. N. (1990). *Focus groups: Theory and practice.* Newbury Park, CA: Sage.

Stewart, G., Manz, C., & Sims, H. (1999). *Team work and group dynamics.* New York: John Wiley & Sons.

Stockton, R., Rohde, R., & Haughey, J. (1992). The effects of structured group exercises on cohesion, engagement, avoidance, and conflict. *Small Group Research, 23*(2), 155–168.

Stogdill, R. (1974). *Handbook of leadership.* New York: The Free Press.

Stone, M., Lewis, C., & Beck, A. (1994). The structure of Yalom's Curative Factors Scale. *International Journal of Group Psychotherapy, 44*(2), 239–245.

Stoner, J. (1968). Risky and cautious shifts in group decisions: The influence of widely held values. *Journal of Experimental Social Psychology, 4,* 442–459.

Stouffer, S. (1949). *The American soldier, combat and its aftermath.* Princeton, NJ: Princeton University Press.

Stuart, R. (1970). *Trick or treatment: Who and when psychotherapy facts.* Champaign, IL: Research Press.

Stuart, R. (1977). *Behavioral self-management: Strategies, techniques, and outcomes.* New York: Brunner/Mazel.

Stuart, R., & Davis, B. (1972). *Slim chance in a fat world.* Champaign, IL: Research Press.

Sue, D. W., & Sue, D. (1999). *Counseling the culturally different: Theory and practice* (3rd ed.). New York: John Wiley & Sons.

Sue, S., Zane, N., & Young, K. (1994). Psychotherapy with culturally diverse populations. In A. Bergin & S. Garfield (Eds.), *Handbook of psychotherapy and behavior change* (4th ed., pp. 783–812). New York: John Wiley & Sons.

Sundel, M., Glasser, P., Sarri, R., & Vinter, R. (1985). *Individual change through small groups* (2nd ed.). New York: The Free Press.

Susskind, L., & Cruikshank, J. (2006). *Breaking Robert's rules: The new way to run your meeting, build concensus, and get results.* New York: Oxford University Press.

Swenson, J., Griswold, W., & Kleiber, P. (1992, November). Focus groups method of inquiry/intervention. *Small Group Research, 23*(4), 459–474.

Syz, H. C. (1928). Remarks on group analysis. *American Journal of Psychiatry, 85,* 141–148.

Taylor, D., Berry, P., & Block, C. (1958). Does group participation when using brainstorming facilitate or inhibit creative thinking? *Administrative Science Quarterly, 3,* 23–47.

Taylor, N., & Burlingame, G. (2001). A survey of mental health care provider and managed care organization attitudes toward, familiarity with, and use of group psychotherapy. *International Journal of Group Psychotherapy, 51*(2), 243–263.

Taylor, R. (1903). Group management. *Transactions of the American Society of Mechanical Engineers, 24,* 1337–1480.

Teger, A., & Pruitt, D. (1967). Components of group risk-taking. *Journal of Experimental Psychology, 3,* 189–205.

Thelen, H. (1954). *Dynamics of groups at work.* Chicago: University of Chicago Press.

Thibaut, J., & Kelley, H. (1954). Experimental studies of group problem-solving process. In G. Kindzey (Ed.), *Handbook of social psychology* (Vol. 2, pp. 735–785). Reading, MA: Addison-Wesley.

Thibaut, J., & Kelley, H. (1959). *The social psychology of groups.* New York: John Wiley & Sons.

Thomas, E. (1978). Generating innovation in social work: The paradigm of developmental research. *Journal of Social Services Research, 2*(1), 95–115.

Thomas, E. (1990). Modes of practice in developmental research. In L. Videka-Sherman & W. Reid (Eds.), *Advances in clinical social work research* (pp. 202–217). Silver Spring, MD: National Association of Social Workers Press.

Thomas, E., & Rothman, J. (1994). An integrative perspective on intervention research. In J. Rothman & E. J. Thomas (Eds.), *Intervention research: Design and development for human service* (pp. 3–23). New York: Hawthorn Press.

Thoresen, C., & Mahoney, M. (1974). *Behavioral self-control.* New York: Holt, Rinehart & Winston.

Thorndike, R. (1938). On what type of task will a group do well? *Journal of Abnormal and Social Psychology, 33,* 409–413.

Thrasher, F. (1927). *The gang.* Chicago: University of Chicago Press.

Tolson, E., Reid, W., & Garvin, C. (1994). *Generalist practice: A task-centered approach.* New York: Columbia University Press.

Toseland, R. (1977). A problem-solving workshop for older persons. *Social Work, 22*(4), 325–327.

Toseland, R. (1981). Increasing access: Outreach methods in social work practice. *Social Casework, 62*(4), 227–234.

Toseland, R. (1990). Long-term effectiveness of peer-led and professionally led support groups for family caregivers. *Social Service Review, 64*(2), 308–327.

Toseland, R. (1995). *Group work with the elderly and family caregivers.* New York: Springer.

Toseland, R., & Coppola, M. (1985). A task-centered approach to group work with the elderly. In A. Fortune (Ed.), *Task-centered practice with families and groups* (pp. 101–114). New York: Springer.

Toseland, R., Decker, J., & Bliesner, J. (1979). A community program for socially isolated older persons. *Journal of Gerontological Social Work, 1*(3), 211–224.

Toseland, R., Diehl, M., Freeman, K., Manzanares, T., Naleppa, M., & McCallion, P. (1997). The impact of validation therapy on nursing home residents with dementia. *Journal of Applied Gerontology, 16*(1), 31–50.

Toseland, R., & Ephross, P. (1987). *Working effectively with administrative groups.* New York: Haworth.

Toseland, R., & Hacker, L. (1982). Self-help groups and professional involvement. *Social Work, 27*(4), 341–347.

Toseland, R., & Hacker, L. (1985). Social workers' use of groups as a resource for clients. *Social Work, 30*(3), 232–239.

Toseland, R., Ivanoff, A., & Rose, S. (1987). Treatment conferences: Task groups in action. *Social Work with Groups, 10*(2), 79–94.

Toseland, R., Kabat, D., & Kemp, K. (1983). An evaluation of a smoking cessation group program. *Social Work Research and Abstracts, 19*(1), 12–20.

Toseland, R., Krebs, A., & Vahsen, J. (1978). Changing group interaction patterns. *Social Service Research, 2*(2), 219–232.

Toseland, R., Labrecque, M., Goebel, S., & Whitney, M. (1992). An evaluation of a group program for spouses of frail, elderly veterans. *The Gerontologist, 32*(3), 382–390.

Toseland, R., McCallion, P., Smith, T., Huck, S., Bourgeois, P., & Garstka, T. (2001). Health education groups for caregivers in an HMO. *Journal of Clinical Psychology, 57*(4), 551–570.

Toseland, R., McCallion, P., Smith, T., & Banks, S. (2004). Supporting caregivers of frail older adults in an HMO setting. *American Journal of Orthopsychiatry, 74*(3), 349–364.

Toseland, R., Naccarato, T., & Wray, L. (2007). Telephone groups for older persons and family caregivers. *Clinical Gerontologist, 31*(1), 59–76.

Toseland, R., Palmer-Ganeles, J., & Chapman, D. (1986). Teamwork in psychiatric settings. *Social Work, 31*(1), 46–52.

Toseland, R., & Reid, W. (1985). Using rapid assessment instruments in a family service agency. *Social Casework, 66,* 547–555.

Toseland, R., & Rivas, R. (1984). Structured methods for working with task groups. *Administration in Social Work, 8*(2), 49–58.

Toseland, R., Rivas, R., & Chapman, D. (1984). An evaluation of decision making in task groups. *Social Work, 29*(4), 339–346.

Toseland, R., & Rizzo, V. (2003). Leading telephone caregiver support groups: A manual for a model psychoeducational program (Unpublished Manuscript). Albany, NY.

Toseland, R., & Rose, S. (1978). Evaluating social skills training for older adults in groups. *Social Work Research and Abstracts, 14*(1), 25–33.

Toseland, R., & Rossiter, C. (1989). Group interventions to support family caregivers: A review and analysis. *The Gerontologist, 29,* 438–448.

Toseland, R., Rossiter, C., & Labrecque, M. (1989). The effectiveness of peer-led and professionally led groups to support family caregivers. *The Gerontologist, 29*(4), 465–471.

Toseland, R., Rossiter, C., Peak, T., & Hill, P. (1990). Therapeutic processes in support groups for caregivers. *International Journal of Group Psychotherapy, 40*(3), 279–303.

Toseland, R., Rossiter, C., Peak, T., & Smith, G. (1990). Comparative effectiveness of individual and group interventions to support family caregivers. *Social Work, 35*(3), 209–219.

Toseland, R., Sherman, E., & Bliven, S. (1981). The comparative effectiveness of two group work approaches for the evaluation of mutual support groups among the elderly. *Social Work with Groups, 4*(1/2), 137–153.

Toseland, R., & Siporin, M. (1986). When to recommend group treatment: A review of the clinical and research literature. *International Journal of Group Psychotherapy, 36*(2), 171–201.

Toseland, R., & Spielberg, G. (1982). The development of helping skills in undergraduate social work education: Model and evaluation. *Journal of Education for Social Work, 18*(1), 66–73.

Tracy, E., & Whittaker, J. (1990). The social network map: Assessing social support in clinical practice. *Families in Society, 71*(8), 461–470.

Trecker, H. (1956). *Group work in the psychiatric setting.* New York: William Morrow.

Trecker, H. (1972). *Social group work: Principles and practices.* New York: Association Press.

Trecker, H. (1980). Administration as a group process: Philosophy and concepts. In A. Alissi (Ed.),
Perspectives on social group work practice (pp. 332–337). New York: The Free Press.

Triplett, N. (1898). The dynamogenic factors in pacemaking and competition. *American Journal of
Psychology, 9*(4), 507–533.

Tropman, J. (1995). The role of the board in the planning process. In J. Tropman, J. Erlich, & J. Rothman (Eds.), *Tactics and techniques of community intervention* (3rd ed., pp. 157–170). Itasca, IL:
F. E. Peacock.

Tropman, J. (1996). *Effective meetings: Improving group decision-making* (2nd ed.). Thousand Oaks,
CA: Sage.

Tropp, E. (1968). The group in life and in social work. *Social Casework, 49,* 267–274.

Tropp, E. (1976). A developmental theory. In R. Roberts & H. Northen (Eds.), *Theories of social
work with groups* (pp. 198–237). New York: Columbia University Press.

Trotter, C. (1999). *Working with involuntary clients.* London: Sage Publications.

Trotzer, J. (1999). *The counselor and the group: Integrating theory, training and practice* (3rd ed.).
Pacific Grove, CA: Brooks/Cole.

Tuckman, B. (1963). Developmental sequence in small groups. *Psychological Bulletin, 63,* 384–399.

Turner, M. P., & Pratkanis, A. (1998). Twenty-five years of groupthink theory and research: Lessons
from the evaluation of theory. *Organizational Behavior and Human Decision Processes,
73*(2–3), 105–115.

Tyson, T. (1998). *Working with groups* (2nd ed.). South Yarra, Australia: MacMillan Education.

Vaillant, G. (1995). *The natural history of alcoholism revisited.* Cambridge, MA: Harvard University
Press.

Valacich, J. S., Dennis, A. R., & Connolly, T. (1994). Idea generation in computer-based groups:
A new ending to an old story. *Organizational behavior and human decision processes, 57*(3),
448–467.

Van de Ven, A. (1974). *Group decision making and effectiveness: An experimental study.* Kent, OH:
Kent State University Press.

Van de Ven, A., & Delbecq, A. (1971). Nominal versus interacting group processes for committee
decision-making effectiveness. *Academy of Management Journal, 9,* 203–212.

Vasquez, M., & Han, A. (1995). Group interventions in treatment with ethnic minorities. In J. Aponte &
J. Wohl (Eds.), *Psychological inteventions and cultural diversity* (pp. 109–127). Boston: Allyn
and Bacon.

Velasquez, M., Maurer, G., Crouch, C., & DiClemente, C. (2001). *Group treatment for substance
abuse: A stages-of-change therapy manual.* New York: Guilford Press.

Verhofstadt-Deneve, L. (2000). The "Magic Shop" technique in psychodrama: An existential–dialectical
view. *International Journal of Action Methods: Psychodrama, Skill Training, and Role Playing,
53,* 3–15.

Vinokur-Kaplan, D. (1995). Enhancing the effectiveness of interdisciplinary mental health teams.
Administration and Policy in Mental Health, 22, 521–529.

Vinter, R. (Ed.). (1967). *Readings in group work practice.* Ann Arbor, MI: Campus Publishing.

Vinter, R. (1985a). The essential components of social group work practice. In M. Sundel, P. Glasser,
R. Sarri, & R. Vinter (Eds.), *Individual change through small groups* (2nd ed., pp. 11–34). New
York: The Free Press.

Vinter, R. (1985b). Program activities: An analysis of their effects on participant behavior. In M.
Sundel, P. Glasser, R. Sarri, & R. Vinter (Eds.), *Individual change through small groups* (2nd
ed., pp. 226–236). New York: The Free Press.

Vorrath, H. H., & Brendtro, L. K. (1985). *Positive peer culture* (2nd ed.). Chicago: Aldine.

Vroom, V. H., Grant, L., & Cotton, T. (1969). The consequence of social interaction in group problem solving. *Journal of Organizational Behavior and Human Performance, 4,* 79–95.

Vroom, V. H., & Yetton, P. (1973). *Leadership and decision making.* Pittsburgh, PA: University of Pittsburgh Press.

Wakefield, J. C. (1996). Does social work need the eco-systems perspective? Part I. Is the perspective clinically useful? *Social Service Review, 70*(1), 1–32.

Waldo, C. (1986). *A working guide for directors of not-for-profit organizations.* New York: Quorum Books.

Wall, V. D. , Jr., Galanes, G. J., & Love, S. B. (1987). Small task-oriented groups, conflict, conflict management, satisfaction, and decision quality. *Small Group Behavior, 18,* 31–55.

Wall, V. D., Jr., & Nolan, L. L. (1987). Small group conflict: A look at equity, satisfaction and styles of conflict management. *Small Group Behavior, 18,* 188–211.

Wallach, M., & Wing, C. (1968). Is risk a value? *Journal of Personality and Social Psychology, 9,* 101–106.

Walls, R., Werner, T., Bacon, A., & Zane, T. (1977). *Behavior checklists in behavioral assessment: New directions in clinical psychology.* New York: Brunner/Mazel.

Walters, K., Longres, J., Han, C., & Icard, D. (2003). Cultural competence with gay and lesbian persons of color. In D. Lum (Ed.), *Culturally competent practice: A framework understanding diverse groups and justice issues* (pp. 310–342). Sacramento, CA: Thomson, Brooks, Cole.

Walton, M. (1990). *Deming management at work.* New York: G. P. Putnam's Sons.

Wasserman, H., & Danforth, J. (1988). *The human bond: Support group and mutual aid.* New York: Springer.

Waterman, J., & Walker, E. (2001). *Helping at-risk students, A group counseling approach for grades 6–9.* New York and London: Guilford Press.

Watson, S. R., & Buede, D. M. (1987). *Decision synthesis: The principles and practice of decision analysis.* New York: Cambridge University Press.

Watson, W., Johnson, L., & Merritt, D. (1998). Team orientation, self-orientation, and diversity in task groups: Their connection to team performance over time. *Group & Organization Management, 23*(2), 161–188.

Watzlawick, P., Weakland, J., & Fisch, R. (1974). *Change: Principles of problem formation and problem resolution.* New York: W. W. Norton.

Wayne, J., & Avery, N. (1979). Activities for group termination. *Social Work, 24*(1), 58–62.

Weaver, H. (1999). Indigenous people and the social work profession: Defining culturally competent services. *Social Work, 44*(3), 217–225.

Weber, A., & Friedman, G. (2000). *Managing stress.* Charleston, WV: Cambridge Research Group.

Wech, B., Mossholder, K., Steel, R., & Bennett, N. (1998). Does work group cohesiveness affect individuals' performance and organizational commitment? A cross-level examination. *Small Group Research, 29*(4), 472–494.

Weinberg, H. (2001). Group process and group phenomena on the Internet. *International Journal of Group Psychotherapy, 51*(3), 361–378.

Weinberg, N., Uken, J., Schmale, J., & Adamek, M. (1995). Therapeutic factors: Their presence in a computer-mediated support group. *Social Work with Groups, 18*(4), 57–69.

Weisner, S. (1983). Fighting back: A critical analysis of coalition building in the human services. *Social Service Review, 57*(2), 291–306.

Weissman, A. (1976). Industrial social services: Linkage technology. *Social Casework, 57*(1), 50–54.

Weissman, H. (Ed.). (1969). *Individual and group services in the mobilization for youth experiment.* New York: Association Press.

Wells, R. (1994). *Planned short-term treatment* (2nd ed.). New York: The Free Press.

Welo, B. K. (2001). *Tough customers: Counseling unwilling clients* (2nd ed.). Upper Marlboro, MD: Graphic Communications.

Wender, L. (1936). The dynamics of group psychotherapy and its application. *Journal of Nervous & Mental Disorders, 84,* 54–60.

Wheelan, S. (1994). *Group processes: A developmental perspective.* Boston: Allyn and Bacon.

Wheelan, S. A. (2005). *Handbook of group research and practice.* Thousand Oaks, CA: Sage Publications, Inc.

White, B. J., & Madara, E. (Eds.) (2002). *The self-help sourcebook: Your guide to community and online support groups* (7th ed.). Denville, NJ: St. Clare's Health Services.

White, J. R., & Freeman, A. (Eds.). (2000). *Cognitive-behavioral group therapy for specific problems and populations.* Washington, DC: American Psychological Association.

White, B., & Madara, E. (1998). *The self-help sourcebook: Your guide to community and online support groups* (6th ed.). Nutley, NJ: Hoffman La Roche.

Whyte, W. (1943). *Street corner society.* Chicago: University of Chicago Press.

Widmeyer, W., & Williams, J. (1991). Predicting cohesion in a coacting sport. *Small Group Research, 22*(4), 548–570.

Wiener, L. S., Spencer, E. D., Davidson, R., & Fair, C. (1993). Telephone support groups: A new avenue toward psychosocial support for HIV-infected children and their families. *Social Work with Groups, 16*(3), 55–71.

Williams, O. (1994). Group work with African-American men who batter: Toward more ethnically sensitive practice. *Journal of Comparative Family Studies, 25,* 91–103.

Wilson, G. (1976). From practice to theory: A personalized history. In R. W. Roberts & H. Northen (Eds.), *Theories of social work with groups* (pp. 1–44). New York: Columbia University Press.

Wilson, G., & Ryland, G. (1949). *Social group work practice.* Boston: Houghton Mifflin.

Wilson, G., & Ryland, G. (1980). The social group work method. In A. Alissi (Ed.), *Perspectives on social group work practice* (pp. 169–182). New York: The Free Press.

Wilson, S. (1980). *Recording: Working guidelines for social workers.* New York: The Free Press.

Winer, M., & Ray, K. (1996). *Collaboration handbook: Creating, sustaining, and enjoying the journey.* St. Paul, MN: Amherst Wilder Foundation.

Winterfeldt, D., & Edwards, W. (1986). *Decision analysis and behavioral research.* New York: Cambridge University Press.

Wittman, H. (1991). Group member satisfaction: A conflict-related account. *Small Group Research, 22*(1), 24–58.

Wolf, T. (1990). *Managing a nonprofit organization.* New York: Prentice-Hall.

Woods, M., & Hollis, F. (1990). *Casework: A psychosocial therapy* (4th ed.). New York: McGraw-Hill.

Worchell, S. (1994). You can go home again: Returning group research to the group context with an eye on developmental issues. *Small Group Research, 25*(2), 205–223.

Wright, J. Basco, M., & Thase, M. (2006). *Learning cognitive behavior therapy: An illustrated guide.* Washington DC: American Psychiatric Publishing.

Wright, J., Thase, M., Beck, A., & Ludgate, J. (Eds.). (1993). *Cognitive therapy with inpatients: Developing a cognitive milieu.* New York: Guilford.

Wright, M. (2002). Co-facilitation: Fashion or function? *Social Work with Groups, 25*(3), 77–92.

Wyss, D. (1973). *Psychoanalytic schools: From the beginning to the present.* New York: Jason Aronson.

Yalom, I. (1983). *Inpatient group psychotherapy.* New York: Basic Books.

Yalom, I. (1995). *The theory and practice of group psychotherapy* (4th ed.). New York: Basic Books.

Yan, M. C. (2001). Reclaiming the social in social group work: An experience of a community center in Hong Kong. *Social Work with Groups, 24*(3/4), 53–65.

Yee, R. (1999). *The art of breath and relaxation: Yoga exercises for a more balanced life.* Santa Monica, CA: Living Arts.

Yost, E., Beutler, L., Corbishley, M., & Allender, J. (1985). *Group cognitive therapy: A treatment approach for depressed older adults.* Elmsford, NY: Pergamon Press.

Yukl, G. (2002). *Leadership in organizations.* Upper Saddle River, NJ: Prentice Hall.

Zajonc, R., Wolosin, R., & Wolosin, W. (1972). Group risk-taking under various group decision schema. *Journal of Experimental and Social Psychology, 8,* 16–30.

Ziller, R. (1957). Four techniques of group decision making under uncertainty. *Journal of Applied Psychology, 41,* 384–388.

Name Index

Aaker, D., 350
Abell, M., 180
Abels, P., 40, 41
Abramson, J., 29, 33, 34, 35, 56, 155
Achenbach, T., 228
Adam, E., 363
Addams, J., 46
Agazarian, Y., 472
Al-Assaf, A., 361
Alban-Metcalf, R., 97
Albers, S., 362
Alberti, R., 391
Aldarondo, E., 260
Alemi, F., 181
Alexander, R., 363
Alimo-Metcalfe, B., 97
Alinsky, S., 374
Alissi, A., 45, 52
Allen, A., 180
Allen, J., 481
Allender, J., 282, 283
Allport, F., 54
American Association of Group
    Workers, 46
American Group Psychotherapy
    Association, Inc., 10, 453
American Psychiatric Association,
    219, 400, 406
Anderson, B., 353
Anderson, J., 12, 56, 64, 69
Anderson, L., 348
Antony, M., 52, 200, 257, 259, 280
Aponte, J., 129
Appleby, G., 140, 146
Arenson, S., 327
Arguello, D., 140
Arndt, R., 419
Aronson, H., 113
Arrow, H., 55
Asch, P., 54
Asch, S., 82
Ashby, M., 145, 228
Asher-Svanum, H., 200
Association for Specialists in Group
    Work, 456
Association for the Advancement of
    Social Work with Groups, 458
Atieno Okech, J., 125

Atkinson, D., 134
Avery, N., 392
Avolio, B., 97, 361
Axelson, J., 133, 135

Bacallao, M., 11, 64, 97
Bachrach, P., 329
Back, K., 75
Bacon, A., 229
Bailey, D., 29, 42
Bailey-Dempsey, C., 413
Baker, J., 481
Bales, R., 54, 55, 56, 57, 86, 87, 88,
    167, 202, 239, 241, 330, 409, 423
Balgopal, P., 63
Bandura, A., 60, 75, 98, 268, 289,
    291, 388
Banker, R., 29
Banks, S., 418
Baratz, M., 329
Bargh, J., 176
Barker, L., 335
Barker, V., 66
Barlow, C., 26, 118, 119, 191, 393
Barlow, S., 235, 401, 409
Baron, J., 340
Barrett, K., 386
Barrick, M., 363
Basco, M., 280
Bass, B., 96, 97
Bass, D., 181
Bauer, M., 200, 205, 257, 259, 283
Baugh, S., 141
Bayless, O., 347
Bechler, C., 106
Beck, A., 281, 301, 422, 423
Beck, J., 61, 280, 281, 282, 284
Becker, R., 280
Becker, W., 391
Bednar, K., 64, 93, 94, 170, 382
Bednar, R., 170
Behroozi, C., 272
Beisgon, B., 482
Bell, J., 13
Bellack, A., 217, 229
Bender, E., 23
Benedict, J., 180
Benjamin, J., 372, 373

Benne, K., 231
Bennett, N., 76
Bennett, R., 483
Benson, G., 362
Berdahl, J., 55
Berg, D., 323
Berger, R., 119
Bergeron, L., 9
Bernadett-Shapiro, S., 51, 259
Bernard, H., 59
Berne, E., 59, 391
Bernstein, D., 287
Bernstein, S., 473
Berry, J., 136
Berry, P., 347, 348
Berry, T., 361
Bertcher, H., 166, 167
Bessant, J., 372
Beutler, L., 282, 283
Bieling, P., 52, 53, 257, 259, 280
Bienvenu, J., 382
Bion, W., 59
Birnbaum, M., 384
Birren, J., 482
Bixby, F., 62
Blackmon, M., 39, 330
Blanchard, K., 102
Blatner, H., 268, 294
Blau, P., 62
Blay, S., 257
Blazer, D., 68
Bliesner, J., 75, 201
Bliven, S., 201, 260
Bloch, F., 9
Block, C., 347, 348
Blom, S., 483
Bloom, B., 335
Bloom, M., 224, 225, 415
Blouin, J., 163
Bluedorn, A., 363
Blue Sky Productions, 471
Blumberg, H., 19, 321
Blythe, J., 26, 118, 191, 393
Bobowick, M., 39, 330
Bonito, J., 419
Booth, H., 483
Borba, C., 481
Borba, M., 481

Borgatti, S., 416
Borkovec, T., 287
Borman, L., 17, 266
Bouchard, T., 348, 349
Boudewyns, P., 285
Bowers, R., 327
Bowman, L., 46
Bowman, R., 177
Bowman, V., 177
Boyd, N., 27, 46
Brabender, V., 394
Brackett, J., 46
Bradford, L., 368
Brager, G., 309, 391
Brehmer, B., 360
Brekke, J., 159
Brendtro, L., 62, 258
Brennan, P., 181
Breton, M., 49
Brewer, M., 238
Brilhart, J., 167
Brill, N., 6, 29, 53, 313
Broder, L., 335
Brodsky, A., 124, 208, 209, 274
Bronstein, L., 29, 33, 35, 56, 373
Brook, D., 136, 141
Brooks, M., 397
Brower, A., 419
Brown, A., 128, 134, 145
Brown, B., 144
Brown, L., 51, 471
Browne, K., 260
Browning, L., 99, 102
Brownson, C., 42
Brownson, R., 42
Budman, S., 60, 76, 200, 231, 239,
    260, 381, 409
Buede, D., 340
Bufe, C., 191
Bufiano, K., 75
Burish, T., 285, 386
Burlingame, G., 18, 51, 193, 229,
    401, 419
Burnette, J., 401
Burns, J., 97
Burns, R., 180
Burwell, N., 143
Busa, S., 123
Butler, H., 416
Butler, R., 483
Byers, P., 352

Cambridge Educational, 287
Cameron, R., 428, 429
Campbell, J., 348
Canfield, J., 482

Caplinger, T., 60, 302, 305, 306
Carless, S., 239
Carletta, J., 70
Carroll, D., 28
Carroll, M., 471
Carrell, S., 481
Carron, A., 76, 167
Carter, R., 69
Cartlege, G., 481
Cartwright, D., 55, 62, 75, 76
Casciato, T., 471
Casey, M., 352, 416
Center for Psychological Issues
    in the Nuclear Age, 471
Chait, R., 39, 330
Chapman, D., 33, 99, 340, 356, 361
Chatman, J., 323
Chau, K., 133, 135, 144, 146
Chemers, M., 95, 97, 98
Cheng, L., 134
Cherry, D., 142
Cheung, M., 481
Chiauzzi, E., 386
Chovanec, M., 212
Cicchetti, A., 384
Clark, A., 112
Clark, C., 345, 347
Clark, P., 483
Clarkin, J., 259
Clemen, R., 340
Clements, C., 483
Clifford, M., 51
Cohen, M., 49
Cohen, S., 29, 57, 239, 409, 423
Cole, R., 362
Colon, E., 140, 146
Collaros, R., 348
Commission on Accreditation, 6, 9
Cone, J., 229
Connelly, J., 381
Connolly, T., 357, 422
Conoley, J., 229
Conrad, W., 38
Cook, S., 238
Cooksey, R., 360
Cooley, D., 54
Cooper, C., 76, 167, 241
Cooper, L., 123, 124
Coppola, M., 395
Corbishley, M., 282, 283
Corcoran, K., 229, 422
Corey, G., 9, 18, 242, 471
Corey, M., 9, 18, 242, 471
Corey, S., 368
Costin, H., 362
Cotton, T., 348

Coucouvanis, J., 481
Cox, E., 49
Cox, M., 238
Cox, T., 130, 134
Coyle, G., 47, 64
Craig, T., 397
Craighead, W., 482
Crano, W., 238
Cross, S., 129
Cross, T., 177
Crouch, C., 53
Crowell, L., 165, 167, 314, 319, 339,
    345, 346, 355
Cruikshank, L., 321, 328

Dabney, S., 42
Dailey, J., 347, 356
Dalgleish, L., 340
Damon, L., 482
Dancu, C., 280
D'Andrea, M., 134, 146
Danforth, J., 51
Dansereau, F., 63
Dattillio, M., 280
Davidson, R., 178
Davies, M., 19, 321
Davis, B., 391
Davis, F., 123, 124, 125
Davis, G., 346
Davis, I., 113
Davis, L., 128, 130, 134, 135, 416
Davis, M., 76, 200, 284, 285, 287
Davison, J., 143
Day, G., 350
Debbane, E., 381, 382
DeBernardo, C., 257
De Bono, E., 339
DeCarufel, F., 381
Decker, J., 75, 201
Degenne, A., 296
de Groot, D., 176
Delbecq, A., 353, 354, 355, 356
Delgado, M., 228
Delucia-Waack, J., 229, 235
Demby, A., 60, 76, 200, 381
Denhardt, R., 363
Dennis, A., 357
DeNunzio, D., 191
DePaola, C., 239
Deutchman, D., 482
Devine, D., 76
Devore, W., 128, 135
Diaz, T., 143
Dickey, H., 483
Dickson, W., 54, 55
DiClemente, C., 53, 211

Diehl, M., 429
Dienesch, R., 96
Dies, R., 104
Diller, J., 128, 132, 138
Dillon, W., 352
Dinges, N., 142
Dinkmeyer, D., 258
Dion, K., 76
Dluhy, M., 42, 53
Dobson, K., 280
Dockray-Miller, M., 53
Dodge, K., 139
Doeing, C., 363
Dolgoff, R., 8, 9
Douglas, T., 56
Drum, D., 201
Drummond, L., 282
Drummond, M., 419
Drysdale, J., 372
Dubrovsky, V., 176
Duncan, S., 59
Duncan, T., 481
Dunnette, M., 348
Dustin, R., 481
Dutton, D., 260
D'Zurilla, T., 227, 284, 333, 334, 347

Early, B., 63
Earley, P., 143
Ebbesen, E., 327
Edelwich, J., 124, 208, 209, 274
Edleson, J., 51, 60, 260, 482
Edmonds, M., 26, 118, 191, 393
Edmund S. Muskie Institute
    of Public Affairs, 471
Edmunds, H., 351, 352
Edwards, M., 113
Edwards, W., 358, 360, 361
Egan, G., 106, 116, 208
Ehly, S., 481
Eisenhart, C., 419
Elias, A., 62
Elliott, H., 64
Ellis, A., 51, 61, 282, 391
Emmons, M., 391
Empey, L., 62
Emrick, C., 113
Ephross, P., 53, 313, 324
Erikson, M., 62
Erlich, J., 341
Eshelman, E., 284, 285, 287
Etcheverry, R., 115, 291, 293
Etzioni, A., 94, 348
Evans, C., 76
Everly, G., 428
Ewalt, P., 113

Fair, C., 178
Falck, H., 3, 51
Fall, K., 260
Fallon, A., 9, 394
Farrell, M., 29
Fatout, M., 33, 34, 53, 313
Feil, N., 471
Feldman, R., 60, 302, 305, 306, 401
Feldstein, M., 55
Fenzel, L., 139
Fern, E., 352
Ferrara, M., 481
Fest, T., 335
Festinger, L., 74
Field, J., 29
Fieldsteel, N., 381
Finn, J., 181
Finnigan, J., 361
Firtle, N., 352
Fish, F., 373
Fisch, R., 284
Fischer, U., 143
Fisher, J., 217, 224, 229, 415,
    422, 483
Fisher, P., 483
Fisher, R., 324
Fitzpatrick, D., 284
Flatten, K., 483
Fleming, J., 281, 282
Flippen, A., 327
Flores, M., 140
Foa, E., 280
Fobair, P., 473
Folkman, S., 428, 429
Follet, M., 47
Fondas, N., 33
Ford, B., 145
Ford, J., 260
Forester, J., 329
Foreyt, J., 482
Forse, M., 296
Forsyth, D., 19, 55, 56, 74, 76, 92, 95,
    130, 139, 141, 165, 202, 234, 318,
    321, 322, 323, 326, 327, 401
Fortune, A., 113, 380, 381, 393,
    394, 413
Foster, P., 483
Frances, A., 259
Frank, J., 193
Frankel, R., 483
Fraser-Krauss, H., 70
Freeman, A., 53, 200, 280, 281, 282
Freeman, H., 405, 419
French, J., 94
Freud, S., 58, 59, 327
Friedman, G., 287

Fry, P., 483
Fuhriman, A., 193, 229, 235, 238,
    401, 409
Furman, R., 118, 191

Galinsky, M., 11, 64, 86, 87, 88, 123,
    125, 128, 130, 134, 135, 169, 177,
    178, 180, 231
Gallogly, V., 198
Gambrill, E., 8
Gant, L., 401
Garant, J., 382
Garland, J., 87, 88, 139, 187, 232
Garrod, S., 70
Garvin, C., 49, 55, 96, 167, 242, 267
Garwick, C., 418
Gazda, G., 238
Gebhardt, L., 72
Gentry, M., 42
Gerhaw, N., 481
Germain, C., 58, 99, 393
Gershenfeld, M., 19, 67, 74, 80, 314,
    323, 328, 347, 349
Getzel, G., 131
Gibb, C., 102
Gibbs, L., 8
Gibson, A., 75
Gilchrist, L., 145, 228
Gill, S., 353
Gillespie, D., 418
Gilroy, F., 139
Giordano, J., 8
Gipson, V., 472
Gitterman, A., 51, 58, 99, 198, 393
Glasser, P., 5, 392
Glassop, L., 362
Glassman, U., 12, 51, 198, 260
Gleason, A., 176
Glenn, W., 38
Glisson, C., 419
Glueckauf, R., 180, 181
Gobert, B., 352
Goebel, S., 381, 418, 429
Gold, M., 419
Goldfried, M., 227, 284, 333, 334, 347
Goldman, M., 348
Goldstein, A., 211, 213, 481, 482
Goldstein, H., 104, 119
Goldstein, M., 471
Goldstein, S., 363
Gondolf, E., 260
Goodman, L., 483
Goodman, P., 243
Goodman, R., 42
Goodstein, L., 191, 482
Good Tracks, J., 221

Goodwin, D., 483
Gordon, C., 136, 141
Gordon, T., 258
Gordon, W., 349
Gorsuch, R., 228
Goto, S., 143
Goulding, M., 471
Gouran, D., 335
Grady, J., 363
Graen, G., 96, 141
Craighead, W., 482
Granrose, C., 136, 141
Grant, L., 348
Gray, B., 9
Gray, G., 364
Gray-Little, B., 69, 139, 141
Grayson, E., 60
Green, A., 176
Green, J., 128, 129, 132
Greenbaum, T., 416
Greenwald, H., 202
Griswold, W., 352
Gruen, G., 483
Gruenfeld, D., 34, 134
Guetzkow, H., 323
Guido, M., 136
Gulley, H., 319
Gully, S., 76, 366, 369
Gumaer, J., 481
Gummer, B., 18, 29, 33, 53, 329, 330,
    361, 363
Gustafson, D., 353, 354, 355, 356
Gutierrez, L., 144, 145
Gyr, J., 323

Haas, L., 180
Hacker, L., 23, 28, 201, 390, 395
Hackett, E., 363
Hackman, J., 29, 243
Halpin, A., 95
Halstead, L., 29
Hamilton, J., 140, 146
Hammond, L., 348
Han, A., 128, 131, 145
Han, C., 131
Hanson, B., 260
Hare, A., 19, 48, 54, 55, 71,
    99, 321, 326
Harlow, K., 177
Harmon, J., 361
Harnack, R., 335
Harrison, M., 373
Hartford, M., 5, 71, 87, 155, 169,
    187, 383
Harvey, O., 55
Hasenfeld, Y., 243

Haughey, J., 79
Havasy, S., 483
Hawkins, R., 229
Haynes, R., 471
Hazel, J., 481
Hazlett-Stevens, H., 287
Heap, K., 96
Heimberg, R., 280
Heinemann, G., 29, 230
Helgeson, E., 483
Hemphill, J., 241, 422
Hennessey, M., 483
Henry, S., 87, 253, 255, 392
Hersen, M., 217, 229
Hersey, R., 102
Herzog, J., 124
Hill, P., 105, 217, 241
Hill, W., 217, 241, 409, 422
Ho, M., 8, 227
Ho, S., 8, 227, 361
Hoag, M., 18
Hogan-Garcia, M., 133
Holland, T., 39, 330
Hollis, F., 222
Hollon, S., 285, 386
Holloway, A., 309, 391
Homans, G., 58, 62
Honts, C., 419
Hopkins, K., 421
Hopps, J., 84, 141, 144, 146, 165, 198
Horne, A., 56
Hornung, C., 235, 422
Houten, L., 483
Howard, M., 400
Howard, S., 260
Howe, F., 39
Huber, G., 319, 321, 358, 361
Huffine, C., 397
Hughes, S., 39, 330
Hula, K., 42
Hull, G., 217
Hurley, O., 483

Icard, L., 131
Ingersoll, B., 483
Insight Media, 471
Institute for Mental Health
    Initiatives, 471
International University College, 471
Ivanoff, A., 35

Jackson, S., 131
Jacobs, G., 229
Jacobs, R., 483
Jacobsen, B., 35
Jacobsen, M., 35

Jacobson, E., 429
Janis, I., 76, 170, 327, 472
Janoff, S., 472
Janssen, P., 59
Jenkins, M., 93
Jennings, H., 55, 238
Jenson, J., 400
Jessup, L., 357, 360
Jette, A., 68
Jehn, K., 323
Joastad, K., 348
Johnson, D., 137
Johnson, J., 347
Johnson, L., 217
Johnson, S., 106
Joiner, B., 33
Jones, A., 481
Jones, H., 87, 88, 139, 187
Jones, L., 135, 136, 137, 145, 245
Joyce, A., 18, 51, 60
Joyce, C., 360
Jung, D., 97

Kabat, D., 381, 386
Kadis, P., 471
Kadushin, A., 68
Kadushin, G., 68
Kaduson, H., 52
Kahai, S., 361
Kahn, S., 370
Kamin, J., 483
Kane, P., 229
Kane, R., 33, 229, 408
Kaplan, D., 69, 139, 141
Karakowsky, L., 93, 94
Karras, B., 483
Kaslyn, M., 180
Kates, L., 12, 51, 198, 260
Katten, S., 327, 472
Katz, A., 23
Katzenbach, J., 243
Kaufman, G., 481
Kaul, T., 64, 93, 94, 170, 382
Kazmierczak, T., 163
Keith, R., 29
Kelleher, K., 177
Keller, T., 63
Kelley, H., 62, 75, 77, 326
Kellner, M., 53
Kemp, K., 381, 386
Kendall, P., 350
Kent, M., 19, 321
Kephart, M., 73
Ketterhagen, A., 419
Ketterson, T., 180, 181
Keyton, J., 380

Kiesler, S., 55, 66, 170, 176, 321
Killeen, M., 140
Killeffer, E., 483
Kim, B., 146
King, K., 483
Kinlaw, C., 362
Kinnear, T., 351, 352
Kircher, J., 419
Kiresuk, T., 417
Kirk, S., 220, 413
Kirst-Ashman, K., 217
Kivlighan, D., 11, 97
Klaassen, D., 473
Kleiber, P., 352
Klein, A., 5, 12, 14, 18, 19, 49, 87, 88, 164, 165, 167, 171, 395
Klein, M., 13
Klein, P., 481
Klein, R., 59
Klein, R. J., 481
Kleindorfer, P., 360
Klerman, G., 329
Kline, W., 125
Klosko, J., 280, 281
Knott, J., 200
Knottnerus, J., 63
Knox, G., 327
Kobernick, A., 472
Kobos, J., 180
Koenig, G., 235, 422
Kolb, J., 93
Kolodny, R., 87, 88, 123, 139, 187, 232
Komnenich, P., 140
Koney, K., 42
Konig, K., 59
Konopka, G., 7, 18, 25, 47, 473
Kopp, J., 223
Koss-Chioino, J., 143
Kottler, J., 113, 220, 273, 274, 275, 286
Kramer, J., 229, 422
Kramer, M., 347, 356, 357
Krebs, A., 230
Kristein, M., 420
Krueger, R., 352, 416
Kukkonen, R., 416
Kunar, V., 350
Kunreuther, H., 360
Kuo, C., 347, 356
Kurtz, L., 23, 28
Kutchins, H., 220
Kutz, J., 113

Labrecque, M., 381, 386, 418
Lage, E., 82
Lakey, B., 39, 330

Lakin, M., 11
Lang, N., 52
Langelier, C., 53
Larrabee, J., 180
Lasky, G., 9
Lassen, C., 113
Lauzon, W., 472
Lavitt, M., 181
Lawler, E., 362, 363
Lawson, H., 373
Lazarus, L., 483
Lazarus, R., 287, 428, 429
Lazell, E., 46
Lea, M., 176
Leahy, R., 61, 282, 284
LeBon, G., 54, 327
LeCompte, M., 416
LeCroy, C., 12, 51
Lederman, L., 352
Lee, J., 49, 388
Lese, K., 422, 423
Lesser, J., 483
Leszcz, M., 59
Lev, R., 481
Levenson, J., 423
Levi, D., 29, 33, 34, 56, 83, 131, 360
Levin, H., 420
Levine, B., 123, 198, 231, 394
Levine, J., 6
Levinson, D., 329
Levinson, H., 394
Levitt, J., 228
Lewin, K., 54, 55, 61, 80, 95, 326
Lewis, C., 422, 423
Lewis, E., 145
Lewis, H., 11, 227
Lewis, M., 483
Lewis, R., 8
Licht, L., 347
Liden, R., 96
Lieberman, M., 17, 64, 260, 266, 301, 422
Lifton, W., 472
Lighthouse International, 68, 69
Likert, R., 164
Linehan, M., 472
Lippert, L., 163
Lippitt, R., 55, 61, 62, 95
Lipsey, M., 405, 419
Lobel, S., 130, 134
Loewenberg, F., 8
Lohr, N., 123, 124
Lonergan, E., 119
Long, K., 383
Longres, J., 131

Loomis, J., 180, 181
Lopez, J., 145
Lowe, S., 134
Lowman, F., 483
Ludgate, J., 301
Lum, D., 128, 129, 135, 136, 146
Lushene, R., 228

Macgowan, M., 49, 423
MacKenzie, K., 12, 51, 60, 257, 260, 382
MacLennon, B., 123
MacNair-Semands, R., 422, 423
Madara, E., 28, 259
Madden, T., 352
Magen, R., 51, 419
Magnan, M., 76
Maguire, L., 13
Maheu, M., 180
Mahoney, M., 223, 224, 282, 283
Maier, N., 314, 319, 367, 368, 369
Malekoff, A., 232, 394, 472
Malone, C., 180
Maloney, S., 46
Maltzman, I., 347
Mandell, G., 482
Manderscheid, R., 235, 422
Mann, L., 170
Mannix, D., 482
Manske, M., 346
Manz, C., 29
Maple, F., 166, 167
Marks, M., 363
Marlatt, G., 386
Marsh, E., 229
Marsh, L., 46
Marshall, C., 416
Marsiglia, F., 129
Martindale-Adams, J., 180
Mason, E., 472
Mason, S., 384
Masters, J., 285, 286, 386
Matsukawa, L., 84
Mattessich, P., 373
Maurer, G., 53
Mayadas, N., 392
Mayer, J., 42, 113, 335
Maznevski, M., 143
McBey, K., 93, 94
McBride, L., 200, 205, 257, 259, 283
McCabe, R., 52, 200, 257, 259, 280
McCallion, P., 361, 363, 373, 418, 429
McCarthy, C., 181
McCaskill, J., 46
McClane, W., 96
McClendon, M., 181

McCorkle, L., 62
McDougall, W., 54
McElherne, L. M., 482
McEwan, P., 420
McFarlane, W., 53
McGee, T., 123
McGinnis, E., 482
McGrath, J., 55
McGrath, P., 133
McGuire, T., 176
McHale, S., 482
McKay, G., 258, 259
McKay, M., 200, 259, 284, 286, 287
McKenna, K., 176
McLeod, P., 130, 134
McMorde, W., 483
McRoberts, C., 18
McRoy, R., 129
Meadow, H., 136, 141
Mederos, F., 260
Meeker, B., 235, 422
Meichenbaum, D., 270, 282, 284, 390, 428, 429
Merenda, D., 42
Merritt, D., 130
Merry, J., 76, 200
Merton, R., 340
Meyers, R., 72
Middleman, R., 26, 49, 52, 106, 107, 108, 112, 114, 191, 255, 482
Milbrun, J., 481
Miles, M., 64, 260, 301, 422
Milgram, D., 273, 274
Milgram, S., 82
Miller, N., 76, 335, 345, 369
Miller, S., 258
Miller, W., 212, 213
Mills, T., 56
Milter, R., 340
Minahan, A., 36
Miramontez, A., 145, 228
Mirvis, P., 363
Mistry, T., 128, 134, 145
Mitchell-Enos, V., 129
Mizrahi, T., 42
Mobley, J., 238
Mohrman, S., 362, 363
Mondros, J., 41, 49
Monsey, B., 373
Moore, C., 368
Moore, R., 9
Moos, R., 423
Moreno, C., 136
Moreno, J., 55, 59, 237, 294, 424
Morgan, D., 350, 351, 352, 416
Morganett, R., 482

Moscovici, S., 82
Mossholder, K., 76
Mukherjee, A., 361
Mullen, B., 76, 167
Mullen, E., 246
Mullender, A., 49
Munzer, J., 202
Murphy, M., 257
Murray-Close, M., 373
Myers, D., 327

Naccarato, T., 56, 180
Nadler, D., 70, 331
Naffrechoux, M., 82
Nakanishi, M., 143, 178
Napier, H., 326
Napier, R., 19, 67, 74, 80, 314, 322, 328, 347, 349
Nas, T., 420
Nastasi, B., 416
Natemeyer, W., 102
Nelson, V., 123, 472
Newcomb, T., 55, 82
Newman, F., 423
Newstetter, W., 42, 55
Nichols, L., 180
Nickelson, D., 180
Nixon, H., 55, 81, 95
Nolan, L., 323
Norcross, J., 211
Norem-Hebeisen, A., 482
Northen, H., 52, 64, 65, 86, 87, 194, 380, 473
Nosko, A., 49, 124
Nunnally, E., 258
Nunnally, J., 421
Nye, J., 139
Nystul, M., 134
Nystrom, N., 131

Ochoa, E., 9
Oei, T., 163
Ogrodniczuk, J., 59
Ollendick, T., 229
Olmsted, M., 83
Olsen, M., 56
Omizo, M., 146
Orasanu, J., 143
Oravec, J., 177
Orme, J., 224, 415
Ortega, R., 144, 145
Osborn, A., 344, 345, 346, 347
Osgood, C., 235
Osgood, N., 483
Oskamp, S., 136, 141
Overall, B., 113

Packard, T., 229, 235, 238, 409
Padgett, D., 416
Paleg, K., 200, 259
Palmer-Ganeles, J., 33
Papell, C., 49, 50, 51, 52, 200
Parrillo, V., 130
Parnes, S., 346
Parsons, R., 49
Parsons, T., 56
Pasick, R., 472
Passi, L., 200, 257
Patton, B., 324
Patton, M., 416
Paulson, L., 482
Paulus, P., 327
Payne, L., 482
Payne, M., 56, 287
Peak, T., 18, 105, 217, 241, 381, 386
Pearlingi, B., 380, 393, 394
Pearson, V., 145, 190
Peltz, L., 51, 259
Pennell, J., 49
Pendelton, L., 383
Pepitone, A., 76
Perl, F., 59
Perlman, H., 257
Pernell, R., 49
Perry, S., 259
Pescosolido, A., 75
Peters, A., 131
Peterson, M., 143
Pfeiffer, J., 191, 482
Phillips, H., 473
Phillips, J., 367
Phillips, L., 140
Pickett, T., 180, 181
Piggins, C., 484
Pillari, V., 130
Pincus, A., 36
Pinderhughes, E., 84, 128, 141, 144, 146, 165, 198
Piper, W., 18, 51, 59, 60, 93, 102, 381, 382, 472
Pope, A., 482
Postmes, T., 176
Powell, T., 23, 259
Prapavessis, H., 76
Pratkanis, A., 327
Pretzer, J., 281, 282
Prigmore, C., 42
Prince, G., 349
Prochaska, J., 211
Proctor, E., 128, 400
Pruitt, D., 327
Public Broadcasting Video, 472
Pudney, W., 482

Purcell, R., 372
Purdy, J., 140
Purdon, S., 9
Putnam, R., 3, 48
Pyle, J., 363

Raab, M., 347
Ramey, J., 401
Ramos, B., 135, 136, 137, 145, 245
Randel, A., 143
Raskin, D., 347
Rathjen, D., 482
Rathus, J., 280
Rauch, J., 229
Raven, B., 94
Ray, K., 42
Reagan-Cirinicione, P., 360
Reamer, F., 9
Reardon, K., 11, 64
Reder, P., 238
Redl, F., 47, 59
Reichling, G., 76
Reid, K., 51, 52
Reid, W., 113, 119, 228, 267,
    275, 413
Reilly, R., 60, 200, 381
Reinecke, M., 280
Research Press, 472
Reyes-Watson, E., 483
Rhode, R., 70
Rice, C., 59
Richards, T., 348
Richmond, M., 47
Ricker, M., 134
Riess, H., 53
Riessman, E., 28
Rimm, D., 285, 386
Rittenhouse, J., 145
Rittner, B., 143
Riva, M., 9, 163
Rivas, R., 53, 99, 119, 340, 347,
    356, 361
Rivers, R., 129
Roback, H., 9, 319
Robert, H., 364, 366
Roberts, A., 400
Roberts, R., 52
Robinson, J., 229
Robson, M., 361
Rochelle, C., 380, 393, 394
Roffman, R., 53
Roethlisberger, F., 54, 55
Rohrbaugh, J., 340, 357, 360, 361
Rohde, R., 79
Rohling, C., 482
Rokeach, M., 6

Roller B., 123, 472
Rollnick, S., 212, 213
Rooney, R., 158, 212, 213, 273, 275
Rose, S., 5, 11, 12, 33, 34, 35, 49, 51,
    53, 60, 64, 97, 119, 200, 224, 257,
    259, 260, 267, 268, 280, 287, 288,
    299, 302, 313, 387, 390, 409, 411,
    412, 424, 472, 482
Rosen, A., 400
Rosenthal, B., 42
Rosenthal, H., 352
Rosenthal, R., 56
Rossi, P., 405, 419
Rossiter, C., 18, 105, 217, 241, 429
Rossman, G., 416
Rosswurm, M., 180
Rothman, B., 49, 50, 51, 52, 178, 200
Rothman, J., 341, 405, 413
Round Table Films, 472
Rounds, K., 178
Rozensky, R., 180, 181
Rubin, H., 246, 371, 372, 373
Rubin, I., 246, 371, 372, 373
Rubin, J., 273, 274
Rusinak, R., 140
Russell, L., 419
Rutan, J., 59, 282
Ryan, D., 373
Ryland, G., 155, 406

Sakhel, K., 176
Salazar, A., 80
Sanchez-Ayende, M., 140
Sandberg, C., 472
Sanderson, W., 280, 281
Santhiveeran, J., 180
Sarri, R., 5, 86, 87
Saunders, D., 260
Sax, G., 421
Schachter, S., 75
Schaefer, C., 52
Scheidel, T., 165, 167, 314, 319,
    339, 345, 346, 355
Scheidlinger, S., 472
Scheneul, J., 416
Schiemann, W., 96
Schilder, P., 46
Schiller, L., 87, 89, 139
Schlenger, G., 483
Schlenoff, M., 123
Schlesinger, E., 128, 135
Schmele, J., 361
Schmidt, W., 361
Schmitt, M., 29
Schoemaker, P., 360
Scholtes, P., 33

Schopler, J., 11, 42, 64, 87, 88, 123,
    125, 128, 130, 134, 135, 169, 179,
    180, 231
Schreiber, B., 257
Schriver, J., 143
Schroeder, R., 29
Schulberg, C., 483
Schumaker, J., 481
Schuman, B., 123
Schuman, S., 357
Schwartz, W., 47, 51, 207
Seaberg, J., 418
Seashore, S., 76, 231, 239
Seely, H., 362
Segal, Z., 280
Seligman, L., 259, 310
Selltiz, C., 238
Sexton, T., 134
Shapiro, B., 113
Shapiro, J., 51, 200, 259
Shaver, P., 229, 422
Shaw, C., 54
Shaw, M., 55, 70, 87
Sheats, P., 231
Sheldon, B., 61, 282, 284, 298
Sheldon, J., 481
Shelton, M., 9
Shepard, C., 57, 61, 62
Sherif, C., 55
Sherif, M., 54, 55, 82
Sherman, E., 201, 260, 483
Sherman, J., 481
Sherman, R., 417
Shils, E., 55, 56
Shimanoff, S., 93
Shipley, R., 285
Shoemaker, W., 257
Shulman, L., 12, 51, 99, 105, 114, 158,
    190, 198, 210, 231, 232, 258, 270,
    302, 384, 472
Siegel, J., 176, 419
Silbergeld, S., 235, 422
Silver, W., 75
Silverman, A., 483
Silverman, M., 401
Simeone, P., 60, 200, 381
Simon, S., 347
Simons, K., 281, 282
Simons, L., 482
Sims, H., 29
Singer, D., 59
Sinha, K., 29
Siporin, M., 7, 18, 58, 99, 115,
    216, 291
Skolnik, L., 9
Slavson, S., 27, 46, 47

Sluyter, G., 361
Smith, A., 27, 46
Smith, D., 243
Smith, G., 18, 349
Smith, H., 363
Smith, K., 323
Smith, M., 8, 113, 418, 482
Smith, P., 87
Smith, T., 176
Smokowski, P., 11, 64, 97, 177
Smucker, M., 280, 281, 282, 283, 284
Snead, R., 472
Soldz, S., 76, 200
Sommers, M., 473
Sonkin, D., 260
Sosik, J., 97, 361
Soweid, R., 42
Spears, R., 176
Spencer, E., 178
Spiegel, D., 473
Spielberg, G., 116
Spielberger, C., 228
Spink, K., 76, 167
Spitz, H., 51
Spitz, S., 51
Sprakin, R., 481
Staecker, K., 260
Staples, L., 40
Starak, Y., 123
Starzecpyzl, R., 473
Stattler, W., 335, 345, 369
Steckler, N., 33
Steel, R., 76
Stein, L., 178
Steinberg, D., 23
Stern, R., 282
Stevens, L., 178
Stewart, G., 29
Stockton, R., 70, 79
Stoddart, G., 419
Stogdill, R., 113
Stone, M., 422, 423
Stone, W., 59, 282
Stoner, J., 327
Stouffer, S., 55
Streibel, B., 33
Strube, M., 134
Stuart, R., 223, 246, 391
Stuecker, R., 482
Suchan, C., 484
Suci, C., 235
Sue, D., 69, 128
Sue, D.W., 69, 128
Sue, S., 134
Sundel, M., 5
Susskind, L., 321, 328

Sween, J., 362
Swenson, J., 352
Syers, M., 51
Syz, H., 46

Tachiki, D., 362
Tackett, M., 163
Tannenbaum, P., 235
Tarrant, J., 11, 97
Taylor, B., 39, 330
Taylor, D., 347, 348
Taylor, J., 351, 352
Taylor, N., 51
Taylor, R., 54
Teasdale, J., 280
Teger, A., 327
Teolis, B., 482
Terdal, L., 229
Thase, M., 280, 301
Thelen, H., 167
Thibaut, J., 62, 75, 77, 326
Thomas, E., 400, 412, 413
Thoresen, C., 223, 224
Thorndike, R., 99, 100
Thrasher, F., 54
Thurman, T., 484
Timms, N., 113
Tobin, S., 113
Todar, K., 11, 64
Tolman, R., 260
Tolson, E., 267
Torrance, G., 419
Torres de Ardon, E., 140
Toseland, R., 18, 23, 28, 33, 35, 53,
    56, 75, 97, 99, 105, 113, 115, 116,
    119, 135, 136, 137, 145, 160, 161,
    174, 176, 180, 201, 217, 228, 230,
    241, 245, 260, 291, 303, 313, 340,
    347, 356, 361, 381, 386, 390, 395,
    405, 418, 429, 484
Train, A., 346
Trecker, H., 47, 87
Triplett, N., 54
Tropman, J., 19, 39, 53, 313, 315, 317,
    335, 341, 380
Tropp, E., 49
Trotter, C., 210, 211, 274
Trotzer, J., 400
Tuckman, B., 87
Tumblin, A., 413
Turner, M., 327

Ury, W., 324

Vagg, P., 229
Vahsen, J., 230

Vaillant, G., 386
Valacich, J., 357, 360
Van de Ven, A., 353, 354, 355, 356
Van den Pol, R., 482
Vasquez, M., 128, 131, 145
Vassil, T., 53, 63, 313, 325
Velasquez, M., 53
Verhofstadt-Deneve, L., 293
Vinokur-Kaplan, D., 318, 330
Vinter, R., 5, 49, 255
Vorrath, H., 62, 258
Vroom, V., 348

Wackman, D., 258
Wakefield, J., 51
Waldo, C., 39
Waldo, M., 134
Walker, E., 53
Wall, V., 323
Wallace, R., 124
Wallach, M., 327
Walls, R., 229
Walters, K., 131
Walton, M., 361
Ward, D., 49, 377
Wasserman, H., 51
Waterman, J., 53
Watson, S., 340
Watson, W., 130
Watts, R., 372
Watzlawick, P., 284
Wayne, J., 392
Weakland, J., 284
Weber, A., 287
Weaver, H., 129
Wech, B., 76
Weinberg, H., 177
Weinstein, M., 420
Weisner, S., 42
Weissman, A., 397
Weissman, H., 48
Wells, H., 482
Wells, R., 60, 267
Welo, B., 212, 213
Wender, L., 46
Werner, T., 229
Wheelan, S., 87, 401
Whiston, S., 134
White, B., 28, 259
White, J., 53, 55, 200
White, R., 55, 61
Whitehouse, E., 482
Whitney, D., 76
Whitney, M., 381, 418, 429
Whitten, P., 180
Whitton, J., 180

Whyte, W., 54
Widmeyer, W., 76
Wiener, L., 178
Wilcox, J., 352
Wilhite, B., 483
Williams, J., 76
Williams, M., 280
Williams, O., 133
Williamson, S., 57, 239, 241, 409, 423
Willis, S., 483
Wilson, G., 14, 27, 155, 406, 473
Wilson, M., 484
Wilson, S., 41, 49, 406
Winer, M., 42
Wing, C., 327
Winter, B., 383
Winterfeldt, D., 360

Wittman, H., 323
Wodarski, J., 60, 302, 305, 306
Wohl, R., 129
Wolcott, A., 484
Wolf, T., 38, 39, 330
Wolosin, R., 327
Wolosin, W., 327
Wood, G., 52, 107, 108, 112
Woods, M., 222
Worchell, S., 86
Wray, L., 56, 180
Wright, J., 280, 301
Wright, M., 125
Wrightsman, L., 238
Wyss, D., 59

Yalom, I., 18, 59, 64, 72, 76, 106, 123, 124, 159, 165, 167, 168, 169, 171,

189, 198, 242, 260, 301, 382, 422, 423, 473
Yan, M., 47
Yeager, K., 400
Yee, R., 287
Yost, E., 282, 283, 285, 299, 300
Young, K., 134
Yukl, G., 92

Zajonc, R., 327
Zander, A., 55, 62
Zane, N., 134
Zane, T., 229
Zeiss, A., 230
Zerfoss, L., 367
Zgola, T., 484
Zhang, J., 180
Ziller, R., 327

Subject Index

Action skills, 111–118
Actual power, 94
Adult Leadership, 53
Advice, 113–114
Advocacy, 40–48, 144, 272
Agency context. *See also* Environment
    of group
    assessment, 244
    and evaluation, 402
    and group culture, 83–85
    and leadership, 101
    and opening statement, 193
    and potential membership
      assessment, 160–162
    sponsorship assessment, 155–157
    and values, 6
Agendas. *See also* Procedures
    beginning stage, 201–202
    board of directors, 38–39
    committees, 36–37
    task group, 327
    treatment groups, 258–259
Alcoholics Anonymous (AA),
    168–169
Alliances. *See* Coalitions
American Group Psychotherapy
    Association (AGPA), 9
Analyzing skills, 111
Announcements, 474–475
Arbitration, 116–118
Assessment, 216–250
    definition of, 216–217
    environment of group, 241–246
    group as a whole, 229–241
    group members, 221–229
    group vs. individual, 217–218
    and intervention, 246–248
    leadership skills, 119–123
    potential membership, 157–160
    process of, 216–221
    sponsorship, 155–157, 242–244
    standardized instruments,
      228–229
Association for Specialists in Group
    Work (ASGW), 9
Association for the Advancement of
    Social Work with Groups
    (AASWG), 11, 48

Attending skills, 106
Attributed power, 93
Autodrama, 295–296

Bales' Interaction Process Analysis,
    423–424
Bargaining, 374
Beck Depression Inventory
    (BDI), 228
Beginning stage,187–215. *See also*
    Assessment
    confidentiality discussion,
      195–197
    contracting, 205–206
    goal setting, 203–205
    introductions, 189–193
    member motivation, 207–211
    obstacles, anticipating, 213–214
    purpose definition, 193–195
    structure, 201–202
    task vs. socioemotional focus,
      202–203
Beliefs About Structure Scale
    (BASS), 121
Board of directors, 38–39
Bonding, 14
    emotional, 71
    treatment vs. task group, 15
Bootstrapping, 371
Boundary clarification, 333–334
Brainstorming, 344–349
    effectiveness, 347–348
    procedures, 345–346
    uses, 346–347
    variations, 348–349
Broker role, 272
Buddy systems, 267
Buzz groups. *See* Phillips' 66

Cabinets, 37–38
Capacity–building strategies,
    372–373
Case examples, 427–451
Case study evaluation methods,
    416–417
Casework, 47
Chairing, 293–294
Charting, 223–224

Choreography, 294
Clarifying content, 108
Classical conditioning, 60
Coaching, 115–116
Coalitions, 41–42
Coding systems, 409
Cognitive–behavioral approaches,
    59–61
Cognitive imagery techniques,
    285–286
Cognitive restructuring, 283–284
Cognitive self–instruction, 284
Cohesion. *See* Group cohesion
Coleadership, 123–126
Collaboration, 374
Committees, 36–37
Communication, 65–74. *See also*
    Self–disclosure
Community environment,
    assessment, 244–246
    and group culture, 83–86
    interventions, 310
    resources in, 396–397
    and values, 83
Computer groups, 180–181
Confidentiality, 195–197
Conflict resolution, 116–118, 323–326
Confrontation, 116
Consulting pairs, 267
Contingency management, 298–300
Contracting, 171–173, 270–271
    beginning stage, 205–206
    and evaluation, 412
    planning stage, 171–173
Council on Social Work Education, 48
Countertransference, 119
Cues, 71, 281–282
Cultural diversity. *See* Diversity
Cultural sensitivity, 129–133
    practice principles, 146–148
Culture. *See* Group culture
Curative factors scale (YALOM), 423

Data collection, 218–219, 338–339
    and evaluation, 402–403
    focus groups, 349–352
    leadership skills, 109–111
    and problem solving, 338–339

Decision making, 326–328
Delegate councils, 43
Democratic values, 6
Describing skills, 109
Developmental evaluation, 412–413
Developmental research. *See*
     Developmental evaluation
Diagnosis. *See* Assessment
Diagnostic and Statistical Manual of
     Mental Disorders, 219, 405–406
Diagnostic labels, 219–220
Diaries, 224
Directing, 113
Discrimination, 133–144
Diversity, 128–148
     and assessment, 133–139
     and communication, 142–143
     and cultural sensitivity, 129–133
     and group composition, 133–134
     and interventions, 139–146
     and leadership, 128–129
     and member recruitment, 165–166
     and values, 8
"Door knob" communications, 258,
     384
Doubling, 295
Dynamic equilibrium, 57

Educational groups, 23–24
Emotional bonds, 71
Empowerment strategies, 144,
     261–262
Enabler role, 272
Ending stage, 379–399
     change maintenance/generalization,
          386–392
     feelings about, 393–395
     future planning, 395–396
     and group cohesion, 392–393
     meetings, 383–385
     referrals, 396–397
     termination types, 380–385
Environmental interventions, 295,
     307–310
Environment of group
     assessment, 241–242
     financial support, 175
     and group culture, 84–85
     interventions, 300–301
     planning, 173
ERIC, 404
Ethics, 9–11, 453–470
Ethnic competence, 139–146. *See also*
     Diversity
Evaluation, 400–426. *See also*
     Monitoring

case study methods, 416–417
developmental, 412–413
effectiveness/efficiency, 417–420
measures, 420–424
and monitoring, 405–412
and planning, 403–405
reasons for, 401
single system methods, 413–415
Excursion, 349
Expressive skills, 106–107

Feedback, 17
     and communication, 66–67
     and problem solving, 332–333
Field theory, 61–62
First Annual Symposium for the
     Advancement of Group Work, 48
Flooding, 285
Focus groups, 349–352
     effectiveness, 361
     procedures, 352
     uses, 351–352
Focusing, 107
Follow–up sessions, 389–390
Force field analysis, 208–209
Formed groups, 13
Free–floating interaction, 70
Freewheeling, 345
Freudian theory. *See* Psychoanalytic
     theory

Gender, 131, 134, 145–146, 165
Getting to Yes, 324
Goal attainment scaling, 417–418
Goals, 263–269. *See also* Contracting
     awareness of, 263–265
     beginning stage, 203–205
     problem solving, 337
Governance groups, 26–27
Group, The, 53
Group as a whole,
     assessment, 235–241
     ending, 385
     interventions, 301–307
     and leadership, 101–102
     planning, 163–170
Group Atmosphere Scale, 412
Group cohesion, 62, 74–77
     assessment, 237–238
     beginning stage, 197
     and cultural diversity, 136–139
     ending stage, 77, 392–393
     evaluation, 423–424
     interventions, 296–298
     principles for practice, 77
Group composition, 163–170

Group culture, 83–86
     assessment, 239–241
     and cultural diversity, 83–85
     interventions, 306–307
     principles for practice, 85–86
Group development, 86–90, 103.
     See also specific stages
     guidance of, 197–202
Group dynamics, 64–91, 103
     assessment, 229–241
     cohesion, 74–77
     communicative and interaction
          patterns, 65–74, 235–237
     group culture, 83–85
     historical development, 53–55
     influential theories, 55–63
     interventions, 307–315
     social integration, 78–83
     stages of group development,
          86–91
Group Environment Scale, 423
Group feeling, 393–395
Group member assessment, 221–229
     reports by others, 228
     self–observation, 222–225
     standardized instrument, 228–229
     worker observation, 225–228
Group members. *See* Individual
     interventions
     assessment of potential, 154–156,
          221–229
     goals, 203–205
     and leadership, 102–103
     prior relationships among, 191–192
     recruitment, 160–162
     reluctant, 207–211
     screening, 171
Group processes. *See* Group dynamics
Group Psychology and the Analysis of
     the Ego (Freud), 58
Group Therapy Interaction
     Chronogram, 238–239
Group think, 76, 170, 327
Groupwork Engagement Scale, 423
Group work
     definitions of, 11–13
     focus of, 4–6
     vs. individual work, 16–19
Growth groups, 24–25
Guided Group Interaction, 62

Habilation, 19
Harvard Community Health Plan
     Group Cohesiveness Scale, 239
Helper–therapy principle, 17, 266
Helping networks, 112–117

Hemphill's Index of Group
     Dimensions, 422
Heterogeneity of membership, 164
     and group cohesion, 197
     and planning, 164
Hill Interaction Matrix, 235, 422
Historical developments, 45–63
     casework, comparison with, 46–47
     social science research, 56
     theories, 56–63
     treatment groups, current trends,
          49–51
Hitchhiking, 345
Homogeneity of membership
     and planning, 163
Hot seat, 70
How Members Achieve Change Scale,
     122–123
Human Group, The (Homans), 58
Humanistic approach, 198

Identifying skills, 280–281
Implosion, 285–286
Individual interventions, 279–301
     environmental, 295–301
     interpersonal, 288–295
     intrapersonal, 279–288
Individual vs. group focus, 16–19
     assessment, 217–218
Information requesting, 109–110
Informed consent, 10
Instructions, 113–114
Interactional model, 98–104
Interaction patterns, 70–74
     assessment, 235–237
     and cultural diversity, 141–143
     and evaluation, 422–424
     interventions, 302–303
     and physical arrangements, 73
     principles for practice, 74
     and size, 73
     and structure, 258–261
     subgroups, 72
Interaction Process Analysis, 59, 413
Interest alliances, 71
Interorganizational environment, 244
Interpersonal interventions, 288–295
Interventions. *See also* Individual
     interventions; Treatment group
     foundation method
     and assessment, 246–247
     and coleadership, 123–126
     and communication patterns,
          302–303
     and diversity, 139–140
     environment of group, 307–310

group as a whole, 301–307
     levels of, 279
     and structure, 258–261
Intrapersonal interventions, 277–278
Introductions, 189–193
Involuntary clients, 211–214
Involving members, 194–195

Judeo–Christian values, 6

Language diversity, 141–143
Lateral thinking, 338–339
Leadership, 92–127. *See also*
     Interventions; Leadership skills;
     Worker roles
     coleadership, 123–126
     and diversity, 128–148
     and environment of group,
          101–102
     and group as a whole, 100–101
     and group leader, 103–104
     and group members, 102–103
     influences on, 96–97
     interactional model, 98–104
     and power, 93–95
     and problem type, 99–100
     and purpose, 99
     style, 119–123
     theories, 97–98
Leadership Comfort Scale (LCS),
     120–121
Leadership skills, 104–119
     action, 111–118
     data gathering and assessment,
          109–111
     group dynamics facilitation,
          105–109
     learning, 118–119
Learning theory, 59–61
Logs, 224

Mainstream model, 52
Majority rule, 328
Mandated clients. *See* Involuntary
     clients
Manual of Parliamentary Practice
     (Jefferson), 364
Maypole, 70
Mediator role, 272
Medical model, 25
MEDLINE, 404
Member expectations
     and leadership, 102–103
     and opening statement, 194–195
     and problem solving, 320–321
Member motivation. *See* Resistance

Middle stage. *See* Task group
     foundation methods; Treatment
     group foundation methods
Minority groups, 127–148
Mirror role playing, 295
Mobilization for Youth, 48
Mobilization strategies, 370–371
Modeling, 289–291
Monitoring, 405–412
Monodrama, 293–294
Multiattribute utility analysis,
     357–361
     effectiveness, 361
     procedures, 357–361
     uses, 360–361
     variations, 360–361
Multicultural, 128–148

National Association of Social
     Workers (NASW) code of
     ethics, 9
National Training Laboratory in Group
     Development, 48
Natural groups, 13
Naturalistic observation, 54–55,
     225–226
NCJRS, 404
Needs assessment, 404–405
Nominal group technique (NGT),
     353–357
     effectiveness, 356–357
     procedures, 351–352
     uses, 354–356
Norms, 79–80. *See also* Status

Observational learning, 289–291
Observational measures, 222–229,
     423–424
On–the–spot interview role playing,
     294
Open vs. closed groups, 86, 168–170
Operant conditioning, 60
Organizational context. *See* Agency
     context
Orientation, 170–171
"Own role" role playing, 293

Parent Effectiveness Training
     (PET), 258
Parliamentary procedure, 364–367
     effectiveness, 367
     procedures, 364–366
     uses, 366–367
Partializing skills, 110
Phillips' 66, 367–370
     effectiveness, 369–370

procedures, 368–369
uses, 369
Physical arrangements, 174–175
Planning, 134–135, 149–183
    contracting, 171–173
    environment, 173–175
    and evaluation, 403–405
    group composition, 163–170
    member orientation, 170–171
    member recruitment, 160–162
    models for, 152–153
    potential membership assessment,
        157–160
    and purpose, 153–154
    sponsorship assessment, 155–157
    virtual groups, 175–181
    written proposals, 181–182
Positive Peer Culture, 62
Power, 93–95
Pregroup training, 170–171
Prejudice, 143–144
Pretraining, 170–171
Primary group, 54
Probing skills, 109–110
Problem cards, 224
Problem solving, 331–341
    data collection, 338–339
    goal setting, 337
    group versus individual, 326–327
    identifying a problem, 332–337
    plan development, 339
    plan implementation, 340–341
    plan selection, 339–340
Problem type, 99–100
Procedures
    contracting, 173
Process recordings, 406
Professional ethics, 9–11
Program activities, 227–228, 255–277,
        481–484
    and assessment, 227–228
    beginning stage, 197
    culturally appropriate, 145–146
Program materials. *See* Program
        activities
Progressive muscle relaxation,
        287–288
Psychoanalytic theory, 58–59
Psychodrama, 278
Psychodynamic theory, 58–59
PSYCLIT, 404
Purpose, 13–14
    beginning stage, 193–194
    and leadership, 99
    and orientation, 170
    and planning, 153–154

Quality circles (QCs), 361–363
    effectiveness, 363
    procedures, 362
    uses, 362–363
Quality improvement teams. *See*
        Quality circles
Questioning, 109–110

Race. *See* Diversity
Rapid assessment instruments,
        228–229
Rational emotive therapy, 391–392
Reciprocal model, 51
Recreation groups, 27
Recruitment, 160–163
Redefining, 112
Referrals, 296, 396–397
Reframing, 112, 284–285
Rehabilitation, 19
Rehearsing, 115–116
Reinforcers, 71, 298
Relaxation, 287–288
Reliability, 421
Remedial model, 49
Resistance, 272–275. *See also*
        Involuntary clients
Resources, providing, 114
Responding, 107
Reverse brainstorming, 348
Risky shift, 327
Robert's Rules of Order (Robert),
        319–320, 363–366
Role playing, 115, 226–234, 291–295
Role reversal, 292
Roles, 80–81, 231–234
Round robin, 70, 190–191
Rules, 117, 196–197
Rules for Radicals (Alinsky), 374

Scanning, 106
Scapegoats, 72, 231–232
Sculpting, 294
Selective perception, 67
Self–anchored rating scale, 225
Self–disclosure
    beginning stage, 197–198
    dangers of, 18
    and diversity, 141
    and information development, 322
    treatment vs. task groups, 15
Self–help groups, 27–29
Self–instructional training. *See*
        Cognitive self-instruction
Self–monitoring, 222–225, 422–423
Self–report measures, 422–423
Semantic differential scale, 235–237

Service technology, 104
Setting. *See* Physical arrangements
Settlement houses, 45–46
Sharing, in role playing, 295
Simulation tests, 226
Single–system evaluation methods,
        413–416
Size of group, 73, 101, 166–168
    and interaction patterns, 73
    planning, 166–168
Social action groups, 40–41
    and community assessment,
        244–248
    methods for, 373–374
Social Darwinism, 6
Social Diagnosis (Richmond), 47
Social exchange theory, 62–63
Social goals model, 49
Social integration, 78–83. *See also*
        Norms; Power; Roles; Status
    assessment, 231–234
    interventions, 305–306
    principles for practice, 82–83
Socialization groups, 26–27
Social judgment analysis (SJA),
        360–361
Social learning theory, 59–61
Social mapping, 132
Social networks, 296–298
Social Process in Organized Groups
        (Coyle), 47
Social skills groups, 26–27
Social Work with Groups, 123
Socioeconomic status. *See* Diversity
Sociometry, 237–239
Soliloquy role playing, 294
Spirituality, 142–143
Staff development groups, 35–36
Stages of development. *See* Group
        development
Standardized instruments,
        228–229
Status, 73–74
    assessment, 231–232
    and cultural diversity, 137
    and interaction patterns, 81–82
    and norms, 78–79
Strait Trait Anxiety Inventory, 228
Strength perspective, 140–141
Structure, 201–202, 257–261
Subgroups, 71–73
Suggestions, 113–114
Summarizing skills, 110
Summary recording, 400
Support groups, 20, 23
Supporting skills, 111–112

SYMLOG (Systematic Multiple Level Observation of Groups), 57, 235, 235–239, 423–424
Synectics, 349
Synthesizing skills, 110–111
Systematic desensitization, 288
Systematic Training in Effective Parenting (STEP), 258
Systems theory, 56–59

Task group foundation methods, 313–343
    conflict resolution, 323–326
    decision making, 326–328
    information development, 321–323
    information sharing, 318–320
    meeting preparation, 315–318
    member involvement, 320–321
    monitoring and evaluation, 330–331
    and political functions, 329–330
    problem solving, 331–341
Task groups. *See also* Task group foundation methods; Task group specialized methods; specific group types
    composition, 163–166
    confidentiality, 195–196
    goal setting, 203–205
    historical development, 53–56
    political functions of, 329–330
    size of, 166–168
    structure, 201–202
    typology, 30–32
Task group specialized methods, 344–376
    brainstorming, 344–349

capacity building, 372–373
    community groups, 370–382
    focus groups, 349–352
    mobilization strategies, 370–371
    multiattribute utility analysis, 357–361
    nominal group technique, 353–357
    parliamentary procedure, 363–367
    Phillips' 66, 367–370
    quality circles/improvement teams, 361–363
    social action strategies, 373–374
    social judgment analysis, 360–361
Task recording, 269
Teams, 33–36
Telephone groups, 177–180
T–groups, 61–62
Therapeutic factors inventory, 323
The Human Group, 58
Therapy groups, 25–26. *See also* Treatment groups
Thought stopping, 284
Time limits, 101
"Top secret," 190
Total Quality Management (TQM), 361–363
Transference, 119
Transformational leadership, 97–98
"Treasure hunt," 191
Treatment conferences, 34–35
Treatment group foundation methods, 253–278
    contracting, 263–265
    goal awareness, 263–265
    meeting preparation, 254–257
    member motivation, 261–263

monitoring and evaluation, 275–276
    resistance, 272–275,
    structure, 257–261
    treatment plans, 269–272
    worker roles, 272
Treatment groups. *See also* Treatment group foundation methods; specific group types
    current trends, 49–53
    vs. individual work, 16–19
    size of, 166–167
    typology of, 19–20
Treatment plans, 269–272
Trigger groups, 348–349

Universalizing, 100, 189

Valence, 61
Validity, 421
Values, 6–8
Vertical thinking, 338
Virtual groups, 175–181
Videotapes, 408–409
Visual disability, 69

Worker roles. *See also* Interventions; Leadership
    advocate, 272
    broker, 272
    educator, 272
    enabler, 272
    mediator, 272
Working stage. *See* Task group foundation methods; Treatment group foundation methods
Written proposals, 181